THE BUSINESS INSURANCE HANDBOOK

THE
BUSINESS INSURANCE
HANDBOOK

COMPILED AND EDITED BY

Gray Castle, Esquire
New York, New York
Of Counsel To Pepper, Hamilton and Scheetz
(Formerly Senior Vice President and General Counsel,
INA Corporation)

Robert F. Cushman, Esquire
Pepper, Hamilton and Scheetz
Philadelphia, Pennsylvania

Peter R. Kensicki, D.B.A., CLU, CPCU
Director of Producer Education
The American Institute for Property and Liability Underwriters, Inc.
Malvern, Pennsylvania

INA SPECIAL EDITION

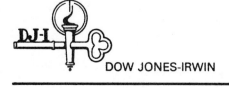

DOW JONES-IRWIN   Homewood, Illinois   60430

ISBN 0-87094-237-9
Library of Congress Catalog Card No. 80-70437
Printed in the United States of America

2 3 4 5 6 7 8 9 0 K 8 7 6 5 4 3 2

INTRODUCTION

John R. Cox,
President, Insurance Company of North America

It is a pleasure to present this special INA edition of the Dow Jones *Business Insurance Handbook*.

There has long been a need for a definitive work such as this, which addresses all of the key facets of insurance as it relates to the needs and interests of business people.

Because of INA's position of leadership in the world of insurance and particularly in matters of insurance education and training, we were asked to prepare two chapters in this text.

In Chapter 21, John C. Morrison, President of INA Special Risk Facilities, Inc., and Executive Vice President of the Insurance Company of North America, analyzes one of the most frequently used combination policies, the Special Multi-Peril Policy. This flexible policy was designed to simplify the task of dealing with the major insurance aspects of a business (property, liability, crime, boiler and manufacturing coverage) and serves to reduce the possibility of gaps in coverage between these various policies.

In Chapter 16, Peter H. Foley, Former Executive Vice President of INA Special Risk Facilities, Inc., investigates the liability exposures of corporate executives. The chapter focuses upon their obligations and the protection the Directors and Officers Policy provides. Additionally, the chapter develops Fiduciary Liability Insurance, so important now since the passage of the Employee Retirement Income Security Act of 1974 (ERISA), as well as Kidnap and Ransom Insurance, and Political Risk Insurance.

At INA, through our agents and brokers across the United States and around the world, we are prepared to provide almost every kind of insurance coverage that is needed by businesses, institutions, and individuals.

I trust that all businessmen who read this book will find it a very useful and illuminating experience in providing them with a background of information needed to help them handle the insurance aspects of their business responsibilities.

John R. Cox

ABOUT THE EDITORS

GRAY CASTLE, Esquire

Mr. Castle is Counsel to the law firm of Pepper, Hamilton & Scheetz. Prior to joining the firm, he was Senior Vice President and General Counsel of INA Corporation. Earlier, he served as Vice President, Secretary and General Counsel of NL Industries and Counsel, Headquarters Operations and Managing Attorney of Xerox Corporation.

The founder and first president of the Westchester-Fairfield Corporate Counsel Association, Mr. Castle is a frequent lecturer at American Bar Association, Practicing Law Institute and Conference of American Legal Executives programs. He is a member of the Corporation, Banking & Business Law, Antitrust Law and Tort and Insurance Practice sections of the American Bar Association, and is on the advisory board of the Southwestern Legal Foundation.

Mr. Castle is a graduate of Washington and Lee University and its law school where he was an editor of the *Law Review*.

ROBERT F. CUSHMAN, Esquire

Mr. Cushman, a partner in the Philadelphia lawfirm of Pepper, Hamilton & Scheetz, is a recognized specialist and lecturer on all phases of building construction and insurance law. He serves as legal counsel to numerous trade associations, construction companies, and fidelity and surety companies. Mr. Cushman is the editor and co-author of *The McGraw-Hill Construction Business Handbook*, the editor and co-author of *The Construction Industry Formbook*, published by Shepard's Citations, Inc., and the editor and co-author of *The Businessman's Guide to Construction*, published by Dow Jones-Irwin.

Mr. Cushman, who is a member of the International Association of Insurance Counsel, has served as executive vice president and general counsel to the Construction Industry Foundation and as regional chairman of the Public Contract Law Section of the American Bar Association.

Mr. Cushman is currently editing *The Businessman's Guide to Real Estate*, which will be published by Dow Jones-Irwin in 1982.

PETER R. KENSICKI

Dr. Kensicki is Director of Producer Education for the American Institute for Property and Liability Underwriters and the Insurance Institute of America. He received his B.B.A. at the University of Cincinnati (1966), M.INS (1968), and Doctor of Business Administration (1972) from Georgia State University. He has received three insurance professional designations: CLU (1972), FLMI (1977), and CPCU (1980). Dr. Kensicki has been an insurance agent, insurance regulator, and director of the first statewide consumer program for the state of Georgia. He also was assistant professor of finance at Ohio University and assistant vice president of the Cincinnati Insurance Company. He has published many articles in academic journals and the trade press. He has general editorial responsibilities for a series of three textbooks to be published by the Insurance Institute of America and is a co-author for all the texts.

CONTENTS

SECTION I
CONTROLLING BUSINESS INSURANCE COST

1. **Risk management—ways to reduce costs,** *Carroll E. Henkel,*
   John M. Harrington,   Joseph E. Johnson, Ph.D. **2**

   Role of risk management: *Risk identification, analysis, and evaluation.*
   New ventures or new construction. Existing operations. Risk control:
   Avoidance. Reduction. Case histories. Other loss control activities. Sep-
   aration. Combination. Risk financing: *Retention. Retention with outside*
   funding. Captive insurance companies. Service organizations for reten-
   tion. Transfer: By contracts, leases, purchase orders, and similar agree-
   ments. Additional insureds. Transfers through divestiture or acquisi-
   tion. The use of limited noninsurance transfers. Transfer: By the pur-
   chase of insurance. Claim adjustments. Buying insurance from direct
   writers. The insurance markets: *Property insurance. Casualty insur-*
   ance. Marine insurance. Miscellaneous insurance. Rating. Selecting a
   broker. Conclusion. Notes.

2. **Risk management and obtaining risk management services,**
   Peter R. Kensicki, B.B.A., CLU, CPCU **32**

   When to hire a consultant. Risk management techniques. How to use a
   consultant. "Consulting Firms Fill Needs—For A Price." Directory of
   firms.

3. **Your major business exposures,**
   Frederick R. Hodosh, Esquire, Ph.D., J.D., CPCU **56**

   Property exposures. Liability exposures. Specialized exposures. The
   coordination and combination of insurance coverages. Providing for business continuation through insurance and selected employee benefits.
   Unique exposures. Data processing insurance.

SECTION II
CONTROLLING PROPERTY EXPOSURES

4. **Direct damage to buildings and fixtures,**
   Theodore W. Flowers, Esquire,   Thomas D. Rutherfoord, Jr.,
   Thomas J. Ziomek, Esquire **82**

   Real property exposures—an overview. Legal concepts: *Contractual re-*
   quirements. Lapse. Cancellation. Principles of insurance contracts: *In-*

demnity. Insurable interest. Actual cash value. Co-insurance. Warranties and representations. Subrogation. Standard fire policy and general property form: Property covered. Property not covered. Extensions of coverage. Co-insurance. Deductible. Perils insured against. Exclusions. Valuation. Other provisions. Special forms, policies, and insurance markets: All-risk coverage. Flood. Earthquake. Nuclear contamination. Operation of building codes. FAIR Plan. Excess and surplus lines markets. Insurance limits relative to property valuation: Insurance to value. Deductibles. Blanket limits. Property insurance rates: Specific and class rates. Blanket rates. Loss engineering. Occurrence of loss: Occupancy and vacancy. Dealing with a loss.

5. **Direct damage to contents,** *Patrick F. Carton,*
   Joseph A. Bambury, Jr., Esquire **112**

Exposure of the business: Ownership. Care, custody, and control. Contractual exposure. Identification of contents: Fixtures. Inventory. Supplies and equipment. Special assets. Property off the premises. Customary policy forms: "Named peril" versus "all-risks". Standard fire policy. Exclusions. Blanket coverage. Valuation at loss. Increase in hazard, vacant premises. Package policies. Other exposures to loss. Additional contents coverage: Stock reporting. Manufacturers output policy. Transit insurance. Commercial property floater policies. Electronic data processing policies. Federal flood program. How to handle claims.

6. **Loss of profits—indirect damage,** *Leo Kling* **134**

Time element coverages: Types of time element coverages. The protection of Business Interruption coverages. The major time element coverages: Gross Earnings Forms coverages. Earnings insurance. Contingent Business Interruption coverages. Extra expense insurance. Similarity in forms—major clauses: Actual loss sustained. Resumption of Operations Clause. Contribution Clause. Expenses to reduce loss. Interruption by civil authority. Limitation—media for electronic data processing. Special exclusions. Pro rata clause. Normal. Loss clause. Alterations and new buildings. Electrical Apparatus Clause. Liberalization clause. Nuclear exclusion. Common endorsements: Premium Adjustment Endorsement. Agreed Amount Endorsement. Extension of period of interruption. Other time element coverages: Rental Value coverage. Leasehold Interest coverage. Blanket coverage.

7. **Dishonesty losses,** *Frank L. Skillern, Jr., Esquire* **154**

Types of policies available. Risks covered: Dishonesty. Other coverage. Who is covered. Exclusions: Acts of the insured. Inventory exclusions. Knowledge of fraud or dishonesty. Conditions for recovery: Notice and proof of loss. There must be a loss. Other provisions and issues: Limits liability. Valuation and subrogation. Joints insureds. Danger of libel or slander. Riders. Risk management.

SECTION III
CONTROLLING LIABILITY EXPOSURES

8. **General liability insurance,** *Prof. James W. Bowers,*
B. C. Hart, Esquire **182**

General liability risks: *Automatically covered risks. Extra coverage for additional general liability risks.* Special forms of general liability insurance contracts. How to read the CGL policy: *The declarations. The basic policy. The endorsements. The policy jacket.* What the policy covers: *The insured—who is protected. What claims are covered: "Caused by an occurrence". What claims are covered: Bodily injury. What claims are covered: Property damage. What claims are covered: Personal injury.* How you pay for coverage: *Rate bases. Manual rates, rating classifications, and audits. Experience rates. Composite rates. Retrospective rating plans.* What to do when trouble comes: *Giving notice. Insurer's duty to defend you. Conflicts of interest. Your duty to cooperate.* What to ask your insurance agent or broker.

9. **Commercial automobile liability and physical damage,**
Frank L. Eblen, Vice President, Robert S. Smith, J.D., CPCU **218**

The businessman's exposure to loss through the operation of automobiles: *Statutory requirements.* Risk handling by noninsurance methods: *Avoidance or elimination of risk. Loss control—accident prevention. Self-assumption. Transfer by noninsurance.* Risk transfer through insurance: *Liability Insurance coverage. Limits of liability. Exclusions. No-fault coverage. Medical Payments coverage. Uninsured Motorists coverage. Physical Damage coverages. Covered autos. Business Auto Policy (BAP) options.* Premium computation.

10. **Truckers liability and garage risks,** *Charles T. Bidek,*
James C. Blanton, Esquire **246**

What are the exposures? *Bodily injury and property damage liability. Cargo exposure. General Liability coverage. Workers' compensation.* Optional coverages and exposures (required in some states): *Uninsured Motorists coverage. No-fault personal injury protection insurance. Physical Damage (Fire/Theft, Specified Perils and Collision).* Policy construction and rating. What the general liability-automobile policy gives the insured: *Policy terms most often used. Who is covered under the insuring agreement. Coverage provided. Major exclusions. Special exclusions by endorsement.* Cargo insurance: *Available protection. Handling cargo claims.* Special governmental regulations. Safety departments of insurance companies. What to do when an accident occurs. How trucking insurance is marketed. The garage policy: *Bodily injury and property damage coverage and exclusions. Garagekeeper coverage and exclusions. Physical damage insurance and exclusions. Medical Payments coverage.*

11. **Workers' compensation and employers' liability,**
Robert Needle, Esquire, J.D., Frank E. Raab, Jr. **266**

Coverage in general: *Historical perspective. Requirement on employer to secure exposure. Relationship giving rise to the exposure. Benefits provided.* Analysis of the policy: *Insuring agreements. Exclusions. Conditions. Modifications and extensions through endorsements.* Risk management techniques: *Guaranteed cost insurance; dividends, premium discounts, and experience rating. Participating plans. Retrospective rating. Self-insurance.*

12. **Products liability insurance,** *Sheila L. Birnbaum, Esquire*
Diane S. Wilner, Esquire **288**

Modern trend in products liability law. Products liability coverage. A typical policy: *Policy territory. Applicable limits. Occurrence.* Products hazard clause: *What are products? Injury or damage away from premises. Possession must be relinquished.* Completed operations clause: *Completion of operations. Exclusions to completed operations clause.* Products liability exclusions: *Sistership exclusion. Injury to products exclusion. Injury to work performed exclusion. Business risk exclusion.* Punitive damages. Summary. Conclusion.

SECTION IV
CONTROLLING SPECIALIZED EXPOSURES

13. **Surety bonds,** *George L. Blick, Charles H. Carman* **310**

A surety bond is not an insurance policy. License and permit bonds. Construction and related contract surety bonds: *Bid Bonds. Performance Bonds. Payment Bonds. The Maintenance Bond. Subdivision Bonds.* Judicial bonds: *Replevin Bonds. Lien discharge Bonds.* Public official bonds. Court fiduciary bonds. Miscellaneous surety bonds: *Lost instrument Bonds. Tax Bonds. Financial guaranty Bonds. Lease Bonds.* The decision to bond.

14. **Ocean marine and aviation,** *James E. Goulard,*
Charles N. Shepherd, W. B. Harwood, Jr. **320**

Ocean marine insurance: *Ocean cargo insurance. Hull Insurance. Protection and Indemnity Insurance. Additional insurances. Markets. Negotiations and your agent or broker.* Aviation insurance: *Aviation insurance "ground rules." Aircraft liability. Aircraft physical damage. Summary.*

15. **Professional liability,** *Francis E. Shields, Esquire,*
Sherryl R. Perry, Esquire, Penrose Wolf, Esquire. **352**

History and general trends: *Negligence defined. Malpractice problems.* Specific professions covered and recent developments: *The medical and health service providers' professional liability. Attorneys' professional liability. Accountants' professional liability. Architect's and engineers' professional liability.* Professional liability protection and insurance: *Medical and health service providers' professional liability. Attorneys' professional liability. Accountants' professional liability. Architects' and/or engineers' professional liability.* Professional liability of a corporation. Miscellaneous.

16. Executive exposures, *Peter H. Foley* **396**

The age of liability. Directors and officers liability: *The growing need for D&O coverage. The obligations of directors and officers. The D&O policy. International considerations.* Fiduciary liability insurance. Kidnap and ransom: *Introduction. Loss prevention. Insurance. Type and availability of coverage. Who can be covered. Scope of coverage. Conditions of coverage. Premium considerations.* Political risk insurance.

17. Miscellaneous coverages, *Kenneth J. Kelly, Esquire* **418**

Boilers and pressure vessel coverage. Machinery coverage. The boiler and machinery policy: *Definitions. Exclusions. Conditions. Indirect coverage—Business Interruption. Inspection and suspension. State laws. Risk management techniques. Questions to ask the agent or broker.* Glass insurance. Credit insurance. Valuable papers insurance.

18. Title insurance, *John E. Flood, Jr.* **434**

The risks covered by title insurance. Interests in real estate that may be covered by title insurance. Scope of coverage; limitations on coverage: *The standard coverage policy. The extended coverage policy. Exclusions from coverage. Endorsements.* Term of the policy; continuation of coverage. The title insurance commitment. The amount of insurance; the cost of title insurance. Availability of title insurance.

SECTION V
PACKAGING EXPOSURES INTO ONE POLICY

19. Rounding out the insurance program,
George B. Flanigan, Ph.D., CPCU, Richard Turner, CPCU **454**

Excess liability coverage: *Use of the excess. The unlimited magnitude of the liability exposure.* The commercial umbrella policy: *History of the umbrella. Purpose of the umbrella. Primary coverage required by umbrella underwriters. Limits of liability required on underlying policies. Self-insured retention. Limits of liability. The insuring agreement. Exclusions. Conditions. Professional umbrella coverage.* The difference in conditions policy: *What can be covered. Perils covered. The deductible. Important coverages afforded. Co-insurance. Other insurance provisions. Indirect losses. Filling in the gap: An example. Conclusions and summary.*

20. **The businessowner's policy,**
Edward M. Glenn, Ph.D., CPCU, CLU **470**

Eligibility for the businessowners' policy. Property coverages: *Standard policy form. Special policy form.* Liability coverages: *Business liability. Medical payments. Definition of the insured.* General conditions and other provisions: *War Risk, Governmental Action, and Nuclear Exclusions. General conditions. Conditions applicable to Section I. Conditions applicable to Section II.* BOP rating. Summary and questions for the agent or broker: *Summary. Questions you might ask your agent or broker.*

21. **The special multi-peril policy,** *John C. Morrison* **498**

Development of the package concept: *Reduced cost. A single policy contract. History of the package. The present SMP policy.* A summary of SMP coverages: *Property insurance. General liability insurance. Optional coverages available. Crime coverage. Boiler and machinery insurance.* Businessowners' program—a comparison. Detailed review of coverages available: *Property insurance—Section I. General liability coverage—Section II. Crime coverage—Section III. Boiler machinery insurance—Section IV.* Conclusion.

22. **Insurance for farmers,** *James A. Carter* **518**

The Farmowners' (farm package) Policy: *Basic Perils coverage. Broad Perils coverage. All-risk coverage. Property requiring specific insurance. Additional features and extensions. Liability coverage.* Workers' compensation and employers' liability. Crop hail insurance. Livestock mortality insurance. Safety, loss control, and insurance to value.

SECTION VI
PROVIDING FOR BUSINESS CONTINUATION
THROUGH INSURANCE AND SELECTED EMPLOYEE BENEFITS

23. **Providing for business continuation through insurance**
and selected employee benefits—for the sole proprietor,
Arthur Gowell, CLU, Gordon K. Rose, CLU **538**

Health insurance: *Blue Cross-Blue Shield. Comprehensive Hospital-Surgical-Major Medical coverage. Optional coverages available with group plans.* How to buy. Disability: *Policy considerations.* Life insurance: *Mututal or stock company. Term or permanent. Beware of the twister. Nonforfeiture provisions. Options and riders. Use of dividends.* Retirement. Disposing of the business: *Disability. Death. Retirement. Necessary provisions in the buy-sell agreement.* The estate plan of the sole proprietor.

24. **Providing for business continuation through insurance and selected employee benefits—for partnerships,**
Richard W. Ledwith, Jr., CLU, Robert S. Price, Esquire 556

The use of the partnership vehicle. Description of the partnership vehicle: *Continuity of life. Centralization of management. Limitation of liability. Free transferability of interests.* The decision to use a partnership: *Tradition. Business. Taxation.* The partnership as an aggregate. Tax considerations in selecting the partnership vehicle: *Starting up. Operating. Termination.* Income splitting. Compensation and fringe benefits. Keogh plan. Buy-sell agreements: *Partner valuation. Book value. Sales of interests. Capitalization of income. Capitalization from assets. Purchased goodwill.* Disability insurance for the partnership. Miscellaneous insurance: *Group term life insurance. Health insurance. Fringe benefit insurance.*

25. **Providing for business continuation through insurance and selected employee benefits—for corporations,**
William J. Kane, CLU, MSFS 580

Nature of close corporation business continuation. Transfer of ownership. Buy-sell agreements: *Advantages. Details. Funding the buy-sell agreement. Beyond the buy-sell agreement.* Life insurance products. Partial corporate redemptions. Valuation of closely held corporations: *Market value. Intrinsic value—earnings. Intrinsic value—other considerations.* Your value.

26. **Providing fringe benefits for key personnel,**
Wendell J. Bossen, CLU, Mel J. Massey, Jr., Esquire 592

The objectives of the benefit program. Pension and profit-sharing plans. Employee stock ownership plans. Funding the plan. The individual retirement account. The simplified employee pension plan. Tax-deferred annuities and the non-profit organization. Deferred compensation plans: *Tax aspects. Funding the plan through life insurance. Funding the plan through annuities. Funding the plan through mutual funds. Including majority stockholders.* Group life insurance: *Prefunding through group permanent insurance. Prefunding through a retired lives Reserve plan.* Cafeteria plans. Employer financed insurance: *Paying the premium as a bonus. Split-dollar insurance.* Interest free loans. Executive health plans. Medical reimbursement plans. Planning for the receipt of fringe benefits at retirement. Planning for the receipt of fringe benefits at death. Selecting the agent or broker and choosing the program. Introduction to and follow up with the employees. Summary.

27. **Fringe benefits for general personnel,**
Charles H. Stamm, III, Esquire 622

Group insurance benefit plans. Regulation of insured employee benefits. Choosing among available benefit plans. Basic group benefit plans available: *Group life insurance benefits. Group health insurance benefits. Group disability income coverages. Group dental insurance.* Health Maintenance Organizations (HMOS): *Basic benefits and exclusions.* Risk management techniques. Emerging fringe benefits: *Group legal. True group auto. Vision care.* Employer packaging assistance available. Key questions to ask your agent or broker.

28. **Insured pension and profit sharing,**
    Charles H. Stamm, III, Esquire, Thomas F. Shea, Esquire **644**

Defined contribution plans—in general. Defined benefit plans—in general. The advantages and disadvantages of the defined contribution plan. The advantages and disadvantages of the defined benefit plan. The tax qualified plan concept. ERISA—Employee Retirement Income Security Act: *Reporting and disclosure. Minimum standards. Other ERISA requirements. Fiduciary duties. Plan termination insurance.* Insured pension plans. Insured group pension products: *Deposit administration contracts. Immediate participation guarantee. Separate accounts.* Questions to ask the agent or broker.

SECTION VII
UNIQUE EXPOSURES

29. **Computer facility (data processing) insurance,**
    Guy R. Migliaccio **660**

Developing the disaster plan. Data processing equipment insurance: *Understanding the lease clauses. General data processing policies. The Difference-in-Conditions Policy. User or employee negligence.* Data storage media insurance: *Determining media values.* Accounts receivable insurance: *Determining media values.* Accounts receivable insurance. Business interruption insurance. Extra expense insurance. Data processors' (third-party) errors and omissions liability insurance: *Sources of loss.* Recommended course of action. APPENDIX: RISK AND INSURANCE SURVEY FOR DATA PROCESSING.

30. **Business legal expense insurance and tender offer defense expense insurance,** *Sydney Aronson* **682**

Business legal expense insurance: *The need. Highlights of the coverage. Exclusions. Eligibility. Plans available. Examples of how this insurance has been utilized. Business legal expense insurance summary.* Tender offer defense expense insurance: *Background on tender offers. Covered expenses. Benefits limits available. Optional coinsurance. Deductibles and policy period. Significant exclusions. Significant definitions in the policy. How the insurance works. The significance of the range of limits and deductibles. Special considerations. The premium. Public policy considerations.*

31. Environmental impairment liability insurance,
Lynne M. Miller,   Michael J. Murphy **698**

Statutory and regulatory requirements: *Resource Conservation and Recovery Act, Comprehensive Environmental Response, Compensation, and Liability Act. Motor Carrier Act.* Common law liability: *Strict liability. Nuisance. Negligence.* Insurance availability and markets. Risk assessment techniques: *Inherent hazard potential. Environmental pathways. Potentially exposed population. Facility-specific considerations. Summary of the risk.* Reducing risks.

SECTION VIII
APPENDIX: RISK MANAGEMENT CHECKLIST

Risk management checklists **716**
Aetna Plan Questionnaire **723**

INDEX **741**

CONTROLLING BUSINESS INSURANCE COST

CHAPTER 1

RISK MANAGEMENT— WAYS TO REDUCE COSTS

ROLE OF RISK MANAGEMENT
Risk identification, analysis, and
evaluation
New ventures or new construction
Existing operations

RISK CONTROL
Avoidance
Reduction
Case histories
Other loss control activities
Separation
Combination

RISK FINANCING
Retention
Retention with outside funding
Captive insurance companies
Service organizations for retention
Transfer: By contracts, leases,
purchase orders, and similar
agreements

Additional insureds
Transfers through divestiture or
acquisition
The use of limited non-insurance
transfers
Transfer: By the purchase of
insurance
Claim adjustments
Buying insurance from direct writers

THE INSURANCE MARKETS
Property insurance
Casualty insurance
Marine insurance
Miscellaneous insurance

RATING

SELECTING A BROKER

CONCLUSION

Carroll E. Henkel
Chairman of the Board, Insurance Buyers' Council, Inc.
Baltimore, Maryland

Carroll E. Henkel is Chairman of the Board of Insurance Buyers' Council, Inc., and is in his 19th year as an independent Risk Management Consultant. With 40 years' experience in the insurance business, he is also engaged in speaking and contributing articles on risk management subjects. Mr. Henkel is a member of the Institute of Risk Management Consultants and the Society of Fire Protection Engineers. He has the CPCU (Chartered Property and Casualty Underwriters) and ARM (Associate in Risk Management) designations and is a Professional Engineer in fire protection engineering.

John M. Harrington
Assistant Treasurer and Director, Risk Management,
    NL Industries, Inc.
New York, New York

John M. Harrington has been involved in Risk Management for the past 20 years, having previously held insurance positions at Morgan Guaranty Trust Company and Eastern Airlines. He has been active as a committee member of the American Bankers Association, the International Transport Association and the Manufacturers Chemists Association. He has an MBA degree from Fordham University and a BBA degree from the College of Insurance.

Joseph E. Johnson, D.B.A.
Department of Business Administration
University of North Carolina
Greensboro, North Carolina

Joseph E. Johnson, Professor of Business Administration, serves as Head of the Department of Business Administration, School of Business and Economics, at the University of North Carolina at Greensboro. He is also President of the North Carolina Insurance Education Foundation. He received his undergraduate degree from UNC-Chapel Hill and his Master's and Doctor of Business Administration from Georgia State University. He is a CPCU.

Dealing with exposure to financial loss is a daily challenge to the businessman. Some who have assets which may by chance be destroyed or in some way reduced in value, assume that insurance is their sole answer. But insurance is, in fact, only one of many techniques to address these exposures. Indeed, some exposures are not insurable (wear and tear); and some exposures, though insurable, may be more economically handled by using a noninsurance technique.

Risk management is a topic broader than but including insurance management. Perhaps the most important concept in this introductory chapter is that alternatives to insurance can and should be considered. The process of considering these alternatives is risk management.

Risk management is the effective and intelligent use of money, materials, and man to best protect business financial interests, to produce maximum profits, and to assure the continuity of business. A full definition is in Chapter 2.

Risk management evolved from the insurance management process. Still an emerging discipline, risk management is gaining acceptance by business organizations, insurance companies, brokers, and agents as its value is realized. Its techniques fall into two broad categories—risk control and risk financing.[1] Within risk control, the approaches of avoidance, reduction, separation, and combination are used. Risk financing includes insurance, noninsurance transfer, and retention.

ROLE OF RISK MANAGEMENT

With increasing insurance premiums, expanding employee benefit requirements, and continuing inflation, management is taking a closer look at costs involved in their insurance programs. Alternate means are being considered to protect assets and future income. Many corporations and nonprofit organizations have their own Risk Managers. Moderate-sized and small organizations are seeking the assistance and expertise of consultants, agents, brokers, or insurance companies.

Risk identification, analysis, and evaluation

At whatever level risk management is practiced, the same basic processes are used (although there are some differences in terminologies and approaches observable among available texts and courses). Initially, risk management *identifies* exposure to loss. These exposures may be expected to produce losses of the following types: (1) direct or indirect property losses, (2) income losses, (3) statutory or legal liability losses, and (4) personnel losses.

Significant research and investigation is necessary to complete the risk identification process properly. The steps may vary among Risk Managers, but it is necessary to become intimately familiar with the operations of the organization. A company's financial statement presents a wealth of information relating to the activity and financial strength of the business, as does the Securities and Exchange Commission 10-K report required of public companies.

Contained in the financial statement under "assets information" are original costs, depreciated values, or book values of all owned buildings, equipment, and all types of contents. (Valuation for insurance purposes, however, considers a different source.) Accounts receivable and accounts payable balances are also identified, including reserves set aside for growth.

By examining a series of financial statements, the Risk Manager can determine the history of the business and the patterns established to provide guidelines in considering risk control.

Of extreme importance to the Risk Manager is a physical inspection of owned and leased properties. Reviewing operations with departmental or supervisory personnel will help him gain insight into the business. Attitudes of employees as they relate to safe working habits, housekeeping, and general care of the premises should be observed. A well-designed questionnaire, prepared prior to the visit, will be helpful. Ideally, the questionnaire should be designed to elicit detailed financial, operating, and management information. This information should permit the identification and analysis of the business's exposure to loss. Questionnaires can be obtained from insurance companies, the American Management Association, and risk management or insurance organizations. A number of consultants have prepared their own survey forms based on the type of business to be reviewed. In addition, two complete questionnaires will be found in Chapter 2.

Sales brochures, flowcharts, and quality control methods data also will provide additional insight into the operations when the business is of sufficient size that it will use such material and data. A professional appraisal and accurate inventory information will provide excellent information to establish values of property and indicate the exposure involved.

New ventures or new construction

When a new venture or new construction is planned, the Risk Manager should have the opportunity to review plans and specifications for the proposed project. Many times financial savings are possible in both the short and long run.

Consider these typical cost saving examples:

1.   A new administration office and laboratory building is planned. The Risk Management Consultant meets with the architects and the insurer. After consultation, it is agreed that if a superior fire-retardant ceiling is used and a thicker insulation installed on the roof support structure, a different type roof with lighter secondary supports can be used. This results in a savings of $100,000 in construction costs.

2.   Architects for a new hospital are confronted with the additional costs involved in increasing the interior fire protection since the height of the building is in excess of state and local codes for public fire-fighting apparatus. The contour of the ground varies considerably. In meeting with the governmental personnel and the state fire marshal, the Risk Management Consultant suggests having an access road at the top contour level where sodding had been planned. The change is accepted. This revision saves $150,000 in the cost of the project.

3.   In reviewing plans and specifications for a new plant, the Risk Management Consultant notes the installation of automatic sprinklers is not planned. After comparing the property damage insurance rates on a sprinklered and on an unsprinklered basis, it is found the cost of the sprinkler system could be amortized in slightly over a three-year period based on the annual insurance premium saved following the installation of the sprinkler system. Thereafter, a pure annual savings is realized. Not only is there a financial gain, but the probability of a severe fire loss is materially reduced.

As can be seen, failure to consider new ventures or new construction from a risk management perspective may cause management to miss the opportunity for substantial monetary savings and improved protection.

Existing operations

After the desired inspections on existing operations are completed and the requested information obtained, the analysis can begin. At this point, detailed loss experience for the particular business and, if available, that of similar businesses is extremely helpful. The frequency and severity, and the type of loss experienced, present an historic picture and provide information for projecting losses. The indirect costs in relationship to workers' compensation accident costs should be reviewed from available records. In some instances these indirect costs can be far greater than the direct cost.

With this wealth of information, the Risk Manager can prepare flowcharts of the operating processes. This layout is invaluable in analyzing and evaluating the exposure.

Examples of a citrus cooperative in Florida serve to show the value of flowcharts (Exhibits 1-A and 1-B).

The physical movement of all materials can be traced from the points of origin to and through the cooperative and then to the various destinations of the finished product (Exhibit 1-A). The physical assets can be easily reviewed as well. Exhibit 1-B presents the administrative and financial operations. The members of the cooperative depend upon the accuracy and protection of vital records to assure their share of the profits at the end of the season.

With these flowcharts depicting financial, operational, and personnel data, the exposures can be evaluated. With regard to exposure identification, the following key questions arise:

1. What events can interrupt this flow?
2. What is the probability of such disruptive events?
3. What types of losses may result from these disruptive events?
4. How large are the resulting losses likely to be?
5. What steps need to be taken to best protect the assets and resources as well as assure the continuity of the business?

Next, meetings should be held with executive management, including the chief financial officer. The insight gained as to the guidelines and philosophy under which the business has been operating will be of value to the Risk Manager in making his recommendations.

A determination can be made regarding a reasonable retention level through self-insurance or deductibles. At some point there will be an aversion by management to increasing the level of retention. This decision will be based on both financial and psychological considerations. The groundwork can be prepared for the full backing and ongoing cooperation of the executives.

Not to be overlooked in the study is the attorney for the business. He should have valuable background information on the company's business. His knowledge of the leases and contracts to which the company is a party also should be helpful. Changing legal concepts of the doctrine of negligence to that of strict liability and the anticipated growth of absolute liability must be given serious consideration. Under these strict and absolute liability doctrines, negligence need not be proven as the cause of the incident.

After digesting all of the information, data, and thoughts of those with whom the Risk Manager has been in contact, the plan of attack for protection of assets and resources can now be developed. There should be a clear and concise understanding of the objectives and the methods to be pursued to accomplish the desired results of maximizing profits and assuring continuity.

A well-planned risk management program will attack the various exposures to risk and encompass procedures to secure optimum profits and continued operation. It also will include means for protecting against possible adverse situations that could cause unnecessary loss of the assets or resources.

To the degree risk management is effectively used to achieve desired goals, it should result in a reduction in costs with minimum interruption of the business.

RISK CONTROL

Risk control methods may be used individually or in combination, depending upon the situation. Risk control methods are designed to minimize, at the lowest possible cost, the losses sustained by an organization. These methods include avoidance, reduction, separation, and combination.

Avoidance

Risk avoidance is simply removing any exposure to loss. By not entering into a new relationship, companies avoid any danger of loss associated with the proposed arrangement. By discontinuing certain practices or changing some procedures, companies also can avoid loss.
Some examples:

A company is planning to manufacture a special line of furniture. When it is found that the plastic intended for use burns easily and while burning emits large amounts of smoke and toxic fumes, the idea is abandoned.

After examining several auto lease agreements, a lessee's Risk Manager discovers one lessor requires an absolute hold-harmless and indemnification provision by the lessee. The lessee could be held responsible for negligence of others, including lessor. Recognizing the potential exposure, the Risk Manager suggests auto leasing contracts be awarded exclusively to those firms which do not require such an assumption of liability, thereby avoiding this difficult-to-manage risk.

The decision as to when to avoid risk is a relative one, depending on a number of factors, including the economic health of the business. Ideally, the Risk Manager makes *conscious and deliberate* decisions as to which risks to avoid in order to minimize operational and revenue disruptions.

An area of risk avoidance, possibly the most painful, is divestiture of an operation. Financial analysis may lead to a decision that divestiture is desirable. For example, accelerating workers' compensation claims together with the liberal tendencies of state workers' compensation officials in some states may make it prudent to close down an operation rather than to continue in an environment where the cost of workers' compensation has the company at a break-even or negative income point.

There are other situations where government emission restrictions or compliance with Occupational Safety and Health Act (OSHA) standards make an operation unprofitable overnight. Prudence, in such a case, dictates closing the plant. It is imperative that any new venture or acquisition be examined from a risk management perspective and risk management costs be included in return on investment calculations before final decisions are made.

The point is some loss exposures are so potentially costly that the most attractive alternative is to avoid the exposure altogether.

Reduction

The purpose of loss reduction (or loss prevention) is to reduce the frequency and/or severity of losses. Loss prevention activities are an essential element in operating any business.

Safety programs can be most effective in reducing workers' compensation injuries. Proper training, indoctrination of employees, and improving the workplace all play an important part. Establishing and reviewing loss records is a must to determine the experience.

Loss records should include:

Employee's name

Date of accident

Time of accident

Place of accident

Cause

Type of injury

Estimated amount of indemnity (paid or set aside as a reserve for possible future payments)

Medical payments (paid and reserved)

The prevention program should call for scheduled safety meetings with supervisors. The size of the business will govern the type and frequency of such meetings.

Consider these facts from a nationwide study of on-the-job accidents:

> Medium-size companies—those with 50 to 1,000 employees—had a heavier concentration of on-the-job accidents than larger or smaller companies. About 43.5 percent of these medium-size businesses reported injury and illness incidents of 1 to 10 per 100 full-time workers. One in four had an injury and illness rate of 10 to 20 per 100 workers.[2]

These facts reflect what loss control specialists in the insurance industry have observed for some time: When it comes to controlling work-related injuries and illnesses through an organized job safety and health program, medium-sized businesses have a serious communication problem.

Apparently, job safety in a medium-sized company becomes lost in the shuffle as the owner becomes more removed from daily operations. His first concern is staying in business. Unless he is aware of how he can cut expenses and increase his profit margin through loss control, he may let safety take a back seat.

If the business expands still further, however, a more formal management structure typically develops. The owner may be able to afford a safety supervisor or at least assign the task of maintaining safety standards to several of his middle managers. As the statistics reflect, injury and illness records improve when a firm's work force goes over 1,000.[3]

Insurance companies writing workers' compensation insurance will provide engineering services and loss control programs to assist insureds, if requested. Case histories have shown that time after time positive results in reducing both injuries and costs are obtained when a loss prevention program is adopted and has the continued backing of executive management.

Case histories

Several cases will show the value of cooperative efforts. Each of these insureds retained a risk management consulting firm to study their problems.

A dairy had an unsatisfactory experience which caused an increase in premium for workers' compensation insurance. There was no formal safety program in effect nor had the insurance company given any assistance. Recommendations were made to implement a safety program headed by a qualified safety director. Insurance was subsequently purchased from a different insurer providing engineering services and monthly loss experience runs. In the space of three years, management implemented the safety program. An amazing safety record was achieved—500,000 hours without a lost-time accident. The results—major decreases in the cost of insurance and a lowering of production costs as a side benefit.

A second example involves a cooperative. The workers' compensation insurance rates were 89 percent higher than manual premiums because of the cooperative's poor loss experience. Investigation disclosed there was no real communication between the insured and the engineering department of the insurance company. Meetings were held by the management of the cooperative with local management of the insurance company. A safety program was established, and good communications developed. Monthly printouts of losses were provided. It took time, but each year showed an improving loss record, with the insurance rating reduced to a 20 percent credit in six years.

Depending on the size of a business, the Risk Manager may plan all safety activities or his duties can be delegated to a Safety Engineer. In either case, loss control includes employee training aimed at the development of good work habits. This can be aided by the dissemination of procedure manuals, safety bulletins, and other materials. Such information may be discussed and handed out at weekly safety meetings to the foremen and supervisors who will post the information on bulletin boards, or, if convenient, may be given directly to the employees. Safety must be a continuing educational process to be effective.

Suggested memos or bulletins are shown in Exhibits 1-C and 1-D. One memo relates to driving, and the other one instructs retail store employees with respect to precautions which should be taken to avoid robberies. The bulletins are representative of those available from the National Safety Council. They can be ordered in handout or bulletin board size.

Other loss control activities

Quality control of products and the general care and maintenance of the premises should be a vital concern to the Risk Manager. So should driver training programs. All of these exposures can involve possible outside liability as a result of injury to persons or damage to property of others.

An indirect benefit is obtained when employees are well trained in safety and good housekeeping. Not only are they less likely to have accidents at home or on the road, but residents of the household also are likely to have fewer accidents. Employee benefit programs will have fewer claims as a result.

A program of pre-employment physicals also will aid in reducing employee benefit costs to the extent that job applicants with serious disease or internal impairments are rejected as a consequence of such pre-employment physicals.

Sales and products literature should be examined as though they were medical prescriptions, because courts hold manufacturers responsible for omissions in instructions which can lead to possible ill effects to the consumer. All communications between a business and the public must be written to minimize liability. The Federal Consumer Product Safety Act clearly requires all manufacturers to exercise more than reasonable diligence in their written warnings and instructions to the consumer. To the extent management insists upon legal review of all business communications, it has taken the first real step in loss prevention.

Adequate property conservation programs and engineering are an essential requisite for a loss control program. Too often the purchase of insurance leads to a reduction of internal property conservation and other loss control practices. The maintenance and seaworthiness of a vessel are far more important than lifeboats and lifesaving apparatus.

Many industry associations have established insurance committees to share loss experience and underwriting information, as well as loss control techniques. Wherever available, such information should be reviewed. For example, the cost of fire losses should be allocated to the division involved and be included in the managers' incentive program if the losses were preventable.

A manual of operations, including emergency plans, should be prepared for each facility and plant. Periodic audits should be employed to check plan efficiency. Physical inspections should be made to assure continuity of protection programs.

Loss control information for plant and equipment exposed to fire loss is plentiful. There is no excuse for any business to be without an in-house property conservation program. Too many serious fire losses are the result of human failure. Moreover, it could be considered grossly negligent (perhaps even criminal) for a company to be without a minimum Emergency Plan.

It is not necessary to be a registered engineer to recognize blatant fire hazards. Organize a weekly inspection of facilities and plants to improve maintenance and housekeeping. Appoint a foreman or manager as a fire warden, with specific instructions to follow in the event of a fire. There are major companies today that have not established in-house responsibility for response to an emergency, inspection of premises, maintenance of fire equipment, checking of sprinkler valves, storing of combustibles away from exposed areas, and so forth. These companies do not practice loss control. The installation of automatic sprinkler systems, improved protection of premises, maintaining fire first-aid equipment, and testing of equipment are part of the fire prevention activities.

A well-maintained automatic sprinkler system with an adequate water supply will either extinguish or control a fire. The system is designed to check a fire in its incipient stage. Thus, losses normally are small and cleanup operations are simple. There should be little interruption to business.

On the other hand, unsprinklered premises would be seriously damaged or totally destroyed in the event of a fire. This could cause a suspension of the business and loss of earnings. Statistics have shown that nearly half of those businesses suffering a severe fire loss never get back into business on a profitable basis.

A secondary benefit of having an automatic sprinkler system is an insurance rate reduction. Depending upon the credit by the insurance company, the cost of an automatic sprinkler system can be recovered in three to ten years with the business owner usually amortizing this investment in six to seven years.

Prudent risk management should look beyond the immediate monetary benefits as the only criteria for installing a sprinkler system. Delay in getting back into business can be devastating, particularly in a competitive market. Building materials may be difficult to obtain. The replacement of special machinery could take many months. Damaged or smoke-laden stock might be useless.

In smaller businesses, fire detection systems can be installed to transmit an alarm to the fire department. Prompt response will serve to control the amount of damage. A credit is given in determining the premium for a fire detection system when the installation is accepted by rating authorities.

Proper placement of approved fire extinguishers aids in putting out a fire before it gets beyond the initial stage. Employees should be trained in their use.

Special systems for the control of fire are available for valuable equipment such as electronic data processing equipment and for the storage of fine arts or valuable papers and records. Many of these systems use Halon, an extinguishing agent that will not adversely affect humans. Carbon dioxide, dry chemical, or special water or inert gas systems may be considered for hazardous areas, including deep-frying equipment, paint spraying and dipping, and similar operations.

In all instances, fire protection equipment must be well maintained and inspection and testing procedures should be developed as part of the risk management program.

Separation

Separation or dividing valuable equipment, stock, or finished goods among several locations reduces the loss exposure. Masonry fire walls can be installed to divide a structure, or more than one geographic location can be considered.

A plumbing wholesaler contracted to erect a new warehouse. It was planned to install a double gypsum board wall to divide the warehouse into two areas. His Risk Management Consultant recommended that an 8-inch masonry wall be built in accordance with Insurance Services Office (ISO) standards. There were two reasons for this. First, a 10 percent credit in the fire rate would be allowed by the ISO. Second, since part of the area would be leased, the masonry wall would prevent easy entry into the owner's section. The gypsum wall would be subject to damage from forklift trucks, and would require continuing maintenance and earlier replacement than the masonry wall. As a further consideration, it was suggested that an Underwriters Laboratories' approved door frame be installed in the wall as it was being built. This would reduce future costs when the owner expanded to the entire building. The decision was promptly made to install the masonry wall.

Combination

The combination (or diversification) technique embodies the duplication of similar type units, normally at different locations, or increasing the number of exposure units.

Another example of combination is the duplication of valuable papers and records, dies, patterns, plans, or vital master tapes or media used in electronic data processing. The duplicates should be stored in fire-rated cabinets or vaults at another location. In the event of loss at one location, the duplicates could be obtained promptly and work could proceed with little delay.

RISK FINANCING

Risk financing utilizes the risk management techniques of risk retention or risk transfer to secure or maintain sufficient funds to pay for losses. Risk transfer includes insurance.

Retention

Whether a business is small or large, some level of retention should be considered:

a. Full retention (funded or unfunded) without insurance.
b. Purchase of insurance subject to a deductible.
c. Retention of losses other than those of a catastrophic nature, with excess insurance being purchased for large loss exposures.
d. Other means to fund losses such as the creation of a captive insurer.

Where losses can be predictably measured and their occurrence will not materially affect resources or assets, they should be retained. Such losses can be paid as an operating expense or from a special fund maintained for such a purpose. For example, breakage of glass or loss of small sums of cash may be assumed in full without insurance.

Collision losses for a large fleet of vehicles with a good loss experience are often retained or insured subject to a deductible. Deductibles are usually adopted where credits are given in insurance rates or where losses are small and frequent. In certain instances, insurance companies impose a mandatory deductible.

Thorough analysis of exposures may reveal opportunities for formal retention, if (1) there is a high degree of predictability of the occurrence of loss, (2) loss and expense loading under existing policies are considered to be excessive, or (3) necessary excess insurance to protect against catastrophic loss is available at reasonable cost. Funded retention may be selected if total cost is about equal to estimated premiums of an existing, fully insured program, simply because the insured will have use of the premium which otherwise would be paid to an insurer.

The risk retention decision is analogous to a person's reaction to pain. Each person's threshold of pain is different, not in accordance with physical size or financial well-being but through sensitive nerve-brain-anatomy relationships. The same applies to business. If financial loss is equated with pain, it is possible to evaluate the degree of pain a company can endure in order to measure how much and which risks should be retained.

Small businesses can endure some financial loss, but obviously to a lesser extent than larger businesses. The size of the business, however, is not the criterion; continuity of operations is. If a retained loss would have the effect of closing the business, that loss must be transferred. That "door closing" point can be used as a departure point to determine the tolerable level of financial loss. Other barometers or guidelines, such as capitalization mix and earnings, should be considered in making the decision.

If a given loss level is projected to have a serious impact on earnings, only a portion of that loss should be retained. There are some businesses that decide on a percentage of aftertax earnings as a retention level; for example, 5 percent of annual aftertax net income. Others decide on the basis of the amount of "uninsured loss" they are willing to show on the financial statement. Some determine retention levels as a function of a debt covenant requiring "allowable retention of loss" to be a percentage of current assets or working capital.

Unless there are internal funding programs for business-wide levels of risk retention, some divisions might elect lower retention levels because of their particular internal cash flow situation. Cyclical industries must wrestle with the degree of loss they can assume during the downturn of sales and profitability. There is no precise formula available, but general recommendations can be made. Minimum levels of loss retention should be set as a function of losses. Wherever severity and frequency are predictable, consideration should be given to some level of retention. The losses would either be expensed as they occur or funded through an accounting mechanism. Predictability can be based on a three-year average, discounting any large or unusual claim. Since predictable loss levels that are insured must include insurance companies' overhead, it may be less expensive to retain these losses if in-house funding can be arranged. Administrative cost may be less, and other factors such as employee or public relations should not be affected adversely. There is a cash flow advantage also as these losses are paid when they occur rather than being prepaid in the form of a premium.

As the loss scale moves from predictable and small losses to fortuitous, large, and infrequent losses, retention should be limited to a percentage of net income. At that point, businesses should be prepared to increase costs by staffing with competent claims and engineering professionals. Businesses should consider the cost of these services as part of loss retention expenses.

The higher the retention level, the greater the need for in-house engineering and safety expertise. A company starting a loss retention program should not embark upon a planned retention level above its historical severity and frequency pattern unless there is internal control proficiency established as part of the corporate structure (quality control, safety programs, or property conservation). If these internal controls are not available, they may be contracted for—either through an agent, a broker, an insurance consultant, or an insurance company. An insurer's claims and engineering service, without insurance, may be purchased under a "fronting" form of contract or a pure service arrangement.

As a business increases its self-insured retention and thereby exposes itself to a greater degree of financial loss, it becomes prudent to justify the retention level by probability studies based on industry experience, potential exposure, historical loss levels, interest earnings, assumptions, and trending assumptions. Comparisons should be made between expected losses (minus cash flow and interest benefits) and the probable cost of insuring the same losses.

Loss probability studies, whether conducted in-house or outside by a consultant (generally a preferable course because of greater objectivity from the outsider), should include statistical confidence levels of projections. Percentage of likely deviations from the "best case" and "worst case" should be identified. The science of predicting losses and related funding requirements is not exact, and consequently the data used must be examined to determine if it is complete and "credible" permitting its use as the basis for predicting probability of loss projections three to five years in the future.

Most corporations do not have accurate historical loss data. A data base of from three to five years should be developed *before* any sizable retention is contemplated. Yearly updating of the probability studies is required as is annual evaluation of actual results and comparison with original projections. A new acquisition or discontinuance of a product line can change the projections materially.

In large multi-divisional firms, discussions should be held regularly with division management for the purpose of reviewing loss projections. The Risk Manager should review the liability reserves with counsel to assess accurately any pending settlement of a claim. Whenever retention levels are funded in-house, annual cash projection requirements should be furnished the controller to insure that claims requirements are funded adequately.

Retention with outside funding

It is possible for a business to fund losses externally, either through a banking arrangement or a captive insurance company. In either case, the same planning and retention evaluation is necessary. The claims fund need only be kept at a prescribed level in order to pay expected claims and compensate the bank for administrative expenses. Some banks will pay interest on this type of loss fund, while others will credit the amount against compensating balance requirements on debt instruments.

Captive insurance companies

Captive companies require more expertise, not only in their management but also in developing retention levels and determining necessary capitalization and adequate reinsurance programs. The level of retained losses in a captive should be in excess of the predicted loss levels; otherwise the additional cost for incorporation and management fees is wasted. The majority of corporations that form captives retain losses in excess of predictable levels.

An extensive discussion of the advantages and disadvantages of a captive is beyond the scope of this chapter. However, there are definite advantages to a corporation that wishes to retain a large loss level. A working level might be described as the level or limit under which most losses usually occur before insurance coverages are involved. The amount will vary from $100 to $500 million depending on the nature and size of the business and loss exposures.

When a captive is formed, adequately capitalized (with a ratio of at least $1 in capital to $3 in premium), has a reasonably profitable class of the parent's business and the proper reinsurance program, including an aggregate stop limit, then, together with a professional probability study of loss forecasting, the captive is probably the most efficient method for funding risk. Through such a captive, underwriting profits and investment income will be generated from premiums paid. Should the captive be funded improperly, or should projections be inaccurate, the company will not derive any underwriting profit and might not be able to meet its obligations.

Every business's risk retention should not be funded through a captive. Rather, if high levels of retention are contemplated, a "feasibility study" should be made either by a broker or a consultant to determine if the expenditures for incorporation, capitalization, and management is worthwhile relative to the anticipated underwriting income, predictability of losses within retention level, and interest earnings.

There are serious federal taxation questions concerning the deductibility of premiums paid to a captive which should be reviewed. Many corporations, however, form captive subsidiaries despite the taxation uncertainties solely as a method of funding retained loss exposures, earning additional income, and having access to reinsurance.

Some captives sell insurance coverage to third parties in addition to accepting the parent's risks. This can be a source of profit for a well-run captive and an insurance market for other companies. At a minimum, loss retention at high levels will require the use of a service organization for either forecasting or administrative functions.

Service organizations for retention

What type of servicing organization should be considered? The size of an organization, measured in terms of sales, number of people, number of branches, or number of clients, is not indicative of the quality of either its products or services. Cases can be cited where the smaller service firm has excelled over seemingly insurmountable competition from larger competitors. This is not due alone to luck or competitive zeal. Success is attributable to the one asset that makes all corporations equal in the eyes of the consumer—the individuals operating the firm. This is especially true for insurance service organizations. As would any well-informed buyer, a business must prepare a list of the qualifications it seeks and examine the accomplishments of the service organizations in light of these qualifications.

Transfer: By contracts, leases, purchase orders, and similar agreements

It is often possible to transfer a loss exposure by mutual agreement to a third party, thereby eliminating the need for insurance. For example, agreements referred to as *indemnity* or *hold-harmless* agreements are noninsurance transfers. They are frequently found in contracts such as purchase orders, leases, and construction agreements. Noninsurance transfer agreements vary both in the degree of risk transferred and in style.

Assumed indemnity or hold-harmless agreements (Exhibit 1–E reflects a broad hold-harmless clause favoring the lessor) represent a serious exposure to any corporation, regardless of size, and should be reviewed very carefully by counsel as well as the Risk Manager. Unfortunately, businesses often accept risk transfers from other businesses without having appropriate insurance protection or prefunded capacity and without considering that this exposure could lead to bankruptcy if the indemnified loss is substantial. Noncontrolled indemnity acceptance is one of the most serious risk management failures.

Risk management should seek to uncover any contract of indemnity or assumption of liability that is excessive relative to probability and risk of loss. Ideally, a business should limit indemnification to its own "negligent acts."

In fact, a company with a controlled indemnity or hold-harmless program will establish procedures whereby *all* contracts entered into by *anyone* in the corporation are reviewed by risk management *and* counsel before they are signed.

If the contemplated contract's transfer of a loss exposure is considerably beyond existing liability insurance limits, the Risk Manager should recommend either a limitation clause or advise against signing the contract. Such a recommendation may be overruled for "business reasons," but that should not deter the Risk Manager from pointing out the danger in accepting the transfer of risk.

Other transfer agreements are quite specific as to particular areas of liability, either assumed or transferred. For example, one might deal only with workers' compensation, transportation loss, or property damage. Each category in any indemnity agreement must be reviewed carefully, and where possible, specific evidence of insurance coverage of the indemnification should be called for (with certificates of insurance exchanged between parties).

One of the most onerous types of indemnity agreements is that in which one party seeks to transfer the risk of loss for his own negligent activity. This type of agreement should be avoided whenever possible. Courts have disallowed such transfers (sometimes pursuant to legislation) when either economic coercion was used (refusing to deal unless the other party agrees to such a provision) or where a court believed that such an agreement was contrary to public policy. Nevertheless, most agreements involving transfer of risks, in fact, do prevail, providing they are specific in intent and reasonable in matter.

Additional insureds

Another noninsurance transfer is to be a named insured under another party's insurance coverage. Here, it is important that knowledge of the agreement be given to the insurance company prior to execution of the contract so the insurer will not deny a claim.

The inclusion of another financial interest as an additional named insured dilutes coverage for the insured under most liability programs. It may be preferable to have each party rely on its own program without exposing individual coverage to dilution and adverse loss experience not related to normal operations. In property insurance, however, it is quite common and sensible to have another party included, either as an additional insured or loss payee, if the other party has a financial interest in the property. Some examples are found in lease, construction, and consignment agreements.

Similarly, businesses sometimes request a "waiver of subrogation" which has the effect of precluding insurance companies from taking legal action against a negligent party named in the waiver. Again, this type of transfer must be communicated to the insurer.

Transfers through divestiture or acquisition

Transfer also may occur in an acquisition/divestiture situation. Since liability policies are generally written on an occurrence basis (the occurrence of the loss must take place during the policy period), it is not uncommon to have a divesting company assume all responsibility for losses occurring before the date of sale of their subsidiary or division, and the acquiring company assume liability for losses that occur after the date of sale. Insurance policies can be extended to cover these situations, providing the Risk Manager has an opportunity to review the transfer wording and make proper arrangements prior to divestiture.

If there is doubt whether a transfer of risk being proposed is covered under existing insurance programs, the proposed transfer contract should be reviewed by the insurance agent or broker and underwriter. When an exposure is to be transferred, each party should review the exposure transferred, the funding, and the insurance or noninsurance techniques available for the transfer to be certain there is mutual understanding of the risk transferred.

The use of limited noninsurance transfers

A modified transfer is an alternative in risk transfer situations. Here, one party indemnifies the other up to a specific limit. This type of contract is generally more acceptable to the transferee or indemnitee, as the liability is fixed, which will be reflected favorably in his insurance premium. The indemnitor or transferor also gains since by transferring some of his exposure he can arrange for insurance at a reduced cost to cover only exposures in excess of the limit.

Given the present upward trend in liability awards, a noninsurance transfer should be very carefully reviewed. A compromise transfer can be a solution to large risk transfer problems. In such an arrangement each party agrees to transfer the risk to an established account funded by both participants or supported by a Letter of Credit, from which any loss would be paid regardless of whose negligence is involved.

These are but a few ways to utilize noninsurance transfer.

Transfer: By the purchase of insurance

After a business has analyzed its exposures to loss, evaluated appropriate levels of retention, initiated loss control procedures, selected service programs which complement self-retained coverage, and transferred exposures where possible under noninsurance contracts, there remains the transfer of remaining exposures to an insurance company. This final stage, often the least rewarding in terms of cost control, can be the single and most important decision a Risk Manager makes.

The selection of an insurance company is generally based on many factors—price, reputation, service capacity, claims ability, engineering, loss prevention; all enter into the equation. Premium expense relative to exposures transferred does have a dominant role in the selection process. However, the smaller the premium a company pays, the less selective it can be and the more dependent it will be on insurance brokers to market and place insurance coverages. Nonetheless, good and accurate information can help to reduce insurance costs. Also, selection of the appropriate type of insurance is important to cost control.

In considering property damage insurance, a comparison should be made between replacement cost and actual cash value forms. Advantages and disadvantages of each must be weighed since replacement cost coverage eliminates depreciation if damaged property is restored. The best means for establishing such values is a professional appraisal for insurance purposes—not for market or sales purposes.

Proper job description classification of all workers and correct classification of liability exposures is essential to assure the lowest premiums and broadest liability coverages.

Claim adjustments

Adjustment of losses may be the most important service received from an insurer. When and if a loss occurs, it is important to have clear procedures for prompt settlement and restoration. Good risk management plans for such a contingency. Reputable insurance companies, whether stock, mutual, or reciprocal, are anxious to cooperate:

> Generally speaking, all good insurance companies want the adjustment of a loss claim completed without any delay. They want satisfied policyholders and continued patronage. This requires, however, that policies be originally written in a manner which will fully protect a policyholder's interest. How policies are written before the loss determines how they will pay after the loss. Satisfy yourself before a loss that your policies will actually provide the protection you expect after a loss.
>
> Many businessmen fail to give their property damage insurance policies any serious consideration—until after a loss occurs. This is a

serious mistake. The insurance service they receive before a property loss, such as fire, is of even greater importance than the adjustment service after the fire. Such adjustment must obviously be made on the actual provisions of the policy contract as previously written.

That is why it is so important that the original policy forms be properly worded with adequate amounts of insurance under the policy conditions, in order that a satisfactory adjustment will be possible.

Expert precautionary service and an intimate knowledge of the specific requirements from the insurance policy standpoint are necessary in order to give the best possible coverage.

It is only when a loss occurs that the great value of adequate protection, clear and concise wording and proper coverage under your insurance policies becomes wholly apparent.

You can feel secure if you know that expert care and knowledge have gone into the preparation of your policies, and that no effort has been spared to provide the most satisfactory protection.

Your interest should come first and there should be no conflicting problems to work against the equitable and prompt settlement of your claim.

Such a settlement should be further assured by the financial responsibility of your insurance carrier. There should be ample funds available for the exclusive payment of claims, and also an established reputation for satisfactory loss payments.

Your insurance is too important to be handled in any haphazard manner, or by those who are not qualified by experience and technical knowledge to look after your interest efficiently.[4]

Buying insurance from direct writers

The larger the exposure transferred the easier it is for an insured to deal directly with an underwriter. Some companies may have sufficient in-house expertise to deal effectively with "direct writers" (companies that do not engage the services of brokers or agents). Theoretically, insurance costs should be less when using a direct writer because there are no agent or broker commissions paid. The savings, however, may prove illusory when it comes to negotiating a claim without the assistance of a broker.

The choice between a direct writer and an agency company must be viewed in the context of the adequacy of in-house expertise. Some of the large accounts use brokerage companies for a portion of their insurance program simply for the purpose of keeping abreast of developments in the insurance marketplace.

THE INSURANCE MARKETS

The market for unique or special risks is sometimes limited to a few insurers. Over the years, many special risks have been written at

Lloyd's of London where capacity to insure virtually every type of risk seemed to be available (at a price). In the very recent past, the American market has provided new and flexible capacity, and today practically any risk can be placed domestically.

The property and liability insurance business consists of four separate markets: (1) property, (2) casualty, (3) marine, and (4) miscellaneous. Another classification is (1) primary, (2) excess, (3) surplus lines, and (4) reinsurance. Each line involves its own underwriting expertise and marketing techniques.

Property insurance

A direct market exists in the property insurance market which does not require a broker nor a minimum premium size, the so-called highly protected risks (HPR). HPRs require sprinkler protection and evidence of a superior facility from a fire protection standpoint. The rates for this HPR protection are the lowest available, due to the low probability of loss as compared with a "nonengineered" facility.

Some property insurance companies write HPR insurance business through brokerage firms. Even with the commission added to the preferred rates, the rates are still lower than non-HPR rates, and it gives the businessman brokerage claims expertise in the event of a difficult claim. For certain types of property losses, such as business interruption, smaller businesses without insurance departments may be better off with their property coverage written through brokers.

Casualty insurance

Casualty insurance includes automobile, all types of liability, and workers' compensation insurance. Most casualty companies deal through brokers, although some are direct writers.

Casualty companies have unique liability insurance underwriting practices; and, consequently, smaller businesses should use brokers or consultants who can package the insured's exposure to reduce premiums and broaden coverage. This is especially true when dealing with excess underwriters where the average insured or insurance manager is out of his element. The excess and reinsurance markets require a degree of expertise not often found in corporate insurance departments.

Marine insurance

Marine companies truly are specialists, handling some of the largest values and risks in the world. With rare exception, marine companies do not deal with the public. Marine markets, because of their international exposure, tend to be less structured in underwriting and premium and rating practices. The market consists of *wet marine*, covering most waterborne exposures, and *dry marine*, covering inland transit, transportation, and communication facilities. The marine insurance market is dependent on brokers and agents as a consequence of the unique policy language and claim settlement procedures. Rates are almost entirely a function of loss experience and the shipping exposures.

Of special importance in the selection of a marine insurance company is the claims representative surveyor. A prospective insured should review the surveyor list with his broker and evaluate the surveyor's ability to service the insured's account as well as the insurer's claims payment reputation.

In recent years, marine companies insuring cargo shipments have offered engineering services for packaging and shipping to effect better loss control. Before selecting a marine company, review their loss control procedures since this factor could reduce losses and future premiums substantially.

Miscellaneous insurance

The miscellaneous markets generally provide specialty coverage through one or several insurers. Policy form, price, and competition are restricted. Here, adequate brokerage support is essential.

Aviation liability, nuclear exposures, Employee Retirement Income Security Act (ERISA) liability, directors' and officers' liability, and political and kidnapping risks are examples of specialty coverages, with only a few insurance companies willing to compete for business. The reason for the limited market is high severity exposures without predictable loss trends to set premium levels. With the possible exception of aviation, industry loss statistics are limited. As a result, premium development becomes an exercise in pre-loss exposure evaluation, requiring detailed questionnaires designed to inform the underwriter as to the probable loss potential of the prospective insured.

Premium negotiations and potential loss adjustments require a great deal of expertise and knowledge of the marketplace and a broker versed in these critical areas should be selected before any of the specialty coverages is placed.

RATING

A clear understanding of various rating processes is helpful for risk managers.

Changes in conditions or experience will cause changes in rates which, of course, affect the cost of insurance. Loss control will produce a savings in premium, both in the short run and in the long run.

Rapid strides in rating methods have been made in recent years, particularly in the property damage and automotive areas. The computer age has brought about more accurate procedures for establishing actuarial data for employee benefit programs used to determine rates and premiums.

A number of "bureaus" are in existence for the purpose of establishing insurance rates, primarily with regard to property damage and liability insurance. In 1971, six national rating bureaus merged into a single organization known as the Insurance Services Office (ISO). This rating organization has developed a uniform rating plan for property damage insurance adopted by at least 38 states. It has expanded its program to include automobile rating and comprehensive general liability rating.

The National Council on Compensation Insurance is a national workers' compensation rating organization operating in most of the United States. Some of the states have established their own rating plans. Organizations and businesses within states having a state workers' compensation fund must obtain their insurance from the state funds.

There are no rating bureaus for life, accident, health, and disability insurance. However, virtually all companies follow the same basic principles and make extensive use of actuarial tables or loss experience data which have been developed for such purposes. Rating methods will be discussed in later chapters.

SELECTING A BROKER

In making the decision to use the services of a broker, the business must use many of the criteria for selection of insurance companies. However, since the services of agents and brokers do not include the payment of losses, the selection process must concentrate on "the people side" of the broker organization. Questions to be answered include:

1. Are the individuals involved in the business able to represent the insured adequately to the underwriter?
2. Do they have the essential experience to handle a "delicate" loss?
3. Are their regional offices staffed sufficiently to service the business's subsidiaries?
4. Who will be assigned to the account?
5. Will they do the job in marketing, service, claims, and engineering?

6. Do they have the professional credentials?
7. Is the broker worth the cost?

Disregard titles; vice presidents in brokerage houses are commonplace, and often those with up-to-date market knowledge are the non-vice presidents, the troopers in the field who handle the accounts.

There is no "best method." Businesses should interview the brokerage personnel who will be assigned to the account as they would a prospective employee. Generally, insurance brokers know their way around insurance markets and are paid for their ability to negotiate on behalf of their clients.

It may be that the commission paid (normally a percentage of premium) is out of proportion to the actual services comtemplated. Under such circumstances, a reduced commission may be negotiated or a fixed fee agreed on. Many brokers, large and small, are willing to accept a fixed-fee arrangement.

A fixed fee allows the broker to be totally objective in recommending additional insurance protection. It is usually negotiated every year and based on the past year's activity and expected future costs. Some brokers resist the fee concept because in inflationary periods when insurance needs and premiums rise, the fee does not rise proportionately as would a commission.

CONCLUSION

Recently an executive in charge of an insurance company's claim and loss prevention departments retired. He was asked to distill his many years of experience into one single all-important recommendation which would have the widest applicability to the greatest number of property owners. He stated:

> Probably the strongest loss control measure available to anyone in business is genuine, effective commitment of top management to a real interest in Loss Control, both property conservation and employee protection. There is no substitute for such a positive control program. All the details fall into place when it is consistently implemented.[5]

Such commitment should apply to all phases of risk management to assure its success. However, risk management cannot be a one-time venture but must be a continuing process. The Risk Manager or Risk Management Consultant must be continually aware of changes in business operations, as well as changes in the insurance market, both as to coverages and to premiums. Risk control must have the backing of executive management over the long term and all activities carefully watched as results affect future insurance premiums and the availability of insurance.

An example of such alertness is the recent experience of a small manufacturer. A Risk Management Consultant had made a study of the company and recommended a number of changes in the insurance program. A delay had occurred in implementing this plan. Later, the consultant was called to meet with the agent and owner to review the premiums and coverages. It was learned the owner had contracted the work of assembling a special machine to an outside firm. The owner only did minor finishing work. In view of this, the Risk Management Consultant recommended the purchase of contingent business interruption insurance. But more importantly, this closed a gap in the insurance program and eliminated a possible loss exposure. The consultant then suggested that the contractor do the entire work on the machine. This was accomplished. As an expected result, the product liability basic rate was reduced to 10 percent of the previous premium since the owner was no longer a manufacturer. In addition, risk control was implemented with the elimination of the manufacturing operation.

The sophisticated use of risk management techniques requires expertise in all risk management areas. Most smaller firms do not have this expertise in-house and must acquire these services from brokers, agents, consultants, or engineering and safety organizations. Larger firms can develop staffs to provide expertise and often succeed in eliminating some middleman costs.

The risk management and insurance environment is dynamic. Business, in order to survive in this setting, must be ever alert to the new and changing exposures as well as to alternative techniques for the treatment of these exposures. The risk management job is never completed—it is a never-ending process.

NOTES

1. Dr. George L. Head, Ph.D., CPCU, CLU, *The Risk Management Process* (New York: The Risk and Insurance Management Society, Inc., 1978), p. 53.

2. Reprinted from the April 30, 1979, issue of *The Journal of Commerce.*

3. Ibid.

4. Reprinted by permission of Warner Insurance Company, Chicago, Illinois, 1970.

5. Reprinted by permission of Claude M. Westerman.

Exhibit 1–A
CITRUS COOPERATIVE OPERATIONS

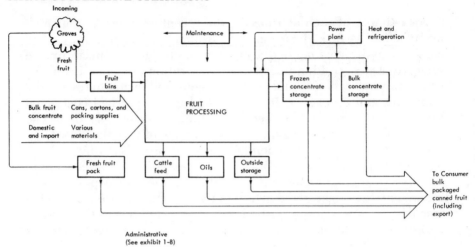

Exhibit 1–B
CITRUS COOPERATIVE OPERATIONS

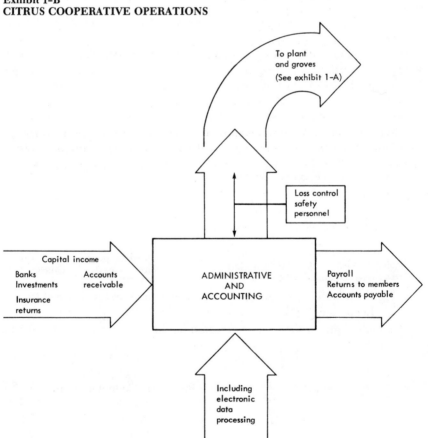

Exhibit 1–C
SAFETY MEMO

TO: Drivers of company vehicles
FROM: C. E. Hiden, Jr.

RE: Safe driving

INATTENTION

Two Hands on the Wheel

Too many drivers ignore a basic defensive driving fundamental of "two hands on the wheel." Here are a few examples of what results:

- □ Reaching for cough drops .... a head-on
- □ Shuffling papers .... into ditch
- □ Reaching for cigarette lighter .... right-angle collision
- □ Dropped lighted cigarette on seat .... right-angle collision
- □ Trying to open ashtray .... another rear-ender
- □ Searching for match .... bang, bang
- □ Thumbing through notes for next stop ..... hit parked car

And, so it goes.

Driving is a Full-Time Job

Just as you should keep two hands on the wheel, also have your mind on driving at all times—every second. Good driving—safe driving—requires constant attention and complete concentration. Here are a few examples of accidents caused by split-second inattention:

- □ Looking for street address .... wham at intersection
- □ Thinking about next call .... slid into car in front
- □ Checking house numbers .... hit car backing out of drive
- □ Bee in vehicle .... zingo, off the road

Increase attention and reduce the risk of an accident by practicing the two we've been talking about:

1. Keep both hands on the steering wheel at all times.
2. Keep your mind on your driving.

Remember, pride, prestige, *profits,* and public relations are influenced by "how" you drive—*everytime you drive.*

Courtesy of Capitol Milk
Producers Cooperative, Inc.

Exhibit 1-D
SAFETY MEMO

TO: All stores
FROM: C. E. Hiden, Jr.

ROBBERY PRECAUTIONS

Robberies continue to be a problem to many retail businesses, and are a major concern because of the threat to our employees' personal safety. Listed below are some guidelines which should be followed by store employees to further reduce the robberies in our stores.

1. Watch for suspicious automobiles parked on the parking lot or near the store for long periods of time.
2. Keep as little money as possible in the register.
3. No guns in the store—it is against our company policy, and could result in further harm.
4. Greet every customer who comes into the store.
5. If a customer lingers long in the store—ask if you can be of assistance.
6. Don't block the view of the cash register area—place signs so it can be seen from outside.
7. If you're alone with a suspicious customer, get out from behind the cash register.
8. Keep store looking safe and active.

What to do if robbery occurs:

1. Let robber know if someone is in back room—dangerous if robber is surprised.
2. Don't argue or fight with the robber—do what he says!
3. Don't lie to robbers about the fake security devices.
4. Observe as much of the robber as you can. An accurate description of the robber is most helpful to the police. Enclosed is a copy of a form they have developed. Please review this with all employees and post where it is readily available if needed.
5. Try to get description of any vehicle used by robber.
6. Call police immediately—then the Store Supervisor.
7. Do not reveal or estimate amount of money lost.

Courtesy of Capitol Milk
Producers Cooperative, Inc.

Exhibit 1-E
EXAMPLE OF BROAD HOLD-HARMLESS CLAUSE

Lessee shall protect, defend, *indemnify, and save harmless* the Lessor from and against any and all claims, demands, and causes of action of any nature whatsoever, for injury to or death of persons, or loss of or damage to property occurring on the premises or in any manner growing out of or connected with Lessee's use and occupancy of the premises, whether or not such injury, death, loss, or damage is caused or contributed to by the negligence of Lessor or is deemed the responsibility of Lessor by operation of law.

Lessee hereby assumes all duties and obligations of an Owner and Lessor with relation to the premises and the use and manner of use thereof, so that no matter from what source arising, if anything shall be ordered or required to be done on, upon or about the premises, the building and improvements thereon, or the appurtenances, equipment, appliances, utilities, or conveniences thereof, all shall be done and fulfilled at the expense and as the responsibility of the Lessee, without expense, liability, or obligation to or on Lessor.

CHAPTER 2

RISK MANAGEMENT
AND OBTAINING
RISK MANAGEMENT SERVICES

WHEN TO HIRE A CONSULTANT

RISK MANAGEMENT TECHNIQUES

HOW TO USE A CONSULTANT

"CONSULTING FIRMS FILL NEEDS—
FOR A PRICE"

DIRECTORY OF FIRMS

Peter R. Kensicki, D.B.A., CLU, CPCU
Director of Producer Education
American Institute for Property and Liability Underwriters, Inc.
Malvern, Pennsylvania

Peter R. Kensicki is Director of Producer Education for the American Institute for Property and Liability Underwriters and the Insurance Institute of America. He received his BBA at the University of Cincinnati (1966), M. Ins. (1968), and Doctor of Business Administration (1972) from Georgia State University. He has received three insurance professional designations: CLU (1972), FLMI (1977), and CPCU (1980). Dr. Kensicki has been an insurance agent, insurance regulator, and director of the first statewide consumer program for the state of Georgia. He also was Assistant Professor of Finance at Ohio University and Assistant Vice President for The Cincinnati Insurance Company. He has published many articles in academic journals and the trade press. He has general editor responsibilities for a series of three textbooks to be published by the Insurance Institute of America and is a co-author of two of the texts.

While this Handbook will answer many of the reader's questions concerning insurance and risk management, it is not intended to be a substitute for expert advice focused on the specific situation and needs of an individual business. Consequently, even with a thorough understanding of the concepts outlined in this book, it still will be necessary for an individual businessman to discuss his specific risk management needs with an expert. If these needs extend only to insuring his business, he need look no further than his broker or agent.

WHEN TO HIRE A CONSULTANT

On the other hand, if a businessman is at all interested in a more sophisticated approach to the resolution of his risk management problems, he should consider the employment of a Risk Management Consultant. There are at least three situations in which a Risk Management Consultant should be considered:

1. Where there is no in-house risk management capability but the business does have sufficient assets to make the use of risk management techniques other than insurance desirable.
2. When a firm has a risk management capability but needs a periodic "objective" audit of its risk management program.
3. Where a firm wishes to enter into sophisticated and complicated loss control or risk transfer arrangements.

RISK MANAGEMENT TECHNIQUES

Risk management techniques fall into two areas: loss control and loss financing.

Loss control measures are designed to prevent or minimize losses. Specifically, these measures include:

☐ Risk avoidance to eliminate the possibility of loss.
☐ Loss prevention to reduce the probability of loss.
☐ Loss reduction to reduce the severity of loss.
☐ Segregation to reduce the concentration of assets exposed to loss.
☐ Noninsurance transfers to eliminate *responsibility* for loss.

Loss financing is the generic term used to describe those ways in which a business may finance losses through some form of retention or transfer. Retention financing techniques include:

☐ Expensing losses—meeting losses from current operational income.

☐ Establishing funded or unfunded reserves—an accounting technique to charge losses against the reserve much like a Reserve for Bad Debts account.

☐ Borrowing—establishing lines of credit to meet loss payment requirements.

☐ Setting up a captive insurer as a wholly owned subsidiary—an option which should be considered only by large corporations.

☐ Transferring as a means of loss financing. This includes:

     ☐ Traditional insurance purchase which transfers this risk to insurers.

     ☐ Noninsurance transfer which is using a noninsurer, such as party to a contract, to accept responsibility through indemnification for losses.

For many smaller businesses, the insurance transfer loss financing technique is the most economical, but insurance is only one of an array of risk management techniques. As the business grows, other loss financing techniques may make sense and should be considered. However, in the area of loss control, size of a business is no barrier to implementation. The smallest firm can and should exercise some loss control management. As would be expected, the complexity of loss control grows with the size of the firm. The greater the complexity the greater the desirability of retaining a Risk Management Consultant.

HOW TO USE A CONSULTANT

But which Risk Management Consultant? Consultants are specialists and, in fact, hold themselves out as professionals. They should be employed as any professional. At the outset, the businessman should give the consultant a statement of the services which the consultant is to provide. (This Handbook will enable the businessman to identify in a general way what he wants from the Risk Management Consultant.)

It is not enough to have a firm with a good reputation. Find out who within the firm will perform your work. Will it be a principal or a junior associate? Whoever will be in charge of your work should be interviewed to establish his level of expertise, his ability to meet your time parameters for completion of the work, and his capability to interact effectively with your organization.

Most desirably, the Risk Management Consultant you will employ will be able to service your company as it grows. Therefore, it is important to establish that the capabilities of the Risk Management Consultant extend beyond your present needs. For example, would the Risk Management Consultant be able to organize a captive when you have grown to sufficient size to justify consideration of a captive? Will other services provided by the Risk Management Consultant provide a conflict of interest with his risk management services? In other words, does he sell the insurance he recommends? In the final analysis, if you are sufficiently concerned with having an effective risk management program to hire a consultant, pick the best. In any event, monitor the consultant's progress and costs.

With this as background we direct your attention to two articles from *Business Insurance* reprinted here.

Business Insurance is a national news weekly devoted to loss prevention, risk financing, and employee benefit management. The first article, "Consulting Firms Fill Needs—for a Price," discusses the wide range of risk management services available. These extend from exposure indemnification to sophisticated self-insurance programs employing captive insurers. The second article, "52 Risk Consultants List Their Services," contains a *representative* listing of risk management consulting firms, their addresses, telephone numbers, description of the services they provide, and in most cases the fee structure followed. It should be emphasized that the firms listed in the article are fine firms. There are, however, other firms throughout the country of comparable ability, many of which specialize in a particular facet of insurance consultation, who do not appear on the list. One such specialty firm, Clement Associates, Inc. of Washington, D.C., has developed a unique multi-disciplinary approach to assessing risks which is used by many of the present markets offering environmental impairment liability insurance (see Chapter 31).

CONSULTING FIRMS FILL NEEDS—FOR A PRICE*

LOS ANGELES—At $50 to $200 an hour, risk management consulting doesn't come cheap.

Hourly rates vary from $50 to $200 with most companies charging $75 to $100. Daily charges range from $150 to $750, and a single job can cost as much as $50,000 or more. Some firms also bill clerical services separately.

Finding the best value for your consultant dollar is no easy chore. Almost all firms have a mix of clients on retainers and those charged on an hourly basis. Some, such as Insurance Consulting Associates of Teaneck, N.J., have all retainer clients, while others, such as the insurance consulting department of Towers Perrin Forster & Crosby, work strictly on a fee-for-service basis.

Many consultants are reluctant to discuss hourly fees, insisting they are misleading. Certainly it is useless to compare fees without knowing how much time the firms think will be required to do a job. Most consultants specify a range of high and low estimates in advance. Many will even guaran-

---

* This story is based on reporting by Rhonda L. Rundle and Stuart Emmrich. It was written by Ms. Rundle.

tee the high figure as a maximum cost to the client, absorbing cost overruns as long as the scope of the assignment is not enlarged.

Hennessy & York work exclusively on a contingency basis with major U.S. corporations. There are no upfront fees or expenses. They charge 50 percent of the actual cost savings to the client achieved through their services, calculated annually for a two-year term.

One other consulting firm, RIMCO Risk Management Consultants in Dallas, mentions that it sometimes works on a contingency fee basis.

But consultants' fees don't seem to curtail demand for their services. Corporate America, trying to plug the insurance/loss cost drain, keeps turning to consultants.

Risk management consulting firms are so flush with success that their biggest beef is the shortage of consultant talent for hire to lighten their loads and boost their bottom lines.

"Everybody is looking for someone 25 years old with 50 years of experience," quips Frank Alderson, executive vp of Insurance Audit & Inspection Co. in Indianapolis.

Growth may be limited by the personnel problem, but the top firms eager to expand report a healthy 15 percent to 20 percent rise in revenues during 1979. Some smaller, newly formed companies are celebrating heavy income increases of 100 percent a year and more.

And they predict boom times ahead. Eventually consultants will be retained like outside CPA firms to routinely and periodically audit a company's risk management program, contends William Peet, president of William Peet Co. in St. Paul.

The greatest source of real growth seems to be more business from existing accounts, agree most of the more than 50 consultants surveyed by *Business Insurance*. New firms are springing up too, as ambitious consultants break away from established companies to start their own.

Alternative risk funding vehicles, including self-insurance, captive insurance companies, and sophisticated cash-flow plans, are a tremendous boon to consultants because they create demand for unbiased counsel and expertise in lieu of insurance salesmanship.

"Self-insurance is growing by leaps and bounds," enthuses Ray Rich, chairman of Corporate Policyholders Counsel. That means clients' access to risk management is no longer through a broker or insurer but through a consultant, he explains.

Consultants say their clients are more sophisticated than ever before. Eager beavers demand feasibility studies for state-of-the-art risk funding, even when self-insurance or a captive is really not the way to go. Some risk managers and corporate insurance buyers may not know a paid-loss retro from a compensating balance, but they've heard the lingo and they want to learn more.

To be sure, the bread-and-butter services of risk management consultants are still exposure identification, portfolio auditing, and program recommendations. Many firms, however, offer much more than advice. They don't sell insurance, but they do provide claims administration, computer loss reporting, and other services traditionally piggybacked on insurance.

Captive management specialists, such as Chanslor Risk Management in Texas and Risk Treatment Services in Colorado, literally perform as insurance companies, providing full administration and accounting to their corporate customers.

This tendency toward marketing services could begin to blur previous distinctions between independent and affiliated consultants, vigorously promoted by the Institute of Risk Management Consultants. Many firms that do not sell insurance may sell services—and that gives them a real stake in the fate of their recommendations.

The independent versus affiliated controversy still burns brightly, however. When asked what the most important criteria should be for selecting a consultant, nearly every independent consultant declared that the commercial buyer must retain an unbiased, disinterested adviser.

"Some people are misled into thinking that a broker can do what a consultant does," said Bernard Salwen of S. B. Ackerman Associates of New York. "Even if a broker says he will not place insurance and that is written into the contract, there is still going to be subtle pressure from insurers, especially if he is dealing with an important client."

Keith Kakacek at RIMCO Risk Management Consultants put it even more strongly: unless insurance is sold, the broker is either working for free or overcharging other paying clients, he contended.

"The critical factor is how well the services are provided, regardless of where they come from," argues Charles L. Ruoff, senior vp at the Continental Insurance Co., which is mobilizing a major marketing effort to attract more clients to its risk-related services division.

Insurers and big brokerage firms like Marsh & McLennan and Alexander & Alexander are bolstered by a formidable staff of technical consultants and assistants, as well as other financial resources.

"We are out there to do the best job possible for our clients and we do it without any bias," insists Richard Lapham, senior vp of Commercial Union Risk Management Inc. an affiliate of Commercial Union Assurance Co. "I don't think we get any pressure, subtle or otherwise," he added.

The independent consulting firms range in size from EBASCO Risk Management Consultants Inc. in New York with 105 consultants to several one-man operations, sometimes former risk managers, brokers, or agents working out their own homes.

Consultants with smaller staffs stress their close personal contacts with clients, creating long-term relations and steadfast confidence. Some individual consultants could be described as multi-client risk managers, since they fulfill that function on a part-time basis for two or more companies.

Larger firms such as The Wyatt Co. tout their team approach, giving a customer access to a wide range of staff specialists trained to handle specific problems in their field. If a client corporation grows through diverse external acquisitions, for example, its loss exposures may change rapidly. Even a sophisticated risk manager may desperately need advice from such a consultant.

Although most consulting firms prefer not to be pegged as specialists in a particular risk exposure or by type of business activity, a few deliberately narrow their clientele.

A Louisiana company, Insurance Analysis Inc., specializes in consulting with clients in the oil industry.

Risk Sciences Group Inc. programs a client's loss history, banks it in a computer, and then runs the data through different loss forecasting models. Besides forecasting future losses, the system facilitates comparison of a wide variety of alternative funding models. The only other companies offering these services are Marsh & McLennan and Alexander & Alexander's Anistics division, says Joseph A. Destein, president of the young Santa Monica, Calif.-based company.

DIRECTORY OF FIRMS: 52 RISK CONSULTANTS LIST THEIR SERVICES*

A

S. B. Ackerman Associates
605 Third Ave., New York, N.Y. 10016; 212-599-1717

With offices in New York, Philadelphia, and Pittsburgh, Ackerman's staff of 25 consultants and 10 support personnel last year consulted for about 100 firms, 5 percent to 10 percent of which were in the Fortune 1,000, said senior managing partner Bernard Salwen.

Almost 95 percent of the clients pay an annual retainer, which can run from $2,000 to $200,000, while others pay hourly fees of $30 to $150. Mr. Salwen declined to release the company's revenue figures for 1979.

Although the firm provides a wide range of services and its clients cover various industries, Mr. Salwen said most people probably think of Ackerman in terms of its work in the medical malpractice area. "We are the acknowledged best in malpractice," Mr. Salwen said. "In fact, other consultants have referred clients to us in that area." The firm is also heavily into providing services to municipalities and schools.

J. H. Albert International Insurance Advisers Inc.
161 Highland Ave., Needham Heights, Mass. 02194; 617-449-2866

With a staff of 11—seven consultants and four support personnel—this firm services about 100 clients on retainer and last year completed 15 to 20 projects for additional clients, said assistant vp Frederic Shultz.

Fees range from $3,000 to $50,000 per client, with an average customer paying $4,000 to $10,000, Mr. Shultz said. He estimated last year's revenues at about $700,000.

Although 12 years old, this firm has experienced sudden growth in the past few months. Two junior consultants were just hired upon graduation from the

---

* This directory is based on interviews with the consultants conducted by *Business Insurance* associate editors Stuart Emmrich and Rhonda L. Rundle.

Using the membership rosters of the two consultants' societies as a starting point (Institute of Risk Management Consultants and Insurance Consultants Society), *BI* tried to make the listing as complete as possible. Omissions may indicate unresponsiveness from a few consultants contacted.

Independent consultants—those who are not affiliated with any company that brokers or sells insurance or insurance-related services—are listed first, alphabetically. Consultants affiliated with brokers, insurers, or other sellers of services are listed at the end of the independent consultants directory.

Reprinted with permission, *Business Insurance*, February 18, 1980.

University of Georgia and one more junior consultant is expected to join the staff within the next few weeks, Mr. Shultz said.

Aldrich & Cox. Inc.
274 Delaware Ave., Buffalo, N.Y. 14120; 716-856-2991

Nine consultants and four support staff last year serviced approximately 100 clients, almost 95 percent of which contracted with Aldrich & Cox on a retainer basis.

All fees are hourly and are determined by the type of services rendered, president Herbert Cox explained. For management of a client's entire risk management program, the company charges $40 an hour. It charges $50 an hour for providing outside services to a company's insurance manager, $60 an hour for pure consulting work, and $70 an hour for those clients who purchase project-by-project services.

The firm recently added a full-time consultant who specializes in employee benefits, Mr. Cox said.

All Risk Ltd.
294 Broad St., Red Bank, N.J. 07701; 201-741-3450

This one-consultant firm specializes in providing insurance "second opinions" to local retailers and manufacturers in a semirural county on the outskirts of New York City. Hubert Farrow, president, is also experienced at preparing insurance specifications.

His list of about 20 clients includes several public entities and some small firms for which he supervises risk management. He works with a research assistant and a medical claims assistant. Although most of Mr. Farrow's clients are based within a 50-mile radius of his home, he "would just as soon go farther away."

Depending on the job, Mr. Farrow charges either an hourly fee of $50 or a flat fee for the assignment. A trip to a client's office or place of business costs a minimum of $250.

B

D. A. Betterley Risk Consultants
Worcester Plaza, 446 Main St., Worcester, Mass. 01608; 617-754-1704

About 40 percent of last year's 80 clients kept this staff of six—four consultants and two support personnel—on retainer contracts. Most were small and medium-sized companies with sales of $25 million to $100 million a year, said Richard Betterley, vp and principal consultant. The firm also has a large number of clients in the public sector—school districts, municipalities, and hospitals.

Fees are hourly—$85 for a senior consultant, $60 for a principal consultant, $50 for a staff consultant, and $35 for a risk analyst, Mr. Betterly said, adding that an average fee runs about $400 per job. He declined to release revenue figures for last year.

Like other broad-based consulting firms. Betterley reviews risk management programs and has recently strengthened its data management capabilities, offering clients the option of setting up a data processing system to handle payment of claims. Heading the firm is Delbert A. Betterley.

George Betterley Consulting Group
200 Clarendon St., Boston, Mass. 02116; 617-367-4300

Sparked by an annual growth rate of 25 percent to 33 percent during the last few years, according to executive vp Charles Tagman Jr., this firm has added four new consultants in the past two years and now employs eight full-time consultants and five support staffers. The firm services about 100 clients, one fourth of which are among the Fortune 1,000.

All fees are charged on an hourly basis, ranging from $40 to $100 an hour, depending on the expertise of the consultant. Although 65 to 70 of the clients contract for services on an annual basis, they do not pay a flat retainer fee. Instead, the firm tries to estimate how much work will need to be done and gives an estimate of what the charges might run, Mr. Tagman said. "A normal project for us might run about $3,000, although it might cost a Fortune 500 company between $30,000 and $60,000 for a full risk management audit." Revenues last year ran in the "high six figures," Mr. Tagman said.

Clients of this Boston firm represent the paper industry and industrial concerns. Few municipalities are serviced by the company. Principal is George M. Betterley.

Blades & Macaulay
2444 Morris Ave., Union, N.J. 07083; 201-687-3735

Blades & Macaulay performs risk management audits and studies of related problems including identification of exposures and operational hazards. "We are not pension consultants," points out John J. Crout, one of three partners and senior consultants.

The 57-year-old company surveys eight to 10 corporations annually. Another 20 clients are on retainer, and the firm also takes on two or three special risk management assignments every year.

Fortune 500 companies pay $20,000 to $35,000 for a full-scale survey depending on the scope of the job. Medium-sized entities pay $5,000 to $12,000, and a small account with just one location might be charged $2,500 to $3,500. Audit clients are charged on a fixed flat fee that represents Blades & Macaulay's estimate of their cost to do the work, Mr. Crout reports.

T. E. Brennan Co.
250 E. Wisconsin Ave., Suite 1503, Milwaukee, Wis. 53202; 414-271-2232

T. E. Brennan Co. consults on property and casualty exposures with special expertise in property loss adjustment and business interruption counseling. It does not advise clients regarding their employee benefit programs.

Company president John Hayes estimates the firm's client list at more than 200, including several Fortune 500 companies. Nine staff consultants include an attorney, fire protection engineer and CPA. They work nationwide out of

Milwaukee and a recently opened Chicago office. The firm has also added a word processing system for internal use.

Nearly 95 percent of T. E. Brennan's clients use the consulting firm on a continual basis, but none is billed on retainer. Hourly fees vary from $50 to $85, depending on the consultant.

Founded in 1895, T. E. Brennan Co. says it is the oldest insurance consulting firm in the country.

Larry W. Buck & Associates
4801 Woodway, Suite 300E, Houston, Tex. 77056; 713-961-4223

This one-consultant firm acts as risk manager for about 20 small and medium-sized companies that don't employ their own. Larry W. Buck, president, says he usually works directly with an owner, president, or chief financial officer.

Most of his clients are based in the Houston market area and run the full gamut of commercial activities including wholesale distribution, real estate development, architectural contracting, and manufacturing as well as government. Mr. Buck's hourly fee is $100 plus expenses.

C

Corporate Policyholders Counsel
20 N. Wacker Dr., Chicago, Ill. 60606; 312-372-8225

This 82-year-old company uses a team approach, combining the expertise of three or four consultants on a job. An account supervisor heads up each project, but other consultants are available to handle client queries.

Corporate Policyholders Counsel lists approximately 100 clients, a quarter of which are Fortune 1,000 companies. Nine staff consultants advise on the full range of property, casualty, and employee benefit programs. They do not provide engineering or loss prevention counseling, however.

After a proposal is written, the firm quotes a probable cost range, including a maximum figure. "We'll generally abide by our maximum," says Ray Rich, chairman. Senior consultants bill their time at $100 an hour, which includes all support services.

Crain, Langner & Co.
20575 Center Ridge Road, Rocky River, Ohio 44146; 216-333-7622

"Highly conservative" Crain, Langner provided services for about 100 clients last year, over 80 percent on a retainer basis. The firm employs four consultants.

Fees are charged by the hour and average about $75. Retainer charges are based on how much time the firm estimates will be needed by a client over the year. The company declined to release 1979 revenue figures.

The 41-year-old firm goes out of the way to cultivate a "very low key" reputation, said Mary Lou Kirk, a consultant. Principal is David A. Langner.

D

Kevin F. Donoghue & Assoc.
190 High St., Boston, Mass. 02110; 617-482-7015

With a staff of nine, including five consultants, this Boston-based firm last year consulted for 55 clients, approximately 70 percent of which were on a retainer status, president Kevin Donoghue said.

Hourly rates run $50 to $80, with an average rate estimated at $62.50 by Mr. Donoghue. He declined to release 1979 revenue figures.

Only a few of this firm's clients are in the Fortune 1,000 category; most are small to medium-sized retailers or municipalities.

E

EBASCO Risk Management Consultants Inc.
Two World Trade Center. New York, N.Y. 10048; 212-785-2200

One of the largest risk management consulting firms in the country, EBASCO last year provided services for approximately 250 clients, more than 50 percent of which are in the Fortune 1,000 category, according to senior vp Bruce Suter. The staff of 120, which includes 105 consultants, operates out of EBASCO's main New York office and its branches in Newport Beach, Calif., Chicago, Atlanta, and Hamilton, Bermuda.

Fees are charged both on annual basis, for the approximately 100 clients on retainer status, and hourly. The average fee for a client usually runs about $150 to $750 per day of work. EBASCO's revenues last year were in excess of $4 million, Mr. Suter said.

The spread of clients and the range of services provided are wide. The company has been stressing computer capabilities for projections as an impetus for continued growth at an average rate of 20 percent a year.

F

First Risk Management Co.
835 Glenside Ave., Wyncote, Pa. 19095, 215-927-3404

This 20-year-old firm was retained by approximately 60 clients last year and performed one-time projects for an additional 10. A staff of 13 includes 6 consultants.

Fees are charged on an hourly basis, with work performed by executive consultants billed at $150 an hour, by technical staff at $100 an hour, and by clerical staff at $15 an hour, said executive vp Alvin Mangold. The average fee for a project ranges from $8,000 to $10,000. Revenues for 1979 reached about $500,000.

Clients of this consulting firm include heavy representation of supermarket, hotel, banking, and light manufacturing industries. Only a couple are among the Fortune 1,000, Mr. Mangold said. President is Leonard J. Silver.

Fleming, Marceau & Associates
313 Foothill Blvd., La Canada, Calif. 91011; 213-790-8714

Partners Ed Fleming and G. David Marceau teamed up about 18 months ago to specialize in claims consulting and auditing for self-insurers. They also prepare self-insurance feasibility studies and design loss data reporting systems for self-administered programs.

The firm does a lot of public sector business, listing several municipalities, school districts, and water districts among its 40 clients. Mr. Fleming and Mr. Marceau are assisted by two technical consultants and three support staffers. They also use an in-house computer to provide claims data experience reports to self-insured clients.

Mr. Marceau says the firm helps many public entities in California prepare reimbursement applications for increased workers' compensation costs under the state-mandated local cost reimbursement program. When the legislature put a cap on certain local revenues in 1973, it agreed to reimburse public entities directly out of state coffers for increased costs.

Hourly consulting fees vary from $45 to $64, Mr. Marceau says. Claim audits calculated on a project basis usually cost $2,500 to $3,500 for a basic sampling. An initial setup fee of $500 or more is charged for claims data experience reports. Thereafter each claim costs $10 to $15 to track until the case is closed.

H

H&W Risk Management Services
19752 MacArthur Blvd., Suite 150, Irvine, Calif. 92715; 714-851-9122

H&W Risk Management Services works exclusively with agents and brokers who require special expertise on a project to serve a major account. If an agent's client acquires a new exposure, for instance, the agent may seek professional expertise, counseling, and support to retain the client.

This newly founded firm, affiliated with H&W Insurance Services headquartered in Encino, Calif., prepares alternative risk funding feasibility studies, provides claims auditing services, and researches special problems to meet an agent or broker need.

Three staff consultants typically work on about ten assignments at any time, estimates David R. Hoskins, president. Hourly consulting fees range from $60 to $100. Special research projects are priced according to their salability to future clients and could vary from $500 to $7,500.

Thomas J. Hammond & Co.
3701 Wilshire Blvd., Suite 1038, Los Angeles, Calif. 90010; 213-480-3833

Thomas J. Hammond & Co. is a two-consultant firm with approximately 35 to 40 clients on monthly retainer and another dozen for which the firm performs special assignments.

Self-insurance feasibility reports, audits, and financial studies are the firm's consulting mainstays. "We've deliberately chosen to remain small," says executive vp Joan Morris, "so as not to dilute our close personal relations with clients. They think of us as employees."

Ms. Morris was reluctant to discuss fees because she said they vary based on the risk management sophistication and expertise required by a particular account. Average fees run in the vicinity of $75 an hour, she said.

Hennessy & York Inc.
358 Nassau St., Princeton, N.J. 08540; 609-921-0050

Hennessy & York, a husband-wife team, specializes in working for major U.S. corporations to make their property, casualty, and employee benefits programs more cost effective. The firm, founded in May, has seven clients; all are Fortune 1,000 companies, four with more than $1 billion in sales.

Fees are charged as 50 percent of the actual cost savings to the firm achieved through the services of Hennessy & York, calculated annually for a two-year term. There are no upfront fees or expenses. When presenting its recommendations, Hennessy & York agrees with the client on how present costs and subsequent savings will be measured. The largest savings to a client so far has been $2 million, says G. P. York, chairman.

"Our company was founded on the assumption that hundreds and hundreds of millions of dollars are being wasted each year by the Fortune 1,000 companies in the insurance area alone," says Mr. York, former risk manager for the Northrop Corp. Sharon Hennessy-York is a former employee of RIMS.

"We work directly with the chief executive officer or chief operating officer, rather than the risk manager," Mr. York says. To coordinate a savings program, however, Hennessey & York work closely with the risk management and employee benefits departments.

I

Insurance Analysis Inc.
4809 Wichers Dr., Marrero, La. 70072; 504-340-7601

Insurance Analysis Inc. specializes in providing risk management counseling and auditing worldwide to clients in oil-related industries, with emphasis on diving, drilling, and transportation exposures. Three staff consultants also testify in court as expert witnesses for attorneys in maritime matters.

Ninety-eight of the firm's approximately 100 clients are on an annual retainer. Fees are figured at $80 to $100 an hour depending on the legwork required. "If our estimate of hours needed to do the job falls short, we absorb the loss," says Burnett J. Tappel II, president.

Insurance & Financial Consultants
21 Baldwin Road, Warwick, R.I. 02886; 401-822-0256

For the last four years, John Fitzgerald has been providing risk management consulting services for small to medium-sized companies that do not have their own full-time risk managers. Last year he had approximately 90 clients, about 25 on an annual retainer basis.

Mr. Fitzgerald's fees average $60 an hour and brought him revenues in the "low six figures" during 1979.

Insurance & Risk Management Services
Suite 225, Russo Building, Fredonia, N.Y. 14063; 716-673-1777

The one-man staff of Warren McPherson last year provided risk management consulting work for about 18 clients, 13 on an annual retainer. Most clients had annual revenues of $4 million to $5 million, with the two largest both pushing the $15 million mark, Mr. McPherson said.

Fees are charged by the hour, with the average charge running about $45 per hour, he said. Mr. McPherson declined to release 1979 revenue figures for his five-year-old operation.

Almost all of Mr. McPherson's consulting work is in the property/casualty area. He doesn't design any pension plans or captive feasibility studies and says he advises on some employee benefit options, "but not on a sophisticated level."

Insurance Audit & Inspection Co.
5425 East 82nd St., Suite 206, Indianapolis, Ind. 46250

This closely held firm performs risk management audits and full-scale program evaluations except for captive insurance company feasibility studies, which are subcontracted. Its approximately 300 clients include small and medium-sized companies as well as half a dozen corporate giants.

The 79-year-old firm employs 11 consultants and 6 other staffers working in Indianapolis and in field offices in St. Louis, Charlotte, N.C., and Columbus, Ohio.

The firm charges a flat fee for all services. About 80 percent of the company's clients pay an annual retainer ranging from $2,500 to $10,000. A big job with lots of travel might be billed at $25,000 or more, figured on an individual consultant's billing rates of $500 to $800 per day.

Insurance Buyers Council
22 West Road, Baltimore, Md. 21204; 301-828-1656

This 35-year-old firm has a client list of 200 to 250 companies, estimated president William P. Davis III. About 70 percent of that number contract with the consultant on an annual retainer basis. The staff includes nine senior consultants, three associate consultants, and six support personnel.

The range of hourly fees for clients, including a lot of government entities, is $50 to $60. He estimated 1979 revenues at about $1 million.

Insurance Consultant Associates
4848 Guiton St., Houston, Tex. 77027; 713-627-9823

Jack Culbertson advises half a dozen clients regarding their property and casualty risks. He examines their exposures, evaluates coverage, and recommends insurance.

After 40 years in the insurance industry as an agent, general manager of an insurance agency, and insurance company officer, Mr. Culbertson founded his own business in 1966.

He works alone and bills his services at $50 an hour.

Insurance Consulting Assn.
P.O. Box 1296, Teaneck, N.J. 07666; 201-836-9595

All of this firm's approximately 100 clients pay annual retainers that give them continuing access to the six consultants and ten support staff, partner Barron S. Wall said. The New Jersey-based company has three branch offices—one in New York City and two on Long Island.

Retainer fees range from $2,000 to $50,000, with the average client paying $10,000 to $15,000, Mr. Wall said. He declined to release 1979 revenue figures.

Besides clients in the food industry, this company depends on Canadian firms for a lot of its consulting work, Mr. Wall said.

Insurance Management Consultants Inc.
4113 W. Inman Ave., Tampa, Fla. 33609; 813-877-3360

Otto Lee Henderson is president of this one-consultant firm that performs insurance audits, designs new risk management programs, and assists clients with claims handling. Although his 50 clients are engaged in a wide variety of business activities, Mr. Henderson specializes in wrap-up and builder's risk coverage for airports of all sizes.

His hourly fee is $50 and he sets a minimum charge of $250. In 1979, Insurance Management Consultants grossed approximately $60,000 in revenues, Mr. Henderson reports.

K

Robert A. Krause & Associates
Route 1, Townville, S.C. 29689; 803-287-4477

This firm specializes in worldwide arbitration of disputed claims, representing either policyholders or insurers. Robert A. Krause, president, says other consultants sometimes retain his company for advice on how to best represent their clients with a disputed loss claim.

"We obtain most of our clients after they've already been burned by a bad underinsured loss," Mr. Krause says. "They find they've been improperly covered and want to set their house in order."

Four consultants and 10 support staffers serve about 75 clients, 10 percent of which are Fortune 1,000 companies. The firm is headquartered in South Carolina and maintains field offices in Southfield, Mich., and Atlanta, Ga.

Consulting fees are $150 hourly and $750 daily. The firm sets a minimum retainer fee of $7,500 per job, based on ten days' work.

L

John Liner Insurance & Risk Management Advisers Inc.
555 Washington St., Wellesley, Mass. 02181; 617-235-8450

This four-consultant firm advises primarily on property and casualty risks and performs insurance portfolio audits. A large support staff of 14 provides technical as well as clerical services.

A second office in New York goes by the name of John Liner Associates Inc. Massachusetts licensing laws require the firm to use "insurance" in its name but "we are strictly advisers and do not sell insurance," declares Dwight Levick, president.

Mr. Levick declined to discuss the firm's clientele or fees. "We are well aware of what other consultants are charging and our fees are comparable and equitable," he said.

M

Miller & Gilbert
407 Sansome St., San Francisco 49111; 415-398-3993

Miller & Gilbert, a professional excess/surplus lines claims adjustment firm, has recently begun offering a wide range of consulting services, including full-line insurance portfolio reviews and claims auditing. M&G consultants will also train in-house claims administrators and provide third-party administration for self-insurers.

The California firm has offices in San Francisco and the Los Angeles area and plans a third location in Seattle next summer, reports Frederick J. Fisher, vp. Eight consultants and 5 support staffers serve 11 corporate clients, he adds.

Consulting services are billed at $75 hourly, $500 daily, $2,300 weekly, or $9,000 monthly. Claims supervision is generally billed at $35 hourly, although the firm has one client charged on a per claim basis.

Mund, McLaurin & Co. of Los Angeles
600 S. Commonwealth, Los Angeles, Calif. 90005; 213-385-3201

"We sell time and expertise to evaluate and design risk management programs," declares William J. Pickney, vp of Mund, McLaurin & Co. The firm also advises clients regarding risk management staffing.

A five-consultant staff serves about 85 to 100 continuing clients, including 30 to 35 in the Fortune 1,000, Mr. Pickney says, "We sell 38 years of background and experience," he added. Mr. Pickney declined to discuss consultant fees except to say they are calculated on hourly and flat monthly bases.

N

P. D. Norman Associates Ltd.
8331 River Road, Richmond, B. C., Canada, V6X1Y1; 604-273-3033

Working out of its offices in Richmond and Toronto, this staff of two consultants and three support personnel last year provided consulting work to 22 clients, six on retainer.

Fees average more than $100 an hour, said president Peter Norman, who estimated 1979 revenues for his firm at $300,000 to $500,000.

In the last ten years, Norman Associates has built a reputation for handling clients needing advice on professional liability, Mr. Norman said.

P

William Peet Co.
2156 Inglehart Ave., St. Paul, Minn. 55104; 612-645-1845

Risk management consulting services offered by the William Peet Co. include claims audits, preparation of insurance specifications, coverage evaluation, problem-solving, expert testimony, and advice to management on consolidations and mergers.

The two-consultant firm consists of William Peet, president, and Jeffrey Isenberger, an attorney. The corporation grosses approximately $30,000 a month in revenues, Mr. Peet reports.

Consulting services are usually billed at $75 an hour but may go higher under special circumstances such as a meeting with the client's board of directors.

H. Russell Perry
P.O. Box 611, Concord, Mass. 01742; 617-263-2226

About 20 clients came to Mr. Perry for consulting work during 1979, half on a retainer basis. The typical client, Mr. Perry said, is a small manufacturing firm with sales of less than $50 million a year.

Mr. Perry charges clients an average of $60 an hour, with retainer fees based on the estimated number of hours needed to provide the contracted services. Last year's revenues were between $50,000 and $100,000, Mr. Perry said.

Neil E. Pritchard
325 E. Prospect St., Marquette, Mich. 49855; 906-228-6932

Neil E. Pritchard is sole proprietor of this four-year-old consulting business with 23 clients on retainer. He prepares loss evaluation surveys, writes insurance specifications, and evaluates quotations.

Mr. Pritchard was risk manager for five years with a university, and today many of his clients are educational institutions. Most of his consulting is in Michigan, but he also takes on out-of-state clients.

In Michigan a consultant cannot charge for services without a written agreement, so Mr. Pritchard puts all new clients on a minimum annual retainer. Subsequently, he charges $30 per hour plus expenses, which may be deducted from that minimum retainer.

R

RIMCO Risk Management Inc.
10300 N. Central Expressway, Bldg. V, Suite 350, Dallas, Tex. 75231;
214-363-2451

RIMCO Risk Management lists its most popular services as exposure identification, insurance program evaluation, alternative funding studies, claims reviews, and captive feasibility studies. Three out of 13 staff consultants specialize in oil and gas exposures. Construction and medical malpractice are other areas of special expertise, says Keith Kakacek, president.

Approximately 10 percent of the firm's 200 clients are Fortune 1,000 companies. RIMCO also assists agents and brokers in getting licensed in various states.

"We require $1,500 to open a file," Mr. Kakacek reports. Hourly fees vary from $40 to $100 for consultants and run about $20 for clerical services. The 13-year-old firm also is willing to discuss compensation on a contingency basis. Revenues last year totaled about $1.5 million.

Risk Consultants Inc.
2915 Providence Road, Charlotte, N.C. 28211; 704-364-2600

This ten-year-old firm, with offices in Charlotte, Dallas, and Denver, provided services for about 175 clients last year, 50 of them on annual retainer. The company added three consultants in the past two years, bringing the total staff to 15 consultants and 7 support staffers. The company opened the Denver office three years ago, said president William Brown.

Fees for retainer clients range from $1,000 to $40,000, with the average running about $10,000 to $20,000. Hourly charges are $12.50 to $75.

Although about 10 percent to 15 percent of this consultant's clients are among the Fortune 1,000, Mr. Brown said his firm specializes in providing services to companies not large enough to have their own full-time risk management department.

Risk Management Consultants Inc.
250 W. 57 St., New York, N.Y. 10019; 212-582-2214

More than 50 companies, most of them small businesses without their own full-time risk managers, came to this consultant for services last year, says president Ezra Lipshitz, who heads a staff of three consultants and two support personnel.

About 90 percent of the clients are on a retainer arrangement, paying between $1,500 and $10,000 a year, Mr. Lipshitz said. Hourly fees range from $50 to $100 an hour, with the average fee estimated at $60 an hour.

Formed in 1957, this company provides a wide range of risk management advice, but stays away from captive studies and the more sophisticated self-insurance plans.

Risk Planning Group
722 Post Road, Darien, Conn. 06820; 203-655-9791

At any one time, this Connecticut-based consulting firm will be under contract to about four firms and completing individual projects for an additional 20 companies, president Felix Kloman estimated. Last year, Risk Planning Group was retained by 20 firms and performed consulting work for another 100, he said. The staff includes ten consultants and five support personnel.

Hourly fees range from $35 to $140, Mr. Kloman said, adding that 1979 revenues were in the "very high six figures."

A broad range of available services is what Mr. Kloman stresses to potential clients, adding that he deliberately hasn't tried to specialize in any one area.

Risk Sciences Group Inc.
524 Colorado Ave., Santa Monica, Calif. 90401; 213-393-0507

Most of this firm's 25 active clients are Fortune 500 companies seeking computerized risk management information systems. The client's loss data history is programmed and stored in a computer system that is then run through different loss forecasting models. Besides forecasting future losses, the system facilitates comparison of a wide variety of alternate funding models.

Risk Sciences Group president Joseph A. Destein founded the Anistics division of Alexander & Alexander, then broke away two years ago to go into competition with his former employer. The eight-consultant staff includes persons with Ph.D.s in mathematics and probability, as well as M.B.A.s and CPAs.

Mr. Destein estimates initial computer programming charges at $2,500 per source of data (usually an insurer), plus an average annual charge of $1 per record in the data base. That figure varies according to the types of services and information required by the client. Hourly fees range between $25 and $125, averaging $50 to $60. The firm's projected revenues through fiscal 1979, ending March 31, are $500,000.

S

E. W. Siver & Associates
3535 First Ave. N., St. Petersburg, Fla. 33733; 813-822-9335

"We provide risk management, insurance and employee benefits consulting services to the public and private sector," declares Edward W. Siver, president of this ten-year-old firm. Risk management audits are popular with clients, he says, because they explain "what you've got, what's wrong with it and what to do about it." Property appraisals and claims auditing are farmed out, he adds.

Eight consultants and seven support staffers in the firm bill their time at $20 to $100 depending on their experience and educational designations.

T

R. Maynard Toelle
703 Thunderbird Ave., Sun City Center, Fla. 33570; 813-634-4975

Consultant R. Maynard Toelle evaluates loss exposures and history to determine if a client's insurance portfolio is adequate to meet his needs.

Working in his home in a small town south of St. Petersburg, Fla., Mr. Toelle retains six clients and serves as executive secretary of the Institute of Risk Management Consultants.

Billing is more an art than a science; he says, since an assignment may often be more complicated than the client or the consultant originally contemplated. His standard hourly rate is $65.

Towers, Perrin, Forster & Crosby
1500 Market St., Philadelphia, Pa. 19102; 215-563-4500

The insurance consulting department of TPF&C last year added 40 clients to its rosters, many of which came to the Philadelphia-based division for financial analysis and actuarial services, said Richard Delaney, vp and principal. A staff of ten includes six consultants and four support personnel.

Fees are hourly—no clients are assigned a retainer status—and the range of fees runs from $40 to $150 an hour, plus expenses, Mr. Delaney said. He declined to release 1979 revenue figures.

Although primarily known as an actuarial firm, TPF&C has been providing risk management consulting services since 1969, Mr. Delaney said.

W

Warren, McVeigh & Griffin
1420 Bristol St. N., Newport Beach, Calif. 92660, 714-752-1058

This full-service risk management consulting firm claims about 100 active clients, a majority of which are Fortune 1,000 corporations. The most common assignments are claims audits for self-insurers, design of in-house claims administration systems, comparisons of risk funding alternatives, information systems surveys, and captive feasibility studies, says Bud Griffin, president.

The firm also performs captive insurance company management audits that evaluate accounting, claims handling, funding, reinsurance.

Warren, McVeigh & Griffin employs 11 consultants including an actuary, plus 6 support staffers assisted by a word processing system. Two former principals, David Warren and Donn McVeigh, recently sold their interests in the 12-year-old West Coast firm.

Most WM&G clients are billed on an hourly rate ranging from $35 to $120, depending on which consultant does the work. The firm will quote prospective clients a price range and maximum cost on a job.

Wyatt Co.
233 S. Wacker Dr., Sears Tower, Suite 5600, Chicago, Ill. 60606; 312-876-1616

The Wyatt Co.'s risk management consulting division maintains an active list of about 250 clients, including a substantial number of Fortune 1,000 companies. Founded in 1973, the division employs 30 consultants in its offices in Chicago, Washington, Detroit, Dallas, and San Francisco.

Consulting services include audits of property and casualty insurance programs, preparation of specifications for competitive bidding, captive and self-insurance feasibility studies, and actuarial evaluations.

The firm favors a team approach, with a project manager and other specialists on each assignment. There are three actuarial consultants on staff, as well as others with backgrounds as risk managers, brokers, and rating bureau officials. More than 100 of the company's clients are hospitals.

Consultant fees average $80 hourly, ranging from $60 to $125. Clerical services are billed separately at $20 to $25 and analysts' time at $35 to $45 hourly.

DIRECTORY OF FIRMS: AFFILIATED RISK CONSULTANTS

AIG Risk Management
70 Pine St., New York, N.Y. 10005; 212-770-6360

A separate division of the huge American International Group insurers, AIG Risk Management consulted for risk management departments of 12 companies last year, said president Joseph Smetana. Clients have no obligation to purchase insurance from AIG. About half the clients contract on a retainer basis.

Mr. Smetana normally has a staff of five consultants, although work done on an ad hoc basis, for a Fortune 500 company might necessitate reaching into other AIG departments to put together a temporary working team of perhaps ten people.

Fees are based on time plus expenses, with hourly fees ranging from $30 for clerical work to $150 for work performed by consultants. He declined to give 1979 revenue figures.

Anistics
640 Fifth Ave., New York, N.Y. 10036; 212-840-8500

This risk management consulting subsidiary of Alexander & Alexander provided services for about 120 clients last year, with about 10 percent of them contracting with the firm on a retainer basis, said Robert Gielow, A&A senior vp. The staff of 70 includes 15 consultants, located in Anistics' offices in New York, Palo Alto, Calif., and Denver.

Fees are hourly or at a project rate, with the range estimated by Mr. Gielow of $2,500 to $100,000 per project. He declined to give a revenue figure for 1979.

Anistics is strongest in forecasting potential losses for its clients, as well as developing financial alternatives to insurance, such as captives or creative pooling arrangements, Mr. Gielow said. President is Peter Densen.

Chanslor Risk Management Inc.
10101 Fondren, Houston, Tex. 77096; 713-777-3561

Chanslor Risk Management specializes in organizing and managing association captive insurance companies in Texas. It offers all the ancillary services generally provided by an insurance company, including claims management, loss prevention, audits, accounting, and supervision of litigation.

Bill Chanslor, president, works with seven technical assistants and four clerks to manage two captives and provide claims administration to four corporate self-insurers.

Captive management costs are a percentage of premium income. Self-insurers are charged a percentage of premium based on manual rates. The firm's approximately 25 other clients are billed at $100 to $125 hourly for general consultation.

Continental Insurance Co.
80 Maiden Lane, New York, N.Y. 10038; 212-440-2727

The Continental Insurance Co. is undertaking a major marketing drive to emphasize sales of risk-related services separate from insurance, reports Charles L. Ruoff, senior vp.

Salaried account executives who do not earn commissions from insurance sales advise clients regarding self-insured retentions, safety, claims administration, and other services. Continental also provides claims administration, loss control engineering, and computer services to clients on a variety of negotiable fee structures. Other services, already routinely available to insurance clients, may soon be added to the risk-related services group.

"There is no set compensation formula," Mr. Ruoff notes. "We can work on a contract, flat fee, or per claim percentage of paid or incurred losses," he said.

CU Risk Management Inc.
600 Atlantic Ave., Boston, Mass. 02210; 617-725-6010

CU Risk Management is owned but separately operated by Commercial Union Assurance Cos. and has grown in its three years to where it handles about 75 clients, said senior vp Richard Lapham. About 40 percent of them are in the Fortune 1,000.

The Boston-based staff includes 11 consultants and 11 support personnel. Hourly fees usually run from $30 to $40, said Mr. Lapham, who declined to give 1979 revenue estimates. He said the firm grew 67 percent last year.

Among the firm's strengths, Mr. Lapham said, are advising clients on claims management, loss control engineering, and data processing. President is Ross C. Cowan.

Marsh & McLennan Client Services
1221 Avenue of the Americas, New York, N.Y. 10020; 212-997-2000

Marsh & McLennan offers a wide range of technical services available to major client businesses on a fee basis. Major categories include loss prevention and security, environmental control, claims management services to self-insured client companies, and captive insurance companies domiciled in Colorado, Tennessee, or offshore.

The gigantic insurance brokerage firm is staffed to undertake almost any special project, including multinational insurance services, nuclear consulting and analysis of cash-flow benefits of various insurance, and self-insurance options.

"Fee work is based on the nature of the assignment, the professional qualifications of the people who do the work, and is negotiated with the client," says Philip J. Brown Jr., executive vp and head of the Client Services Group. The vast majority of M&M's clients, however, prefer to work with the firm on an annual retainer rather than an hourly basis, he added.

M&M declined to discuss its fees more specifically, explaining that they are too varied to enumerate.

Risk Treatment Services Co. Inc.
3025 S. Park Road, Suite 825, Aurora, Colo. 80014; 303-752-4912

This firm's major activity is management of captive insurance companies. One of the five captives presently managed by RTS was the first formed under Colorado's enabling legislation, reports Gary R. Nelson, vp. The domestic company is also affiliated with Risk Treatment Services Ltd. in Bermuda.

The firm offers a number of ancillary services, including captive and self-insurance feasibility studies, claims administration, financial and accounting services, investment management and consulting, and determination of insurance policy premium levels, "but we are not brokers and we do not sell insurance," Mr. Nelson says.

Fees are charged on a time and expense basis ranging from $25 to $75 hourly, depending on which of four consultants and three technical assistants works on the project. One association captive pays a set percentage of premium for RTS's management services.

Scor Risk Management Inc.
1201 Elm St., 52d Floor-First International Building, Dallas, Tex. 75270; 214-748-1100

A newcomer to the risk management consulting field, formed in July 1979, Scor has a client list of about 20 firms, most of them in the Fortune 1,000 category and all on a project basis. The staff of six includes five consultants and one support person.

Fees range from $30 to $100 an hour, with the average charge estimated at $80, said executive vp Tom Miller. Mr. Miller, acknowledging that as a new firm "we have more money going out than we have coming in," projected 1980 revenues might reach $300,000.

The Dallas-based firm, a subsidiary of Scor Reinsurance Co., specializes in captive management and feasibility studies, Mr. Miller said. President is Alain B. Ellet.

CHAPTER 3

YOUR MAJOR
BUSINESS EXPOSURES

PROPERTY EXPOSURES

LIABILITY EXPOSURES

SPECIALIZED EXPOSURES

THE COORDINATION AND
COMBINATION OF INSURANCE
COVERAGES

PROVIDING FOR BUSINESS
CONTINUATION THROUGH
INSURANCE AND SELECTED
EMPLOYEE BENEFITS

UNIQUE EXPOSURES

DATA PROCESSING INSURANCE

Frederick R. Hodosh, Ph.D., J.D., CPCU
Secretary, General Counsel, and Director of Legal and Claims
  Education
American Institute for Property and Liability Underwriters
Malvern, Pennsylvania

Frederick R. Hodosh is Secretary, General Counsel, and Director of Legal and Claims Education of the American Institute for Property and Liability Underwriters and the Insurance Institute of America. In addition, he is Chairman of the Board of Ethical Inquiry of the American Institute. Dr. Hodosh received his college education in Hungary and Austria, obtaining his Ph.D. degree in Political Science and International Law at the University of Innsbruck, Austria. Subsequently, he received his Juris Doctor degree (with distinction) from the University of North Dakota School of Law and has been admitted to the Bar in North Dakota, Michigan, and Pennsylvania. Before joining the American and Insurance Institutes, Dr. Hodosh spent some 15 years in the insurance industry both in claims and in corporate legal positions. He is a member of the American, Pennsylvania, and Michigan Bar Associations and the Society of CPCU. Dr. Hodosh is also an Adjunct Professor of Law at Delaware Law School. He is a co-author of the text *The Legal Environment of Insurance* and the author of several articles published by insurance and legal journals on the role of the claim function, the licensing of adjusters, and accident reparations.

It is the purpose of this book to identify the potential sources that may result in a loss of assets by a business and to discuss the various types of insurance available to deal with each form of loss. In reviewing the potential risks of loss, consideration should be given to three major areas, all vital to the survival and success of the enterprise:

1. The cost of loss or damage to tangible and intangible property.
2. The cost of indemnification of others due to the conduct of business resulting in legal liability.
3. The cost of loss of productivity due to death or disability of those individuals who are involved in the operation of the business.

Loss of property may involve the actual loss or damage to buildings, machinery, and any other physical property needed in the business resulting in an expenditure to replace or repair such property itself. It may also mean the loss of profits due to the destruction of buildings, factories, workshops, and other means of production. Asset loss due to dishonesty of others can also be classified as falling into this area.

Business, just as an individual, may incur loss by virtue of liability to indemnify others due to business activity. Generally the reason for claims of this type is negligence in the conduct of some specific aspect of the business operation.

The sources of loss based on negligence may be derived from occurrences caused by a specific instrumentality or by a specific activity such as the negligent operation of a vehicle; from thousands of business activities which result in liability, such as the manufacturing or distributing of the product; from liability to workers; and from exposures which stem from various executive and professional actions of those connected with the business.

A business enterprise can become severely crippled and unable to function if the men and women responsible for its successful operation are removed or incapacitated because of death or disability. This is true whether or not the business is a sole proprietorship, a partnership, or a corporation. Moreover, these risks can severely endanger the value of a person to the business whether or not the individual works in a management capacity or as an employee involved in production, marketing, administration, or other areas.

The reader paging through this book will find an examination of all these areas focusing on the availability and extent of insurance protection. The aim of this chapter is to furnish an overview of these major business risks, to describe them briefly, and to refer the reader to the chapters in which these groups of exposures and their insurance treatment are described in more detail.

PROPERTY EXPOSURES

Property losses may arise from a large variety of causes, such as fire, explosion, lightning, windstorm, vandalism, dishonesty of employees, or theft. They are often classified in two groups: direct and indirect losses. If a building housing manufacturing operations of a company is damaged by fire, there is direct loss to the building. If a tornado destroys or damages a truck, the owner of the truck sustains direct damage to his property. If an explosion renders the premises unusable, the cost of repair or replacement is a direct loss as is the loss sustained when a safe is burglarized, both to the extent of any damage to the safe itself and of the loss of money or other valuables taken.

Indirect losses are associated with or follow from direct ones. When a business is forced to shut down for repairs due to a direct fire loss to its premises, it will, in addition, sustain loss of revenue and profit until the direct damage is repaired and normal business life is resumed. Moreover, during this period, while a business may not have to incur certain noncontinuing expenses, other items of normal overhead may have to be paid for the period of suspension which negatively affect profit. Continuing expenses and net profit not earned may be considered "indirect" losses.

Further examples of indirect loss might be the spoilage of goods under refrigeration when electrical failure occurs, or where the work product of data processing equipment is lost because of storm damage sustained by an electric transformer perhaps some distance away from the insured premises. Undamaged portions of a building may have to be torn down because of a building code requirement where a substantial portion has been damaged and cannot be rebuilt except with more modern and more expensive methods.

Many of the direct losses can be insured by a fire insurance policy supplemented with "forms" and "endorsements" to cover direct damage to the insured property by a number of additional perils. Most states have developed "standard" fire insurance policies which, in addition to granting specific coverage against fire, lightning and removal, incorporate provisions that are designed to govern the relationship between the insurance company and the policyholder. The next chapter examines these in detail. The discussion includes the parties to the contract, their interests in the property insured, the amount of coverage and premium rate, the description of the property insured, and types of losses covered by the policy, called perils. These perils may include, in addition to fire and lightning, hail, tornado, earthquake, riot, windstorm, explosion, damage caused by automobiles or airplanes, smoke, vandalism, falling objects, water damage, freezing, glass breakage, and collapse. The policy also lists perils that are not covered and the type of property that is excepted from coverage. As all insurance policies, it contains provisions for the inception and termination of coverage, describes duties of the insured, and sets forth the procedure for making claims. This contract entered into by the insurance company and the policyholder is the basic document to which various "forms" and "endorsements" may be attached. The endorsements contain additional contract provisions specifically applicable to the property insured. Thus, for example, a "building and contents" form enables the insured to purchase separate amounts of insurance on the building, on personal property contained therein, and on the improvements and betterments.

Chapter 5 discusses exposures to contents which may include owned furniture, fixtures, machinery, equipment, stock, and other personal property. Fixtures, alterations, and additions which become part of the described building when installed by the tenant may be separately insured to protect the tenant's financial interests.

Personal property, such as products or stock of the business, may also be exposed to transportation perils. Inland marine policies are designed to furnish insurance coverage against this type of loss. Chapter 5 examines property insurance on goods in transit by railroad, truck, aircraft, or by express or U.S. mail. Such property in transit may also be the subject of insurance taken out by businesses and organizations engaged in transporting the property of others to afford protection against liability arising from their operations to the owner of the goods. The business firm shipping merchandise or equipment will often purchase an annual transportation policy which insures shipments for which it is responsible. This policy covers property while it is in the custody of railroads, motor vehicle common carriers, as well as air and land transportation companies. The insurance applies from the initial point of shipment to the point of delivery, and it often protects against "all risk of physical loss or damage." If the policy covers transportation over water, it might include coverage for perils ordinarily insured against by ocean marine insurance policies, such as perils of the seas, fire, and acts of persons both on and those not on the vessel.

Direct physical loss to insured property also can result in consequential losses to a business. These include the loss of income and profits that cannot be earned while the business is not functioning. Chapter 6 reviews the exposures of the business enterprise to such losses and the insurance protection available to protect against them. An indirect loss may follow direct physical loss to insured property and may be every bit as great or greater than the fire or storm damage caused to the insured building. A resulting loss of income may threaten the business's existence if it cannot meet its obligations; it may result in the suspension of dividends, the inability to pay valued employees, and otherwise create a severe disruption in the life of the business. To guard against this danger, the business interruption insurance form was devised. It indemnifies the policyholder for loss of potential future income resulting from interruption of business due to physical damage by an insured peril at the location described in the policy to the extent of the continuing expenses and the anticipated profit. An often used policy is the so-called Gross Earnings Form which promises to pay the insured the loss in gross earnings during the period the business cannot function minus noncontinuing expenses or, stated in another way, the loss of net profits plus continuing expenses. The policyholder's recovery for losses is limited to the actual loss sustained—as required by the principle of indemnity—by the face amount of the policy, the time required for restoration of the damaged premises with the exercise of due diligence, and by coinsurance provisions. The latter require the insured to carry insurance in the amount corresponding to a certain percentage of the annual gross earnings during the policy period. If the insured fully complies with the provision, losses will be paid in full; otherwise, he will have to bear a percentage of the loss. The cost of payroll may or may not be included as a continuing expense, as desired.

Chapter 7 analyzes asset losses to the business due to dishonest acts of humans. These include burglary, robbery, theft, forgery, embezzlement, misappropriation, and the like. Insurance policies may combine coverage for several of these crimes. The culprit may or may not be an employee of the business enterprise. The chapter deals for the most part with broad dishonesty coverages and does not address the more limited coverages available.

A common policy form is the Mercantile Open Stock Burglary Policy. It requires, in order for the insurer to be liable, a felonious entry during nonbusiness hours and the use of force and violence evidenced by visible marks left upon the exterior of the premises at the place of the entry by explosives, tools, electricity, or chemicals. Similar provisions are found in safe burglary policies. In addition to loss caused by burglary as defined, the policy covers damage to the building or premises. The property covered includes stock of merchandise whether in the open or enclosed. In order to protect money and securities, however, it is necessary to purchase mercantile robbery insurance, safe burglary insurance, or some combination of these policies. Generally, employee dishonesty is not covered in any of these policies.

Losses by business due to forgery are many times greater than those caused by burglars and robbers. Forgery involves not only counterfeiting of signatures but any type of unauthorized change of figures or data committed with a criminal intent. The most frequently used insurance policy to protect against forgery is the Depositors Forgery Policy and, for banks, the addition of forgery and alteration coverage to their fidelity bond.

Losses sustained by a business due to dishonest acts of employees are usually covered by fidelity bonds. A bond is a guarantee by the surety to the "obligee" (insured) that if an individual employee's dishonesty results in financial loss, the surety will make it good in his behalf. The dishonest acts include larceny, theft, embezzlement, forgery, misappropriation, wrongful abstraction, willful misapplication, or other fraudulent or dishonest acts. Although space limitations preclude the development herein, the reader should be aware of the Federal Crime Insurance Program which makes some of the above-described crime insurance coverages available at subsidized rates in states where there is a critical problem of insurance availability at an affordable price.

LIABILITY EXPOSURES

An enterprise may sustain loss by virtue of having incurred legal liability to others. Such a loss can often be of greater magnitude than a loss sustained by direct or indirect damage to property. A substantial portion of this *Handbook* is devoted to identifying and analyzing legal liability exposures of the business and examining the insurance coverages that are available to render protection against losses of this type.

Legal liability is accountability imposed by law on a person or business entity for his or its acts. It consists of a duty to respond by the payment of damages to the injured or damaged by some wrongful act or omission, referred to as a *tort*. Such a "tortious" act or omission may be caused intentionally, negligently, or without any fault. Physically attacking a business competitor in a fit of rage is clearly an intentional, wrongful act constituting the tort of assault and battery creating a civil liability for damages sustained by the victim as well as criminal responsibility to society. Nearly all instances of such liability resulting from intentional acts are not insurable because of public policy. Insurance coverage is designed to protect against liability arising out of fortuitous events causing injury to others due to the actor's negligence or of certain nonnegligent acts or omissions not intended to inflict harm.

Perhaps the large majority of liability exposures facing the business enterprise are based on a negligent act or omission. Negligence is present where a person fails to exercise care not to cause harm to others. It presupposes a duty owed to others, a failure to live up to that duty, injury or damage to the person to whom the duty is owed by failure to exercise the required degree of care, and actual damages sustained by the victim.

In a liability insurance contract the insurance company promises to assume the policyholder's liability to pay damages to third persons damaged by the policyholder's negligence. In addition, in the policy the insurance company promises to defend the policyholder against claims arising from an obligation imposed by law or one assumed by contract. Claims, of course, are not paid "automatically," i.e., on demand. First, the occurrence which gave rise to the claim must be within the coverage of the policy, namely, the activity that is insured and not excluded by the policy. Second, assuming that the claim does fall within the terms of the coverage, the party making a claim against the policyholder must still prove the existence of liability on the part of the policyholder. If there is no legal liability on the part of the policyholder, there is no obligation on the part of the insurance company to pay the claimant. However, in the latter case, the insurer is still obligated to "defend" the insured, with such obligation to defend including the investigation and evaluation of the claim, even though it may be subsequently denied.

A common way of classifying liability loss exposures faced by a business is to group them according to exposures arising out of the ownership and control of real property and exposures originating from the business's operation. Chapter 8 concerns itself with these exposures and the insurance treatment available.

While ordinarily a person or entity must be in control of the land in order to be made subject to liability by those who sustain injury or damage because of some condition on the land, the determination of who was in control at the time of the loss or accident is often a disputed factual question. The owner of the land, even if it is occupied by others, may find himself in the position of having to defend against such a claim. Persons who come on the premises in a business capacity can expect that the owner will exercise reasonable care to prevent injury to them. The duty owed to those on the premises for nonbusiness purposes, or who are present even unlawfully, is a great deal less. The person possessing the land, however, may still be subject to claims and adverse judgments. Depending on the circumstances, the owner/possessor may be guilty of negligence with respect to a failure to maintain the premises where visitors may be expected to come, for creating or allowing dangerous conditions on adjoining roads due to his activities, for the inadequate maintenance of offices and parking lots, even for allowing abnormally dangerous conditions to exist that could be particularly inviting and injury causing to young children who may be on the land without any legal right.

A duty of care extends to those in control of the premises. Thus tenants may be found equally liable for negligence resulting in injuries arising out of a dangerous condition.

Chapter 8 identifies not only land-related but also operations liability of the business enterprise. Any negligent act by anyone connected with the business in the performance of his or her duties triggers liability to an injured or damaged third party. Insurance coverage is available for protecting against both types of liability and includes policies designed for owners, landlords and tenants, manufacturers and contractors, storekeepers, innkeepers, and other specific types of business, as well as so-called general liability policies available to most businesses.

Endorsements to broaden coverage to meet particular needs also receive attention in this chapter.

An example of *strict, nonnegligent* liability, which is discussed in Chapter 12, is the sale of a defective product causing injury to a user even though the producer or seller has exercised due care.

Perhaps no one operation of an instrumentality develops the number of liability ·claims as does the operation of automobiles. Chapter 9 is devoted to detailed discussion of these exposures and the insurance coverage available to protect against them.

It would be difficult to find an enterprise that did not utilize motor vehicles in its business. Operation of a motor vehicle creates potential liability, regardless of whether or not the vehicle is owned by the business; as long as it is used for its benefit by the driver (who may or may not be an owner, partner, or employee of the business), the exposure to liability for damages is there. In most cases liability is predicated upon negligent operation, although in several states which have adopted "no-fault" laws liability may exist without regard to fault.

Liability exposure to damages may be for bodily injury or property damage sustained by another person or entity. Liability must be established by proof of a breach of duty in the form of a violation of common law rules or of statutory enactments. It may arise out of the ownership, operation, maintenance, or use of a motor vehicle.

Chapter 9 examines in detail the business auto policy specifically designed by the insurance industry to meet the coverage needs of the business enterprise. It is a "package" policy in that it combines liability insurance coverage, personal injury protection (or equivalent no-fault coverage), automobile medical payments, uninsured motorist coverage, and physical damage insurance for a vehicle owned by a business. The liability insurance coverage covers and protects the owned, nonowned, rented, or leased vehicle.

An important part of the chapter discusses a liability of an enterprise for the operation of its vehicles by others. The most frequent illustration is the employer/employee relationship which may result in liability on the part of the employer for the employee's negligent operation of the vehicle. Important legal distinctions are drawn between the consequences of the automobile being operated by an employee and by an independent contractor.

Chapter 10 deals with the liability exposures of businesses engaged in operating a garage or a related business, as well as those in the long-haul trucking field. The liability insurance needs of a garage operator are provided by two major types of forms: the garage liability form and the garagekeeper's insurance form. The garage liability form provides for premises and operations coverage similar to other general liability forms, plus contractual liability coverage needed to protect the garage operator from liability he was forced to assume under a repair order; for example, coverage of work done by independent contractors, coverages for products liability and completed operations liability, medical payments insurance for claims originating on the insured premises, as well as automobile liability coverage. Since the garage liability form does not provide protection against claims for damage to cars of customers while being repaired, serviced, or stored, garagekeeper's insurance coverage is needed to hold the insured harmless against claims of the latter variety.

Businesses engaged in long-haul trucking have certain specialized exposures with special insurance coverages to meet them. For smaller trucking firms, the most practical coverage is the Comprehensive Automobile Liability Policy with the "truckmen" specified vehicles form which, as its name implies, identifies specific vehicles to be insured. The premium rate is computed by taking into consideration the weight of the trucks and their radius of operation. On the other hand, for the large trucking firm the detailed description of every vehicle insured could involve a great deal of administrative burden and expense. For this reason, businesses in this category use the truckmen gross receipts or mileage forms where the premium is based on the total gross receipts of the firm or on the basis of the total mileage driven, and there is no requirement of listing of the vehicles themselves. This chapter also discusses other details of the operations of long-haul truckers, their special loss exposures, and other insurance forms developed to meet their needs.

Before workers' compensation statutes were enacted in the United States toward the beginning of the 20th century, injuries sustained by workers on the job created a liability on the part of the employer only if the employer has violated certain "common-law" duties toward the employee, namely the duty to provide a safe workplace, sufficient and competent fellow workers, safe tools and equipment, warnings of work-related dangers known to the employer, and enforcement of safety rules by all workers. Violation of any of these duties constituted negligence resulting in the employer's liability to the injured worker. The employer, however, was not without defenses against such claims, the most important ones being contributory negligence, assumption of the risk of injury by the employee, and proof that injury was due to the negligence of another employee. With the development of more complex and dangerous work processes, there has been a great increase in work-related injuries and diseases, many of which remained uncompensated because the injured worker was unable to prove liability on the part of the employer. Faced with this social problem, many state legislatures enacted workers' compensation laws under which injured employees became eligible to be paid for their expenses and loss of wages by the employer regardless of whether the latter was in any way guilty of negligence in causing the worker's injury. The elements of compensation consist of payment of medical expenses and compensation for total or partial disability which may be temporary or permanent. Payments are also due for certain specific injuries and for death.

While workers' compensation payments are commonly regarded as being based on "strict" liability of the employer, the claim must satisfy certain essential elements. The injury must originate in an accident, and it must arise out of the employment relationship, with the accident occurring in the course of the employee's employment. Chapter 11 is devoted exclusively to the subject of workers' compensation and employers' liability claims with an in-depth discussion of the insurance coverages available to protect against them. Such coverage is sold either by private insurance companies or by workers' compensation insurance "funds" operated by certain states on either a monopolistic or competitive basis with private insurers. The policy provides for holding the insured harmless against claims of this type by promising to satisfy all statutory requirements in the case of workers' compensation claims or any legal liability of the employer in situations where workers' compensation does not apply. The latter coverage comes into play where for some reason the injured worker cannot meet the statutory coverage requirements or the injured worker recovers his claim from a negligent third party who then attempts to recoup its loss by claiming against the employer. The determination of the premium rate reflects a relationship between the claims history of the employer and the size of the payroll. Large employers are rated according to such claim experience. Retention of a certain quantity of the losses is becoming a widely used device to reduce the cost of insurance to the employer who purchases excess insurance for losses over and above the retention limit.

If one sustains injury because of a defect in a product he is using, he will generally have a right of compensation against the seller or the manufacturer of the product. If a contractor agrees to perform a service and upon its completion the other party or a third person sustains injury or damage due to the contractor's negligence in performing the work, legal liability arises on the part of the contractor and in favor of the injured or damaged person. Chapter 12 contains a detailed discussion of the exposures to the business enterprise arising out of products liability and service liability (commonly referred to in insurance terminology as "completed operations" liability).

With respect to liability arising out of defective products, the injured party will usually base the claim on one or more of three legal theories of liability of the seller or manufacturer. The first claim is a *breach of express or implied warranty* in furnishing a defective product and is based on the failure by the seller or manufacturer to live up to the bargain. The second claim is one of *negligence* in designing, producing, or marketing the product. The third claim is based on the theory of liability which is gaining increasing popularity in its use— the theory of *strict liability in tort*. Here, responsibility is placed upon the seller of a defective and dangerous product, even though he has exercised all possible care in the preparation and sale of the product. The advantage on the part of the claimant in basing a case upon the strict liability theory is that there is no need to prove negligence on the part of the seller, nor does the claimant have to be a direct purchaser of the defective product, for he just may be a user or consumer thereof.

Whether the claim is for products liability or for "completed operations" liability, the person injured or damaged is entitled to the repair or replacement of the product, as well as to monetary damages. The Comprehensive General Liability Policy is the most frequently used form to provide coverage for products liability and completed operations exposures. The specially developed Storekeepers' Liability Policy, Garage Liability Policy, and Businessowners' Policy include products liability coverage without additional premium charge. Chapter 12 analyzes in detail the policy provisions dealing with products liability and completed operations and discusses the various sources from which insurance coverage may be obtained.

SPECIALIZED EXPOSURES

Business enterprises engaged in activities where some type of work or service is to be performed may be required to file guaranty or surety bonds to assure performance or completion of that work before they are awarded the job. The function of the bond is to have a financially responsible third party, the surety, to guarantee performance of the work and fulfillment of the contractor's obligations under the contract.

Chapter 13 discusses contract, surety, license, and permit bonds designed to meet this need.

Chapter 14 focuses on aviation exposures together with those resulting from marine operations. A business enterprise may own or operate aircraft and thus be exposed to aviation risks. The risks include damage to the aircraft, either on the ground or in flight—a "direct" damage to owned or leased property—and the risk of liability to others arising out of the operation of the aircraft. Aircraft hull may sustain physical damage when stored in hangars or tied down in the open, due to fire, windstorm, hail, and other perils similar to those that may damage other property. The hull is also exposed to damage or destruction when in flight for reasons ranging from weather conditions through mechanical malfunctions to human error.

The liability to others arising out of the operation or, in some cases, of mere ownership of aircraft runs primarily to two groups: persons injured or damaged on the ground, and occupants of the aircraft. While basically such liability is predicated on common law rules of negligence, many jurisdictions have modified the common law by statute to provide strict or absolute liability on the part of aircraft owners and operators for injury to persons on the ground who might be injured by the aircraft or from falling objects originating from the aircraft. With respect to liability to passengers, the common-law rules of negligence are still the basis of liability, although in some states a higher degree of care may be required of airlines.

Aviation insurance policies are similar to automobile policies in that they frequently combine both hull and liability coverages in the same form. Also, many of the terms and conditions are similar to those in auto policies modified, where needed, to take into account the different nature of the exposure, as illustrated, for example, by the Approved Pilot Clause restricting coverage to instances only when an approved pilot is in charge.

Chapter 14 describes the unique group of loss exposures represented by those involving ocean marine operations. Businesses engaged in marine commerce might be exposed to asset loss in the form of damage to the vessel, to the cargo, and of liability to others for injury or property damage. The most common causes of loss are those specifically associated with the sea: storms, collision, and generally the violent action of elements, collectively referred to as "perils of the seas." In addition, fire and explosion, mishaps while loading and unloading the vessel, and damage to machinery are some of the other perils to which the venture is exposed. The loss to vessel or cargo may be total or partial, and there may be voluntary expenses involved in an attempt to save the property. A diminution or elimination of profit can result from the loss or damage to property, and prepaid charges for carrying goods and passengers may be lost.

The liability exposures generally include liability for the cargo, for injury or death of passengers and crew, as well as liability for negligent collision with another vessel. The most commonly used ocean marine policy is similar to the so-called Lloyd's form developed some 200 years ago in Britain. This basic policy can be adjusted to suit the needs of the individual insured by adding or deleting clauses. The basic form covers only damage to hull and cargo, and while usually it includes collision liability, if general liability protection, termed *protection and indemnity* (P&I) insurance is desired, it is provided under a separate insurance policy. The latter affords protection against liability for damage to bridges, piers, and other structures; liability to passengers, crew, and stevedores; damage or loss to cargo aboard the vessel; and the operator's liability for fines for violation of maritime laws. Liability incurred by negligent pollution is not covered by the protection and indemnity form but may be insured through separate pollution liability policies.

Physicians, attorneys, architects, engineers, insurance agents, and many other professionals may be liable for negligence if in the course of their professional activities they fail to live up to the standard of care that the law requires them to exercise. Often a claim for professional liability is based on a theory of breach of contract claiming that the professional has failed to fulfill assumed obligations to the client or patient. More frequently, however, the basis of the claim is based on tort liability arising out of the negligent failure to live up to accepted standards of conduct resulting in injury or damage to the patient or client. Chapter 15 discusses the liability exposures of professionals and various types of insurance coverages available for their protection.

Claims against physicians most frequently include charges of improper or incompetent treatment, misdiagnosis, surgical mistakes, and the failure to secure the informed consent of the patient before certain medical or surgical procedures are undertaken. Defenses that may be available to a physician consist of simultaneous contributory negligence on the part of the patient, proof that the patient has executed a release of the physician prior to the alleged negligent act or that the patient's consent was a willing one given with the knowledge of all possible consequences. Malpractice insurance policies undertake to protect the insured medical personnel from damages because of injuries sustained by the patient due to acts or omissions by the insured professional or by others for whose acts he or she is responsible. A provision peculiar to professional liability policies requires that the insurance company obtain the insured physician's written consent to settle any claims or lawsuits.

Professional liability claims against architects and engineers often allege faulty design of building plans or improper supervision of construction. The damages may be measured by the cost of repairs or the difference in value of the building as built and the value it would have had without the architect's or engineer's error.

An attorney may be held liable to a client for negligence in the manner in which he represents the client. Such liability may be based on ordinary negligence in that the attorney fails to meet the standard of care ordinarily possessed by attorneys who are similarly situated. A frequent cause for malpractice claims against attorneys involves alleged procedural errors, such as the failure on the part of the attorney to start suit prior to the expiration of the statute of limitations with the result that the client's ability to take his case to court is extinguished. Other claims may involve the failure to properly interpret or locate official documents, giving wrong advice, improper drafting of documents, and mismanagement of the client's funds.

The insurance protection available to attorneys for professional liability claims is largely similar to that of medical personnel and architects with certain exclusions covering situations particularly applicable to legal practitioners.

Another major professional group which has become the target of liability claims consists of insurance agents and brokers. These insurance professionals are intermediaries active in the process of establishing a contractual relationship between the insurance company and the insurance consumer. An agent or broker may owe duties both to the insurer and the insured, the breach of which can expose him to liability. As to liability to the insured, it may result from failure to procure the proper insurance coverage required by the client or failure to renew coverage upon its expiration. An insurance agent may be held liable to the insurance company he represents for failure to follow instructions or other negligent performance of duties which results in damage to the insurer. In his defense, the agent or broker might utilize facts tending to prove the absence of a breach of contract or negligence or the presence of contributory fault on the part of the plaintiff.

The professional liability insurance available to insurance agents and brokers is often called errors and omissions insurance and is designed to apply to claims resulting from a negligent act, error, or omission of the insured agent or broker or from those of his employees. Some of these policies also reserve the right to the insured to disapprove settlements proposed by the insurer.

Chapter 16 investigates the liability exposures of corporate executives. The business and affairs of a corporation are managed by a board of directors while its officers supervise and carry out its day-to-day operations. The exposures to liability of officers and directors consist of claims alleging negligent or illegal acts resulting in damage by persons either outside or inside the corporation. Such claims might involve alleged breaches of the duty of diligence, loyalty, or obedience to the corporate charter or bylaws. Against a charge of negligence in the standard of care an officer or director must prove (1) that he exercised ordinary prudence such as required in the exercise of one's own affairs and (2) that ordinary care of a director or officer of a corporation in a similar position and circumstance has been observed. Charges might include the violation of various statutes, such as antitrust, securities, or criminal laws. A recently emerged fiduciary liability of officers and directors is that under the Employee Retirement Income Security Act of 1974 (ERISA). The director or officer who exercises any discretionary control in the management of employee benefit plans incurs personal liability if he fails to act solely in the interest of the plan participants or to exercise the care and skill of a prudent person conducting an enterprise of similar character.

While most jurisdictions allow the indemnification of officers and directors for legal expenses that they incur in defending suits based on their alleged wrongful acts, liability insurance covering officers and directors plays an important role. The premium for such insurance has been held to be deductible by the Internal Revenue Service as an ordinary and necessary business expense of the corporation. With respect to fiduciary liability under ERISA, however, the corporation or the fiduciary himself must obtain a "recourse" liability policy separate from the usual officers' and directors' errors and omissions policy.

Most businesses using boilers and other pressure vessels and certain machinery are faced with the exposure to asset loss due to explosions and other violent malfunctions. Such accidents can result not only in extensive damage to the pressure vessels and machinery themselves but also in losses due to the interruption of the business and in liability to the property or person of others. Chapter 17 discusses these exposures and their insurance treatment. It describes the typical boiler and machinery insurance coverage which covers loss involving accidents caused by these instrumentalities. It examines the insuring agreement which extends coverage to the insured's property damaged by the accident, the extra cost of temporary repair that may be involved in putting the damaged equipment back into operation, liability for damage to others, and optionally, bodily injury liability to third parties.

The chapter also focuses on some specific exposures to which many business enterprises are subject, namely, glass breakage, the loss of valuable papers and records, and financial losses inherent in credit risks.

While the exposure to loss by glass is largely due to its susceptibility to breakage, glass damage could arise from the interaction of chemicals or by the mechanical means of abrasion. Sand or dust storms damaging a plate of glass are an example of the latter. To protect against such losses comprehensive glass policies are available which often list the specific glass panels insured, together with any inscription, lettering, or design on the glass since it, too, would be replaced if damaged. This is one of the few insurance contracts where the loss does not have to be "accidental." Intentional glass breakage to overcome the obstacle of a locked door would be covered.

Valuable papers and records insurance is available to cover loss or damage to deeds, maps, blueprints, and other documents. Those capable of replacement are covered on a blanket basis, while unique items must be listed specifically with a listed amount of insurance available in case of their loss or destruction.

There are few business enterprises that do not extend some type of credit to their customers and, therefore, are not exposed to the possibility of sustaining financial loss because of the inability to collect payments when due. Insurance coverage has been developed to protect primarily a manufacturer and wholesaler who has relatively large amounts involved in credit accounts. In view of the fact that all businesses can normally expect to sustain a certain number of credit losses, the coverage is designed to protect against credit losses of extraordinary magnitude where the debtor becomes "insolvent," such term encompassing, in addition to financial inability to repay his obligations, the death or insanity of the debtor, his absconding, or the attachment or other lien on his stock. Retail sellers of merchandise have available credit insurance policies to cover installments due from purchasers that are not forthcoming because of death or disability of the purchaser. Credit transactions arising out of the exporting of merchandise may be insured by the Foreign Credit Insurance Association.

A unique form of insurance is available to protect legal title to real property. This is described in detail in Chapter 18. The value of such title depends greatly on whether it is free and clear of any liens, encumbrances, or claims of others. Title insurance companies specialize in examining the history of the title representing ownership of land and in issuing title insurance policies whereby they agree to assume the cost of legal procedures including litigation that might be necessary to eliminate competing claims. Title insurance policies are often issued to protect the interests of mortgagees as well. A one-time premium payment is made at the time title is acquired. The policy remains in effect as long as the insured owns the property or has a security interest in it.

THE COORDINATION AND COMBINATION OF INSURANCE COVERAGES

Even though the prudent business person has obtained all the protection against asset loss that is available by the selection of appropriate basic insurance coverages, he or she may realize that there is still a need to safeguard the enterprise from catastrophic loss. Inflation and other economic, social, and legal developments may represent a threat to the business in the form of loss potentials not covered, or only partially covered, by basic insurance protection, even though the limits of the latter have been maximized. Chapter 19 explores such excess exposures and identifies the measures that can be taken to minimize their impact.

Conceptually, loss to the business enterprise reasonably well protected by basic insurance may arise under two sets of conditions: (1) the existing insurance coverage is *quantitatively* inadequate in that there is a reasonable possibility of the loss exceeding the amount of the coverage, and (2) the basic insurance coverage is *qualitatively* insufficient because it furnishes no coverage whatsoever against certain types of losses. Chapter 19 focuses on certain specialized insurance policies designed to eliminate or lessen the consequences of the loss potential in this area.

Umbrella liability insurance has been devised both to furnish protection against catastrophe losses and against losses of unusual nature. In its first function it requires the existence of a certain amount of basic insurance coverage for the same type of loss and steps in only when the coverage limits of the basic coverage have been exhausted. In its second function it extends coverage, subject to a self-insured retention, "from the first dollar up" for unusual types of losses not covered by primary insurance. In this manner, the umbrella policy affords relief for both the qualitative and quantitative shortcomings of existing basic insurance protection. Because of its high limits, commercial umbrella liability insurance protection is the chief line of defense against the rapidly growing number of "jumbo" verdicts secured by individuals with severe bodily injury claims.

Such excess insurance policies are different in scope with respect to property losses. The best-known policy of this type is the Difference in Conditions (DIC) Policy, the purpose of which is to protect the insured's property against most of the perils not covered by basic property insurance policies such as fire and extended coverage. While it is often termed an *all-risks* coverage, it does exclude coverage already afforded by other forms in that it is designed to fill the gap in existing insurance protection. Furthermore, *unlike* the umbrella liability policy, it *does not* increase the amount of coverage quantitatively by adding higher limits on top of those of the existing policies. In this respect, it could be considered yet another basic policy which is excess only in the sense of giving protection against additional perils.

Chapter 20 undertakes to analyze the special policy designed to accommodate several of the property insurance needs of the small to medium-sized nonmanufacturing business. As characteristic of many combination policies, the Businessowners' Policy represents a package in which a number of basic coverages are combined with a few optional ones that may be added by endorsement. For the business enterprise eligible for the Businessowners' Policy there is a choice between a named peril form and a so-called special form which grants coverage on an all-risks basis. In order to be eligible the business must not exceed certain physical limits expressed in square feet. The property that is insured consists of real and personal property of the business and of the loss of income that may be sustained because of damage to physical property. Optional coverages available are fidelity insurance protecting against employee dishonesty; burglary and robbery; damage to exterior signs and glass, boilers, air-conditioning equipment; and damage due to earthquake.

Owners of commercial farms and ranches are eligible to purchase farm owners—ranch owners insurance discussed in Chapter 22. These policies insure the farm dwelling and household personal property, as well as the farm personal property, barns, buildings, and other structures for physical damage and afford personal liability coverage together with medical payments. This chapter also includes a discussion of crop hail insurance and other coverages of importance to a farming enterprise.

Chapter 21 analyzes one of the most frequently used combination policies, the so-called Special Multi-Peril Policy. This combination policy was developed because there was a need for convenience and efficiency both from the viewpoint of the insurance company in reducing administrative work, policy printing, procedures, and rating, and for the insured in simplifying the task of dealing with the insurance aspects of his business. More importantly, it reduced the possibility of gaps in coverage between various policies. There is added advantage in its flexibility and adaptability to the needs of the insured, for beyond certain minimum required property and liability coverages, there is a wide variety of additional protection that may be selected. Business groups eligible for the Special Multi-Peril Policy are apartment complexes, construction operations, motel and hotel operations, industrial and processing enterprises, institutions, mercantile businesses, offices, and service firms. The major sections of the policy are property coverage, liability coverage, crime coverage, and boiler and machinery coverage. Only the first two are mandatory. In addition to the latter two, other optional coverages are available by endorsement. Becuase of this flexibility, the better protection, and the convenience, the Special Multi-Peril Policy is an attractive insurance form steadily gaining in popularity.

PROVIDING FOR BUSINESS CONTINUATION THROUGH INSURANCE AND SELECTED EMPLOYEE BENEFITS

A business enterprise can face substantial losses and the possibility of termination of its existence when its managers and employees are exposed to the hazards of advanced age, illness, and death. Certain employees may occupy a position of critical importance for the success of the firm. The death or disability of these individuals can easily result in reduced income, increasing costs, adversely affecting the credit rating of the enterprise, and ultimately, the liquidation of the business. It may influence the morale and attitude of the employees by creating uncertainty about their future. Chapters 23 through 26 describe the details of these potential losses and offer some solution by means of insurance and other techniques. Chapter 23 begins the discussion of insurance and risk management of human assets. Health insurance, disability income, and retirement income are discussed in the early portions of the chapter. These are coverages usually assumed, at least in part, by an employee. Since the business affairs of the sole proprietor are also personal affairs, the chapter examines insurance policies that are essentially policies for individuals applied to the circumstances of the sole proprietor. Chapter 23 also deals with the consequences of the death of the owner-manager of the business. Often after the sole proprietor-manager dies, if no plans have been made, the economic death of the business shortly follows. The personal representative of the owner's estate must liquidate the business in the absence of previously arranged continuation plans. Sometimes, there is an immediate need to convert business assets into cash in order to pay the costs of last illness, funeral expenses, taxes, and the expenses of administering the estate. Chances are that such quick liquidation will result in a substantially lower return for the assets.

In order to avoid financial loss, arrangements can be made for continuing the business provided there is legal authority and well-laid plans such as those that are generally developed in a trust agreement or a buy-sell agreement prior to the death of the proprietor. Buy-sell agreements are entered into between the owner and a willing buyer to go into effect upon the owner's death. Most such agreements are funded by life insurance that the prospective purchaser owns on the life of the owner. The advantage of such an agreement is that the heirs of the owner will receive the going-concern value of the company rather than a diminished liquidation value; the sale is accomplished promptly and with a minimum of arguments concerning business value, and creditors and employees will feel more secure as they are assured of the continuation of the business. For the buyer, who is often a trusted employee, there is more job security and the ability to plan for the future.

In case of disability of the sole proprietor, the buy-sell agreement may provide that after a certain length of time, the prospective buyer must be offered ownership.

After reviewing the advantages and disadvantages of the partnership form of doing business, Chapter 24 discusses partnership business continuation problems and their solutions. Unless there is an agreement among the partners, the death of a partner dissolves the partnership and the partnership's business must be liquidated. Once again, a buy-sell agreement might prove to be the solution. Life insurance on the lives of the individual partners payable either to the surviving partners or to the partnership itself is the preferred funding method.

Chapter 25 focuses on business continuation, stock valuation, and transfer problems that face the closely held corporation upon the death of a key owner. Even though the death of the stockholder of a closely held corporation does not automatically terminate the corporation's existence as it is in the case of death of a partner, important management talent can be lost with adverse effects on the morale of employees and the confidence of creditors. In addition, a need for immediate liquidity is frequently encountered. A well-designed buy-sell agreement can in this instance provide for the remaining stockholders to purchase the stock of the deceased. Life insurance would guarantee the funding of the agreement. This is called a *cross-purchase* plan. If a *stock redemption* or entity plan is used, the agreement is between each stockholder and the corporation, with the latter required to purchase and retire the shares of the deceased stockholder. The chapter includes an examination of life insurance used in funding buy-sell agreements.

Chapters 26, 27, and 28 deal with the subject of employee benefits. Salary, wages, and other monetary compensations are not the only way employees are rewarded. An equally important part of employee compensation consists of having benefit plans which provide for income maintenance at times when regular earnings are interrupted or terminated because of accident, sickness, retirement, unemployment, or death. Other important employee benefit plans are designed to meet medical expenses incurred because of injury or illness. The three chapters differentiate between key personnel and the remaining employee force. However, both groups have many common benefit needs and are provided such benefits by the same or similar plans. The three chapters discuss employee benefit plans involving individual and group life insurance, pension planning devices, and health, accident, and disability plans.

An important role in devising benefit plans for executives of the firm is played by tax considerations. As high-income employees, they are interested in receiving part of their compensation in the form of deferred income which becomes payable after retirement and at a time when presumably they are in a lower tax bracket.

Life and health insurance is an important part of employee compensation in that it provides for lost income, as well as coverage for additional expenses at the time when the employee is incapacitated or after his death. Such life and health insurance protection is often afforded on a group basis benefiting the entire group of employees. The vast majority of group life insurance plans where the premium is paid by the employer use the term life insurance variety which does not develop a cash value and is payable only in case of death. Due to a change in the tax law in 1966, however, it has become possible to furnish group *ordinary* life insurance with employer contributions under Section 79 of the Internal Revenue Code. An employee under such a plan can change his term insurance coverage to permanent cash value life insurance and under certain conditions the employer's contributions toward the cost of such insurance will be tax-free to the employee. Because so many of the employee benefit plans utilize the group insurance principle, there is an examination of the characteristics of group underwriting as it differs from individual underwriting of insurance policies.

There is extensive discussion of disability income insurance, medical expense insurance, and the individual variations of each. Special attention is given to one of the recent developments in commercial health insurance plans called the Health Maintenance Organization (HMO). By making certain periodic payments to such an organization, the participants are eligible to receive preventive and remedial medical care from a panel of medical practitioners who are compensated on a salary rather than a fee basis. The commercial insurer serves as the sponsor of the organization and provides its overall management.

This segment of the book also includes an examination of pension and profit plans for the self-employed and describes methods that physicians, attorneys, accountants, and other professionals can employ to arrange for deferring income as a means of pension planning.

UNIQUE EXPOSURES

The newer coverages available today for businesses are the result of new exposures businesses face or exposures that have grown in importance in recent years. Thirty years ago computers were owned by government agencies, research facilities, or extremely large businesses. Today it is not uncommon to find them in the home.

Chapter 30 is an example of exposures that have grown in significance to the extent new policies have been devised. There are some liability exposures that may not be covered by other policies, such as equal employment opportunity lawsuits and defending unfriendly and undesirable tender offers for control of a business. This chapter describes two coverages: business legal expense insurance, to pay legal expenses for many actions against a business not covered by other insurance; and tender offer defense expense insurance, available to pay many expenses incurred by a business listed on a securities exchange in fighting a tender offer. Both policies are relatively new and potentially significant to eligible businesses.

DATA PROCESSING INSURANCE

Business owners and lessees of electronic data processing equipment are exposed to special risks of loss arising out of the ownership and use of such equipment. This equipment must be maintained in a controlled environment, it is susceptible to damage by fire and other perils, and it is expensive to repair or replace. Computer tapes, disks and cards containing the data, collectively referred to as "media," are subject to loss and destruction resulting in substantial damages to the owner. Chapter 29 is devoted to this subject and examines in detail the Electronic Data Processing (EDP) Policy. It affords all-risks coverage with certain specific exceptions. The property covered is the data processing equipment whether owned, leased, or otherwise under the control of the insured. Each piece of machinery must be specifically listed on the policy. There is a separate coverage for data processing media. The amount of loss to media may be determined either by the cost of reproduction of the data or on a valued basis, i.e., a specific, previously agreed-upon valuation is paid in case of loss. The insured may also purchase, on an optional basis, extra expense insurance covering the cost of the operation of the business while it is being restored after a loss. Other optional coverages are for valuable papers and records, accounts receivable, and business interruption.

Dealing with potential exposures of asset loss by the business enterprise is one of the most important functions of business management. This book is directed to the individual who performs such risk management function whether he or she bears the title Risk Manager or performs the function without the title. In keeping with this philosophy, the Appendix at the end of this *Handbook* contains checklists prepared to aid in identifying the risks facing the business enterprise.

Chapter 31 on Environmental Impairment Liability (EIL) insurance highlights the requirements imposed by statute for insurance coverage against gradual pollution occurrences. The chapter also summarizes the liabilities that all companies face under common law, whether or not they are required to purchase commercial insurance. Specific markets for EIL insurance are discussed, and techniques are provided that allow underwriters and corporate planners to assess the potential for gradual environmental impairment arising from specific operations or facilities.

Our aim is to have the reader refer to the chapters that apply to his or her business situation as well as to examine new loss exposures which are created when a business expands, with a view toward obtaining increased and more complete coverage at a reduced cost.

CONTROLLING PROPERTY EXPOSURES

CHAPTER 4

DIRECT DAMAGE
TO BUILDINGS AND FIXTURES

REAL PROPERTY EXPOSURES—AN
OVERVIEW

LEGAL CONCEPTS
Contractual requirements
Lapse
Waiver and estoppel
Cancellation

PRINCIPLES OF INSURANCE
CONTRACTS
Indemnity
Insurable interest
Extinguishment
Actual cash value
Co-insurance
Valued policies
Warranties and representations
Subrogation

STANDARD FIRE POLICY AND
GENERAL PROPERTY FORM
Property covered
Property not covered
Extensions of coverage
Co-insurance
Deductible
Perils insured against
Exclusions
Valuation
Other provisions

SPECIAL FORMS, POLICIES, AND
INSURANCE MARKETS
All-risks coverage
Flood
Earthquake
Nuclear contamination
Operation of building codes
FAIR Plan
Excess and surplus lines markets

INSURANCE LIMITS RELATIVE
TO PROPERTY VALUATION
Insurance to value
Inflation Guard Endorsement
Replacement Cost Endorsement
Agreed Amount Endorsement
Deductibles
Blanket limits

PROPERTY INSURANCE RATES
Specific and class rates
Blanket rates
Loss engineering

OCCURRENCE OF LOSS
Occupancy and vacancy
Dealing with a loss

SUMMARY

Theodore W. Flowers, Esquire
Partner
White and Williams
Philadelphia, Pennsylvania

Theodore W. Flowers is Chairman of the Commercial Litigation Department of the firm of White & Williams. He is a member of the Third Circuit Judicial Conference, past Chairman of various committees on litigation involving federal procedures and commercial transactions, with emphasis on SEC, antitrust, and general corporate litigation. Mr. Flowers has been lecturer on trial practice techniques, management of complex litigation, and class action procedures at various universities and professional societies, including Court Practice Institute at the University of Chicago, University of Pennsylvania, and University of Colorado under the auspices of the American Bar Association.

Thomas D. Rutherfoord, Jr.
Executive Vice President
Thomas Rutherfoord, Inc.
Alexandria, Virginia

Thomas D. Rutherfoord, Jr. is Executive Vice President of Thomas Rutherfoord, Inc., a large regional insurance brokerage with its home office in Roanoke, Virginia. Mr. Rutherfoord manages the firm's Washington office in Alexandria, Virginia. He co-edited the firm's 1973 publication "Bonds and Insurance for Contractors" distributed through the National Association of Surety Bond Producers for which he has served as a director.

Thomas J. Ziomek, Esquire
Partner
White and Williams
Philadelphia, Pennsylvania

Thomas J. Ziomek is a partner in the law firm of White and Williams, engaging primarily, in commercial litigation. He is admitted to practice in Connecticut and Pennsylvania. He is a member of various committees and sections of the American Bar Association and the Philadelphia Bar Association with general emphasis on securities, corporate, and business litigation and manufacturer's liability. He has published and made presentations on complex litigation, professional malpractice (legal and accounting) litigation, and class action procedures.

This chapter deals with damage to buildings and fixtures directly or proximately caused by an insured peril. Buildings and fixtures include machinery, equipment, and other property constituting a permanent part of a building or pertaining to the service of a building. Because this property is typically valuable and represents a significant portion of a business's assets, loss exposures are great. Currently, insurance is the principal mechanism for treating this property loss exposure. Retention of the exposure by a business is generally limited to a tolerable level through deductibles after considering the benefits of marginal premium additions or reductions associated with various deductibles.

This chapter (1) covers questions and considerations to be addressed before insurance covering real property is purchased; (2) discusses insurance policies, endorsements, or extensions of coverage protecting against loss; and (3) highlights many commonplace problems and considerations once a loss has occurred. An insured who is generally aware of potential problems in adjusting a loss will be better prepared and able to understand, discuss, and plan for these contingencies.

REAL PROPERTY EXPOSURES—AN OVERVIEW

In order to make a reasonable decision about what property to insure and to what extent, the businessman must analyze his company's properties and determine their values subject to loss. He must measure the degree and nature of loss exposures based on potential loss frequency and severity. A well-developed property survey, including loss histories, will facilitate and improve insurance decisions. This is true because loss frequency and severity are key elements of an exposure considered by insurance underwriters in agreeing to terms of coverage. A typical analysis should begin with preparation of a schedule of all physical properties showing for each property the type of construction, location, occupancy, exposures to perils (potentially leading to loss) and hazards (increasing the risk of loss), replacement cost, and depreciation (taking into consideration a realistic replacement value and useful life).

Certain perils cannot be insured—war, intentional losses, neglect by the insured, and wear and tear, for example. Certain other perils may be fully or partially insured, or may not be insured at all, depending on the nature of the property and its location. Water damage, flood, and earthquake are good examples.

A businessman and his insurance counselor should consider the potential of loss from perils which can be insured along with those which may not be insured, recognizing both frequency and severity of probable and possible losses. In cases where more than one location is involved and the exposures are treated as a group, the maximum probable loss can be considerably less than the maximum possible loss from any one occurrence. While probable loss is an important consideration in premium negotiation, possible loss is the determining factor in retention versus insurance decisions. The costs of retaining the somewhat predictable, tolerable losses should be weighed against the costs of insuring the more fortuitous but possible losses to arrive at a well-balanced insurance program. By retaining portions of the risk, a business may effect significant savings in policy premiums. For their part, insurers not only pay losses but provide significant services in safety engineering, inspection, and loss adjustment, among others.

Proper planning for new facilities (or for changes in existing facilities), utilizing construction techniques and materials for fire protection, such as sprinklering a building, along with other safety and security measures, will reduce loss frequency and severity and therefore insurance premiums. Risk control can and should be an important part of any analysis of real property and a determination of what to insure.

LEGAL CONCEPTS

Prior to discussing the basic procedure for negotiating and executing an insurance policy, it is helpful to understand the basic legal principles underlying the relationship between a businessman and his insurer. When a claim is filed, the first action by the insurer is to ascertain the nature and extent of insurance coverage. In other words: Was a policy in force? Is the loss covered? Are there any applicable exclusions? Proper interpretation of the insurance policy and its parties' relationship, responsibilities, and mutual intent goes a long way toward answering questions prior to a loss, and reduces the likelihood of problems after a loss.

Contractual requirements

An insurance policy is a contract, in legal definition, and requires the existence of certain elements in order to be effective and binding. In its most elementary form, a contract is an agreement between two or more parties and consists of mutual promises on the part of each— promises the law will enforce. Like all contracts, an insurance policy consists of an agreement which not only provides benefits but also imposes obligations. In the case of a policy insuring buildings and fixtures, the contract consists of a promise on the part of the businessman to pay premiums in exchange for the promise on the part of the insurance company at its option to pay, repair, rebuild or replace the damaged property after a loss. For purposes of an insurance contract, it is necessary that there be mutual assent to the agreement by knowledgeable parties who understand the nature of the agreement. There must be consideration—the legal term for the inducement to enter into the contract. For example, the businessman agrees to pay the premiums and the insurer agrees to and is obliged to pay a covered loss. The parties to the contract must have legal capacity which, for purposes of this discussion, means that the individual acting on behalf of the business must be authorized to so act, and must have the power to bind the business. The general nature of the understanding and assent on the part of the businessman usually is set forth in the application for insurance. As stated, the consideration offered by the businessman is the payment of premiums to the insurer. For its part, the insurance company offers coverage, evidenced by either an insurance policy, a binder of insurance, or a conditional receipt for the premium tendered. Two particular problems which can affect this arrangement are the effect of nonpayment of the premium or consequent cancellation of the policy.

Lapse

A question that sometimes arises concerns whether or not there is coverage during the time interval between the insured's payment or tender of premiums and the insurer's delayed processing of an application. Another question concerns what happens upon the nonpayment of scheduled premiums when due.

Some courts have refused to recognize claims in favor of the businessman against an insurer when there is an allegation by the businessman that the insurer unnecessarily and/or negligently delayed processing an application for insurance. This problem can be avoided by the use of binders or conditional receipts, either of which may be issued by the agent, broker, or insurance company as evidence of coverage.

As to the question of coverage when there has been a lapse in the payment of premiums, generally the policy will state that when the policyholder fails to pay the required premium, the policy terminates—or lapses. Usually a policy will provide for the payment of premium in advance of the period of coverage. At the time of a loss where the question of lapse is an issue, the insurer generally takes the position that the payment of the premium is a *condition precedent* to the effectiveness of the policy, that is, there is no coverage under the policy and the policy does not exist unless and until the premiums have been paid. Two doctrines of law that work in favor of the businessman in this situation are those of waiver and estoppel.

Waiver and estoppel. If an insurer acts in a manner, or enters into a course of conduct, which is inconsistent with insistence upon strict compliance with policy terms, and that conduct is communicated to the insured, the insurer *waives* its right to argue the policy has lapsed. For example, retention of premiums by the insurer after a policy default can result in a decision that the insurer has waived its right to argue the policy has lapsed.

Estoppel is a corollary argument to that of waiver and generally means that an insurance company is prohibited (estopped) from denying the effectiveness of an insurance policy if it has acted in such a way as to create the impression, upon which the insured relied to his detriment, that the policy is in effect. Stated more simply, if the businessman can demonstrate the insurer acted as if the policy was in effect, and the businessman so understood the policy to be in effect and therefore did not take other precautions, the doctrine of estoppel may be applicable.

Cancellation

When is notice of cancellation an effective argument for the insurer to deny coverage? As might be expected, the issue of cancellation and notification generally arises after a loss has occurred, a claim submitted and denied. Depending on the facts and circumstances of each cancellation situation, the insurer presents the argument the policy had been cancelled with proper notification to the businessman prior to the occurrence of the loss, and therefore (1) the cancellation was effective, (2) the loss was not covered, and (3) payment is not due or owed the insured. The key issue is the effectiveness of cancellation. It depends to a great extent on the facts of each case, so business procedures of the insured and documentary evidence are critical to the preservation and advancement of the businessman's rights. Prior planning is obviously essential.

Every insurance policy has a provision setting forth the terms and conditions for cancellation. For example, the standard fire policy, discussed later in this chapter, requires the insurance company to give the insured five (5) days written notice of cancellation (or such longer period if extended by statute or endorsement). This notice may be with or without immediate tender of any return premium (if the return premium is not tendered, it will be refunded upon demand of the insured). The cancellation issue most often revolves around the question of whether the insured actually received notice of the cancellation. If the insurance company can establish that notice of cancellation was mailed, as a general rule, it is presumed that the insured received the notice. This presumption of receipt of notice may be rebutted by the insured. Often the only evidence offered by the businessman is oral testimony that notice was not received.

Prior planning and establishment of procedures for handling insurance matters are effective aids to the insured in presenting evidence of nonreceipt. A businessman should establish a system where all correspondence, notices, and documentations of any type from the insurance company are kept in a file. Then he has the advantage of being able to testify that in the ordinary course of business, his business keeps and retains notices and other documents received from the insurance company and, in the particular instance involved, his file does not contain notice of cancellation. Note that the businessman is in the position of attempting to show that something did not happen. It is also helpful, if it can be established, that the businessman continued to deal with the insurance company after the alleged cancellation of the policy. For example, documentary evidence showing that the insured continued to correspond with the insurance company without any contrary return correspondence or notification that the policy had been cancelled is helpful. Also, continued payment of premiums establishes the continued effectiveness of the policy (doctrine of estoppel). The insurance company cannot deny the policy is effective under circumstances in which it continues receiving and accepting premiums for the payment of the policy. Proof of premium payment, whether in the form of cancelled checks, correspondence, or whatever, is the insured's best evidence.

PRINCIPLES OF INSURANCE CONTRACTS

Indemnity

The principle of indemnity is the foundation of insurance. For purposes of property damage and insurance, indemnity simply means making one whole for the damages to the buildings and/or fixtures. The purpose of the insurance policy is not to place the insured in a better position than prior to the loss. This policy against wagering is a foundation for another requirement for the validity of an insurance policy, insurable interest.

Insurable interest

It is essential to have an interest in the insured property in order to have an enforceable contract. Anyone obtaining insurance must have some stake in the property being insured in order to avoid wagering and, more importantly, to avoid a situation in which that person would be tempted to seek the destruction of the premises rather than take precautions against harm to the premises. If no insurable interest exists, the contract of insurance is contrary to public policy and considered void. The general rule is that an insurable interest exists when the person or persons applying for insurance obtain profit, advantage, or benefit by the continued existence of the property or will sustain a loss from damage to the property. It is an either-or situation: that is, the requirement is satisfied if there is continuing benefit by the existence of the property or if there is loss from damage.

Indeed, the principle of law has developed that a lessee and lessor can each have an insurable interest in the same property because each has separate and distinct interests and would have paid separate premiums for separate coverage. Clearly, an owner has an interest in the continued preservation of his property, and a tenant has such an interest when the continued preservation also means his ability to conduct business without interruption.

Extinguishment. It is possible for an insurer to contend that a contract of insurance is voidable if the person (or business) who originally took out the insurance no longer retains an insurable interest in the property at the time of loss—that is, when an interest in the property has terminated or been extinguished. The majority rule is that an insured must have an insurable interest at the time of loss. The theory is someone who has lost, sold, or transferred his interest in the property has nothing to gain from its continued existence.

A full understanding of the principle of indemnity—making the insured whole—requires a brief explanation of some further doctrines involved in determining not only what was owned and has been destroyed but also how much it was worth and what a businessman can expect to happen in the process of recovering for the loss.

Actual cash value

In reading an insurance policy, the average insured may encounter terms he does not fully understand, including *actual cash value* (ACV). This term has a particular definition and is significant to an insured because actual cash value determines how much money will be paid for a claim. There are several interpretations throughout the United States of the term *actual cash value,* including the strict rule, the so-called liberal rule, and the intermediate rule.

The strict rule adopted by approximately one third of the states in the United States provides that actual cash value means the replacement cost of an article less physical depreciation. This rule does not take into consideration market value, cost of repairs, or any other factor other than the actual replacement cost. For example, an insured who suffers a fire loss at an old building—typical of some factory buildings found in large cities—a building constructed of 18-inch fieldstone walls, with high ceilings, obsolete elevators, and other features which could not possibly be reproduced under today's conditions—is entitled under this ACV rule to the cost to replace that building as it stood before the fire, less physical depreciation, or wear and tear.

The so-called liberal rule permits evidence of any facts which concern themselves with value to be considered in arriving at the actual cash value. Obsolescence, neighborhood, market value, illegality, and any other factor which has any bearing at all on the "worth" of the building can be taken into account.

The intermediate rule is a combination of both strict and liberal construction. Some elements, market value and obsolescence, for example, would be permitted, but other such factors such as neighborhood or illegality might not be admitted. It is important to know exactly what rule is applicable at the property's location because ACV effects the co-insurance clause.

Co-insurance

One of the most important parts of the insurance contract is the co-insurance clause. As the word itself indicates, it means a sharing of the insurance by the insurance company and the insured. To a degree this is true, but co-insurance has a more limited and restricted meaning within the insurance business. The mandatory and minimum amount of co-insurance is usually 80 percent. Illustrating the co-insurance clause by example best explains its meaning and application. To comply with the co-insurance clause, a business insuring property with an actual cash value of $100,000 must carry insurance on at least 80 percent of the value of the property. In this case, $80,000 would be the minimum coverage required to avoid penalty in the event of a loss. If, for example, this same insured were to carry $60,000 worth of coverage in lieu of the required $80,000, he would be carrying only three fourths of the minimum coverage demanded by the co-insurance requirement. In this instance, the insured would suffer a penalty should a loss occur. In the event of a $1,000 loss, exclusive of all deductibles, the insured would receive not $1,000 but three fourths of the loss, or $750. In the event of a total loss, however, the insured would be able to collect the full face value of the policy, or $60,000. Since the property was valued at $100,000 before the loss, the insured is still penalized for not having insured sufficiently. The co-insurance clause is taken very seriously in the insurance business, and an insured who does not adhere to its requirements can expect to suffer a penalty when faced with a loss.

When purchasing insurance, the businessman should obtain a commitment from the agent or the insurance company concerning the meaning of ACV applicable at the property's location, and it is suggested that examples be used to explore the situation. Otherwise, a businessman may be dismayed to find that the term *actual cash value* has been used in his policy to his detriment.

Valued policies. The valued policy, which is available only in states which have enacted valued policy laws, makes it possible to specify a set value for the property insured so that upon the occurrence of a total loss and in cases a partial loss, it is not necessary to produce evidence of replacement costs, market value, salable value, or depreciation. When an insured purchases a valued policy actual cash value is no longer the important determination. A value must be specified as the courts require clear and express language showing an intent to value the property at a specific amount. If it is clear that the policy involved is a valued policy, the valuation set in the policy is conclusive and binding at the time of loss provided there has been no fraud, misrepresentation, mistake, or accident.

Warranties and representations

Another determination necessary in valuing a loss and determining whether a businessman will be made whole is the question of whether any warranties, which become part of the insurance policy, were breached. As a general proposition and for purposes of property insurance, a warranty is a statement by an insured which serves as the basis of the insurance contract. The validity of the insurance contract depends upon the literal truth of or compliance with the warranty by the insured.

Warranties can be either affirmative or promissory. An affirmative warranty means that a businessman has warranted the existence of a fact at the time the policy is entered into, and that warranty is binding upon him. If it was not so, the contract is not valid. A promissory warranty is one which requires something to be done or not be done after the policy is in effect. An oversimplified example of an affirmative warranty is the representation that a building, at the time of the execution of the policy, is used for the operation of a printing business. A contract covering the loss to that building and its fixtures will not be valid if it is determined that the building was in fact being used for the production of explosives. A promissory warranty, on the other hand, would be a statement that the building would not be used as an explosives factory. If it was converted to explosive manufacturing, the policy may be void.

Warranties may refer to many different representations in fact but most often refer to ownership of or title to the property. It is a valid provision in a policy of property insurance to require the insured to have sole and unconditional ownership of the property. Other provisions are called representations and may relate to the description, use, or occupation of the building or the value of the building, or special matters affecting the risk, such as the danger of incendiarism or the continued occupancy of the building. (See Divisible Contract Clause under headings "Standard Fire Policy and General Property Form: Other Provisions".) A standard provision in property insurance policies specifies that the policy is void (and therefore a loss will not be paid) if the insured has misrepresented or concealed any material fact concerning the insurance or the property or concerning the interest of the insured in the insurance or the property.

Subrogation

One principle which may have an effect on how and when a businessman is to be indemnified under a policy covering building and fixtures is the principle of subrogation. This is, generally, a simplified method of payment, used in part to avoid the necessity of referring a loss or dispute, if there is one, to a lawyer.

Subrogation means the substitution of the insurance company in the place of the businessman upon the occurrence of a loss. It is a standard provision in a policy of property insurance. Typically, if a loss occurs to a businessman's building or fixtures through the fault of another, that businessman has a right of action against the other party for having caused his loss. Through the principle of subrogation, the insurance company pays the loss under the businessman's policy and then succeeds to the rights of the insured businessman concerning any claim that the businessman has against the third party. This corresponds with the duty of an insurer to act in good faith toward his insured when there is a loss, and it results in payment to the insured, followed by the insurance company's attempt to recover against the third party. The businessman himself no longer carries the burden of attempting to establish the negligence or other causative factor on the part of the third party.

STANDARD FIRE POLICY AND GENERAL PROPERTY FORM

A complete property insurance contract is a combination of a fire insurance policy with various forms which describe the insurance coverage in more specific terms. The fire insurance policy consists of Policy Declarations (the "insuring agreement") and Policy Provisions and Stipulations. The declarations are tailored to the individual specifications for each exposure and set forth the parties to the contract—insurer and insured(s), the policy term—inception and expiration dates, the policy number, the property description and location, the perils insured against, the amount(s) of insurance, the premium, and the mortgagee(s) or trustee(s), if any.

Although policy wording is governed by the laws of each state, the benefits to both policyholders and insurance companies of a consistent application of provisions and stipulations (such as those which call for simplified loss adjustment and reduced litigation) have led to standardized wording with only minor variations in less than a third of the states. Standardized wording generally follows the New York Standard Fire Policy adopted in 1943 which has 165 numbered lines of provisions and stipulations. However, it is important to recognize variations where they exist; the Texas Standard Fire Policy, for one, has a structure very different from the New York Standard Fire Policy.

The General Property Form published by the Insurance Services Office (ISO) is the form regularly used to complete the insurance contract covering direct damage to buildings and fixtures (and also contents, discussed in Chapter 5). The form consists of sections describing property covered, property not covered, extensions of coverage, co-insurance percentage, deductible amount, perils insured against, exclusions, valuation, and other provisions. The following discussion of certain parts of these sections and other optional coverages provides a better understanding of the property insurance contract.

Property covered

As used in insurance, the term *building* has a specific meaning. Everyone understands that a house, an office, or a garage is a building, but many people may not realize that certain other items, machinery and its housing for instance, and other items not commonly considered a building in ordinary experience, may be treated as a building for the purpose of insurance. Also, part of the property may consist of "fixtures": items or accessories which become attached to or are used to service the real estate and in effect become part and parcel of the realty. For example, fixtures may consist of the machinery and equipment necessary to the conduct of business in an insured building. Problems concerning fixtures have generally arisen in the context of tenants in an insured property; a dispute develops, for example, over who owns the machinery and equipment that in effect has become attached to the property. Generally, ownership is now specifically spelled out in a lease, but for purposes of property insurance, fixtures are considered part of the property. Policies may have specific provisions excluding coverage for furniture, fixtures, and equipment, and depending on the type of business being operated, these exclusions may cause confusion. Coverage for fixtures should be specifically negotiated and understood in the process of applying for insurance. It is also possible to expressly include particular items through the process of negotiation.

The General Property Form tends to be sufficiently specific in most cases, but if not, or if another form is phrased in general terms, such as one covering "building, equipment, and fixtures," it may be necessary for the court to resort to the legal definition of fixtures. Some courts have held that fixtures which can be removed without injury to the buildings are not covered by a contract with such general language. Other courts have held that because of the physical attachment of items such as machinery and appliances, a policy on a building will cover loss to such fixtures. It is important to note that fixtures differ from contents. Contents coverage, which is usually written together with buildings and fixtures coverage, is explained in the next chapter.

In the event of an insured loss, debris removal expense is covered along with the balance of the loss up to the policy limits. Debris removal coverage does not carry a specific limit and is not included in the actual cash value of the property.

Property not covered

Excavations, foundations, and pilings have a minimal exposure to perils covered under the general property form and therefore are excluded when there is an applicable co-insurance clause. This reduces the amount of insurance required by the co-insurance clause and additionally reduces the premium charge which is based on total values insured.

Extensions of coverage

Newly acquired property, including property under construction, intended for similar occupancy is automatically insured up to 10 percent of the existing amount of coverage, but not more than $25,000, for a period of 30 days unless the policy expires sooner. Because this extension is somewhat limited, it is prudent to report newly acquired property for purposes of endorsement at the earliest opportunity.

Co-insurance

For each property listed in the declarations, that percentage of actual cash value which the business agrees to insure is the co-insurance percentage. Under the co-insurance clause, if the insured maintains less than this required amount of insurance for any property, the insurer's liability for that property in the event of a loss will be reduced by that proportion which the insurance maintained bears to the insurance required.

Deductible

Unless changed by endorsement, a standard $100 deductible applies separately to each building (and its contents) subject to a $1,000 aggregate per occurrence. Premium dollars can be saved by increasing the deductible.

Perils insured against

The standard fire policy insures against all direct loss by fire, lightning, and removal. The General Property Form inlcudes these fire perils and, when indicated in the policy declarations, extended coverage and vandalism and malicious mischief perils.

Basic fire perils

Fire—damage from hostile (that which is out of its intended place) combustion with a flame or glow including consequential damage from such perils as smoke and water.

Lightning—damage from natural discharge of electricity usually resulting in fire.

Removal—damage to insured property while being removed from a building, damaged or about to be damaged by fire or another insured peril.

Selected extended coverage perils

Windstorm or hail—damage caused by severe windstorms (not wind erosion), such as tornadoes, and impact from hail.

Smoke—damage from accidental release of smoke normally vented.

Explosion—damage from explosion of combustion chambers and flues (not steam explosion).

Riot, riot attending a strike, or civil commotion—damage from these perils including pillage and looting.

Aircraft or vehicles—damage from contact of aircraft or objects from aircraft and vehicles not owned or operated by insured or any tenant of insured.

Vandalism and malicious mischief

Willful and malicious damage to insured property excluding glass may be insured against.

Optional perils

By endorsement to the standard fire policy and General Property Form (or in certain situations, by separate policy) certain optional perils may be insured against.

Falling objects—damage to the exterior of a building (from a falling tree, for example) and any resulting interior damage.

Weight of snow, ice, or sleet—damage from accumulation of these perils including structural damage.

Collapse—damage from complete collapse of a building.

Water damage—damage from accidental discharge or leakage of water or steam within its system excluding damage from natural causes and sprinkler leakage.

Glass breakage—damage to glass which is part of the property insured, excluding signs, however caused. Limits are quite low. For a major exposure, Plate Glass coverage (Chapter 17) is necessary.

Sprinkler leakage—damage from an accidental discharge of any part of an automatic sprinkler system.

Exclusions

The standard exclusions contained in the General Property Form include:

1. Damage to electrical apparatus from artificially generated currents.
2. Damage from nuclear reaction, radiation, or contamination.
3. Damage from operation of building codes.
4. Damage from power failure.
5. Damage from war.
6. Damage from flood or other surface water, from water backed up through sewers, and from subsurface water.

These and other exclusions which may be included or contained in endorsements to the policy are used to help delineate the insurer's exposure or liability from which a rate and premium may be developed. To avoid surprises in uninsured losses and unnecessary premium charges, it is in the insured's best interest to fully understand not only those perils insured against but also those perils excluded.

Valuation

The valuation of property insured and the insurer's limit of liability in the event of loss is based on actual cash value unless changed by endorsement or by the statutes of the state in which the property is located.

Other provisions

This last section of the general property form contains other provisions which augment those of the standard fire policy.

SPECIAL FORMS, POLICIES, AND INSURANCE MARKETS

All-risks coverage

Those coverages discussed so far in this chapter are known as *named peril* coverages because the perils are specifically named and outlined in the policy. A recommended alternative to insuring on a named peril basis is insuring on an all-risks basis. This can be accomplished by using an all-risks endorsement, an all-risks policy, or a named peril policy plus a Difference in Conditions (DIC) Policy (explained in Chapter 19). Both an all-risks endorsement, when added to the standard fire policy, and an all-risks policy insure against *all* direct damage or loss *except* for the perils and property specifically excluded. For this reason, all-risks coverage, which in some cases is called comprehensive coverage, is somewhat of a misnomer within the insurance industry.

When an agent or broker states that a policy affords all-risks coverage, it is most important to look with care toward the exclusions. The exclusions in the various all-risks policy wordings differ and can be either of minimum consequence or important. In discussing this property coverage with an agent or broker, pay special attention to the perils excluded. Some typical exclusions are war, wear and tear, neglect of the insured in preserving the property, theft by employees, operation of building codes, flood, earthquake, and nuclear perils. When necessary, it is quite possible that coverage for one or more insurable perils excluded under the "all-risks" can be added by endorsement, deleting the particular exclusion. Several key perils typically not excluded are theft (by other than employees), collapse, and water damage. The broadened coverage from these perils alone is enough to justify strong consideration of insuring on an all-risks basis.

Since all-risks coverage generally increases the exposure underwritten by an insurer due to the many unknowns assumed, this coverage can be more expensive than named peril coverage. But with the increasing preponderance of major property insurance now being written on an all-risks basis, the market tends to be soft to pricing differences, and the additional cost is generally not significant when considering the broader coverage provided. However, when necessary, an insured may effect savings by retaining additional portions of the exposure through increased deductibles and reduced policy limits. Problem perils, flood and earthquake, for example, quite frequently require high deductibles and reduced "sub" limits of insurer liability. Problem locations may be handled similarly. Also, named peril forms may be layered over all-risks forms. Layering provides all-risks coverage up to a predetermined limit over which named peril coverage would respond.

Flood

Flood damage, distinct from water damage by definition, is from a general and temporary condition of partial or complete inundation of normally dry land from the overflow of inland or tidal waters or from the runoff of surface waters or the resulting mudslide and collapse of land. Coverage may be provided in all-risks forms and policies, especially under DIC policies, generally with high deductibles and low limits. When coverage is too costly or not available from the private insurance market, limited coverage may be provided through the National Flood Insurance Program established in 1969.

Flood losses occur with high frequency and severity in concentrated locations and can be predicted with reasonable accuracy over a relatively short time span. Therefore, in many cases the private insurance market has a difficult time achieving an adequate spread of risk for a reasonable premium and the federal program may be the only alternative for insurance. The National Flood Insurance Program is administered by the Federal Insurance Administration through a private servicing corporation, EDS Federal Corporation, which has representatives in each of ten federal regions. EDS handles basic insurer functions under emergency and regular programs with claims and operating expenses backed by U.S. Treasury loans. For a firm to be eligible, the governing community must participate in the federal program, at first on an "emergency" basis and then, when engineering studies are complete, on a "regular" basis. (Studies are generally made and statistics kept by the U.S. Army Corps of Engineers.) The flood insurance contract is made up of a flood insurance policy describing perils and a general property form for flood describing property. Maximum limits applicable to commercial buildings are $100,000 under the emergency program and $250,000 under the regular program. No co-insurance applies. The current deductible is the greater of $200 or 2 percent of the loss, but this is under review and subject to change. Chargeable rates are a fraction of self-sustaining actuarial rates and vary by community, engineering, and so on.

Earthquake

Coverage for damage from earthquake and resulting aftershocks, within 72 hours, may be provided by endorsement to the standard fire policy or all-risks policies or by special all-risks forms and DIC policies. Coverage by endorsement typically excludes resulting loss by fire, explosion, or flood, which may be covered elsewhere. Coverage includes damage to excavations, foundations, and pilings which are excluded under the standard fire policy. When co-insurance applies, the costs for this additional property insured must be considered in setting total values in order to avoid co-insurance penalties.

Deductibles are generally quite high and, depending on property location and construction, range from 2 percent to 10 percent or higher. In certain circumstances an insured may wish to purchase insurance for or "buy out" a large part of a deductible, generally through the so-called specialty or excess and surplus market. This market uses negotiated rates and terms which may differ from those filed and used by the standard market in each state. In either case, rates are determined primarily by the property's location and construction classification.

Nuclear contamination

Radioactive contamination, which is part of the standard nuclear perils exclusion along with nuclear reaction and radiation, may be insured under certain circumstances. Where radioactive substances are used by a business other than a nuclear power facility, coverage for contamination damage to the insured premises may be provided by limited or broad form endorsements to the standard fire policy or all-risks policies.

Operation of building codes

The ordinance or law exclusion in most property policies excludes damage from operation of building codes requiring demolition of partially damaged structures and superior construction in new or replacement buildings. Demolition coverage, which may be included by endorsement to the standard fire or all-risks policies, provides coverage for the cost of demolition and the loss from that remaining portion of the building which must be demolished when required by local ordinance. The Demolition Endorsement is often combined with an Increased Cost of Construction Endorsement which affords coverage for the difference in costs between the original construction damaged and the new construction required by current building codes. Ordinances mandating superior construction are quite prevalent in older cities where fire codes have been changed over the years.

FAIR Plan

Where a business is unable to insure property in riot prone, environmentally hazardous urban areas through the private insurance market, coverage is available through the Federal Riot Reinsurance Program under the FAIR (Fair Access to Insurance Requirements) Plan, a partnership of private insurers and state and federal governments. The plan is managed by the Federal Insurance Administration (HUD) which also provides reinsurance, catastrophe backup, and statistical accumulation and evaluation backed by U.S. Treasury loans. Plans encourage placement first through private or regular insurance facilities where possible, then through regular facilities plus association reinsurance, and last through the insurance placement facility.

Coverage is generally limited to fire, extended coverage, and vandalism and malicious mischief. A building must be otherwise insurable, except for its location in a blighted or deteriorated, "eligible" urban area. Once a property has been inspected and reported to the placement facility, it may be accepted, conditionally accepted, or unconditionally declined (but not for reasons of environmental hazards in urban areas). Maximum limits are $500,000 for commercial property at any one location.

Excess and surplus lines markets

Often the standard insurance market is unable to accept a property risk and charge an affordable price for the coverage. Underwriting guidelines, rating structures, and capacity limits may be too restrictive from time to time for certain types of buildings. The Excess and

Surplus Lines Market is available to a business which has property to be insured against extra hazardous perils, for extremely high values, in hazardous locations, of hazardous occupancies, or even in substandard conditions. "E and S" companies (American and foreign) and syndicates such as Lloyd's of London will provide coverage for just about any type of risk imaginable. The market is approached by agents and brokers through "wholesale" E and S brokers who maintain contacts and underwriting arrangements with various segments of the market. The presence and function of this residual and very flexible market should never be overlooked if needed.

INSURANCE LIMITS RELATIVE TO PROPERTY VALUATION

Insurance to value

An insurance policy will pay no more than the value of the property covered as defined by the policy terms and conditions. Based on the principle of indemnity, if a building is insured for $250,000 and the property's value, defined by the policy as actual cash value, is only $200,000, the insurer generally will pay a maximum of $200,000. However, in valued policy law states, an insured may usually purchase the amount of coverage he desires, even above the known value of the property, and can collect the total loss if indeed there is a total loss. In valued policy states, insurance companies try to prudently monitor insurance to value to avoid potential moral hazards in insuring buildings at values substantially higher than their actual worth. Undervaluing property in either case exposes a business to various problems in covering either a total or partial loss.

In the standard fire policy, valuation is based on actual cash value unless superseded by valued policy laws or endorsements changing the basis of valuation. Under the headings "Principles of Insurance Contracts: Actual Cash Value," this chapter has discussed the concept of actual cash value in insurance. Actual cash value is not defined per se in the policy, but it is taken to mean the current cost to replace a building less the actual physical depreciation of that building. Other than indexing original costs to current construction values, replacement costs can be determined through appraisals. Rule of thumb values per square foot are not recommended other than for rough measures. ACV is generally greater than book value which reflects *original* cost less tax related depreciation (and generally a faster scaled depreciation than is reasonable for insurance purposes). Even so, a property's actual cash value may be substantially lower than its value to the insured. Were a loss to occur, an insured would receive only the depreciated value of the property. In these days of inflation, it is sometimes difficult to keep current with rising property values, but an insured can protect against the inadvertent underinsurance which may result. Among the means available are the Inflation Guard Endorsement, the Replacement Cost Endorsement, and the Agreed Amount Endorsement.

Inflation Guard Endorsement. An Automatic Increase in Insurance Endorsement, generally called an Inflation Guard Endorsement, helps insured property values keep pace with inflation. By this endorsement, the amount of coverage is automatically increased on a quarterly basis at a rate preselected by the insured. Although an Inflation Guard Endorsement can alleviate the problem of inflation to a degree, it should not replace a sound annual review of property values.

Replacement Cost Endorsement. Payment of a loss on an actual cash value basis often can leave a business short of funds where it *must* repair or replace damaged property with identical but more costly property. This exposure may be covered through a Replacement Cost Endorsement which substitutes the term *replacement cost* for *actual cash value* where applicable in the policy, eliminating a deduction for depreciation in property valuation. Subject to policy limits and co-insurance provisions, coverage is limited to either the cost of restoring the property to its original (nondepreciated) condition or the actual cost of repairing or replacing the property, whichever is less. If a building is restored with changes in construction, location, occupancy, or use increasing its cost, the additional cost of restoring the property beyond its original condition must be assumed by the owner.

It is important to note that a policy will pay on a replacement cost basis only if the damaged property is repaired or replaced and within a reasonable time after a loss. Otherwise the policy will revert to an ACV basis. Where replacement may take a significant amount of time, an insured may elect to settle on an ACV basis initially and then after the property has been restored, settle the balance due on a replacement cost basis. In settling a loss under a replacement cost policy, the co-insurance clause applies to a replacement cost valuation only (generally requiring at least 80 percent). This is true even when a loss is settled on an ACV basis. A co-insurance penalty can be especially costly in such circumstances. If a business intends to repair or replace a building after a loss and maintain a sufficient level of insurance, replacement cost coverage should be considered.

Agreed Amount Endorsement. For superior property, an agreed amount clause is another means of protecting against inadvertent underinsurance in an inflationary environment. Through this endorsement, the co-insurance clause is superseded and a specified amount of insurance takes the place of a specified percentage of actual cash value. Whereas ACV is determined after a loss occurs, an agreed amount is established before a loss occurs, eliminating uncertain settlements and co-insurance penalties. Partial losses are paid in full. In establishing limits, a sworn statement of values must be filed annually. A certain percentage of those values, generally not less than 90 percent, must be insured. If an insured fails to file a statement in any year, the co-insurance clause becomes effective at the high percentage of values insured, exposing an insured to possible co-insurance penalties.

Deductibles

In discussing insurance limits, retention decisions generally start with deductibles. Even people with little knowledge of building coverages are familiar with the term *deductible*. The word itself is simple enough to understand, but its application in insurance is often misunderstood. The use of a deductible means that the insured pays the first dollar amount, as specified in the policy for a loss.

Insurance companies are not in business to provide insurance dollars to cover the insured's operating expenses. Small, maintenance-type losses are more readily handled by the insured than by the insurance company. Moreover, when the insured is responsible for paying the deductible and thus has some monetary interest in his program, he is more likely to exercise care to avoid a financial outlay. This approach to deductibles explains why the insurance company is generally willing to consider and even encourage the use of deductibles. When an insured is agreeable to and capable of accepting or increasing a deductible, the exposure to the insurer is reduced. The insured benefits through a corresponding premium credit. Credits for deductibles vary according to the property's insurable value, the size of the deductible relative to the insurable value, the perils covered, the property's physical features, the rating territory (location), and the insurer. It is important to consider not only the dollar amount of a deductible but also its ratio to insurable value. For a given deductible, credits increase as the insurable value decreases while credits decrease as the insurable value increases.

Often when an insured hears the word *deductible*, he assumes that he will be retaining the first specified dollars of every loss and the insurer will be responsible for the rest. In many cases the deductible is used this way, but it is important to be aware that different forms of deductibles are used in different ways. One form, the deductible written on an *occurrence* basis, specifies that for every occurrence leading to loss, there is a deductible related to that occurrence, and that occurrence only. Thus, one fire equals one occurrence, and one deductible applies. Deductibles are not only written for each occurrence of loss in general but also may be scheduled for certain perils or locations individually. This allows flexibility in retention and pricing where an insured may choose to retain a greater share of a risk where the cost of insurance is especially high.

Another form of deductible, the *per claim* deductible, applies to every claim filed, regardless of the number of occurrences. The per claim deductible is somewhat confusing in that one occurrence, such as the fire in the example above, may lead to a number of claims. If this fire were to result in six claims, an insured carrying a $500 per claim deductible would be responsible for six deductibles, or $3,000, before the insurance would enter into payment.

A third form of deductible, the *aggregate* deductible, requires the insured to retain up to a certain dollar amount of losses, after which the insurer pays all else. The aggregate applies either to each occurrence or over a specified period of time where it is generally written on an annual basis. For example, with a $25,000 annual aggregate deductible, the insured would retain a maximum of $25,000 of losses in a given year and the insurer would be responsible for any additional loss payments in that year. The use and application of the deductible may differ from policy to policy. Keeping this in mind, it is also essential to consider the dollar amount of the deductible as it relates to the size and nature of the business and property to be insured. Of course, a large deductible will mean a larger financial outlay in the event of a loss and may mean total responsibility for smaller losses, but it will also result in an immediate premium dollar savings. In these times of concern over cash flow, interest, and investment, it is advisable, and often mandatory, for the insured to ask for and carefully consider the deductible options available.

Other forms of retention might be used to assume various degrees of risk above a property's insured value. Co-insurance and underinsurance or insurance covering a percentage of actual value are several which have been discussed. Also, sublimits are used to cap an insurer's liability for selected perils or locations which may be too costly or difficult to insure for full value.

Blanket limits

Coverage may be provided for multiple locations on a blanket basis where a single limit covers all (or selected) locations. Co-insurance requirements generally start at 90 percent, and many states require filing a statement of values. Though blanket coverage is slightly more expensive than specific coverage, the advantages of insuring on a blanket basis are worth considering. A total loss at any one location would represent only a portion of the blanket limit and would be paid in full, barring any co-insurance deficiencies or required pro rata distribution. This is especially attractive when only 90 percent co-insurance is required. Further, compliance with co-insurance requirements can be more flexible as the number of locations increases. In certain circumstances, co-insurance may be waived altogether and a blanket limit established at a fraction of the total value.

PROPERTY INSURANCE RATES

Specific and class rates

Several types of rating formulas are used in determining the bulk of property insurance premiums. One such type, *specific rating,* indicates that a building is rated on its own merits. The Insurance Service Office or an independent rate making firm inspects and establishes specific rates for a particular building based on its construction, age, occupancy, protection class, and individual features which make it different from other buildings of its type. Safeguards, for example, include loss-conscious management, sprinkler systems, and structural soundness. Incorporating the acquired data, the rate-making firm formulates and determines an individual rate for the building. Insurers then may deviate from filed rates with applicable credits. A less flexible type of rating, *class rating,* applies to a wide group of similar buildings and provides that a building of a given construction and a particular occupancy is charged a predetermined rate based on that construction and occupancy. For example, 22 restaurants of brick construction in the same town would be subject to identical starting rates per $100 of value for building coverage, although the rates would be adjusted upward or downward depending on the individual characteristics of each building.

Blanket rates

A third rating type, *blanket rating,* is used when a building owner has more than one building, preferably four or more. In lieu of treating each building as an individual entity, the rate-making firm establishes a rate predicated on each of the individual rates and exposures at hand, reflecting the characteristics of the entire group of buildings. The resulting average rate then may be reduced by credits for premium size, dispersion of values, and loss experience. With blanket rating, the building owner can insure all his building exposures under one policy, at one rate.

Loss engineering

Uncovering and recommending techniques for the prevention of future losses is a major function of the insurance business. Referred to as engineering, this function may include such things as checking an insured's fire extinguishers, or recommending that an insured install a sprinkler system, change the type of paint he uses, decrease the use or storage of flammable liquids, or exercise tighter work control. Loss prevention engineering has been shown to reduce the frequency and severity of losses, and as a result, often means lower premiums for the insured. Sometimes, though, it may appear to the insured that the insurance company makes too many recommendations and asks for too many changes or improvements after charging so many dollars for the coverage. Despite appearances, engineering can save the insured money. As pointed out earlier, specific rates or class rates serve as a base in determining the cost to insure a particular property. These base rates, however, are reflected upward or downward depending on how the individual risk, its management, its construction, and its other features compare with the normal risk of its class. With loss prevention engineering and its resultant improved loss experience, the individual insured may well find a reduction in his insurance premiums.

OCCURRENCE OF LOSS

The businessman's recovery is determined after the occurrence of a loss. A loss is the catalyst which causes a businessman to come to grips with the question of whether he really knows where he stands when damage occurs to his buildings and/or fixtures. Unfortunately, in businesses where there is no in-house risk management, experience indicates that the businessman does not know where he stands.

The first area of analysis is determining the nature and cause of the loss and establishing that it fits within the policy's coverage. Property and fixtures can be damaged or destroyed by a multitide of perils. Often, unless particular attention has been paid to the possibility of loss from perils such as acts of God (flood, earthquake, lightning, wind), contamination, vandalism, and so on, many of them will have been excluded from coverage. For example, the standard fire insurance policy without any extensions of coverage excludes losses caused by fire and other perils which result from war or rebellion situations, by neglect of the insured in preserving the property, or by theft. There are many other problems concerning the extent of coverage for property which has been destroyed by a particular peril. The discussion of these problems is much beyond the scope of this chapter. Suffice it to say that there are particular types of property insurance available to a businessman, depending upon the location in which his business operates and the type of business he runs. From court cases, general principles of property losses have developed. There are, however, specific problems inherent in particular businesses which are subject to particular insurance coverages. For example, a businessman can specifically insure against loss to property, particularly fixtures, by robbery, theft, or acts of nature, including cyclone, tornado, hail, lightning, or flood. There are also specific problems involved when loss to property is caused by arson or by the conduct of an ultra-hazardous activity. One particular problem specifically dealt with in the standard fire policy is loss attributable to the businessman in some way, whether by acts of commission or omission. For instance, the standard fire policy provides that coverage is suspended when the hazard is increased by means within the control of the insured. One specific example, the subject of litigation, is the question of whether the failure of an insured to maintain a building in accordance with a municipal building code is sufficient cause to suspend coverage within the terms of the policy. Of course, the loss must be attributable to a risk that was increased by failing to properly maintain the building: a fire caused by poor electrical wiring, for example.

Occupancy and vacancy

Another problem concerning recovery for property loss is that of occupancy or vacancy. This problem arises in two situations: (1) when there is a question whether the insured has made any statement as to the occupancy of the building to which the insurance applies; and (2) when the building becomes vacant after the policy is in force. As a general proposition, if there is no particular representation about the specific occupancy at the time the insurance is purchased, the fact that the building is not occupied on that date does not cause a breach. For example, the designation of a building as a "dwelling" has been held to be a general description of the building and not a warranty binding the insured that the building is actually occupied as a dwelling house at the time the insurance goes into effect. In order to avoid ambiguity, the practice should be to designate specifically the purpose or nature of the occupancy of the building.

As stated, the standard fire policy has a provision which suspends coverage while the building is vacant or unoccupied beyond 60 consecutive days. A breach of this occupancy requirement will suspend coverage subject to any waiver or estoppel on the part of the insurer.

The general theory behind the provision requiring occupancy is that such a provision will tend to assure the safety of the building. Decisions concerning occupancy or vacancy are usually questions of fact depending on the circumstances of each case. Normally, courts look to whether there was someone intended to be in charge of the premises, someone who would naturally take precautions to protect against loss by fire. For example, custody by a watchman or caretaker, despite no domicile or occupancy by that individual, has been held to be sufficient to constitute occupancy for purposes of the fire policy. Similarly, where operations of a business are halted or suspended during repairs to the plant or installation of new equipment or machinery, the plant is not considered vacant or unoccupied for purposes of policy construction. Generally, the courts will not allow suspension of coverage if there is a mere temporary stoppage of business operations, provided there is some attention paid to the building.

Dealing with a loss

Consider that the businessman has been involved in the negotiation for insurance, has a good understanding of the nature of the coverage, and now suffers a loss. He knows the extent of his loss, but what are his obligations at this point?

Notice. Beginning at line 90, the standard fire policy sets forth the requirements and obligations imposed upon an insured in the case of a loss. Insurance covering loss due to perils other than fire generally imposes similar obligations upon the insured.

A fire policy requires immediate written notice of loss to the insurance company. With immediate notification, the insurance company has the opportunity to promptly investigate the loss to determine its nature, extent, and causes. Also, the passage of time between the occurrence of the loss and the time when the insurance company is notified, and therefore can investigate, may not only allow further damage to occur by reason of exposure to the elements but may also dissipate evidence which would be relevant to determining the cause of the loss.

Although by its express language the policy requires "immediate" notice, this term is not usually literally construed by the courts. Generally, a businessman who has suffered a loss has the obligation to give notice within a reasonable time having acted with due diligence. As a practical matter, notice of the loss should be given with as little delay as possible to avoid this problem.

The problem of notice is important. If the businessman does not provide early notice of a particular loss, the question of how much time is reasonable may have to be determined through litigation. The insurer may take the position that notice was not given either immediately or within a reasonable time. Therefore, a promissory warranty was violated and the policy was not in effect. The old rule of law stated that giving notice as prescribed in the policy was a condition precedent to the effectiveness of the coverage. The developing trend and the majority rule at present is that when a question of late notice to the insurance company arises, the insurer has the obligation to show that it was prejudiced by the late notice. In practical terms, prejudice to an insurer means that due to the passage of time, witnesses or evidence are no longer available. In the case of a property damage loss, the passage of time without notice to the insurance company usually presents an easier case showing prejudice to the insurer than in other types of insurance, since the passage of time has a direct effect on the determination of the cause of the loss, the status of the occupancy, and use of the building at the time of the loss, and since it affects other warranties and representations in the policy.

Salvage. The standard fire policy also requires that the insured use all reasonable means to save what is left of the building and fixtures after the loss has occurred and to protect the property from further damage. The policy specifically requires the insured to separate damaged goods from undamaged goods and to prepare and supply an inventory applicable to the loss. Basically, the inventory is an itemization of property before and property left after the loss, broken down according to quantity, cost, cash value, and depreciation.

Proof of loss. The insured must also submit a sworn proof of loss to the company. Further detail and documentation supporting the amount of the loss, the proof of loss also gives reference to various representations previously submitted by the insured, checking that the insured has complied with these warranties—that is, has the insured increased the risk, changed the use of the building, or continued the occupancy of the building properly under the policy provisions? The standard fire policy gives a detailed outline of what the insured must furnish to the company. The information to be supplied is as follows:

1. The time and cause of the loss.
2. The interest of the insured in the property and the interest of any other individuals in the property.
3. The actual cash value of each item of loss and the amount of loss to each item if it is less than a total loss.
4. All incumbrances or liens on the property.
5. The existence of other contracts of insurance on the property.
6. Any changes in title, use, occupation, location, possession, or exposures of the property.
7. The actual occupancy and use of the building at the time of loss.

It is also helpful to present to the insurance company any existing itemization for fixtures (machinery, for example) that were destroyed. In addition to the affirmative obligations listed above, the insured also is obligated to submit to agents of the insurer, upon request, books of account, invoices, or any other documentary evidence supporting the loss being claimed.

Errors in the proof of loss. What happens if the businessman submits a proof of loss in which he gives erroneous information or has omitted or forgotten other items of loss? Generally, the insured is entitled to amend his proof of loss and may supply information previously omitted unless there is indication of deliberate concealment or unless some estoppel is working against him. Consider, for example, that a material difference exists between information submitted about an item on the original proof of loss and that given a subsequent attempt at amendment. If in the time passing between submission of the original proof of loss and submission of the amendment the item has been destroyed or salvaged so that the company has no opportunity to make any investigation into its actual value, the doctrine of estoppel may work against the insured. Again, this is a question of fact based on the circumstances of each individual case.

If some items normally required in the proof of loss are not set forth in the proof as submitted, it is generally the duty of the insurer to point out the defects or the omissions to afford the insured an opportunity to correct them. The businessman who refuses, for whatever reason, to furnish information after having been notified of defects in the proof, runs the risk of not recovering. This is particularly true if the matter ever comes to litigation in the form of a suit against the insurer.

It is also true that information submitted in the proof of loss is subject to further explanation. However, if there is a material difference between the originally submitted information and a subsequent explanation, the insured may be precluded from recovering, particularly if the insurer has acted upon the initial information. The insurer generally is not a party to the proof of loss and is not bound by the statements set forth therein. A proof of loss prepared by an adjuster hired by the insurance company, however, is strongly construed against that insurer, and the insured is not estopped at a later date from challenging the correctness of information in such a proof.

Cooperation. In addition to the affirmative duty of supplying specific items of information, the insured also has the duty of cooperating with the insurance company investigating the loss. This means not only making the premises available for inspection but also producing documents, invoices, vouchers, and books and records which may be requested by the insurance company as a necessary avenue of investigation in documenting or determining the amount of the loss.

Holdback. One practice that has developed in the adjusting of property damage losses is the use of a holdback system. Under this system, a loss is adjusted by the insurance company holding back a certain percentage of the proceeds due under the policy until a certain percentage of the work or replacement is actually completed. The theory behind this practice is that it serves as a check against turning a loss into a profit by submitting a very high estimate of repair or replacement cost, then making a profit on the loss, for example, using different materials or labor or a combination thereof to repair or replace the property at a much lower cost.

Appraisal. The standard policy also provides for the use of appraisal in the event of a controversy or dispute concerning the value of the property. The procedure is set forth in the policy to reduce litigation, and requires that, upon disagreement, there be a written demand for appraisal by either the insured or the insurance company. Each party then selects an appraiser to consider the issue, and the two appraisers in turn select a third disinterested appraiser who acts as an umpire, if necessary, to determine the value of the loss.

In some states, the appraisal clause once was considered unenforceable and consequently raised the question of the insurance company's liability to pay without litigation. This rule has changed generally, so that now there is a question of the dollar amount of the loss only; appraisal upon demand is binding.

SUMMARY

The most basic business insurance is for property, in this case for buildings and fixtures. Because insurance is a contract, certain legal principles apply. Also, the insurance contract contains unusual provisions because it attempts to indemnify an insured after the contract is in force.

The most basic property insurance is provided by the so-called standard fire policy and the General Property Form. Other forms or endorsements are added to make insurance fit individual business property exposures. Some special perils, like flood, need further endorsements or separate insurance.

The balance of the chapter addressed adequacy of insurance, rates, and obligations in the event of loss.

Any contract requires good faith among the parties. An insurance contract, if anything, requires extraordinary good faith between the insurer and insured. A businessman should know his rights under the contract but should also understand and perform his obligations at time of loss. It is always difficult to suffer a loss, but good faith and performance on the part of the businessman and his insurer at loss is essential.

CHAPTER 5

DIRECT DAMAGE
TO CONTENTS

EXPOSURE OF THE BUSINESS
Ownership
Care, custody, and control
Contractual exposure

IDENTIFICATION OF CONTENTS
Fixtures
Inventory
Supplies and equipment
Special assets
Property off the premises

CUSTOMARY POLICY FORMS
"Named peril" versus "all-risks"
Standard fire policy
Exclusions
Blanket coverage

Valuation at loss
Increase in hazard,
    vacant premises

PACKAGE POLICIES

OTHER EXPOSURES TO LOSS

ADDITIONAL CONTENTS COVERAGE
Stock reporting
Manufacturers output policy
Transit insurance
Commercial property floater policies
Electronic data processing policies
Federal flood program

HOW TO HANDLE CLAIMS

Patrick F. Carton
Senior Vice President
Corroon & Black Company of New York, Inc.
New York, New York

Patrick F. Carton is a Senior Vice President for Corroon & Black Company of New York, Inc. He has responsibility for Property/Casualty Loss Control, Risk Management Services, and New Account Marketing. During the past 25 years he has had extensive experience in client services including insurance program design and loss control for large national and international industrial corporations. A graduate of Iona College, New Rochelle, New York, with a degree in Business Administration, Mr. Carton obtained additional formal education at the College of Insurance and the Factory Mutual Training Center for Loss Control Management. Mr. Carton has been a lecturer for the American Management Association and a panel member for the American Paper Institute's seminar on property insurance. In addition, he has made presentations to chapter meetings of the Risk and Insurance Management Society and the Corporate Practice Institute of the Wisconsin Bar Association.

Joseph A. Bambury, Jr., Esquire
Vice President and General Counsel
Royal Insurance
New York, New York

Joseph A. Bambury, Jr., is Vice President and General Counsel of Royal Insurance. He has served on various insurance industry committees and is presently Chairman of the Law Committees of the National Council on Compensation Insurance, New York Property Insurance Underwriting Association, and the Medical Malpractice Insurance Association (New York). A member of the American Bar Association, New York State Bar Association, New York County Lawyers Association, and the New York Catholic Lawyers Guild, he has been active in numerous civic and political affairs and is an adjunct associate professor at The College of Insurance, New York. He was graduated from Holy Cross College and received a J.D. degree from Columbia Law School.

This chapter outlines the coverage available for the contents of offices, factories, and stores. It will also describe the Inland Marine coverages for movable property and equipment, as well as goods in transit.

Direct damage to insured property may be defined as losses proximately and effectively caused by an insured peril. Consequently, once it is established that the insured property has been physically damaged (loss of use of insured property resulting from damage to another property is not covered here), it is necessary to determine the cause of loss. Use of the word *direct* does not mean that the peril insured against must be the sole or immediate cause of loss. It is sufficient if the loss is proximately caused by the peril. This concept of proximate cause can be illustrated by the following example.

The standard fire policy provides coverage for direct loss by fire and specifically excludes coverage for loss resulting from theft. The policy further requires the policyholder to take all reasonable means to safeguard the property from loss. Assume a fire started in the insured premises and the policyholder attempted to save a valuable piece of furniture by moving it out of the burning premises. Assume that while attempting to save other property, a thief makes off with the first piece of furniture. A literal interpretation of the words of the policy would lead to the conclusion that the loss was in fact caused by theft and not by the fire. However, many courts have held the proximate cause of this loss of the piece of furniture was the fire which precipitated its removal. Of course, the further in time and distance from the fire that the furniture is when stolen, the less likely it is that the fire will be considered the proximate cause of loss.

There will always arise grey areas where it may be difficult to determine if the peril insured against was the direct cause of loss. Consider, for example, a policy covering loss resulting from windstorm but not water damage. Courts have not been reluctant to find in situations where a windstorm has blown the roof off, and a torrential rain has followed before steps could be taken to make repairs, that the damage caused by the water was proximately caused by the windstorm. The courts take a long look to the time interval between the windstorm and the water damage as well as the availability of means by which protection for the property could have been provided in reaching their decision.

For purposes of this chapter, we will consider direct damage as damage which results proximately and effectively, both as to time and space, from the peril insured against.

EXPOSURE OF THE BUSINESS

The businessman must be concerned with damage to the contents he owns, to those contents which he does not own but for which he has a responsibility imposed by law, and for those nonowned contents for which he has assumed responsibility under contractual provision.

Ownership

The concept of ownership can be nebulous. For purposes of this chapter, ownership should be thought of as a relationship to property where the businessman bears the risk of loss if the property is destroyed. Ownership encompasses all contents where the businessman has absolute ownership and those contents where he has ownership even though there remains some obligation to fulfill before ownership becomes absolute, such as payment of a security interest or a chattel mortgage.

Ownership would also relate to those contents where ownership may not yet have been transferred, either absolutely or conditionally, but where the risk of loss has passed under a sales contract. As a general rule, the risk of loss passes to the purchaser of personal property when he has the ability to exercise control even though he may not receive possession. Practically, the purchaser has an insurable interest as soon as he has a risk of loss.

Care, custody, and control

Before the Uniform Commercial Code, liability of a businessman for damage to property of others in his care, custody, and control was determined by the law of bailment. In most commercial transactions, the property of others was held under a mutually beneficial bailment relationship where the risk of loss remained with the bailor (owner) and the bailee (custodian) was liable for damage to the property only if he failed to exercise reasonable care.

The Uniform Commercial Code changed this law in connection with sales made by the businessman who for some reason retains possession of the goods. This Code requires that the buyer actually receive the goods from the businessman before the risk of loss passes to him. In a nonbusiness situation, the Code requires that the seller tender (offer) the goods to the buyer in order to transfer the risk of loss. Let us suppose a customer orders a piece of equipment from a dealer and that after it has been received by the dealer and tendered to the customer the customer requests certain modifications to his specifications. Under bailment law, the customer would have the exposure while these modifications were made. The Uniform Commercial Code, however, places the exposure with the dealer while the modifications are being made and until the customer receives the equipment.

The changes effected by this new concept of the traditional view of the custodian's legal liability are significant. Where a businessman once had the option of insuring customers' property in his care, custody, and control (for goodwill purposes as opposed to legal liability purposes), he now must insure all sales transactions where possession is retained.

Contractual exposure

A third source of exposure arises from the terms of lease agreements. These fall into two general categories: real estate leases and equipment leases. In the area of real estate leases, the lease agreement itself must be reviewed to determine the businessman's exposure. The lease may provide that both the landlord and tenant have the benefit of each other's insurance and each holds the other harmless for loss to his property caused by certain perils. These agreements may even go so far as to provide that even the negligence of one party, say the landlord, will not subject him to liability to the tenant if the tenant had, or could have obtained, insurance to cover damage to the tenant's property. A real estate lease must be reviewed further to determine if the tenant assumes any liability for the fixtures or other property of the landlord.

In connection with equipment leases it is not uncommon to find a requirement imposing almost absolute liability upon the tenant for damage to equipment from any cause. The larger and more sophisticated the equipment, the more frequently such a clause is found.

In determining what property is to be insured, the businessman should bear in mind that his exposure can arise from the several sources outlined. It is important to remember that the parties can agree between themselves as to which should bear the risk of loss. The courts will generally enforce this agreement if it is fair and expressed in clear and unambiguous terms.

IDENTIFICATION OF CONTENTS

The identification of contents may appear to be self-evident. Everyone knows the contents or personal property he has within his premises. The classification of property, however, often depends on several extraneous points. If a piece of a tenant's personal property is permanently affixed to premises which are leased, is it still the property of the tenant or does it become a fixture and thus the property of the landlord? Which of them is responsible for its replacement in the event of loss? Machinery placed within a leased premises and then permanently affixed to the structure may be converted into a fixture and, in the absence of contract or lease provisions, become the property of the landlord. As such, its destruction would be a loss to the landlord, but this legal nicety does the tenant little good if the landlord refuses to replace it.

Fixtures

Traditionally, the test of what is a fixture is a three-pronged analysis. If the personal property has been attached to a building in a manner whereby it cannot be removed without causing substantial or material damage to the leased premises, it is considered a fixture. If the personal property has been attached in a manner whereby it has lost its identity, it becomes part of the building such as brick which is made a part of the building wall. If personal property is specially made for the building, it is usually considered a fixture. The intent of the party who affixed the personal property is also a test in identifying property as a fixture, although it is difficult to apply the intent test in the absence of mutual agreement. This again points up the importance of agreement prior to a loss. Care must be taken in preparing real estate leases to clarify in detail whether it is intended that machinery, equipment, and other personal property are to become fixtures and who is to be responsible for replacement in the event of damage.

The normal real estate lease provides that improvements become the property of the landlord. However, it is not uncommon to insert a provision that they remain the property of the tenant and must be removed at the termination of the lease by the tenant at his own expense.

Trade fixtures, showcases, and other improvements necessary for the conduct of a tenant's business are usually deemed to remain the property of the tenant, and the tenant is responsible for their removal at the termination of the lease.

The time to reach an understanding for insuring and replacing personal property is before a loss—at lease time. After a loss the insurance company may not be amenable to a loss-sharing agreement. Moreover, there will be questions of adequate coverage if one of the parties did not fully appreciate the extent of his exposure.

Inventory

Probably the most significant item of contents coverage facing the mercantile establishment is the insurance of inventory or stock in trade held for resale. Certainly, while it remains inventory, the businessman has no hesitation about the need for insurance coverage. But, what about insurance after it has been sold to a customer?

Generally speaking, the businessman retains an insurable interest in stock until such time as it is fully paid for. This presents no problem in situations where the stock is paid for by the customer at the time of sale. However, if the stock remains on hand after it has been sold to the customer, for example, in those situations where further processing or modification might be necessary, the businessman should consider continuing to insure. If the customer is extended credit, the businessman may wish to consider insurance either in his own name or as an additional insured under the customer's policy.

With respect to goods held by the businessman on consignment from others, either for resale or processing, the same principles outlined in connection with care, custody, and control apply.

Supplies and equipment

Supplies are an essential ingredient to the businessman's continuing success and the inclusion of these items as part of his contents should not be overlooked. Here, questions of valuation may come into play, mainly whether they should be valued at cost to the businessman or at projected replacement cost in the event of destruction.

Office equipment used by a businessman is an essential element to the continuing efficient conduct of the business. Some of the equipment may be held on lease while some may have been purchased outright. The previous comments with respect to equipment leases should be reviewed for the leases may contain specific provisions concerning insurance. Once again, the question of valuation comes into play. The businessman should recognize that most policies will only provide for coverage on an actual cash value basis which will invariably be less than the original cost and in all likelihood far less than replacement cost.

In the areas of electronic data processing equipment there are several components to be considered and direct damage to the main frame may cause considerable expense. This large item is undoubtedly foremost in the businessman's mind, but he should be as concerned with respect to the peripheral and support equipment and wiring pertaining to the operation of his computers. The question of software should also be considered. All of these items are covered in this Handbook in Chapter 29 on data processing.

Special assets

The accounts receivable and other valuable papers of the businessman are worth no more than the paper they are printed on insofar as coverage under a policy of direct insurance is concerned. However, other coverages are available to compensate for their loss. This subject is covered in Chapter 17.

The successful businessman may well have some valuable paintings placed around his office, and even if he considers these to be contents, he may find that his insurance company does not or that it severely limits the amount of loss recoverable under standard forms of contents insurance. He should seriously consider specifically insuring them under the appropriate forms as discussed later in this chapter.

The businessman may have occasion to ship his contents either to an ultimate purchaser or for eventual return. The typical inland marine transit policy will provide coverage while the goods are in transit and until they reach their destination. This should be adequate in those situations where the goods are delivered to the purchaser at destination. Where, however, the goods are to be stored or eventually returned to the businessman, he should be alert to the fact that the transit policy does not provide coverage once the trip ends unless this coverage is specifically included.

While the situation is the same with ocean marine insurance, there is an important distinction—the ocean marine insurer will normally not extend his policy beyond coverage while the goods are in the course of import and export. Of course, the businessman can obtain coverage after the trip is completed, but he should be aware of this distinction between inland and ocean marine policies.

Property off the premises

Frequently, the businessman will place his property in the possession of others in locations off the insured premises. This can happen when property is stored in a public warehouse or is on consignment to others or is being held by a subcontractor. The liability of a public warehouseman is, generally speaking, fairly limited; and while a warehouseman may carry insurance to protect his liability in the event of damage to this property, the businessman would be well advised to continue his own coverage just as he should where he is holding property of others.

Often an insured will place his property off his premises under a subcontract so that it may be processed or fabricated. The terms of the subcontract should be examined to determine if insurance is to be provided by the insured or his subcontractor, for in the absence of a covering provision the only liability of the subcontractor will be that of a bailee.

Generally speaking, where the insured has the care, custody, and control of the property of others, if the insured is not negligent in causing damage to such property, he will have no legal liability for its destruction. Of course, he may well feel it is to his advantage from the point of view of continuing customer relations to provide as extensive an insurance program to protect this property as he has for his own property. Again, in a sales transaction, the traditional definition of bailee legal liability is expanded by the Uniform Commercial Code.

CUSTOMARY POLICY FORMS

There is a proliferation of property insurance policy forms each designed for the segment of the market the particular insurance company wishes to penetrate. Because of the variety of insurance contracts available, it is important to the businessman that all insurance contracts be reviewed in detail to obtain a clear understanding of the protection afforded by the insurance policies purchased.

"Named peril" versus "all-risks"

Conceptually, there are two basic approaches to insuring contents: "named peril" or "all-risks." The named peril approach lists the perils insured—for example: fire, lightning, explosion, wind, or hail. In order to be reimbursed by the policy there must be damage. The damage must be the result of direct loss by the perils enumerated in the policy. The all-risks alternative states that the perils insured against are "all-risks" of direct physical loss or damage. Reimbursement under this type of policy does not require the claimant to prove the loss was caused by a specific peril. There are policy exclusions applying to both the named peril and all-risks approaches which modify the extent of protection provided in either case. Simply stated, the named peril approach places on the insurance buyer the burden and responsibility of selecting the perils to be insured. He must pick and choose. The all-risks approach relieves the buyer of selecting perils. Of course, the all-risks approach can be expected to generate higher costs.

Standard fire policy

The standard fire policy provides insurance against "all direct loss by fire, lightning and by removal from premises." Additional specified perils such as windstorm, civil commotion, smoke, hail, aircraft, vehicles, explosion, riot, vandalism, malicious mischief, and sprinkler leakage are added by attaching forms to the standard fire policy.

Exclusions

The policy does not cover accounts, bills, currency, deeds, evidences of debt, money, or securities. Nor, unless specifically named, bullion or manuscripts. The policy, if requested, may be extended to cover these types of property.

There is no liability for loss if caused directly or indirectly by *(a)* enemy attack or armed forces, *(b)* invasion, *(c)* insurrection, *(d)* rebellion, *(e)* revolution, *(f)* civil war, *(g)* usurped power, *(h)* order of a civil authority, *(i)* neglect of insured to use all reasonable means to save his property at or after a loss, nor *(j)* loss by theft.

Blanket coverage

It is not uncommon for businessmen to insure all of their contents on a blanket basis. If this approach is followed, the policy would include protection for stock (including merchandise, materials, stock, and supplies), furniture, fixtures, machinery, equipment, improvements and betterments, and other personal property. The contents of several locations may be included (blanketed) in one policy. Although there are several methods of insuring property at various locations, it is usually recommended that all locations be insured in a single item with the amount of insurance provided on a blanket basis.

Valuation at loss

The standard fire insurance policy provides for reimbursement to the extent of "actual cash value" of the property at the time of the loss but not exceeding the amount which it would cost to repair or replace the property with material of like kind and quality within a reasonable time after the loss. *Actual cash value* is generally defined as being replacement cost at the time of the loss, less depreciation. The amount of depreciation is subject to many variables including the age of the property, physical condition, and estimated remaining useful life. Policies may be amended to respond on a different basis; for example, on replacement cost, on scheduled value, on inventory at cost plus a fixed percentage, or on any other basis that is reasonable.

Replacement cost insurance eliminates the factor of depreciation in a settlement of a loss. The intent is to permit the insured to replace the damaged property without adding funds from sources other than the proceeds of the insurance policy. Certain property such as obsolete machinery and equipment or property which is of special design or which has unique use can be insured based upon values which are scheduled in the policy. Inventory can be valued in many ways including sales price, cost, cost plus a fixed percentage, or any other reasonable way which would reflect the insured's financial interest in the inventory.

Increase in hazard, vacant premises

There is one condition in the policy which is often overlooked or ignored. The policy states that insurance is automatically suspended or restricted while the hazard is increased by any means within the control or knowledge of the insured or while a described building (whether intended for occupancy by an owner or tenant) is vacant for more than 60 consecutive days.

This policy condition places upon the insured the obligation of notifying the insurance company of the increase in hazard or when the property is vacant or unoccupied. One difficulty here is there is no definition for the term *increase in hazard,* and there are many borderline situations. Because it is the responsibility of the insured, it is in his best interest to report each and every instance of a possible hazard or where there is a change in occupancy.

The conditions regarding the premises being vacant or unoccupied refer to two separate conditions. Vacant means a premises without contents. Unoccupied refers to premises, with or without contents, where there has been no human visitation for a period of time. When it is anticipated that a building will be vacant or unoccupied, it should be reported to your broker or insurance company. The policy coverage can be amended so that the usual 60-day limitation is extended.

PACKAGE POLICIES

Package policies have been developed to bring together in one insurance contract the property and casualty coverage commonly required by business organizations. The purpose is to streamline coverage, avoid duplication and overlap, broaden the insurance protection, and reduce the total cost.

A package policy can include personal property, real property, business interruption, extra expense, boiler and machinery coverage, fidelity coverage, and comprehensive general liability coverage. It can be extended to include fine arts insurance, accounts receivable, valuable papers, and builders risk insurance.

The property section can be written on either a named peril basis or on an all-risks basis. The coverage can include rain and sleet damage to property in the open, seepage, backup of sewers and drains, theft from unattended vehicles, marring and scratching, and damage caused by changes in temperature. The policy can also be designed to include provisions for the elimination of co-insurance. The property insured can include glass and signs. It may also be extended to include, up to a specified amount, personal property of others in the care, custody, and control of the insured. Improvements can be insured up to the full replacement cost or full actual cash value, based upon the valuation clause in the policy. Newly acquired buildings can be insured up to an amount of $100,000 or more for a period of 90 days or more.

In addition to the advantages of broad protection through the facilities of a single underwriter providing a complete and fully integrated program of protection, the package policy affords the businessman substantial price discounts. These package policies are discussed again in Chapters 20 and 21.

OTHER EXPOSURES TO LOSS

The businessman often assumes responsibility for property of others in his care, custody, and control. In addition, it is possible that the peril of fire, explosion, water damage, and so on, can damage buildings and personal property of a third party. He can be held legally liable for such damage.

In the first instance, it is a relatively simple matter to endorse the property or package insurance policy to include reimbursement for damage to property in his care, custody, and control caused by those perils insured in that specific policy.

With respect to property not in a businessman's care, custody, and control there is some element of protection provided by the general liability policy. Additional protection can be obtained in our property insurance policy to include damage done to property of third parties which is not in his care, custody, and control.

Changes in processes or technological improvements can make existing machinery and equipment obsolete. As a result, at the time damage occurs which requires machinery replacement, there is an increased cost because of technological improvements. The policy can be specifically designed so that it will pay the full cost of the modern, more costly machinery or equipment capable of performing the same function.

Automatic coverage under the personal property insurance schedules can include protection for the newly acquired property for a period of 90 days following the date of acquisition or until more specific insurance has been placed, subject to limits of liability. Personal property can be insured automatically up to an amount of $25,000 or more for each newly acquired location which is owned by, leased by, or occupied by or controlled by the insured. If newly acquired property is valued higher than the automatic limit provided in the policy, it is imperative that the businessman notify his broker and/or insurance company immediately so that adequate limits can be provided.

ADDITIONAL CONTENTS COVERAGE

Following is a summary of other policy forms which have wide application for contents coverage.

Stock reporting

The stock reporting form was devised for those businesses which have wide fluctuations in the value of their stock during the period of the policy. Under conventional insurance policy forms the businessman, in order to protect himself against loss when the value of his stock is at its high point, would normally use the highest value anticipated as the basis for selecting limits in buying insurance. If he follows this approach he is paying too much premium for his average exposure over the course of the year. His alternative would be to buy a lesser amount of insurance and become a co-insurer if loss occurs when a stock is at the high point.

To eliminate this dilemma the stock reporting form was developed. The operating principle behind the form is simple. The insured selects a limit of liability sufficient to cover his maximum exposure to loss. A provisional premium is developed based upon estimated values and the rate for the location or locations involved. The limit of liability may be increased or decreased during the term of the policy. During the term of the policy, usually monthly, the insured reports the values for that particular reporting period. At the end of the policy the monthly reports of values are averaged and a final premium adjustment is made. The final premium is based on the average of the values reported in the periodic statements of values. The result is the insured has adequate limits in accordance with the limit of liability selected;

however, he only pays premium based upon average values exposed to loss. Property insured under the stock reporting form is not limited to stock. It can include materials, supplies, furniture, fixtures, machinery and equipment, and improvements and betterments.

Manufacturers output policy

The manufacturers output policy is a policy form designed to cover property of the insured away from manufacturing premises. Although the form may be modified, coverage is extended to cover all personal property owned by the insured, the insured's interest in improvements and betterments to buildings not owned by the insured, his interest in and legal liability for personal property of others in his actual or constructive care, custody, and control. It includes property of others sold by the insured where he has agreed to insure such property.

The policy does not insure currency, money, notes, growing crops, or standing timber; property covered under import and export ocean marine policies; animals, aircraft, and watercraft; properties sold by the insured under conditional sale or deferred payment plans; and loss resulting from interruption of business.

The manufacturers output policy is designed to insure against all risks of direct physical loss or damage from any external cause. It is important to review the perils excluded; mainly, earthquake or flood.

The exclusion of the perils of earthquake and flood does not apply to licensed automotive vehicles, rolling stock, and similar property of a mobile nature not intended for sale. It does not apply to property which is in the due course of transit, or imports or exports or property in the custody of a processor, nor damage caused by ensuing fire or theft, nor explosion following an earthquake or a flood. Underwriters will consider eliminating the earthquake and flood exclusion for additional premium charges. Loss caused by the explosion or rupture of steam boilers, steam pipes and steam turbines, and machinery derangement on equipment owned or operated by the insured is excluded. A boiler and machinery policy is required to cover this exposure. Loss or damage caused by collision or overturning of automobiles, automotive trucks, and trailers which were being operated under their own power or towed is also excluded. Additional exclusions include loss of market, loss of use, wear and tear, and damage caused by dampness of atmosphere, dryness of atmosphere extremes, or change of temperatures, loss of weight, plus contamination, unless such damage is caused by specified perils. Also excluded are losses sustained by property while actually being worked upon and any unexplained loss or mysterious disappearance.

The policy usually applies to property within the Continental United States including property in transit and is extended to include Canada while property is in due course of transit originating or terminating in the United States.

The businessman is required to identify his exposure to loss and to select limits of liability which will apply during the term of the policy. The three areas where you must select limits of liability are property at any one location, property in any one conveyance in transit, and property at any convention or fair. The limits of liability selected should cover the maximum exposure to loss. In determining the limit of liability it is important that there be an understanding of the valuation of the property which becomes the basis for adjustment for loss. The valuation clause can vary by the type of the property.

The valuation clause can be changed to suit specific needs; for example, stocks and merchandise are valued at actual cash value while improvements and betterments are valued at replacement cost less physical depreciation at the time and place of loss if actually replaced. If not replaced, improvements and betterments are valued at the unamortized value. Accounts, manuscripts, mechanical drawings, and other records or documents are valued at the value of the document blank, plus the cost of transcribing. Exhibitions and displays are valued at cost. Patterns and dyes are valued at replacement cost if actually replaced (there is no depreciation here). If not replaced, the patterns and dies are valued at the actual cash value. Finally, automobiles, trucks, machinery and equipment, and any other property not otherwise specified are valued at actual cash value.

A unique feature of the manufacturers output policy is the method by which the premium is computed. The policy requires regular reports of value. Most forms require that within 60 days after the end of each month the insured report to the insurance company the total value of all of the property insured under the policy. This report is due monthly. In addition, once during the calendar year the insured must report to the insurance company the values of all property covered by location. The report also must include, as a separate item, the value of goods in transit. At the end of each policy year, the premium of the policy is adjusted based upon the monthly values reported and the monthly policy rate as specified in the contract. The monthly rate can be modified in accordance with rating plans established by the insurance company.

Simply stated, the policy starts off with a provisional premium based upon estimated values. At the end of the year the premium on the policy is adjusted based upon the actual values reported. In effect, the insured is paying only for his real exposure to loss. However, the limits of liability selected do not play a part in the premium adjustment aspect of the policy. The limits of liability only determine the maximum that can be paid in event of loss under the policy. As a final consideration it should be noted that the policy usually is subject to a minimum annual premium specified in the policy.

Transit insurance

Property in transit may be covered under a manufacturers output policy or as part of an all-risks program of insurance protection. If not insured as part of one of these insurance contracts, property in transit can be insured under a separate transit insurance policy. (This review will not include coverages for policies available for those businesses which ship or receive goods from overseas. Ocean marine coverages and exposures are reviewed separately in Chapter 14.)

Transit insurance can apply to any property in transit by rail, truck, or airplane, or over inland waterways, practically anything moveable or under instruments of transportation (or communication). Included within this exposure coverage are goods in the course of transportation located in warehouses and other locations.

If you are an occasional shipper and require insurance only for individual shipments, a special trip policy can be purchased to cover the one shipment. A premium is paid based upon this specific shipment. It is more usual to purchase an "open policy" intended to cover all shipments for which the businessman has liability and/or financial interest for a specified term—usually one or three years. The premium is generally based upon the values to be shipped and insured and may be paid in a variety of ways. The most frequent way is to establish a deposit premium at the inception of the policy. Reports of values are submitted to the underwriter monthly or semiannually. At the end of the policy period, or at the end of each year, a premium is developed based upon the actual value of the insured goods shipped.

A businessman who relies on the common carrier to provide insurance while his property is in transit may not recover for damage caused by acts of God, riots, or strikes. Questions pertaining to valuation and extent of damage, need to replace and repair, and so on, can delay payment. Attempts to transfer risk of loss can have legal complications and lead to delay and large collection fees. The advantage of a transit insurance policy is that after a careful analysis of all exposures, the policy can be designed and tailored to eliminate many of these potential problems of the businessman with his suppliers, carriers, or customers in loss situations. A transit policy provides for prompt payment of losses even though another party may be liable. The transit insurance company will pay the loss and recover, if recovery is possible, from the third party. It eliminates the need for litigation and attorneys' fees which many times are expenses which cannot be recovered. The policy also covers losses where the third party is not normally liable such as flood, earthquake, and other acts of God. Finally, it reimburses the insured based upon an agreed valuation method.

A transit policy may be designed either on a specified peril basis or on an all-risks basis. Since it is not possible for the businessman to determine in advance what can happen to damage his goods, it is recommended that coverage be designed on an all-risks basis. The policy should be designed to be as broad as possible so all exposures inherent in the operation of the business are covered automatically during the term of the policy. Consider requiring the use of the following phrase: "This policy covers all goods and property usual and customary in the conduct of the insured's business."

It is important to carefully review and change, if necessary, the valuation clauses of the policy. Note the difference between actual cash value, replacement cost, selling price, and invoice valuation. You may also want to include a factor to cover the additional time and expense incurred as a result of the loss. If the nature of the property in transit lends itself to a frequency of small claims, it would be wise to consider a deductible to eliminate the handling necessary in processing these claims. In reality they are a business risk and should be handled as such. Passing small claims on to insurers can increase the cost of insurance. In addition, in some instances, a frequency of small claims can lead to policy cancellation.

All transit policies have a specified limit of liability. There is usually a limit of liability specified per shipment and a specified limit for any one occurrence. It is possible for a catastrophic event such as a windstorm, a flood, or earthquake to destroy property in separate conveyances scattered over a large geographical area.

It is the intent of most transit policies to provide coverage of the goods shipped until they are delivered to their destination. Transit contracts should be examined and amended to assure coverage in situations where goods are delivered to their destination and are refused or returned.

It is not usual to insure a business interruption loss suffered as a result of damage to goods in shipment. It is possible that property damage in shipment could cause a business interruption loss. For example, a machine being returned from a repair facility could be damaged by collision. The plant cannot start up in time because of this damage. Where such exposure looms, extensions in coverage can be designed to pick up this indirect loss.

Attempts should be made to avert or reduce transit losses. For example, a shipper of goods with high value or goods which are easily disposable such as gold, diamonds, or high-fashion clothing should make sure that the packaging of material does not clearly identify the contents. Delicate scientific equipment should be securely packed. Labels for special handling should be displayed, and shipping routes should be carefully selected. Over the long term, a businessman pays for his own losses. Anything he can do to reduce transit losses will help control the cost of his transit insurance.

Commercial property floater policies

In addition to the insurance protection available through fire policies, package policies, transit, and manufacturers output policies there are specialized insurance contracts covering business related property. These policies are termed *floater policies.* They include pattern and die floaters; contractors equipment floaters; exhibition policies on property while on exhibition and in transit to and from such exhibitions; installation floaters covering machinery, equipment, and supplies being used during the course of installation, building, renovating, or repairing; machinery and equipment floaters covering specified property of a mobile nature; installment sales and leased property floaters, garment contractors floaters, accounts receivable policies; valuable papers and records floaters. In addition, there are "floor plan" policies which cover property for sale while it is in the possession of a dealer and which support a loan from a bank or lending institution.

The coverage provided under these commercial property floater policies can be either a named peril policy or an all-risks policy. It may also include business interruption. The specific policy form varies in term and conditions by the type of property to be insured.

These policies usually contain the clause that in the event of a loss the insurance company will pay the actual cash value of the property. This may be amended to pay on the basis of repair or replacement. Additionally, you may select the option to have the policy pay claims on the basis of a specific schedule which is included as part of the policy. Just as there are special policy forms for each type of property insured, there are specific sets of exclusions for each policy form.

Careful attention should be given to the exclusions. For example, under the contractors equipment floater there are three classes of property which cannot be insured. They are motor vehicles designed for highway use, aircraft, and watercraft. In addition, plans, blueprints, designs, or specifications are excluded. Also excluded is property located underground and property which has become a permanent part of a structure. Steam shovels, hoists, cranes, drag lines, and other equipment of a similar nature have specified designed capacity.

Loss or damage caused by lifting weights in excess of the designed capacity is generally excluded.

Most floater policies contain a co-insurance clause. In addition, it is necessary for the businessman to select limits of liability. When a loss occurs, the burden of proving the loss falls upon the insured. It is imperative that the insured understand the provisions of the co-insurance clause, as well as the values insured, so that at time of loss the policy will properly respond to pay the insured on a basis which will make him financially whole.

Electronic data processing policies

The new world of electronic data processing has presented to the businessman new exposures to loss which may not be adequately covered under the conventional commercial insurance policies. Specialized insurance policy forms have been developed to insure the EDP equipment, media, extra expense arising out of loss to such equipment, business interruption, valuable papers, and accounts receivable. This specific coverage is discussed in Chapter 29.

Federal flood program

The peril of flood may be covered under a Difference in Conditions Policy (Chapter 19), a manufacturers output policy, or under transit coverage. The Flood Disaster Protection Act of 1973 provides an alternate source of flood insurance protection. This is particularly important for businessmen in areas subject to flood as the program may be the only flood insurance available for real and personal property. The coverage available under the act of 1973 is provided through the National Flood Insurance Association, a pool of private insurance companies.

Banks insured under the Federal Deposit Insurance Corporation and federally regulated banks and savings and loan associations are prohibited from making loans on property in flood prone areas where flood insurance is available unless flood insurance is carried.

The standard policy form defines *flood* as a general and temporary condition of partial or complete inundation of normally dry land areas from:

1. The overflow of inland or tidal waters.
2. The unusual and rapid accumulation or runoff of surface waters from any source.
3. Mud slides which are proximately caused or precipitated by accumulations of water on or under the crown.

In addition, the definition includes the collapse of subsidence of land along the shore of a lake or other body of water as a result of erosion or undermining caused by waves or currents of water exceeding the cyclical whole levels which result in flooding as defined above.

The definition of flood as it appears in the federal program is different from the definition of flood which may appear in commercially available policies.

There are two flood programs available. The first program, termed *the regular program,* is available in communities where a federally recognized flood management program exists. The second program, *the emergency program,* is available in communities not eligible for the regular program but which have adopted preliminary land use measures in accordance with federal regulations. In both cases a $100,000 limit of liability is available for small-business buildings, small-business contents, other nonresidential buildings and contents in nonresidential properties. Under this program, the rates charged are subsidized by the federal government. Also under the regular program, additional limits are available up to a maximum of $300,000 at rates not federally subsidized. The federal program has limitation, exclusion, and deductible requirements which must be reviewed prior to melding this program into an overall program of business insurance protection.

HOW TO HANDLE CLAIMS

The prompt, equitable settlement of insured losses is a major reason for the existence of the insurance industry. How does the businessman handle a loss? What should he do when a loss occurs?

As soon as practicable, every occurrence which may be a claim under an insurance policy should be reported to the insurance company or its agents. Losses involving burglary, arson, and malicious mischief should be reported promptly to the police. The initial report of loss to the insurance company or its agents may be by way of telephone, but a written record of the report should follow either by a telegram or letter.

All insurance contracts place an obligation on the insured to conserve and salvage the property involved in the loss. He must take all reasonable precautions both at the time of the loss and after the loss to prevent further damage and he must promptly separate the damaged property from the undamaged property. The insured is obligated to make temporary repairs if necessary. The insurance company is liable for reasonable expenses incurred by the insured to minimize the insured loss. This would include but not be limited to such items as boarding up windows, plastic covers, temporary roofing, and overtime charges for labor engaged in salvage work.

Whether or not there is insurance, the businessman wants to get back into operation as soon as practical. If he does insure his income, there is a time limitation for which the insured may claim a business interruption type loss (Chapter 6). This time limitation is referred to as "the minimum restoration period" and is defined as the time span starting at the time of loss or damage to the time when with due diligence and care the property damage could have been restored and made ready for normal operations. The insured may wish to make changes in plants and equipment as part of the repairs. Any extension past the point that the facility "could have been restored" is not compensable under the business interruption policy. Generally, it is in the businessman's best interest to get back into operation as soon as possible.

Most policies contain a proof of loss provision similar to the following:

> Within 60 days after the loss, unless such time is extended in writing by the insurance company, the insured shall render to the insurance company a proof of loss giving the time and origin of loss, the interest of the insured and all others in the property, and the value of each item and the amount of loss, all encumbrances and information on all contracts of insurance whether valid or not covering any of said property, any changes in the title, use, occupation, location, possession, and exposure of such property since the issuing of said policy, by whom and for what purpose, any building insured was occupied at the time of loss.

The standard policy forms also contain a clause dealing with concealment of fraud similar to the following:

> This entire policy shall be void if whether before or after a loss the insured has wilfully concealed or misrepresented any material fact or circumstance concerning this insurance or the subject thereof or the interest of the insured therein or in case of any fraud or false swearing by the insured relating thereto.

In preparing, handling, or settling his claim, the businessman may want to consider seeking outside help. This help is available through many sources: principally his accountant, his lawyer, his insurance broker, the insurance underwriter, or a public adjuster. In preparing the claim, a claims adjuster, attorney, broker, or underwriter needs the same information you would develop yourself as, for example, contractor's invoices giving a description of the repair work to be performed including a breakdown as to how the costs are developed.

The costs for the claim should be divided into sections such as clean-up costs, labor, material, and outside services such as rented cranes and public truckmen. The costs of labor should be divided between the labor supplied by outside contractors and use of the businessman's own labor force. Materials supplied by the insured should be stated and described separately. In those cases where competitive bids have been obtained copies of the unsuccessful bids or estimates should be incorporated as part of the records.

A claim involving stock and supplies should be broken down into three general areas: First, the raw materials, supplies, and stock not manufactured by the business; second, the work or stock in process; and last, the finished goods manufactured.

Generally, losses to property can be identified and claims prepared with a minimum of difficulty because the loss is to a tangible item. Business interruption claims on the other hand can become complicated because they deal with potential, that is, loss of net profit and fixed charges which would have been earned had the business been able to operate. Generally, the policies require the businessman take whatever action he deems necessary to reduce the business interruption loss. This expense to reduce loss is insured under the policy. Sometimes a question can be raised as to whether these expenditures equal the savings. Where there is any question in this regard, it is prudent to obtain the agreement of the insurance company before incurring that expense.

It is important the businessman understand his exposures to loss. He should regularly review these exposures with his insurance broker or agent and work with him to develop a program of insurance protection to adequately cover his financial loss in the event of a claim. Since, in the every day course of events, the needs of a businessman change, policies must be regularly reviewed and amended to reflect these changing needs.

CHAPTER 6

LOSS OF PROFITS— INDIRECT DAMAGE

TIME ELEMENT COVERAGES
Types of time element coverages
The protection of Business
Interruption coverages

THE MAJOR TIME ELEMENT
COVERAGES
Gross Earnings Forms coverages
Earnings insurance
Contingent Business Interruption
coverages
Extra expense insurance

SIMILARITY IN FORMS—MAJOR
CLAUSES
Actual loss sustained
Resumption of Operations Clause
Contribution Clause
Expenses to reduce loss
Interruption by civil authority
Limitation—media for electronic
data processing

Special exclusions
Pro Rata Clause
Normal
Loss Clause
Alterations and new buildings
Electrical Apparatus Clause
Liberalization Clause
Nuclear exclusion

COMMON ENDORSEMENTS
Premium Adjustment Endorsement
Agreed Amount Endorsement
Extension of period of interruption

OTHER TIME ELEMENT COVERAGES
Rental Value coverage
Leasehold Interest coverage
Blanket coverage

SUMMARY

Leo Kling
GAB Business Services, Inc.
New York, New York

Leo Kling began his career as an adjuster with GAB, now GAB Business Services, Inc., in Albany, New York, in 1940 where he remained until entering the Army during World War II. Shortly after the war, he rejoined GAB in Newark, New Jersey, as an adjuster in 1948. Subsequently, and until 1961, he was Branch Manager of General Adjustment Bureau at Parkersburg, Wheeling, West Virginia, and Jackson Heights and Hempstead, New York. In 1961 he was appointed General Adjuster in the New York City Controlled Loss Department and served in that capacity until January 1967 when he was assigned to the then Eastern Departmental Office. The latter office in 1971 was identified as the New York District where he remained until June of 1972. He was elected a Secretary of GAB Business Services, Inc., in May 1976 and his present assignment as Executive General Adjuster involves him in the handling of property and business interruption losses on an international basis.

A manager of a business protects the value of the business's physical assets by the purchase of insurance. Property insurance is designed to mitigate the adverse effects of the destruction of buildings, equipment, fixtures, stock, or other physical properties from identified perils. Liability insurance protects the owner from the negative effects of his employees' negligent acts or responds to the failure of products to meet express or implied warranties. Although an evaluation is made of insurance needs, costs, and budget limitations, both of these coverages are purchased rather routinely.

In addition to the protection of the physical assets of the business, the income from the use of the physical assets also should be protected from the same identified perils.

TIME ELEMENT COVERAGES

All of the coverages addressed in this chapter relate directly to the passage of time. Normally, time element insurance forms contain a phrase that limits the coverage to the period of time, frequently called the period of suspension, for "not exceeding such length of time as would be required with the exercise of due diligence and dispatch to rebuild, repair or replace . . . the described property."

Types of time element coverages

The coverages that relate to the interruption of business, originally called use and occupancy insurance (and still identified that way by boiler-machinery insurers), are now commonly referred to as business interruption insurance. They are:

Gross Earnings Form—Mercantile and Service Risks (sometimes called non-manufacturing).

Gross Earnings Form—Manufacturing Risks.

Earnings insurance.

Contingent forms.

Extra expense.

There are additional coverages available such as Rental Value, Leasehold Interest, Selling Agents Commission, Tuition Forms, and the like. These relate to highly specific needs and will not be explored here.

The protection of Business Interruption coverages

Business Interruption coverages are designed to do for the owner of the business exactly what the business would have done had the interruption not occurred. These coverages will return, subject to the application of any Contribution Clause, the same net profit the business would have produced during the period of suspension had no loss occurred. In addition, these coverages will pay the expenses which necessarily continue during the interruption. They will not go beyond that point.

The coverages are not intended to guarantee the same set of customers the business enjoyed prior to the occurrence, nor can they assure the insured's market or the insured's share of the market. The coverages cannot prevent customers from going elsewhere nor can they guarantee the return of those customers once the period of suspension or interruption has ended and the business is back in operation. As a practical matter, loss of customers or market shares defy any rational attempt to place a monetary value on them.

An integral part of the protection of income is paying, and therefore retaining, the employees who contribute to the generation of the operation's income. These coverages provide for this payment. Moreover, an Extra Expense coverage is available (with some limitations) for businesses which must continue to function without pause in operation.

Business Interruption coverages cannot guarantee the continuance of a particular business or industry due to economic conditions. For example, should a gas station lose additional business during a loss suspension as a result of a lack of available fuel, the policies will not respond.

Throughout this chapter reference will be made to the Contribution Clause and "expenses that would have been earned." The Contribution Clause makes the insured share in otherwise covered losses if underinsured. "Expenses that would have been earned" means those normal business expenses of a firm that have been covered by revenue. If a firm is earning a profit, all expenses have been earned. If a firm is operating at a loss, all expenses have not been earned.

THE MAJOR TIME ELEMENT COVERAGES

Gross Earnings Forms coverages

The largest volume of Business Interruption coverage written is on one of the two Gross Earnings Forms. The two forms are:

1. Gross Earnings Form—Mercantile and Service Risks (sometimes called non-manufacturing).
2. Gross Earnings Form—Manufacturing Risks.

For mercantile and service risks the term *gross earnings* is defined in the policy as "the sum of total net sales and other earnings derived from operations of the business, less the cost of merchandise sold, including materials therefor, materials and supplies consumed directly in supplying the services sold by the insured, and services purchased from outsiders (not employees of the insured) for resale, which do not continue under contract." Further, "no other costs shall be deducted in determining gross earnings."

In an adjustment of a loss, this definition is followed to determine the actual loss sustained. The definition, however, does relate to the Contribution or Co-insurance Clause which may then modify the dollar amount of the insurer's loss payment. For all losses, gross earnings are based upon the revenue that would have been earned had no loss occurred during the 12 months immediately following the date of damage to or destruction of the described property.

The definition of gross earnings in the manufacturing form policy is "the total net sales value of production plus total net sales of merchandise and other earnings derived from operations of the business, less the cost of raw stock from which such production is derived (less the cost of), supplies consisting of materials consumed directly in the conversion of such raw stock into finished stock or in supplying services sold by the insured, (less the cost of) merchandise sold including packaging materials therefor, and (less the cost of) services purchased from outsiders (not employees of the insured) for resale which do not continue under contract." As in the non-manufacturing form, the policy states that no other costs shall be deducted in determining gross earnings.

There is a provision that contemplates the possibility that a manufacturer might also be involved in selling merchandise. It therefore provides for the exclusion of cost of sales but anticipates including as income the sales of such merchandise.

The other difference in the two forms pertains to finished stock. This is an important concept for the purchaser of Gross Earnings coverage for a manufacturing operation. The insurer does not intend to be liable for any loss resulting from damage to or destruction of finished stock nor for the time required to reproduce the finished stock. The policy insures the net sales value of production. Finished stock can be insured under a physical damage policy on an actual cash value basis which would not include profit or it can be insured for its selling price.

An example of the earnings and gross earnings mercantile non-manufacturing coverages. Assume the sales of a retail establishment for the preceding fiscal/calendar year were:

January $25,000	May $31,000	September .... $ 26,000
February 23,000	June 30,000	October 30,000
March 22,000	July 26,000	November 46,000
April 25,000	August........ 28,000	December 48,000
		Total $360,000

What follows in Exhibit 6–A is a realignment of the profit and loss statement, a "restructured" income statement, in accordance with the definition of gross earnings in the Mercantile/Service/non-manufacturing Risks coverage form.

Exhibit 6–A
A RETAIL ESTABLISHMENT

Gross sales		$360,000
Less returns and allowances ....$	720	
Discounts	1,260	
Bad debts	360	
Freight and shipping....................................	4,860	
	$ 7,200	7,200
		$352,800
Less opening inventory ....$	95,000	
Purchases	260,000	
Purchases discount	(5,600)	
Freight-in	4,200	
Merchandise available for sale ....$	353,600	
Closing inventory	119,600	
	$234,000	
Wrapping and packaging supplies	1,800	
	$235,800	235,800
		$117,000
Other income—franchise		5,000
Gross earnings..		$122,000
Less operating expenses:		
Salaries ....$	46,000	
Wages	11,500	
Payroll taxes and benefits	13,300	
Taxes	2,400	
Rent	18,000	
Depreciation	5,000	
Truck and auto	4,800	
Advertising...	2,400	
Insurance	2,800	
Heat, light, and water	800	
Postage and stationery	600	
Charity donations	400	
Accounting and legal..................................	1,100	
Miscellaneous	400	
	$109,500	109,500
Net income...		$ 12,500

Note that the first step is the identification of net sales. Those items deducted from gross sales represent funds not available for use in the purchase of merchandise or for the payment of operating expenses.

The next group of figures represents the pure cost of the merchandise necessary to produce the net sales for the period. "Purchases discount" is considered as a reduction in the cost of merchandise which follows the definition "earnings" and "gross earnings" in the forms being discussed. Wrapping and packaging supplies are directly related to sales and therefore will also be subtracted from net sales.

"Other income" tracks with the insured definition. But if "other income" is not derived from operations, it is not intended to be insured.

The figure of $122,000 in the example then is the item insured under both the Earnings coverage and the Gross Earnings coverage. It is a vital figure because:

a. Within the Gross Earnings coverage this item is the amount against which the Contribution Clause is applied.
b. The $122,000 figure includes $12,500 of net profit that would have been earned and the $109,500 of operating expenses that would have been earned if the interruption had not occurred.
   1. Assume for a moment that the profit and loss statement reveals salaries, wages, payroll taxes, and benefits that amounted to $85,000 total instead of $70,800.
   2. The total operating expenses would be $123,800 rather than $109,500. Instead of a net profit there would be a net loss of $1,800 ($122,000 − $123,800 = $1,800 net loss).
   3. The $122,000 is still earnings by definition as it represents the sum of the total net profit, payroll expenses, taxes, interest, rent, and all other operating expenses *earned* by the business.

(Note: Noncontinuing and nonincurred expenses during a period of suspension are not intended to be insured.)

Sales value of production.   Nowhere in the forms under discussion has the accounting term *gross profit* been used. It is not the intent to insure gross profit as such but to insure gross earnings (a term not found in accounting terminology) as defined in the forms.

So, too, as the form is used to insure manufacturing operations, the term *net sales* is not used but the term *net sales value of production*. The distinction is made that the insurance is for a reduction in earnings for an unknown period of suspension that might occur during the manufacturing cycle. The insurance is not for net sales only but for a reduction in net sales value.

When the product manufactured is sold as it comes off the production line, there is essentially no difference between net sales and net sales value of production. On the other hand, if a manufacturer produces for inventory, the definitions differ. Consequently, in the preparation of a business interruption work sheet to establish values for the coverage or for determining values for a year after a loss, there should be added to net sales, the year-end inventory of finished goods at net sales value and the beginning inventory should be deducted. Following is an example of determining net sales value of production for any fiscal period:

Gross sales		$ . . . . .
Less:	Bad debts, commissions, discounts, freight-out, returns and allowances, etc.	. . . . .
Net sales		$ . . . . .
Add:	Year-end inventory of finished goods at net sales value	. . . . .
Subtotal		$ . . . . .
Deduct:	Beginning inventory of finished goods at net sales value	. . . . .
Net sales value of production		$ . . . . .

Ordinary payroll exclusion. The Gross Earnings Forms include all payroll expenses including taxes, vacation pay, and the like. In a manufacturing operation a businessman may not want to insure the ordinary payroll of the business. The reasons might be that local labor can be trained quickly for the particular manufacturing process involved or the necessary premium costs to insure ordinary payroll are expensive. In mercantile operations the same general conditions may exist. The operator of a mercantile or service business may not wish to pay the premium required to insure ordinary payroll for an extended period of time.

The Gross Earnings Forms automatically insure *all payroll* to the extent necessary to resume operations with the same quality of service which existed immediately preceding the loss. The forms can be endorsed, however, to exclude ordinary payroll completely or to limit the coverage to 90 days with additional increments of 30 days permissible. Consideration at the same time must be given to the effects of this endorsement, as they relate to the amount of insurance required and the resulting ultimate cost of coverage.

Earnings insurance

Earnings insurance was specifically designed for the new or smaller business. This coverage is especially appealing to the smaller specialty shops found in shopping centers, the average merchant in the small city, and to service-type operations such as gas stations, restaurants, laundromats, and dry cleaners.

The form has a less complicated definition of *earnings* than the Gross Earnings Form and the added advantage of not having a Contribution or Co-insurance Clause. Depending upon the jurisdiction in which the policy is written, recovery under the Earnings Form is limited to a stated percentage of the total amount of insurance purchased for each 30 consecutive calendar-day period of suspension.

The majority of the coverage is written with a 25 percent limitation. This means that the amount of insurance carried should be at least four times the amount of coverage the owner of the business requires for any given 30 consecutive days. The basis for selecting the amount of insurance should be the income of the most significant 30 consecutive days of business operation.

Other limitations written are on a 16.67 percent or 33.33 percent of total insurance purchased basis. Consequently, the policy limits should be six (in the event of a 16.67 percent limitation), four (a 25 percent limitation), or three (a 33.33 percent limitation) times the anticipated monthly needs of the business. For retail shops, the amount of coverage and limitation selected should comprise the Christmas selling season. Should an owner determine coverage in this manner, it is possible that a slightly excessive amount would be purchased. Since the most important period covered would encompass the Christmas selling season, however, it would be false economy to save a relatively small amount of premium and sacrifice a portion of a potential claim.

The monthly limitation needs are determined by the earnings generated by the business as defined within the form. Earnings are defined as "the sum of the total net profit, payroll expenses, taxes, interest, rents, and all other operating expenses *earned* by the business." If no net profit would have been earned, there may well have been some portion of the expenses that likewise would not have been earned. Consequently, the policy in the case of an interruption or suspension from an insured peril provides payment only for the portion of the expenses that would have been earned by the business had there been no loss.

Privacy of financial information. There is no requirement in Earnings coverage that an insured furnish financial information to the insurer at the time of purchase of the coverage. The companies recognize that most "earnings" insureds jealously guard their modus operandi and generally consider all accounting information as proprietary. The insured can withhold disclosure of costs, gross profit, and, in fact, all information at the time of purchase. The owner of the business simply makes a judgment of the amount of coverage required to meet business needs. Should there be an interruption of the business by an insured peril, however, the insured will be required to furnish the insurer all accounting information necessary to support and evaluate the claim.

The provisions within the earnings form which spell out the latter are contained in the paragraph entitled "Requirements in Case Loss Occurs" and require among other things the insured furnish all books of account, bills, invoices, and other vouchers as may be reasonably required.

Contingent Business Interruption coverages

Generally, for an insured to sustain an insured loss, the property owned by the insured must have sustained damage from an insured peril. Contingent Business Interruption coverages, however, provide reimbursement for loss of income that results from the damage to or destruction of property owned by others. Two types of coverage are available.

Contributing Property coverage is available for insureds who depend on the operations of a supplier or manufacturer for material to use in their manufacturing process. This coverage protects the insured if their supplier is affected by an insured peril from the resultant loss of profit and the earning of other expenses until a new supplier can be found.

Recipient Property coverage is available for insureds who depend upon a customer to purchase the product they manufacture. In situations where an insured might produce an item solely and exclusively for one customer, should the premises of that customer be affected by an insured peril, the insured would have no other avenue of sales available and the consequences would be a loss of profit and other expenses.

Businesses which depend on the continuation of another's operation need contingent coverage. Contingent coverage can only be obtained when the insured does not have a financial investment in the other operation. It cannot be a subsidiary of the insured or a "sister" corporation. If it is, blanket business interruption coverage should be considered.

Magnet Properties coverage is relatively new and owes its genesis to shopping centers. Many large centers contain one or more major department store or supermarket units which are in fact the centers' major attraction. In the event of a curtailment of operations of the major or "magnet" operation, the satellite properties (the small merchants and service businesses within the center) may experience a curtailment of their sales even though their premises have not been affected.

Extra expense insurance

Extra expense insurance is for the business which, by its nature, must continue to function despite the destruction or damage to its physical properties. The most notable are newspapers, banks, dairies, and similar service businesses. This coverage is not intended to respond to a loss of profit or the continuing expenses of the business. It responds to extra expenses defined as "the total cost incurred during the period of restoration chargeable to the operation of the insured's business, over and above the total costs that would normally have been incurred."

Depending upon the type of business involved, consideration should be given to the purchase of this coverage in combination with a Gross Earnings Form. In some jurisdictions a combination form is available. Where available, it is certainly recommended.

SIMILARITY IN FORMS—MAJOR CLAUSES

The forms used to provide the coverage for losses resulting from interruption of business contain clauses which limit coverage and define the duties and obligations of the insured as well as the insuring company.

Each of the clauses referred to is usually identified by a numerical designation, followed by a boldface print title or description of the clause. There then follows an elaboration of the descriptive title. Some of the more important clauses follow.

Actual loss sustained

The words *actual loss sustained* appear in boldface type in all forms discussed in this chapter and are intended to require a provable loss resulting from the interruption of business. The mere fact that an interruption of business has taken place as a result of physical damage to the insured's property is not in and of itself evidence that there has been a loss under the policy.

During the riots of the 60s, sales lost by many merchants were the result of fewer customers venturing on the streets, not damage to the properties of the insured merchant. Similarly, during catastrophe situations, such as a hurricane or tornado alert, business may drop off dramatically. It is not the intent of the contract to cover the loss of business that occurs at that time. However, should the property sustain physical damage so that the business cannot operate after the storm has struck, coverage will apply.

From the insurers' point of view, the boldface words also act to preclude an attempt to collect for a loss that was not in actuality realized.

For example,

When payroll expense is insured, in order for the insured to collect there are two considerations that must be met: first, coverage will respond only if the payroll *is necessary* to resume operations (with the same quality service as before the loss); and, second, the payroll must, in fact, have been paid.

Payroll is the prime example, but the requirement that the expenses be *earned, incurred,* and *paid* is within the scope of the words *actual loss sustained* whatever the expenses are.

Resumption of Operations Clause

The Resumption of Operations Clause is designed to place the insured under an obligation to use all available facilities in order to reduce the loss. Generally speaking, this is applicable to all insurance. An insured has an obligation and a duty to mitigate a claim whenever possible.

The Resumption of Operations Clause states this principle as a condition. If the insured could have reduced the loss by using other facilities and did not, the reduction will be taken into account in arriving at the amount of the loss. An insured is clearly under an obligation to resume partial or complete operations by using damaged, undamaged, or any other facilities available.

Contribution Clause

The Contribution Clause does not appear in the Earnings Form but does appear in the Gross Earnings Forms. The Contribution Clause is, in effect, a Co-insurance Clause. While the verbiage is not identical to Co-insurance Clauses in other policies, it has the same result insofar as the collectibility of a claim is concerned when there is an insufficient amount of insurance to meet the requirement. Contribution or Co-insurance Clauses are devices utilized by the insurance company to balance the premium and the risk.

These clauses create the greatest difficulty in adjustments between insurers and insureds. Disputes can be avoided if proper attention is given to the amount of insurance purchased. When the contract contains such a clause, it is usually identified on the declarations page of the policy with a notation regarding the percentage of insurance required to the value at risk. In effect, the amount of insurance carried must be equal to or greater than the stated percentage of the item insured.

A definition of the item to be insured is contained elsewhere in the form. For instance, if gross earnings are anticipated to be $200,000 and the policy contains an 80 percent Contribution Clause, the insured must buy *at least* $160,000 of coverage to avoid a Contribution Clause penalty. The insurance is written and the Contribution Clause applied against the operations of the business for a 12 month period following the occurrence of the loss. Restating the effects, should the businessman/owner/insured not purchase an amount of insurance equal to or greater than the amount required by the percentage shown, the business must bear a part of the loss that occurs. It becomes a coinsurer of the loss.

It follows that it is extremely important to pay strict attention to the progress of the business insured in order to prevent the negative effects of the Contribution Clause in the event of a loss. In times of inflation, an increase in the amount of insurance may be in order to meet the requirements of the Contribution Clause which is measured against the business operations for the year following the loss. Likewise, in the case of a falling economy, adjusting limits downward can prevent payment for an excessive amount of insurance.

It is wise, therefore, in these inflationary times to consider the purchase of a greater amount of insurance than current operations indicate because the measurement of recovery relates to the gross earnings that *would have been* earned during the 12 months immediately following the date of damage or destruction of the described property.

In order to conclude an adjustment under any business interruption form containing a Contribution Clause, it is necessary for the owner of the business and a representative of the insurer to agree upon the results that the business would have produced for the 12 months following the incident had the loss not occurred. Agreement on the particular amount requires considerable discussion and review of current conditions, the nature and movement within the insured's accounts, and accounting records. The need is for a complete understanding and agreement between the adjuster and insured in order to project what the business would have done for the 12 months following the incident. As the adjustment of losses under these coverages is far from an exact science, the relatively limited amount of litigation concerning Time Element coverages is remarkable (particularly in today's litigious climate).

Expenses to reduce loss

> This policy also covers such expenses as are necessarily incurred for the purpose of reducing loss under this policy (except expenses incurred to extinguish a fire), but in no event shall the aggregate of such expenses exceed the amount by which the loss otherwise payable under this policy is thereby reduced. Such expenses shall not be subject to the application of the Contribution Clause.

The intent of this paragraph is to reduce the period of interruption. Considerable judgment must be exercised in deciding whether an expenditure should be made and what the positive effect will be upon the reduction of the claim. As a practical matter, the owner/operator of a business usually has the information that enables a qualified judgment to be made of whether or not an expenditure of funds will reduce a loss. Usually the insurer's representative and the owner will work together, but the presumption exists that the owner of the business is more knowledgeable of the operation than a third party.

There are times too, that the owner will make a decision to get back into operation quickly, but the result will not serve to reduce the claim under the policy. The decision, however, will enable the operator to serve his customers. These expenses will need extra expense insurance in order to be covered.

The final sentence of the "Expenses to reduce loss" paragraph indicates that these expenses will not be subject to the application of the Contribution Clause. These expenses in fact are affected by the Contribution Clause in that the limit of the policy is the amount that would have been paid if these expenses had not been incurred. The policy will pay any expenses necessarily incurred so long as the total claim is reduced.

For example:

Assume the insured is a retail operation and has been operating at a profit. Assume also that as a result of an insured peril there will be a relatively short period of suspension of six selling days (Monday through Saturday). Assume anticipated sales to be $12,000 for the week and that following the definition of "earnings" there will be a reduction in earnings of 33.33 percent of sales. In all probability there would be no expenses that could be discontinued. Were the suspension allowed to go the full six selling days, the reduction in earnings would be $4,000.

By the use of overtime labor amounting to $1,000, the suspension could be reduced to three days. There would, therefore, be a loss of sales of $8,500. The reduction in earnings then would be 33.33 percent of $8,500 or $2,833 which, when added to the $1,000 of expenses to reduce the loss, would produce a total claim of $3,833. The expenditure of $1,000 would result in a reduction of the claim from $4,000 to $3,833 and would be honored. The example assumes, of course, that the amount of insurance carried meets the requirements of the Contribution Clause and that there are no noncontinuing expenses.

Interruption by civil authority

This coverage does not require direct damage to the insured's property but extends coverage for a period of time, not exceeding two consecutive weeks, when the insured's business is interrupted as a consequence of direct damage to property adjacent to the insured's premises and access to the insured's premises is prohibited by order of civil authority. A classic example is when the police or fire department close off a street because of damage to property other than that owned by the insured. Access to the insured's premises is then impossible.

This extension of coverage is designed to reimburse the insured for the results of a loss of business for a period not exceeding two weeks. It should be noted that access to the premises must be prohibited as a result of an insured peril.

Limitation—media for electronic data processing

The insurance business recognizes the value of media for electronic data processing. However, at the time this coverage was introduced, experience was limited and insurers limited the business interruption loss sustained to any 30 consecutive days of interruption or the length of time that would be required to rebuild, repair, or replace the damaged or destroyed property, whichever is less.

The loss must be to the insured's property, at the location named within the contract and for the perils insured against. It is possible to extend the period of time beyond the 30-day limitation within the form or to totally eliminate the 30-day limitation with an increase in the rate.

Special exclusions

Most insurers disclaim liability for any increase in loss resulting from "enforcement of any ordinance or law regulating the uses, construction, repair or demolition of buildings or structures. . . ." It is the insurers' intent to avoid loss that results from zoning regulations or building codes.

Insurers disclaim liability for any loss resulting from "interference at the described premises, by strikers or other persons, with rebuilding, repairing or replacing the property or with the resumption or continuation of business. . . ." It would be a serious question of fact whether or not the strike or other interference referred to would have taken place whether or not the loss had occurred.

The next designated special exclusions is a disclaimer of liability resulting from "the suspension, lapse or cancellation of any lease, license, contract or order unless such suspension, lapse or cancellation results directly from the interruption of business, and then this company shall be liable only for such loss as affects the insured's earnings during, and limited to, the period of indemnity covered under this policy; . . . ." Insurers attempt to avoid liability for situations considered uninsurable or not caused by an insured peril.

The remaining special exclusion is an omnibus exclusion disclaiming liability for any other consequential or remote loss.

Pro Rata Clause

This clause appears in all fire insurance forms and is an attempt to avoid duplicate or excess payment for any loss. The clause requires the insurer to contribute to the payment of a loss in the same proportion that the individual policy bears to the total of insurance in existence at the time of the loss (whether or not the loss under the other contracts is collectible).

It is important for an insured to be certain that all insurance policies intended to cover the same property contain the same clauses. In order to avoid the possibility of only a partial recovery of a loss, all policies must be identical in nature.

Normal

"The condition that would have existed had no loss occurred." Loss payments are based on interrupted "normal" operation.

Loss Clause

"Any loss hereunder shall not reduce the amount of this policy." At one time property insurance policies (including business interruption coverage) were automatically reduced by the amount of the payment of any loss. It was then necessary to reinstate that amount of insurance by the payment of an additional premium. Today most policies are automatically reinstated without any additional premium. The Loss Clause makes that reinstatement automatic and is beneficial to all insureds.

Alterations and new buildings

The lengthy clause relating to alterations and new buildings states that the policy insures any loss resulting from the damage or destruction to alterations, additions, or new buildings that are made in or added to the described premises. As in the Loss Clause above, this particular clause has an historic connotation. Formerly, property damage policies did not respond to changes made in any exposure without specific endorsement once the policy was written. The effect of the alterations clause is the elimination of the need for endorsements every time any change, alteration or addition is made to the insured premises. The clause does not waive or modify any conditions of the Automatic Sprinkler Clause if such a clause is attached to the policy.

Electrical Apparatus Clause

The Electrical Apparatus Clause is contained in most property policies. It reflects the insurer's intent to avoid losses resulting from or damages caused by a short circuit unless a fire ensues. It is excluded here because it is intended to be a subject of insurance under a boiler machinery policy.

Liberalization Clause

This particular clause provides for the automatic modification of an insurance policy without endorsement if there is a change that broadens or extends the coverage without an increase in premium.

Nuclear exclusion

It is not the intent of a business interruption policy to insure for any loss caused by nuclear reaction, radiation, or contamination and this clause has been included in business interruption forms to clearly exclude any such loss.

COMMON ENDORSEMENTS

Premium Adjustment Endorsement

This endorsement is designed to minimize the possibility of the adverse effects of insufficient insurance on coverage that is subject to a Contribution Clause. It is a reporting form type of coverage and, as in all reporting forms, strict attention must be paid to the reporting requirements.

Values are reported at the inception of the endorsement and periodically thereafter. Eliminating the effects of a Contribution Clause is accomplished by the purchase of a greater amount of insurance than appears to be required. However, the endorsement provides for a refund of the excess premium when the insured reports actual gross earnings at the required time if the original amount of insurance was in excess of actual requirements.

Agreed Amount Endorsement

The Agreed Amount Endorsement eliminates any contribution penalty. Check with your agent or broker, as this may not be available in your state.

Extension of period of interruption

All the standard coverages addressed in this chapter have related to the loss in the "time required, with the exercise of due diligence and dispatch, to rebuild, repair or replace such part of the property described as has been damaged or destroyed." When the property has been repaired or replaced, the suspension period has ended and the payment under the policy ceases. The Extension Clause acknowledges that business does not always return immediately to the same profitability level as existed immediately prior to the loss. With this endorsement, an additional amount of coverage can be purchased for the period of time during which the insured's business is returning to normal.

The extension can be purchased in 30-day increments. It should be noted that regardless of the additional time period or periods purchased, the form still limits recovery to actual loss sustained. This means that even though an insured might have purchased an extension of two additional 30-day periods, it would be necessary in the event of a loss to be able to demonstrate precisely when the business returned to its normal operation. The mere fact that the coverage exists does not make a payment under the form automatic.

OTHER TIME ELEMENT COVERAGES

Rental Value coverage

Rental Value coverage is provided under standard Homeowners' Policies. It pays for any increased cost to rent alternate facilities. Under Business Interruption Policies, rent is an operating expense and is an insured item under the Earnings and Gross Earnings Forms to the extent earned. For the owner of an apartment house or a commercial building, rental value or rental income is an item that should be insured.

Loss recovery under the form caused by an insured peril has the same *actual loss sustained,* due diligence and dispatch, noncontinuing expense clauses as other business interruption forms.

Leasehold Interest coverage

The prime candidate for Leasehold Interest coverage is the lessee of premises on a long-term lease that is especially valuable. If the premises were destroyed or so damaged that the Fire Clause could be exercised by the lessor, the lessee would need comparable quarters but the cost of the new premises could far exceed the fixed costs under the original lease. Others who might need this coverage are tenants who have an advance rental payment lease or who had purchased a lease from a prior tenant.

The coverage is also a tool to protect extensive improvements to a premises by a tenant. Leasehold Interest coverage protects the value of the improvements when the provisions of a Fire Clause of the lease can be enforced by the owner, even though the improvements might not have been damaged by the insured perils.

Blanket coverage

Blanket is an insurance term that means that one or more geographic locations or types of property are insured. Blanket Business Interruption coverage is available to the business that operates from more than one location.

SUMMARY

The loss of profits or the requirement to honor contractual expenses can force a business out of business. Business interruption insurance can be designed to meet this need. It is as vital to business as sick pay is to an individual.

CHAPTER 7

DISHONESTY LOSSES

TYPES OF POLICIES AVAILABLE

RISKS COVERED
　Dishonesty
　Other coverage

WHO IS COVERED

EXCLUSIONS
　Acts of the insured
　Inventory exclusions
　Knowledge of fraud or dishonesty

CONDITIONS FOR RECOVERY
　Notice and proof of loss
　There must be a loss

OTHER PROVISIONS AND ISSUES
　Limits of liability
　Valuation and subrogation
　Joint insureds
　Danger of libel and slander
　Riders

RISK MANAGEMENT

Frank L. Skillern, Jr.
General Counsel
Federal Deposit Insurance Corporation
Washington, D.C.

Prior to accepting the position in 1979 of General Counsel of the Federal Deposit Insurance Corporation, **Frank L. Skillern, Jr.** was a partner in the Dallas, Texas, law firm of Strasburger and Price, where he specialized in handling fidelity claims. Mr. Skillern is a past Chairman of the Fidelity and Surety Committee of the Section of Tort and Insurance Practice of the American Bar Association and Chairman of the American Bar Association National Institute on the Bankers Blanket Bond in 1978 and on Financial Institution Blanket Bonds in 1979. While in private practice, Mr. Skillern was special counsel to the Federal Deposit Insurance Corporation on the fidelity claims involving three of the four largest bank failures in the history of the country.

Perhaps the most disturbing and demoralizing type of loss that a business can suffer is a defalcation by a trusted employee. Cases of this kind are almost always personal tragedies for the employee and his family. Most businessmen must trust their associates and employees and even those with a cynical view of human nature are astonished when such a fraud is discovered. Over the past 10 to 20 years, the financial community has been jolted by a series of well-publicized losses due to insider fraud, some involving tens of millions of dollars. Many of these cases involved fraud by senior level officers. In fact, the lesson that has been painfully learned by the insurance industry is that the major risk of a large loss is from the acts of senior executives. Accompanying this trend has been a tendency by the courts to expand the traditional definition of dishonesty, ultimately resulting in the insurance industry attempting to narrow coverage by policy provisions.

TYPES OF POLICIES AVAILABLE

There are several types of dishonesty or fidelity coverage which are currently available to businesses. They fall into two categories:

1. Specialized policies for particular industries, such as the banking industry, the savings and loan industry, the brokerage industry, and the insurance industry itself. These policies are generally designated as "blanket" bonds (e.g., Bankers Blanket Bond, Savings and Loan Blanket Bond, etc.) and cover risks in addition to fidelity.
2. Nonspecialized policies for general business concerns.

The principal nonspecialized policies are called the Blanket Crime Policy and the Comprehensive Dishonesty, Disappearance and Destruction Policy (known in the industry as the Three-D Policy). There is also a policy referred to as a Commercial Blanket Bond, though this form has not been used much in recent years. Generally speaking, the fidelity part of each of these policies covers all employees of the insured. In addition, it is possible to purchase a policy which covers a specifically named individual or whoever is acting in a specifically designated position, such as a treasurer. The Three-D Policy has two employee dishonesty coverages, Form A, which has a total limit of liability for each loss applicable to all employees, and Form B, which applies the limit of liability to each employee.

This chapter is concerned principally with the nonspecialized policies, which will be referred to as "Commercial Policies." Reference will be made to the specialized policies when appropriate. The specialized policies will be referred to as the Financial Institution Bonds.[1] The use of the word *bond* when describing certain of these policies is a holdover from early days of fidelity coverage, when the undertaking by the company was actually a bond, with the insurance company (the surety) guaranteeing the performance of an individual (the principal) to the individual's employer (the obligee). However, current policies are just insurance policies, and the law of insurance, not the law of principal and surety, is applicable to their interpretation. Most policies refer to the party issuing the policy as the "Company" or the "Underwriter" and the party to whom the policy is issued as the "Insured." In this chapter that nomenclature will be followed.

RISKS COVERED

Dishonesty

Everyone thinks he knows what dishonesty means. Indeed, in many ways, dishonesty is like pornography—a precise definition is difficult, but most people think that they "know it when they see it." Many dictionaries define dishonest as "not honest" and equate the quality with lying and cheating. However, a satisfactory definition for insurance purposes eluded the courts for decades. As early as 1930, one of America's great judges, Justice Cardozo, held that dishonesty was not a term of art but involved acts whose purpose would "be fairly characterized as dishonest in the common speech of men."[2] In other words, "I know it when I see it."

To understand the coverage currently available, it is necessary to trace the history of dishonesty or fidelity insurance, as it is sometimes called. Fidelity coverage goes back to the late 19th century, with the earliest form indemnifying the insured against loss through the fraud or dishonesty of a particular employee or the person holding a particular position, such as cashier. In the first decade of the 20th century, a policy designated as a "blanket" bond was made available by Lloyd's of London. A few years later, American companies issued a somewhat similar policy. These early policies had coverages other than fidelity (hence the term *blanket*), but the primary coverage indemnified the insured against loss "through any dishonest act of the Employees wherever committed, and whether committed alone or in collusion with others." The insurance companies believed that a "dishonest" act under these policies was an act that the employee intentionally committed with the knowledge at that time that the act was wrongful. Although the companies never seriously attempted to limit coverage to acts which were violations of criminal statutes, they generally believed that the same type of intent was necessary. Several early cases held that a dishonest act, as that term was used in a fidelity bond, was broader than a criminal act and it was not necessary for the employee to intend to personally profit from the transaction for the insured to recover. However, most of the claims involved classic dishonesty and the companies had no real reason to be concerned.

In the 1930s, a series of cases substantially expanded on the insurance companies' belief in the meaning of its coverage, with some courts using language which seemed to equate dishonesty with gross negligence. In those years, the losses were not too great, and though the insurer began to be concerned, the concern was not too serious. In fact, during this same time, the words *fraudulent* and *criminal* were added to the word *dishonest* in most policies, so that by 1936, the insuring agreement in most policies indemnified the insured against loss "through the dishonest, fraudulent or criminal act of any of the Employees. . . ."

As later cases were decided, the following general statements of law became more or less accepted in fidelity insurance cases:

1. The conduct in question did not have to be criminal.
2. The person involved did not have to personally profit from the transaction.
3. Negligence, carelessness, or stupidity were not sufficient.
4. Except in a case of clear criminal involvement by the employee, the question of dishonesty was one of fact to be decided by a jury (or the judge if the case was decided without a jury).

Various factors were considered by the courts in analyzing these cases. The most important factor which argued in favor of dishonesty was, of course, personal gain by the employee. Absent this fact, the courts viewed secrecy and concealment by the employee as evidence of dishonest intent. Also significant was the knowing violation of internal rules, the length of time involved in the questionable activity, and the size of the loss.

In the 1960s and early 1970s, a number of cases were decided against the insurance companies. Many of them involved fact situations in which it did not appear that the employee had the dishonest intent that the companies believed necessary to invoke the coverage. In one case, a court held that a technical violation of a state statute which made it a misdemeanor to solicit the sale of unregistered securities was a "criminal" act covered by the policy.

Other developments during this period resulted in a dramatic increase in claims (both in number and amount) and payments by the companies. These developments included a series of bank failures and a significant increase in the number of claims involving senior corporate executives. The companies' concern became serious, and they finally decided to respond. In 1976 a rider was issued which modified the dishonesty coverage by defining it as follows:

> Dishonest or fraudulent acts as used in this Insuring Agreement shall mean only dishonest or fraudulent acts committed by such Employee with the manifest intent:
>
> *a.* To cause the Insured to sustain such loss; and
> *b.* To obtain financial benefit for the Employee, or for any other person or organization intended by the Employee to receive such benefit, other than salaries, commissions, fees, bonuses, promotions, awards, profit sharing, pensions or other employee benefits earned in the normal course of employment.

An industry spokesman has made the following statement with regard to this new definition:

> This definition emphasizes the fundamental characteristics of the act insured against—intent to harm coupled with intent to profit. Both must be present. Numerous other human failings may have one of these two earmarks—but these undesirable traits are usually described by some term other than "dishonest." Included in that category would be revenge, negligence, failure to disclose an honest error, exceeding one's limit of authority and others.[3]

The basic elements of the new definition are a manifest intent:

1. To cause the insured to sustain the loss and
2. To obtain financial benefit (other than benefits earned in the normal course of employment)
   a. For the employee or
   b. For any other person or organization intended by the Employee to receive such benefit.

This definition will answer some of the questions which were previously left to the courts. However, some problems remain, although most of these problems involve the type of claim usually made by a financial institution. The main problem involves the fact that under the definition, an employee need only have the intent that some other person or organization obtain the financial benefit. Some of the most difficult cases have been the cases involving loan officers exceeding their authority. In these cases, even if the employee does not intend to get a financial benefit himself, he naturally intends that some other person or organization (the borrower) receive such benefit (the loan proceeds).

However, this new definition should clearly tell business entities exactly what coverage the companies think they are selling and should eliminate a large number of claims that otherwise might have been made.

Other coverage

The Commercial Policies have four coverages other than employee dishonesty. These coverages are:

a. *Inside the Premises coverage* covering various losses within the insured's premises (defined as "the interior of that portion of any building which is occupied by the insured in conducting its business"). This coverage includes loss of money and securities by destruction, disappearance, or wrongful abstraction; loss of other property by safe burglary or robbery; loss of a locked cash drawer, cash box, or cash register by felonious entry; and damage to the premises by a safe burglary, robbery, and so on, provided that the insured owns the premises or is liable for the damage.

b. *Outside the Premises coverage* covering loss of money and securities by destruction, disappearance, or wrongful abstraction and loss of other property by robbery while being conveyed by a messenger or an armored car company.

c. *Money Orders and Counterfeit Paper Currency coverage* covering loss due to the acceptance of post office or express money orders not paid upon presentation or loss due to the acceptance of counterfeit currency in the regular course of business. For this coverage, the insured must have accepted the item "in good faith." This phrase is not defined. The few cases that have considered the issue seem to equate lack of good faith with bad faith or fraud. It is clear that negligence on the part of the insured will not prevent recovery.

d. *Depositors' Forgery coverage* covering loss through forgery or alteration of a check or similar instrument made or drawn or purportedly to be made or drawn by or upon the insured, or by one acting as its agent. This coverage is for the benefit of the insured and the insured's bank. If the bank pays a forged or altered instrument under conditions that result in the insured bearing ultimate loss, the insured is entitled to the recovery. If the insured sustains the loss and is reimbursed by its bank, the insured still can make the claim, but the payment is made directly to the bank. If suit is brought against the insured or the bank alleging a forged or altered instrument, the company is liable for reasonable attorneys' fees in defending the suit.

The term *forgery* is not defined in any of the policies. Some courts look to the definition in the criminal statute of the jurisdiction involved. Other courts look to the common-law definition. Still other courts look to dictionary definitions and the general understanding of the word. A typical definition of forgery is "the fraudulent making or altering of a writing to the prejudice of another."

Coverages *(b)* and *(c)* above have several detailed exclusions which should be carefully reviewed.

WHO IS COVERED

The dishonesty coverage applies to acts of employees. The word *employee* is defined in the Commercial Policies to mean:

> Any natural person (except a director or trustee of the Insured, if a corporation, who is not also an officer or employee thereof in some other capacity) while in the regular service of the Insured in the ordinary course of the Insured's business during the Policy Period and whom the Insured compensates by salary, wages or commissions and has the right to govern and direct in the performance of such service, but does not mean any broker, factor, commission merchant, consignee, contractor or other agent or representative of the same general character.

Under General Agreement A, there is also coverage for acts of persons who become employees through consolidation or merger with or purchase of assets from another concern, provided the insured gives the company notice 30 days after the fact and pays an additional premium.

The definition of *employee* in the Commercial Policies is somewhat different from the definition in the Financial Institutions Bonds. For instance, the definition in the Bankers Blanket Bond includes "attorneys retained by the Insured to perform legal services for the Insured and the employees of such attorneys while such attorneys or the employees of such attorneys are performing such services for the Insured." Each specialized policy should be reviewed carefully to determine exactly who is covered and who is excluded.

Most of the cases in which the issue of whether the person involved was an employee have turned on the question of control. If the insured compensates and has the right to direct and control the person's activities, he is usually an employee. The following factors have been considered, though no one factor is conclusive:

1. Does the insured withhold from the employee's pay for income tax purposes?
2. Does the insured make social security contributions for the person involved?
3. Is the person listed as an employee for purposes of workers' compensation or unemployment compensation?
4. Is the person entitled to fringe benefits such as health and life insurance?
5. Is the person entitled to participate in the insured's pension program?

6. Did the person have set working hours?
7. Did the person work exclusively for the insured?

After weighing factors such as these, the cases are still divided on the issue of control.

The definition of employee makes it clear that a director per se is not an employee and his or her acts are not covered by the policy. This coverage is consistent with the general law that a director has no individual power of action and must act through the collective action of the board of directors. Of course, if the director is also an officer, his or her acts are covered, but not if the acts are committed in the person's capacity as a director. Certain of the Financial Institution Bonds provide coverage for acts of directors who are not officers, but only when performing acts coming within the scope of the usual duties of an employee or while acting as a member of a duly elected committee.

A very important part of the coverage in Commercial Policies is coverage for loss caused by unidentifiable employees. The part of the clause outlining this coverage is as follows:

> If a loss is alleged to have been caused by the fraud or dishonesty of any one or more of the Employees and the Insured shall be unable to designate the specific Employee or Employees causing such loss, the Insured shall nevertheless have the benefit of [the Employee Dishonesty coverage] . . . provided that the evidence submitted reasonably proves that the loss was in fact due to the fraud or dishonesty of one or more of the said Employees. . . .

This coverage is limited by the Inventory Exclusion Clause (which will be more fully developed later in this chapter), which states that a claim for loss caused by an unidentifiable employee cannot be based solely on an inventory computation or a profit and loss computation. A possible claim of this type could involve a claim for property missing from an area which only employees had access.

One final problem should be mentioned. Some of the so-called alter ego cases have held that persons who are in effect the alter ego of the insured corporation are not employees, even though the books and records of the insured reflect that the person was elected to the position of an officer, usually president. This concept is discussed in detail under the section on exclusions. However, for purposes of this section, it should be remembered that by definition an employee is one that the insured has the right to govern and direct in the performance of his duties. For a corporation, the insured for these purposes is its board of directors. If the board does not function and abrogates its duties by allowing one person, in effect, to become the corporation, there is no longer the requisite right to govern and direct the performance of his duties.

EXCLUSIONS

The Commercial Policies have three major exclusions. Certain of the Financial Institution Bonds have exclusions that are included because of particular industry problems (e.g, the paid against uncollected funds exclusion in the Bankers Blanket Bond and the trading loss exclusion in the Brokers Blanket Bond), but these exclusions are not discussed, as they do not apply to any other type of business.

Acts of the insured

The Commercial Policies exclude "loss due to any fraudulent, dishonest, or criminal act of any Insured or a partner therein, whether acting alone or in collusion with others." This exclusion is based on the proposition that one cannot obtain insurance that will pay oneself for losses resulting from one's own dishonesty. Public policy would prevent this insurance from being effective. If the insured is an individual, this rule is easy to apply. However, the insured is usually a corporation, and the rule is not always so easy to apply.

This exclusion is related to a series of cases generally referred to as the alter ego cases. These cases are confusing, but persons seeking fidelity coverage should be aware of the principles involved. In one case, coverage was denied because the dishonest persons were principal officers and the only directors of the insured and owned all of its stock, directly or indirectly.[4] In another case, the court implied that there would be no coverage for the acts of persons who controlled substantially all of the activities of the insured corporation.[5] These results are by no means uniform, and other courts have reached the opposite result. A recent case found coverage, even though it was undisputed that the dishonest person was the sole stockholder, alter ego, and chief executive officer of the insured.[6] However, in this case, it was clear that the company knew this fact when the policy was issued and the court was obviously influenced by this fact.

Except in very unusual circumstances, there issues arise only after an insured has been taken over by a receiver. However, to avoid problems of this kind, consideration should be given to the following:

1. A full disclosure should be made as to the ownership and management of the company seeking the insurance at the time of the application.
2. If the insured is a corporation, it should be operated as a corporation, with the activities of the board of directors being carefully recorded.

Inventory exclusion

The Commercial Policies exclude:

> loss, or to that part of any loss, as the case may be, the proof of which, either as to its factual existence or as to its amount, is dependent upon an inventory computation or a profit and loss computation; provided, however, that this paragraph shall not apply to loss of Money, Securities or other property which the Insured can prove, through evidence wholly apart from such computations, is sustained by the Insured through any fraudulent or dishonest act or acts committed by any one or more of the Employees; . . .

Generally, an inventory computation is an inventory arrived at by taking a beginning inventory, adding purchases and deducting the cost of merchandise sold. Generally, a computed inventory loss would be arrived at by deducting an actual inventory from the inventory computation.

The Inventory Exclusion Clause has resulted in a substantial amount of litigation. The following scenarios are typical of the cases: Assume that a physical count reveals $100,000 less goods than reflected in the inventory records. Even if no one but employees had access to the goods, most courts would deny recovery—there is no independent evidence of employee dishonesty; the only evidence as to the loss and its amount is based on an inventory computation.

However, assume that an inventory computation reveals goods missing which have a value of $100,000. After an investigation, an employee confesses to having stolen $10,000 worth of the goods. No other direct evidence of dishonesty by that employee or any other employee is uncovered. Can the insured introduce the inventory records to support a claim of loss of $100,000 or is the insured limited to a recovery of $10,000?

Prior to 1970, most of the cases allowed the use of inventory comparisons only to corroborate independent evidence of dishonesty. Under these cases, no inventory records could be introduced to establish the amount of the loss even though there was some direct evidence of employee dishonesty. Applying these cases to the example, recovery would be limited to $10,000. Some cases refer to this result as the "majority" rule.

Since 1970, however, the cases have tended to allow the insured to prove the full amount of its loss by inventory computations if there is some evidence of employee dishonesty. Applying these cases to the above example, a jury verdict of $100,000 would be upheld. Some cases refer to this result as the "minority" rule, although it probably represents the majority rule in cases decided since 1970.

Also, in recent cases, there has been a seeming relaxation of the evidence necessary to establish employee dishonesty, with some courts allowing the case to go to the jury on circumstantial evidence of dishonesty plus inventory computations.

There are few absolute statements that can be made about the use of inventory computations. The trend has been noted, but it should be emphasized that it is only a trend. The cases in a particular jurisdiction must be examined with care.

One court has drawn a distinction between an inventory "computation" and an inventory "enumeration."[7] A men's clothing store kept a record of suits in a swatch book. When suits were purchased, a record was entered in this book showing the number, sizes, and so forth, together with a swatch of material. When the suits were received at the store, sleeve tickets were attached to each suit showing the book number. A notch was made in the book when the suit was displayed, and the sleeve ticket was removed when the suit was sold. At the end of each day, the tickets were checked against the swatch book and each one sold was lined out. The court held that the swatch book was not an inventory but an enumeration, and the computation of the loss based on this book was not an inventory computation.

The following are suggestions for a businessman faced with a claim involving proof of some dishonesty but a much larger inventory loss:

1. Have your lawyer determine whether your jurisdiction has ruled on the meaning of the Inventory Exclusion Clause.
2. Prepare an analysis of the inventory procedure to demonstrate that the system produces an accurate inventory count if correctly used.
3. Make a careful review of factors other than employee dishonesty which could explain the loss. These factors include:
   a. Negligence or incompetence of employees.
   b. Theft by persons other than employees, including shoplifting.
   c. Poor management.
   d. Errors in procedure to establish inventory or physical count itself.
   e. Inventory shrinkage.

If employees had previously been dismissed for negligence or incompetence, the company may argue that their conduct, not covered by the policy, contributed to the loss. Likewise, if persons other than employees had access to the missing items, figures for losses from shoplifting in prior years should be collected. Also, the accuracy of prior inventories should be established. Shrinkage usually can be determined by a comparison of the inventory discrepancy with sales figures.

The insured's goal is to establish that employee dishonesty is the only reasonable explanation for the inventory shortage. The insured's most important witness in developing the claim is an accountant. In many instances, an accountant helped develop the inventory system and usually makes an ideal witness.

Knowledge of fraud or dishonesty

The Commercial Policies provide that the coverage of the policy shall not apply:

> to any Employee from and after the time that the Insured or any partner or officer thereof not in collusion with such Employee shall have knowledge or information that such Employee has committed any fraudulent or dishonest act in the service of the Insured or otherwise, whether such act be committed before or after the date of employment by the Insured.

These policies further provide that if any prior fidelity coverage had been cancelled as to any employee and the employee had not been reinstated, then the employee is not covered unless the company agrees to such coverage.

These provisions tie in to the cancellation section, which provides in part that the policy shall be deemed cancelled as to any employee:

> immediately upon discovery by the Insured, or by any partner or officer thereof not in collusion with such Employee, of any fraudulent or dishonest act on the part of such Employee. . . .

These provisions are logical and reasonable. An insured should not expect to have insurance to cover loss resulting from acts of an employee that the insured knows has committed a dishonest act, either in prior employment or for the insured. These facts normally would be revealed in the application for the insurance, but new employees hired after the insurance is issued automatically come under the coverages without any notice to the company.

It is important to note that this coverage does not apply after such knowledge by the insured "or by any partner or officer thereof not in collusion with such employee." The Financial Institution Bonds do not have a similar exclusion, but the termination clause provides for termination or cancellation as to any employee "as soon as the Insured shall learn of any dishonest or fraudulent act on the part of such Employee. . . ." The difference in language is significant if the insured is a corporation. Under the Financial Institution Bonds, the discovery must be by the "Insured," which has generally been interpreted to mean the board of directors of the insured.[8] Under the other types of policies, discovery need only be by another officer, even if the officer does not report his discovery to the insured's board of directors. However, under certain circumstances, if the officer learns of an employee's dishonesty and fails to report it, the officer also may be guilty of dishonesty (at least prior to the new definition) and thus would be in collusion with the defaulting employee and his discovery would not terminate coverage. It has long been the rule that a person acting dishonestly has an adverse interest to his employer and his knowledge of his own dishonesty or of the dishonesty of a co-conspirator would not be imputed to the employer.[9]

How much knowledge is required by the partner, officer, or board of directors to trigger the exclusion or cancellation? Generally speaking, it is the same knowledge that is necessary to require the insured to give notice to the company and start the time running for the proof of loss to be filed—knowledge of facts which would cause a careful and prudent man to accuse another person of dishonesty. This subject is discussed in detail in the section of this chapter on the notice and proof of loss requirements.

It should be noted that the company may agree to cover an employee even if the employee is known to have committed a dishonest act. These situations generally arise in the case of a person who committed a relatively minor offense in his or her youth. If the person has demonstrated his honesty over a substantial period of time, many companies will agree to cover the person. However, even if the offense seems relatively minor and is in the employee's distant past, the company should be notified and specific coverage requested; otherwise, the insured has no coverage for loss resulting from the employee's dishonesty.

CONDITIONS FOR RECOVERY

Notice and proof of loss

All fidelity and crime policies contain some provisions requiring notice to the company and the filing of a proof of loss. The language in these provisions is extremely important. In the Financial Institution Bonds this provision states:

> At the earliest practicable moment after discovery of any loss hereunder the Insured shall give the Underwriter written notice thereof and shall also within six months after such discovery furnish to the Underwriter affirmative proof of loss with full particulars.

Both the notice and proof of loss provisions relate to "discovery of any loss" under the policy. This language has been interpreted by the courts to require actual knowledge of loss through employee dishonesty on the part of the insured, rather than suspicion of such loss. This rule was first stated by the U.S. Supreme Court in 1898.[10] In the second opinion in that case, the Court stated that the insured was required to give notice "only when satisfied that he [the employee] had committed some specific act of fraud or dishonesty likely to involve loss to the company." This rule has been followed consistently since that opinion, though there have been many cases which involved a dispute over when the insured became so satisfied. Another way of stating this rule is that the insured discovers loss under the policy when it becomes aware of facts which would justify a careful and prudent man in accusing another person of dishonesty. Though this rule may seem relatively simple, its application can be very complex, particularly in claims which involve elaborate schemes to defraud. Some of these claims require many months of investigation and the review of thousands of documents. It is difficult to say at what point the insured obtains sufficient knowledge to charge the former employee with dishonesty. Under the Commercial Policies, loss must be discovered within one year from the end of the policy period.

The problem is even more difficult when coupled with the rule stated by a few courts that "knowledge is what a reasonable person should have concluded from known facts" and a careful and prudent man is justified in charging another with dishonesty "when he learns those facts which are later asserted to constitute acts of dishonesty." In this regard, it is imperative to review the particular policy language applicable to the claim. The Commercial Policies contain the following provisions:

> Upon knowledge or discovery of loss or of an occurrence which may give rise to a claim for loss, the Insured shall: *(a)* give notice thereof as soon as practicable to the Company . . . ; *(b)* file detailed proof of loss, duly sworn to, with the Company within four months after the discovery of loss.

The time for giving the notice and filing the proof of loss under these policies begins upon discovery of "an occurrence which may give rise to a claim for loss." This provision arguably requires notice and proof of loss earlier than the provision in the Financial Institution Bonds, which requires "discovery of loss." However, it is intended to mean the discovery of facts which may not involve a current loss but which subjects the insured to exposure for loss; even under this language, the insured should not be required to give notice or file a proof of loss based on a mere suspicion of dishonesty.

This interpretation makes sense, as the proof of loss under the Commercial Policies must be under oath. It would not make sense to charge another person with "suspicion of dishonesty" under oath.

The notice and proof of loss provisions are important to the insured as they initiate the company's claim procedure, allow it to investigate the claim, possibly minimize its loss and establish the statutory reserves.

The time limits themselves are as follows:

a. *Notice*—"as soon as practicable" under the Financial Institution Bonds. This language has generally been interpreted to mean "within a reasonable time, having in view all of the circumstances of the case."[11] A delay of five months and longer has been held to be not "at the earliest practicable moment."
b. *Proof of loss*—four months under the Commercial Policies and six months under the Financial Institution Bonds.

In connection with both the notice and proof of loss requirements, state statutes should be carefully consulted. All Fidelity Policies provide that if any limitation period in the policy is prohibited by the controlling law, then the limitation period is deemed to be the shortest period of time permitted by such law. Also, all endorsements to the policy should be carefully reviewed. In some states, the standard limitations are amended by statute or insurance department rule and these new time limits are reflected by an endorsement.

None of the policies involved require any particular form for the proof of loss. Under the Commercial Policies, it must be "detailed" and "duly sworn to." Most companies have a form for proof of loss. However, use of the company's form is generally not mandatory. The following is a checklist of items to include in a proof of loss:

a. Name of insured.
b. Policy number.
c. Date of policy.
d. Name and position of defaulting employee.
e. Total amount of claim.
f. Date and amount of each transaction making up total claim and a brief description of each transaction.
g. Any credits to the claim.
h. Any security for the claim.
i. A clear unequivocal statement that the insured sustained the loss through the insured peril.
j. A statement that the company may have full access to the insured's books and records involved in the claim.
k. A statement reserving the right to amend or supplement the proof of loss.

For a relatively simple claim, the company's form should be used, as the company can later complain about its own form. However, in complex claims, the form usually is inadequate as more detail should be provided. It is helpful to attach copies of the most important documents to the proof of loss.

Most courts are reluctant to deny recovery solely because of the insured's failure to comply with what are perceived to be "technicalities." A "substantial compliance" rule has been adopted with regard to proof of loss requirements. Generally, this means that a proof of loss need only state the facts known to the insured at the time of filing, even if the insured does not know the "full particulars" at that time. Practically speaking, it means that it is almost impossible to lose the case based on an insufficient proof of loss. However, the preparation of the proof of loss is the most important single act of the insured in making a fidelity claim. Consequently, the insured should spend whatever time is necessary to carefully investigate the claim and preparing the proof of loss. In many instances, the company's first real contact with the facts of the claim will come from the proof of loss. Even if the claim is a good one, a poorly prepared proof of loss will result in an initial negative reaction from the company. This may make ultimate resolution more difficult. In a complex case, if the investigation cannot be completed within the time limits set out in the policy, the insured should request an extension of time to file the proof of loss. Many companies will grant such an extension, without prejudice, of course, to any rights or defenses which it may have at the time of the request. However, if the request is denied, the insured should include in the proof of loss whatever it knows at the time the proof is prepared. Usually, this will be sufficient.

In a further effort to prevent a total forfeiture of the insurance proceeds, courts in different jurisdictions have adopted rules (in some instances, these rules have been codified into statutes):

1. *Prejudice.* In some states, the defense of late notice and/or late proof of loss can be successfully asserted only if the company was prejudiced by the lateness. Prejudice has been a difficult concept for the courts to define. The easiest case for a finding of no prejudice would be a situation in which the dishonest employee has stolen a sum in excess of the policy limits, spent the entire amount prior to the time of discovery, and has no other assets. A late notice or proof of loss could not prejudice the company. The easiest case for a finding of prejudice is one in which the employee has stolen a substantial amount prior to discovery but still has most of the stolen money; then, prior to the notice, the employee disposes of the money. A late notice or proof of loss clearly prejudices the company. However, most cases are not black or white but fall somewhere in between.

2. *Waiver.* It has been held, in most, if not all, states, that certain

acts by the company constitute a waiver of the company's right to assert the timeliness of the notice and/or proof of loss as a defense. Acts of the company which have been held to constitute waiver include:

a. Acceptance of notice or proof of loss which is defective or late.
b. Investigation.
c. Denial of liability.
d. Conduct.

Typically, the cases involving waiver apply common sense rules. For example, it would not be fair to allow the company to accept a proof of loss without saying anything about it, wait for the time limits to expire, and then deny liability based on a defective proof of loss. On the other hand, a company should be able to investigate a claim in good faith without running a risk of waiver. Most companies which issue these types of policies have professional claims departments that treat the insured fairly and handle the claim on its merits unless the facts are so flagrant that the use of a so-called technical defense is necessary to prevent a clear injustice.

One final limitation period should be noted—suit limitation. The Commercial Policies provide that suit may not be brought for a certain period after the proof of loss is filed (60 to 90 days) and after a maximum time has elapsed (2 years after the insured discovers the loss). These contractual provisions are usually held to be valid, but the same comments previously made regarding local statutes modifying the time limits and waiver are equally applicable to these limitations. The shorter period is to allow the company sufficient time to make its investigation and respond to the claim.

An insured should take the following steps when it discovers facts which indicate a fidelity claim:

a. Carefully review the policy to determine the notice and proof of loss deadlines.
b. Consult an attorney to determine if these limitations are modified in any way by statute or case law.
c. Immediately determine who will conduct the investigation and promptly begin the investigation.
d. Notify the company if the policy involved requires notice "upon knowledge or discovery of . . . an occurrence which may give rise to a claim for loss." However, care should be exercised, and the form of notice should use those words, without naming the suspected individual or individuals (unless there is specific evidence of dishonesty on the part of an individual). On the other

hand, if the policy involved requires notice "after discovery of loss hereunder," the investigation should continue until the insured has more than a mere suspicion of dishonest conduct.

e. Request an extension if it becomes apparent that the insured cannot fully complete its investigation prior to the proof of loss deadline. (Remember that you have one year after the policy expires to discover loss.)

f. Prepare the proof of loss carefully—it will probably be the most important single document in the claim.

g. After the proof of loss is filed, allow the company full access to the documents and witnesses and fully cooperate in its investigation. The Commercial Policies contain a provision requiring the insured to cooperate with the company "in all matters pertaining to loss or claims with respect thereto."

h. If the company has had sufficient time to investigate and respond to the claim and has not done so, set a deadline, and if the deadline is not met, file suit.

There must be a loss

It might seem axiomatic that it is necessary for the insured to have a loss before a claim can be successfully presented. One court has clearly stated that "Dishonesty in the abstract cannot be compensated in damages, and in a suit to recover on the bond, the dishonesty must have resulted in pecuniary loss." This rule is a simple one and one with which most people would agree. There are many instances of dishonest conduct by an employee without a loss to the employer. One example would be a situation in which an employee steals money from the employer but pays it back. Another instance would be the making of false entries in bank records, which is a crime but which, by itself, does not involve a loss. As one court stated, a theoretical or bookkeeping loss is not covered. However, though this rule seems simple, its application has not been without complications, particularly when the issue of causation is involved in the same claim. The causation rule, simply stated, is: The risk insured against (dishonesty in these policies) must have caused the loss. Unfortunately, until recently, none of the policies discussed in this chapter used the words "caused by" or "resulted in" to describe the requirement of a necessary relationship between the act and the loss.

Prior to the 1976 definition of dishonesty, the insuring agreement in the Commercial Policies read in substance that the company agreed to pay the insured for:

> *Loss* of money, securities or other property which the Insured shall sustain *through* any fraudulent or dishonest act. . . . [Emphasis added.]

The word *through* was revised in 1976, so that by rider most fidelity coverages now provide for indemnification for:

> *Loss resulting directly from* one or more dishonest or fraudulent acts of an Employee. . . . [Emphasis added.]

Some of the confusion in the cases prior to this change can best be illustrated by a few examples. Assume that a bank officer takes a kickback in connection with the granting of a loan but the bank has sufficient collateral from the borrower to repay the loan in full. Has the bank sustained a loss? The courts have generally held that it has and not required the insured to pursue any collateral or rights against third parties as a condition to a successful claim.[12] The courts have viewed the parting of money by the bank to the borrower as the loss. Upon payment of the loss, the insurance company would have the right to recover from the borrower pursuant to the contractual provision of subrogation.

Now, let's add a twist. Assume an unsecured loan to a customer without any dishonesty, but the loan officer takes a kickback in connection with the renewal of the loan at a time when the customer has no assets. The bank will sustain a loss, but except for the amount of the kickback the loss resulted from the original loan and not the renewal.

Put the kickback or bribery situation in the context of a commercial enterprise: Assume that an employee of a construction company takes a bribe from a bidder on a construction project and awards the contract to the person who gave the bribe. If the party awarded the contract was not the low bidder, the company's loss is easy to determine; it is the difference between the accepted bid and the low bid. But, even if the person awarded the contract as a result of the bribe is the low bidder, the cases allow recovery by the insured for the amount of the bribe. The rationale for this result is found in the corporate legal principle that an employee who receives a bribe owes it to his employer.

Problems of loss and causation occur in relatively few claims, and the insurance industry hopes that the new language in the 1976 rider will further clarify the coverage in this regard.

OTHER PROVISIONS AND ISSUES

Limits of liability

The Commercial Policies contain several sections which define the company's dollar exposure in a variety of situations. The first place to look is in the declarations. In the Blanket Crime Policy, one figure is given for the "Total Limit of Liability." This figure is the maximum amount the insured can collect under most circumstances. The Three-D Policies have a separate table of limits of liability for the different coverages; also, the limit on the Employee Dishonesty coverage under Form A applies to all employees for each loss, whereas the limit on the same coverage under Form B is for *each* employee.

All of the Commercial Policies have the following limitations:

1. The total limit of liability is not cumulative from year to year; if the limit is $100,000 and the policy continued for five years and five premiums are paid, the limit is still $100,000.
2. Payment of a loss does not reduce the limit of liability; if the limit is $100,000 and the insured sustains a loss of $50,000 through the dishonesty of an employee and the loss is paid, the insured still has a limit of $100,000 for other employee dishonesty.

Except as to Form B of the Three-D Policy, this last rule is applicable if more than one employee is involved unless the same employee was "concerned or implicated" in each of the dishonest acts. Therefore, assuming a limit of $100,000 and a fraudulent scheme involving four employees in a series of dishonest acts, with one employee being the ringleader, and a loss of $100,000 resulting from the acts of each employee, the company's exposure would be $100,000. However, with the same limit of $100,000 and four separate fraudulent schemes involving four employees acting independently and a loss of $100,000 resulting from the acts of each employee, the company's exposure would be $400,000. As previously stated, under Form B of the Three-D Policy, the limit of liability is applicable to each employee, and with this form, the recovery would be $400,000 in both instances.

There is a separate provision governing the company's limit of liability if its issues a new policy to the same insured. The Commercial Policies are "loss sustained" policies in that the loss must occur during the policy period and must be discovered during that period or within one year thereafter. This provision is unlike the Financial Institution Bonds, which are discovery policies, in which loss can occur at any time if it is discovered during the policy period; however, the Financial Institution Bonds do not have one year for discovery added on to the end of the policy period, though such additional discovery period can be purchased under some circumstances.

These provisions can result in some interesting fact situations. Assume that the insured has a Commercial Policy with a limit of $100,000 which expires on December 31, 1981, and the same company issues a new policy on January 1, 1982, with a limit of $200,000. Further assume that an employee stole $100,000 in December 1981, and another $100,000 in January 1982. How much could the insured recover? The answer is $200,000; the Commercial Policies provide that in the event that the insured sustains a loss partly during the current policy period and partly during the period of the preceding policy issued by the same company to the insured and under which the period for discovery had not expired, the liability of the company does not exceed the amount of the coverage under the current policy or the amount of coverage under the prior policy, whichever is larger. Therefore, if the new policy was for $50,000, the insured could recover $100,000, the amount of the prior policy. Under these circumstances, the insured could not recover $150,000, even though it sustained a loss of $100,000 during the first policy period and discovered it within one year after it expired and a loss of over $50,000 during the second policy period.

If the insured has other insurance available covering any part of its loss, the coverage under the Commercial Policies is treated either as excess coverage or prorated, depending on the wording in the other policy.

Valuation and subrogation

In the event that the insured proves that it sustained a loss covered under one of the insuring agreements, the amount to be paid must be determined. In addition, the priority of rights against third parties must be established.

The rules regarding valuation are relatively simple. If the loan involves money, the amount speaks for itself. If the loss involves securities, the company is liable for the actual cash value at the close of business on the business day immediately prior to the day that the loss was discovered. If the loss involves property, the company is liable for its actual cash value at the time of loss or for actual cost of repairing it or replacing it with property of like quality and value.

The most difficult problems involve losses in connection with loans. Assume that the insured makes a loan of $100,000 in a transaction involving employee dishonesty. The loss is $100,000, the amount of money paid out by the insured. However, assume that the insured gets collateral worth $100,000; has the insured sustained a loss? The case law says "Yes," reasoning that the insured should not have to collect the debt or realize on the collateral to recover its loss. Of course, the insured cannot make a profit; if the company pays the loss, it becomes subrogated to the insured's rights against at least the following: *(a)* the dishonest employee, *(b)* any person in collusion with the person in default, *(c)* the debtor, and *(d)* the insured's lien on the collateral.

The Commercial Policies contain a subrogation clause, which is also a general statement of the law. In addition, the policies require the insured to execute and deliver instruments necessary to secure such rights. No such instruments are necessary under the law, except proof of payment. However, it is customary for the company to take an assignment from the insured.

Generally speaking, the company's rights of subrogation do not concern the insured, particularly if the loss is less than the limits of liability and the insured has been paid in full. However, the issue becomes relevant when the loss is in excess of the coverage. Assume a loss of $200,000 and a policy limit of $100,000, and recoveries are made from a third party of $50,000. The Commercial Policies specifically provide that the insured is entitled to all such recoveries (except for recoveries from such sources as insurance) until it is fully reimbursed, less the cost of effecting such recoveries, with the remainder going to the company.

Joint insureds

If there is more than one insured under the policy, the joint insured provision must be carefully reviewed. Under this provision:

a. The first named insured is required to act for itself and all other insureds named in the policy.
b. Knowledge possessed or discovery made by any insured or any partner thereof constitutes knowledge or discovery by every insured for the purposes of the prior fraud section, the notice and proof of loss section, and the cancellation section.
c. Cancellation of the insurance as to any employee applies to his position with each insured.
d. The company can pay the first named insured for any loss under the policy and the first named insured can sign a release.

Generally speaking, only companies that have common ownership or some other close relationship should be joined in the same policy.

Danger of libel or slander

Any insured that contemplates accusing another person of dishonesty should be aware of the danger of a retaliatory claim of libel or slander by the accused person. An allegation of dishonesty, if written, is libel or, of oral, slander. However, as a general rule, the communication by an insured to its insurance carrier is a privileged communication. The privilege is conditional and is not actionable unless motivated by malice.

The following steps should be taken by insured to protect itself against such a claim:

a. An attorney should be hired to investigate the claim and advise the insured concerning the factual and legal implications of the claim; the insured should act on this advice in making its decision on whether or not to file the claim.
b. The accusation of dishonesty should be made in the proof of loss only and should not be otherwise disclosed (unless a report to law enforcement authorities is required).
c. Discussion of the claim should be confined to the group involved in the investigation and the insured's board of directors, if a corporation.
d. All documents in connection with the investigation should be marked "Confidential."

Riders

All riders to the policy should be carefully examined. State law or regulations of the state insurance department may result in special riders being used in a particular state.

The new definition of dishonesty is contained in a rider, which is made a part of all commercial policies. This rider adds a provision excluding certain types of loss and expenses. They are:

1. Potential income, including interest and dividends, not realized by the insured because of a covered loss.
2. All damages for which the insured is legally liable except "direct compensatory damages" arising from a covered loss.
3. All costs, fees, and other expenses incurred by the insured in establishing the claim.

Potential income and damages always were regarded as too speculative by the companies, but, in a few cases, the courts had found or suggested coverage. It is clear that the insured must pay for the cost of proving the claim. Under certain policies, this exclusion can be deleted for an additional premium, and the cost covered.

RISK MANAGEMENT

Risk management for dishonesty insurance involves two distinct phrases: pre-employment and post-employment.

1. Pre-employment. For all prospective employees, the following should be required: *(a)* a written application, *(b)* a personal interview, and *(c)* a verification of all references. In addition, for middle management, the insured should use *(d)* psychological testing and *(e)* stress analysis. Finally, for top management and all financial officers, the insured should have *(f)* a security check and *(g)* a detailed examination of the prospect's financial background and his or her family background. If these procedures are followed, many potential problem employees can be identified before they are ever hired.

2. *Post-employment.* Ideally, the insured should have an internal auditor, who is responsible directly to the board of directors, and have an outside annual audit by a certified public accountant. One of the purposes of an outside audit is the detection of fraud. In addition, the following steps should be considered, depending upon the particular business of the insured:

a. A system of checks and balances should be effected by the use of position and responsibility rotation, where appropriate.

b. All employees should be required to take at least two weeks' vacation, preferably to include a month-end to permit audit.

c. Bank accounts should be rotated periodically, with special reconciliations prepared.

d. Two signatures should be required on all checks.

e. All systems of internal controls should be periodically reviewed by outside experts for adequacy.

f. The board of directors should appoint an audit committee.

g. All sensitive data processing material should be duplicated and stored off premises.

h. Surprise audits should be conducted of all departments.

In the final analysis, a clever employee can circumvent the best system of checks and balances—at least for a short time. However, a large loss can result in a very short time. It is for this reason that every business should carry insurance protecting it against loss resulting from dishonesty.

NOTES

1. In July, 1980, the Bankers Blanket Bond, the major Financial Institution Bond, was substantially revised.

2. *World Exchange Bank* v. *Commercial Ins. Co.*, 173 N.E. 902 (N.Y. 1930).

3. Weldy, "A Survey of Recent Changes in Financial Institution Bonds," 12 *The Forum* 895 (Spring 1977).

4. *Kerr* v. *Aetna Casualty & Surety Co.*, 350 F.2d 146 (4th Cir. 1965).

5. *Phoenix Savings & Loan, Inc.* v. Aetna Casualty & Surety Co., 381 F.2d 245 (4th Cir. 1967) and 427 F.2d 862 (4th Cir. 1970).

6. *Fidelity and Deposit Co. of Maryland* v. *USAFORM Hail Pool, Inc.*, 463 F.2d (5th Cir. 1972) and 523 F.2d 744 (5th Cir. 1975).

7. *Sun Insurance Company of New*

York v. *Cullum's Men's Shop, Inc.*, 331 F.2d 988 (5th Cir. 1964).

8. *Fidelity and Deposit Co. of Maryland* v. *Courtney*, 186 U.S. 341 (1902).

9. *American Surety Co.* v. *Pauly*, 170 U.S. 133 and 170 U.S. 160 (1898).

10. Id.

11. *Fidelity & Deposit Co. of Maryland* v. *Courtney*, 186 U.S. 342 (1902), interpreting the word *immediate*. The 1980 edition of the Bankers Blanket Bond requires notice "at the earliest practicable moment, not to exceed 30 days, after discovery of loss." This policy also defines discovery to occur "when the Insured becomes aware of facts which would cause a reasonable person to assume that a loss covered by the bond has been or will be incurred, even though the exact amount or details of loss may not then be known."

12. *Fitchburg Savings Bank* v. *Massachusetts Bonding & Ins. Co.*, 174 N.E. 324 (Mass. 1931).

CONTROLLING LIABILITY EXPOSURES

CHAPTER 8

GENERAL LIABILITY INSURANCE

GENERAL LIABILITY RISKS
  Automatically covered risks
  Extra coverage for additional general
    liability risks

SPECIAL FORMS OF GENERAL
LIABILITY INSURANCE CONTRACTS

HOW TO READ THE CGL POLICY
  The declarations
  The basic policy
  The endorsements
  The policy jacket

WHAT THE POLICY COVERS
  The insured—who is protected
  What claims are covered: "Caused
    by an occurrence"
  What claims are covered: Bodily
    injury
  What claims are covered: property
    damage

What claims are covered: Personal
  injury

HOW YOU PAY FOR COVERAGE
  Rate bases
  Manual rates, rating classifications,
    and audits
  Experience rates
  Composite rates
  Retrospective rating plans

WHAT TO DO WHEN TROUBLE
COMES
  Giving notice
  Insurer's duty to defend you
  Conflicts of interest
  Your duty to cooperate

WHAT TO ASK YOUR INSURANCE
AGENT OR BROKER

Professor James W. Bowers
Texas Tech University
Lubbock, Texas

James W. Bowers is Associate Professor of Law at Texas Tech University Law School. He teaches business and commercial law subjects. Prior to becoming a law professor, he was in private practice for ten years. One of his principal specialties is insurance law. He is a graduate of Yale University (B.A. 1964) and Yale Law School (LL.B. 1967).

B. C. Hart, Esquire
Briggs and Morgan
St. Paul, Minnesota

B. C. Hart is the President of the law firm of Briggs & Morgan, located in Minneapolis and St. Paul. He is a specialist in insurance law with particular emphasis on liability, fidelity, and surety law. He is nationally known as a construction attorney representing all phases of the industry, including architects, engineers, contractors, subcontractors, building suppliers, and sureties. Mr. Hart is a graduate of the University of Iowa (B.A. 1947) and Harvard Law School (J.D. 1950). He is a member of The International Association of Insurance Counsel, The Federation of Insurance Counsel, The American College of Trial Lawyers and the American Board of Trial Advocates.

Whatever your business, you probably own a Comprehensive General Liability (CGL) Policy. If not, you probably should. This chapter discusses what the CGL policy covers and why you may need it. It also points out what the policy does not cover. Finally, it tells how the insurer computes your premiums, and what to do if a claim is made against you.

As the title indicates, a CGL policy covers *liability* risks. Unlike the property policies discussed in previous chapters, it pays nothing to you. It only compensates third parties for injuries you cause. The word *comprehensive* in the policy name is a technical term referring principally to the manner in which your premiums will be computed. Finally, the policy covers only "general" liability risks. Special liability risks must be covered by other policies. At the outset it is necessary to understand what these general risks are.

GENERAL LIABILITY RISKS

The CGL policy is designed to protect you automatically against four specific general liability risks. In addition, there are two other kinds of general risk which are frequently added to the policy's coverage by endorsements. If your business faces any of them, you may need General Liability coverage.

Automatically covered risks

Generally speaking, the *automatic* coverage you purchase when you buy a CGL policy protects against suits which may be brought against you by third parties who claim that you have caused or contributed to their bodily injury (BI) or property damage (PD). You may need this protection because your business faces one or more of the four following risk-creating situations:

You own or occupy real estate. One part of the automatic protection is referred to as *Premises* coverage. Sometimes it is called Owners', Landlords', and Tenants' or OL&T coverage. It applies when people who fall into holes, slip on waxed floors, walk through glass doors, or trip on stairs sue you for their injuries. Premises coverage also covers some suits against you for certain kinds of property damages.

For this protection you will normally pay a "rate" multiplied by a "rate base," which is normally the number of square feet of real estate you own or occupy. The more people who come and go from your property, the more the risk. The more the risk, the higher the rate. The higher the rate, the higher the premium. Premises protection, like all the other coverages in the policy, is subject to a number of exclusions which are discussed below.

You conduct risk-creating business operations. Much of this risk is covered by other special policies and will be excluded from your CGL coverage. If you use trucks, automobiles, aircraft, or watercraft in your business, you will have to buy separate automobile, aircraft, or watercraft liability policies. If you have employees, the risk that they may sue you for their injuries must be covered by a workers' compensation and employers' liability policy. If you are a "professional" (which includes, these days, not only lawyers, doctors, accountants, and architects, but also insurance agents, barbers, sex counselors, ministers, and many other service businesses), your "malpractice" exposure will have to be picked up by a special professional "errors and omissions" (E&O) policy. Except in these "special" cases and except for excluded claims which will be discussed later, the CGL policy covers claims against you for injuries you or your employees may cause in the conduct of your business. This protection is called *Operations* (or Operations in Progress) coverage. Sometimes it is called Manufacturers and Contractors or M&C. The premium is usually calculated by multiplying a rate times your payroll, your gross sales, or other figure that varies in proportion to your business activity. The riskier your business, the higher the rate and therefore the premium. Since all businesses conduct operations and most occupy some real estate, you usually get both Premises and Operations coverage under the CGL policy. Your premium will be based on the real estate measure if that is the best measure of the risk, and on the operations rate base if business activity risk outweighs the real estate risk.

You may have contracts employing others who may injure someone. Some of the claims against you asserted by persons injured by your independent contractors are covered by the CGL policy. This part of the coverage is called *Independent Contractors* or sometimes "protective" or "contingent liability" coverage. The premium for this policy is calculated as a percentage of the total dollar volume of your independent contracts. For businesses who employ contractors or subcontractors, this protection can be extremely important. Some Manufacturers and Contractors (M&C) forms of general liability insurance do not include this independent contractors' protection.

You make or sell products or perform work that may injure somebody after the sale or after the work is done. For manufacturers, distributors, and retailers of goods, this protection is called *Products Liability* coverage. For contractors, repairmen, mechanics, or similar sellers of services rather than goods, the risk that someone may sue you for bodily injury or property damage caused by your faulty workmanship after the work is done is called the completed operations hazard, and is covered in the CGL policy by the *Completed Operations* coverage. If defective products or workmanship cause claims before the sale (or before the work is finished), it is the Operations coverage, not the Products or Completed Operations coverages that provides protection. Products or Completed Operations coverages, although they cover past rather than present defects, usually have a premium calculated by multiplying another rate times your current sales or payroll.

Extra coverage for additional general liability risks

The above four liability risks are the general liability risks which (except for several excluded claims) the CGL policy automatically covers. You may, however, choose to save premiums by electing not to buy coverage for one or more of the covered risks. In that case the insurer will add an endorsement to your policy which excludes coverage of the risks you decide not to buy. There are two other general risks which can be *added* to your CGL policy by endorsement. These specially purchased general coverages are appropriate in the following two circumstances:

You have agreed to hold someone else harmless against bodily injury or property damage claims. Leases and easement agreements frequently require tenants or users to indemnify and defend landlords (or owners) from claims of injured third parties. Railroads and elevator companies require similar indemnity agreements from businesses with whom they have sidetrack or elevator maintenance contracts. Sometimes municipalities issuing permits make similar requirements of businesses to whom permits are issued. Bodily injury or property damage claims brought against you under hold-harmless clauses in the above types of contracts (called incidental contracts in the policy) are automatically covered by standard form CGL policies. However, if you rent equipment (anything from photocopiers to draglines), you may have to hold the lessor harmless. Franchisees are also often required to hold franchisors harmless. Subcontractors and suppliers often agree to defend and indemnify contractors, and contractors may have similar agreements with owners or architects. These latter agreements are not "incidental" contracts, and claims brought against you under the hold-harmless clauses in them are not automatically covered. To obtain protection for this risk (called *contractual liability*) you must buy separate coverage in the form of an endorsement to your CGL policy. For this extra protection, you will pay a rate (based on the likelihood you will have to indemnify someone, which may vary with the breadth of the hold-harmless clause) times a dollar volume figure such as the rent under the equipment lease or the subcontract price.

Two types of Contractual Liability coverage are typically sold. One type covers designated hold-harmless clauses only. The other type is called blanket contractual. It covers any hold-harmless contracts into which you may enter. Both versions contain a number of exclusions.

You face risks for claims other than for bodily injury or property damage. The liability protection provided under the CGL coverages described above applies only to claims that you caused someone "bodily injury" or "property damage." What if you libel or slander someone, invade their privacy, commit a trespass, or mistakenly accuse someone of shoplifting or theft, and they sue you? For an extra premium you can purchase a special *personal injury* endorsement that gives limited protection from some claims of this type.

SPECIAL FORMS OF GENERAL LIABILITY INSURANCE CONTRACTS

Every business is exposed to some of the general liability risks covered by a CGL policy. The coverage may have different names depending on how the underwriter fits it into your insurance program. Your contract may, as noted, be called an OL&T or M&C rather than a CGL program. It may be one part of a Special Multi-Peril (SMP) contract which provides other special liability or property coverages as part of a larger package. Another type of general liability policy is an Owner's Protective Policy. It is simply a CGL policy purchased by a contractor which protects his owner-customer against the general liability risks associated with a single project. On some large projects the owner may buy CGL protection for contractors and subcontractors on that single project under what is called a wrap-up program. Sometimes manufacturers buy products liability insurance which protects their wholesaler and retailer customers as well. In that form, the CGL coverage is called vendor's liability.

By whatever name, these other insurance contracts contain (although perhaps only in part) what is called general liability insurance. In most cases, the carriers all use standard or "boiler-plate" forms which contain uniform language adopted by rating bureaus, which are trade organizations through which the insurance companies compare loss and cost experience. The wording in the various clauses and exclusions in the insurance contract and endorsements will thus generally be identical wherever you buy coverage.

The rating bureaus change forms periodically. The last major revision was in 1966. Minor changes were made in 1973. It is not surprising that as claims are made under each revised form, risks arise which the underwriters did not foresee. If the policy turns out to cover a previously unforeseen risk, the insurers wish to establish and collect an appropriate premium for it. The revisions are attempts either to close any such loopholes or to permit the insurers to charge extra for them. While you can expect another major revision in the near future, the basic coverages are likely to remain substantially the same. There will be differences in the details.

HOW TO READ THE CGL POLICY

In origin and by evolution the CGL policy has become a complex document. It will normally consist of a jacket, with separate loose pages fastened inside. Among the loose pages will be a printed form called "The Declarations" with specific information (coverages and rates) typed in the blanks. Additional loose pages will consist of the basic CGL policy and endorsements. Here is a recommended method and sequence for reading the policy:

The declarations

Look at the declarations. This page will tell you (by checks in the appropriate boxes) whether you have coverage for premises liability (in which case the property will be described), operations, independent contractors, products and/or completed operations, contractual liability, and personal injury. The declarations will also have blanks filled in with the policy's "per occurrence" and "aggregate" limits of liability for each of the coverages, and will also note the dates between which the coverage will be in effect (called the policy period).

The basic policy

Look at the basic policy page. When you read it, look for:

The insuring clause. The first paragraph on the page tells what the company promises. It states: "The Company will pay . . ." and goes on with some very comforting sounding language including a promise to defend any suit, even groundless ones. Note, however, that certain words in the clause: the *insured, bodily injury, property damage,* and *occurrence* are printed in boldface type.

Definitional exclusions. The boldface words are carefully defined in the policy jacket, and they do not mean what you might think they would. In fact, the definitions are actually exclusions.

Substantive exclusions. Immediately after the insuring clause comes a long list of exclusions.

Other limitations. After the exclusions come three additional sections that further limit the protection afforded by the policy. The Persons Insured section tells *who* will be defended and on whose behalf any payments will be made. The Limits of Liability section tells how various types of claims will be limited by the dollar figures appearing in the declarations. The territory provision of the policy limits coverage to bodily injury or property damage occurring within the "policy territory."

Even though the Premises, Operations, Products, and Independent Contractors coverages, and so on, are the coverages being provided, these terms will not appear when you read the coverage part of the contract itself. Why? Because, the policy does not try to cover those risks directly. The bulk of the policy is devoted to describing *what is excluded!* The policy is structured so that the general liability risks which it actually covers are what is left over after taking out all the excluded risks.

The endorsements

Flip through the remaining loose pages, which will consist of various additions to or subtractions from the basic coverage called *endorsements.* These endorsements will fit into several categories:

Endorsements adding additional exclusions. Some of these you may have ordered in order to save on premiums. Products and Completed Operations coverages that would otherwise automatically have been provided are sometimes endorsed out for that reason. Other exclusions may be added because you have special risks in your business which would be covered by the contract language but which the policy was not designed to cover. For example, if you are a professional you will find an endorsement that excludes from CGL coverage any claim for professional malpractice.

Endorsements adding coverage for additional general liability exposures (e.g., contractual liability or personal injury). These will take the form of basic policies, with their own special insuring clauses, definitional and substantive exclusions, and other limitations much like the basic contract. Another example is so-called Premises Medical Payments coverage under which the company agrees to pay certain medical bills incurred by persons injured on your premises or by your operations whether or not you are legally liable to the injured person.

Endorsements adding back coverage that has been otherwise excluded. These are, in principle, just like the contractual liability and personal injury contracts noted above. They take a different form, however. They do not look like separate contracts. Rather, they simply delete (in whole or in part) portions of the exclusions in the main policy, or replace the broad standard exclusions with narrower ones. Typical examples are:

Host liquor liability. For some insureds, the basic policy excludes claims for injury caused by persons to whom the insured has provided alcoholic beverages. Several states impose this "dram-shop" liability on businesses which serve alcoholic beverages when entertaining customers, suppliers, clients, or friends. This risk can be covered (at a small additional charge) by deleting the basic exclusion with a host liquor liability endorsement.

XCU coverage. The basic policy may exclude certain risks called the explosion, collapse, and underground property damage hazards. For contractors who need coverage for those risks, the XCU exclusions can be deleted (for an extra premium) by endorsement.

Broad form property damage liability. The basic policy excludes claims for damages to certain kinds of property. Those broad basic exclusions can be deleted and replaced by this narrower one.

Fire legal liability. If you rent real estate and negligently burn it down, part of your landlord's claim against you would be excluded by the basic policy. You can buy an endorsement adding back this coverage in limited amounts. (Since standard fire insurance policies permit you and your landlord to waive subrogation against each other and thus rely on fire insurance, this protection is generally unnecessary.)

Endorsements relaxing other policy restrictions. The basic policy can be cancelled by the company upon ten days' notice to you. You can sometimes bargain for an endorsement which gives a longer notice period. If you wish to have other persons become "insured" (commonly by making your employees additional "insureds"), or wish to be protected from claims for injuries which occur outside the "policy territory," you can do so by buying an endorsement which relaxes the standard policy limitations, all for an extra premium.

Many of these extra endorsements are sold routinely. There is even a so-called Broad Form Comprehensive General Liability Endorsement which bundles a number of them together into one document. It includes a version of all those mentioned above except for the XCU deletion and any special additional exclusions.

The policy jacket

Read the policy jacket itself. As noted above, the jacket contains several *definitions* which are really exclusions. Some of the words defined in the jacket may not even appear in your policy. They are nevertheless put there because the defined words are used in some common endorsements. An endorsement may also contain additional definitional exclusions which apply only to that endorsement. The jacket will also contain a Nuclear Energy Liability Exclusion. The jacket contains two other important sections:

Supplementary payments. In this section the insurer promises to pay certain expenses that arise in connection with any covered claims—including attorneys fees, court costs, interest on any judgments, and premiums for appeal bonds. Under these provisions the company also promises to pay first-aid expenses you incur at an accident helping the injured party. The company also will pay up to $25 per day for your own time (which you are obliged to spend), cooperating with them in investigating or preparing to defend against any claims.

Conditions. Even if your policy has the appropriate coverage and the claim is within the policy limits, you still may not be covered unless you comply with the requirements in this section of the policy jacket. The most important of these are:

You must pay the premium.

The policy must not have been cancelled.

You must give the insurer prompt notice of any claim.

You must cooperate fully with the insurer in any investigation of or defense of the claim against you. *You cannot pay the claim yourself and then expect to look to the insurer for reimbursement,* even though you might like to do so, for example, to preserve good relations with a claimant who happens to be a good customer.

You must not release anyone else whom the insurer might sue to recover back any money that it pays out.

You must give truthful information to the company about your business when you apply for the policy in the first place.

WHAT THE POLICY COVERS

In explaining the exposures for which CGL coverage is generally purchased, and in explaining how the policy is put together and how it should be read, two principal points have been made. First, you discover what the policy covers by finding out what it does not cover. Thus while we indicated that the policy covered *some* "premises" or "operations" or "products" or "completed operations" risks and the like, the interesting question remains: What parts of those risks are not covered? Second, the coverage the policy gives will vary with the additions and deletions in the various endorsements which you may be required to accept or which you elect to buy. Whether a particular claim against you will be covered may thus depend on unique features of your own policy. Selecting proper coverage is something you will have to take up with your insurance agent or insurance counsellor and your lawyer (in that order). Nevertheless, if you have tried to read the policy and do not understand it, you may be better able to get the help you will need if you have some insight into the policy structure and details.

The insured—who is protected

The Insuring Clause of the policy promises that:

> The Company will pay on behalf of *the insured* all sums which *the insured* shall become legally obligated to pay as damages because of
>
> *bodily injury* or
> *property damage*
>
> to which this insurance applies, caused by an *occurrence* and the Company shall have the right and duty to defend any suit against *the insured* seeking damages on account of such *bodily injury* or *property damage*. . . .

Obviously, the company will defend against and pay claims only if they are for *bodily injury* or *property damage* and then only if they are "caused by an *occurrence*." Just how those defined terms limit coverage will be discussed below. Even if the claim would otherwise be covered, however, the company promises only to defend claims against (and pay them on behalf of) *the insured*. The obvious first question must be: "Who is the insured?"

The term *insured* is one of those boldface defined words. The definition of that word in the policy jacket refers the reader to the Persons Insured paragraphs in the coverage itself. The definition also states, however, that "The Insurance afforded applies separately to each insured against whom claim is made or suit is brought, except with respect to the limits of liability." This rather cryptic sounding sentence is sometimes called the severability clause. It suggests that each *insured* will be treated as if he were issued a separate policy, except for the liability limits. It also suggests that there may be several different "insureds." That is frequently true.

Turning to the Persons Insured section as the definition directs, you will find that "the insured" can mean several people:

> The *named insured* (identified in the declarations) is of course an "insured." The *named insured* will normally be the entity in which you conduct business, be it a proprietorship, partnership, or corporation. There is an important exception, however. If your firm is a partner in a partnership or joint venture and only your business is named in the declarations, but not the partnership or joint venture, you will not be covered for claims that arise out of the partnership or joint venture activity.
>
> *Proprietors, partners, officers, directors, and shareholders.* If the *named insured* entity is a proprietorship, the proprietor and his or her spouse are also *insureds*. If it is a partnership the partners are also *insureds*. (Their spouses can be named as additional *insureds* by endorsement). If the named insured is a corporation or similar organization, then the executive officers, directors, and stockholders are also designated as *insureds*. Finally, your real estate managers (who are not mere employees) are also *insureds*. All of these *insureds* are covered only against claims that arise out of the activities of the

named insured's business. They must cover any liability exposure arising from the conduct of their personal lives separately.

None of the foregoing may appear startling until you tie it together with some of the exclusions and the severability clause noted above. Several of the exclusions are written referring to "the insured." For example:

Intentional injuries are excluded in the definition of the word *occurrence* which is defined to mean injury neither expected nor intended from the standpoint of *the insured.*

Bodily injury claims asserted by employees of *the insured* are excluded on the theory that workers' compensation coverage should be separately provided.

Property damage claims for property in the care, custody, or control of *the insured* are also excluded.

Suppose that an injured employee of the named insured company sues an officer personally. The claimant is an employee of the company but he is *not* an employee of the *insured* officer. Or suppose that an employee intentionally injures someone and the injured party sues a director or shareholder personally. The injury was not intended from the standpoint of that director or shareholder. Or suppose that the company has care, custody, or control over someone else's property which gets damaged and the owner sues one of the extra insureds who did not personally have care, custody or control. Many courts have held that because the severability clause treats each insured as though he had bought a separate policy, the main policy will protect you personally if you are among the other insureds *even though it excludes your company itself.*[1]

Employees. Most claims against your business will result from the negligent acts of employees. In most of these cases the claimant will sue your business, but he can sue your employee personally as well. Unless the employee is also an officer, director, partner, or shareholder, the insurance company is not obligated either to defend or to pay any judgment rendered against the employee. (Employees who operate "mobile equipment," which generally means unlicensed off-the-road vehicles like forklifts or bulldozers, will be deemed *insureds* for injuries caused by those operations, except for injuries to fellow employees or for damage to property in the care, custody, or control of their employer.) Of course, if the insurer, in defending the business, pays the claim, there is nothing left for the plaintiff to collect from the employee.

Nevertheless, most employees will be shocked on learning that they may, at their own personal expense, have to hire individual defense counsel. Even worse, *once the insurer pays the claim,* it can sue the employee to recover what it had to pay on behalf of the business. This power to sue the employee, the primary wrongdoer in this case, is called the right of subrogation. You may recall the earlier discussion of the conditions of the policy (paying the premium, giving prompt notice of claims, and the like). One of those conditions provides that you can lose all coverage if you prejudice the right of the insurer to recover back from other parties any dollars it pays out. You dare not, therefore, interfere with the insurer's suit against your employee, on pain of not being covered yourself.

The serious morale problem which results when your employees discover you have covered yourself but not them can be easily avoided. Endorsements naming employees as additional *insureds* for claims arising in the course of their employment are routinely sold. Most of those endorsements, unlike the coverage given to partners, officers, and the like, do not give the employee coverage when coverage for the employer has been excluded.

Newly acquired organizations. Suppose you form or buy another business while you have a CGL policy in force. Since it is not a "named insured" or another "insured," claims against it will not be covered by your policy. Endorsements are routinely sold, however, automatically making newly acquired or formed organizations "insureds" for 90 days after they are acquired or formed. After that, of course, you will have to add them to your policy or get other insurance.

What claims are covered: "Caused by an occurrence"

In the insuring clauses of the CGL policy and the contractual liability policy or endorsement, the company promises to defend the *insured* against and to pay claims only for damages because of *bodily injury* or *property damage* "caused by an *occurrence*." Policy limits are also expressed in terms of dollars "per occurrence." The significance of the boldface defined term *the insured* has been considered. How the bodily injury and property damage definitions limit coverage is discussed below. However, since no insured is protected against any claim unless it is *"caused by an occurrence,"* the meaning of that strange sounding phrase must be developed.

The definition states that:

> *occurrence* means an accident, including continuous or repeated exposure to conditions which results in *bodily injury* or *property damage* neither expected or intended from the standpoint of the insured.

In general, this means that claims against you for damages are covered only if they were caused by accident. Just what injuries are accidentally caused has been widely litigated. The subject is too complex to be covered in detail here. As a guideline, however, there are three typical types of cases in which the "occurrence" definition is relevant.

First, clearly when you intentionally hurt someone, his claim against you will not be covered. Second, and more troublesome, are potential injury-creating conditions you are aware of like a pothole in your parking lot, a glass door without any warning decals on it, or a piece of defective merchandise you have sold or workmanship you have performed. While you might not intend those circumstances to cause anybody harm, when someone's car is damaged by falling into the pothole, or their face is cut walking into the glass door, or their building is damaged by your unrepaired workmanship, the injury or damage is not "unexpected" from your standpoint. It may not, therefore, be "caused by an occurrence" and the claim against you for the damages which result will not be covered. Finally, however, suppose you intentionally do something not realizing that it might hurt someone. In that case, the damages are not expected, and the injury is usually held to be accidental, and therefore "caused by an occurrence."

What claims are covered: Bodily injury

Except when you buy personal injury coverage (discussed below), the basic CGL policy (and your contractual liability policy covering your hold-harmless clauses) will defend you against and pay only two types of claims—those for *bodily injury* and *property damage*. Those two terms are defined in the policy jacket.

What bodily injury includes. The definitions say that:

> *"bodily injury"* means bodily injury, sickness, or disease sustained by any person which occurs during the policy period, including death at any time resulting therefrom.

The definition of what bodily injury is has not been particularly troublesome, although interesting questions could arise about whether psychological disturbance could be said to be bodily injury, or sickness or disease, particularly if physical symptoms result. The more controversial aspect of this definition has been its time limitation. To be "bodily injury," the injury, sickness, or disease must occur during the policy period. If it does, the claim for wrongful death which occurs after the policy expires will still be covered.

There are nevertheless some problems. Suppose claimants are exposed to injurious conditions (like asbestos or coal dust, chemical fumes, or radiation) over a long period of time. They may be injured a little bit more every day over the entire period. Now suppose, say over a five-year period, the insured has, each year carried CGL policies with bodily injury policy limits of $100,000 per occurrence. If the bodily injury could be said to have occurred over five years and if the claim is for $500,000, how much does the insurer owe? If there were five different insurers, a lawsuit to resolve coverage issues among them is virtually inevitable.

The bodily injury claim stemming from such exposures is clearly "caused by an *occurrence*" because the jacket defines *occurrence* to include "continuous or repeated exposure to conditions which result in bodily injury." Furthermore, the Limits of Liability section of the policy says that: "For the purpose of determining the limit of the company's liability all bodily injury and property damage arising out of continuous and repeated exposure to substantially the same general conditions shall be considered as arising out of one *occurrence*." The insurer will therefore argue that it pays no more than $100,000, the "per occurrence" limit of liability. Some courts, however, have held that because bodily injury is defined as injury occurring *during the policy period* and since the injury could be said to have occurred during each of the five-year periods involved, the policy limits for each of the five years are payable. The insurers have argued that this result gives the insured what were in effect half million dollar limits on this sort of bodily injury claim even though premiums were paid for limits of only $100,000. Because the insurers have lost that argument, you can expect the rating bureaus in future revisions of the policy forms to handle the problem differently.

What bodily injury claims are excluded. Once you determine that a claim against you is for bodily injury and is "caused by an occurrence," as the policy defines those terms and assuming you are an insured and have paid the premium, cooperated, and met the other policy conditions, there is one more place to look to see whether you have coverage: the substantive exclusions. Some risks are so potentially catastrophic that they are simply uninsurable. For that reason, bodily injury claims are excluded for:

Pollution. If your business activity creates a discharge of contaminating fluids or fumes into the air or water, bodily injuries (or property damage) caused by the discharge are excluded, unless the discharge was sudden and accidental. For most businesses the nonaccidental pollution exposure is uninsurable.

Promises to hold others harmless from war risks. This risk is not covered under any incidental contract. Even if you desire to become your landlord's insurer against war risks, your insurer does not wish to join you in that effort.

Because the CGL policy is designed to cover only "general" liability, not surprisingly, most of the remaining exclusions refer to bodily injury (and property damage) claims which can be covered under separate "special" policies. Of course, those separate policies will have their own definitions, exclusions, and conditions, so that even if you own them you may still not be covered. It is an unfortunate fact of life that not all liability risks are insurable, even special risks. Subject to that caveat, however, the principal bodily injury claims which should be specially insured against, because they are excluded in your CGL policy, are:

Automobile, aircraft, and watercraft risks. Bodily injury (and property damage) claims arising out of the ownership, maintenance, operation, use, and loading and unloading of automobile, aircraft, and watercraft are excluded (with some minor exceptions). Those risks are separately insurable under automobile, aircraft, and watercraft liability policies. The principal problem with those exclusions arises when there is a dispute over when and where loading and unloading begins and ends. The best way to avoid the problem is to buy your automobile, aircraft, or watercraft policy from the same insurer that has your CGL coverage (and in the same policy limits). That way you avoid any possible suits between your CGL and your automobile, aircraft, or watercraft liability insurer over which one should pay the claim.

Snowmobiles and stunts with mobile equipment. Snowmobile liability must be covered elsewhere. So must coverage for any racing, demolition, or speed contests using mobile equipment and any practices for such contests.

Liability to employees. Bodily injury claims by employees should be covered separately under a workers' compensation and employer's liability policy. They are excluded under the CGL policy except perhaps when the claim is made against an officer, director, partner, or shareholder who is protected under the policy's severability clause as noted above.

Liquor liability. If you are in the business of making, selling, or serving alcohol, or if you own or have rented property to someone who conducts such a business from your property, you have what is termed a *dram-shop* exposure. If you or your tenant serve alcohol to someone who is obviously intoxicated (or to a minor even if he looks older) and the person served injures someone, in some states you can be sued by the injured person. That exposure should be covered separately under a Liquor Liability Policy. If you claim you are not in the liquor serving business but want to avoid disputes over whether entertaining your customers and friends puts you in the business, a host liquor liability endorsement which adds back the coverage taken out by this exclusion is available for a nominal additional premium.

Contractual liability. Claims for bodily injury (and property damage) which are asserted against you because you assumed them under a hold-harmless clause in a contract are not covered by the basic policy.

Claims brought under hold-harmless clauses in "incidental contracts" like leases of real property, railroad sidetrack agreements, and
so on, as noted are not automatically excluded, but are subject, of
course, to all the other exclusions in the policy. To be covered for
claims brought against you under hold-harmless clauses in any nonin-
cidental contracts you must buy a separate contractual liability policy
or endorsement. Of course the contractual liability coverage you specially purchase will have its own exclusions. Some of these (like the
exclusion for war risks, liquor liability, or for claims that would be
covered under a workers' compensation policy) are similar to the bodily injury claims excluded in the main policy itself. Two others are
unique to the contractual coverage itself. These are:

Claims arising under contracts to indemnify architects and engineers for
their professional errors and omissions. If you agree to hold an architect
harmless from such claims, you agree in effect to become his malpractice
insuror. While you may desire to do so, your contractual liability insurer does
not want you to put it into the architectural malpractice insurance business.

Claims by third-party beneficiaries on public contracts. When you contract to supply goods and services to any governmental agency, many members of the public stand to benefit. If you agree in your contract to hold
members of the public harmless and are sued by a member of the public who
claims that your contract authorizes him to sue you directly, the policy
excludes that claim. If the public agency itself sues you, you are covered
however, so long as the claim is not otherwise excluded. This exclusion in the
contractual liability policy can be eliminated or narrowed by buying a special
endorsement.

Surprisingly, the other specially insured bodily injury exclusions in
the main CGL policy do not appear in the contractual liability endorsement. Thus, you are covered for bodily injury and property damage claims that are asserted against you under hold-harmless clauses
in your contracts even though those claims arise out of the operation of
automobiles, aircraft, and watercraft, snowmobiles, and stunting activities, or which are caused by polluting discharges (so long as such
claims are not excluded for other reasons). You can anticipate that
when the policy forms are next revised, these contractual liability
claims that might have been separately insured against will be
excluded.

What claims are covered: Property damage

The basic policy covers only one type of claim other than for bodily
injury. That type is the claim for property damage. Taken in its ordinary meaning, the term *property damage* when coupled with bodily
injury would seem to cover the field. Whatever negligent injury you
are likely to cause a potential claimant, if not to his body, would be

almost by definition to his "property." Unfortunately for CGL policy owners, the coverage does not go that far. The words *property damage* are among those defined in the policy jacket in a way that renders the definition into a significant exclusion.

What property damage includes. The jacket defines property damage as follows:

> "Property damage" means (1) physical injury to or destruction of tangible property which occurs during the policy period, including the loss of use thereof at any time resulting therefrom, or (2) loss of use of tangible property which has not been physically injured or destroyed provided such loss of use is caused by an occurrence during the policy period.

The same definition applies not only to claims under the basic policy but also to claims brought under any hold-harmless clause covered by a contractual liability policy or endorsement. The definition excludes all claims for lost profits, lost investments, loss of goodwill, loss of favorable contract opportunities (by interference with contract), and a host of similar possible claims that might be made against you. How is this exclusion achieved? The policy, by way of the property damage definition, covers only claims for damages to *tangible* property, thus excluding claims for damage to *intangibles*.[2]

Moreover, the damage that must occur to the tangible property must be either *physical* injury or loss of use "caused by an occurrence."

The "caused by an occurrence" limitation on loss of use claims, as we have seen, because of the definition of the term *occurrence* generally means "caused by accident."

The property damage definition has been most troublesome when it is combined with some of the substantive exclusions which cut out coverage of claims for damage to certain kinds of property. One such problem is this: Suppose you furnish goods or materials or work which are incorporated into a larger entity such as a building or large piece of machinery or equipment. (Persons furnishing lumber or carpentry service to contractors or those supplying parts for appliances or equipment are examples.) Suppose further that the part you supply is defective. If the defect in your part causes the large item to be ground up in little pieces or to burn up, your customer's claim for loss of the large item is for *physical* damage to tangible property and would, therefore, not be excluded in whole or in part by the property damage definition. (It may be excluded, in whole or in part, by other provisions in the policy.)

However, what if the defect in your product or work only reduced the value of the large item of which it has become a part? Can it be said that the larger whole has been physically injured by your defective part? What happens, for example, if you supply defective plaster which cracks when put onto the interior walls of a building. Over 30 years ago this problem arose with precisely those facts in the case of *Hauenstein* v. *St. Paul Mercury Indemnity Co.*, 242 Minn. 354, 65 N.W. 2d 122 (1954). There was then, and there is now, a substantive exclusion denying coverage for damage to the plaster itself. The Minnesota Supreme Court decided that since the building was damaged as well as the plaster, the owner's claim against the plaster supplier for the cost of repair was covered.

The term *property damage* has been redefined twice since then in attempts by insurers to reverse the *Hauenstein* result. The courts have remained split, however, on the question whether the economic damages in this kind of case are covered "property damages."[3] The requirement that the building be "physically" injured represents the latest such attempt. It remains to be seen, however, even with the present definition, whether courts will find that a building is not physically damaged by cracking plaster or other failing component.

What kinds of property damage claims are excluded?

Property damage to the named insured's own products or work. The kind of claim which falls within the definition of property damage is also important in cases where a small part of the insured's workmanship or products become part of a larger end product having nondefective parts. Even if the defect in the product or work of the insured does not physically injure or destroy the other products, the definition may exclude the claim because the policy contains three significant other provisions excluding claims for:

> Property Damage to premises alienated by the Named Insured arising out of such premises or any part thereof;
> Property Damage to the Named Insured's Products arising out of such products or any part of such products; and
> Property Damage to work performed by or on behalf of the named insured arising out of the work or any portion thereof, or out of materials, parts or equipment furnished in connection therewith.

Because of these exclusions, you can anticipate that when trouble comes your carrier will offer to pay only the labor cost for physical damage and perhaps the cost of taking apart and putting back any "other property," but none of the cost of taking out and putting back any defective parts or work you supplied.[4]

Property damage to property in the care, custody, and control of the insured. The exclusion of claims for damages to your own product or work are normally important only for products liability or completed operations risks (which succeed your premises or operations risks after the product is sold or the work is done). If you still have care, custody, or control over any property or work when the damage occurs, neither the claims for damage to your own property or work nor claims for the damage to the "other" property will be covered. The policy excludes claims for:

> Property Damage to property owned or occupied by or rented to the insured, property used by the insured, or property in the care, custody or control of the insured or as to which the insured is for any purpose exercising physical control. . . .

The exclusion applies to claims for damages to any real estate and personal property you own. You cannot be liable to yourself if you damage your own property, however, and in any case your CGL insurance covers only claims brought by others. Excluded property in your care, custody, or control, however, may also consist of property you rent, even though you may be liable for the property damage to the lessor. You may have other property in your care, custody, and control in your possession which belongs to someone else. Contractors work on somebody else's buildings; some businesses may hold other people's goods on consignment or for storage. Other firms may have outsider's goods on hand while repairs or services or modifications are being performed. If you fit in any of those classes, it is quite possible that you have a great deal of other people's property under your care, custody, or control. If you injure it, the owners' claims against you for damages to it will not be covered because of this exclusion.

There are two reasons why the underwriters exclude claims for damages to property in your care, custody, or control. The reasons relate to two kinds of events which can cause the damage.

> The first kind of event is a loss which is not your fault—like fire, rainstorm, windstorm, vandalism, and the like. You can normally buy fire and extended coverage or even all-risk property insurance which will pay you the value of the lost property or the cost to repair it. While the amount of this payment will not necessarily be the same amount as your liability to the owner, it will give you some protection. The first reason for the exclusion relates to this fact. Since you can buy special protection elsewhere in the form of property insurance policies, the risk is excluded in your General Liability and Contractual Liability coverage. Fire legal liability insurance noted above, which is available by endorsement, is the only exception to this particular underwriting aim.

> The second kind of event which may cause damage to property in your care, custody, or control is injury caused by your failure to take care of it. The underwriters view your obligation to live up to any express or implied promise to take care of someone else's property as a business risk much the same as they view your obligation to repair or replace any of your own defective products or work at your own expense. They do not intend to insure you or your customer against your breaches of contract.

The principal problem in applying the care, custody, and control exclusion occurs when several people arguably have care, custody, or control. The hardest cases usually involve construction sites with many owners, contractors, subcontractors, and suppliers working in and about the property which gets damaged. The question of which of the many parties has care, custody, or control (and therefore has no CGL coverage) has been heavily litigated.[5] The cases turn largely on complex and often unique facts, which means that in case of a dispute you may need to consult your lawyer.

Additional coverage added back by the Broad Form Property Damage (BFPD) Endorsement. The care, custody, and control exclusion and the exclusion for damages to the insured's own work (but not the exclusion for damages to the named insured's own products) in the CGL policy and the Contractual Liability Policy (or endorsement) can be narrowed in part by the purchase of a Broad Form Property Damage (BFPD) Endorsement. The endorsement itself is complex. It supplies additional protection only to businesses which perform work *away from their principal places of business.* For firms doing repair or service work outside their own shops and for contractors and subcontractors who fit into that class, the additional protection the endorsement gives can be substantial. The endorsement can be vital for those businesses in two circumstances:

Operations by insureds working on or having care, custody, and control over large end products. Suppose a general contractor who controls an entire project performs a small piece of defective foundation work which causes the building to collapse, or starts a fire while welding a small piece of reinforcement. The care, custody, and control exclusion in the contractor's CGL policy and in his contractual liability coverage would arguably exclude the entire loss. Likewise, since the entire project (including work done by his subcontractors) represents "work performed by or on behalf of the insured," and the damage "[arose] out of the work or any portion thereof, or out of materials, parts or equipment furnished in connection therewith," the "work itself" exclusion arguably cuts out coverage of the owner's claims for all of the loss.

The BFPD Endorsement changes that result. *So long as the damage occurs before the whole job is finished,* the endorsement adds back coverage of claims for all the damages *except* for the small portion of the work which was defective and caused the loss. In our example, the claim for loss of the defective foundation ȯr the reinforcing upon which welding was being performed would be excluded. Under the BFPD Endorsement the insurer would pay for the rest of the loss unless it is excluded elsewhere in the policy. If the contractor had uninstalled material on the site or had rented tools and equipment from others which was destroyed, claims for loss to that equipment or those materials remain uncovered. Builders risk or installation floater coverage must still be obtained to cover them.

Completed operations for suppliers of portions of the work in large end products. If a completed piece of faulty workmanship damages a building or large pieces of equipment which have been serviced away from the insured's premises, the entire loss would be excluded by the "work itself" exclusion in the insured general contractor's CGL and Contractual Liability coverage. A version of the BFPD Endorsement is available applying to "completed operations" which restricts that exclusion. The standard policies exclude claims for damage to work performed *"by or on behalf of* the insured arising out of the work or any portion thereof. . . ." That means the general contractor is not covered if the defective work was done by a subcontractor.

The BFPD Endorsement, in the version which includes completed operations, eliminates the "by or on behalf of" phrase. When the damage which occurs is within the completed operations coverage (i.e., if it happens after the job is done), the elimination of that phrase means two things:

First: If the loss was caused by defective work done by a subcontractor, the general contractor's CGL or contractual policy covers the entire claim.

Second: If the loss was caused by the general contractor's own defective work, he does not get coverage of claims for damages to the rest of his *own* work, even the part that was not defective. (There is a rare version of the BFPD called Lloyd's Form B which would cover the nondefective parts of his own work, but it is very expensive and hard to obtain.) However, the BFPD Endorsement does give the General Contractor coverage for damages to any of his subcontractors' work which, because of the "on behalf of" clause would have been otherwise excluded under the standard exclusion.

Claims for loss of use of tangible property. You may recall that the definition of the term *property damage* included both claims for physical injury to tangible property *and* loss of use of tangible property caused by an "occurrence." However, not all loss-of-use claims are covered. The policy excludes claims for:

> loss of use of tangible property which has not been physically injured or destroyed resulting from:
>
> > a delay in or lack of performance by or on behalf of the named insured or any contract or agreement, or the failure of the named insured's products or work performed by or on behalf of the named insured to meet the level of performance, quality, fitness or durability warranted or represented by the named insured;
>
> but this exclusion does not apply to loss of use of other tangible property

resulting from the sudden and accidental physical injury to or destruction of the named insured's products or work performed by or on behalf of the named insured after such products or work have been put to use by any person or organization other than an insured. . . .

Failure to deliver on time or failure to deliver goods or perform work up to the standards you have promised may give rise to claims for loss of use (measured by the amount of delay in delivery or the time to correct any of the defects). The underwriters class those claims as business risks. On the other hand, should your defective product or work physically damage "other" property, the loss of use claim for the time needed to repair or replace the other property, is covered.

Product recalls and the "sistership" exclusion. Suppose you discover or receive notice from your first customer that you have sold some defective products or performed some work defectively. Suppose in addition that the rest of your customers have not yet been injured or that one poorly built column of 50 identical ones in a project constructed by you fails and you reasonably expect the rest of them may be about to fail. If you do nothing and someone's body or property are later injured you will get sued, *but* your insurer will say that you should have expected the injuries and will deny the claims because those later injuries were not "caused by an occurrence." You must, therefore, act to recall or repair the defects before any further damage is done. If you make the needed repairs or if your customers make them and bill you, are those recall or repair expenses covered? Arguably those claims are for "property damage caused by an occurrence." Nevertheless, the insurers have disposed of that argument by a substantive exclusion called the sistership exclusion because it deals with "sister failures" to the one you are aware of. It excludes claims for:

damages claimed for the withdrawal, inspection, repair, replacement, or loss of use of the named insured's products or work completed by or for the named insured or of any property of which such products or work form a part, if such products, work or property are withdrawn from the market or from use because of any known or suspected defect or deficiency therein; . . .

XCU risks. If you are in the construction business, your CGL policy will probably contain three extra exclusions for property damage claims arising from the explosion (X), collapse (C), and underground property damage (U) hazards. The XCU exclusions may have been left out or deleted by a further endorsement if you paid extra for the additional coverage. The policy provisions excluding these risks are quite complex. However, the exclusions, when properly understood, are much narrower than they may seem when first read. Excluded property damage claims are those:

arising out of blasting or explosion; for collapse or structural injury to structures caused by earth-moving, pile driving or coffer-dam and caisson work or demolition work; and for damage to buried pipes, wires, and tanks caused by earth-moving or pile driving operations.

None of those claims are excluded if they arise from the work of your independent contractors or if they are being made against you under a hold-harmless clause insured by your contractual liability endorsement. If the explosion, collapse, or underground hazard occurs after the job is done (i.e., the claims are for completed operations, and you have completed operations coverage), the claims are not excluded.

Finally, the exclusion will apply only if the claims arise in connection with a long list of specifically described (or "coded") construction activities. The coded activities will be set out in the exclusions or in the declarations. If any noncoded activity causes an X, C, or U claim for property damage caused by an occurrence and the claim is not otherwise excluded (e.g., because the work damaged was your own, or was under your care, custody, or control), it will be covered despite the XC&U exclusions.

Other property damage claims which are uninsurable or are insurable under other special liability policies. Before leaving the subject of property damage claims, it should be noted that several specially insurable areas which were referred to in discussing bodily injury exclusions apply to property damages as well. Thus, because you can secure Property Damage Liability coverage under automobile, aircraft, and watercraft liability policies, any property damage claims resulting from those risks are excluded from your CGL policy (although *not* in the contractual liability endorsement). If you have agreed to hold someone harmless from those risks, claims under those indemnity agreements are covered by your contractual liability endorsement. Liquor liability property damage claims, like those for bodily injury, while they are excluded in the standard form CGL and contractual policies, can be added back by endorsement. The standard exclusions discussed in connection with bodily injury claims relating to pollution risks and agreements to indemnify someone for war risks apply to property damage claims as well.

What claims are covered: Personal injury

As we have seen, the standard General Liability and Contractual Liability Policies cover claims against you only for bodily injury and property damage. You can also buy protection from certain other claims which underwriters call claims for *personal injury*. That term, as used in the policy, means something different than you may ordinarily have understood it to mean.

What personal injury includes. "Personal Injury" as used in the insuring clause of your personal injury policy or endorsement, is defined as:

> injury sustained by the claimant arising out of the conduct of the named insured's business caused by one of the following:
>
> Group A—False arrest, detention or imprisonment, or malicious prosecution;
>
> Group B—the publication or utterance of a libel or slander or of other defamatory or disparaging material, or a publication or utterance in violation of an individual's right of privacy; except publications or utterances in the course of or related to advertising, broadcasting, or telecasting activities conducted by or on behalf of the named insured;
>
> Group C—wrongful entry or eviction, or other invasion of the right of private occupancy.

You pay a separate premium for each of the groups of coverage. That means that you can buy less than the entire amount of available "personal injury" coverage if you wish to self-insure or if you feel that one or two of the three types of claims against you are not likely to occur. The coverage is frequently sold on a participating basis under which the insurer agrees only to pay a fixed percentage of any personal injury claim brought against you.

Excluded claims for personal injury. By reason of the personal injury definitions under the group B covered risks, you will have to buy advertising liability coverage separately if you desire protection against claims that your advertising has defamed anyone. Limited extra advertising liability protection is sold by endorsement which covers you against certain claims that your advertising violates the rights or privacy of someone, or infringes on their copyrights or trademarks, or constitutes unfair competition. Otherwise, the specifically excluded claims are few. The primary ones are:

> Claims for defamatory statements first made prior to the policy period.
>
> Intentionally false statements.
>
> Claims resulting from willful violation of any law or ordinance.
>
> Claims relating to your employees—as for example claims by fired employees, and claims by ex-employees who are displeased by any unfavorable reference you may have given to another prospective employer.
>
> Contractual liability. You cannot ordinarily get coverage for personal injury claims brought against you under any hold-harmless clauses.

Most of the misunderstandings about this coverage concern claims that result when you misdescribe products or prices in advertising and claims that you have discriminated against certain racial, religious, ethnic or perhaps sexual groups. You can expect your insurer to resist defending or paying such claims.

HOW YOU PAY FOR COVERAGE

Rate bases

The price you pay for each of the General Liability insurance coverages depends upon the amount of risk the insurer thinks it will bear if it sells you the protection. For most of the coverage, that risk will vary depending on the amount of business activity you conduct during the policy period. Your premiums are therefore based in part on various measures of activity which fluctuate with the risk. Thus, for example:

Premises coverage is often written based on the number of square feet (or frontage feet) of real estate you occupy during the policy period.

Operations coverage is likewise frequently written based upon your sales (or sometimes your payroll) on the theory that the more you sell (or the more employees you have) the higher the level of your business's risk-creating activity.

Your "independent contractors" exposure similarly is thought to vary with the cost of subcontracts you enter into. The more independent contractors you employ and the larger their contracts, the more the risk.

Products and completed operations risks are also linked with your current sales (or gross receipts).

Your premiums for each of the coverages will be computed by multiplying your rate base for each coverage (e.g., payroll, sales, or square footage) times the appropriate rate. At the beginning of the policy period, of course, neither you nor the insurer know for sure just what your rate bases will add up to at the end of the year. At the outset, you will have to give the insurer an estimate and will be charged what is termed a "deposit premium." At the end of the year you must supply the actual final figures upon which your final premium will be computed. If the actual rate bases turn out to be larger than the initial estimate, you will receive a bill for the extra premium due. If the rate bases turn out to be smaller, you should correspondingly receive a refund. This feature of the coverage, as noted in the introduction to this chapter, is why the coverage is called comprehensive.

In order to maintain the integrity of this flexible method for determining premiums, the company reserves the right to audit your books for three years after the coverage expires.

Manual rates, rating classifications, and audits

The rates by which your various rate bases will be multiplied to determine your preliminary and final premium bill also vary with the risk involved in the business activity which the policy covers. The insurance industry collects loss statistics on various kinds of risks from which so-called manual rates are computed. If your Premises coverage covers only a quiet office space, your manual rate will be low. If it covers busy retail space it will be higher. Likewise the independent contractors rate you pay covering your janitorial service contract will be lower than the rate you pay for contracts employing demolition subcontractors. Your total premium will be computed by applying separate rates to each appropriate rating classification. At the end of the policy year, the insurer's audit of your books will thus look not only at your total sales or square footage figures, but will break them down to make sure you pay the high rate on the high risk portion of each rate base.

If your premiums are substantial, it is worth your while to have someone representing you look over the insurer's final premium audits. Unless you keep records which distinguish low risk sales or square footage or subcontract costs from high risk ones the insurer's auditor will lump them all together and charge you the high rate for the entire activity.

Experience rates

Insurance buyers commonly believe that since the insurance business is regulated, the rates they actually pay are fixed by law. In fact, the rates may be negotiable. "Dividends" and "discounts" are commonly available. More importantly, however, once your premium reaches a minimum size you do not pay the manual rate. In figuring your premium, the underwriter starts with the manual rate and then raises it or lowers it depending on your past loss experience. The formulas used in this process (called experience rating) are designed to penalize accounts with histories of many small claims, but which assure that a single huge loss does not raise your experience rate forever after. The past "loss" figures which the underwriter uses to adjust your manual rate are not necessarily just losses actually paid but also included estimates of future payments that will have to be made (called loss or claim reserves) on claims which are still pending. Obviously, the experience rating process requires the underwriter to make several "judgment calls" when he figures your rates. For larger insurance buyers, someone who knows the business who represents you in negotiating the rates can save you substantial amounts of premiums simply by seeing that all of the judgment calls are not made heavily in the insurer's favor. Experience rating has one other significant meaning to you. If you have claims against you this year, next year's rates will be higher. It thus pays you to avoid having claims even if loss prevention programs cost you something.

Composite rates

Normally your total premium will be computed in applying several different experience rates to the several different rating classifications in your various rate bases, and adding up the products of those multiplications. Suppose, however, for internal cost accounting or bidding purposes you would like to be charged based on a single rate applied to a single rate base (like payroll or sales). You can negotiate with the insurer to be charged for all of the CGL coverage with a single "composite" rate. It is computed by estimating what the total premium will be when figured normally and then dividing the result by the single composite measure you prefer, to arrive at the composite rate. So long as the composite rate base you choose remains relatively stable from year to year, and so long as you have someone knowledgeable on your side representing you when the composite rate is negotiated, this simplified technique can be useful in your internal bookkeeping and may even save you money. The process is sufficiently complex, however, that you should employ it only under expert guidance.

Retrospective rating plans

Once your experience rate or composite rate is determined when you buy the policy, the final premium will be computed using those rates no matter how many or how few claims the company must defend or pay under the policy. In other words, the rate is normally "guaranteed" for the policy period. Sometimes, however, you can negotiate to pay for the coverage on a nonguaranteed or "retrospective" basis.

Under retrospective plans your deposit premium (called the standard premium) is computed the same as it would have been for a guaranteed plan. However, if at the end of the policy period, your actual loss experience turns out to be much less costly than anticipated, you are entitled to a refund. On the other hand, should the insurer's losses be greater than anticipated, you will receive a final bill computed using even higher rates. In a sense, retrospective plans are a sophisticated form of partial self-insurance. The plan will incorporate provisions for a minimum premium even though your losses are zero, and will also provide for a maximum limit on the size of the end-of-the-year bill which the insurer can send you. In between these high-low limits, you end up sharing part of the loss with your insurer.

If you are in a particularly hazardous business, sometimes the only way you can obtain coverage is under a retrospective plan. If you are not obliged to buy insurance on a retrospective basis, you should consider it only when:

You are financially solvent enough to afford a large additional premium if you incur a major loss. If things start to go wrong you will not be able to cancel out in mid-term without having to pay a substantial penalty premium.

You have expert guidance. Among other things, the additional bill you may have to pay will be based not just on loss payments the insurer actually incurs but on reserves it sets for those losses. If the actual claim payment is less than the amount reserved you will eventually get some of your money back. But unless you negotiated for it in advance, the insurer may hold your money without interest for the long period over which the claims are pending.

If you have just suffered a catastrophic loss which makes your experience rates very high, or are getting out of some of the riskier aspects of your past business or are planning on introducing more effective loss prevention measures, you have good reason for believing that your future losses will be substantially lower than your past ones. On the other hand, if you are expanding and adding inexperienced employees, you should probably stick to guaranteed rates.

WHAT TO DO WHEN TROUBLE COMES

Giving notice

One of the conditions of the policy is that you give prompt notice *both* of any accident or occurrence *and* of any claim or suit brought against you. The policy provides:

Insured's duties in the event of occurrence, claim or suit: In the event of an occurrence, written notice containing particulars sufficient to identify the insured and also reasonably obtainable information with respect to the time, place and circumstances thereof, and the names and addresses of the injured and of available witnesses, shall be given by or for the insured to the company or any of its authorized agents as soon as practicable.

If claim is made or suit is brought against the insured, the insured shall immediately forward to the company every demand, notice, summons or other process received by him or his representative.

If you fail to give reasonable notice you may be shocked to find that the company's obligations to defend you and pay any claim have been forgiven. Notice is normally given by contacting the agent or broker who sold you the policy. To protect yourself it is wise to give notice in writing or to get written confirmation from the agent acknowledging that he has received your notice. If there is any question in your mind whether the policy covers the claim, you may be wise to consult your attorney first and have him assist you in giving notice to the insurer. A poorly drawn notice may prompt the insurer to deny coverage rather than to investigate and pay the claim.

Insurer's duty to defend you

The insuring clause of the policy provides not only that the company will pay any covered claims for bodily injury or property damage (or personal injury where appropriate) but also that the company:

> shall have the right and duty to defend any suit against the insured seeking damages on account of such bodily injury or property damage, even if any of the allegations of the suit are groundless, false or fraudulent and may make such investigation and settlement of any claim or suit as it deems expedient, but the company shall not be obligated to pay any claim or judgment or to defend any suit after the applicable limit of the company's liability has been exhausted by payment of judgments or settlements.

In many cases this right to be defended against claims is the most important thing you get when you buy the policy. Particularly when there are many claims of doubtful merit or where the claims are complex, defense costs alone can be a significant drain on your net worth.

Most efficient claim departments will start to investigate any claims as soon as you give notice. Many claims may be settled by the insurer's claims adjusters before you get sued. However, the company may tell you that it has no duty to investigate and pay claims before an actual suit is commenced. It is therefore worth your while to ask about the quality of a particular company's claims service before you buy the policy in the first place. The lowest premium does not always represent the best buy. In any case, if your insurer seems to be ignoring or evading a claim, you should consult your own attorney.

Once you get sued by the claimant (and have given notice), the insurer will normally hire an attorney of its choice to represent you in the ensuing litigation. The insurer may refuse to do so, however, if it believes the claim may not be covered by the policy. Whether you are entitled to a defense and whether the insurer is entitled to control the defense is a complex question of the facts in each case and the particular law of your jurisdiction. There is substantial disagreement among the courts of various states, but in general the rules are these:

> Whether the insurer must defend you, in the first instance depends upon the allegations in the complaint or petition which was served upon you to start the action. If the allegations appear to allege a claim for property damage or bodily injury caused by an occurrence, the insurer is usually obliged to undertake your defense. This is true even though the claim against you is baseless. It does not matter that the allegations are untrue. All that counts is that they have been asserted against you.

Even if an occurrence which caused bodily injury or property damage is alleged, it may also be clear in the suit that the claim is excluded (e.g., because it is for damages to your own product, or arose out of operation of an automobile, etc.). A few state courts have held that you are nevertheless entitled to be defended even though if the suit is lost the insurer would not be obligated to pay the claim. Most states, however, have held that if the alleged claim is excluded in the policy the insurer need not defend. When the policy form is next revised, insurers will probably change the wording to clarify or eliminate the insurer's duty to defend against excluded claims.

If the insurer refuses to defend, you will be obliged to hire your own counsel. This does not mean that you have no further recourse against the insurer. If during the course of preparing to defend yourself you or your attorney discover facts which were not alleged in the suit papers which indicate that some or all of the claims are in fact covered by the policy, you can again put the insurer on notice, at which time it will be obliged to take up the task of defending. You may also be able to sue the insurer for indemnity and for other relief for a wrongful refusal to defend you.

Conflicts of interest

Normally, once the insurer starts to defend you, it must follow through and must pay any judgment that the claimant obtains against you. If the insurer suspects, however, that it may not be liable under the policy for any judgment but must nevertheless defend, it will do so under what is called a "reservation of rights" which is simply a notice to you stating in effect: "We will defend you now, but if the defense is unsuccessful we reserve the right to refuse to pay the claim." If you receive such a notice, you should consult your own lawyer promptly and be guided by his advice.

In a routine case your interest and that of the insurer defending you will coincide. Both you and your insurer wish to defeat or minimize the amount of any claim against you. However, when the insurer defends "under reservation" possible conflicts may develop between what is best for you and what is best for the insurer. That is why you will need independent advice and perhaps independent representation. The conflict most often occurs in two kinds of cases:

When the claim is asserted on several grounds, some of which are within policy coverage and some which are excluded. If coverage is arguably applicable to one ground, most courts hold that the insurer must defend you not only on that ground but on all of them. Nevertheless, it may better serve the insurer's interests to devote its efforts to proof that the claim arose on the excluded ground rather than to defend against the claims on their merits or to reduce the amount of the claim.

When the claim exceeds the policy limits. If the insurer is unable to settle the claim except at or near the policy limits it has little to lose and everything to gain by refusing to settle and going all the way to a verdict. If the verdict comes in below the policy limits the insurer reduces its loss. If the judgment is in excess of the limits the insurer has nothing to lose—but you do.

One way to better assure that your interests are being adequately protected by the insurer's appointed counsel when there is a defense under reservation of rights is to have your own lawyer available to monitor and police the conduct of the defense by appointed counsel. It may even be necessary for you or your lawyer to participate in the defense in order to assure proof of facts having an important bearing on insurance coverage issues.

Your duty to cooperate

Once the claim is made you will not be able to turn it over to the insurer and forget about it. One of the last provisions in the "Conditions" in the policy jacket requires that:

> The insured shall cooperate with the company and, upon the company's request, assist in making settlements, in the conduct of suits and in enforcing any right of contribution or indemnity against any person or organization who may be liable to the insured because of injury or damage with respect to which insurance is afforded under this policy; and the insured shall attend hearings and trials and assist in securing and giving evidence and obtaining the attendance of witnesses. The insured shall not, except at his own cost, voluntarily make any payment, assume any obligation or incur any expense other than for first aid to others at the time of accident.

Should you fail to cooperate as the policy requires, the company may refuse to defend or pay any of the claims against you.

There are two situations involving your duty to cooperate which are typically troublesome:

The first is when you want the insurer to pay the claim but it does not desire to do so. Frequently claimants end up being your suppliers, customers, or friends, or even family members whose goodwill (and future business) you value. Under such circumstances you may not wish to help your insurer defeat the claim against you. When you face these situations you have an unfortunate choice to make. Either you must cooperate with the insurer in resisting the claim or you may pay the claim yourself. If you fail to cooperate, the insurer will probably deny coverage.

The second is the conflict of interest situation described above involving the duty to defend. When you give information to the insurer's claim agents or the attorney it has retained to defend you, they may ultimately use it not to defend you but rather to build a case for denying coverage. Generally, information given to the insurer-designated attorney cannot be disclosed to the insurer for use against you unless the attorney makes it clear in advance that he will not treat your statements as confidential. However, once he learns from you that the insurer has a possible policy defense he may be forced to withdraw from the case. The insurer will then suspect that the coverage issues exist and will question you itself. If you fail to answer completely or truthfully, the insurer may deny the claim for your failure to cooperate. It therefore behooves you, if you have any reason for believing that the claim is not clearly within coverage, to obtain independent advice from your own attorney, and to follow his advice on how to proceed.

WHAT TO ASK YOUR INSURANCE AGENT OR BROKER

By now you have discerned that understanding general liability insurance is largely a problem of learning about what risks are insurable and knowing the special vocabulary the industry uses to describe them. The checklist offered below reviews some of the material we have discussed in the form of questions which you may wish to ask your own agent or insurance counselor.

1. Do you have general liability coverage of your own, and are you covered by any policies purchased by others?
2. Does the form of policy you own cover:
    All your premises exposure?
    All your operations exposure?
    All your independent contracts?
    Products liability?
    Completed operations?
3. Do you have endorsements or separate policies covering:
    Your contractual liability?
    Your personal injury liability?
4. Do you need to cover your employees, spouses, joint ventures, partnerships, your customers, or any newly acquired entities as additional insureds?
5. Do you need any of the routine additional coverages provided by endorsement including:
    Host liquor liability?
    Fire legal liability?
    XCU coverage?
    Broad Form Property Damage Liability?
6. Do you have special policies to cover the risks excluded by your general liability policies including:
    Automobile, watercraft, or aircraft liability carried by the same insurer?
    Property coverages on all property in your care, custody, and control?
    Workers' compensation and employers' liability?
7. Do you understand what various rate bases the insurer proposes to use in calculating your premium?
8. Could you keep additional records which segregate lower risk rate bases and thus save premiums?
9. Should you consider composite or retrospective rating plans?
10. What is your insurer's history of claims service?

Your workers' compensation or professional liability coverages may in fact be the most important (and most expensive) insurance policies you own. Your comprehensive general liability insurance, however, is the most complex. No other policy attempts to cover so many different and hard to measure and understand risks which may occur in your business activity. For that reason, the CGL policy is the cornerstone for your entire liability insurance program. If you can understand its most important features and limitations, you can deal more knowledgeably with insurance agents, counselors, and risk managers to whom you must turn to obtain coverage that meets both your needs and your budget. Once you know what rights the policy gives you, we hope you will be able to deal more effectively with both the insurer and with your own legal advisor when the really troublesome questions about coverage arise.

NOTES

1. Courts are split over this issue. See, e.g., *Zenti* v. *Home Ins.*, 262 N.W.2d 588 (1978), CCH Fire & Cas. Cases 627 (1978).

2. See annotation: "Liability Policy Providing Coverage for Damages Because of Injury to or Destruction of Property as Covering Injury to Investments and Goodwill," 92 ALR3d 525.

3. The history of the dispute over whether coverage applies when defective goods or workmanship are incorporated into a larger end product is analyzed in detail in Bowers, "General Liability Insurance Coverage for Defective Materials and Workmanship," in B. C. Hart, ed., *Construction Litigation* (New York: New York Law Journal Seminars Press, 1979). See also Henderson, "Insurance Protection for Products Liability and Completed Operations—What Every Lawyer Should Know," 50 *Neb*. L.Rev. 415 (1971); and Annotation, "Products Liability Insurance Coverage as Extending Only to Product-Caused Injury to Person or Other Property, as Distinguished from Mere Product Failure," 91 ALR3d 921.

4. The underwriting theory behind the property damage exclusions is this: Whether you sell quality products or do good work, or if you sell a building, whether it is as good as you promised your customer it would be, is a question of business risk, not insurance risk. Keeping your customers happy and standing behind your work or product is your own prob-

lem. The underwriters only intend to protect you against claims that your product or work accidentally injures some *other* property.

In the *Hauenstein*-type case, insurers have argued that the plaster supplier is liable to replace his own defective plaster. The insured has always argued that the defective plaster did damage "other" property—that is, the building in which it was installed. (Note that if the plaster was installed by the general contractor, his policy would not cover the claim in any case because there is no "other" work from his standpoint. The entire building was his own "work" not the work of others.)

The reason insurers have twice revised the definition of "property damage" since *Hauenstein* was to clarify just what the difference is between damage to the insured's own work or product (which is excluded), on the one hand, and damage to "other" products or work (which they intend to cover), on the other. The latest definition attempts to make this distinction by requiring that in order to qualify as "property damage," the injury must be a "physical" injury. As we have suggested, it is not that clear that cracked plaster does not "physically" injure other property.

Only one case has been decided construing the current definition. In that case, *Wyoming Sawmills, Inc.*, v. *Transportation Ins. Co.*, 578 P.2d 1253 (Ore. 1978), the insured supplied 2X4 studs which warped when installed in a building. The insured's customer spent $17,000 in labor to replace the studs. The insurer denied the claim for labor on the grounds that it had not been shown that the rest of the building had been *physically* damaged or that the whole $17,000 had been spent repairing that damage. The Oregon Supreme Court upheld the insurer's position and remanded the case for more detailed fact findings. In a hopelessly ambiguous opinion the court suggests three tests for whether "property damage" has occurred under the new definition:

> If the "other" property (i.e., the building) can be completely repaired by merely replacing the defective studs, there has been no "property damage" and there is, therefore, no coverage;

> If on the other hand other parts of the building must be torn out and put back in the process of replacing the studs, the stud supplier's policy will cover that cost;

Most importantly, however, the court also stated that if the *only* way to repair the damage to the rest of the building was to install new studs, the labor cost of that installation might be covered.

While the first two tests suggested by the court seem to accept the insurer's theory that the damage must be to "other property," the third test seems to hold the reverse and for most *Hauenstein*-type cases return to the position that the loss is covered. (It is clear that the lumber cost of the new studs is excluded in any case.)

As an insurance buyer, where does all this confusion leave you? Probably in the hands of your lawyer when trouble finally comes.

5. Many of the cases are collected in an annotation: "Scope of Clause Excluding from Contractors' or Similar Liability Policy Damage to Property in the Care, Custody, or Control of Insured," 62 ALR2d 1242.

CHAPTER 9

COMMERCIAL AUTOMOBILE LIABILITY AND PHYSICAL DAMAGE

THE BUSINESSMAN'S EXPOSURE TO
LOSS THROUGH THE OPERATION OF
AUTOMOBILES
   Statutory requirements

RISK HANDLING BY NONINSURANCE
METHODS
   Avoidance or elimination of risk
   Loss control—accident prevention
   Self-assumption
   Transfer by noninsurance

RISK TRANSFER THROUGH
INSURANCE
   Liability Insurance coverage
   Limits of liability

Exclusions
No-fault coverage
Medical Payments coverage
Uninsured Motorists coverage
Physical Damage coverages
Covered autos
Business Auto Policy (BAP) options
Premium computation

QUESTIONS TO BE ASKED THE AGENT
OR BROKER

Frank L. Eblen, CPCU
President
Corporate Energy Resource Services
Corroon & Black Corporation
New Orleans, Louisiana

Frank L. Eblen joined Corroon & Black in August 1981 to create and develop the new Energy Resource Services division. After 31 years in the insurance business, Mr. Eblen's career includes underwriting, engineering, brokerage in property, casualty and marine areas, risk management administration, self-insurance, captives, and other related fields. Mr. Eblen is a member of American Management Association's Insurance and Benefits Planning Council, holds the designation of "Certified Licensed Insurance Consultant" in the State of Connecticut, is Chairman of many AMA Seminars, and is a frequent speaker at RIMS and other industry groups.

Robert S. Smith, J.D., CPCU
College of Business
Florida State University
Tallahassee, Florida

Robert S. Smith is an Adjunct Professor of insurance at the College of Business, Florida State University, and Staff Director of publications and continuing education for the Florida Association of Insurance Agents. He has been a local agent and in various underwriting positions for major insurers. He also has extensive background in advisory and consultant relationships in the legislative and regulatory areas. Mr. Smith has written and published numerous technical service books for the industry, manuals, and articles for professional journals.

This chapter is divided into three sections: the businessman's exposures to loss through the operation of automobiles,[1] how these risks might be handled utilizing "noninsurance" methods, and risk transfer through purchased insurance.[2]

THE BUSINESSMAN'S EXPOSURE TO LOSS THROUGH THE OPERATION OF AUTOMOBILES

In today's commercial world it is virtually impossible to envision a business which does not, at some point in time, having something being done on its behalf through the use of an automobile. Under the broad legal doctrine of vicarious liability, a party whose interest is being served by a vehicle is considered to have liability exposure. Moreover, financial responsibility laws; no-fault insurance laws; compulsory insurance laws; requirements of federal, state, and local governmental agencies such as Departments of Transportation; and public utility commissions extend the businessman's automotive risks even further. With risks ranging from nearly unrecognizable to highly visible, each commercial auto exposure must be carefully identified, analyzed, and addressed for each represents potential catastrophe to the unwary.

The increased use of leased automobiles (a lease arrangement of 12 months or longer) by business has created additional risk management considerations. In the following description of various commercial auto exposures, the business may be the owner or the lessee of the vehicles, and the basic or primary protection on the leased units may be provided by either the lessee or the lessor.

Commercial auto risks are divided into classifications based on the type of equipment. The Commercial Auto category includes private passenger cars, trucks of all types which either carry the owner's own merchandise or the property of others (businesses transporting property of others are commonly referred to as truckers, movers, common carriers, contract carriers or specialized haulers, and are subject to Federal Department of Transportation and/or State Public Utility Authority rules and regulations), and the large miscellaneous group of ambulances, police and security, fire trucks, and other special-use vehicles. Mobile equipment such as power shovels, cranes, graders, and rollers may be included from an insurance standpoint. For some of these specialized vehicles, liability insurance is usually provided under a general liability policy and Physical Damage coverage under an inland marine type of policy.

The Public Automobile category includes vehicles used to transport people for a charge. Taxicabs, private and public livery, general passenger buses, and school buses are typical examples of public automobiles. Under common law, the highest degree of care is required on the part of the for-hire provider of public transportation. Public carriers (common or charter) are subject to this high care standard. A new phenomenon in this category is the "bus van" now used by many businesses. Due to the gas shortage, business owners have started providing transportation for their employees, as a private livery. This arrangement appears to come under the transportation for-hire classification subject to the extreme care doctrine, and this has created exposure problems not normally encountered in the usual commercial risk. If the employee-passengers are not covered under the state's workers' compensation statute, the additional exposure can be extremely costly, as insurance rates are high for public carriers.

Garage Risks are another distinct classification of commercial auto risk. This class includes automobile and truck dealers, repair shops, service stations, storage garages, and public parking facilities. Since garage and trucking risks represent an important and large segment of the commercial auto risk, Chapter 10 has been entirely devoted to this subject.

The greatest concern of businessmen should be the exposure of liability from bodily injury and property damage to others. This exposure includes legal damages resulting from negligent acts of drivers, as well as costs of defense against claims and suits. Investigation and litigation can involve substantial sums to disprove or minimize damages.

A second exposure is the direct loss of a vehicle by fire, theft, windstorm, collision, or other peril—generally referred to as "physical damage." While normally this exposure is not one of major consequence, highly valued units or a concentration of units at a single garaging or parking location can produce a serious exposure. Related to direct loss by physical damage perils is the "loss of use" exposure. How this type of loss would effect the financial stability of the business depends upon the results of a thorough program of exposure identification and analysis.

Another exposure concern is injury to occupants in a vehicle where an owner is not legally liable. Many businessmen feel a moral obligation to provide some degree of protection when an occurrence takes place involving nonemployees (such as guests, family members, salesmen) or employees off the job (workers' compensation covers employees "while on business"). This exposure is most prevalent in small family owned businesses where family private-passenger cars are often registered in the company's name. Medical, accidental death, or dismemberment and other benefits must be considered even though there is no legal obligation.

When vehicles are rented or leased, the exposures may depend upon contractual obligations set forth in the lease agreement. In short-term rentals (as with Hertz, Avis, National, etc.), the owner normally provides insurance for the primary liability and physical damage exposures, *without* any option to decline the provided coverage. For example, the Hertz rental contract provides insurance for bodily injury liability of $100,000 each person and $300,000 each accident, and property damage liability of $25,000. Physical Damage coverage is provided subject to a collision or upset deductible of $250. This collision damage deductible can be eliminated for an extra charge per day. Also *included* in these types of rental agreements are compliance with statutory requirements such as no-fault and financial responsibility laws. Generally, all rental agreements contain provisions pertaining to who can drive the vehicle with the lessor's permission (such as lessee's immediate household members over 21 years of age who are duly licensed) and what vehicle uses are prohibited (such as "can't be used for illegal purposes, racing or testing" or carrying persons or property for hire).

In long-term lease agreements most leasing companies make insurance available as an option. If insurance is provided by the lessor, the same restrictive type clauses referred to above are usually included. However, depending on the number of vehicles and the circumstances involved, lease conditions can and should be negotiated. For example, an executive assigned a leased vehicle may have a teenage driver in the family. Although the vehicle will be principally driven by the executive on business, there may be an occasion where the teenager will drive. From the businessman's viewpoint, the lease agreement should provide that insurance coverage will be valid in case of an accident involving the teenager and any other family member.

All vehicles, whether leased or owned, should be subject to the same risk management analysis. By treating all of the vehicle exposures in the same manner, continuity, elimination of gaps, and avoidance of overlapping or unwanted coverage can be achieved.

The most serious exposure from automobiles neither owned nor leased is from employees driving their *own* vehicles on behalf of the business. When an employer asks an employee to perform a duty utilizing the employee's own vehicle, the employer becomes vicariously liable. Generally, however, the *insurance covering the non-owned vehicle is primary*. This means the vehicle owner's insurance policy responds *first*. Any other applicable insurance such as the operator's or that of the business in whose behalf the vehicle was used pays *after* the vehicle owner's insurance limit is exhausted. This excess insurance will cover the vicarious liability of the business held responsible for its use.

Many businesses which require employees to use their own vehicles on company business attempt to cover their liability by requiring certificates of insurance showing minimum limits such as bodily injury—$100,000 each person, $300,000 each accident; property damage—$50,000 each accident. Employers imposing this requirement on employees are not always successful. Limits may be lower than desired, and policies can be cancelled without notification to the employer. An employer is well advised not to rely on insurance purchased by others.

In addition to the employer-employee relationship, a nonemployee vehicle use creates the same exposure of liability under the law of agency. Example: A salesman calls on the manager of the X Corporation. After a successful sale, the manager asks the salesman if he would drop off a package at a nearby location. On the way to this drop-off location the salesman hits a pedestrian. Regardless of the final outcome of this claim, the X Corporation could be a defendant as the entity responsible for the use of the vehicle causing the accident. Again, the X Corporation would be protected under the nonemployee vehicle's insurance to the extent of its limits. The corporation needs its own insurance, however, for judgment or settlement over the nonemployee's limit.

Statutory requirements

Financial responsibility laws are in effect in 47 states and the District of Columbia (compulsory liability insurance laws have been passed by the remaining three). These laws attempt to establish the vehicles' owners' or operators' ability to pay for injury and damage to others resulting from negligent driving of automobiles.

Financial responsibility laws are similar in principle, but vary in detail. In general they require that when a motorist is involved in an accident causing bodily injury or property damage or is convicted of a major traffic violation (such as driving under the influence or leaving the scene of an accident), he must provide a guarantee of his ability to pay damages. An automobile liability policy equal to the required minimum limits is accepted as proof of this ability.

Compulsory insurance states require an insurance company certification before a vehicle can be registered.

No-fault laws of varying types are in force in approximately half the states. These generally provide for the injured party to be reimbursed for medical expense and lost income without having the burden of proving negligence or fault. Funding is generally secured through a medium of insurance called Personal Injury Protection.

Uninsured Motorist (UM) Protection may also be mandatory in certain states. UM permits an innocent victim to make a claim against his own insurance company for damages (usually, for bodily injuries only) caused by a negligent uninsured motorist.

A businessman may also be subject to statutory requirements of state and federal public utility commissions if his business includes public transportation of persons or property. Usually, limits of financial responsibility prescribed by statute must be shown before a license to operate is issued.

RISK HANDLING BY NONINSURANCE METHODS

The noninsurance risk management techniques for handling automobile liability and physical damage exposures are often ignored by businessmen who tend to rely solely on insurance.

Avoidance or elimination of risk

Many business owners have avoided auto risks simply by *not owning* any vehicles. Under long- or short-term leasing agreements, the lessor provides the required protection for the liability and other exposures of the user. The businessman should consider the need for his own catastrophic coverage over the insurance provided by the lessor. (See Chapter 19, umbrella policy.) When the leasing company provides insurance, the user should insist that the policy include Drive Other Car coverage for all persons (and their family members) who are furnished a lease car and who do not have personal auto insurance on autos which they own. This form of insurance protects for use of borrowed cars.

Some businesses that own their passenger cars have found the cost of owning and *insuring* one or two trucks was greater than long-term leasing which includes insurance protection provided by the lessor. A comparison of costs should be made between insurance coverage furnished by the businessman's own company (for the leased vehicles) as opposed to the lessor providing the insurance coverage. Generally, the leasing company's insurance premiums which are passed onto the user are higher. These costs may vary substantially depending on the number of vehicles in a fleet, the type of the vehicles, the radius of operation, total mileage, and the garaging locations.

Through the utilization of contract truckmen or common carriers, a businessman can avoid the automobile exposures of owning delivery trucks.

Loss control—accident prevention

Risk reduction through the use of loss control techniques may be used in conjunction with other risk management methods. Loss experience (the amounts paid to claimants as a result of auto accidents in relation to insurance premiums paid) will largely determine the ultimate cost of the automobile insurance. Insurers use plans which recognize not only loss experience but also current safety programs and vehicle maintenance practices. Depending upon the size of a fleet, available personnel, and the priority given loss prevention by management, some or all of the loss control measures discussed in this chapter may be utilized in a fleet safety program to reduce automobile exposures and eventual costs.

The safety or loss control function should be assigned to one individual who must be given authority consistent with the responsibility of the job. In a business consisting of a passenger car fleet and few trucks, the risk manager or insurance buyer usually takes on these duties, assisted by loss prevention specialists employed by the firm's insurer. In a large trucking fleet, a full-time fleet safety supervisor should be appointed. In order to achieve the maximum results from a loss control program, management should develop a fleet safety policy. A written statement signed by the business principal or corporate president should outline management's goals, what is expected in the achievement of these goals, who is responsible for the direction of the program, accountability for accidents and investigations, accident review board authority and its function, and similar subjects. The distribution of the policy statement should be to *all* involved in the program. This action will make it clear what top management expects from participation in the fleet safety program.

The human and mechanical elements are key factors in any fleet safety program. Most automobile accidents are caused as a result of human error and should be the first consideration.

The most important human error control begins with driver selection. This process usually consists of:

1. Completion of an employment application.
2. Investigation of the driver's record and background.
3. A physical examination.

Like most businesses involved with truck fleets which have developed a special employment application for driver applicants, all firms should require personnel who will be driving company vehicles to fill in an information form on their past driving record—accidents, traffic convictions, and current driver's license information. Motor vehicle records should be obtained and matched with the applicant's statements before hiring. (Insurance underwriters will require the driver's name, license number, and date of birth in order to obtain motor vehicle records for themselves.) If the driver's record is undesirable, the insurance company might request that the driver be relieved of his driving duties or cancel the policy. Safety directors can secure additional background information by utilizing credit agency reports and checking with past employers.

Today, pre-employment physicals are standard operating procedure for many employers. A physical examination could be particularly helpful in determining whether the driver-applicant has the requisite health and physical requirements. If a company is regulated by Federal Department of Transportation regulations, a physical exam is mandatory.

Driver training programs can be used in varying degrees depending upon job requirements and facilities available. Programs can range from formal classroom and behind-the-wheel instruction for large trucking firms to informal safety films and defensive driving courses for passenger car fleet drivers. Road patrols may be used to observe vehicle operation on the highways. These patrols can be run by the business, a private road patrol company, or an insurance company specializing in fleet risks. Finally, an incentive or driver reward plan can be instituted to reduce accidents.

The "mechanical" element in fleet safety refers to equipment maintenance. Although the majority of accidents result from the human element, maintaining the vehicles in the safest possible condition is vitally important. A system of regular fleet maintenance should be installed. This program should include the use of master vehicle records, driver vehicle condition reports, and periodic review of all records to comply with the recommended standards modified for operational conditions.

Procedures for accident reporting and investigating must be thoroughly understood and complied with by all involved. Accident records and driver records are an integral part of a fleet safety program.

Assistance in establishing, administering, and monitoring safety and loss prevention programs can be elicited from many insurance companies and some brokers and agents.

Related to loss control and risk reduction is control of corporate vehicles. Every business should have a written policy establishing regulations for the business and personal use of all company vehicles (governed by management's overall corporate philosophy of "employee benefits"). This corporate policy should specifically outline by whom, when, and where the vehicle may be used. Issues which should be addressed are the operation by employees' spouses, children, relatives, friends; mileage driven; use of campers and boat trailers; whether the vehicle may be taken out of the country.

Self-assumption

Often, if the steps of identification and analysis of the risk management process are properly applied, some exposures can be either partially or totally assumed. The first area many businesses consider for self-insurance is auto physical damage. The value of the vehicle is a known quantity, and the total loss possibilities are predictable. The size of the self-assumption level is therefore dependent upon several factors: first, the financial capabilities of the firm to absorb loss; second, the spread of exposures (how many vehicles are subject to one loss); and finally, review of the firm's claim experience.

For instance, Company A with a private passenger fleet normally had vehicles each valued new between $6,000 and $9,000. These units were usually garaged at the salesmen's homes thereby creating a wide "spread of risk." Experience for this firm showed only one total collision loss in a five-year period. There was no concentration of vehicles to produce a catastrophic risk for fire. This company felt it prudent to completely assume the risk of collision and purchased only fire and theft insurance subject to a reasonable deductible.

Bodily injury and property damage liability exposures are not usually self-insured by the average business because of statutory requirements (financial responsibility, no-fault, uninsured motorist, etc.) and catastrophic loss potential. However, many fleet operators partially assume (by deductibles) the first $250 to $10,000 of any one loss. To assume no-fault, uninsured motorist or other types of mandatory coverage may not be feasible. For instance, New Jersey has unlimited personal injury protection requirements. In addition, in practically all no-fault situations, there is no chance of any recovery against others.

Loss responsive type insurance plans (retrospective, retention) are partial self-insurance devices wherein an insurer is paid a basic premium to provide its services and guarantee against catastrophic losses, with loss costs charged back to the insured within a minimum-maximum range. Sometimes automobile exposures can be combined with general liability and workers' compensation under a combined loss responsive program in order to use the increased total applicable premium for a more attractive plan.

Transfer by noninsurance

The discussion under the heading "Avoidance or elimination of risk" indicated that by leasing vehicles, the automobile exposures might be avoided. This concept appears somewhat similar to a noninsurance transfer, that is, making someone else (transferee-leasing company) responsible for the negligent acts of drivers. This arrangement may only transfer the financial risk since the ultimate legal responsibility still remains with the transferor (the business).

A complete transferring of the ultimate legal responsibility would take place if the business used a common carrier for transportation of its goods. The public truckman becomes the transferee of virtually all of the loss exposures to which the business (transferor) would have been subject had the business undertaken or continued to make deliveries with their own vehicles. All vehicle leases, contract cartage agreements, and other equipment contracts which may have an element of automobile liability exposure should be closely examined.

RISK TRANSFER THROUGH INSURANCE

When the risk of automotive liability and property loss is transferred through purchase of insurance, the "standard" policy contract used by most insurers is the Business Auto Policy (BAP). Independently designed contracts by large insurers differ in detail, but the essence of coverage is the same as BAP.

BAP is a relatively new contract which is written in readable style, replacing previous legalistically worded policy forms. By comparison, there are fewer words, larger type and greater spacing, and informal wording (the insurer is "we" and the named insured is "you"). It is intended that precision not be sacrificed in the simplification, but the contract form is too new for the courts to have developed any body of interpretive case law.

The BAP is composed of (1) a declarations section which personalizes the details of applicable coverage; (2) the printed policy conditions which contain the insuring agreements, exclusions, and conditions; and (3) endorsements to add special provisions.

Declarations: In the declarations, there are three particular points of importance for the policyholder to understand and check. First is the identification of the named insured. It is important to set forth *all* legal entities for whom protection is desired. Affiliated or subsidiary companies are not protected unless they are named. If the business is a partnership, protection is not provided to the partners as individuals for their own vehicles or nonpartnership activities unless the partners are named as individual insureds.

The declarations list the coverages (liability, collision, etc.) available and the limit of protection afforded. Only the coverages for which a premium charge is shown are applicable. If no premium or an incorrect limit is shown for a desired coverage, a correction is indicated.

A symbol number system is used in the declarations to designate what are "covered autos" for each coverage. Entry of correct symbol numbers is critical to the properly tailored protection. An explanation of which vehicles are "covered autos" is best deferred until each of the policy coverages is defined.

Liability Insurance coverage

Liability Insurance coverage is the first coverage listed in the declarations and the one of primary importance to a business owner. This coverage pays, up to the policy limit, sums which the insured is legally obligated to pay because of bodily injury or property damage to others arising out of an accident with a covered auto. In addition, the insurer must defend insureds against claims for which there is policy coverage. Those with the status of "insured" to receive the liability protection include the named insured stated in the declarations, without qualification, and certain others on a limited basis. "Insured" means anyone using a covered auto with permission *except* (1) autos hired or borrowed from employees or their family members; (2) an automobile sales or service business for use of a covered auto (expected to have its own coverage for pickup, delivery, parking, etc., of its customers' autos); and (3) interests other than the named insured's employees, or a lessee or borrower (or their employees) of a covered auto, as to property being moved to or from the auto. Finally, anyone vicariously liable for conduct of any insured described above is also an insured, but not the owner of a covered auto which has been leased, hired, or borrowed from another (owners are expected to have their own liability protection).

Limits of liability

The limit of liability stated in the declarations is the maximum amount payable for liability claims in addition to the cost of defending against claims. BAP design contemplates a single limit for all liability in a single accident. In most states, the minimum limit is $25,000, but higher limits are more common; for example, $50,000, $100,000, $300,000, $500,000, or $1 million. Alternately, by special policy endorsement, a "split limits" approach is available. A first limit applies to the claim of each person for bodily injuries, and a second for the claims of all persons in a single accident. Separately, a limit applies for all property damage in one accident. The most common split limits required to comply with state laws are $10,000 per person and $20,000 per accident for bodily injury liability and $5,000 for property damage liability, commonly expressed as "10/20/5." Common higher split limits are 25/50, 50/100, 100/300, 250/500, 500/1,000, or higher for bodily injury and $10,000, $25,000, $50,000, $100,000, or higher for property damage.

The questions of adequacy and whether single or split limits are preferable cannot be answered in a general way because of differing needs of individual firms. It is difficult to accept, however, the concept that the smallest of businesses should operate with limits lower than $300,000 single of 100/300/50 split. If a Commercial Umbrella Policy is carried, as is recommended for most businesses (Chapter 19), the usual course is to carry the lowest limits acceptable to the umbrella insurer, as primary protection. A common umbrella requirement is for primary limits of not less than $500,000 single or 250/500/50 split. If such is the case, cost of the split limits is less than the single limit.

Exclusions

The broad grant of coverage in the insuring clause for liability insurance is modified by the exclusions. The principal function of the exclusions is to avoid coverage under the BAP for situations in which other kinds of insurance are appropriate. The contract excludes liability (1) under a workers' compensation or similar law or for injuries to an employee of the insured (for which workers' compensation and employees' liability insurance is required—Chapter 11); (2) for damage to property transported by or in the insured's care, custody, or control (inland marine cargo insurance—Chapter 5); and liability assumed under contract (contractual liability insurance—Chapter 8).

The remaining BAP exclusions remove coverage for (1) liability of an employee of the insured for causing bodily injury to another employee; (2) accidents, as to loading or unloading, before the property is accepted for loading and after completion of unloading, or from mechanical devices not attached to the vehicle; and (3) nonaccidental pollution or contamination. The first of these may cause some concern and is discussed later.

An additional provision of note in the BAP Liability Insurance section provides the policy will automatically be construed to comply with the requirements of any compulsory insurance, financial responsibility or no-fault law, when a covered auto is in a different state than the one in which licensed. Thus, the policyholder need not worry about the liability limits or no-fault law requirements of other states or Canadian provinces (the BAP applies to accidents and losses anywhere in the United States, its territories or possessions, Puerto Rico, and Canada).

No-fault coverage

The second listed coverage in the BAP declarations is Personal Injury Protection. This is the name of a mandatory coverage usually provided for under no-fault laws. If the business maintains vehicles in a no-fault state, and those vehicles are of a type subject to the law, this coverage must be included. Because each state's no-fault law is different, provisions for this coverage are not built into the BAP; a unique endorsement is available to meet the requirements of the individual state. Typically, coverage is for reimbursement of medical costs and loss of income, without regard to fault.

Medical Payments coverage

The next listed coverage is Auto Medical Payments which also requires an endorsement to the policy if the protection is desired. The coverage is for reasonable expenses incurred within three years from the date of an accident, for medical and funeral services of persons injured while occupying a covered auto (if the named insured is an individual, coverage extends to that person and relatives while occupying or if struck by another vehicle). The limit shown in the declarations applies "per person," and those available are $500, $1,000, $2,000, $5,000, $10,000, or higher. If Personal Injury Protection applies, Medical Payments coverage is normally excess over such coverage, to avoid duplication.

There are several exclusions for Auto Medical Payments, but the one of primary interest to the business owner excludes occupational injuries to employees. This exposure is covered by workers' compensation and employees' liability insurance.

The need for Auto Medical Payments coverage varies. If the only exposure is trucks and similar equipment, operated only by employees and only on the job, there is little justification for the coverage. If employees are permitted personal use of company cars, or if company cars are used to transport nonemployee guest passengers, Medical Payments coverage on these vehicles will be inexpensive and worthy of consideration.

Uninsured Motorists coverage

Uninsured Motorists insurance (UM) is the next listed coverage in the declarations, also requiring an endorsement to the BAP because of state variations. In some states the coverage is mandatory; in others, it is optional; and in others it is automatically included with liability insurance unless the insured specifically rejects it.

The intent is to place covered individuals who are injured through the fault of one who carries no liability insurance in a position to recover what would have been payable by a liability insurer. A few states cover property damage losses as well. Limits available are usually the same as those for liability (single or split).

Benefits are triggered by injuries having been caused by an "uninsured motor vehicle," which is actually a shorthand term. It means (1) a vehicle without liability insurance, or (2) a vehicle insured by an insolvent insurer, or (3) an undiscovered hit-and-run vehicle. Further (optionally in some states and basically included in others), protection is included for "underinsured motorists," which means a vehicle with liability insurance limits lower than the policyholder's UM limits. For example, if one with a $300,000 UM limit is injured by a vehicle subject to a $100,000 liability limit, the UM insured has $200,000 available as excess over the liability proceeds. If the other party's liability limit is equal to or higher than the UM limit, there is no response under UM coverage.

The persons subject to UM benefits are essentially the same as for Medical Payments—occupants of covered autos, the named insured (if an individual), and relatives if occupying or struck by other autos. Provisions are included to avoid duplication with Personal Injury Protection, Medical Payments coverages, and workers' compensation insurance. In making a claim for UM benefits, if the insurer and insured cannot agree on the question of entitlement to or measurement of tort right damages, settlement is by arbitration.

While the decision of whether or not to purchase UM coverage (if optional) is similar to the criteria for purchasing Medical Payments coverage, most buyers place a higher emphasis on UM. If a principal, employee, or guest passenger is seriously injured through the fault of one who is not insured or inadequately insured, a substantial fund for damages can be established with UM coverage.

Physical Damage coverages

There are four Physical Damage coverages listed in the BAP declarations: Comprehensive, Specified Perils, Collision, and Towing. The latter is of little interest to business owners and will not be considered further.

Comprehensive pays for loss to covered autos from any cause not excluded, except collision or overturn. Specified Perils is an alternate to Comprehensive, covering against specified perils of fire, explosion, theft, windstorm, hail, earthquake, flood, mischief, vandalism, and the sinking, burning, collision, or derailment of a conveyance transporting the auto. Collision covers loss by collision with another object or overturn.

Physical Damage coverages normally apply a limit of "actual cash value" of the covered auto, subject to a selected deductible. Unlike most forms of property insurance, wherein a specific dollar limit applies to the subject property, the limit for each covered auto is its actual cash value at time of loss, or the cost to repair or replace, whichever is less. A wide range of deductibles is available; typically $100 to $500 or higher.

Physical Damage exclusions of principal interest are wear and tear, freezing or electrical breakdown, and road damage to tires. Although coverage basically applies to all attached equipment of covered autos, loss to sound reproducing equipment such as tape decks (if not permanently installed) tapes and records are excluded. Additionally, citizen's band radios, two-way radios, telephones, and scanning monitor receivers are not covered unless permanently installed in the dash or console opening normally used by the manufacturer for the installation of a radio.

Covered autos

The description of "covered autos" is highly technical, and it is recommended that symbol selection be discussed with the agent or broker. A numerical symbol identifies each coverage. The term *auto* in the BAP means "a land motor vehicle, trailer or semi-trailer designed for travel on public roads" but does not include vehicles defined as "mobile equipment." Mobile equipment includes off-road equipment such as bulldozers, cranes, and road construction vehicles, those which are solely to provide mobility to permanently attached special equipment, unlicensed units, and those used solely on the insured's premises. These are normally covered by general liability insurance (Chapter 8) for liability and by inland marine insurance (Chapter 5) for physical damage.

There are ten covered auto symbols defined briefly as:

1. Any auto (owned, hired, leased, borrowed—literally, every auto in existence).
2. All owned autos (autos of every type owned by the named insured).
3. All owned private passenger autos (sedans, station wagons).
4. All owned autos other than private passenger types (trucks, trailers, buses, motorcycles, etc.).
5. All owned autos subject to a no-fault law in the state where they are licensed or principally garaged.
6. All owned autos subject to a compulsory uninsured motorists law.
7. Specifically described autos—those identified in the policy declarations, with 30 days' automatic coverage provided on replacements, and if the insurer covers all owned autos, 30 days' automatic coverage on newly acquired units.

8. All leased, hired, rented, or borrowed autos (except from employees or their relatives).
9. Autos not owned, leased, hired, or borrowed (except from employees and their relatives, used in connection with the named insured's business).
10. Any special category, as defined by the insurer in the policy (this could be used, for example, if a coverage were desired on owned private passenger and pickup or panel trucks but not heavier equipment, as there would be no way to make such an identification with symbols 1 through 9).

A typical BAP covering a business entity might specify in its declarations:

Liability—symbol 1.

Personal Injury Protection—symbol 5.

Auto Medical Payments—symbol 3.

Uninsured Motorists—symbol 3.

Physical Damage—Comprehensive—symbol 3.

Physical Damage—Specified Perils—symbol 4.

Physical Damage—Collision—symbol 7.

The reasoning behind such covered auto symbol selections might be:

Symbol 1:	Liability—the need to be covered for all liability, direct or vicarious, arising from existence of any auto.
Symbol 5:	Personal Injury Protection—to comply with a no-fault law for all vehicles which come under the law.
Symbol 3:	Medical Payments and UM—to cover executives, salesmen, and guest passengers in private passenger autos only; the trucks in the fleet being occupied solely by employees in the course of their duties and therefore covered by workers' compensation.
Symbols 3&4:	Comprehensive and Specified Perils—the former being applied to private passenger autos to cover "all-risks;" the latter narrower coverage (at substantially lower cost than Comprehensive) being adequate protection for commercial vehicles.
Symbol 7:	Collision—certain highly valued units identified for the coverage, the risk retained on lower valued vehicles.

What possibilities should the businessman consider? For liability insurance, the available symbols are 1, 2, 3, 4, 7, 8, and 9. It is difficult to imagine any business accepting coverage under any symbol other than 1. While covering only certain hazards is a sensible approach to other coverages, every business should take a blanket approach to its liability exposure (excepting only the largest firms which are qualified self-insurers). With symbol 1, coverage automatically applies to new vehicles acquired and discontinues earning premium on those disposed of, besides covering the variety of loss possibilities from autos owned by others. Symbol 1 includes all vehicles which would be included in all of the other symbols combined.

If a no-fault law must be complied with, symbol 5 is the only symbol which should be considered. It assures blanket compliance with the law.

The available symbols for Auto Medical Payments are 2, 3, 4, and 7. Symbol 2 might be considered if all units in the fleet are subject at any time to being occupied by persons other than employees while engaged in their occupational duties. As stated in the preceding example, 3 is a common selection to leave out commercial equipment. Symbol 4 could be an unusual choice (covering commercial vehicles but not private passenger types). Symbol 7 would be appropriate, for example, to cover only specified autos furnished to certain executives or others for their personal use.

For Uninsured Motorists, symbol 6 is the proper selection if there is a compulsory UM law in the state. Otherwise, the same possibilities and approach may be used as described for Auto Medical Payments.

The available symbols for the Physical Damage coverages are 2, 3, 4, and 7. In this area the businessman should carefully consider various possibilities on which coverages should be applied to which vehicles, and the deductible amounts to be applied. Physical Damage premiums generally comprise a significant portion of the total policy cost. Relative savings for different deductible variations are discussed later. In a sizable mixed fleet of new and old, high- and low-valued units, symbol 2 (all owned autos) might be appropriate for Specified Perils but would probably be a poor choice for Comprehensive or Collision. Without deductibles, the cost of Comprehensive is nearly double that for Specified Perils, although the less-expensive coverage includes the main noncollision perils which cause loss: fire, explosion, theft, wind, hail, earthquake, flood, and vandalism. Collision is the most expensive of the Physical Damage coverages, and retention of risk should be considered for, at least, those units with diminished values. When only certain specified units are identified for a coverage (symbol 7), it should be remembered that newly acquired additional units are not automatically covered, and 30 days' automatic coverage only applies to newly acquired replacement units. Thus, prompt action in notifying the insurer is needed when the coverage is desired on a vehicle not appearing in the policy schedule.

The following chart illustrates some choices of covered auto symbol selection for various coverages for different kinds of businesses. It is emphasized that the symbols stated are not necessarily those recommended for the described business. They are only examples of choices which might be made.

Coverage	Covered auto symbols			
	*A	*B	*C	*D
Liability	1	1	1	1
Personal Injury Protection	—	5	5	—
Auto Medical Payments	2	3	—	—
Uninsured Motorists	2	2	—	6
Comprehensive	2	3	—	3
Specified Perils	—	4	2	4
Collision	2	2	7	7

*A—A service firm owning four sedans only, no no-fault law.

*B—A retailer with two sedans and four delivery trucks in a no-fault state.

*C—A contractor with 12 trucks in a no-fault state.

*D—A manufacturer with 10 sedans and 40 trucks and trailers in a state with a compulsory UM law but not a no-fault law.

Business Auto Policy (BAP) options

Consideration is now given to options which should be considered by the buyer of commercial automobile insurance, including relative costs. The BAP coverages as basically designed are intended to meet normal, usual needs. Many businesses should consider variations.

For liability insurance

1. Limits. Base rates contemplate a single limit of $25,000 per accident. For an idea of the relative cost of higher limits, following are the increases over base rates chargeable in one representative state for trucks and trailers:

PERCENTAGE PREMIUM INCREASE OVER BASIC 25,000 LIMITS

Limit	Auto not subject to no-fault	Auto subject to no-fault
$50,000	27%	30%
$100,000	46	51
$300,000	77	86
$500,000	91	101
$1 million	112	124

These percentages vary by state and by vehicle type. If split limits are employed rather than the single limit per accident, the increases are relative. For example, limits of 250/500/100 cost more than $300,000 but less than $500,000 single limit.

2. Deductibles. Liability insurance is normally issued without deductibles. For smaller businesses, this is usually the preferred basis. Large firms, staffed with personnel qualified to adjust minor losses with claimants, may use deductibles as a premium-saving retention of risk device. Typical premium credits which apply only to the portion of the premium charged for $25,000 basic limit:

| | Premium |
Deductible	credit
$250	8%
$500	12
$1,000	17
$5,000	31
$10,000	42

3. Drive Other Car coverage (DOC). When a partner, officer, or employee operates a vehicle owned by the firm, protection is afforded to such individual by the firm's BAP liability insurance. If the individual owns a vehicle, the liability insurance on the vehicle provides protection for operating that vehicle and those owned by others. The gap which exists is a person associated with the business who does not own an automobile but may operate vehicles owned by others, not in the firm's business activities. Such individuals may be named on a Drive Other Car Endorsement to the BAP and be individually protected. Two examples: (1) an officer is furnished a company car and does not own one in his own name; and (2) an individual incorporates his small business, principally for tax purposes, and registers all vehicles in the corporate name including his personal car. When an individual is named for coverage in the DOC Endorsement, coverage also applies automatically to the spouse, if they reside together. If the individual has children or other relatives on whom coverage is desired, they must be separately named. The DOC Endorsement may include, in addition to liability insurance, Auto Medical Payments, UM, and Physical Damage.

4. Partnerships. If a partnership entity is the named insured in the BAP declarations, the policy will contain an endorsement which provides that no coverage is afforded for an auto owned personally by partners or members of their households unless a premium is charged. This restriction applies even if symbol 1 (any auto) is shown in the declarations. Liability insurance which the partners have on their own cars extend to protect the firm. It is recommended, however, that the firm include protection under its own BAP because of possibilities of inadequate limits or lapse of the policies individually held by the partners. This coverage is called Partnership Nonownership Liability and protects the firm but not the partners or their families. Thus, the coverage being provided to the firm in the BAP does not eliminate the need for the partners to individually insure.

5. Fellow-servant exclusion. BAP liability insurance covers the personal liability of employees for operation of company cars. It does not, however, cover an employee for causing bodily injury to a fellow employee while on the job. Workers' compensation provides a remedy for the employee so injured and insurers do not want to create a liability fund which would invite a lawsuit. Suppose, for example, the sales manager of the firm takes some salesmen employees to lunch in a company car and negligently injures them. Whether or not the BAP protects the manager, the salesmen may elect to exercise their common-law rights against the manager for negligence. There is no "standard" option provided, but deletion of the fellow-employee exclusion may frequently be negotiated with the insurer, and should be considered to protect key personnel.

Optional variations in Physical Damage coverages

1. Deductibles. Important premium savings may be achieved through thoughtful consideration of higher-than-standard deductibles, consistent with the firm's ability to fund or budget for the absorption of losses lower than the deductibles. The possibilities can best be demonstrated by examples of premiums. Following are base annual premiums in one territory for a new truck which costs between $20,000 and $25,000:

PREMIUMS FOR PHYSICAL DAMAGE INSURANCE WITH VARIOUS DEDUCTIBLES FOR A SELECTED TERRITORY

Coverage	Deductible	Premium
Specified Perils	None	$ 60
Comprehensive	None	113
	$ 50	79
	100	73
	250	68
	500	57
	1,000	51
Collision	100	166
	250	161
	500	135
	1,000	94

No standard basis is provided for deductibles applicable to Specified Perils, but they can be negotiated with the insurer and savings should be relative to those shown for Comprehensive. Note that coverage offered might be Comprehensive with no deductible and Collision with $100 deductible, for which the annual premium would be $113 + $166, or $299. Assuming Specified Perils would constitute adequate protection for noncollision perils, and deductible credits for Specified Perils may be secured at the same rate as those for Comprehensive, the annual premium for Specified Perils with $250 deductible and Collision with $500 deductible would be $36 + $135 or $171, which is $128 less. Depending upon usage, size, territory, and other factors, the Physical Damage premiums might be considerably higher than those illustrated, but premium differences would remain proportionately the same.

2. Limited Specified Perils. To achieve further savings on Physical Damage premiums, there are four bases to insure against noncollision perils, narrower than Specified Perils:

a. Fire, explosion, and transportation perils to a conveyance transporting the covered auto.
b. The coverage in *(a)*, plus theft.
c. The coverage in *(b)*, plus windstorm, hail, and earthquake.
d. The coverage in *(c)*, plus flood (this includes everything in Specified Perils except mischief and vandalism).

Compared to Specified Perils coverage, the cost compared to Specified Perils premiums is 35 percent for the perils in *(a)*, 60 percent for *(b)*, 70 percent for *(c)*, and 90 percent for *(d)*. For an example of maximum savings, assume an owner of a large fleet can retain the risk of loss up to the value of any single unit, that terminals are maintained where many units are garaged at one time, that none of the terminals is located in a floodprone area or where extensive damage from windstorms is expected, and that the main causes of loss are fire and explosion. In this example situation the savings to insure for fire and explosion alone would, of course, be substantial.

3. Stated amount insurance. As an alternate basis to covering each auto for its "actual cash value" under Physical Damage coverages, each auto may be insured for a specified dollar limit. There is no coverage benefit in using this approach because the insurer's maximum responsibility remains the actual cash value of the loss. However, the stated amount basis might yield some premium savings. The commercial auto insurance buyer may consider placing a dollar amount on each vehicle which would be an acceptable settlement in case of a total loss, and ask the insurance representative for an alternate quotation on that basis. If premium savings are relatively small, the actual cash value basis should be elected.

4. Sound equipment.   Special coverage may be purchased to cover automotive equipment excluded under BAP Physical Damage coverages such as citizen's band radios, two-way mobile radios, phones, and scanning monitor receivers (including antennae and other accessories) if such equipment is not permanently installed in the dash or console opening normally used by the manufacturer for installation of a radio. There is a high incidence of theft on this type of equipment, and some firms have substantial investments in these items. Optional coverage includes protection up to the actual cash value of the equipment, and no deductible otherwise applicable applies. Tapes, records, and other media used with sound reproducing equipment may also be covered, but this option is normally of little interest to the commercial insurance buyer.

5. Rental reimbursement.   Any or all of the Physical Damage coverages may be extended to cover costs for rental of a substitute vehicle when a covered auto is damaged by a covered peril. A selection is made of a desired limit to apply per day and the number of days that coverage is to apply, subject to $10 and 30 days' limit. The period for recovery begins 24 hours after the loss and continues until the vehicle can be repaired or replaced, subject to the maximum number of days selected. Only expenses which are necessarily and actually incurred are reimbursed, and the coverage does not apply if the insured has spare or reserve autos available at time of loss. The BAP Comprehensive and Specified Perils coverages basically include reimbursement of up to $10 a day for 30 days for covered autos of the private passenger type only and only for the peril of theft.

Premium computation

It is useful for the commercial auto insurance buyer to have some knowledge of how premiums are computed. One reason is that rating data for a vehicle often appears in the policy declarations and the insured may be able to detect and have corrected an error in rating which favors the insurer. Another is that in dealing with the insurer's representative, emphasis should be placed on those factors which will result in most premium favorable treatment.

Most insurers use the same rating methods, although some have independent rating plans. In most states insurers use the same base rates. Areas of flexibility which exist in the systems, however, result in sharply different final pricing. The following description applies to the "standard" method of pricing.

Owned vehicles are divided into four different rating categories:

1. Trucks, truck-tractors, trailers, and semi-trailers.
2. Private passenger types.
3. Public transportation (buses, taxis, limousine service, etc.).
4. Special types (motorcycles, ambulances, emergency vehicles, rental cars, driver training, similar special types and uses).

The information below applies to rating of Liability and Physical Damage coverages. Medical Payments and Uninsured Motorists are usually rated at simply a flat premium per vehicle; Personal Injury Protection is typically rated with the same criteria as for Liability.

1. Trucks and trailers. Rating is based on Radius Class, Size Class, Business Use Class, Special Industry Class, and Rating Territory, separately determined for each covered auto.

a. Radius class. There are three classifications, Local (not over 50 miles), Intermediate (51–200 miles), and Long Distance (over 200 miles), based on the straight-line distance from point of principal garaging to which the vehicle regularly operates. "Regularly" is not defined, giving an area of flexibility for the underwriter. A moderate interpretation would be to recognize the farthest point involving 50 percent or more of the vehicle usage, but to rate for longer distance in any event if there are four or more trips per month. Thus, if it is determined that Intermediate or Long Distance rating has been applied to a vehicle which irregularly or infrequently goes beyond a 50-mile radius, corrective action should be sought. When providing information to underwriters, make certain that limitations on operations beyond 50 or 200 miles are understood.

b. Size class. Rating for type and weight of the vehicle is wholly objective, based on gross vehicle weight or gross combination weight (the heavier the vehicle, the higher the premium).

c. Business use class. There are three classifications. The lowest rated, "Service," means no transporting of property except as incidental to the vehicle's primary purpose of carrying personnel, tools, equipment, and supplies to and from job locations. "Retail" means picking up or delivering property to individual households. Commercial includes all others and for most Size Classes is the highest rated. Again, an area of flexibility exists. Rules require rating a vehicle for its highest rated usage, but if 80 percent or more of the usage is in a lower rated class, such class applies. Thus, if a vehicle is used incidentally for retail or "commercial" deliveries and has been rated as such by the insurer, when something like 80 percent of usage qualifies for Service, it is again time to discuss corrective action.

d. Special industry class. Vehicles used by manufacturers to haul raw or finished goods, public truckers, wholesale distribution of food products, delivery subject to time constraints (newspapers, mail, film, armored cars), and those used in waste disposal are all subject to special increases from base rates. Vehicles used in farming receive a reduction. This system of classification permits another opportunity for the insurer to make an error. Note, for example, that *all* vehicles owned by a manufacturer are not subject to this higher rating—only those used to haul raw or finished products. In addition, the "80 percent rule" applies (the special higher rating should not be applied if the usage is less than 20 percent of total usage).

e. Rating territory. The street address where the vehicle is principally garaged dictates the rating territory to be applied (except in the case of Long Distance, wherein rates for the territories at terminal points are considered). Rates vary widely by territory (including those adjacent to one another) so it is important that the determination of the principal garaging point be made properly.

f. Cost and age. The original cost new and age of the vehicle enter into development of Physical Damage premiums. These criteria, of course, relate to the value of the vehicle.

As an indication of how important it is to be certain the insurer is rating on full information, assume a manufacturer with a medium-sized truck, in response to the insurer's question, responds it is used for trips up to 150 miles to deliver goods. Actually, trips over 50 miles are infrequent and the truck is mainly used for utility, nondelivery purposes around the plant. If rated at Intermediate radius, Commercial usage, and "manufacturer hauling goods," the premium will be 180 percent higher than the Local-Service-"no Special Industry Class" rating which would actually be proper.

2. Private passenger types. Rating depends only upon rating territory, original cost new, and age.

3. Public transportation. Rates vary by type of vehicle (taxi, bus, etc.) and by seating capacity, in each rating territory.

4. Special types. These vehicles are "flat rated" in each rating territory, based on type of usage. For example, an ambulance is subject to a higher rate and farm equipment carries a very low rate.

Supplemental to the basic rating described above, underwriters employ "individual risk rating plans" which provide broad flexibility in pricing. All but the smallest of businesses are eligible for rating under these plans as they typically permit application to ownership of as few as five vehicles.

An "experience rating plan" provides reductions or increases for the prior loss history of the business. A "schedule rating plan" allows the underwriter to recognize features such as management practices, preventive maintenance, and driver safety programs (or lack thereof) with premium *reductions* or *increases* up to 25 percent. While on the surface these plans seem to apply objective criteria to establish a final premium, their application leaves fairly complete freedom for the underwriter to charge what he wishes. For a profitable account, that means a price which the underwriter hopes will be competitively attractive to the prospect.

Businesses which pay substantial auto insurance premiums may also consider a "retrospective rating plan," sometimes called cost-plus insurance. A basic premium is guaranteed to the insurer, to which is added losses and loss adjustment expense to determine the final premium, subject to an agreed minimum and maximum. The operation of retrospective rating plans is discussed in Chapter 11 as they are most commonly applied for workers' compensation insurance.

Finally, premiums for the BAP are subject to audit. That means the insurer may, but is not required to, look at the operations as they apply to the BAP annually to adjust the premium. The BAP automatically covers some autos, depending on the symbol selected. The audit may *increase* or *decrease* the initial premium.

QUESTIONS TO BE ASKED AGENT OR BROKER

I. Exposure and coverage
  A. Liability
    1. Are all vehicles (owned, leased, hired, borrowed, nonowned) covered?
    2. Are all "entities" included as "named insureds"? "Entity" means all subsidiary and/or affiliated companies, lessors, and all others having an insurable interest.
    3. Are all compulsory state requirements met—Uninsured Motorist, Personal Injury Protection, NoFault, Compulsory Liability?
    4. Are statutory filing requirements (DOT, PUC, Others) complied with?
    5. Is there any family need for Drive Other Car coverage?
    6. Are limits adequate? This question applies to (a) underlying requirements when an umbrella policy is written over the primary BAP or (b) if there is no umbrella or excess policy and the BAP provides the entire protection program. The usual minimum requirements for (a) would be either $300,000 or $500,000 CSL (Combined Single Limit) and (b) $1,000,000 CSL.
  B. Physical Damage
    1. What is the actual cash value of each vehicle? Is there a concentration of vehicles (garaging location) subject to one large loss?
    2. Is Comprehensive coverage needed? Can more limited

Specified Perils coverage be purchased instead of Comprehensive?

3. Does Collision exposure present a catastrophic risk?

C. Other

1. Is medical payments coverage needed (employee personal usage, nonemployee guest, passengers)?

II. Retention and rating

1. Where are there areas for potential savings? What are the premium reductions for deductibles (retention) in bodily injury and property damage? Can the Physical Damage deductible be increased for greater assumption of risk? Does the past loss record help in determining various retention levels? Is there any duplication of coverage? (Medical Payments versus workers' compensation.) Is there any coverage that can be completely self-assumed (retained)?

2. Is the current BAP policy experienced rated? What is the rating? Credit or debit? How does this compare to the actual premiums versus losses for the past four years?

3. Is any type of "loss responsive" plan available, either separately for automobile or combined with general liability and/or workers' compensation, retrospective, dividend-loss ratio, and so on?

III. Loss control

1. Has an individual been appointed to be responsible for fleet safety operations?

2. Are personnel files maintained for each driver? Do files contain a copy of the Motor Vehicle Record for each driver? Is there a regular driver selection procedure?

3. How regularly are the vehicles serviced? Are driver defect reports used?

4. Are fleet safety engineers available for guidance from your insurance company and/or agent/broker?

NOTES

1. "Automobiles" and "Auto" used through this chapter refer to all types of vehicles which could be used by businesses such as private passenger cars, station wagons, vans, pickups, panel trucks, campers, motor homes, straight trucks, tractors, trailers, semi-trailers, buses, and others.

2. The insurance policy description and coverage analysis refers to the Business Auto Policy (BAP). This policy was introduced in 1978 by Insurance Services Offices and is in use by most insurers.

   The BAP has been approved for use by insurance companies in every state; however, some specialty markets issue policy forms of their own design. Since the BAP is so widely accepted by the great majority of insurers, it was chosen for discussion here.

CHAPTER 10

TRUCKERS LIABILITY AND GARAGE RISKS

WHAT ARE THE EXPOSURES?
  Bodily injury and property damage
    liability
  Cargo exposure
  General Liability coverage
  Workers' compensation

OPTIONAL COVERAGES AND
EXPOSURES (REQUIRED IN SOME
STATES)
  Uninsured Motorists coverage
  No-fault personal injury protection
    insurance
  Physical Damage (Fire/Theft,
    Specified Perils and Collision)

POLICY CONSTRUCTION AND RATING

WHAT THE GENERAL
LIABILITY–AUTOMOBILE POLICY
GIVES THE INSURED
  Policy terms most often used
  Who is covered under the insuring
    agreement
  Coverage provided

Major exclusions
Special exclusions by endorsement

CARGO INSURANCE
  Available protection
  Handling cargo claims

SPECIAL GOVERNMENTAL
REGULATIONS

SAFETY DEPARTMENTS OF
INSURANCE COMPANIES

WHAT TO DO WHEN AN ACCIDENT
OCCURS

HOW TRUCKING INSURANCE IS
MARKETED

THE GARAGE POLICY
  Bodily Injury and Property Damage
    coverage and exclusions
  Garagekeeper coverage and
    exclusions
  Physical damage insurance and
    exclusions
  Medical Payments coverage

Charles T. Bidek
Assistant Executive Director
Insurors of Tennessee
Nashville, Tennessee

Charles T. Bidek is Assistant Executive Director of Insurors of Tennessee, a producer trade association. He has taught insurance at Bowling Green State University, Ohio State University, and the University of Tennessee. Mr. Bidek holds a B.S. and an M.B.A. from Ohio State University.

James C. Blanton
President
Carolina Casualty Insurance Company
Jacksonville, Florida

James Cleveland Blanton, Jr., is President and Director of Carolina Casualty Insurance Company, Jacksonville, Florida. He attended Wingate College, Wingate, North Carolina; University of South Carolina where he received a B.A. degree; and also attended the University of South Carolina School of Law. He attended the Mississippi College of Law, Jackson, Mississippi, where he received a L.L.B. degree. He also did special studies at the University of Maryland. Mr. Blanton is a member of the Mississippi Bar Association, the American Bar Association, the Federation of Insurance Counsel, and the International Association of Insurance Counsel. He is a member of the Jacksonville, Florida, Chamber of Commerce, as well as a member of the Committee of 100. He is a member of the Meninak Club, Jacksonville, Florida. He is a Director and Past-President of the Florida Insurance Council, Tallahassee, Florida; and he is President and Chairman of the board of Commercial General Agency, Jacksonville, Florida. Mr. Blanton is on the Board of Directors of The Sun Bank of Jacksonville, Florida. He is a Governor of the International Insurance Seminars and is Past-President of the Truck and Heavy Equipment Claim Council. Mr. Blanton started his insurance career with Allstate Insurance Company in Jackson, Mississippi. He joined Carolina Casualty in 1962 in the Legal Department.

The coverages for long-haul trucking are basically the same as for other commercial vehicles, although long-haul trucking, from an insurance standpoint, is different and often unique. Insuring a long-haul trucking operation can be a complex and sometimes perplexing task. This chapter will explain the coverages afforded the long-haul trucker by the insurance industry and discuss some of the complexities unique to this particular area.

The differences between the terms *long-haul trucking, intermediate trucking,* and *local trucking* are almost self-explanatory except for rating purposes. A truck that transports commodities in excess of 300 miles radius from its point of garaging is considered a long-haul truck. Vehicles hauling between 50 and 300 miles are rated intermediate, and those less than 50 miles are considered local operations. The types of vehicles vary according to the commodity being transported as well as the distance traveled, which are important when determining exposure.

WHAT ARE THE EXPOSURES?

Although the basic insurance coverage in a long-haul trucking operation is the same as for regular commercial vehicles, the coverage required can be unique in that the exposure is usually subjected to jurisdictional requirements of the different states in which the trucker travels as well as the requirements of the Interstate Commerce Commission. State requirements vary, particularly in the area of uninsured motorists, no-fault coverage, and limits required. Some of these exposures, particularly those having to do with public safety, are required by law to be insured. In contrast, physical damage exposures are a personal loss and therefore insurance is not required. If a mortgage exists, however, the mortgagee will most certainly require Physical Damage coverage to protect its financial interest. There are other coverages available which provide protection against a variety of other exposures. They provide protection for the public as well as protection against personal loss while affording a number of insurance options depending upon the needs of the insured.

Bodily injury and property damage liability

Primarily, this is damage to a third party, either through injury or damage to his property. Liability is the most serious exposure faced by the trucker to the public. This simply means that if the trucker's vehicle is involved in an accident and there is injury to a person or persons or property, the trucker can be held responsible if legally liable. Even if liability is questionable, the trucker is subject to suit, and the question of liability is determined by a jury or a judge. Most states, and the Interstate Commerce Commission, require that this exposure be insured. The limits vary among the states, but are uniform with the ICC. The most common required limits are $100,000 for each person injured, $300,000 for all injuries suffered in the accident, and $50,000 for property damage, or 100/300/50 as it is also known. Most insurance companies write far higher limits based on the desires and needs of the insured. The trend in most states is toward higher statutory limits. For example, the state of California requires limits of 250/500/100.

Cargo exposure

A trucker hauling goods for others is responsible for these goods and is required by some states and the ICC to insure this responsibility. Evidence of this insurance must be filed with the state and with the ICC. Most states do not require filings on "exempt commodities" such as produce, grains, and fruits, although there are some exceptions. If a long-haul trucker maintains terminals and stores cargo, Cargo Terminal coverage is required.

General Liability coverage

This is liability arising out of the operation of the trucker's premises, such as a terminal or office. The coverage can extend to independent contractors and employees of the trucking firm.

Workers' compensation

Most states require by law that truckers have workers' compensation coverage. This covers an employee while he is involved in the scope of his employment. The number of employees usually determines whether workers' compensation is required.

OPTIONAL COVERAGES AND EXPOSURES (REQUIRED IN SOME STATES)

Uninsured Motorists coverage

This coverage is for the benefit of the insured. It covers the insured and the occupants of his vehicle when they are involved in an accident with an uninsured auto. This coverage usually applies only to the bodily injury of the occupants. Property damage is usually insured optionally, but in some states it is required.

No-fault personal injury protection insurance

This is a fairly new coverage and is not always required on commercial vehicles, depending on the state of operation. It covers injury or death to the occupants of the insured vehicle. The amount of coverage and limitations are determined by the laws in a given state.

Physical Damage (Fire/Theft, Specified Perils and Collision)

This coverage is optional and is written freely by most insurers. Lien holders of the insured's equipment usually require some Physical Damage coverage. The amount is determined by the value of the vehicle. The coverage is written with varied deductibles, for example, $250, $500, and $1,000.

POLICY CONSTRUCTION AND RATING

Most long-haul trucking insurance, other than cargo, is written on the General Liability–Automobile Policy or a close variation. Some companies use policies that are specially designed for a particular trucking firm. All coverages permissible under the policy are shown on the face or declarations sheet. Those coverages applicable under a given policy are shown by a charge on the face sheet. Coverages are explained separately by endorsements attached to the policy. The face sheet of the policy, in addition to showing the coverages included, shows the name and address of the insured, the policy number, the dates of coverage, and the form of business venture in which the insured is engaged (an individual, partnership, corporation, joint venture, etc.). The policy must be signed by an authorized representative of the company as well as countersigned by an agent in the state of issue.

A policy can be written in three different ways, the difference being the way in which the policy is rated for premium purposes:

1. *Specified car.* This type of policy lists all equipment owned or leased, and the premium is charged on each individual power unit. There is a separate charge for the trailer, usually 10 percent of the charge for the power unit.
2. *Reporting form.*
   a. *Gross receipts.* The premium is based on a percentage of each $100 gross revenue on all owned or leased equipment.
   b. *Gross mileage.* The premium is based on the number of miles driven (loaded or unloaded) on all owned or operated equipment.
3. *Retrospective.* The premium is calculated by using either the

specified vehicle or the reporting form basis, but the final premium is determined by the loss experience of the account (claims and expenses paid).

WHAT THE GENERAL LIABILITY-AUTOMOBILE POLICY GIVES THE INSURED

The insuring agreement of the policy states the terms and conditions of the policy and defines specific terms that are used extensively in the policy. An understanding of these terms is of great importance. The insuring agreement clearly states the obligations and rights of the insured and the insurance company; it shows what is insured, the limits of coverage, who is insured, and the definition of the terms, as well as the exclusions contained in the policy.

Policy terms most often used

1. *Automobile.* A land motor vehicle, trailer, or semi-trailer designed for travel on public roads.
2. *Bodily injury.* Bodily injuries, sickness, disease, or death sustained by any person during the policy period arising out of the use of the automobile.
3. *Named insured.* Person or organization named in the declaration of the policy.
4. *Occurrence.* An accident, including continuous or repeated exposures to conditions which result in bodily injury or property damage neither expected or intended from the standpoint of the insured.
5. *Property damage.* Physical injury to, or destruction of, tangible property which occurs during the policy period, including the loss of use of this property. This property must belong to a third party and must not be under the care, custody, or control of the insured at the time of the accident.
6. *Temporary substitute automobile.* An automobile not owned by the named insured or any resident of the same household, while temporarily used with the permission of the owner as a substitute for an owned automobile when withdrawn from normal use for servicing or repair because of its breakdown, loss, or destruction.
7. *Newly acquired automobile.* An owned automobile, newly acquired by the named insured during the policy period, provided (a) it replaces another owned automobile, or (b) the company insures all automobiles owned by the named insured on the date of such acquisition, and the named insured notifies the company within 30 days thereafter of his election to make that and no other

policy issued by the company applicable to such automobile and pays any additional premium required because of the acquisition of the new vehicle.

Who is covered under the insuring agreement

1. The named insured, meaning the insured shown on the face of the policy.
2. Any partner or executive officer of the named insured.
3. Any other person while using an owned automobile or temporary substitute vehicle with permission of the named insured.
4. With respect to bodily injury or property damage arising out of the loading or unloading, such other persons shall be an insured only if he is a lessee or borrower of the vehicle or an employee of the named insured or such lessee or borrower.

Coverage provided

1. *Automobile Medical Payments (Med Pay) coverage.* Covers the insured or any family member while occupying or, while a pedestrian, when struck by any truck or automobile. The policy also covers anyone else occupying a covered vehicle or temporary substitute for a covered vehicle. Med Pay coverage pays reasonable expenses incurred for necessary medical and funeral services to or for an insured who sustains bodily injury caused by accident.
2. *Automobile Physical Damage (Fleet Automatic) coverage.* This coverage is specifically designed for fleet operations and provides a designated limit on newly acquired vehicles wherein numerous changes make coverage difficult to control. It maximizes values and controls catastrophic loss limits.
3. *Automobile Physical Damage (Nonfleet) coverage.* This coverage provides a specific limit of liability for each scheduled vehicle. This is generally used for the smaller trucking operation.
4. *Basic Automobile Liability Insurance coverage.* This form of coverage usually provides liability insurance for the smaller trucking operation. The perils covered are specified and limited to vehicles scheduled in the policy.
5. *Comprehensive Automobile Liability Insurance coverage.* This form of liability insurance is primarily used for the large fleet operations. It provides automatic coverage for all owned and operated vehicles used in the business of the insured. This form of coverage generally lists vehicles by category rather than specifically scheduling each unit. It is usually found in the reporting form or retrospective rated-type policy.

6. *Owner, Landlords, and Tenants Liability and Manufacturers and Contractors Liability Insurance coverage.* This is a form of general liability insurance. Protection provided is typical to a fleet operation. It provides coverage for the insured's premises in much the same way as a Homeowners' Policy applies to a homeowner. Coverage is afforded for accidents which arise out of the existence of the insured's property (automobile excluded) such as terminals, offices, and so on.

Major exclusions

The General Automobile–Liability Policy has several general exclusions. There are sometimes special exclusions added by endorsement to the policy.

1. The liability portion of the policy does not insure for liability assumed by the insured under any contract or agreement. *Special attention should be paid to this exclusion when a trucking firm is either lessor or lessee.*
2. Any obligation for which the insured or any other trucking firm, as his insured, may be held liable under any workers' compensation, unemployment compensation, or disability benefit.
3. Bodily injury to an employee of the insured arising out of the course of his employment by the insured.
4. Property owned or being transported by the insured, or property rented to the insured or in his care, custody, or control.
5. Bodily injury or property damage due to war, civil war, insurrection, or rebellion or revolution.
6. Bodily injury or property damage arising out of the ownership, maintenance, or operation of a vehicle when used as a public or livery conveyance unless specifically declared and described.
7. Bodily injury or property damage arising out of discharge and release of smoke unless sudden or accidental.

Special exclusions by endorsement

1. Most policies exclude by endorsement the hauling of explosives unless specifically underwritten.
2. Refrigeration units unless specifically described.
3. Bodily injury or death to a passenger.
4. Drivers specifically excluded. Drivers can be excluded due to a bad driving record.
5. Wrong delivery of liquid products (such as, delivering a load of gasoline to the wrong storage tank).

Note: All special exclusions by an insurance company should be filed and approved by the state insurance department in the state in which they plan to use the exclusion. If the exclusion is not approved, its validity is questionable.

CARGO INSURANCE

The importance of adequate and proper motor truck cargo insurance should be of paramount concern to the management of the trucking firm. The purpose of cargo insurance is to cover the liability assumed by the trucker under a bill of lading, shipping receipt, or lease, while goods are in the care, custody, and control of the trucker from the point of shipment to their ultimate destination or receiver. Further, it is intended to provide protection while shipments are held by the trucker at its warehouse or terminal. Clearly the individual trucking firm should seek to secure adequate protection for all risks that it assumes while in possession of the goods of others.

Available protection

The protection available varies from coverages applicable to the individual units owned or operated by a firm under a specified peril basis, to all-risks coverage where any type of loss is insured against while the cargo is on any vehicle owned or operated by the trucking firm. The trucking firm should confer with the Risk Manager or the appropriate insurance representative to be certain that the coverages under the insurance contract adequately and uniformly protect the type of goods carried and the exposures assumed. In addition, the appropriate selection of deductible clauses and the election to self-insure part of the cargo by co-insurance provisions should be discussed and evaluated in light of the benefits each would have to the specific firm.

Handling cargo claims

A working relationship between the trucking firm and a knowledgeable insurance agent should be established so that each party is aware of procedures necessary for appropriate handling of cargo claims. In this manner, each will be working for the maximum benefit of the other, and dialogue will mitigate many disagreements. Most disagreements in the handling of claims arise from the lack of communication between management, the firm's agent or broker, and the representative of the insurance company. If each understands that their primary concern is to establish the cargo damage, protect the interests of the trucking firm, and pay the appropriate cargo claim, then all other tangential questions can be easily and quickly answered. After all, it is the establishment of a good working relationship that aids the processing of any claim presented by either the shipper or the receiver.

The insurance company should be made aware of the type of business operation conducted by the trucking firm so that the needed information at a time of loss can be handled with the minimum of delays. Generally, in order to handle a claim from the shipper or consignee, the trucking firm and the insurance company need the same information, which usually can be obtained from the original invoice, the statement of claim, or the freight bill.

The insurance company, in order to properly handle a claim, will require two additional documents: the bill of lading or shipping receipt, and the lease agreement, if applicable.

Once all this information is supplied, the trucking firm, as well as the insurer, will be able to process any claim presented against the trucker. Many shippers and consignees, because of the size and scope of their operation, have, pursuant to Interstate Commerce Commission (ICC) rules, nine months to present a claim. It may therefore be necessary for the trucking firm to hire an independent adjuster to verify the damages to protect its interests when a claim is presented.

The cargo insurance contract is an indemnification policy and is intended to reimburse the trucking firm for claims which it has paid. Generally, each claim is subject to an individual deductible which is elected by the trucking firm at time of inception of the policy. The liability of the insurance company is to the trucking firm and not to the shipper or consignee making the claim. However, in many instances, the insurance company may reserve the right to settle any claims presented against the insured by dealing directly with the claimant.

The importance of adequate and appropriate protection cannot be over emphasized. Trucking firms not only have a duty to the general public (as a bailee in charge of goods) but in addition, the Interstate Commerce Commission has established insurance requirements for trucking firms which must be met.

SPECIAL GOVERNMENTAL REGULATIONS

All truckers hauling interstate are subject to the rules and regulations of the Interstate Commerce Commission with the exception of truckers hauling exempt commodities. The ICC requires that truckers have insurance coverage by a company approved by the Commission with limits of liability no less than $100,000 for each person injured in an accident, $300,000 for all persons injured in a single accident, and

$50,000 property damage. Evidence of liability coverage must be filed directly with the ICC by the trucker's insurance company. Evidence of cargo insurance coverage is also required in most circumstances and must be filed directly by the insurance company.

All truckers hauling in a given state are subject to the rules and regulations of the Public Utilities Commission in that particular state. The required limits for liability exposures vary in each state. Half of the states require minimum liability limits of 100/300/50 with some states requiring higher limits. Minimum limits must be determined by specifically checking each state.

The State Departments of Transportation are interested primarily in safety on their highways. Truckers hauling interstate are subject to the rules and regulations of these agencies and are subject to fines or other penalties for failure to adhere to these standards.

SAFETY DEPARTMENTS OF INSURANCE COMPANIES

Most insurance companies insuring truckers have safety engineering departments. These departments work directly with insureds in an effort to prevent losses and to improve overall safety programs. Cooperation with these safety engineers is beneficial to a trucker in that loss ratios most often determine rates charged.

The engineer can aid the insured in setting up a complete and detailed safety program, but in order for a safety program to be successful, it must have the full support of the management of the trucking firm. With management support the engineer can assist the insured by conducting safety meetings, furnishing road observation reports, making equipment inspections, and developing detailed accident analyses.

WHAT TO DO WHEN AN ACCIDENT OCCURS

When an accident or loss occurs, it is the responsibility of the insured or the driver to report the occurrence as quickly as possible. This is extremely important since it is a condition of the insurance policy that all accidents or losses, regardless of severity, be reported to the company. It is also important to understand the reasons behind this reporting requirement.

All too often, what appears to be a minor or insignificant loss is ignored by the trucker and a prompt report is not given to the insurance company. When this happens, the initial evidence and testimony is not available to the insurance company's claim department. The result is that the insurer's ability to properly investigate and protect the interests of the trucker is severely hampered. When an accident or loss occurs, it is important to follow a strict practice of reporting any and all accidents regardless of fault or severity and to obtain as much information as possible at the scene of the accident. With this assistance from the insured, insurance companies can make a prompt and proper determination on all losses.

It is important to remember that a condition of the policy is that insureds cooperate fully with the company in all aspects of that investigation. Failure to report accidents or provide the necessary cooperation when dealing with a claim department may serve to jeopardize the policy coverage. The insurance company claim department has the insured's best interest at heart. Open exchange of relative information is important to all parties.

When an accident occurs:

1. Gather as much information at the scene as possible, recording names and addresses of all parties involved plus names and addresses of witnesses.
2. Immediately report the accident or loss to the insurance company claim department or one of its authorized representatives.
3. Give complete cooperation to the insurance company claim adjuster or investigator in all aspects of their investigation.
4. If a lawsuit is filed, it is a condition of the policy that all documents be immediately forwarded to the insurance company. It is suggested that they be forwarded by registered mail.

HOW TRUCKING INSURANCE IS MARKETED

Trucking insurance is written by most large casualty insurance companies, as well as several specialty companies specializing in the long-haul trucking or transportation business. These companies market insurance through four different methods:

1. *By local agents.* Local agents are those who deal primarily in trucking insurance (or other specialized lines) and have contracts directly with insurance companies. These agents can bind coverages as well as issue policies. Local agents are self-employed.
2. *By general agents.* General agents never deal directly with the insured. General agents usually represent several different companies for many different lines of insurance. Most general agents who handle trucking insurance are well versed in their specialty lines but accept trucking insurance business only from local agents or brokers. The general agent has authority to bind the company and usually authority to issue policies.
3. *By a broker.* A broker represents only the insured and deals either

with a general agent or directly with the company. Brokers do not have authority to bind and do not issue policies.
4. *By a direct writer.* A direct writer (Insurance Company) deals directly with the trucker through its own employee agents.

Trucking insurance is a highly specialized business. Truckers are urged to deal only with representatives and companies who understand the complexities of the trucking insurance business. Bodily injury, property damage, physical damage, and cargo insurance are the lifeblood of a trucker. Coverages not written correctly and exposures not covered properly can result in unexpected and severe financial loss.

THE GARAGE POLICY

The term *garage risks* is applicable to automobile dealers, commercial garages, repair shops, service stations, and parking facilities. The modern garage policy is a package designed to cover most liability situations arising from auto accidents and situations particular to garage operations. Additionally, the garage policy makes it possible to insure physical damage to the business's automobiles. This package combination of automobile and general liability is unique. The purpose of this combination is to avoid duplication of coverage and intercompany disputes over which the insurer is liable for a specific accident. The policyholder benefits from this package policy if the policy is written to handle garage risks the individual needs.

Specific needs are addressed by specific policy sections and additional endorsements are required. The majority of garage risks needs are addressed in policy sections of Bodily Injury and Property Damage, Garagekeepers Insurance, and Physical Damage Insurance. Additionally, most garage policies are endorsed with a Medical Payments section.

Bodily Injury and Property Damage coverage and exclusions

This coverage, referred to as BI and PD, provides coverage for liability situations arising from garage operations and automobiles. Coverage provided for automobile accidents is essentially the same as that provided by any automobile policy—coverage is provided for situations where the insured is found to be legally liable.

The options available to an insured are for coverage from owned autos only or for all autos whether owned or nonowned. Although intuition suggests that there be little need to insure against nonowned exposures, practice dictates otherwise. It is imperative that the businessman secure coverage for autos which are not owned. An illustration of a nonowned exposure is where a service station owner asks an employee to use his personal car to pick up parts. While enroute, the employee has an accident. It is possible that liability for the accident (or part of it) can be attributed to the service station owner. Even if the suit proves groundless, the legal defense could prove costly. Few, if any, garages are immune from nonowned auto expenses.

In addition to automobile liability coverage provided in the Bodily Injury and Property Damage Coverage section, coverage is also provided for any acts resulting from garage operations. General Liability and Products Liability coverage is provided by this section, but coverage is provided only for incidents arising from garage operations. Businesses operated in conjunction with garage operations are not covered. For example, a service station along an interstate highway adds a gift shop. The garage policy would cover accidents occurring in the garage area but not in the gift shop. To cover the liability exposure in the gift shop, separate policies are needed.

It is important to describe the entire business operation to your agent or company representative so that uninsured gaps are not left in your insurance program. Should any changes be made in the business operation, it is wise to contact your agent or company to ascertain whether coverage is provided by the policy or a special endorsement or new policy is required.

Exclusions are common to all insurance policies, and the BI and PD section of the garage policy is no exception. Most of the garage policy's exclusions deal with situations where an insured's employee is injured. These exclusions should not cause concern because this exposure is usually insured by workers' compensation or employers' liability insurance, which is often mandated by state law and purchased separately. In addition to the "employees" exclusions, there is an exclusion for damage to property left in the care, custody, and control of the business. This is a crucial exclusion to all garages, service stations, dealerships, and parking facilities. Fortunately, this coverage is available on a "buy-back" basis as a separate policy section.

Three major exclusions not usually available on a buy-back basis and that can result in an uninsured exposure are liability assumed under contract, racing exclusion, and autos leased or rented to others.

Liability assumed under contract is when a businessman signs or verbally agrees in advance to accept liability that may arise from a particular situation. For example, assume a dealer agrees to pick up vehicles at the factory, which will be owned by the manufacturer. If while delivering those vehicles, an accident occurs, there would be no coverage if the dealer had agreed in advance with the manufacturer that the dealer would accept all responsibility. An agreement such as this, known as hold-harmless agreements, will need a special policy or endorsement for coverage to be provided. It is wise not to sign or enter into an agreement of this type without submitting the entire agreement to legal counsel, as well as your agent and/or insurance company for possible coverage implications.

The racing exclusion deals with automobiles that are being used in racing or stunt events or being prepared for such events. Numerous dealerships and garages allow their names to be associated with this type of vehicle or in some cases actually own vehicles of this type. If this is the case, a separate policy should be secured. The advantages of advertising and goodwill can dissipate quickly in the face of an uninsured loss.

If the garage operation leases or rents cars to others, separate coverage is required. However, this exclusion does not apply if the leased or rented automobile is provided while a customer's auto is being repaired or left for service. The purpose of this exclusion is to separate pure leasing operations into a separate category where a separate policy or a special endorsement is required, together with an additional premium. It is suggested that whenever a garage risk considers leasing or renting automobiles, notice be given to the agent or company representative.

The amount of coverage should be carefully selected, and the amount of insurance purchased should be discussed with the agent or company representative. Where higher limits are desired than the limits obtainable from the garage policy insurer, it may be necessary for your agent to secure an additional layer of coverage, often referred to as an excess or an umbrella policy. Here the company writing the upper layer will dictate the amount of insurance to be written.

Garagekeeper coverage and exclusions

The care, custody, and control exclusion of the BI and PD section of the garage policy creates the need for this section of the contract. Garagekeepers' coverage, formerly known as garagekeepers' legal liability, is an optional coverage available in the garage contract. In a sense it can be thought of as buying back the care, custody, and control exclusion in the BI and PD section.

Although the section is a liability coverage, it resembles Physical Damage coverages purchased for automobiles. The coverage is designed to provide Physical Damage coverage on automobiles left by customers on the premises for repair, storage, and so forth, which the businessman can be held legally liable for. For an additional premium, the business can secure coverage not only for acts that the business is legally liable for but also for acts it is not legally liable for that occur while the automobile is in the business's care, custody, and control. To illustrate, a customer might leave his car overnight at a dealership for service the next day. During the night a hailstorm damages the auto. It is doubtful that the car's owner could prove legal liability against the dealer. However, for public relations reasons, the dealer might want to pay for the damage that resulted. This option to the policy is known as direct coverage and is available in two forms. One form (the less expensive) pays only if there is no other insurance covering the loss. The other form makes the direct coverage primary and replaces any other available insurance. It is advisable to consider direct coverage, for removing the question of legal liability often results in speedier claim payments from the insurer.

To offset the additional cost of direct coverage it is wise to consider the largest deductible that businesses' cash flow can withstand for large premium credits are available for deductibles. Deductible pricing does not follow a linear progression.

The coverages available under the Garagekeepers' section are Specified Perils, Comprehensive, and Collision. Collision coverage pays for losses caused by collision with another object and includes upset. For an additional premium, the business can add Collision coverage for other than the auto (i.e., articles contained in the auto).

Specified Perils and Comprehensive coverage insurance offer two ways to handle noncollision losses. Specified Perils covers damage caused by fire, explosion, theft, mischief, or vandalism. Comprehensive coverage covers for all situations except those specifically excluded. Since theft and vandalism constitute many losses at parking facilities, garages, dealerships, and so forth, many businesses find the reduction in premium an inducement to purchase Specified Perils coverage. Before purchasing either Comprehensive or Specified Perils coverage, it is wise to secure a quote for each and, with the help of the insurer, evaluate the needs of the business.

The exclusions to the Garagekeepers' section are few but nonetheless noteworthy. Assuming liability under a contract (a hold-harmless agreement) is excluded. You must be certain that any type of bailment certificate given to your customer does not accept liability, and your form of ticket should be reviewed with counsel.

Additional exclusions state that the insurance company is not liable for theft losses by anyone associated with the garage. Fidelity coverage is available to handle this exposure if desired.

An exclusion which cannot be handled through the insurance mechanism is the one that excludes faulty work performed by the garage. Faulty parts and materials are likewise excluded. The rationale for these exclusions is to ensure the continued interest on the part of the business operator to perform satisfactory work.

Particular items which have demonstrated special theft exposure are likewise excluded. Citizen's band radios which are not installed in the normal dash opening for a radio, and tape players (not permanently installed) and tapes are excluded from coverage. These coverages are available from some insurers on a buy-back basis, but most insureds find the cost prohibitive. Many garages attempt to alleviate this problem by having customers remove these articles prior to leaving the vehicle.

The premium a business pays for garagekeepers insurance will depend upon whether the direct coverage option or the Specified Perils or the Comprehensive option is selected, as well as the size of the deductibles selected. In addition, it will depend on a host of variables over which the insured may not have control. For example, concentration of values is a variable that the insured may have little control over, but will affect the premium. Concentration of values is the average worth of the vehicles received in bailment and the number of locations. In general, the higher the concentration of values in a single location, the higher the premium.

Storage environment and ignition key control are two variables the business does have some control over. Since vandalism and theft are the most frequent losses to garagekeepers, meaningful modification to the storage environment usually develops the largest policy credits. A well-lighted and fenced area patrolled frequently by police is desirable. It makes sense to check with the insurance company as to what reductions in premium are available for certain storage environment modifications. Often the cost of these modifications can be partially offset by premium reductions. It is imperative to work closely with insurers on these changes as insurers can be very particular over what type of modification qualifies for a credit, as for example, the height of the fence.

Ignition key control is another variable that an insured often has some control over. Good key control is essential in large garage risk particularly in urban areas. More and more garages are requiring positive identification before returning the vehicle to the customer in an effort to achieve better key control.

Physical damage insurance and exclusions

To this point, we have been developing situations whereby the garage operator is held liable for various actions or desires to voluntarily assume losses to others. Physical damage insurance is designed to protect the garage's own vehicles. Coverage is available on a specified car or an all-vehicle basis. Specified car coverage is used when the number of vehicles insured remains relatively stable and the vehicles insured remain the same (i.e., a service station with two trucks). However, when a used car lot or a new car dealership is insured, they are usually insured for all vehicles on the basis of value. Rates are quoted per $100 of value.

The coverages available are similar to those discussed in the Garagekeepers' section: Collision, Comprehensive, and Specified Perils coverage. Specified Perils coverage is expanded to cover wind, hail, and earthquake. Additionally, coverage is provided if an auto is damaged while being transported. Just as in the Garagekeepers' section, fire, theft, vandalism, and explosion are covered. Because of premium differences, many businesses tend to accept Specified Perils coverage rather than Comprehensive. It is suggested that price quotations be acquired for both coverages. Various deductible strategies can reduce premium payments.

Since inventories of vehicles change, the prices charged for physical damage insurance are subject to audit. That is, the premium paid for the coverage is merely a deposit (hence called deposit premium). At the end of the policy period the business's records are examined for the average amount of inventory and the deposit premium is credited to a final charge which is made by the rendering of an additional bill or a refund. In order to avoid shocking bills at audit, it is wise to estimate as accurately as possible the anticipated average values with an allowance calculated for price increases and dealership growth. Using the past years data often results in a net amount due at the end of the period. When comparing quotes between agents or companies, be certain the average values used are similar or you will not be obtaining comparable quotes.

This section excludes coverage for tape players and there is no coverage for leased vehicles unless it is leased to a customer whose vehicle was left for repair. Moreover, cars used in racing or stunts are likewise excluded from coverage.

Other exclusions are similar to personal automobile policies. For example, wear and tear, freezing, and mechanical or electrical breakdown are not covered. Tires are only covered for blowouts, punctures, or other road damage connected with another loss covered by the policy. Should a tire be damaged in an accident, it would be covered but a simple blowout would not be covered.

Although theft is covered with Specified Perils or Comprehensive coverage, there is no coverage should someone cause you to voluntarily part with an auto by trick or scheme. This coverage is available on a buy-back basis.

Dealerships have additional exclusions that do not apply to other types of garage risks. Expected profit from the sale of a vehicle is not included under the Physical Damage section. Special policies are however available for this situation.

Sometimes dealers leave vehicles at other than their regular place of business. Here coverage is limited for physical damage for 45 days. For coverage in excess of 45 days, an endorsement must be secured. A situation that might result in this exclusion being applied is when an auto is left past 45 days in an airport area.

Occasionally, dealers find themselves delivering cars to customers. There is an often overlooked exclusion which removes collision coverage if the auto is being delivered more than 50 miles. Should coverage be desired for such deliveries, a special endorsement must be issued.

Medical Payments coverage

Although not a part of the garage policy per se, Medical Payments coverage is an often utilized endorsement. This endorsement bears no relationship to legal liability, as was seen in the BI and PD section. Rather this coverage may be thought of as a payment regardless of fault.

Medical Payments coverage is optional, and a separate endorsement must be added to the policy to make it effective. Most agents and insurers strongly recommend this coverage. Their recommendation stems largely from their desire to prevent possible lawsuits that would need to be defended and perhaps paid under the BI and PD section of the contract. Since this section, known as Med Pay, pays regardless of fault, it is hoped that paying necessary medical expense to insured parties will diminish the number of lawsuits. It is beneficial to the business to avoid lawsuits even if there is insurance coverage. Adverse publicity can be generated by suits of this type as well as the possibility that the limits of the policy might be exceeded. Many businesses purchase this coverage as a result of humanitarian spirit. They recognize that their customers deserve reasonable care and consideration.

It is important to remember that there is no policy coverage afforded to employees who should be covered under workers' compensation and employers' liability. It is, however, possible in some circumstances to cover executive officers and their families with this coverage. Before accepting this option, consideration should be given to the necessity of this coverage in light of individual and group health insurance contracts.

Coverage is limited to medical expenses that are necessary and the amount is limited to so much per individual. Usual available limits are

$500, $750, $1,000, $2,000. It is possible to secure higher medical payments limits but the risk will have to be specifically rated by the company. The reason for these seemingly low limits is that often, when these amounts of medical expenses are exceeded and there is a question of fault, a claim will usually be covered by the BI and PD section of the contract. Medical Payments coverage can be thought of as health insurance for situations that probably will not result in a lawsuit.

When insuring med pay, the business has the option of selecting coverage applying to automobiles use only, garage operations only, or both. Selection should be made on the basis of exposure rather than the premium. For example, a garage risk that owns no autos or only autos which are occupied by employees, might select coverage for garage operations only. On the other hand, a dealership may need both auto exposure as well as garage operations.

The cost of this additional coverage is determined by the amount of coverage desired and the amount of payroll. Payroll is used as the determining variable even though no coverage is afforded to employees. The rationale for this is the larger the exposure probable the larger the payroll. In comparison to the premium charges for the garage policy itself, most insureds find med pay charges small.

WORKERS' COMPENSATION AND EMPLOYERS' LIABILITY

COVERAGE IN GENERAL
  Historical perspective
  Requirement on employer to secure
    exposure
  Relationship giving rise to the
    exposure
  Benefits provided

ANALYSIS OF THE POLICY
  Insuring agreements
  Exclusions

Conditions
Modifications and extensions through
  endorsements

RISK MANAGEMENT TECHNIQUES
  Guaranteed cost insurance;
    dividends, premium discounts
    and experience rating
  Participating plans
  Retrospective rating
  Self-insurance

Robert Needle, Esquire
Assistant Vice President
Mid-Atlantic Region
Alexander & Alexander
Philadelphia, Pennsylvania

Robert Needle received his B.B.A. and M.B.A. from Temple University with a concentration in insurance and risk. He received his J.D. from Temple University School of Law and is a member of the Pennsylvania Bar Association. Prior to joining Alexander & Alexander Inc., Mr. Needle was an Associate with the Philadelphia law firm of Harvey, Pennington, Herting & Renneisen, Ltd. He has held the position of Assistant Director of Legal and Claims Education for The American Institute for Property and Liability Underwriters and Insurance Institute of America. Mr. Needle is currently an Assistant Vice President with the Mid-Atlantic Region Risk Management Services Group of Alexander & Alexander.

Frank E. Raab, Jr.
President
Allianz Insurance Company
Los Angeles, California

Frank E. Raab graduated from the University of California at Berkeley in 1943 with a Bachelor of Science Degree. He went directly into the Navy and served from 1943 to 1946. After the war, he stayed with the Reserve program and in 1968 was promoted to Rear Admiral. Mr. Raab has been in the property and casualty insurance business since 1946. He was President of Pacific Employers in 1968; in 1973 he was elected President of the Insurance Company of North America. He is currently Chairman, President, and Chief Executive Office of Allianz Insurance Company. He is a past National President of the Chartered Property and Casualty Underwriters, and is past Chairman of the Loman Foundation. Mr. Raab is a past President of the Los Angeles Safety Council. Presently, he is on the Board of Governors of the New York Insurance Exchange and a member of the Executive Committee of American Nuclear Insurers.

COVERAGE IN GENERAL

Employers' liability and workers' compensation exposures arise out of the employment relationship. Workers' compensation is a statutorily imposed obligation. When an employee sustains an injury arising out of the workplace or suffers an occupational disease to which a workers' compensation statute is applicable, the employer is subject to absolute liability. That liability generally extends to medical benefits and statutorily defined indemnity benefits.

Historical perspective

Prior to the enactment of workers' compensation statutes, the liability of the employer to the employee was based on English common law which place on the employer certain legal duties and obligations to his workers. These duties were developed and clarified by our courts into a body of case law requiring the employer to:

1. Provide a reasonably safe workplace.
2. Provide reasonably safe tools, equipment, and other instrumentalities.
3. Provide the employee with reasonably competent fellow employees.
4. Provide the employee with a reasonably sufficient warning of work-related dangers of which the employee would be unaware.
5. Develop and enforce reasonable safety rules.

The courts held that the violation of one of these duties was an act of negligence and the basis of a lawsuit against the employer.

In response to such action, the employer could rely on certain defenses: First, if the employee's negligence contributed to the injury, the employee could not recover; contributory negligence was a complete defense. Second, the employer could defend an action on the basis that the employee assumed the risk of injury. This defense required the employer to prove that his employee was aware of the danger and proceeded, thus accepting its existence. Last, the employer was not liable for injury resulting from an act caused by a reasonably competent fellow employee. When an employee was fortunate enough to obtain a court award, the delay in receiving actual dollars, inherent in the system, caused most injured employees financial hardship. This adversary system, with all its complications and uncertainties, could not help but create unnecessary antagonism between labor and management.

These problems, coupled with an inordinate amount of accidents occurring at the turn of the century, led to the enactment of workers' compensation statutes in each of our states. Federal statutes were also enacted to cover employees not covered by the state statutes or subject to state jurisdiction.

In general, workers' compensation statutes require that the employee relinquish his right to bring a common-law action against his employer. When an injury is work related, the employer's liability is absolute. A determination of contributory negligence or assumption of risk is irrelevant as the employee receives statutorily defined wage and medical benefits.

Requirement on employer to secure exposure

The legislation which created this statutory liability to injured workers also required that employers secure the payment of compensation benefits to the injured worker. This security requirement varies from jurisdiction to jurisdiction. In general, it can be accomplished by (1) the purchase of insurance through a private insurance company, (2) retaining the risk by becoming a qualified "self-insurer," or (3) purchasing coverage through a state workers' compensation fund.

Not all of these alternatives are permitted in all jurisdictions. For example, self-insurance is currently not permitted in North Dakota, Texas, and Wyoming. Additionally, there are currently six states where coverage written through private insurers is prohibited (Nevada, North Dakota, Ohio, Washington, West Virginia, and Wyoming). Here coverage must be purchased through the state fund, or, as an alternative in Ohio, West Virginia, Nevada, and Washington, be self-insured.

Relationship giving rise to the exposure

Employer-employee. To determine whether workers' compensation is applicable to a given injury, the first question to examine is the existence of the employer-employee relationship. To do this, one must examine the state statutes and the definition of the terms *employer* and *employee* in state workers' compensation statutes. The Pennsylvania Workers' Compensation Act defines employer as synonymous with "master" and includes all natural persons, partnerships, joint stock companies, profit, nonprofit and municipal corporations, the Commonwealth, and all governmental agencies. This statute is typical in that it specifies that any entity, public or private, is an employer. The Pennsylvania statute defines employee as synonymous with "servant" and includes all natural persons who perform services for another for a valuable consideration.

In general, the legal standards considered in determining the employer-employee or master-servant relationship are (1) the right to control the means and methods of the work, (2) the right to fire, (3) payment for the work, and (4) whether the work performed is part of the employer's regular business.

The issue as to whether an employment relationship exists most often arises in the context of determining whether one is an employee or an independent contractor. An independent contractor is not subject to the control of the "master" as to the means of the work. The independent contractor represents the "master" or principal only as to the results to be accomplished. An independent contractor is not eligible for workers' compensation benefits and can only recover for any injury on a negligence basis.

Many states have, either by statute or judicial interpretation, created other employment relationships for workers' compensation purposes. For example, a general contractor may be responsible for the employees of an uninsured subcontractor.

Employments covered.   Depending on the state, there may be employments excluded from workers' compensation. Some typical exclusions are employers with less than a stipulated number of employees such as three or five, farm laborers, and domestic servants. The current trend is to make state workers' compensation laws more inclusive.

If an employee is not subject to the workers' compensation law, he retains the right to bring a negligence action against his employer. An employer with nonsubject employees should cover this exposure through the purchase of employers' liability coverage. An option which may be available to some employers is to attempt to bring their employees under the workers' compensation law by means of voluntary workers' compensation.

Injuries covered.   For an injury to be subject to the absolute liability imposed by workers' compensation laws, it must arise out of and in the course of employment. This means that the injury must occur while the employee is engaged in work-related activity, or activity causally related to the employment.

In the majority of cases, this determination is not difficult. One can look to a number of factors to determine if an injury is work related. The most obvious situation is where an employee is engaged in specified duties at a work location. Other factors which tend to signify a work-related injury are (1) the occurrence of the injury while on the premises, (2) injury while traveling in the course of employment or where transportation is furnished by the employer, or (3) injuries while the employee is engaged in activities that benefit the employer. Note that an injury to an employee while traveling to and from work or while away from premises during lunch or coffee breaks, is usually not considered work related.

Diseases covered. While a work "accident" or injury can be analyzed as compensible or not compensible with relative ease, occupational diseases present differing and more difficult questions. Obviously, not all diseases contracted in the course of employment are "occupational diseases" and attributable to the work environment. There must be a cause and effect relationship between the occupation and the disease. There is considerable variance among jurisdictions as to coverage of various occupational diseases as well as the substantive and procedural methods available to an employee to demonstrate that an illness is an "occupational disease." Also, in some jurisdictions the occupational disease statutes are separate from the workers' compensation statutes.

Most occupational disease provisions provide a list of specific diseases covered such as silicosis, asbestosis, and anthracosilicosis. Most of these statutes also contain a catch-all provision such as:

> All other diseases (1) to which the claimant is exposed by reason of his employment, and (2) which are causally related to the industry or occupation, and (3) the incidence of which are substantially greater in that industry or occupation than in the general population.

A particular difficulty with many occupational diseases is the long-term nature of development and discovery as, for example, asbestosis may not be discovered and diagnosed for 25 years. Consequently, many state statutes provide additional periods of time for employees to discover and file a claim.

Benefits provided

The objective of workers' compensation is to indemnify the employee for loss of earnings and expenses. The benefits under workers' compensation statutes relate to these two areas. The employer is obligated to pay for the reasonable cost of medical, surgical, hospital, and nursing services as required. The injured employee is also entitled to weekly compensation payments for the length of the disability. In some situations, such as loss of use or severance of certain limbs, the injured employee is entitled to additional payments or indemnity as provided by statute. Where the injury results in death, payments are usually required to be made to the deceased workers' dependents.

Medical benefits. In most states, payment of medical expense is required without regard to dollar limit or duration and the injured worker is entitled to all necessary medical treatment arising out of the injury. Medical treatment must be provided if required, regardless of whether the injured worker returns to work. "Medical treatment" is usually considered to be services rendered by a duly licensed practitioner of the healing arts. There are distinctions in some states regarding services performed by those outside the typical medical community. Included within the cost of medical expenses are all medicine and supplies, and orthopedic appliances and prostheses.

In most states the injured worker is entitled to select their own physician while in others the injured worker can select a physician from a designated panel. Many states also have specific provisions in their statutes pertaining to rehabilitation, as, for example, providing for special rehabilitation funds. Federal funds are available to aid states in this area of rehabilitation under the Federal Vocational Rehabilitation Act.

Indemnity benefits—earnings loss. The largest area of exposure is the weekly indemnity benefit designed to replace lost earnings. For an injured worker to receive this benefit, the injury must produce "disability" resulting in a loss of earning power. This loss of earning power is measured by comparison with pre-injury wages. In most states, disability includes not only physical injury and limitation but also mental conditions arising from and affecting employment.

Unlike medical expenses which usually are payable without limitation, the rate of compensation for lost earnings is fixed by statute. Here, benefits are limited to a fixed percentage, such as 66.67 percent of the employee's average weekly wage, subject to a weekly dollar maximum. On this point there is considerable variance among states, and in many, the weekly dollar maximum has not kept pace with the escalating cost of living. Some states have provided a sliding scale based on the average weekly wage earned by employees in the state. Under this method the maximum figure will change yearly.

As an example of the workings of the sliding scale system, Pennsylvania determines the Statewide Average Weekly Wage for 12-month periods ending June 30. Prior to January 1 of each year the new wage figures are published for application in the coming year. In Pennsylvania the maximum has risen from $171 in 1975 to $242 in 1980. In addition to maximum amounts set by statute, most states also provide for minimum weekly payments.

A common provision found in most workers' compensation statutes is a "waiting period." Typically, such provisions provide that compensation will not be paid for the first 7 days after the disability arises, but if the disability lasts 14 days or more, compensation is to be paid for the first 7 days. The intent of waiting period provisions is to eliminate proportionally high administrative costs involved in minor claims.

Death benefits. When an employee dies as a result of a work-related injury, benefits usually are payable to his dependents. Death cases give rise to two types of benefits: payment for funeral expenses and weekly benefits as defined in the state statute. A typical statute will provide for benefits for a dependent spouse until remarriage and dependent children until attaining the age of majority. Some statutes provide for payments to parents, brothers, or sisters under the prescribed circumstances. In the event there are no dependents some states require a payment to a rehabilitation or similar fund. Some states place a maximum amount on total death benefits.

Many statutes provide that death resulting from the work-related injury must occur within a specified time. For example, the Pennsylvania statute provides that for death benefits to be received, death must occur within 300 weeks of the date of the injury.

Schedule injuries or specific losses. Most compensation statutes contain provisions providing specific benefits for enumerated injuries. These provisions usually contain provisions fixing the amount of compensation where there has been a permanent injury to a certain member of the body, either by amputation or loss of use, as in loss of hearing or sight. Most schedules set forth a specific number of weeks of compensation which is to be paid to the injured worker. The amount is usually fixed without regard to whether the injury has actually affected the workers' earning capacity.

Typical disability classifications. Since compensation is paid for the inability to work due to injury, payments are made whether the injury renders the worker partially or totally disabled and whether the condition is temporary or permanent.

Where there is permanent total disability, that is where the injured employee is unable to do any type of work (and it is anticipated that this condition will continue for his or her lifetime), benefits will continue for life in most states. However, a few states still limit maximum payment to specified number of weeks of compensation.

Where there is a temporary total disability (the injured employee is unable to perform work for a limited period of time but it is anticipated that he or she will recover), the injured employee will receive indemnity benefits for the period of disability.

When an employee is temporarily partially disabled and capable of some work but is unable to perform at full capacity and receive full earnings, the injured employee is usually entitled to receive a percentage of the difference between the amount which is now being earned and the wages which were earned prior to the disability.

When an individual has sustained an injury which is permanent in nature but one which only partially affects his or her performance of duties and earning capacity, he is considered permanently partially disabled. Here payments are intended to pay for the effect of the injury on the employee's future earning capacity. Many of these types of injuries are "schedule" injuries where the injured worker is allocated statutorily specified number of weeks of compensation payments because of his or her reduced ability to effectively compete in the labor market. When an injury is of the nonschedule variety, many states will determine compensation on the basis of actual loss of earnings capacity.

ANALYSIS OF THE POLICY

The Standard Workers' Compensation and Employers' Liability Policy provides, as primary coverage, the statutorily defined workers' compensation obligation and, in addition, provides employers' liability coverage. The following analysis of this policy will include examination of the insuring agreements, exclusions, and conditions. Modifications and extensions of the policy through endorsement will also be considered.

Insuring agreements

Coverage provided. Section I of the insuring agreement sets forth the coverage provided. It is divided into Coverage A—Workers' Compensation and Coverage B—Employers' Liability. Under Coverage A, the insurer agrees to pay all compensation and other benefits required of the insured by the workers' compensation law. The law which applies is defined in Section III of the insuring agreement as the workers' compensation law and any occupational disease law of the state designated in item 3 of the declarations.

The coverage provided is unique in that the policy contains no limit of liability. The insurer agrees to pay whatever is required by statute. Effectively, the limit of liability is contained in the applicable statute and not the insurance policy. The statute prescribes the amount of weekly indemnity benefits and mandates required medical expenses, usually without limitation. This unique aspect of workers' compensation distinguishes it from most other insurance coverages.

Coverage B provides employers' liability coverage which protects employers from their legal liability to an employee for injury arising out of and in the course of employment which is not covered under the workers' compensation law. For example, in some states, there could be situations where death, injury, or specific diseases do not fit within the scope of the compensation statute, or where suits are permitted by dependents of employees.

A further exposure facing the employer is an action instituted by a third party. This could arise where an injured employee sues and recovers from a legally responsible third party such as the manufacturer of machinery. This third-party manufacturer may in turn seek recovery from the employer, contending, for example, that the employer negligently maintained the machine.

One of the considerations under employers' liability coverage is the geographical scope of coverage. This coverage applies to states designated in the declarations, and where "necessary or incidental" to these operations while within the United States, its territories or possessions, or in Canada. Coverage also applies worldwide for an employee who is a citizen or resident of the United States or Canada, if temporarily outside of the United States, its territories or possessions, or Canada.

Employers' liability coverage, in contrast to workers' compensation coverage, is subject to a specified limit of liability. This is customarily written at a limit of $100,000. It is advisable to have this coverage scheduled on the umbrella or excess liability policy to assure that the higher umbrella limits apply.

Defense, settlement, supplementary payments. The provisions concerning defense, settlement, and supplementary payments are similar to that found in most liability policies. Under these provisions the insurer agrees to defend any suit or proceeding brought against the insured in connection with the coverage afforded by the policy, even if the suit is groundless, false, or fraudulent. The insurer has the right to investigate, negotiate, and settle any such suit or claim as it deems expedient. The insurer also agrees to pay or reimburse for all reasonable expenses incurred.

Definitions. The insuring agreement of the policy contains four definitions intended to clarify the scope of coverage.

The definitions of workers' compensation laws provide that the law which applies is that of the state or states designated in the declarations.

As further amplification, *state* is defined as any state or territory of the United States or District of Columbia. This effectively excludes coverage under federal laws such as the Longshoremen's ane Harbor Workers' Compensation Act. Such exposure can be covered by endorsement.

Also defined is *bodily injury by disease* and *bodily injury by accident*. The intent of these definitions is to distinguish between both terms so that no single injury can be both an accident and disease.

The definitions also specify that under employers' liability coverage, *assault and battery* shall be deemed an accident unless committed by or at the direction of the insured. The purpose of this definition is to provide coverage for the employers' liability unless such was committed or openly sanctioned by the insured.

Exclusions

The Standard Workers' Compensation and Employers' Liability Policy contains six exclusions. These exclusions serve to define and limit the coverage afforded by the insuring agreement. The rationale of the exclusions are to exclude coverage not intended by the insurer and to prevent overlapping coverage with other insurance. Of the six exclusions, four relate only to employers' liability coverage, while two relate to both coverages.

Other insurance or self-insurance. This exclusion relates to both coverages. It excludes coverage for workplaces not described in the declarations if the insured has other insurance or is a qualified self-insurer for such other operations. Note that there would be coverage for all operations in states specified in the absence of other specified coverage or specific exclusion.

Domestic or agricultural employment. This exclusion also applies to both coverages. It excludes coverage for domestic or agricultural employment unless required by applicable law or voluntarily covered.

Contractual liability. This exclusion applies to the employers' liability coverage and specifies that liability assumed by the insured under contract is not covered. An example is a contractual assumption of liability to reimburse a third party for a work-related injury. This would be the subject of contractual liability insurance.

Punitive or exemplary damages. Many workers' compensation laws include provisions relating to illegal employment, such as employment of minors in hazardous occupations. When injury results to an illegally employed person, some states provide for additional compensation. The Conditions section of the policy provides that the insured reimburse the insurer for any such excess benefits required under the workers' compensation law. This exclusion applies to employers' liability coverage and excludes punitive or exemplary damages. Thus, punitive or exemplary damages are the obligation of the employer.

Timing of claim. This exclusion relates to employers' liability coverage and requires a claim be made or suit brought prior to 36 months after the end of the policy period.

Workers' compensation exclusion. This also relates to employers' liability coverage and is intended to prevent application of employers' liability coverage to any situation which is properly within the workers' compensation exposure.

Conditions

The Standard Workers' Compensation and Employers' Liability Policy contains various conditions which enumerate the duties and obligations of the insurer and the insured employer. Following is a brief explanation of the conditions found in the policy:

Premium. This condition relates to premium calculation. In workers' compensation, premiums are calculated on the basis of payroll in each rating class. At policy inception, it is not possible to precisely determine payroll for each rating class. This condition provides that the final premium is calculated according to the payroll or exposure which actually existed during the policy period. Thus, the insured is required to keep and furnish records to permit the insurer to compute actual earned premium.

Long-term policy. When a policy is written for more than one year, each year is considered separate, and all provisions of the policy apply separately to each 12-month policy period. If rates are changed, the premium for periods after the first year are revised.

Partnership or joint venture as insured. If the insured is a partnership or joint venture, the policy does not cover the operations of an individual partner or member of a joint venture which are not operations of the insured partnership or joint venture.

Inspection and audit. Under this provision, the insured agrees to permit the insurer and any rating authority having jurisdiction to inspect the operations of the insured covered by the policy. This provision also states that such inspection does not constitute an undertaking by the insurer to determine or warrant that such workplaces or operations are safe, or are in compliance with law.

Finally, the insurer must be permitted to examine payroll records and other books which may be necessary to determine or verify the amount of remuneration applicable for rating purposes.

Notice of injury. When injury occurs, the insured is required to notify the insurer as soon as practicable. Such notice must contain reasonably obtainable information relating to the time, place, and circumstances of the injury.

Notice of claim or suit. If a claim is made or suit is brought against the insured, the insured agrees to forward all particulars to the insurer immediately.

Assistance and cooperation of the insured. Under this condition the insured agrees to cooperate with the insurer in giving and securing evidence, attending hearings and other proceedings, and assisting in effecting settlements.

Statutory provisions for workers' compensation coverage. This condition essentially contains three key provisions. First, it incorporates into the policy all provisions of applicable workers' compensation laws. Further, it states that bankruptcy or insolvency of the insured does not relieve the insurer of its obligations under this coverage. Additionally, the other significant provision relates to excess or additional benefits. Where the insurer is required to pay any punitive damages, the insured is obligated to reimburse the insurer for any additional amount.

Limits of liability—employers' liability coverage. This provision states the existence of a specific limit of liability for the employers' liability coverage. The application of this coverage and limit of liability has been previously discussed.

Action against company—employers' liability coverage. This provides that an action by the insured against the insurer is not valid unless the insured has fully complied with the terms of the policy, nor until the amount of the insured's obligation to pay is fully established. This further provides that the bankruptcy or insolvency of the insured shall not relieve the company of any of its obligations under the employers' liability coverage.

Other insurance. If two or more policies cover the same loss, each insurer will be called upon to contribute pro rata, to the payment of the loss.

Subrogation. In the event of any payment, the insurer is subrogated to all of the insured's rights of recovery. The insured must do nothing that would prejudice these rights. A typical application of this clause is an employee injury caused by unsafe machinery or equipment. Under such circumstances, the insurer will pay compensation benefits and seek recovery against the manufacturer of the unsafe instrumentality.

Changes. Changes in the policy are permitted only by endorsement.

Assignment. Assignment of interest is possible only with the written consent of the insurer. Death of the insured is exempted from this requirement.

Cancellation. The policy may be cancelled by the insured at any time by mailing to the insurer written notice stating when the cancellation shall be effective. The insurer may cancel by giving not less than ten days' written notice, unless state law provides otherwise.

Terms of policy conformed to statute. Any terms of the policy which are in conflict with the applicable compensation laws are amended to conform to such laws.

Declarations. The insured agrees that the statements in the declarations are representations and that the policy is issued in reliance upon these statements.

Modifications and extensions through endorsements

The Standard Workers' Compensation and Employers' Liability Policy is sufficiently broad to require a minimum amount of modification through endorsement. Common endorsements used are the Broad Form All States Endorsement, Voluntary Compensation Endorsement, and the Longshoremen's and Harbor Workers' Endorsement.

Broad Form All States Endorsement. The workers' compensation policy provides coverage only under the laws of the state(s) listed in the declarations. If a claim is filed under the laws of a state not listed under the declarations, there will be no coverage for that claim. The Broad Form All States Endorsement provides coverage for this contingency. It provides automatic workers' compensation and employers' liability insurance in all states not listed in the declarations.

Voluntary Compensation Endorsement. The purpose of the Voluntary Compensation Endorsement is to extend workers' compensation benefits to employees who are not eligible for mandatory coverage under state law. This endorsement provides for the voluntary payment of benefits to a specified group of employees, such as "all employees" or "all executives." This endorsement also requires designation of the state of operations and the designated workers' compensation law that applies.

It should be noted that an employee not covered by compulsory compensation can elect not to accept voluntary compensation and may bring suit against the employer. If an employee does accept the voluntary statutory benefits, the employee must release the employer from further liability.

United States Longshoremen's and Harbor Workers' Compensation Act. The standard workers' compensation and employers' liability coverage does not provide coverage for federal obligations such as that contained in the Longshoremen's and Harbor Workers' Act. This act is a federal compensation coverage which operates in a manner similar to state compensation coverages. The remedy provided against an employer is exclusive. The coverage of the act is for services performed upon navigable waters of the United States, including any adjoining pier, wharf, dry dock, terminal, building way, marine railway, or other adjoining area customarily used by the insurer in loading, unloading, repairing, or building a vessel. Here exposure may be endorsed to the policy.

RISK MANAGEMENT TECHNIQUES

The Risk Managers' choice for retaining risk for workers' compensation and employers' liability exposures is limited by the compulsory features of the workers' compensation laws in all 50 states. Three states, New Jersey, South Carolina, and Texas, have "Elective" laws under which the employer may accept or reject the act. If the act is rejected, the employer loses the common-law defenses—assumption of risk, negligence, so in effect, all states are compulsory. All 50 states require insurance, 6 in State Funds, as enumerated earlier, 12 in either a competitive State Fund or private insurance companies. "Qualified" self-insurance is permitted in 47 states.

Unlike some other exposures, the Risk Manager cannot legally choose noninsurance or large deductibles for workers' compensation exposures. However, there are a number of methods of insurance and retention or risk-sharing programs which can be applied, both simple and complex, such as discounts, experience rating, participating (dividend) plans, retrospective rating plans, and self-insurance.

Guaranteed cost insurance: dividends, premium discounts, and experience rating

Workers' compensation insurance involves a statutory policy to cover a statutory exposure. A Workers' Compensation Bureau for each state establishes classification codes for all types of business and industry and the rates for each classification, which apply to each $100 of payroll. The rates are subject to approval by the state department of insurance and are used by all companies. A copy of every policy must be filed with the bureau and is subject to their approval of the classification and rate charged. The premium for the policy is based on estimated payroll and is subject to audit and adjustment to actual payroll at the end of the policy period.

As the name implies, the premium on a "guaranteed cost" policy does not fluctuate based on loss experience. Rather, a premium, established by application of manual rates to payroll provides the employer with (statutory workers' compensation) coverage without dollar limitation.

However, in addition to the application of manual rates to payroll, other factors can affect the cost. The most significant adjustment to cost or manual premium is the application of experience rating. Experience rating utilizes the loss experience of the insured over a period of time to adjust the class rate either upward or downward. A factor, usually termed an experience modification, will be generated for the insured's account. For example, an insured with a manual premium of $50,000 and an experience modification of 1.50 would have a modified manual premium or "standard premium" of $75,000.

Experience rating is applicable for all qualifying insureds. Eligibility requirements differ by bureau, but in most states served by the

National Council on Compensation Insurance, a risk shall qualify for experience rating:

a. If the payrolls or other exposures developed during the last year or last two years of the experience period produced a premium at manual rates of at least $1,500, or

b. . . . during an experience period of more than two years produced an average annual premium at manual rates of at least $750.

The experience period is three years, beginning four years prior and ending one year prior to the date of the policy to which the experience modification applies.

If your losses have been few and experience rating has not been applied, have your agent or broker make inquiry to the company. He should also check the rating for accuracy if there appears to be a discrepancy.

Experience rating is an incentive for applying loss control measures and training employees in the safe way to do their job and providing them a safe environment in which to do their work.

In addition to the application of the experience modification, premium discounts and dividends may affect ultimate cost. Most states have premium discounts based on the size of the manual premium (which reflects the insurance company's savings in expenses on policies with larger premiums). The percentage of discount varies in some states, but the usual discounts are:

Premiums	*Stock companies*	*Nonstock*
First $5,000	0	0
Next $9,500	9.5%	2.0%
Next $400,000	11.9	4.0
Over $500,000	12.4	6.0

Participating plans

Additionally, most insurance companies, whether stock or nonstock, have participating plans designed to share profits by means of dividend payments to the insured. It is important to recognize that dividends are not guaranteed and are available only if a company has the available surplus level to declare them. There are two types of plans prevailing, sliding scale and fixed amounts. The sliding scale varies dividends with the size of the premium and the loss ratio. The dividend increases as the premium becomes higher and the loss ratio lower. When the loss ratio exceeds 65 percent, usually the dividend disappears. The fixed amount dividends are lower returns, ranging from 5 percent to 15 percent, but are not dependent on the loss ratio. Participating plans apply in addition to premium discount and experience rating, thus, good loss experience can result in substantial savings for the small businessman.

Retrospective rating

There is a wide range of modified "cost-plus" programs available to the medium-sized and larger risks called retrospective (Retro) rating plans. Retro Plans are complicated and are only briefly mentioned here to give you some idea of the elements involved in selecting a Retro Plan.

Usually, months after the policy term has expired, the premium is recalculated based on the factors contained in the Retro Plan selected. The Retro formula is basically the same for all plans:

Retrospective premium (subject to upper and lower limits) =
[(Basic premium factor × Standard premium) +
(Losses × Loss conversion factor)] × Tax multiplier

A definition of retrospective rating terms aids in understanding the concept:

1. *Standard premium* is manual premium after the application of the experience rating modification, but without the reflection of premium discount (which does not apply when a Retro Plan is used).

Retrospective rating utilizes the loss experience of the insured for a given policy period to adjust the premium after the policy period.

2. *Basic premium* is the portion of the standard premium retained by the insurance company. It contains the necessary cost elements for administration, acquisition, contingency costs, and profit. It also contains an additional ingredient called the insurance charge.
3. *Insurance charge* is an actuarially computed charge based on a charge/savings formula reflecting the degree of loss containment in the plan, depending mainly upon the maximum and minimum factors selected.

    Example: High maximum—reduces insurance charge.
    High minimum—reduces insurance charge.
    Low maximum—raises insurance charge.
    Low minimum—raises insurance charge.

    The charge moves up or down, according to the advantage received by either the insurer or insured.
4. *Maximum premium factor* is the maximum (Maximum factor ×

Standard premium) premium that can be charged the insured, based on losses incurred during the plan.

5. *Minimum premium ratio* is the minimum (Minimum factor × Standard premium) premium the insured can pay for the plan. In some cases the basic premium is also the minimum paid when there are no losses.
6. *Loss conversion factor* is a factor that is applied to incurred losses as a charge for the claims function.
7. *Tax multiplier* is the charge used to collect necessary state premium taxes and varies by state.
8. *Excess loss premium factor* is the charge for limiting the size of an individual loss that will be used in determining the Retro earned premium, to a specific amount per occurrence. This loss limitation factor is not available on standard premiums under $25,000, but for up to $50,000 a limitation of $10,000 may be selected; up to $75,000 − $15,000; up to $100,000 − $20,000. For standard premiums over $100,000 the rule is that the loss limitation cannot exceed 25 percent of the premium. The cost for the loss limitation is substantial, and it is seldom used on premiums under $100,000.

The Workers' Compensation Tabular Retro Plans A, B, C, and J contain pre-calculated tables of Retro factors for all levels of Standard Premium and apply in all jurisdictions under the National Council on Compensation Insurance. A comparison of the factors at the $25,000 standard premium level will allow comparison of the wide range of trade-offs available.

	Retro Plan			
	A	B	C	J
Basic premium factor	40.4	28.0	38.5	31.8
Minimum	77.1	61.3	—	68.2
Maximum	100.0	143.0	143.0	121.5
Standard premium	$25,000	$25,000	$25,000	$25,000
Basic premium dollar	10,100	7,000	9,625	7,950
Minimum premium	19,275	15,325	10,105	17,050
Maximum premium	25,000	35,750	35,750	30,375

The loss conversion factor to be applied to losses is the same in each plan, 112.5 percent. The tax multiplier varies by state with most falling in a range of 4 percent to 7 percent, though a few are higher.

Plan A is the most conservative with a maximum premium equal to the standard. Remember, premium discount does not apply to Retro rating. On a $25,000 premium, the discount is $3,316 for a guaranteed cost premium of $21,684. Thus, in Plan A there is a possible additional savings of $2,409 at the minimum of $19,275. If the insured's expected losses are under $7,300 a year, he will achieve the minimum premium.

Plan B has a lower basic and minimum premium in exchange for the higher maximum premium factor of 143.0. This plan would be selected if more than minimal losses are expected making the lowest possible basic premium attractive.

Plan C has a higher basic premium than Plan B, but the minimum premium is the basic premium with tax applied. It is attractive to the buyer who expects less than minimal losses which would produce a much lower premium than the 61.3 percent minimum premium ratio in Plan B.

Plan J is a moderate plan with all factors ranging in between those of B and C. All these plans apply only to workers' compensation premiums.

There is a fifth Retrospective Plan—Retro Rating Plan D—which can be applied separately or in combination for workers' compensation, automobile liability and physical damage, general liability, burglary, and glass insurance. Plan D is an extremely flexible plan. The insured and his agent negotiate with the insurance company the best feasible maximum factor, minimum factor, and loss conversion factor. The basic premium factor will be actuarially adjusted up or down, reflecting the advantage to the insured or the insurance company as the factors are adjusted.

Paid Loss Retro.   Short of self-insurance for the large insured, the only means currently available to legally recognize "cash flow" principles for workers' compensation is by use of a Paid Loss Retrospective Plan. The Retro Plan is established as previously described. The difference is that a Paid Loss Retro provides a means of financing the premiums due on the difference between paid losses and total incurred losses. The latter include both paid and reserves on unpaid losses. This financing is accomplished by an agreement to bill the insured on a mutually agreed schedule, usually quarterly, for the next period's deposit premium and the previous period's actual earned retrospective premium, both based on paid losses only. The difference between incurred loss calculated premium and paid losses premium should be secured by an interest-bearing note receivable and supported by an irrevocable letter of credit. The "cash flow" advantage is that the loss portion of the Retro premium is not remitted to the company until the loss is actually paid.

It should be noted that because the insurer relinquishes investment income under a Paid Loss Retro, an additional charge may be added to the basic premium.

Self-insurance

In many instances, self-insurance is an extremely attractive alternative for handling the workers' compensation exposure. Self-insurance can minimize cost by maximizing the insured's cash flow. Since workers' compensation losses are paid out over a period of years, the employer retains the use of the reserve funds, and thus the investment income. Self-insurance also minimizes cost by reducing expenses for insurance company overhead items. However, it must be recognized that the expected lower (reduced) costs must be measured against any increased risk involved.

The workers' compensation exposure lends itself to a self-insured approach because of the relative higher loss frequency, which affords greater loss predictability. Further, as noted earlier, loss severity, or the indemnity benefits provided statutorily, are predetermined.

Since an insurance company performs such services as claims adjusting and safety engineering, an employer desiring to self-insure must purchase these services independently (the employer may want to consider the cost of establishing his own service department internally). When such services are purchased from an outside service company, self-insurance poses no additional administrative burden.

All jurisdictions require the self-insurer to prove financial ability to carry their own risk. A prospective self-insurer should seek advice from their broker or consultant for the legal requirements to qualify and to determine the financial obligations they assume. Consultation with their attorney or accountant is mandatory. Most states require the self-insurer to post a surety bond or other form of guarantee.

Few employers are large enough to fully self-insure their workers' compensation exposure. It is usually desirable and/or required by the state of operation that excess insurance be purchased. There are basically two types of excess workers' compensation coverage available. One form is referred to as specific excess insurance, and the other is aggregate excess. These coverages pay losses over a specified retention.

Specific excess insurance operates on a per occurrence basis. Coverage is provided for loss in excess of a retained limit on one occurrence. For example, an employer who purchases a specific excess policy with a limit of $1 million and a retention of $200,000, must pay the first $200,000 of losses resulting from any one occurrence. Thus, if the employer sustained a $300,000 loss from one occurrence, the excess insurer would pay $100,000.

An aggregate excess policy insures the employer for losses that exceed a specified aggregate of all losses incurred within one policy year. Of course, this policy also includes a limit of liability.

Note that these coverages can be purchased separately or in combination. The selection of appropriate retention levels and limits is, of course, dependent upon many factors such as retention of the firm, state benefit levels, loss experience.

The decision to self-insure should, of course, be preceded by a detailed study by your agent broker or insurance consultant.

Captive insurance company. Another alternative available to fulfill certain specialized needs is a captive insurance company. In essence, this is an insurance company owned or controlled by an employer or association group. The specific advantages and disadvantages of the captive alternative are dependent upon the particular facts involved. Most businesses are too small to consider a captive and should rely on insurance or self-insurance to cover the workers' compensation exposure.

CHAPTER 12

PRODUCTS LIABILITY INSURANCE

MODERN TREND IN PRODUCTS
LIABILITY LAW

PRODUCTS LIABILITY COVERAGE

A TYPICAL POLICY
Policy territory
Applicable limits
Occurrence

PRODUCTS HAZARD CLAUSE
What are products?
Injury or damage away from
premises
Possession must be relinquished

COMPLETED OPERATIONS CLAUSE
Completion of operations
Exclusions to Completed Operations
Clause

PRODUCTS LIABILITY EXCLUSIONS
Sistership exclusion
Injury to products exclusion
Injury to work performed exclusion
Business risk exclusion

PUNITIVE DAMAGES

SUMMARY

CONCLUSION

Sheila L. Birnbaum
Professor of Law
New York University School of Law
New York, New York

Sheila L. Birnbaum is a Professor of Law at New York University School of Law and of counsel to the firm of Skadden, Arps, Slate, Meagher & Flom. She has lectured and written extensively in the products liability field. She is Chairperson of the Products, General Liability, and Consumer Law Committee of the Torts and Insurance Practice Section of the American Bar Association and a member of the Products Liability Committee of the New York State Bar Association. Professor Birnbaum writes a column on products liability for the *National Law Journal.*

Diane S. Wilner
Skadden, Arps, Slate, Meagher & Flom
New York, New York

Diane S. Wilner, as a litigator with Skadden, Arps, Slate, Meagher & Flom, practices in the fields of product liability, toxic substances and insurance, and has lectured and published articles in these areas. She is President of the New York Woman's Bar Association, and a member of the Science and Technology and Torts and Insurance Practice Sections of the American Bar Association. Prior to practicing law, she was a biologist, having served as an educator and research scientist.

Under traditional rules of contract law which stem from the customs of ancient marketplaces, manufacturers and sellers of products were essentially responsible only to their immediate purchasers for injuries caused by their defective products. Thus, a third party who either obtained the product from the purchaser or suffered injury as a bystander could not recover from a retailer or manufacturer as a result of this privity barrier.

Only within the last two decades has an injured third party with no direct relationship (privity) to a manufacturer, distributor, or seller of a product been able to recover for damages sustained as a result of a defect in that product. It is this expansion of products liability law that has given rise to a need for products liability insurance coverage.[1]

MODERN TREND IN PRODUCTS LIABILITY LAW

The law recognizes that manufacturers, distributors, and sellers owe certain duties to anyone who foreseeably may come in contact with their products. Parties may recover damages for their injuries based upon various theories of liability including fraud, misrepresentation, negligence, breach of warranty, and strict liability in tort.

A manufacturer owes a duty to exercise reasonable care in designing, testing, manufacturing, and packaging its product. The manufacturer also has a duty to warn of any risks or dangers inherent in its product that are not obvious. Any breach of these duties, or the negligent performance of them, may result in liability.

Warranties may be express or implied. Any affirmation of fact or promise made by the seller that relates to the product and is part of the basis of the bargain creates an express warranty that the product will conform to such affirmation or promise, even though the seller does not use formal words such as *warranty* or *guarantee*. An implied warranty of fitness for a particular purpose arises when the buyer makes known to the seller the particular purpose for which the product is to be used and that the buyer is relying upon the seller's skill and judgment to select or furnish a suitable product. When a merchant sells goods, an implied warranty of merchantability arises that the goods are fit for the ordinary purposes for which such goods are used. An injured party can recover for bodily injury or property damage resulting from a breach of any of these warranties.

An injured user or consumer may also recover damages from a seller of a defective product based on a theory of strict liability in tort. This theory generally permits recovery for injuries caused by defective and unreasonably dangerous products even though the seller has exercised reasonable care in the preparation and sale of the product.

PRODUCTS LIABILITY COVERAGE

Present products liability insurance coverage had its beginnings in the mid 1920's. As the privity barrier fell and theories of strict products liability were expanded, products liability insurance coverage adapted to meet the needs of industry, with modern revisions to the standard policies occurring in 1966 and 1973.[2]

Products liability coverage is usually contained in a Comprehensive General Liability Policy. However, this coverage may be included in other types of policies such as druggists' or storekeepers' liability insurance. In rare instances, some businesses may prefer to obtain only that form of products liability coverage available separately as Products—Completed Operations Liability. Most insurers, however, are reluctant to write this insurance without Premises and Operations coverage.[3]

The basic purpose of products liability insurance is to provide coverage for damages imposed upon an insured, by reason of law, for injuries arising out of the insured's product, if such injuries occur after the insured has completed the product or work out of which the occurrence arises. Two operative provisions are necessary to implement this purpose: Products Hazard coverage for bodily injury or property damage away from the insured's premises arising out of the insured's product after the insured relinquished possession; and Completed Operations coverage for bodily injury or property damage arising after the insured's work has been completed. Although possession of the product and location of the occurrence may be irrelevant to the question of whether the injured party will ultimately recover damages from the insured, they can become significant factors regarding the question of whether the insured is covered for the damages claimed under the insurance policy.

Essentially, the Products Hazard provision gives the insured coverage for occurrences arising from products. Completed Operations provides coverage for occurrences arising out of completed work or services. Depending upon the specific needs of the insured, it may not be necessary to purchase coverage for both risks.

In order to comprehend products liability coverage, it is necessary to understand some general provisions contained in the typical Comprehensive General Liability Policy. The policy contains the following parts: declarations, insuring or coverage agreements, definitions, conditions, exclusions, and endorsements. Those risks actually insured can only be determined by evaluating, not only what is given, but what is excluded. Certain risks may be either specifically included or excluded. Although coverage for a particular risk may appear to be given by the insuring agreement or a declaration, the insured may find there is no coverage because the risk does not fall within an applicable definition, is subject to a condition that has not been met, falls within an exclusion, or has been "endorsed off the risk" (specifically excluded by an endorsement).

Moreover, you get what you pay for. Products liability coverage may be automatically included in some standard forms of Comprehensive General Liability Policies. Absent payment of a specific premium, however, such coverage may well be "endorsed off the risk." In other forms of policies where the risks regarding Products Hazard and Completed Operations are within the policy exclusions, products liability coverage may nonetheless be secured by endorsement and payment of an additional premium.

Generally an insured's business will automatically be covered for a new product or line that arises during the policy period.[4] The insured, however, must pay an additional premium for this coverage. Thus, the insured should understand that the premium for products liability coverage may increase during the policy period if new products are marketed.

A TYPICAL POLICY[5]

While each business should have a policy tailored to its own needs and each policy should be read carefully, there are some provisions common to most policies.

A typical policy provides:

> The company will pay on behalf of the insured all sums which the insured shall become legally obligated to pay as damages because of:
>
> > bodily injury or
> > property damage
>
> to which this insurance applies caused by an occurrence . . . the company shall not be obligated to pay any claim or judgment or to defend any suit after the applicable limit of the company's liability has been exhausted by payment of judgments or settlements.

The phrase "to which this insurance applies" points to the fact that in order for the insured to be indemnified by its insurer, the policy must contain a provision pursuant to which the risk has been insured, and even if there is a general provision providing such coverage, the specific risk must not have been excluded by any other provision of the insurance policy. For example, a drug manufacturer may have specifically purchased Products Hazard coverage, but the policy may contain an endorsement providing that there is no coverage for injuries arising out of the sale, manufacture, or distribution of any oral contraceptive. Accordingly, the drug manufacturer will not have insurance coverage for losses arising out of oral contraceptive drugs because such coverage has been specifically excluded by the endorsement.

Policy territory

The Comprehensive General Liability Policy provides coverage for property damage and bodily injury occurring within the policy territory, which generally encompasses the United States of America, its territories and possessions, and Canada. Coverage also generally extends to international waters and airspace if the damage or injury does not occur during transportation or travel to or from a foreign country.

Businesses that produce products for foreign markets or perform operations abroad may need to expand the general coverage provided. By way of endorsement, the policy territory can be expanded to include foreign countries, and the insured may obtain worldwide coverage if necessary. However, since a typical condition of such endorsement is that claims or lawsuits be brought or enforced in the United States, manufacturers with facilities in foreign countries should consider obtaining special insurance tailored to their particular needs.[6]

Applicable limits

The insurance coverage purchased by an insured is, of course, limited. Since the potential financial exposure associated with some products may be in the multi-million-dollar range or higher, a business should attempt to estimate the potential financial exposure arising from its products.[7] This may be a difficult if not impossible task. A manufacturer may be unable to predict and measure the probability or severity of injury from a product before actual injury occurs. Thus, the applicable policy limits can be significant, particularly where one product causes serious injury to a substantial number of people.

The applicable limits of a company's liability are usually contained in an endorsement. Coverage is generally limited in two ways: a limit of liability for each occurrence and an overall limit regarding the amount of money the insurer will pay on behalf of the insured in any given year during the policy period. By way of illustration, such endorsement may provide:

Coverage	*Limits of liability*
A. Bodily Injury	$25,000 each occurrence
	50,000 aggregate
B. Property Damage	5,000 each occurrence
	25,000 aggregate

In this example, the insurance company is liable for a maximum of $25,000 per occurrence for bodily injury and $5,000 per occurrence for property damage, regardless of the ultimate liability of the insured to those who are damaged by the insured's product. In other words, if three people each recover $10,000 in damages for bodily injuries arising out of one accident or occurrence involving the insured's product, the insured cannot recover the total of $30,000 from the insurance company pursuant to the policy, but may only recover $25,000. On the other hand, if three people recover $10,000 in damages for bodily injuries arising out of three separate accidents or occurrences involving the insured's product, then the insured can recover the full $30,000 from the insurance company.

Once the aggregate limit has been reached, coverage is exhausted. The aggregate limit is usually applicable to each year during the policy period. By way of illustration, if six people each recover $10,000 for bodily injury from the insured for six separate accidents or occurrences in the same year, the insurance company is responsible to indemnify the insured for only $50,000. The aggregate limits may become especially significant when one of the insured's products causes substantial injury.

A determination of whether there is one or more occurrence when a product causes injury is important in determining the limits of coverage. Where a product causes many injuries, does the "per occurrence" limit apply or is the "aggregate" limit applicable? For example, contaminated bird seed was sold to eight retailers who in turn sold it to customers. After the deaths of many birds, the question arose as to whether the eight sales of the contaminated product was one occurrence or eight occurrences. An interpretation that it was eight occurrences required the insurance company to indemnify the insured for a sum up to the aggregate limit. It has been suggested, however, that a 1973 revision to the standard policies should make it clear that continuous or repeated sales (or production) of a contaminated product may be considered as one occurrence, requiring the insurance company to pay up to the "per occurrence" and not the aggregate limit.

This problem, however, has not been completely resolved by the 1973 revision. A question that may be litigated in the future is whether the "per occurrence" limit can be stacked. Asbestosis and other asbestos related lung diseases are illustrative of this problem. One court found that a person with one of the asbestos related diseases was injured each time he inhaled asbestos fiber which impacted upon his lung tissue. The court held that each impact upon inhalation of asbestos fiber was an occurrence within the meaning of the insurance policy. Assume the injured persons recovers $500,000 from the insured and that the applicable insurance policy provides $250,000 per occurrence and $1 million aggregate. Since the injured person has experienced many occurrences, will the insurer be responsible for the full $500,000? On the other hand, since only one injured person is involved, should the "per occurrence" limit apply? These questions have not yet been answered by the courts.

Occurrence

A typical policy provides: "The company will pay . . . damages . . . caused by an occurrence. . . ." Most liability policies in use today are "occurrence" policies.[8] Occurrence is defined as:

> an accident, including continuous or repeated exposure to conditions, which results in bodily injury or property damage neither expected nor intended from the standpoint of the insured.

The definition of "occurrence" specifically excludes the infliction of intentional or expected injury. Thus, there is no coverage for marketing a product the insured knows will cause damage.

For coverage to attach, the injury must occur within the policy period. It is the injury, rather than the negligent act or mistake that created the product defect that is significant. The injury may be to persons or property. The injury may be sudden or the gradual result of repeated exposure. By way of illustration, assume a component of an automobile is defective. A customer drives out of the showroom and is injured when he loses control of the car because of the component's malfunction. This is a "sudden" occurrence. Or, assume the customer drove the automobile out of the showroom and the car appeared to handle properly. As the customer drove the car, however, the component gradually eroded and weakened. After the car was driven 5,000 miles, the defective component caused the driver to lose control of the car and injured him. This too is an occurrence. As long as the injury occurred during the policy period, the insured may recover. The definition of occurrence makes it unnecessary to determine the specific time of the injury causing event, as long as the injury occurs during the policy period. Thus, in our last example, it would be unnecessary to determine when the component part became sufficiently weakened to cause the injury.

When terminating a business, a manufacturer should continue its products liability insurance because there may be a defect in a product that causes an occurrence after the business has been terminated.[9] For corporations, the insurance should be maintained at least through the statutory "winding up" period provided by the applicable state's corporation law.

Since an "occurrence" during the policy period triggers coverage, the interpretation of "occurrence" will determine whether the damage in question is covered by the policy. The meaning to be given the term *occurrence* is being considered by several courts where injured persons have been exposed to asbestos products over a substantial period of time. In many of these cases, an injured plaintiff was diagnosed as having lung disease more than 20 years after initial exposure to asbestos. Assuming the injured claimants recover damages from the manufacturers, the critical question to be determined from the standpoint of insurance is "when did the injury occur?" Did the injury occur upon exposure to one asbestos fiber? Many asbestos fibers? Did the injury occur when the first cell change took place in the injured party's lung? Did it occur at or near the time of diagnosis?

To date, the federal appellate courts that have addressed this issue agree that each inhalation of asbestos caused impact upon lung tissue and is an "occurrence" within the meaning of the insurance policy. The meaning of *occurrence* is apt to continue to be of importance to manufacturers because it appears that more persons, including workers and consumers, are seeking damages for injuries claimed to have been caused by hazardous products manufactured and sold many years before diagnosis of illness.

PRODUCTS HAZARD CLAUSE

The jacket definition of Products Hazard in the Comprehensive General Liability Policy states:

> "products hazard" includes bodily injury and property damage arising out of the named insured's products or reliance upon a representation or warranty made at any time with respect thereto, but only if the bodily injury or property damage occurs away from premises owned by or rented to the named insured and after physical possession of such products has been relinquished to others.

Providing the insured pays the requisite premium, this clause provides insurance coverage for damages arising out of the named insured's products. Insured damage includes both bodily injury and property damage. Coverage is also provided for damages or injury arising out of reliance upon a representation or warranty (e.g., implied warranty of fitness for a particular purpose, implied warranty of merchantability, and express warranty) made regarding the insured's product. To assure that there is coverage for such warranty claims, the provision excluding liability assumed by the insured under any contract has been modified to except from such exclusion product claims based on warranty.

For Products Hazard coverage to attach, all of the following factors must be present: (1) a product or reliance on a representation regarding a product has caused injury or damage; (2) the injury or damage occurred away from the insured's premises; and (3) the insured gave up physical possession of the product before the injury or damage occurred.

The Products Hazard provision has been interpreted broadly. For example, a mail-order house negligently sold a teargas device to a minor. The insurance company argued that the Products Hazard provision should be limited to defective products as opposed to negligent sales. The court rejected this argument. The broad construction given to this clause by the court indicates that the insured is covered for injury caused by the manufacture (including defective design, improper workmanship, and inadequate testing), sale, handling, or distribution of the product. Thus, a retailer should be covered if he negligently sells a product to a minor, mistakenly delivers the wrong product, or fails to warn of a danger inherent in the product.

In order to understand fully the Products Hazard Clause, it is necessary to review other definitions contained in the policy.

What are products?

Products are defined as follows:

> "Named insured's products" means goods or products manufactured, sold, handled or distributed by the named insured or by others trading under his name, including any container thereof (other than a vehicle), but "named insured's products" shall not include a vending machine or any property other than such container, rented to or located for use of others but not sold.

A product is usually a tangible substance in which one trades. However, it need not be the item one primarily trades in. In one case, a bottled gas dealer provided gas cylinders to his customers at no charge. When a cylinder exploded, it was held to be "goods" within the Products Hazard Clause.

Under the Products Hazard Clause a product includes any container holding the product, other than a vehicle. Most policies, however, specifically state that a product does not include vending machines, or any products that are rented, leased, or bailed but not sold. Accordingly, one engaged solely in the business of leasing or renting equipment does not generally need Products Hazard protection. However, such a business should consider obtaining a policy with a Premises and Operations provision.

Injury or damage away from premises

Products Hazard coverage is provided "if the bodily injury or property damage occurs away from premises owned by or rented to the named insured. . . ." This language is intended to effectuate the purpose of product liability coverage, which is to provide insurance for losses arising after the product has been completed and put into the stream of commerce.

For certain businesses, however, such as a restaurant, where products are consumed on the premises, the typical Products Hazard coverage would be of no benefit to the insured. Such businesses should obtain a standard endorsement that redefines Products Hazard whereby coverage attaches "after physical possession has been relinquished." The phrase "away from premises" thus would be omitted in a standard restaurant endorsement.

Possession must be relinquished

Not only must the occurrence take place away from the insured's premises, but Products Hazard coverage attaches "only if the bodily injury or property damage occurs . . . after physical possession of such products has been relinquished to others."

The legal distinction between "custody" and "possession" and the passage of legal title to the product is insignificant for the purpose of products liability coverage. The transfer of physical possession is the critical event.

For example, assume an insured is a retailer engaging in a promotional scheme to sell appliances. A potential customer takes the appliance home on a special ten-day trial offer, actually intending to return it at the end of the trial period. The appliance explodes in the potential customer's kitchen, causing serious bodily injury. Since the occurrence took place away from the retailer's premises and the retailer relinquished physical possession of the appliance, coverage is provided under the Products Hazard Clause. For the purpose of products liability coverage, it is unimportant that legal title to the appliance remained with the retailer.

COMPLETED OPERATIONS CLAUSE

Under modern tort law, one may be held liable for damages arising from services or work performed carelessly. This liability can be imposed long after the completion of the work in question. Building and construction contractors are obvious examples of businessmen who should purchase Completed Operations coverage.

The Comprehensive General Liability Policy jacket defines this clause as follows:

"Completed operations hazard" includes bodily injury and property damage arising out of operations or reliance upon a representation or warranty made at any time with respect thereto, but only if the bodily injury or property damage occurs after such operations have been completed or abandoned and occurs away from premises owned by or rented to the named insured. "Operations" include materials, parts or equipment furnished in connection therewith. Operations shall be deemed completed at the earliest of the following times.

1. When all operations to be performed by or on behalf of the named insured under contract have been completed,
2. When all operations to be performed by or on behalf of the named insured at the site of the operations have been completed or
3. When the portion of the work out of which the injury or damage arises has been put to its intended use by any person or organization other than another contractor or subcontractor engaged in performing operations for a principal as a part of the same project.

Operations which may require further service or maintenance work, or correction, repair or replacement because of any defect or deficiency, but which are otherwise complete, shall be deemed completed.

Completed Operations coverage is similar to Products Hazard coverage in that (1) bodily injury and property damage are covered; (2) the damage in question may arise out of either the insured's operations or reliance upon a representation or warranty in connection therewith; (3) coverage is provided only if injury or damage occurs after completion or abandonment of the operations; and (4) if the occurrence takes place away from the insured's premises. While Completed Operations coverage is aimed at insuring exposures arising out of completed work or services, it includes materials, parts, or equipment furnished in connection with such services or operations.

Completion of operations

There is a fine line between Premises and Operations Liability coverage and Completed Operations coverage. The insurance policy contains three clauses defining when operations are considered complete.

Operations are deemed to be complete when any one of the following events takes place:

1. The contract terms have been met; or
2. All work at the site of operations is finished. (Where a project involves work at many locations, the Completed Operations

Clause applies to each site or location as the work is finished at that location. Thus, if the same type of accident occurs at two different locations, and the operations are incomplete at the first location and complete at the second, theoretically, Premises and Operations coverage should apply to the former and Completed Operations coverage should apply to the latter.); or

3. "When the portion of the work out of which the injury or damage arises has been put to its intended use. . . ." (By way of illustration, where a tenant moves into a completed floor of a building still under construction, and that tenant suffers injury as a result of the negligent services that went into constructing that floor, operations will be deemed complete, even though the entire building has not been completed. However, if upon completion of that one floor, the contractor stores materials there before a tenant moves in and an injury arises out of the work performed on that floor, Completed Operations coverage does not apply. Such injury should be covered by Premises and Operations Liability coverage.)

The operations are deemed complete at the earliest happening of any of the three events listed above. Completed Operations coverage attaches even if further service is required by the insured, providing that service is in the nature of maintenance work, correction, repair, or replacement because of any defect or deficiency. Thus, an insured who must repair defective work should not be concerned regarding his Completed Operations insurance coverage. For example, where a contractor must return to a finished building to replaster a defective ceiling, he will still be covered by the Completed Operations provision if the ceiling falls and injures someone.[10]

Exclusions to Completed Operations Clause

The definition of Completed Operations contains three specific exclusions.

The completed operations hazard does not include bodily injury or property damage arising out of

a. Operations in connection with the transportation of property, unless the bodily injury or property damage arises out of a condition in or on a vehicle created by the loading or unloading thereof,

b. The existence of tools, uninstalled equipment or abandoned or unused materials, or

c. Operations for which the classification stated in the policy or in the company's manual specifies "including completed operations."

Damage or injury arising out of operations in connection with transportation of property is excluded. However, where the injury or damage arises out of a condition created by the loading or unloading of a vehicle, the Completed Operations insurance coverage is applicable.[11] An example of the second exclusion is where a contractor finished a building, turned it over to the owners and a tenant was injured by uninstalled materials left at the building by the contractor. This type of injury, as well as damage arising out of operations in connection with transportation of property, falls within the Premises and Operations Liability Clause. The third exclusion to the Completed Operations Clause refers to damage or injury arising out of those operations included in the Premises and Operations Liability Clause by the policy itself or the insurance company's manual.

PRODUCTS LIABILITY EXCLUSIONS

The purpose of products liability insurance is to indemnify the insured for losses incurred as a result of property damage or bodily injury to a third party (e.g., consumer, user, bystander) arising out of the insured's products or services. Products liability insurance is not intended to provide coverage to the insured for (a) losses incurred because the insured has to recall defectively designed products, (b) injury to the insured's products or work, or (c) losses resulting from the failure of the insured's work to serve the purpose or function intended. While the insured may be legally liable for such losses, they are not covered under products liability insurance.[12]

Sistership exclusion

It is not unusual these days to read or hear that a manufacturer or distributor is recalling a product from the market. For example, according to figures compiled by the National Highway Traffic Safety Administration, almost 9 million vehicles and more than 250,000 tires were recalled for safety defects in 1979. Domestic manufacturers recalled 7 million vehicles in 205 recall campaigns. The cost of recalling a product may be extremely high. In 1971 the Food and Drug Administration required Bon Vivant to remove 4 million cans of soup from the market when it was suspected that some cans of soup caused botulism. Following the recall costs and adverse publicity, Bon Vivant filed for reorganization under the Bankruptcy Act. When an engine fell off an American Airlines jet in 1979, all DC-10s were grounded for inspection. The inspection costs, economic loss from grounded planes, cancelled reservations, and other losses from adverse publicity had a considerable impact upon the airline industry.

A governmental agency may compel or influence a manufacturer to recall a product or the manufacturer itself may initiate the recall. It may be unwise for a manufacturer to delay recalling a product where there is reason to expect that the product may cause injury. Pursuant to the definition of "occurrence," products liability insurance does not provide coverage for "expected" bodily injury or property damage. Accordingly, where a manufacturer has reason to know that one of its products can cause injury, it may be necessary to recall the product in order to maintain products liability coverage for that product.

Although a manufacturer or distributor may be under an obligation, legal or otherwise, to recall, inspect, replace, or repair its products, most liability policies do not provide coverage for these risks, which are excluded by the sistership exclusion. In most liability policies the sistership exclusion states:

> This insurance does not apply to damages claimed for the withdrawal, inspection, repair, replacement, or loss of use of the named insured's products or work completed by or for the named insured or of any property of which such products or work form a part, if such products, work or property are withdrawn from the market or from use because of any known or suspected defect or deficiency therein.

This exclusion applies to both products and completed work, and excludes expenses incurred by the insured or anyone else (e.g., the insured's buyer). This exclusion applies whether the expenses are incurred in connection with withdrawing products or work from the market or in connection with the loss of use of products before they are actually marketed. Furthermore, the exclusion is applicable to products recalled because of a suspected as well as a known defect.

This exclusion also applies to those situations where the defective work or product is only a part of the ultimate product. For example, assume that the insured utilizes a component part in manufacturing its product. Further, after the insured's product is marketed, it is discovered that the component part is defective. As a result, the insured must recall the entire product from the market. This loss may not be recovered pursuant to either the insured's policy or the component part manufacturer's policy because of the sistership exclusion. However, some courts do not interpret the sistership exclusion in this manner and may allow coverage for the component part manufacturer who is sued by the manufacturer of the product for the costs of recalling the product.

In summary, the sistership exclusion is intended to exclude expenses incurred in connection with withdrawing a product from the market. This exclusion is not applicable to bodily injury or to damage to *other* tangible property caused by the insured's product.

Manufacturers who need recall insurance may be able to obtain it from some insurance companies. It should be specifically requested by the insured and would require an additional premium. When requesting recall insurance, management should consider all of the expenses that could arise from the recall and seek appropriate coverage. Examples of expenses incident to product recall are: telephone, telegraph, radio, television, and newspaper announcements; costs of stationery, postage, and printing of announcements; personnel costs, including additional personnel and overtime for regular personnel; costs of inspection; and costs of returning nondefective products to the customer. Since product recall insurance is likely to cover only products in the United States and Canada, those businesses servicing international markets should be cognizant of their individual insurance needs.

Injury to products exclusion

Products liability insurance is intended to provide coverage for bodily injury or property damage arising from the insured's products, but it is not intended to provide coverage for expenses incurred in connection with the replacement or repair of the insured's products which themselves become damaged. The insured must bear any losses associated with repair or replacement of defective products, regardless of whether the defect was caused by the manufacturer or the supplier of a component part.

The following exclusionary language appears in most general liability policies to cover such situations:

> This insurance does not apply to property damage to the named insured's products arising out of such products or any part of such products.

Where an insured, in manufacturing a product, utilizes a component part that is defective, and if as a result the insured's product is inoperable or damaged, the exclusion applies, and the insured cannot recover for any losses incurred in the repair or replacement of the product. Moreover, the supplier of the component part will not be covered under its policy for replacement of the defective component part. However, the question arises as to whether there is coverage under the supplier's policy where the component part causes damage to the manufacturer's product. The answer should be in the affirmative because the supplier's product has caused property damage away from the supplier's premises after the supplier has relinquished possession of the component part. In one case, this exclusion did not preclude coverage where a hot water heater installed on a boat caused damage to the boat. The court reasoned that the hot water heater was the product out of which the accident occurred.[13]

Injury to work performed exclusion

The obligation of the insured to repair or redo defective work is specifically excluded:

> This insurance does not apply to property damage to work performed by or on behalf of the named insured arising out of the work or any portion thereof, or out of materials, parts or equipment furnished in connection therewith.

Thus, where an insured must repair a ceiling it installed, it may not recover the replacement cost from its insurer. This exclusion applies whether or not the insured's operations are completed.

Business risk exclusion

The business risk exclusion is based upon an intention to exclude coverage for damage claims arising out of the product's failure to perform the function or purpose intended by the manufacturer if such failure arises out of a defect or mistake in design, formula, plan, advertising material, or printed instruction prepared by the insured. It should be noted that this clause does not exclude coverage for claims of bodily injury or damage to property caused by the insured's product.

The business risk exclusion states that the policy does not apply:

> to loss of use of tangible property which has not been physically injured or destroyed resulting from
> 1. A delay in or lack of performance by or on behalf of the named insured of any contract or agreement, or
> 2. The failure of the named insured's products or work performed by or on behalf of the named insured to meet the level of performance, quality, fitness or durability warranted or represented by the named insured;
>
> but this exclusion does not apply to loss of use of other tangible property resulting from the sudden and accidental physical injury to or destruction of the named insured's products or work performed by or on behalf of the named insured after such products or work have been put to use by any person or organization other than an insured. . . .

This exclusion does not distinguish between management and employee error or design and production error. The exclusion is designed to eliminate insurance coverage for those risks more appropriately shouldered by the insured in the normal course of its business.

Where an insured is responsible for constructing a building and fails to complete the building by the time specified in the contract, the insured may be liable for losses arising from its delay in performing its contractual obligations. However, the insured will not be able to recover this loss pursuant to subsection (1) of the business risk exclusion.

Subsection (2) would exclude losses such as those incurred as a result of the failure of a boiler to heat an amount of water as represented by the insured. Any loss of use of the building from this failure to perform as represented should not be covered by the policy. However, this exclusion contains an exception. If the boiler accidentally and suddenly breaks down, causing no other injury, and is essential to the building, this loss of use of the building is covered. (This loss of use falls within an exception to an exclusion from coverage.)

PUNITIVE DAMAGES

A person instituting a products liability lawsuit usually seeks compensatory damages to restore or compensate for the loss. In some instances, injured plaintiffs have succeeded in recovering punitive damages in addition to compensatory damages. Punitive damages are awarded to punish a defendant for his outrageous, wrongful conduct and to deter the defendant and others from engaging in similar wrongful acts. In states that permit a punitive damages award in a products liability case, it must generally be established that the seller recklessly disregarded the safety of product users.

Where punitive damages are awarded, the question arises as to whether an insured may recover for such expenditures pursuant to its products liability insurance. This question has been answered both affirmatively and negatively by courts.

In resolving this issue, courts have been called upon to interpret the insurance policy to determine whether punitive damage awards are within the provided coverage. In making such determination, it is necessary to look to the specific policy language in question. In some instances, courts have been called upon to interpret an insurance policy which provides coverage for damages awarded "because of bodily injury" or "because of property damage." This language has been construed to exclude punitive damages. On the other hand, where the insurance policy provides coverage for "all sums for which the insured is legally liable . . . as damages," it can be argued that punitive damages are included in the term *all sums*. Accordingly, this language has been construed to provide coverage to the insured for punitive damages.

Beyond the policy language in question, courts are also confronted with questions of public policy in deciding whether an insured may recover for punitive damages under an insurance policy. Awards of punitive damages are based on various rationales, which include, among others, punishment of a wrongdoer and deterrence of others from engaging in similar conduct. These public policy reasons may be undermined by permitting a wrongdoer to pass off the assessed punishment to its insurer. Accordingly, even where punitive damages arguably fall within the coverage of an insurance policy, a court may not permit an insured to recover such loss from the insurer on the grounds of public policy. In some instances, however, public policy may not be offended by permitting an insured to recover from its insurer for a punitive damage award. For example, a business may be held liable for punitive damages for an act done by one of its employees. Where the business did not take part in the wrongdoing and is only vicariously liable, neither the "punishment" nor "deterrence" purpose of awarding punitive damages is affected by permitting insurance coverage.

Recently, as punitive damage awards began to increase in frequency and size, some insurers endorsed punitive damages off the risk, specifically excluding them from insurance coverage. Consequently, although a manufacturer obtains product liability insurance, he should not expect all damages associated with his product to be covered by insurance. The best "insurance" against punitive damage awards may be pre-marketing and post-marketing efforts to reduce the risk of injury or damage from a product.

SUMMARY

While product liability insurance is in a state of flux, it has evolved sufficiently to provide management with some general guidelines. Consider the following examples:

1.   John Innovator designed a new type of automobile powered by solar energy. He intends to manufacture and market it next year. He plans to begin the business in his garage but is hopeful that the business will be successful enough to permit him to build a manufacturing plant within five years. Does he need products liability insurance? Since Mr. Innovator has not manufactured any product yet, he does not need products liability insurance. However, once he manufactures and sells his product, he would be well advised to obtain this insurance.

2.   Sally Cola's business involves the sale and distribution of bottled softdrinks. One of her customers complained because a bottle exploded in the customer's home injuring her seven-year-old son. Is Ms. Cola covered for this claim? If she has Products Hazard coverage, Ms. Cola may recover from her insurer since the "container" is included within the definition of "product."

3.   A toy manufacturer has been requested by the Consumer Products Safety Commission to recall a specific toy that is hazardous to children because of a design defect. Can the cost of this recall be recovered from the insurer? No. The sistership exclusion to products liability insurance precludes coverage for these expenses.

4. You have just installed a new heating system in your customer's house and learn that your employee incorrectly installed it. Can you recover expenses incurred as a result of having to go to the customer's home and reinstall the system yourself? No. These expenses fall within the work performed exclusion.

5. After installing a new heating system in your customer's house, the system malfunctions, explodes, and damages one wall of the house. Can you recover expenses incurred in repairing the damage to the wall? Yes, assuming you have products liability coverage.

CONCLUSION

Products liability insurance, like products liability law itself, is in a state of evolution. In view of the rapid expansion of products liability law, a manufacturer or seller must have sufficient products liability insurance, both in amount and coverage. A substantial product defect, if not covered by insurance, could bankrupt a small company and significantly affect the financial stability of even a large company. Management would be well advised to consult with insurance brokers, risk managers, and attorneys in order to be certain that their insurance needs are adequately met.

NOTES

1. Products liability coverage apparently had its earliest beginnings in England in 1890, when policies were written to insure bakers against the accidental addition of roach powder to dough.

2. Only those revisions presently in effect are discussed in this chapter.

3. Since Premises and Operations coverage protects a manufacturer against loss from injury or damages to a third party arising from an occurrence *during* the period in which the product is being manufactured and products liability coverage protects the manufacturer for damage or injury to a third party *after* the product production process is complete, it may be desirable for a manufacturer to obtain both coverages.

4. Some policies, however, contain a provision requiring the insured to notify the insurer within 90 days of marketing a new product.

5. Although some general guidelines can be enunciated regarding products liability insurance, it should be noted that in most instances, insurance policies differ from business to business. No business has the exact same insurance needs as another business, even if they are within the same industry. In addition, insurance policies may differ depending upon, among other things, (1) which insurer issues the policy, (2) the insurance broker used, and (3) the state in which the policy is issued. Therefore, statements made within this chapter are intended to be used as educational guidelines. Management would be well advised to consult appropriate professionals for guidance.

6. By way of illustration, a manufacturer with a foreign plant designed to produce products for use in that foreign country may find itself amenable to a claim or suit in that foreign country. Such claim or suit would not ordinarily be covered pursuant to a standard worldwide coverage endorsement.

7. Inasmuch as there can be multimillion-dollar risks associated with

some products, it is necessary for some companies to obtain layered coverage, which spreads the risk among many insurance carriers. For example, it was reported that one automobile manufacturer, for the period December 15, 1977, through December 15, 1978, had the following insurance: it retained the first $2 million as a self-insurer; one carrier provided $5 million excess of primary; seven insurers provided $15 million excess of $5 million; eight carriers provided the next layer of $30 million excess of $20 million; nine carriers provided the next $25 million excess of $50 million; and seven carriers provided $25 million excess of $75 million.

8. Earlier policies provided coverage for "accidents." Some policies today, such as medical and legal malpractice policies, provide coverage for "claims made." An "occurrence" includes an accident. While the occurrence must take place during the policy period for coverage to attach, a claim can be made after the policy period.

9. Because the statute of limitations runs from date of discovery of the injury in some states, one may not receive notice of a lawsuit regarding a product manufactured by a terminated business until several years after termination of that business.

10. However, the insured will not be covered for the cost of repairing the ceiling. This expense is subject to an exclusion.

11. This is an example of an exception to an exclusion from a clause providing coverage. In other words, the clause provides coverage, the exclusion takes it away, and the exception gives it back.

12. Expenses arising out of the situations falling within the specific exclusions to the Completed Operations Clause are usually covered by other insurance. On the other hand, expenses incurred as a result of events falling within the general products liability exclusions are usually not covered by any other insurance and must be borne by the insured.

13. In other words, the product (hot water heater) caused injury to other property (the boat). Had the court viewed the boat as the product out of which the accident occurred, the injury would have been to the insured's product and excluded. The definition of "product" can be significant with regard to this exclusion.

CONTROLLING SPECIALIZED EXPOSURES

CHAPTER 13

SURETY BONDS

A SURETY BOND IS NOT AN
INSURANCE POLICY

LICENSE AND PERMIT BONDS

CONSTRUCTION AND RELATED
CONTRACT SURETY BONDS
  Bid Bonds
  Performance Bonds
  Payment Bonds
  The Maintenance Bond
  Subdivision Bonds

JUDICIAL BONDS
  Replevin Bonds
  Lien Discharge Bonds

PUBLIC OFFICIAL BONDS

COURT FIDUCIARY BONDS

MISCELLANEOUS SURETY BONDS
  Lost Instrument Bonds
  Tax Bonds
  Financial Guaranty Bonds
  Lease Bonds

THE DECISION TO BOND

George L. Blick
Assistant Vice President
Aetna Casualty & Surety Company
Hartford, Connecticut

George L. Blick attended DePaul University and DePaul University Law School. A Major in the U.S. Marine Corps Reserve, Mr. Blick commenced his employment with the Aetna Casualty & Surety Company in 1959 as a claim representative in the Chicago Office. In 1964 he was transferred to the home office in Hartford as Senior Claims Analyst. Mr. Blick was appointed Claims Manager in 1971 and Assistant Vice President in 1980. As such he directs all fidelity and surety claim matters of the largest fidelity and surety company in the country.

Charles H. Carman
President
National Association of Surety Bond Producers
Washington, D.C.

Charles H. Carman is Chairman of the Board of Charles H. Carman, Inc. & Carman Brokerage Corporation, New York, N.Y. He serves presently as President of the National Association of Surety Bond Producers having served as Past Chairman of National Insurance Producers Council. Mr. Carman is a member of the New York Small Business Administration Advisory Council, the N.Y. Building Congress, the Building Contractors Association, the American Subcontractors Association, and the Greater N.Y. Insurance Brokers Association.

A SURETY BOND IS NOT AN INSURANCE POLICY

Unlike a Fidelity Bond which is purchased by one who desires protection against the acts of others, a Surety Bond is purchased by a party who has agreed to perform a stated obligation, for the purpose of guaranteeing the performance of that obligation.

The Surety Bond or "Guarantee Bond" is in fact a contract of performance between a Principal (the individual, corporation, partnership, or joint venture who is obligated to perform a contractual commitment) and an Obligee (the entity to whom the commitment has been made), and in addition, a third party to the contract, a Surety (who guarantees fulfillment of the Principal's undertaking). Should the Principal not perform the obligations stated in the bond and its underlying documents, which together set forth the obligation of the Principal and the duties of the Surety, the Surety is required contractually to respond to the Obligee.[1]

Surety bonding is often misunderstood for a Surety Bond is not an insurance policy—it is merely an extension of credit—more akin to an irrevocable bank line of credit than an insurance policy. In corporate suretyship the Surety acts as a guarantor of credit up to a certain amount (the bond penalty).

Just as a bank when it agrees to make a loan presumes that no loss will occur, so too does the Surety underwriter who charges a fee for the extension of credit (the Surety guarantee) based on an analysis of the financial data and an acceptance of the nature and amount of indemnity supplied by the Principal. The fee charged by the Surety is an amount which is based on covering its costs of administration and underwriting as opposed to the charge made by an insurance underwriter which is based on the probability of loss.

Insurance, on the other hand, does presume that a loss will occur, and its cost is based on the statistical probability of that loss and the dollars required in the satisfaction of that loss made from the total pool of premiums paid by all insureds.

The most acceptable risk to the Surety is the one which will cause the least risk of loss, the Principal who in adverse times will be able to respond to his obligation. Economic wealth means little to the insurer; it means far more to the Surety. Financial statements will seldom, if ever, be required of the applicant for an insurance policy. Conversely, they will almost always be required of the applicant for a Surety Bond.

Insurance policies are generally cancellable upon notification. Bonds are less easily cancelled, and sometimes they cannot be cancelled at all. Construction Bonds cannot be cancelled once they have been executed in connection with an award of a contract even if the

Surety Company has not received its premium from the contractor, or even if fraud had induced the Surety to write the bond. This represents additional expense to the Surety, for it must continuously monitor the Principal and the bonds written for that Principal, particularly when an ongoing program of suretyship is provided.

The general categories of Guarantee Bonds are License and Permit Bonds, Construction and Related Contract Bonds, Judicial Bonds, Public Official Bonds, Court Fiduciary Bonds, and Miscellaneous Bonds.

LICENSE AND PERMIT BONDS

Many businesses are required to obtain a license or permit prior to commencing operations; for example, gasoline dealers and distributors, collection agencies, electricians (most skilled tradesmen), retail and wholesale liquor dealers, real estate brokers and agents, automobile dealers, livestock, produce and milk dealers, restaurant and warehouse operations, and so forth. So too are practically all businesses which are required to collect sales taxes, and all businesses which are subject to revenue taxes and customs duties.

The Obligee (the entity to whom the commitment is made) is generally the agency or authority which issues the necessary license, permit, or required combination thereof. In some cases, however, the obligation runs not to the license issuer but with whom the Principal deals (the customer), and an injured party can make a claim directly against the Surety when the Principal fails to conduct its business as required by ordinance, regulation, or statute.

Failure to obtain proper licenses can have serious consequences. For example, an unlicensed construction contractor in many states is precluded from suing to collect contract funds to which he may well be entitled. Further, fines and penalties may be assessed for failure to obtain appropriate licenses and permits. Competent counsel is imperative prior to commencing operation both to the license and permit requirements of the authorities which regulate the particular business enterprise and to the licensing and other filing requirements of the appropriate taxing authorities.

CONSTRUCTION AND RELATED CONTRACT SURETY BONDS

There are five types of Construction Bonds: Bid Bonds, Performance Bonds, Payment Bonds, Maintenance Bonds, and Subdivision Bonds.

Bid Bonds

In situations where contractors are competitively bidding, Bid or Proposal Bonds are usually required. These Bid Bonds are in effect contracts of indemnity which guarantee to the owner of a construction project that if the contractor (the Principal of the Bid Bond Surety) is selected for award of the contract, the contractor will enter into the construction agreement, and in the event that the contractor refuses to accept the award, that the contractor has the capacity to compensate the owner for damages resulting from that refusal. In addition, it gives project owners some security that a construction Surety has examined its contractor's bid and in effect prequalified it by investigating the contractor's ability to complete the project successfully.

The Bid Bond penalty is often an amount equal to a stated percentage, as for example, 5 percent of the amount of the bid. Generally, however, the bond is conditioned to pay the owner's actual damages as a result of the contractor's failure to enter into the agreement. Depending on the terms of the bond (as required by the owner or the statutory requirements if furnished in accordance with a public law), the Surety whose Principal has failed to execute the construction agreement or tender the required Performance and Payment Bonds may be required to forfeit the bond penalty, or may be required to pay the difference between the amount of the winning low bid (its Principal's) and the cost of reletting to another contractor up to the dollar limit of the Bid Bond.

Performance Bonds

This bond guarantees to the owner of a construction project that the construction project will be completed by the contractor to whom the contract has been awarded in accordance with the plans and specifications and other contract documents, and that in the event of default by the contractor in the performance of the work, the Surety can be called upon to intervene in response to the contractor's nonperformance. This bond is generally co-extensive with the obligation of the contractor under the construction agreement and imposes upon the bonding company all of the obligations imposed upon the contractor by his contract or by law with respect to the contract.

The Surety has options when a default is declared, which are usually detailed in the contract and/or the bond. Generally, the Surety can either (and at its discretion) tender the bond penalty and walk away, arrange for completion of the project through another contractor (or contractors), rest on its contract suretyship by responding in damages for the default within the penalty of the bond (the owner completes and looks to the Surety for its loss), or finance its Principal (in the event the Principal is insolvent) in the completion of the contract.

Defenses are at times raised by the Surety to an owner's Performance Bond claim alleging default by the construction contractor. These defenses and attempts to be discharged of its Surety Bond obligations are generally based on one of the following positions:

a. A substantial violation by the owner of a part of the construction agreement to the prejudice of the Surety, as for example, the failure to carry builders' risk insurance.
b. A substantial overpayment to the contractor.
c. A material change in the contract above and beyond the scope of the original agreement.

Payment Bonds

The Payment Bond guarantees to the suppliers of labor, services, and material who are defined as claimants under the terms of the bond, that if they comply with the requirements of the bond as to "notice" and as to "time for suit" that, in the event they are not paid for the supply and performance of their work, they will be remunerated by the Surety.

The Maintenance Bond

The construction contract may require the contractor to deliver a Maintenance Bond following acceptance of the project (or a portion of it) by the owner. The bond secures the owner that the contractor will return to the job to perform maintenance or correction work to a state specified by the contract documents during the contract guarantee period. The Maintenance Bond Surety guarantees the performance of this obligation.

Subdivision Bonds

These bonds guarantee that a developer or builder who is subdividing or otherwise preparing land for (speculative) development will perform his work to completion and in conformity with local codes and required conditions. For example, paving and grading within the site, necessary sewage connections and hookups, sidewalks as required, connection of streets within a subdivision with existing streets, and the completion of other offsite improvements.

JUDICIAL BONDS

The small business should have little use for Judicial Bonds, for it can ill afford them. Unfortunately, however, some may be necessary from time to time. Two of the basic Judicial Bonds are the Replevin Bond and Lien Discharge Bond.

Replevin Bonds

The legal action of replevin (sometimes called *claim and recovery* of *sequestration*) is one which is instituted for the recovery of assets in the physical possession of another which property is alleged to be the legal property of the claimant. The claimant must post a bond which guarantees that the asset (if not the property of the claimant to which it is returned) will be delivered at the end of litigation to the true owner in its original condition, together with any loss sustained by the rightful owner in the interim because of deprivation of use of the property.

Lien Discharge Bonds

A lien filed against real estate discourages those who may wish to purchase the real estate. The Lien Discharge Bond removes this cloud upon the real estate and allows an adverse judgment against the Principal to be satisfied from other assets of the Principal of alternatively from the proceeds of the Lien Discharge Bond.

PUBLIC OFFICIAL BONDS

Public Official Bonds guarantee (to a greater or lesser extent) that public official will perform the duties required of their office. The bond is frequently a hybrid document, depending upon the office held and the bond involved. Various coverages may be obtained and can range from "faithful performance" to "performance in accordance with the required duties and customary standards of the office-holder" to protection of the obligee that there be no dishonesty on the part of the office-holder. The range is vast and the consequences equally so.

COURT FIDUCIARY BONDS

In legal situations where the highest standards are imposed by law and equity ("what's right") upon an individual, Court Fiduciary Bonds are required. These situations range from one serving in the capacity of overseeing the administration of a deceased friend's or relative's estate to assuming the responsibilities of guardianship of a minor or being the conservator of an incompetent's estate. The names of the bonds differ, but the responsibilities inherent are generally descriptive in their titles. Fiduciary Bonds generally require the highest standards of meeting set rules and abiding by a competent attorney's advice. Recordkeeping may be entailed, and hiring an accountant may be necessary. Failure to meet deadlines can lead to varying degrees of grief and disaster.

MISCELLANEOUS SURETY BONDS

These run the gamut and include those required to be posted by organizations which use federal property to bonds required of those who import foreign automobiles which do not but must eventually meet environmental standards. The most common of these miscellaneous bonds are discussed below.

Lost Instrument Bonds

When a stock certificate has been lost, misplaced, stolen, or destroyed, an issuer generally requires, prior to delivering a replacement certificate, that the applicant tender a Lost Instrument Bond. This bond guarantees that in the event the certificate re-appears, that the issuer will suffer no loss by having replaced the original certificate. The major underwriting considerations are the moral character of the applicant, his financial capacity, and the degree of negotiability of the lost item.

Tax Bonds

Tax Bonds are posted to defer the collection of a questioned tax obligation where if collected without a deferral would result in undue hardship.

Financial Guaranty Bonds

Financial Guaranty Bonds guarantee the payment of a sum of money.

Lease Bonds

Lease Bonds are bonds given to a lessor which guarantee that the lessee will perform the covenant of the lease including (1) the payment of rent, taxes, and expenses; (2) the return of the property in good condition at the expiration of the term and the replacement of any property removed, altered, damaged or destroyed; and (3) the keeping of the property in satisfactory repair and covered by the insurance requirements of the lease.

THE DECISION TO BOND

Like material suppliers and banks who extend credit, the Surety underwriter relies basically on the character, the capital, and the capacity of its Principal to perform its contractual commitment before issuing its bond. In construction and related contract Surety bonding, most bonds are written by a limited number of specialized agents who have developed relationships of confidence with Surety underwriters, as well as knowledge of their particular approaches to an underwriting presentation.

Once assured that the Principal has the experience and qualifications, the management capacity, and the financial soundness (and in construction situations, the belief that the contractor can complete the contract without default), the Surety formalizes its legal relationship with its Principal by requiring the execution of the Agreement of Indemnity. Often for purposes of further security, the Surety requires Indemnity Agreements not only from its Principal (usually a corporation) but also from the individuals who are the Principal owners as well as their spouses.

The Indemnity Agreement broadens the Surety's common-law right that its Principal reimburse it for any loss it may incur by further providing that:

a. The Principal and indemnitors indemnify the Surety against all liability for losses and expenses of every kind (including attorney and expert fees).
b. The Surety be permitted to make final and binding determinations on settlements and defenses.
c. That in construction situations the Surety have upon default of its contractor Principal,
  □ Right, title, and interest in the contractor's supplies, equipment, and material.
  □ Right to the proceeds of the construction contract.
  □ The right to complete performance of the project.
  □ The right to control the performance of the Principal.
d. That the Surety has the right to demand the deposit of collateral.
e. The right to look to the individual indemnitors for reimbursement of its losses.

Sometimes the Surety may require collateral in an amount which it deems adequate before issuing its bond. While the collateral of the Principal (or the one providing the collateral) is still the property of the Principal, the collateral cannot be disposed of by the owner without the Surety's consent. Since the proceeds of the sale of collateral will be used by the Surety in the event it has to satisfy a claim under its bond, liquid assets, such as cash, certified or cashier's check, assignment or joint control of a savings account passbook are required. In some cases, an irrevocable letter of credit from a bank in a form satisfactory to the Surety may be used. Because the collateral reduces the Surety's chances of loss, a reduced premium for the bond can sometimes be negotiated.

When a Surety refuses to write a bond, it is generally keyed to the premise that a Surety expects no loss and that the analysis of the experienced underwriter who reviews the presentation believes that a loss could occur. The addition of a strong third party indemnitor (one whose financial assurance the Surety would not otherwise have) may result in acceptance of the risk. Another factor which may be the basis of a refusal to bond may be an economic trend which indicates doom to the future of a particular business or endeavor. The Surety may have reservations about assuming liability in this potentially weak area. Perhaps it already has a "book of business" in this area and believes the assumption of further risks of the same nature would be unsound.

In the early and mid-1970s there were unprecedented losses, tantamount to crisis in the surety industry. Many companies curtailed writing many forms of Guaranty Bonds. Some companies failed. As a result Surety companies have become most stringent in writing Surety Bonds. We close this chapter with an expression of hope that the parallel economic conditions of today to those of the crisis days of the 1970s do not lead to similar unprecedented losses.

NOTE

1. This discussion presumes a paid corporate surety. In modern practice it is a rarity to find an individual assuming the role of a Surety.

CHAPTER 14

OCEAN MARINE AND AVIATION

OCEAN MARINE INSURANCE
   Ocean cargo insurance
   Hull Insurance
   Protection and Indemnity Insurance
   Additional insurances
   Markets
   Negotiations and your agent or
     broker

AVIATION INSURANCE
   Aviation insurance "ground rules"
   Aircraft liability
   Aircraft physical damage
   Summary

James E. Goulard
Executive Vice President
Frank B. Hall & Co.
International Aviation Division
New York, New York

James E. Goulard is an Executive Vice President of the International Aviation Division of Frank B. Hall & Co., formerly Parker & Co. International, Inc. The company has specialized in the aviation insurance brokerage field for over 60 years. Mr. Goulard is a graduate of Dartmouth College, where he obtained a B.A. degree in 1964. Since that time, he has served as an Account Executive for industrial corporations and airlines.

Charles N. Shepherd
Managing Vice President
Manager—Ocean Cargo Department
Frank B. Hall & Co. of New York, Inc.
New York, New York

Charles N. Shepherd, CPCU is a Managing Vice President of Frank B. Hall & Co. of New York, Inc., and Manager of the Ocean Cargo Department. A hull and cargo underwriter for over 20 years, he has been in charge of Hall's Ocean Cargo Department for the past 15 years.

W. B. Harwood, Jr.
Vice President
Marine Department
Frank B. Hall & Co. of New York, Inc.
New York, New York

W. B. Harwood, Jr., has been engaged in the marine insurance business since joining the Insurance Company of North America (New York City) in September 1939. After 4 years of wartime service, he worked for Johnson & Higgins for 22 years, leaving as a Vice President in 1967 to join Frank B. Hall & Co. of New York, Inc., in a similar capacity.

OCEAN MARINE INSURANCE

Ocean marine insurance is steeped in tradition. Its archaic hallmark, "ancient wording," contrasts sharply with modern insurance parlance.

> Touching the Adventures and Perils which the Underwriters are contented to bear and take upon themselves, they are of the Seas, Men-of-War, Fire, Lightning, Earthquake, Enemies, Pirates, Rovers, Assailing Thieves, Jettisons, Letters of Mart and Counter-Mart, Surprisals, Takings at Sea, Arrests, Restraints and Detainments of all Kings, Princes and Peoples, of what nation, condition or quality soever, Barratry of the Master and Mariners and of all other like Perils, Losses and Misfortunes that have or shall come to the Hurt, Detriment or Damage of the Vessel, or any part thereof, excepting, however, such of the foregoing perils as may be excluded by provisions elsewhere in the Policy or by endorsement thereon.

The famous Perils Clause quoted above introduces you to Marine Insurance, which had its origin in the earliest days of trade—days when mariners and merchants together ventured across perilous and unchartered waters in fragile craft to deliver their cargoes, frequently surviving untold risks.

There were many times, however, when in order to save the venture, cargo and/or equipment of the vessel had to be sacrificed by jettisoning. From this there arose the practice of the surviving parties at interest contributing to those interests who suffered loss. General Average, as this practice is known, continues to this day in all forms of waterborne trade.

The ancient practices and terminology undoubtedly have caused many to perceive an air of mystery about marine insurance. In truth, the insurance concepts applicable to marine operations are essentially the same as those applicable to shoreside operations. There is property to be insured against the same perils that affect shoreside property, such as fire, lightning, and explosion, plus perils of the seas. There are liabilities by statute or contract to be insured arising out of business operations. Marine "property" can be a passenger vessel, a mammoth tanker, a tugboat, or any one of a host of miscellaneous craft operating either offshore, along the coast, or on inland waters together with the cargo carried on vessels.

The liabilities faced by early shipowners were of little consequence. As commerce increased so did responsibilities and obligations, leading to development of contracts of carriage. The Bill of Lading—the contract between the shipowner and cargo owner—became subject to Carriage of Goods by Sea Acts (COGSA, also known as the Hague Rules), which sets forth the basic rights and immunities of the ocean carrier and the cargo owner. Charter parties and Contracts of Affreightment, although private contracts, will usually include (by reference) COGSA. Furthermore, maritime nations have enacted legislation not only regulating trade but also enunciating seamen's benefits (in this country, the Jones Act) and, most recently, relating to pollution of waters over which they have jurisdiction.

To provide protection for marine property and liability exposures, there are a number of standard policy forms. What follows are the principal policy forms utilized to insure the primary parties involved in the movement of cargo on an ocean-going vessel:

Policy form	*Insured*
Cargo insurance policy	Cargo owner (shipper and/or receiver)
Hull, machinery, etc. (American Inst. Hull)	Shipowner (and demise or bareboat charterer)
Protection and indemnity insurance	Shipowner (and demise or bareboat charterer)

Ocean cargo insurance

Ocean cargo insurance is available for all legally shipped cargoes in foreign trade by vessel, aircraft, truck, rail, or mail.

The exporter who is not paid for his shipments until they arrive or are accepted by the consignee(s) and the importer who buys abroad have a risk of financial loss that may be covered by ocean cargo insurance from the time of shipment until the goods are received. The risk involves the outlay to repair, replace, and ship the goods and may well include profit or anticipated profit.

Cargo insurance forms. Cargo insurance is available in two basic forms:

1. *Special Cargo Policy*—Negotiable in character—covering a single shipment. Coverage passes from the buyer to the seller, as title and risk of loss passes, if required.
2. *Open Cargo Policy*—A continuous contract covering all export or import (or both) shipments of the insured. The policy format, while containing a number of standard printed clauses, is designed for manuscript amendment so as to meet fully the needs of the insured. The insured is provided with a supply of "certificates" to be used in conjunction with the Open Cargo Policy. These certificates contain printed insuring conditions reflecting the Open Policy coverage. They provide negotiable evidence of insurance on shipments where the intention is to provide coverage that will pass, with title, to the consignee, or buyer, who may

claim directly against the Open Cargo Policy insurer—rather than go back, through the shipper, to recover claims for loss or damage to the goods. When it is not necessary to provide negotiable evidence of insurance, reports of shipments may be made to the insurer by "declaration" on an individual basis or by monthly or quarterly reports—and, in some cases, in a single annual report (as a time and laborsaving device).

Cargo insurance normally provides coverage from warehouse to warehouse, that is, from the time goods leave the shipper or suppliers' warehouse at the point of origin (suitably packed so as to insure delivery, under normal transit methods, to final destination) until the goods arrive at the consignee's premises—or until the consignee accepts delivery, whichever occurs first. It is anticipated that the truckers, ocean carriers or airlines carrying goods to or from the ocean vessels (or airports) will deliver the goods without unreasonable delay and in accordance with provisions of the contract of carriage. This "flow" of goods in transit is known as "due course of transit."

The policy covers goods "in due course of transit" only. Any *voluntary* interruption of movement on behalf of the insured will terminate the insurance on the goods at the moment transit is "interrupted," unless permission to make such interruption is mutually agreed by the insured and the insurer. When such an agreement is entered into, an "additional premium" is usually charged for this extension of the normal "due course of transit" coverage.

Perils covered.   The basic Open Ocean Cargo Policy coverage is limited and is spelled out in the Perils Clause quoted earlier. "Perils of the seas" are those perils peculiar to transportation by water, not something that might happen on land. Collision with other vessels; strandings on reefs, rocks, or shoals; violent action of wind and water (heavy weather); and sinking and contact with floating objects, including ice, are deemed to be perils of the seas. The other perils, frequently referred to as "perils on the seas" are:

1. *Fire*—Both direct and consequential damage whether from smoke or steam or from efforts to extinguish a fire. However, spontaneous combustion occurring in the insured shipment is excluded unless specifically assumed by the underwriter.
2. *Assailing thieves*—That is, a forcible taking of goods rather than a mysterious disappearance or pilferage.
3. *Jettison*—The voluntary dumping overboard of cargo or vessel equipment in order to protect other property from a common danger.
4. *Barratry*—The fraudulent, criminal, or wrongful act of the ship's captain or crew that causes loss or damage to the ship or cargo.

5. *All other like perils*—Perils of the same nature as those specifically mentioned above, but not "all-risks" in the customary usage of the term. Since coverage is "warehouse to warehouse" in duration, this phrase embodies the risks or perils on land that may be like perils occurring during the waterborne portion of a voyage, such as collision or overturn of carrying conveyance.

As mentioned, these are the "basic" perils. Practically no policy, today, is issued without broadening the coverage of the Perils Clause by adding special wording to amplify the coverage to more adequately compensate the insured for the loss or damage to his goods in transit.

Additional named perils most frequently added to basic coverage are:

1. Breakage, including leakage, chafing, and chipping.
2. Sweat of vessels' holds, including fresh water damage.
3. Theft, pilferage, and nondelivery of part or all of each shipment.
4. Contact with fuel or other cargo.
5. Instead of the above, coverage against all-risks of physical loss or damage, from any external cause.

Average Clauses. Many commodities, especially those shipped in bulk, are insured under Free of Particular Average (FPA) conditions:

> Free of particular average, unless caused by stranding, sinking, burning or collision with another vessel.

Superimpose the words *partial loss* for the words *particular average* and the clause indicates (as it is interpreted) that no partial loss is covered *unless caused by* stranding, sinking, burning, and so on. This is the American FPA Clause, also known as FPAAC, Free of Particular Average, American Conditions Clause. Actually, there are two basic forms of the FPA insuring conditions. FPAAC, as described above, and FPAEC, or Free-of-Particular-Average-English Conditions, which reads:

> Free of particular average unless the vessel or craft be stranded, sunk, burnt or in collision.

The courts have interpreted the FPAEC clause as providing coverage for partial losses if the carrying vessel has sustained a stranding, sinking, fire, or collision during the voyage, even though such partial losses are not directly caused by or attributable to such happenings. Needless to say, the broader FPAEC Clause is the more popular of the two, even with American insureds.

Franchises and deductibles. Since the FPA Clauses are so restrictive, insurers took a step further and offered With Average (with partial loss) coverage, or "WA" as it is called in the marine insurance market. WA provides coverage for partial or total loss due to the FPA perils *plus* losses due to seawater damage. Frequently a 3 percent or 5 percent "Franchise" is applied to the WA losses, in which case the coverage is referred to as "3 percent Average" or "5 percent Average," respectively.

The purpose of the Franchise is to eliminate small losses. No losses are payable unless they are in an amount equal to or in excess of the percentage. However, if the claim equals the 3 percent or 5 percent figure, the partial loss claim is paid in full. This is different from a deductible wherein a specific amount is *deducted* from *each* claim—other than a total loss.

In addition to eliminating small claims, the Franchise is a vehicle used by insurers to avoid paying "normal" or anticipated claims on all or most shipments of certain classes of commodities or products. Bagged cargoes might anticipate some broken bags in each shipment, shipments of canned goods can expect *some* denting and some slight rusting, and so on. Since the FPA and WA coverages are on a named peril basis and provide minimal coverage, insurers (for an additional premium charge) will add to those coverages, loss due to Theft, Pilferage, and Nondelivery; Breakage; Leakage; Fresh Water Damage; Sweat of Ship's Hull(s); Contact with Other Cargoes; Contact with (vessel's) Fuel Oil, Jettison, and/or Washing Overboard—any or all of these depending upon the susceptibility of the shipment and the amount the insured is willing to pay.

All-risks coverage. The broadest coverage is, of course, all-risks coverage. Coverage is against all risks of physical loss or damage from any external cause—but excludes the risks of loss or damage due to war, strikes, riots, civil commotions, capture, and seizure. All of these excluded perils may be put back into the policy as a supplementary coverage or insured separately as a War Risk Policy (written by the cargo insurer in conjunction with the Open Cargo Policy—or, for competitive reasons, placed with another insurer).

Two fundamental exclusions of the Cargo Policy are:

1. *Loss due to delay or loss in market.* These are deemed to be "business" losses and may not involve any physical damage to the insured goods.
2. *Loss due to inherent vice.* Loss due to the inherent nature of the product; for example, butter melting and/or becoming rancid when unrefrigerated; deterioration of any perishable product that is exposed to normal temperature changes and not due to any unforeseen or a fortuitous happening or circumstance.
3. Although war risks are excluded under the marine policy and may be put back in as a separate war risks section or supplement, war

risk perils *on land* are excluded completely. War perils, that is, mines, torpedoes, shellfire, bombing, and so on, are only covered while the shipments are waterborne.

Whether the coverage be Free of Particular Average, With Average, or "All-Risks," the Cargo Policy also covers the insured for contributions in General Average and Salvage Charges. These represent voluntary expenses incurred to avoid or minimize loss or damage, and in the case of General Average may not be the result or consequent upon any damage to the insured cargo, itself.

General Average. General Average is the voluntary sacrifice of a portion of the carrying vessel or cargo—or both—made in the face of a real and impending peril, for the preservation of the common interests involved. The "sacrifice" may be in the form of extraordinary expenses as well as physical disposal (jettison, etc.) of vessel parts or part of the cargo. The General Average "action" must be successful. If the sacrifice expenditures are made and the vessel and cargo are lost, the General Average is negated. All parties to the venture contribute to the costs of sacrifice—or the expenses—in direct proportion of the value of their interest in relation to the total value of all of the cargo and the hull after the General Average incident.

Salvage. Salvage charges, also part of the General Average, are monies paid to those who rescue a ship and/or cargo from loss or damage by sea perils and restore it to its rightful owners. While salvage is frequently performed on an agreed basis of remuneration, many salvors work on a "no cure no pay" basis in which case a salvage "award" is made to the salvor based on the following considerations:

1. The degree of danger threatening the property.
2. The enterprise and skill displayed by the salvor.
3. The amount of labor involved.
4. The time occupied by the salvage operations.
5. The value of his property risked by the salvor.
6. The value of the property saved.

Warehouse to warehouse. According to the insureds' needs, as indicated earlier, the cargo insurance coverage commences from the time the goods leave the warehouse at point of shipment until they reach the consignees' warehouse at destination—or are accepted by the consignee, whichever first occurs. This presupposes the goods remain, throughout, "in due course of transit," that is, without interference with the transit by the insured. This coverage is described in the policy in a clause bearing the name, Warehouse to Warehouse.

Deviation Clause. The Deviation Clause states that coverage under the policy will not be invalidated by any unintentional error in describing the vessel, voyage, or subject matter insured. In addition, if for reasons beyond the control of the insured, the vessel deviates from her normal course or itinerary, coverage will remain in effect to destination shown in the insurance certificate or declaration. The Deviation Clause is further amplified by Marine Extension Clauses which reaffirm the continuation of coverage during deviation, delay, forced discharge, reshipment, and other variations of voyages. Marine Extension Clauses further provide for the insurance coverage to continue if the voyage is terminated at some port other than the original port of destination. The insurance then continues until the goods are sold at that port or forwarded to the original destination, or to a mutually agreed upon substitute destination. (Most frequently this occurs during stevedores strikes.)

Valuation.   The usual valuation formula includes the invoice cost, plus all expenses of transportation from sellers' to buyers' warehouses, plus an increment of 10 percent (known as an "advance") to cover the additional administrative or inflationary cost to reorder or replace all or part of the shipment including a possible portion of "profit," as well. Sometimes the "advance" may be 15 percent or even more if the insured so requires. Shipments may be insured at the shipper's selling price, including all transportation costs and all the normal profit. So long as the valuation formula will reflect proper and reasonable indemnification for the insured, the insurer will not question the reasonableness of the formula which will form the basis of the premiums charged and the settlement of claims.

The basic Open Cargo Policy will also contain other clauses providing additional coverage to meet the insureds' specific requirements. These include:

1. *Explosion Clause.* Includes loss or damage due to explosion from any cause.
2. *Inchmaree Clause.* Covers loss or damage to cargo from bursting of boilers, breakage of shafts or through any latent defect in the hull or machinery of the vessel and from errors in the navigation or management of the vessel by the master, mates, engineers, or pilots.
3. *Fumigation Clause.* Covers damage caused by fumigation of the vessel.
4. *Warehousing and Forwarding Charge Clause.* Provides for payment of warehousing and forwarding charges, regardless of Average Clause conditions, if the policy would have been liable for the charges in the absence of an Average Clause.
5. *Loading or Unloading Clause.* Provides coverage for the insured value of any package, piece, or unit totally lost in loading, transshipping, or discharging.

6. *Shore Perils Clause.* This clause provides coverage against fire, lightning, earthquake, cyclone, tornado, typhoon, hurricane, flood (meaning the rising of navigable waters), collision, upset or over-turning of land conveyances, and collapse of docks, wharves, bridges, or similar structures during land transit or elsewhere on shore.
7. *Both to Blame Collision Clause.* Pays for any amount which the cargo owner may be legally bound to pay the shipowner under a "both to blame" clause in the ocean bill of lading.

There are a number of other standard clauses contained in Open Cargo Policies but these serve to illustrate the flexibility available in the cargo insurance coverage and the ability to adapt to the special needs of insureds.

Import/export.   Where Duty is payable on imported goods, it does not usually constitute part of the sales terms between buyer and seller. Usually the buyer pays the Duty separately. The Ocean Cargo Policy will provide coverage on Duty. In practice, the Duty amount is de-clared separately and the insurer charges a lower rate on the amount of Duty insurance than for coverage on the goods themselves. The equity of this is evident when one realizes that if a shipment is lost at sea or arrives in an obviously ruined condition, Duty will not be pay-able at all. In addition, if a shipment arrives in damaged condition and is deemed not usable after the Duty is paid, the amount of Duty may be recoverable from the Customs authorities. In such cases, however, the insured collects the Duty amount from the insurer and, when necessary, assists the insurer in collecting from Customs—with no "penalty" if the recovery efforts are unsuccessful.

Rating.   Historically, ocean cargo insurance premiums have been developed by applying rates—formulated on a basis commensurate with underwriters' evaluation of the exposures, that is, nature of the subject matter being insured, geographical areas of transit, mode of transit (steamer/barge/aircraft), packing, and previous loss experience of similar shipments. Rates are applied to each $100 of insured value. Premiums are only charged on shipments actually made.

While most cargo policies are rated in this manner, a current and growing practice is to develop a "deposit" premium based on prior years' reports of shipments and rates. The "deposit" is paid in quar-terly or semiannual installments with a single annual report at an-niversary date of all shipments covered by the Open Cargo Policy, at a single rate applied to the total values declared. This creates an annual adjustment and assists in establishing a new "deposit" for the follow-ing year.

Since coverage against the risks of war, strikes, riots, and civil commotions is written as a separate section of the Open Cargo Policy, the rating is done separately from the "marine" rating just described. Currently, a trend has been to offer an annual premium basis for this coverage as an alternative to the individual rating basis that has prevailed for many years.

The standard American Open Cargo Policy provides that premiums and losses are to be paid in U.S. dollars. However, by special agreement, insurers may agree to accept some currency other than U.S. dollars. In doing so, the insurer will undoubtedly insist that any claims must be paid in the same currency as that in which the premiums are paid.

One reason why ocean cargo insurance rates have been maintained at "reasonable" levels over the years is that insurers anticipate "recoveries" (known as subrogation) from ocean, air, or common carriers, stevedores, warehousemen, and so on, through whose custody the cargo has passed during the warehouse to warehouse transit. If goods are lost or damaged, the Contract of Affreightment, Bill of Lading, Way Bill or Airway Bill or Warehouse Receipt enumerates the carriers', warehousemen's responsibilities so the shipper, consignee, or (following payment of a claim) the insurer may proceed to obtain reimbursement for lost or damaged cargo from the individual(s) responsible for the loss or damage.

Factors affecting insurance cost. The cost of ocean cargo insurance is not determined by actuarial "science" but rather is based on a series of intangible factors that includes the insurers' experience and/or the respective underwriters' personal experience in dealing with insurance on the type of goods insured, their geographic involvement, the shipping and handling methods used in the foreign transit, and, in addition the following:

1. *Extent of cover desired by the insured.* The importer or exporter may choose policy types ranging from the most limited cover (total loss cover which insures against total loss of the cargo only) up to the most comprehensive coverage against all risks of physical loss or damage from any external cause. The broader, more comprehensive the coverage, the greater the cost.
2. *The commodity—or commodity mix—being shipped.* Fragile goods are likely to have a higher rate than pig iron; refrigerated goods are likely to be higher rated than nonrefrigerated goods—with the same insuring conditions. Susceptibility to loss or damage is a major consideration.
3. *Packing.* Standardization of all export packing has been found to be impractical. Consequently, the type of packing varies considerably with shippers, with resulting variance in rates.
4. *Salvage.* Salvage possibilities vary with the goods themselves, and with locality and economic conditions as well.

5. *Shipping route, length, and duration of voyages.* No two ship- ping routes or voyages present identical risks.
6. *Destination point.* The dissimilarity of destination points will produce differences in the risks of handling, security, weather, traffic, political disturbances, and Customs delays.
7. *Underwriting experience.* Underwriting experience is a valu- able guide in determining whether the rate is adequate, in- adequate, or excessive, but it is not the sole determinant. In con- sidering a new account, an adverse loss ratio indicates the need for careful reconsideration of risk factors. It does not necessarily indi- cate that the rate should be revised. An underwriter considers which of the losses can reasonably be expected to occur in the future. Likewise, he may disregard or largely discount much that has happened in the past if there has been a recent change in packing, transportation methods, or other factors that could be expected to improve the previous claims experience on an ac- count. On an ocean cargo insurance account that has been with the same insurer for some years, the premium and loss "experience" will definitely be a determining factor in the premium charge. Insurers try to keep loss payouts at 70 percent of the ocean cargo premium—although most underwriters would insist that 60 per- cent is closer to a "break-even" point.

As one senior ocean cargo underwriter was known to have ex- pressed on the cargo rating process: "The (cargo) underwriter care- fully reviews the physical characteristics of the goods, the packing, geographical scope, and premium and loss experience in order to de- velop a rate that will produce a profit—then he produces a rate he thinks will get the business." So that after all of the "technical" con- siderations have been taken into account, the competitive world marine insurance markets tend to further influence the cost of ocean cargo insurance. The British (Lloyd's and insurance companies), Bel- gian, French, Dutch, Norwegian, and Japanese insurance markets, plus others, are available to American brokers and are actively com- peting with American insurers and with one another for U.S. ocean cargo insurance business. They are aware of potential U.S. clients through importers and exporters they insure in their own countries.

Because of this international competition and because American goods are in price competition with foreign goods (insured abroad), ocean cargo insurance remains an "uncontrolled" class of insurance. It is not subject to the control of the various state insurance departments in the United States for rates or policy forms.

Risk management techniques. Successful efforts to minimize the risk of loss at the least possible cost are difficult to effectuate where overseas cargoes are involved. Aside from packaging research and development, including use of pallets, containers, and other handling facilities, once the shipper delivers his cargo into the hands of the carrier(s) at commencement of transit and until the shipment is received at destination, there is little either shipper or consignee can do to control the manner in which cargo is handled during transit.

By carefully packing and handling at the shipper's premises and constant monitoring the packaging procedures, with amendments for new or changing products or design as well as frequent checks on handling and shipping practices, the capabilities of the shipping departments can be maintained at optimum levels of efficiency. This may be done with the aid of independent marine surveyors or surveyors' services provided "gratis" by marine insurers—or even by exploiting "in-house" talents and capabilities.

An alternative or at least a supplement to loss control is the use of risk transfer, risk retention, or a possible combination of both. Risk transfer is also effected by way of contracts of carriage, whereby carriers or warehousemen assume full responsibility for loss under contracts of carriage or warehouse receipts. While this practice is not common, the quantum of risks thus transferred helps keep down the cost of risk assumption or professional risk transfer (insurance).

Transfer of risk to a professional insurer is most common. A portion of each risk may be retained by employing a deductible on each claim (or with an annual aggregate amount) at a premium savings over the cost of complete transfer of risk to the insurer.

Transfer to professional insurers usually makes available worldwide claims representation, "subrogation" services (capable of handling recoveries from carrier or warehousemen responsible for loss or damage), and very often services of cargo surveyors for packing, transportation, and claims guidance.

Shippers of sufficient size and volume may have their own "captive" insurance company. The captive may insure all of each risk, or only an increment (only the first $25,000, $50,000, or $100,000 of each loss)—with the remainder—up to the maximum limit required—carried by a commercial marine insurer.

In some cases the captive insures a share (percentage) of each risk as reinsurance of—and parallel with—the commercial insurer.

The effectiveness of any risk management program will depend on regular review of cost and loss control implementation so as to insure a favorable "experience" on behalf of management. As an absolute minimum, a full reevaluation of the program should be done once a year.

All changes in corporate activity that will involve the need for insurance coverage should be conveyed to the insurance broker or agent. Poor communications—or lack of proper communication—has been the cause of more cargo claims being declined than any other single factor.

The Open Ocean Cargo Policy can be tailored to meet the insured's needs. In fact, in recent years Ocean Cargo Policies have been "extended" to include coverage on goods in warehouses—whether or not such goods were ever imported, or intended for export; coverage on "inland" transit moves, wholly within the United States or within foreign countries, via truck, rail, or "Domestic" aircraft; Business Interruption coverage caused by damage to or destruction of goods and/or machinery, during transit and other special coverages— otherwise not considered strictly ocean marine—incorporated so as to minimize any gaps or lack of continuity of coverage in the conduct of the insured's business. If the broker or agent is not fully aware of an insured's complete operations, and kept advised of changes, as they occur or are about to occur, the ocean cargo insurance may fail to provide proper coverage. It is prudent for a cargo insured to "monitor" his traffic/import/export departments to insure that the dollar size of shipments and monthly warehouse values are within the limits prescribed in the policy. At a minimum, an annual or semiannual review of the entire ocean cargo insurance program should be discussed between the insured and his broker.

The broker should be expected to provide periodic reports on premium and loss experience figures since these figures tend to affect the policy rating structure. Information on changes in the insurance market practices that may broaden or influence the insured's existing insurance program should be provided without waiting for the periodic "review." The same applies to changes in world political conditions, methods of transportation, new or unusual hazards of transportation as they develop, or any changes in the world affecting international trade that may affect the insured's insurance coverage. The marine insurance broker or agent should make this "input" a normal part of his service to the insured.

Most large marine insurance brokers have a staff of trained cargo claims people who assist insureds in the presentation of necessary claims documentation (to insurers) and in obtaining prompt payment of claims. Size, of itself, of course, does not necessarily insure a high quality of service from any broker.

Hull Insurance

Although the following discussion of some of the principal clauses in the Hull Policy applies only to an ocean cargo carrier, many of the clauses are found in policies covering tugs, barges, and other commercial vessels.

Assured and Loss Payable Clauses.   Most vessels are financed by a lending institution. The loan agreement will set forth not only what insurance the owner is required to carry but will also specify who must be named as an insured (or assured as they are known in marine insurance) and to whom losses will be paid.

Duration of risk/policy term.   Policies are written for a period of not exceeding one year and are noncancellable except by mutual agreement, contrary to most nonmarine contracts. Exceptions to this are found in the Change of Ownership Clause, which provides among others that a change of ownership of a ship without the prior agreement of the insurer will automatically terminate the policy. Failure to pay premium when due will also give the insurer the option to cancel.

Rate.   The rate is determined by negotiation between the owner's broker and insurers and is based on the owner's experience. The number of vessels in a fleet, their age, type, and trade will influence the rate.

Each fleet is individually rated based on the loss ratio arrived at by contrasting net premium earned by the hull insurer with losses sustained. The policy rate has two components: the first takes into account the total loss exposure (which effectively is a class rate based on type of craft and age and value); and the second reflects the partial loss exposure, which in turn reflects the individual's loss experience. Payment of premium is usually quarterly.

Deductible.   The aggregate of all claims, arising out of each separate accident, is subject to a negotiable deductible. Thus, if the total claim is $100,000 and the deductible is $10,000, the policy will pay $90,000. The deductible does not apply to a total loss. The amount of the deductible will have an influence on the premium.

Perils.   From the Perils Clause cited, the policy insures the vessels against perils of the sea and all other like perils.

There is also an Additional Perils (Inchmaree) Clause which extends coverage to include specified accidents which had been held by the courts to be excluded from the Perils Clause such as certain machinery breakdowns and damage done to the vessel through the negligence of charterers, repairers, or crew. This clause has a proviso that excludes any such loss or damage if it resulted from want of due diligence by the assured, owner, or manager. A broader clause, the Liner Negligence Clause, may be substituted in certain fleet policies, subject to the prior agreement of the insurer.

Deliberate damage.   As a consequence of the severe damage to the environment caused in recent years by stranding and other losses to tankers, the policy has been extended to include "loss or damage to the vessel directly caused by governmental authorities acting for the public welfare to prevent or mitigate a pollution hazard, or threat thereof; resulting directly from damage to the vessel for which the underwriters are liable"—provided such act of governmental authorities has not resulted from want of due diligence by the assured.

General Average and Salvage. To review, particular average is a term used to refer to partial losses whereas General Average is a voluntary sacrifice made by the vessel and/or cargo to preserve ship and cargo in the face of an imminent peril. If the sacrifice is successful, all parties contribute to the loss to ship and/or cargo resulting from the sacrifice as the value of each individual interest bears to the total of the contributing values. The Hull Policy will respond for the vessel's contribution less the applicable deductible. However, if the insured value of the vessel is less than the contributory value as determined by an independent surveyor, the insurer will be liable only for his proportion of the contribution, or:

$$\frac{\text{Insured value}}{\text{Contributory value}} \times \text{Contribution Due} = \text{Insurer's Contribution}$$

Salvage is an award due a salvor for services rendered when a vessel and/or her cargo are in distress. The famous and most commonly used Lloyd's Open Form is a "no cure, no pay" contract. Thus, if the salvor's efforts are not successful, there is no award or "no pay." This type of contract has been supplanted in some instances by a more specific contract which spells out the fee to be received by the salvor whether or not his efforts are successful. In either instance the vessel owner should get the prior agreement of his insurer to the form of contract if time permits. Insurers will contribute to the salvage award or salvage charges similar to a General Average contribution.

Total loss. Obviously, the policy will pay in the event of the total loss of the vessel from a peril insured. Such a claim occurs, for example, when a vessel has sunk or been stranded in waters that make salvage impossible or impractical. The policy will also pay in the event of a constructive total loss which occurs after an accident when the expense of recovering and repairing the vessel exceeds the insured value.

Sue and labor. "In the case of Loss or Misfortune, it shall be lawful and necessary for the Assured, their Factors, Servants and Assigns, to sue, labor and travel for, in and about the defense, safeguard and recovery of the Vessel. . . ." In other words, the assured must take whatever action is necessary to minimize a loss, and insurers will contribute to any expenses so incurred in accordance with policy conditions.

Collision liability. "And it is further agreed: *(a)* if the vessel shall come into collision with any other ship or vessel . . ." and the vessel is held liable or partially liable for the damage to the other vessel, the insurers will reimburse the assured for a liability incurred not in excess of the insured value. Since collision with another vessel is a peril of the seas, his insurers will reimburse the owner for damage incurred by his vessel. This clause extends the policy to cover his liability for damage to the other vessel. In many instances it may be advantageous to restrict liability under the Hull Policy to three fourths and insure the remaining one fourth under the Protection and Indemnity Policy for reasons that will be discussed. Irrespective of the damage to the insured vessel reimbursed by the insurers, they will also pay damages to the other vessel up to the insured value. For example, if the insured vessel was held to be 100 percent liable:

Insured value	$1,000,000
Damage to insured vessel less deductible	500,000
Damage to other vessel	1,000,000

Underwriters will pay $500,000 plus $1,000,000 or a total of $1,500,000. Collision liability is, in effect, a separate contract.

Pilotage and towage.   Many pilotage and towage contracts restrict the liability of the pilot and/or tower. Insofar as these contracts are in accordance with established local practice, hull insurers agree to waive their right of subrogation against the pilot and/or tower. When the contract to be signed is not in accordance with established local practice, the prior approval of the insurers must be obtained.

Additional insurances.   The Hull Policy restricts the amount of additional insurance the assured, owners, managers, operators, or mortgagees may take out against the risk of total loss of the vessel to 25 percent of the insured value.

The clause further restricts the amount of insurance that can be placed on collect freight, anticipated freight, time charter hire, and premiums. But the clause gives the owner permission to place insurance irrespective of amount against risks of War and Strikes, General Average and Salvage Disbursements.

War, Strikes, and Related Exclusions.   You will recall the Perils Clause quoted at the beginning referred to such risks, which are excluded by this clause. Separate insurance must be placed if such coverage is required.

Claims.   The policy makes some general provisions as to the procedure to be followed in the event of damage to the vessel.

However, the presentation of a claim to the insurer is usually prepared by a loss adjuster, who in the United States is usually an employee of the insurance broker and a member of the Association of Average Adjusters. The Association sets forth certain rules that must be followed in preparing the loss adjustments.

Trading warranty.   The area in which the vessel will be permitted to trade will be specified in the policy.

Protection and Indemnity Insurance

P&I provides the liability insurance required by a vessel owner and might otherwise be called a Vessel Owner's Liability Policy. Virtually all P&I insurance on ocean cargo vessels is underwritten by the Mutual P&I Associations (or Clubs), who protect and indemnify their members (owners) against third-party liability claims. Although most of the major maritime nations have a domestic P&I Association (in the United States, the American Steamship Owners P&I Association), the majority of the Clubs are of English origin, and although they may be now domiciled in Bermuda or Liechtenstein, the daily operations are handled by the Clubs' managers in London.

Premiums.   A Mutual Club differs from a fixed premium insurance placed with an insurance company or with one or more Lloyd's syndicates in that the members of the Club (the vessel owners) at the beginning of the policy year (usually February 20th) pay an advance call (premium) based on each Club's estimate of what the total claims will amount to during the policy year. Several months or even several years after the end of the policy year when the Club has been able to make a more accurate assessment of the actual claims and the liabilities accruing therefrom, a supplementary call (premium) is made being a percentage of the advance call.

The advance call is a rate per Gross Registered Ton of each vessel entered by an owner and is based on the total tonnage entered by the owner as well as his record of paid and estimated claims.

P&I insurance on smaller commercial vessels is, more frequently, placed at a fixed premium with an insurance company.

Coverage.   Among the liabilities covered by the rules (terms and conditions) of the Mutual Clubs are:

1. Loss of life or personal injury to or illness of any person other than a seaman but excluding liability under any Workmen's Compensation Act or Employer's Liability Act.
2. Loss of life or personal injury to or illness of any seaman while on board or proceeding to or from the entered vessel, arising under statutory obligation or other contract of employment.
3. Expenses incurred in repatriating an ill or injured seaman.
4. Loss or damage to cargo.
5. Damage to docks, buoys, bridges, cables, and other fixed or floating objects (other than a vessel).
6. One fourth of an owner's liability for collision damage to any

other vessel, assuming the Hull Policy covers only three-fourths collision liability.

7. Damages caused other than by collision such as wash damage.
8. Fines and penalties.
9. Quarantine expenses.
10. Wreck removal.
11. The proportion of general average or salvage charges not recoverable from cargo.
12. Expenses in defending unfounded claims.
13. Customary towage contracts.
14. Pollution caused by oil or hazardous substances.

Some liabilities not insured are:

1. Those arising as a consequence of deviation such as stowing cargo on deck with an underdeck bill of lading. However, this may be covered with the prior agreement of the insurer or placed independently of the P&I insurance.
2. Contractual liability (including a passenger ticket) unless previously sighted, approved, and agreed by the insurer.
3. Those incurred with the privity of the assured such as knowingly sending an unseaworthy vessel to the sea as a consequence of which there is loss to life to the crew and damage to cargo.

Limits of liability and claims. There is no limit of liability as such in a mutual P&I entry except entries in the American Club. However, most countries permit a vessel owner to limit his liability for loss of life, and so on, and for property damage in the absence of privity on his part. The exception to this is that the Clubs presently limit their liability arising out of oil pollution claims to $300 million for any one occurrence.

If the insurance is placed with an insurance company, there must, of necessity, be an agreed limit of liability. If the owner deems this amount to be insufficient, there is no restriction on the amount of excess liability insurance he can buy, assuming the cost is practical.

The Clubs maintain a network of claim facilities located in the principal ports of the world. If necessary, the Master or agent of a vessel can contact a local claim representative for advice and guidance. In the event it becomes necessary for an owner to put up a guarantee to avoid his vessel being arrested, liened or otherwise detained, most claimants and governmental authorities will accept a Club's letter of guarantee in lieu of a bond. P&I insurers in the American market offer the same facilities although only the American Club has an international claims organization.

The Clean Water Act of 1977[1] requires that owners of all Flags calling at U.S. ports (including Puerto Rico, U.S. Virgin Islands,

Panama Canal, Hawaii, and the Trust Territories of the Pacific) file with the Federal Maritime Commission (FMC) evidence of insurance (or other financial guarantee), demonstrating compliance with the financial requirements of the act. The Mutual Clubs will furnish such evidence; but as most American insurance companies exclude pollution liability from their P&I policies, the Water Quality Insurance Syndicate was formed to provide a market and to provide the necessary evidence of insurance to the FMC.

Although P&I Clubs and insurers through their claims agents or correspondent lawyers will negotiate settlements on behalf of and subject to agreement by their assured, your broker should be in a position to offer advice and guidance and, if necessary, negotiate with the Club or underwriter on your behalf.

Additional insurances

Some additional forms that may be required or considered follow.

War risks and strikes. For a vessel engaged in international trade this is, if not essential, required by all lenders/mortgagees. Written at present for a very nominal annual premium, it permits the vessel to trade to any port or place in the world excluding those ports or places which may be considered unusually dangerous because of existing or possible military action or political tension. Vessels calling at such ports or places must obtain the agreement of war risk insurers to extend coverage for an agreed period of time for which an additional premium may be required. Depending on the locale and situation such additional premium can be insignificant or substantial. War Risk Policies also include a provision that the insurance will be automatically terminated:

a. Upon and simultaneously with the hostile detonation of any nuclear weapon of war wheresoever and whensoever such detonation may occur.
b. With the outbreak of war between two of the five major powers.
c. When the vessel is requisitioned.

The policy, generally, is extended to cover an owner's liability for P&I war risks (excluding any contractual liability to the crew) at no additional premium.

Increased value including excess liabilities. Provides additional insurance in the event of the total loss of the vessel and provides protection against loss of a lucrative charter or a rise in the market value or just additional insurance against total loss.

It also covers General Average, Sue and Labor Charges, and Collision not recoverable in full under the Hull Policy but not exceeding the amount insured.

The rate is less than that required by the hull insurance as the policy does not cover partial losses.

The amount that may be insured on this interest is restricted by the Disbursements Warranty/Additional Insurances Clause of the Hull Policy to 25 percent of the insured value set forth in the Hull Policy.

Loss of hire. Insures against a loss of charter hire due to a partial loss suffered by a vessel. The insurance reflects the daily charter hire and pays for an agreed number of days in excess of an agreed number of days (a deductible of days rather than dollars). Thus, the policy might agree to pay $1,000 per day for 90 days in excess of the first 14 days but not exceeding 180 days in all during the policy year irrespective of the number of accidents. Each accident is subject to a deductible of 14 days.

The policy excludes a claim arising out of the total loss of the vessel and is automatically terminated on expiry or cancellation of the charter unless the vessel immediately enters into another charter.

Charterer's liability. Covers those liabilities assumed by the charterer when he charters (leases) a vessel. These include damage to the vessel itself as well as to the cargo on board and to third parties including loss of life, and so on, and property damage. Your insurance broker and insurer should be furnished with a copy of the charter so there is no misunderstanding of the liabilities that are being covered.

Strike insurance. Is similar in concept to loss of hire insurance except that it covers only the loss of time a vessel may be delayed by a strike, lockout, stoppage, or restraint of labor excluding the ship's crew or officers. A strike by the ship's officers or crew may also be insured but not a lockout.

Insurers agree to pay a daily indemnity equal to the sum of the daily running costs for an agreed number of days in excess of an agreed number of days for each strike.

Markets

An owner should insist that his insurance be placed in reputable markets that are financially sound and pay claims promptly. His broker should have the same philosophy. Certainly the insurance companies in the United States, being subject to the financial requirements and regulation by the various states, qualify. Insurance placed with syndicates at Lloyd's, or members of the Institute of London Underwriters, also qualify. Lloyd's and Institute of London Underwriters maintain trusteed reserves in the United States exceeding $1 billion. For this reason any lender, including the U.S. Maritime Administration, will approve them as security.

There are many other responsible markets in both Europe and the Far East, particularly Japan. Despite the fact they are financially sound, pay claims promptly, and all the major lenders will approve their use, they do not maintain trusteed reserves in the United States and, therefore, will not be approved by the Maritime Administration.

Worldwide capacity is such that at the present time the market for ocean hulls is competitive. The market for smaller commercial vessels is more restricted, owners usually preferring, for a number of reasons, to insure locally.

Negotiations and your agent or broker

When negotiating hull insurance on ocean vessels, it is possible to approach different markets for quotations and to place the insurance in more than one market at the rate quoted by each. Though one market's rate may be higher than the other, it is frequently advantageous to use two or more markets. Experience has shown over the years a pendulum swing in rating approach—the low market this year may be high next year.

The agent or broker you select plays a key role in arranging any insurance program. The relationship between you and your broker should be one of trust and confidence. Just as you must keep your broker aware of your present and future plans, your broker should be working constantly and consistently in your best interests.

The ultimate goal is to achieve a program that will protect the assets and earnings of the corporation and should not be employed to provide coverage against exposures to losses which are within the capacity of the corporation to retain for its own account. Marine insurance is based on the doctrine of utmost good faith. By observance of this doctrine the goal can be achieved. The same can be said for the final topic of this chapter, aviation insurance.

AVIATION INSURANCE

The decision to own or lease long-term a business aircraft is a serious one. The convenience and speed offered by the equipment is accompanied by significant expense and risk.

By its very nature, management of the aircraft becomes a personal matter to the business executive. Simply stated, a serious accident most likely will involve key personnel, important clients, and/or friends or family. Loss avoidance or prevention through excellence in equipment, maintenance, and operational standards and procedures is paramount. Insurance is secondary. High standards will aid the businessman in obtaining the lowest insurance costs. In short, while the price of the aircraft may be right, you cannot "afford" to operate a corporate aircraft unless you:

1. Hire a professional crew. The pilot should have ample experience as pilot-in-command of the type of aircraft you intend to purchase. If the aircraft is a high performance multiple engine type, a full-time professional pilot may be advisable, if not essential.
2. Insist your crew take recurrent training at a professionally run training facility.
3. Make sure the aircraft is adequately equipped with navigational aids, avionics, and so on.
4. Employ highest quality ground servicing and maintenance firms.
5. Remember that the pilot is your "Risk Manager" when preparing for or in flight (i.e., the final "go or no go" decision is his, not yours).

Given a qualified pilot and properly maintained equipment, the purchase of insurance can be arranged through a number of brokers or agents who specialize in aviation insurance. Remember, the more expensive the equipment, the greater the seating capacity, the more you operate in major urban areas, the more insurance you need.

Aviation insurance "ground rules"

Almost everyone has had extensive personal and business experience in buying automobile coverages. The most common mistakes are made in following the natural tendency to apply this experience to aviation. Auto and aviation insurance have aspects in common but the differences are significant:

1. Unlike auto, aviation policy forms are not standardized. They vary in scope of coverage, exclusions, and conditions depending on the insurer. Read your policy and carefully review it with your broker or agent.
2. Aviation policies are not universally available as is automobile. Except for a few major insurance companies, most will refer aviation coverage requests to an underwriting management firm or pool in which each participating company shares a modest percentage of the risks. There are literally hundreds of insurers who will not write any aviation coverages. As in any situation where the source of supply is limited, you, in close cooperation with your agent and broker, must give extra attention to the initial placement and every renewal. If you have recently changed your agent or broker, review the aviation coverages and costs with him at the first opportunity.

3. Your agent or broker has a collection of published rates for a large number of auto insurers. This is not possible in aviation. The premiums charged are dependent upon the insurer's current profitability and his underwriter's judgment as to the quality of your aircraft and crew. Under the circumstances, there is no such thing as a "routine" placement or "automatic" renewal.
4. Do not assume your broker or agent has the authority to accept instant orders for coverage or changes in your aviation policy. Few, if any, have binding authority for aviation insurance. Allow him sufficient lead time to negotiate with the underwriter for precise coverage at a firm cost.

Aircraft liability

Why is aircraft liability a separate coverage? The starting point for a review of aircraft liability is in the Comprehensive General Liability (CGL) Policy form which excludes the operation, maintenance, or use of any aircraft—

1. Owned or operated by any insured, or
2. Rented or loaned to any insured, or
3. Any other aircraft operated (i.e., piloted) by any person in the course of his employment by any insured.

These exclusions encompass practically all aircraft liability exposures (except perhaps for the routine purchase of airline tickets or air cargo service).

Note in the above categories the reference to "any insured." In the CGL policy "Insured" means:

1. If you are the sole proprietor of the business, the exclusion also applies to your spouse.
2. If your business is a partnership or a joint venture, it also applies to your partners or the other members of the joint venture.
3. If your firm is a corporation, it applies to any executive officer, director, or shareholder while acting within the course of his duties.

In addition to excluding liability for the ownership or operation of aircraft, the Comprehensive General Liability Policy excludes maintenance of aircraft and loading or unloading of aircraft. The exclusions are specific and comprehensive. In short, the normal casualty insurance marketplace simply does not wish to underwrite aircraft liability exposures.

Aircraft liability coverage. Basic coverage is provided for the aircraft identified by its FAA registration number for claims due to bodily injury or damage to someone else's property. It also will include bodily injury to the aircraft passengers if you order it. No businessman should omit passenger injury liability on the grounds that he never will have a passenger on board or that the only passengers will be his employees whose sole remedy against him is under workers' compensation coverage.

The aviation "flight rules". Most policy forms (both Aircraft Liability and Physical Damage Policies) apply only when the aircraft—

1. Has a Federal Aviation Administration "Standard" Airworthiness Category Certificate (license) as opposed to "Restricted" or "Experimental."
2. Is operated by the pilots either named or described on the policy as being qualified.
3. Is operated on a noncommercial basis, that is, no passenger or anyone else is being charged for its usage.
4. Is flown only within the geographical areas stated in the policy; for example, the USA only; or the USA, Canada, and Mexico; the Western Hemisphere, and so on. Currently, Mexican law requires Mexican Statutory Liability to be covered by a licensed Mexican insurance company, thus special arrangements are necessary if flights to Mexico are planned.

Who is protected? The following persons and groups are covered by the typical aviation liability policy:

1. The insured named on the policy.
2. Anyone who is using or riding in your aircraft with your permission, that is, your employees, customers, guests, friends, and so on.
3. Any person or organization that is legally responsible for the insured aircraft you are using, that is, the owner/lessor, mortgagee, and so on.

On the other hand, the policy usually will not cover—

1. Any person or organization engaged in aircraft manufacturing, sales, service, repair, rental, and so on.
2. An employee injured by a fellow employee. The injured employee must pursue his rights under your workers' compensation coverage.

Liability claims not covered

1. *Aircraft.* Claims for damage to the insured aircraft are excluded since hull insurance is available for this exposure.
2. *Contracts.* Liability of others you assume under a contract or

agreement is not covered. Some insurers, however, automatically will cover liability assumed in an agreement with a governmental agency permitting you to use its airport. In any case, all agreements under which you have indemnified someone else in connection with the aircraft should be reported to your agent or broker to obtain "Contractual Liability" protection.

3. *Intentional acts.* As is the case with most types of liability coverage, intentional injury to persons or property is not covered. Some aviation liability policies will provide cover for such injuries if they result from an effort to prevent a hijacking or other dangerous interference with the operation of the aircraft.

4. *Employee injuries.* No coverage is afforded with respect to an employer's obligations under workers' compensation, unemployment compensation, disability benefits, or similar laws. Some insurers also will make an exception for claims by "domestic" employees who are not under the protection of a workers' compensation law.

5. *Your property.* Damage to property you own, rent, control, or transport in the aircraft is excluded. As in the case of damage to the aircraft, appropriate property insurance has to be secured. Some Aircraft Liability Policy forms do include liability coverage for the personal effects or baggage of passengers for limits in an amount substantially less than the basic coverage limits.

These five categories are the most typical of exclusions found in Aircraft Liability Policies issued on business aircraft. Your policy may contain broader or more numerous exclusions. The underwriter may have required additional exclusions or limitations because of an unusual aspect of your operation or your desire to have less coverage at a lower cost.

In comparing policy coverages of one insurer with another, it is not enough to merely compare the exclusions. The Insuring Clauses and definitions should be compared as well since they can contain important limitations.

Important extras. All aircraft from time to time are "laid up" for maintenance or repairs. Most insurers, upon request, will extend coverage to a substitute aircraft being used during maintenance to the covered aircraft. The insurer, in some cases, also may be willing to provide automatic coverage for newly acquired aircraft. These extensions of coverage can be most useful since "last minute" or "weekend" coverage arrangements are difficult and may not meet your deadline for takeoff.

There are three more extras which may be characterized as "Good-Will" insurance. Serious injury to or death of a prospective customer, client, or guest is likely to produce a lawsuit. The embarrassment and extended delays in final payment can be offset or minimized by the following:

1. *Voluntary Settlement coverage.* Also called Admitted Liability; provides an opportunity for a quick settlement. Subject to the applicable policy limit, the insured can instruct the insurer to offer a substantial sum of money to the claimant in exchange for a release of further claim or suit.
2. *Medical Payments coverage.* Similar to that found in an auto liability policy; offered by most aviation insurers. It will pay for all reasonable medical, surgical, dental, hospital, nursing, or funeral expenses incurred by the injured passenger or his estate within one year from the date of the aircraft accident.
3. Finally, there is Air Travel Accident. This coverage applies to guests, crews, and employees. While not generally available from aviation insurers, it is widely obtainable from accident and health companies.

Aircraft charter and rentals.   Aircraft liability is written on a designated aircraft basis so that the basic Aircraft Liability Policy does not pick up the "Nonownership" exposures which usually arise when:

1. A member of your firm or employee, who happens to have a pilot's license, rents an aircraft or uses his own aircraft to make an urgent business appointment. Your exposure here is significant because your employee is flying the aircraft in the course of his employment. Most corporations prohibit or tightly control this usage.
2. You charter an aircraft and crew from an aviation service or airline to transport some VIPs or vital business property. Your liability exposure here is not as great as in the first situation since your employees or agents are not involved in the operation of the aircraft. But these arrangements usually involve larger aircraft with multi-million-dollar claim potentials.

Many business ventures need nonownership aircraft liability protection. But those businesses which do own and operate aircraft are those most likely to have employees with a pilot's license or to rely on chartered aircraft as a useful business tool. For these it is a must. It is generally available from your aircraft liability insurer at relatively moderate cost. The cost will depend on:

1. The number of flight hours you anticipate in a year, and/or
2. The frequency of charters, the type of aircraft and whether or not they are to be used for carrying cargo or passengers.

Nonownership don'ts. When you charter an aircraft, do not assume the aircraft owner has liability coverage. Get a certificate or other evidence of insurance from him.

Do not rely entirely on his coverage even if he has agreed to name your firm as an insured on his policy. His limits of liability may be "adequate" in his view, but may not be sufficient to protect your assets.

As in the case of aircraft liability, nonownership liability does not include liability for damage to the aircraft itself. If your employee is flying someone else's aircraft, do not assume he or his insurer will not claim against you for damage or destruction of the aircraft. As a condition to your employee's use of the nonowned aircraft, the aircraft owner should waive his rights of recovery against you and provide evidence of aircraft hull insurance including a Waiver of Subrogation Clause in your favor.

What is an "adequate" limit of liability? The selection of a limit of liability is similar to building a levee around your assets. It should be higher than the worst expected flood. If it is not, your business may be severely damaged, if not washed out entirely. While there is no perfect answer to the question of "How high is up?", in aviation operations the exposures are potentially catastrophic in nature.

Most likely your aircraft will, during the course of the year, be sharing a congested airspace or major airport with $50 million airline aircraft carrying several hundred passengers. If your use of such facilities is on a regular basis, the chance of an eight- or nine-figure lawsuit exists. Because of this, large corporate operators of business aircraft are carrying limits in the $50 to $100 million range. Obviously, small companies with smaller aircraft do carry lower limits but the liability potentials are the same.

Fortunately, a $20 million limit does not cost twice as much as a $10 million limit, but it will cost approximately 40 percent more than the $10 million coverage. The additional cost for each $10 million incremental increase above $20 million declines substantially.

Aircraft physical damage

Loss of or damage to your aircraft is covered by an Aircraft Physical Damage Policy or, as some insurers call it, Aircraft Hull "All-Risks." Most major insurers offer policy forms which combine both aircraft liability and aircraft physical damage in one policy. These hull forms are "all-risks" in that they cover nearly all types of physical loss.

The most common exclusions are the war and confiscation perils. These risks can be covered; the premium will depend upon whether or not the aircraft is operated in troubled areas of the world. Deductibles are found in most forms of property insurance and normally appear in aviation policies as well. The use of deductibles keeps the cost of insurance to affordable levels and provides an incentive to the insured to emphasize loss prevention.

When is a loss covered? In addition to the Aviation Flight Rules listed under aircraft liability (the aircraft license, the pilot, noncommercial flight, and place of the accident), the physical damage insurer requires that your interest in the aircraft, as owner, remains as stated in the declaration of the policy. You may not mortgage or sell a part of your interest unless the underwriter has been notified and has agreed to the change before the loss. A new owner is a new insured. Insurers must know who they are insuring.

Who is protected? Unlike aircraft liability, which covers a wide range of persons and organizations, both named and unnamed on the policy, Aircraft Physical Damage coverage will provide payment only to you or, to you and your mortgagee, or the actual owner, if it is a leased aircraft. As noted, the policy must specifically provide for these other parties. Also keep in mind that where there is more than one interest to be paid for a loss, the insurer will not get involved in distributing the payment but will issue a single check payable to all interests.

How much will be paid? For a total loss of the aircraft, the insurer will pay the amount for which it is insured. As with other property covers, insurance to value is a major consideration. In addition to the forces of inflation, many aircraft are not immediately replaceable but may have to be ordered now at next year's or the following year's delivery prices. Are you insuring at:

1. Depreciated "book value?"
2. Original purchase price?
3. Today's market value?
4. Actual replacement cost?

The differences between each category can run into thousands, or even millions, of dollars.

Of course, as you increase the insured value, your physical damage premium will increase, but not necessarily proportionately. You should review this subject with your agent or broker frequently.

Payment for repairable damage is recoverable for the amounts billed by the repairer provided the parts are of similar kind and quality plus labor (at straight time only) up to the insured value. In addition, necessary and reasonable transportation costs to have the work done are also payable if the aircraft cannot be flown to the repair facility.

What is not covered

1. *Contracts.* A hull insurer is likely to deny payment if he is precluded from recovering from a third party who caused the damage by a contract provision absolving that third party. It is advisable that all contracts affecting the use or operation of the aircraft be reported to the broker or agent so that they can be endorsed onto the policy.
2. *Ownership changes.* Changes in the extent of your ownership or interest in the aircraft should be reported to the insurer to avoid an unpaid loss situation.
3. *Tires.* Tires are not covered unless stolen, vandalized, or damaged in conjunction with another insured peril.
4. *Wear and tear.* No loss is covered if it has been caused by wear and tear, deterioration, freezing, mechanical, or electrical breakdown. Resulting damage is covered, however. Additional limitations are also applied to jet engines since they are subject to unique wear, tear, and ingestion hazards.
5. *Embezzlement.* If someone who is in legal possession of your aircraft (i.e., a bailee) embezzles or "cashes it in" by means of a lease, rental agreement, conditional sale, mortgage, or other "legal" agreement with another party, loss of or damage to the aircraft is not covered by most insurers.
6. *War and confiscation.* There are a variety of confiscation, rebellion, invasion, declared or undeclared war, exclusions common to all policies but some policies also may exclude strikes, riots, civil commotion, and intentional damage, as well. All or part of these exclusions can usually be bought out at reasonable costs either under a War, Confiscation, and Related Risks Policy or by endorsement. The ideal arrangement is to cover the "War, Confiscation, and Related Risks" with your all-risks insurer so that your claim is not delayed while the two insurers decide who is responsible for it.

Valuable extras. Just as in the case of aircraft liability, it is important to obtain automatic property coverage for an aircraft which replaces the one you own or is in addition to it. In the event of a total loss of the aircraft, some policy forms will allow for a return of the "unearned" premium. In a case where the loss occurs in mid-policy term, the dollars returned will equal half of the annual premium. This is a worthwhile feature to have included in your policy since the cost of aircraft physical damage coverage is the largest part of your overall aviation insurance cost.

Summary

These guidelines reflect the general state of aviation insurance in the early 1980s. There is one certainty: Changes will occur from year to year depending upon the frequency of catastrophic aircraft accidents. Despite the inherent fluctuations of this marketplace, those who maintain high standards of maintenance, training and safety in their aircraft operations and a close working relationship with their broker or agent and insurer will achieve the best available protection at the most reasonable cost.

NOTE

1. The Clean Water Act of 1977 which set forth the liability of an owner or operator of a vessel for the cost to clean up pollution caused by the escape or discharge of oil or hazardous substances, has been recently superseded with respect to pollution caused by hazardous substances by the Comprehensive Environmental Response, Compensation and Liability Act of 1980 (PL 96-510). The liability of an owner or operator under PL 96-510 was increased drastically.

CHAPTER 15

PROFESSIONAL LIABILITY

HISTORY AND GENERAL TRENDS
  Negligence defined
  Malpractice problems

SPECIFIC PROFESSIONS COVERED
AND RECENT DEVELOPMENTS
  The medical and health service
    providers' professional liability
  Attorneys' professional liability
  Accountants' professional liability
  Architects' and engineers'
    professional liability

PROFESSIONAL LIABILITY
PROTECTION AND INSURANCE
  Medical and health service
    providers' professional liability
  Attorneys' professional liability
  Accountants' professional liability
  Architects' and engineers'
    professional liability

PROFESSIONAL LIABILITY OF A
CORPORATION

MISCELLANEOUS

Francis E. Shields, Esquire
Pepper, Hamilton & Scheetz
Philadelphia, Pennsylvania

Francis E. Shields is a Senior Partner in the Philadelphia, Pennsylvania, firm of Pepper, Hamilton & Scheetz where he specializes in defense litigation, primarily medical malpractice. Mr. Shields is the Past President of the Medico-Legal Committee of the Philadelphia Bar Association and Past Chairman of the Federal Civil Judicial Procedures Committee of the Philadelphia Bar Association. He is a member of the American College of Trial Lawyers. He is also a member of the American, Pennsylvania, and Philadelphia Bar Associations; the Philadelphia Judicial Council; the Defense Counsel Association; and the International Association of Insurance Counsel.

Sherryl R. Perry, Esquire
Pepper, Hamilton & Scheetz
Philadelphia, Pennsylvania

Sherryl R. Perry is associated with the Philadelphia, Pennsylvania, firm of Pepper, Hamilton & Scheetz. Prior to her entry into the legal profession, she was the Technical Supervisory Editor of *Biological Abstracts* and *BioResearch Index*, the two major publications of BioSciences Information Services. Mrs. Perry is currently an Associate Editor of the *Philadelphia County Reporter* specializing in the areas of Torts and Commercial and Corporate Transactions. In the past she has worked as a metallurgist and an inorganic chemist, and in addition to her law degree she has a B.S. in Biochemistry and an M.A. in English.

Penrose Wolf, Esquire
Hartford Accident & Indemnity Co.
Hartford, Connecticut

Penrose Wolf is an Assistant Secretary in the Claim Department of The Hartford Insurance Group. He is a graduate of the Pennsylvania State University and University of Connecticut Law School, member of the Connecticut and American Bar Associations, Vice Chairman of The Fidelity and Surety Committee, and a member of the Governing Committee of The Forum Committee on the Construction Industry, ABA. He also is an arbitrator of the American Arbitration Association.

In our litigious society there is one thing you can count on—an increase in the number of lawsuits. With the present popularity of taking grievances to court, no professional—be he or she a corporate director or member of the clergy—is immune to suit. Concurrent with this increase in the number of actions against professionals is the increase in large judgments. According to a *Wall Street Journal* article, in 1967 there was only one multi-million-dollar professional liability award. The present average is one such award per week in federal and state courts.

Recent insurance company studies indicate that although doctors and surgeons still account for the largest part of the professional liability insurance business (about $3.3 billion is paid annually in premiums), lawyers, accountants, architects, engineers, actuaries, real estate agents, and insurance agents are paying approximately $1.5 billion annually to protect themselves against allegations of professional error, and corporate officers and directors account for another $150 million in professional liability premiums. The fears of these professionals are real, as there are numerous causes of action which may be brought against them, ranging from actions for negligence to those for breach of contract and fraud.

However, the single most significant cause of action, and the action most readily brought to mind when speaking of professional liability, is malpractice, that form of liability based on "fault." Professional liability by definition arises where a client, patient, or other party, who interacts with a professional, suffers a loss or injury for acts or omissions of the professional in the practice of his particular profession.[1]

The term *malpractice* is somewhat of a misnomer. It is no more than professional negligence or carelessness. Moreover, it is the act of ordinary negligence which occurs with statistical regularity in a random fashion in every professional's daily life and can only be prevented by constant diligence. However, since the tort of malpractice is the spectre most often raised in any discussion of professional liability, this chapter will focus primarily on this particular type of fault-based liability and will only briefly consider other possible causes of action against the professional.

While focusing most heavily on medical malpractice and professional exposures in the health care industry, other professions susceptible to professional liability suits will also be identified and discussed.

Finally, an overview of the protections available by the insurance business will be presented with the view of providing the professional with some means of facing the rising tide of professional liability suits.

HISTORY AND GENERAL TRENDS

Lawsuits based on professional negligence began to grow in number in the early 1960s. Starting with the medical profession, professional liability spread to encompass at least 70 different categories of professionals and other providers of services, including lawyers, real estate brokers, security brokers, accountants, architects, engineers, veterinarians, physicians, physiotherapists, hospitals, educators, and psychologists.[2] By the 1970s the growth in the number of professional liability suits had swelled and the increasing size of damage awards had led to widespread concern for what is presently called the professional malpractice crisis.

There are numerous reasons for this unprecedented increase in lawsuits steming from grievances for professionally rendered services, but perhaps the most significant factors are the change in the attitude of the public augmented by the change in lawyers' attitudes as to the propriety of filing lawsuits against other professionals.[3]

Moreover, changing legal concepts across the country have increased the risk of professional liability exposure by eroding the privity doctrine, expanding and redefining the professionals' duty of care, and by expanding the application of the discovery rule, a rule which provides that the statute of limitations does not commence running until the injured party *knows* or has *reason to know* of the facts or cause of his injury. Thus, security analysts, accountants, and lawyers may face liability exposure from a multitude of unknown investors. School board members and administrators may face liability risks in civil rights, fiscal management, and denial of due process. A physician, surgeon, or architect may be sued ten years or more after his professional-client relationship terminated.

Finally, one of the most important and relevant factors in determining "malpractice" is professional custom. Professional custom provides evidence of professional knowledge of the state of the art. It is noteworthy that the effect of custom is now given greater weight in evaluating the conduct of professionals than in judging other forms of human activities. In most areas of human activity, conforming practice is simply important evidence of what is reasonable, but for professionals, customary practice is presumed to be reasonable. One consequence of this adherence to customary practices in judging the conduct of professionals is that the law requires expert witnesses to set forth and explain what the customary standards are, and swear that these customary standards were violated. Thus, professional custom shows how other knowledgeable individuals in given professions have struck a balance between the costs of accidents and the costs of avoiding them. Today, more professionals are willing to come forward and express their opinion as to the state of the art. Thus, the stage is set for the laymen to judge the professional by the standard of the professional's peers, and in so doing, determining whether or not he has committed malpractice, that is, negligence.

Negligence defined

The traditional phrases for negligence—"conduct which involves an unusual risk of causing damage" or "conduct which falls below the standard established by law for the protection of others against unreasonable risk"—are nonspecific and relatively useless.[4] Perhaps the best definition of negligence was set by Judge Learned Hand more than 30 years ago in *United States* v. *Carroll Towing Co.*, a case in which two boats went down at sea while being towed by a tug that did not have a radio receiver.[5] If the tug had had a radio, it would have received warning of the impending storm and put into port. However, even though radios were known and becoming increasingly popular, and even though the cost of a radio was small when compared to the risk of operating at sea without a current weather report, tugs generally did not have radios. Nonetheless, Judge Learned Hand held that the tug company was negligent and therefore liable for the damage. Negligence occurs, he stated, whenever it would cost less to prevent a mishap than to pay for the damage predicted to result from it.[6]

The key to Judge Learned Hand's rule is that not everyone who is injured is entitled to be compensated; there must be someone who was negligent, and negligent behavior boils down to economics, that is, the failure to invest resources up to a level that equals the anticipated savings in damages.[7]

Malpractice problems

Professional malpractice suits differ from other civil tort problems in a number of ways. First, the issues involved are highly technical, and often even well-instructed juries cannot fully grasp the problems. Second, emotional and subjective elements play a much greater role. For instance, one need only look at the verdicts awarded against a doctor whose negligence caused the loss of an extremity versus the loss of the same extremity in an automobile accident caused by a reckless driver. It is not unheard of for the medical malpractice victim to be awarded $500,000 versus $50,000 for the accident victim.

Further, in professional malpractice cases, emotional bias and the juries' view of the professional as the common adversary have led to extremely high verdicts, thereby increasing the risk of the professional and in turn increasing the cost of malpractice litigation. If this cycle continues, the court processes will bankrupt the professional by forcing him to purchase expensive insurance coverage, not only to protect himself against the escalation of award amounts in high value cases and to cover the awards for settling minor or groundless claims but also to pay defense costs when innocent. The fear in minor suits is that if a low value, questionable case gets to a jury, there is no predicting the size of the verdict.

Finally, spiraling insurance premiums often combined with insurance unavailability have created a sudden crisis for all professional groups and have resulted in an astounding amount of misinformation. For example, the ever increasing number of malpractice suits often has been justified by viewing the suits and the subsequent settlements and awards as both a method of compensating innocent victims and as a means of deterring professionals from negligent behavior. Some say awards send "signals" to professionals informing them of the advisability of exercising more care and time to avoid costly mishaps.[8] It is the thesis of this chapter that such views are overly simplistic, often resulting in less imaginative, creative, and personal professional services. Once again consider the medical profession. The present medical malpractice trend has created a situation where skilled physicians who perform difficult and high-risk treatment are particularly penalized. The result being physicians are deterred from undertaking risky procedures, even when these procedures are, on medical grounds, most appropriate and should be performed. At present a physician realizing the personal cost of a bad outcome, in terms of time, money, and aggravation, may very well deprive the patient of an opportunity for better care. Thus, no one benefits from these high malpractice awards, least of all the client or patient. As the risk of liability and malpractice suits increases, the insurance cost necessary to cover the exposure must rise and, in its turn, the cost of services to the public rises.

Even the proponents of the deterrent theory are becoming concerned that the "signal" to the professional is insufficient for ideal deterrence.[9] Moreover, the signal loses its impact because malpractice insurance premiums are often set for groups of professional practicing as a partnership, or a professional corporation and not for individuals based upon their record of prior malpractice incidents.[10]

SPECIFIC PROFESSIONS COVERED AND RECENT DEVELOPMENTS

The medical and health service providers' professional liability

Professionals in the health care field are entering a new and vicious malpractice cycle, one in which the volume of professional liability suits against doctors and hospitals is increasing, glutting the courts and overwhelming the insurance companies.[11] Although the factors leading to this crisis are numerous and diverse, certainly the difficulty and high cost of insurance coverage, double-digit inflation, increased health care delivery costs, and a higher claims consciousness on the part of the public are all instrumental in precipitating the crisis atmosphere. As a result of this crisis, most states have passed remedial malpractice legislation.

Some medical writers have attributed the dramatic increase in malpractice suits in part to the belief that one half of the all surgical operations in this country " . . . are performed by doctors who are untrained or inadequately trained to undertake surgery."[12]

However, such simplistic evaluations do not adequately state nor explain the magnitude of the current malpractice crisis. The health care provider's risk today is not really different from that of the physician who practiced 4,000 years ago under the Code of Hammurabi. As the Code stated:

> If the surgeon has made a deep incision in the body of a free man and has caused the man's death, or has opened the caruncle in the eye and so destroys the man's eye they shall cut off his fore-hand.[13]

Nonetheless, we are seeing a disproportionate number of professional liability suits brought against health care providers, despite the fact that the standards of medical practice in this country have never been higher, or more strictly adhered to, and the quality and intensity of review of the individual practitioner is unprecedented. To what can we attribute this increase?

These professional liability suits are a product of the growing recognition by patients of their rights and capabilities of seeking reimbursement for elements of health care they feel were poorly provided, combined with an increased awareness of the tendency of patients to sue physicians and the attendant publicity of damage claimed.[14] The problem primarily results from a growing misunderstanding by patients of what modern medicine can do for them, combined with a lack of personal identity and rapport with the treating physician or hospital staff member. The effect of this imperfect perception by the patient and the increasingly depersonalized method of treating patients has in great part produced the vast majority of health care professional liability claims.[15] Additionally, these factors have combined with several important substantive changes in the law regarding physician-patient relationships, with dramatic liberalization of the statutes of limitation, with unavailability or extraordinarily costly professional liability insurance, with lawyers' recognition that malpractice cases can be "big ticket cases" and finally, with the judicial attitude that every case should be settled, thereby insuring that no plaintiff's claim is without value.[16]

Upon close inspection, many of the professional liability claims brought in the health care fields appear to be frivolous suits whose foundation rests upon three elements: a poor relationship with the health care provider, a poor result, and a bill deemed by the patient to be excessive.[17]

Although one often speculates on the random nature of malpractice claims and why some doctors and other health care providers go through life never being sued while some seem to experience a disproportionate number of malpractice claims rendered against them, some experts assert that these claims can be predicted with remarkable certainty. For example, in 1972 the risk of a malpractice claim against a surgeon was 14 times greater if he practiced in California than for a general physician who practiced in New Hampshire.[18]

More incidents of medical malpractice occur than result in damages, and many incidents of malpractice never lead to a claim; some may get as far as a report to the insurance company of a mishap, but then are never pursued by the patient.[19]

Against this background the professional liability exposure of the two major health providers, the physician and the hospital, are discussed.

Physicians' and surgeons' professional liability. Without belaboring the distinction, the physician and surgeon are exposed to vastly different theories of liability including malpractice, breach of contract, and assault and battery. The first and most significant theory of liability is malpractice or professional negligence.

Professional negligence is an outgrowth of the relationship between a physician and his patient, where the physician has departed from some duty arising out of their relationship and in which the departure was deemed to have been the proximate cause of the patient's injury.[20] This legal relationship can be found in the most innocuous circumstances. A relationship which creates a duty or obligation on the part of the physician may arise where few words are spoken, where the fee is not discussed, where no fee is involved, where the services of the doctor were obtained for the patient's benefit, even though the patient did not himself hire the doctor, and even where the relationship was created by an agreement between the doctor and a third party who was not the patient.[21]

Furthermore, not only is the physician liable for his acts, he is also liable for the acts of his employees (including nurses or other physicians).[22] Additionally, if a physician practices medicine in a partnership, he may be held liable for an injury resulting to a patient from the lack of skill or the negligence ". . . of any of the partners within the scope of their partnership business."[23]

Having found the requisite relationship, the courts next focus most heavily on the duty owed to the patient and the breach of that duty.

Through the use of intricate legal philosophy, courts consistently find an obligation and proceed to determine whether this duty or obligation had been breached. The most frequent allegation in malpractice claims is ". . . the physician or surgeon failed to use reasonable care and diligence in the care and treatment of the plaintiff, and failed to use the accepted and proper methods."[24] Perhaps, nowhere is the physician's duty put more succinctly than in *Pike* v. *Honsinger*, considered by many as the leading case expressing the obligation owed by a doctor to his patient.[25] As the Pike court stated:

- ☐ [The doctor is to possess] . . . that reasonable degree of learning and skill that is ordinarily possessed by physicians and surgeons in the locality where he practices. . . .
- ☐ [The doctor is] to use reasonable care and diligence in the exercise of his skill and the application of his learning to accomplish the purpose for which he was employed.
- ☐ [The doctor is] . . . to use his best judgment is exercising his skill and applying his knowledge.
- ☐ [The doctor] . . . is bound to keep abreast of the times.
- ☐ . . . [A] departure from approved methods in general use, if it injures the patient, will render [the doctor] liable however good his intentions may have been.

That is not to say a physician or surgeon is held to possess the extraordinary skill and genius reserved to few men of great endowment, but rather he must exercise that reasonable degree of skill and learning used under the same or similar circumstances by other members of his profession. Thus, the rule requiring a physician to use his best judgment will not hold him liable for a mere error in judgment provided he acted after careful examination and reflection in a manner which he thought best, and provided he did not explicitly guaranty a good result. Additionally, each member of a specialty is held to exercise that degree of skill and knowledge ordinarily possessed by similar specialists, not merely the degree of skill and knowledge of the general practitioner.[26] It must be emphasized that if a general practitioner treats a case which clearly lies within the field of a special branch of medicine, he does so at his own peril, as he will be obligated to use the skill equal to that of the specialist and he will be held liable if he fails to do so.

Physicians and surgeons have been expressly held to owe certain obligations or duties to their patients, among them the duty:

- ☐ To advise patients of the fact that they cannot always accomplish a cure;
- ☐ To make a skillful and careful diagnosis;

☐ To give proper instructions to their patients regarding conduct, exercise, medication, etc.;

☐ To heed the patients complaints and observations;

☐ Not to delegate an operation to another surgeon, when he was personally hired to perform the operation.[27]

Of all the duties physicians and surgeons have been held to, the one fraught with the most danger is the duty to make a frank disclosure to the plaintiff of the risk involved in the procedure recommended or about to be undertaken, often called the theory of "informed consent." This doctrine had its genesis in 1957 in *Salgo* v. *Leland Stanford, Jr. Univ. Bd. of Trustees*,[28] where the court held that a physician violates his duty to his patient if ". . . he withholds any facts which are necessary to form the basis of an intelligent consent."[29]

For present purposes, it is unnecessary to discuss at any length whether the informed consent question is or is not negligence, or whether a physician's treatment in absence of an informed consent constitutes an assault, or an intentional act. Suffice it to say there is a difference in the proof required under the two theories of recovery. Expert opinion concerning community standards is not required in assault and battery cases, whereas under traditional rules it is required in negligence actions. Furthermore, the trend appears to run toward classifying the failure to obtain informed consent as negligence rather than assault and battery.[30] Nonetheless, a small but growing minority does maintain the position that an "informed consent" case can be brought as either a negligence action or an assault and battery action. Thus, it is reasoned that expert testimony, although necessary for certain aspects of the case, may not be necessary on the issue of whether or not the consent is informed.[31]

Until recently a common definition of the physician's duty was that he ". . . make reasonable disclosure [to his patient] of all significant facts . . . [of] the nature of the operation and some of the more probable consequences and difficulties inherent in the proposed operation."[32] Thus, the majority of courts concluded the doctrine of informed consent created a cause of action in professional negligence against a physician when:

☐ There was a collateral side effect to treatment, i.e., a bad result; and

☐ The physician failed to inform the patient properly of that possibility when securing the consent; and

☐ The physician failed to advise the patient of alternative modes of treatment.[33]

Furthermore, the physician's duty of disclosure was fixed as in other types of malpractice cases and measured by the prevailing standards of the physicians practicing in his community.[34] Additionally, expert opinion as to the prevailing community standard was required.

This traditional rule and the law of informed consent is presently undergoing rapid change, and several jurisdictions have recently departed from the traditional rules and have held, among other things, that expert medical testimony is not required to prove a prima facie case of lack of informed consent.

One of the leading cases of this minority view is *Canterbury* v. *Spence,* involving nondisclosure of a risk of paralysis inherent in a laminectomy, a surgical procedure which involves the spine in the area of the spinal cord.[35] The defendant, a neurosurgeon, stated that although paralysis can be expected in approximately 1 percent of all laminectomies, it is not considered good medical practice to so inform the patient. The rationale being that this information might frighten or deter a patient who was in need of such surgery. The court in *Canterbury* held

> . . . the physician's duty to disclose is governed by the same legal principles applicable to others in comparable situations, with modification only to the extent that medical judgment enters into the picture. We hold the standard of measuring performance of that duty by physicians, as by others is conduct which is reasonable under the circumstances.[36]

In departing from the traditional rule, various courts have focused on the patient's right to have the physician's or surgeon's standard set by law rather than by physicians, holding that the ". . . doctor patient relationship is a one-on-one affair . . . [Thus] what is reasonable disclosure in one instance may not be reasonable in another. This variability negates the need of the plaintiff showing what other doctors may tell patients."[37] Thus, a prima facie case is made by the plaintiff showing that the physician ". . . failed to disclose material facts reasonably necessary to form the basis of an intelligent consent and [that] he has been injured as a result of submitting to a surgical procedure,"[38] that is, the primary focus being the patients right of self-determination.[39]

> Risk disclosure is based on the patient's right to determine what shall be done to his body. Such right should not be at the disposal of the medical community. The physician's obligation is to make reasonable disclosure of the available choices and the potential dangers, and the test of such reasonableness is for the jury to decide. The jury should not be bound by the conclusions of the medical community.[40]

Some of those jurisdictions which have broken with the traditional rules have additionally enacted informed consent statutes. These statutes, precipitated by the malpractice crisis, often limit informed consent suits by defining the requisite elements necessary to establish a prima facie case, by specifying the legal force and effect of written consent forms, and by specifying defenses for the treating physician or surgeon.

Among the most commonly accepted defenses to the requirement of informed consent are emergencies; "but for situations," i.e., but for the absence of disclosure the patient would not have had the operation; unexpected risks; "ignorance is bliss" situations, i.e., where a patient informs the doctor that he would prefer to remain ignorant; "peace of mind" situations, i.e., where the patient's peace of mind requires less than full disclosure; commonly known dangers; discovered dangers; nonmaterial dangers; improper performance of a proper procedure; and extremely rarely, nonserious risk.[41]

In the final analysis the informed consent rule remains a legal mine field for both the physician and his insurance company, the full risk being typified in *Ferrara* v. *Galluchio*.[42] In *Ferrara*, the defendant radiologist administered x-ray treatments to the plaintiff, which resulted in chronic radiodermatitis. A dermatologist advised the plaintiff she should be checked every six months because the condition could become malignant. The plaintiff developed cancerophobia and successfully sued the radiologist for causing her neurosis. On appeal the New York Court, in upholding the plaintiff's $26,000 recovery, stated the dermatologist's advice may have increased the plaintiff's mental anguish and neurosis, but it was the radiologist who was responsible for the damages arising from the neurosis, due to his failure to explain the risks inherent in the procedure.

Assuming the plaintiff has established the necessary doctor-patient relationship and the requisite duty and breach of duty, in medical malpractice actions, as in all negligence cases, he must still establish causation. Mere proof that the defendant was guilty of a departure from proper medical practice is not enough. The plaintiff must also show this departure was the proximate cause of the injuries claimed. Therefore, although the patient may already have been treated for some ailment which caused him pain and disability, he must prove it was the defendant's malpractice which caused, precipitated, or aggravated his condition.

Statute of limitations. Since one of the prime factors in the rising tide of malpractice actions has been the liberalization of statutes of limitation, it is worthwhile to briefly review these statutes and their impact on medical malpractice cases.

Statutes of limitations, some pertaining expressly to malpractice actions and others pertaining to tort actions generally, set a time period after the accrual of a cause of action in which a suit must be brought or forever be barred. Although there is considerable variance among the jurisdictions in this county, four general rules relevant to medical malpractice actions can be identified.[43]

The first and most traditional rule is that a malpractice cause of action accrues when the physician's negligent act or omission is committed and injury is sustained. Thus, in *Roybal* v. *White*[44] where a sponge was left in the plaintiff's abdomen and not discovered until ten years after her surgery, a sympathetic appeals court espousing the traditional rule upheld the trial court's dismissal of the action brought over ten years after the surgery was performed.

Subsequent to the traditional rule, the following three rules emerged in the special context of medical malpractice cases, all of which are attempts to mitigate the harshness of the traditional rule: the fraudulent concealment rule, the discovery rule, and the continuing negligence rule.

The fraudulent concealment rule tolls the statute of limitations during the period the defendant withholds information of the plaintiff's cause of action. Thus, the action begins to run only after the patient obtains knowledge of the physician's or surgeon's negligence.[45]

The discovery rule is basically two rules, both predicated on when the patient discovers or should have discovered the negligence of the physician or surgeon. The two prevailing applications are one applying the rule only when the claim alleges discovery of a foreign object within the patient's body[46] and the other, not unlike the fraudulent concealment rule when the claim alleges negligence in the diagnosis or treatment of a disease or condition.[47]

The last rule, that of "continuing negligence," stands for the proposition that a physician's negligence and duty to mitigate continues through the course of treatment,[48] or through the termination of the patient-doctor relationship.[49] For example, in the latter situation, a patient may bring an action 30 years after the alleged malpractice occurred, as long as the action is brought within one year of the termination of the patient-doctor relationship.

The various interpretations and applications of the statute of limitation by courts across the country has in many ways precipitated the medical malpractice crisis currently existing in this country.

By creating virtually open-ended statutes of limitation the courts have mitigated the harshness of the limitations rules for the plaintiff-patient and in its stead have placed an intolerable burden on both the physician and his insurance company. The physician is exposed to liability years after he has rendered his services and his insurance company, having no way of predicting the claims experience necessary for realistic rate making, is forced to resort to excessively high premium as a hedge against the uncertainty of wide ranging suits based on occurrences which took place years before, in fact situations where half of the witnesses may have died or disappeared. The net effect is an economic spiral which first places the increased cost burden on the physician, who, forced to pay expensive insurance rates, passes the cost on to the consumer, who ultimately has the ubiquitous pleasure of paying higher fees.

In an effort to stem this rising tide of stale and often questionable litigation, some states are now in the midst of reforming their limitation statutes by codifying exceptions to the traditional rule and imposing definite time periods in which malpractice actions can be brought. It is too early to determine whether the attempted legislative reform of statutes of limitation will ameliorate the present malpractice crisis. However, it is hoped any effort which brings certainty to the time of accrual of an indefinite cause of action will be helpful.

Breach of contract. As indicated earlier, aside from the physician's potential liability for malpractice, he may also be liable for breach of contract if he agrees to effect a cure or obtain a specific result and fails to do so.[50] The significance of a breach of contract claim becomes most apparent when one considers that actions for breach of contract are governed in all states by a different and generally longer statute of limitation. Thus, where a cause of action for breach of contract is stated, the shorter statute of limitations for malpractice will not bar the claim. Likewise, the dismissal of the malpractice claim is not a bar to the breach of contract claims.[51] Furthermore, the negligence of the doctor is not at issue, for if a physician or surgeon makes a contract to effect a cure and he fails to do so he is liable even if he used the highest possible professional skill. Additionally, most medical malpractice liability insurance policies specifically exclude coverage for breach of contract.

Assault and battery. The surgeon who performs an operative procedure in the absence of an emergency, without the patient's consent, may be held liable for assault and battery. In one of the leading New York cases[52] Justice Cardozo in affirming a judgment against a physician for unauthorized surgery, stated:

> Every human being of adult years and sound mind has a right to determine what shall be done with his own body; and a surgeon who performs an operation without his patient's consent, commits an assault, for which he is liable in damages. . . . This is true except in cases of emergency where the patient is unconscious and where it is necessary to operate before consent can be obtained.[53]

The exculpatory circumstance of an "emergency" has been expanded to create "implied consent" in some situations, for example, a surgeon is authorized to extend an operation to any abnormal condition in the area of the operative site which he deems necessary for the welfare of the patient.[54]

Admittedly, the value of recovery under an assault and battery action has been somewhat limited in effectivity by the courts. For the plaintiff to be entitled to more than nominal damages, it is necessary that he establish that it was the actual assault which was the proximate cause of the patient's injury. Thus, although the action for assault and battery may be easier to establish, the monetary recovery is greatly restricted.

Finally, as in a breach of contract claim, expert testimony is not necessary to prevail in an assault and battery action.[55]

Since actions for assault and battery are generally combined with malpractice claims, most medical malpractice insurance policies provide coverage for these actions.[56]

Hospital and other health service providers' professional liability. With the present trend toward the abolition of charitable immunity, hospitals are finding themselves governed by the general doctrine of *respondeat superior,* insofar as liability for the torts of its employees and agents. Thus, a hospital may be held liable for the medical or administrative acts of its employees, that is, residents, interns, nurses, orderlies, and so on, for the acts of its "specialists," that is, anesthesiologists, radiologists, and pathologists, or even for carrying out the acts of the attending physician if they are unreasonable.

A hospital, like a physician, is now deemed to owe its patients the duty of ordinary care. In the cases of hospitals this duty has been referred to as that degree of care, skill, and diligence exercised by hospitals in the general community, and includes furnishing the patient with skillful care by competent attendants and safe equipment. Accordingly, hospitals have been held liable for:

☐ Prematurely discharging a patient, or improperly moving a patient from one hospital to another.

☐ Leaving a patient unattended in a delivery room so that she fell off a bed which did not have side boards.

☐ Failure to exercise reasonable care in selecting and maintaining equipment and facilities furnished to the patient.

☐ Giving a patient improper medication.

☐ Failure of hospital resident to promptly notify the treating doctor of a significant adverse change in the patient's condition.

☐ Failure to provide adequate personnel to assist an elderly patient to the bathroom.[57]

Whether a hospital can be held liable under the informed consent doctrine is unclear. Normally hospital personnel merely perform the administrative function of obtaining the patient's signature on a consent form, whereas the discussion of the procedure is undertaken by the staff physician or surgeon. Consequently, hospitals are generally not involved in consent cases, unless it can be established the hospital employee was involved in obtaining the consent, or providing the treatment.[58] However, recent cases appear to be expanding the hospital's potential liability. Most significantly, hospitals are now held to have an obligation to supervise private physicians who have staff privileges. With this expansion of liability to entities beyond the treating physician, traced to the case of *Darling* v. *Charleston Community Memorial Hospital,* the hospital's risk under the informed consent doctrine may be greatly expanded.[59]

In *Darling,* the court permitted recovery against a hospital because of its failure to intervene in the treatment of a physician despite obvious indications of malpractice. The court held the hospital had a duty, through its medical staff, to assume certain responsibilities for the care of the patient and *supervise* the specific treatment recommended by the physician.

Interestingly, most courts while espousing the principal of *Darling* have rejected its explicit holding and have limited the hospitals' duty to one of investigation and review of the competence of its physicians and of those who have authority to use their facilities. Thus, since the *Darling* decision the case law has placed three primary duties upon the hospitals with regard to the activities of their facilities:

☐ The hospital must formulate rules to ensure patient safety.
☐ Physicians must not be permitted to violate rules established by the medical staff.
☐ The hospital must supervise the selection and activities of staff physicians.[60]

Almost ten years after *Darling,* in *Corleto* v. *Shore Memorial Hospital,*[61] a trial court judge, held that the medical staff of a hospital could be sued as an entity *or* each member of the staff could be sued individually.[62] In *Corleto,* a medical malpractice suit was brought against a doctor who performed abdominal surgery. An additional claim was made against the hospital, its administration, board of directors, and medical staff on the ground they knew or should have known that the doctor was not competent to perform the surgery and therefore should not have been permitted to do so by the defendants, nor should the defendants have permitted him to remain on the case. The court in refusing to dismiss the claim against the hospital et al. stated that the hospital had a duty to a patient not to admit an incompetent to surgical privileges and to remove a staff member who is incompetent. The court further held that the group of 141 hospital doctors involved were amenable to suit as an unincorporated association.[63]

The immediate lesson of *Darling* and *Corleto* is to underscore the court's tendency to view a hospital much as it would a corporation and to impose liability accordingly. Thus, where agents of a corporation are held personally liable if they fail to carry out or negligently carry out a duty owed to an injured party, so the hospital and, in particular, the members of various hospital staff committees are exposed to liability if there is evidence that a treating physician is, or should have been known to be, incompetent. For every physician found liable for an act of malpractice in a hospital setting, there is a group of some number of other physicians who are also potential defendants: the members of the credentials committee who recommended approval of the physician's application for privileges, or the members of the quality assurance committee that permitted flagrant practices to go on, or both.[64]

Therefore, each link in the chain of hospital responsibility from the medical staff to the committee which evaluates peer competence may suddenly find itself the subject of new and expanded theories which impose liability—the degree of risk being directly proportional to the degree of negligence.

Thus, hospitals have become defendants along with physicians, and at trial, the hospitals and its physician staff members often find themselves dealing not only at arm's-length but often as adversaries.[65] To the extent this situation creates an increased awareness of the duties and responsibilities of each toward the patient and toward each other, the result is positive as it upgrades health care. Unfortunately, this presence of multiple defendants has also contributed to the medical malpractice crisis in this country to the extent that plaintiffs' attorneys will often sue everyone in sight, that is, the hospital, its employees, its peer review committee, and the physicians, in the hope of getting the defendants to point fingers of blame at each other thereby winning the plaintiffs' case by establishing the requisite negligence.

Faced with the rising spiral of malpractice cases, hospitals have focused on risk management programs in an effort to reduce their errors and consequently their liability. Unquestionably the key to the success of these programs is their medical staff, as the vast bulk of all serious malpractice claims involving physicians occur in hospitals (e.g., in Pennsylvania approximately 80 percent of all claims involving physicians occur in hospitals).[66] Moreover, when a physician is sued because of a hospital incurred incident, the hospital is also sued, because after *Darling* it is legally responsible to see to it that physicians are competent and adhere to accepted standards of practice.

As indicated, hospitals may, like physicians and surgeons, face liability under the doctrine of informed consent, as the basic principles which apply to physicians apply equally to hospitals. However, there is one additional protection afforded to hospitals, the standard consent forms which patients sign for the hospital protection. While these forms do not necessarily prove a physician or hospital employee properly informed the patient, they can support a defense against a claim of lack of informed consent, particularly if some notation, handwritten and dated, is made by the physician and appears on the patient's progress notes or at the bottom of the signed consent form.[67] All too often the medical records of patients who allege lack of informed consent do not contain documentation that the physician or surgeon visited the patient pre-operatively; thus it becomes a matter of the surgeon's word against the patient's, and it is no surprise to anyone that of late the patient is winning.

Conclusion. The medical profession's liability picture appears bleak—claims, awards, and premiums are on the rise. However, it is not as black as it appears at first blush. There are many malpractice countermeasures the health care providers can adopt, and simultaneous to these individual efforts there are legislative remedies and other tort reform movements afoot throughout the country including:

☐ Abolition of the collateral source rule in some jurisdictions, most notably California which now permits court inquiry into plaintiffs' sources of recovery other than the malpractice action, e.g., it can now be brought out in court that the plaintiff has received or is eligible for compensation for medical expenses, loss of income, etc.;

☐ Limitation of awards for pain and suffering;

☐ More restrictive statutes of limitation;

☐ Allowance for periodic payments;

☐ Procedural tactics adopted by some states in an effort to rid the courts of meritless litigation require a preliminary review of a medical malpractice claim by a physician or panel of physicians;

☐ New, tougher malpractice acts which set standards defining a minimum day notice of intent to sue, set specific and certain statutes of limitation, set limits for informed consent suits, specify defenses available, some of which specifically protect certain hospital activities.[68]

Attorneys' professional liability

Attorneys' professional liability, once a minor if almost nonexistent problem for the legal profession, surfaced in the 1970s to the extent that legal malpractice now often overshadows medical malpractice. Statistically, eight to ten out of every hundred legal practitioners in the United States can expect to be sued for malpractice.[69] Compared with a decade ago, today aggrieved clients are suing their attorneys two and a half times more frequently and are demanding much higher sums for compensation. While the average loss incurred by defending lawyers is not known, unquestionably the upper limits are steadily rising (recently an Ohio jury awarded over $2.3 million in a legal malpractice action, believed to be among this nation's highest such verdicts).

In this brief overview of the professional liability exposure of the practicing attorney, the primary focus will be on legal malpractice. It is legal malpractice which encompasses the negligent acts and omissions of attorneys, including breach of fiduciary duties, and which currently presents the greatest hazard to the legal profession.

What are the causes of these legal malpractice claims? A recent survey of attorneys' professional liability experience in 13 states and encompassing approximately 60,000 attorneys revealed 34.49 percent of all claims were basically administrative law office errors,[70] for example, failure to meet procedural deadlines, failure to file required papers, failure to comply with statutes of limitation, fee disputes, and finally lost files, documents, or evidence—all nonsubstantive mistakes which over time have dramatically increased professional liability claims and likewise professional liability insurance premiums.

Thus, today, approximately half of all legal malpractice claims arise from either missing deadlines or other minor but costly administrative errors. For example, take the case of an attorney defending a products liability case, who through oversight fails to offer into evidence one of many reports and his client loses the case. The client learning of the oversight and believing the report to be highly significant sues both the lawyer and his firm for malpractice.

Another major area for concern is conflict of interest. A few years ago attorneys' professional liability insurers reported conflicts of interest were the cause of less than 5 percent of all malpractice claims. By 1978, however, the figure had risen to 22 percent and was still growing.[71]

The primary cause for the conflict of interest trap arises in the form of dual representation, for example, where an attorney represents both the lender and borrower, mortgagor and mortgagee, vendor and vendee, insured and insurer, husband and wife, multiple plaintiffs or multiple defendants in a tort action. While dual representation does not guaranty a malpractice claim, such multiple representation increases the risk of one and is extremely costly in time, effort, and emotion.

For example, recently the New Jersey Supreme Court held that a lawyer who represented two parties in a business transaction and thereafter sued one of those clients on behalf of the other warranted a public reprimand, despite the fact that there had been no violation of the Canon of Ethics.[72]

With respect to representation of an insured and insurer in defense of an action under a policy, there are numerous situations where the interests of the defendant and his insurer will become adverse and the attorney will be caught in the middle. For example, in 1973 the Texas Supreme Court sent shock waves into both the insurance business and the legal community, particularly the defense attorneys, when it found an attorney hired by an insurance company had engaged in conduct detrimental to the insured.[73] The attorney had been retained by the insured's insurance company to represent the insured who had been sued as the result of an industrial accident. Simultaneously, while representing the insured, the attorney was also developing information which was subsequently used by the insurance company as a basis for denying coverage. Neither the insurer or the attorney bothered to inform the insured there was any possibility of conflict between the interests of the insured and the insurer. Ultimately, the attorney, upon instruction from the insurer, withdrew from the case. The insured filed a declaratory judgment action. The Court recognizing the obvious conflict of interests, the failure of the attorney or the insurer to notify the insured of the conflict, and the ultimate disservice done to the insured determined that the carrier was estopped from denying the insured a defense.

Subsequently, a number of courts have adopted the same rule, and defense attorneys retained by insurance companies would be well advised to regard their relationship with the insured they are representing as a fiduciary relationship and make certain that their dealings with the insurers do not interfere with these obligations.[74] This warning is particularly relevant to attorneys who regularly represent professionals through their insurance companies, because professionals whose reputations are at stake are greatly concerned in the outcome of lawsuits filed against them and tend to keep a more watchful eye on the litigation process. Their greater interest may possibly be ascribed to the fact that professional liability policies often contain clauses which require professionals to consent to any settlement negotiated by the insurer and because the professional may be required to pay a deductible when a case is settled.[75]

Divorce actions are a last example of the conflict problem. Even the most amiably intended divorce action can give rise to conflicts and exposure to malpractice claims if the attorney continues to represent both parties. Thus, the best advice for an attorney is to avoid a possible conflict of interest situation at the outset by representing only one party.

Commingling of client's funds is another high-risk area which offers a double-edged sword in the context of malpractice. The legal practitioner would be well advised at the outset to institute workable office procedures which assure proper protection and prompt disbursement of a client's funds or property.[76] Such procedures may enable the attorney to avoid some of the many complaints now being brought against lawyers based on fee disputes which incline a client to lodge a malpractice claim or counterclaim for malpractice if the attorney sues for his fee.

Finally, one of the most significant sources of numerous lawsuits against attorneys involved in corporate practice are securities transactions.[77] The high degree of risk in these transactions and the increase in such lawsuits has led some sources of professional liability insurance to refuse to issue securities coverage. Identification of clients, or those who may be treated as clients, is a critical first step in preventing malpractice claims in securities transactions. Where a firm expressly agrees to represent a client, there is usually no problem. However, there are situations in which a firm may find the law imposes an attorney-client or third-party beneficiary relationship. To protect against this possibility the attorney or firm should adopt procedures including nonengagement letters to assure that one who might be treated as a client or third-party beneficiary is on notice that the attorney or firm is not representing them.[78]

As in other areas of the law, conflicts of interest play an increasingly greater role in liability exposure in securities transactions. This is especially true if the conflict involves the purchase or sale of a client's securities. If a firm or one of its members is the beneficial owner of 10 percent or more of the securities in question, exposure is clearly increased under §16(b) of the Securities Exchange Act of 1934. Even if the purchase is relatively nominal, disclosure may be required under the SEC Registration Guide 56.[79] Thus, firms should prohibit their members, associates, and employees from purchasing or selling a client's securities, except perhaps through mutual funds. Additionally, firms should set up formal guidelines to prevent both intentional and unintentional disclosure of confidential information. Restricting access to information to a need-to-know basis, numbering important documents restricting copying of such documents, and prohibiting discussion of information relating to securities transactions in nonprivate locations, which may include general areas of the law firm itself.[80]

Finally, the issuance of legal opinions may be potentially the most hazardous and high-risk aspect of securities transaction for the corporate lawyer.[81] In public offerings, wise attorneys refrain from issuing opinions except as to the due and valid issuance of the securities in question. However, private placements frequently involve opinions by lawyers which do present significant exposure. Therefore, where firms are engaged in a practice which requires issuance of opinions in securities transactions, the following risk management guidelines are suggested:

- ☐ Engagement letters;
- ☐ Preparation and preservation of written records;
- ☐ Investigation of the facts and a summary of the reason reliance is placed on particular facts;
- ☐ Recitation in the opinion letter of precautions taken and restrictions placed on the opinion letter;
- ☐ A formal review by a partner other than the one in charge of the opinion letter; and
- ☐ Periodic review of the opinion letter to determine if it is still valid.[82]

Before concluding this section on attorney malpractice it is worthwhile noting the recent trend of some courts to adopt the discovery rule in legal malpractice cases.[83] As in medical malpractice cases, the courts are now beginning to hold that the statute of limitation does not begin to run until the client sustains damages as a result of the attorney's malpractice *and* discovers or should have discovered the cause of action against the attorney.

As this brief review of legal malpractice shows, many of the claims to which lawyers are subjected, and which result in, among other things, great stress, loss of valuable time, and possible damage to their professional reputation can be avoided or, at the least, substantially curtailed by assiduous attention to detail, deadlines, and potential conflict of interest situations. Admittedly, however, the most effective control measures cannot prevent those malpractice suits attributed to faulty judgment or counsel, and unfortunately it is these suits which often result in the multi-million-dollar professional liability claims against attorneys. The only protection for the attorney practicing in these areas is ample malpractice insurance.

Accountants' professional liability

The public accountant may be the target for a host of professional liability actions including malpractice actions and actions for breach of contract, fraud, false, or misleading statements in a statutory prospectus and actions for filing false statements with regulatory authorities. As there has been an enormous increase in the cases brought against accountants in the last ten years,[84] many premised upon the securities laws whose nuances are impossible to discuss in this chapter, the following text is intended to serve only as a general outline of causes of action which could be brought against the accountant.

Malpractice actions against accountants generally are predicated on the *Restatement of Torts* 2d §522 which provides:

(1) One who, in the course of his business profession or employment, or in a transaction in which he has a pecuniary interest, supplies false information for the guidance of others in their business transactions, is subject to liability for pecuniary loss caused to them by their justifiable reliance upon the information if he fails to exercise reasonable care or competence in obtaining or communicating the information.

This type of common-law tort action may be brought by a wide range of individuals including clients or persons who, while not in privity with the accountant, were known or should have been known by the accountant to be relying upon his report at the time he either undertook the assignment or prior to his rendering of the report.[85]

In order to prevail in his malpractice action, the plaintiff must prove the accountant had a duty to the plaintiff (generally contractual or statutory in nature); this duty was breached either intentionally or negligently, and the breach was the cause of the plaintiff's damages.

Alternately, the accountant can be sued by his client-employer for breach of contract, usually premised upon his engagement letter which sets forth his duties and responsibilities. Just as a building contractor may be held liable for a breach of his services contract, so too may an accountant be held civilly liable for a breach of his engagement. The right to bring such an action runs not only to the client,[86] but also to those who stand in the shoes of the client, for example, persons for whose benefit the accountant was engaged under a third-party beneficiary theory.[87] Thus, a stockholder can bring an action against a public accountant who has been retained by a corporation for damages resulting from the accountant's negligence. The mere fact that the stockholder was not a direct party to the contract between the corporation and the accountant is deemed irrelevant, as the stockholder is regarded as a third-party beneficiary to that contract and therefore entitled to a claim against the accountant. Moreover, an engagement agreement whether oral or written, whether signed by both the client and the accountant, or only by the accountant, also can form the basis for an action for breach of contract.[88]

Finally, the largest and most significant risk of professional liability for the accountant lies in the area of fraud. Fraud actions are generally brought under the antifraud sections of the federal securities laws, in particular Section 17(a) of the Securities Act of 1933, as amended and Section 10(b) and 14(e) and Rule 10b(5) of the Securities Exchange Act of 1934.[89]

There is no express provision for civil liability under the antifraud provisions of the 1933 and 1934 acts. However, it has long been held that a private right of action exists under Section 10(b).[90] Moreover, while there have been decisions questioning the existence of a private right of action under Section 17(a) of the 1933 act, most courts have upheld an implied private right of action based upon this provision.[91]

Actions under Section 10(b) and Rule 10b(5)of the 1934 act are limited to persons who incurred damages in connection with either a purchase or sale of securities.[92] Whereas, actions under Section 17(a) of the 1933 act are restricted to a purchaser of securities.

Section 14(e) of the 1934 act similarly has been invoked in private actions. However, a Section 14(e) action is generally coupled with claims premised on Section 10(b) and Rule 10b(5). These actions are limited to fraud committed in connection with a tender offer and may be asserted either by the target company, its shareholders (irrespective of whether or not they tendered their shares), the company soliciting tenders, or by a competing suitor.[93]

Thus, actions based upon the antifraud provisions of the 1933 and 1934 acts may be brought by a broad variety of persons who suffered damages by reason of, or as a result of, violations of those provisions irrespective of their relationship to the defendant accountant. Many commentators believe it is this breadth of potential classes of plaintiffs which has, in large measure, been responsible for the large number of suits brought under these provisions, as such actions may be brought not only against those who violated those provisions but also against those persons including accountants who may have conspired with, or aided and abetted, the principal violator of these provisions.[94]

Additionally, fraud claims may be brought under numerous other antifraud provisions of the federal or state securities laws and statutes which cover among them actions for false registration statements and prospectuses[95] and actions for filing of false statements,[96] and on a common-law fraud basis.

The complexities of these actions are beyond the scope of this chapter and will not be discussed. However, the accountant today must conform to an extraordinarily high standard of care, as often the degree of culpability necessary to be found negligent or guilty of violating the federal or state securities laws is quite minimal. Moreover, it will not be sufficient for the accountant to exculpate himself. He must additionally prove he acted in good faith, a burden which is often difficult to meet. "Good faith" is often predicated on proof that the accountant had no reason to believe or suspect a filing was misleading.

Architects' and engineers' professional liability

Like the accountant, the architect or engineer is exposed to potential legal liability not only to their clients with whom they contract to render services but also to third parties who are not privy to those contracts but who may be injured or suffer damages as a result of a defect found in the architect's or engineer's designs or construction of a structure. Additionally, like the accountant, an action against an architect or engineer can be found to sound in tort or contract. However, in the case of these professionals the determination of whether to bring a tort or contract action is generally determined by the statute of limitations governing the action, which in turn is predicated on the date when the action accrues. It may well be in a particular action the shorter statute of limitations governing tort action has run, whereas the longer statute of limitations for contract actions has not run. The plaintiff will then frame his complaint against the architect or engineer to allege some breach of contract, thereby taking advantage of the longer period of limitations for contract actions.

Generally, action accrual dates for architects and engineers can be lumped into three period: the time of design and construction; the time when damage or injury first occurs; and the time when the damage is discovered, or with reasonable diligence, could have been discovered.[97] Thus, the professional architect or engineer is exposed when he submits his plans; when he is negligent; when he breaches the contract; when the structure is substantially completed; when the structure is completed and is inspected; when the structure is occupied, used, or accepted; when damage occurs; or finally when the damage or injury is discovered. Although the bulk of cases discussed focus on architect's liability, the term *engineer* might just as easily be substituted, as both parties furnish similar services and are prone to similar liability suits.[98]

A cursory review of the literature indicates the standard of care imposed upon an architect or engineer vis-a-vis his client is much like that which rests upon the lawyer or physician, or for that matter any professional who holds himself out to possess some skill and ability in some special area of employment and who then offers his services to the public based on his special skills.[99] In the particular case of the architect, it has been said he implies:

> . . . that he possesses skill and ability including taste, sufficient to enable him to perform the required services at least ordinarily and reasonably well; and that he will exercise and apply, in the given case, his skill and ability, his judgment and taste reasonably and without neglect. But the undertaking does not imply or warrant a satisfactory result.[100]

Having said that, the courts in recent years have tended to hold the architect and engineer to a more exacting measure and while not requiring absolute perfection have tested the architect or engineer by an ever increasingly higher standard of care.

One of the primary areas of potential liability for the architect or engineer is error in the preparation of plans or specifications. Not only must the architect exercise his skill, ability, judgment, and taste reasonably without neglect, but further he is held to responsibilities ranging from initial cost estimates to preparation scheduling, to construction phase services, including supervision and certification.

Thus, estimates as to cost of construction and failure to prepare plans and specs within the cost of construction specified by the client have given "rise" to difficulties between architects and engineers and the owner, and have been known to lead to liability suits which have cost the professional his compensation. Moreover, while the issue of an architect's liability for negligently preparing estimates of construction cost is a jury question, this issue is most often raised as a defense to an architect's suit for fees.[101] Finally, a false representation as to the cost of construction may be tantamount to fraud which may subject the architect or engineer to liability and entitle the owner to recover the excess or some portion thereof above the sum which was to have been invested in the structure for a profitable return.[102]

Additionally, the architect is duty bound to know all of the building code restrictions which impact on his project, to deliver plans and specifications to the owner in a timely fashion, and above all to submit a design within budget which is not faulty or defective in any manner.

Upon completion of the working drawings, plans, and specs, and following their approval by the owner, the bid completion of contract bidding, the architect or engineer enters into the construction phase of his services which includes awarding the contract, supervision, inspection, and issuance of the certificate of payment. Each step of the construction phase service is fraught with risk. The standard of care to be exercised is similar to that invoked in the design phase in that the architect or engineer must exercise reasonable diligence and care, or risk being liable to the owner for damage proximately resulting from any breach of his duty.[103] Although clearly not an insurer nor guarantor of perfect results, the architect or engineer is subject to some standard between that of "ordinary care" and "extraordinary diligence."

With respect to the liability of architects and engineers to third persons, it is difficult to state a conclusion as to the state of the law and what direction it will finally take, as the courts rarely state precisely what principle they relied upon in reaching their decision.[104] However, it is clear that after *Inman* v. *Binghamton Housing Authority,* the architect clearly can be held liable to third parties.[105] In *Inman* a young child fell from a stoop in the back of her parents' apartment. The parents alleged that the absence of a handrail on the stoop was an error of design for which the architect was liable. The New York Court in finding the architect liable, analogized the case to that of *MacPherson* v. *Buick Motor Company* in which Justice Cardozo disregarded the privity of contract doctrine and held a manufacturer was liable to the user of its product.[106] In following *MacPherson*, the *Inman* Court broke with the previous general rule that an architect had no liability to third parties after he had completed his work, since there was no privity of contract between the architect and the third party.

More recently, in *Navajo Circle, Inc.* v. *Development Concept Corp.*, a Florida appellate court ruled privity of contract is not required in a negligence class action against architectural and construction firms.[107] In *Navajo*, the plaintiffs, a condominium association and an individual owner, brought a class action alleging the contractor negligently constructed the roof of a condominium building and the architects negligently supervised the construction and subsequent repairs. The trial court granted defendants' motion to dismiss based on plaintiffs' failure to allege privity of contract.

The question in *Navajo* was whether the defendants owed plaintiffs a legal duty to use a reasonable degree of care to insure against a foreseeable, unreasonable risk. Citing *MacPherson* v. *Buick Motor Co.*, for the proposition that suppliers of products have such a duty to those who may foreseeably come in contact with their product, the appellate court noted Florida had extended this duty to suppliers of services. As in the defective products cases, privity of contract is not required to support a tort action for negligent performance of a service, even where that service is based on a contractual obligation to another party. The court also rejected the contractor's argument that, absent privity, the plaintiff was required to allege a latent defect which was inherently dangerous or created an unreasonable risk of injury, observing that this argument would be more appropriate where appellants rely on a strict liability theory.

From the aforementioned cases and from a brief review of other cases, certain generalized principles emerge regarding the professional liability of architects and engineers to third parties.

Thus, where the architect has been negligent in the preparation of plans and specs for a building and injury to a third person occurs during the actual construction process, the third party may recover from the architect if he himself is free from contributory negligence.[108] If the injury occurs after the completion of the building and it can be proved the building was designed in such a way as to endanger or threaten the life of a person, the injured third party can recover from the architect. For example, where the architect designed and supervised the construction of a stairway in a bus station, he was held liable to a person who was hurt while using the stairway, even though the injury occurred almost two years after construction of the stairway.[109]

There is some question as to whether an architect or engineer can be held liable for injury to a third person which occurred because of a contractor's poor workmanship. Those cases which tend to impose such liability on the architect do so only where it is clear he knew or had reason to know of the danger created by the contractor and did not take steps to eliminate that danger.[110] The trend in some states is to find the architect liable if he is aware that the plans or specifications are not followed and seeing the danger of the situation, he merely directs the contractor or owner to remedy the situation. The onus is on the architect to see the situation is corrected and the plans are followed, that is, some courts have placed a duty of second inspection upon the architect.[111]

The success of an attempt by the architect to restrict his supervisory duties to one of inspection, to determine that the work was performed in accordance with the plans and specifications, and to thereby reduce his exposure to liability is questionable. Some courts have held that where an engineer is responsible for and signed plans for a project but did not enter into any supervision contract, he may not later be held liable for defects in the execution of the project as he did not assume such responsibility.[112] Likewise, in a similar situation, where a contract specifically limited the architect's job site responsibility to insuring that construction proceeded according to specifications and did not give him the power of supervision or control over the actual manner in which the work was to be performed, the architect was held not to be under a statutory duty to maintain safe conditions and therefore not liable under a state's safe place statute for injuries to an employee of the general contractor.[113]

Finally, although the courts are split, the better rule seems to be that where an architect takes no action (i.e., nonfeasance) and affirmative action might have prevented injury to another, the injured person may not recover if he is a third party to the contract between the architect and the owner.[114] However, if the architect does take some affirmative action during the execution of his duties of supervision and this action causes injury to a third party, that person may recover.[115]

Thus, as the knowledge, ability, and skills of architects and engineers has grown dramatically so has their risk of potential professional liability increased toward both client and third parties, requiring constant vigilance and extraordinarily high standards on the part of the modern practitioners.

PROFESSIONAL LIABILITY PROTECTION AND INSURANCE

So long as we have a system which awards money damages to persons injured by the negligent acts of others, the survival of private professional practice in this country will be dependent upon the availability of professional liability insurance at a reasonable price. Professional people and their organizations are inextricably intertwined with the business of liability insurance.

Medical and health service providers' professional liability

Because of the exposure in the medical and health care providers' areas of malpractice, liability has undergone startling changes, and the availability of coverages for these exposures has changed. As discussed, recoveries in the areas of medical malpractice have sharply increased, thereby affecting the availability of coverage for the individuals and institutions involved. Malpractice exposure is one of low but increasing frequency and high severity, with a "long tail" on the incidents, that is, a relatively long period of time between the incident giving rise to the malpractice claim and the assertion of the claim itself, and an extended period between assertion of the claim and final disposition.

This coverage ordinarily is written for a term of one year, although it may be shorter or longer, depending on the circumstances. Limits also depend on the individual or institution involved, as well as on the location, but commonly are written on an occurrence/aggregate basis, for example, $1 million for each occurrence/$3 million aggregate. The policy also is written either on a per claim basis or a per medical incident basis, the latter being the newer concept. If on a per claim basis, the single limit of coverage applies to each covered defendant involved in the entire incident, subject only to the aggregate policy limit. If the coverage is on a per medical incident basis, the single limit is available only once per incident, no matter how many covered employees or professionals may be involved in that incident.

The primary medical professional liability policy is generally coupled with an excess policy or second layer of insurance. The excess policy is commonly written for hospital exposures and usually in substantial amount, for example, $5/$5 million. The excess policy provides that if the primary policy is exhausted on the aggregate side, the excess becomes primary and picks up exposure from the first dollar, as well as providing the higher limits for a single incident.

In the case of the hospital professional liability exposure, the definition of insured includes not only the named insured but also executive officers, hospital administrators, members of the Board of Directors, Trustees, or Governors, all, of course, acting within the scope of their respective duties, and can be broadened by endorsement to include employees, for example, employed medical doctors, registered nurses, technicians, and volunteers, and still further to include independent contractors, for example, medical doctors who are not employees. As with any other complex area of insurance, this point should be covered quite carefully with your lawyer and insurance broker, so as to be tailored to fit the particular situation.

In the marketplace today, conventional insurance combined with one or more of a number of alternatives often make up the professional liability insurance package. Basically, the coverage is provided by insurers. Beyond this, an institution or association of institutions or individuals can self-insure a portion of the exposure or can consider a captive insurance company, an area which has seen much activity in recent years. Creation of a trust fund arrangement is another possibility, and beyond that, the legislatures of a number of states have provided legislative responses to the need for coverages which take the form of joint underwriting associations, patients' compensation funds, and so on. Again, this is a highly complex area with financial consequences of immense proportions and must be worked out carefully, always in conjunction with a lawyer and insurance agent or broker.

Attorneys' professional liability

The scope and extent of lawyers' exposure to liability for malpractice has expanded substantially in recent years. Lawyers and law firms now are being found liable for the consequences of their actions or inactions in areas which represent a sharp departure from the long held views of liability for malpractice in the legal profession. Adequate coverage, therefore, is essential, expensive, and can be difficult to obtain.

The number of companies writing legal malpractice insurance in the marketplace today is rather small. Perhaps only half a dozen are in the market in any substantial way. As a consequence, this insurance is not readily available and the services of a competent agent or broker are essential, both to know where the markets are and to assure the client of the best possible program for the premium dollar.

Insured. The legal malpractice policy basically covers each lawyer named in the policy declarations and any others who thereafter may become members of the firm. For lawyers who leave the firm during the policy term, coverage can be extended for any acts, errors, or omissions which occurred during their tenure in the firm.

Coverage. Coverage for legal malpractice usually is written with a primary policy and covered by either an excess or umbrella type policy. Primary insurance is the first dollar coverage, up to the maximum limit of liability stated in the policy. Limits are usually expressed as a single limit and an aggregate—$100,000/$300,000—and these, of course, may be increased to whatever limit the company is willing to write. This coverage is subject to a deductible.

The excess liability insurance policy provides limits in excess of those specified in the primary policy and can cover up to the limits desired or obtainable. The policy is subject to a deductible which is the single limit of the primary policy. The excess policy is, in effect, an extension of the coverage under the primary policy; it is not more comprehensive and is in reality another layer of insurance, for higher limits.

The umbrella policy, however, can be broader and more comprehensive than the primary policy and usually will also provide the higher limits by way of the second layer. Further, if the aggregate limit of the primary policy is used within the policy year, the umbrella can be written so as to become the primary policy as to additional claims in that policy year.

The policy. The intention is not to examine in this chapter all of the provisions of a legal malpractice insurance policy. This is a complex area of insurance, the coverages are complicated, and the assistance of a competent agent or broker is essential. The intent is only to give an overview of the points of coverage.

Basically, the policy covers negligent acts, errors, or omissions arising out of professional services rendered or which should have been rendered in the insured's capacity as a lawyer. This may also include coverage for libel and slander, as well as basic liability for third-party bodily injury and property damage caused or which occurred in the insured's offices.

The coverage is written in either of two forms: (1) the occurrence basis, or (2) the claims-made basis.

The occurrence basis policy covers acts, errors, or omissions committed or which occurred during the policy period but without regard to when the claim is presented. Coverage beyond expiration date is not a concern as the policy will respond as long as the act, error, or omission was committed during the policy period.

Under the claims-made basis policy, claims for acts, errors, or omissions must have been presented during the policy periods, or at least the insured must have been aware of circumstances which could give rise to a claim and must have reported this to the insurer. This form can be endorsed to pick up the exposure for prior years, but on an excess basis, that is, excess over any other valid and collectible insurance. The "tail" period, that is, that period which follows expiration date, is very important to the lawyer who is retiring or moving to another firm and whose coverage is on a claims-made basis. Most such policies can be endorsed to provide coverage for the period subsequent to the policy period, although such extension may be for only a limited time.

The claims-made basis, by law, is not written in some states, and in others, the cases have found this form to be invalid, as against public policy.

Which of the forms should be considered, assuming the marketplace gives the choice, must be carefully reviewed and analyzed with a competent agent or broker, a point which must be strongly emphasized.

Exclusions. Several exclusions are to be mentioned, although this very important section of the policy should be reviewed carefully. Most policies exclude coverage for dishonest, fraudulent, criminal, or malicious acts. Some provide innocent partner coverage, which protects those who had no knowledge of the act or omission. Also excluded is coverage for liability with regard to activity dealing with the Securities Act of 1933, as amended, or the Securities Exchange Act of 1934, as amended, or regulations issued thereunder. Some policies extend this exclusion to other statutes and acts, as well.

Accountants' professional liability

Accounting became a full-fledged profession in the last hundred years. Its areas of exposure have expanded from the original, narrow bookkeeping concepts to the standards of today, which literally require an accountant to be a detective or a bloodhound and to expose all wrongdoing by the client's employees. With this expanded scope of operation comes a similar expansion of the accountant's liability to clients and third parties.

There are three principal areas of accountants' professional liability which must be covered:

1. Liability to the client employer or to others who stand in the shoes of the client.
2. Common-law liability to third parties by whom the accountant was not retained and with whom the accountant is not in privity.
3. Statutory liability, especially under the Securities Exchange Act and the Securities Exchange Commission rules and regulations.

As with the comment on the other areas of professional liability, this is intended as an overview of the exposures and coverages available, not an in-depth review, and therefore should not be substituted for the guidance and counsel of your own attorney and insurance agent or broker.

Insured. The Accountants' Professional Liability Policy covers under the term *insured:*

a. The named insured.
b. Any predecessor in business.

c. Any accountant or accounting firm while performing professional accounting services under contract with the named insured.

d. Any person who was, is, or hereafter becomes a partner, officer, director, or employee while acting within the scope of his duties.

Coverage. Coverage is written on an Accountants' Professional Liability Policy, expressly intended to cover the professional liability exposure. With high limits, that is, up to $5 million or so, this may be the only policy necessary, but with lower limits, depending on the market, an excess or umbrella policy is strongly recommended.

The policy. Basically, the policy covers the insured's legal liability caused by acts, errors, omissions, or neglect in the insured's performance of professional accounting services. Generally, the policy excludes:

a. Liability for dishonest, fraudulent, criminal, or malicious acts or omissions.

b. Liability for criminal libel, criminal slander, or defamation of character committed in bad faith or in willful violation of law.

However, these exclusions generally do not invalidate coverage for any insured who did not act with knowledge or consent of the excluded act, omission, and so on. In other words, the innocent members of the firm insured do not lose coverage under the policy for the willful, fraudulent acts or omissions of the guilty.

As with other forms of malpractice coverage, accountants' liability policies are written on either the claims-made basis or the occurrence basis. The distinctions between these two types of policies, noted earlier in this chapter, apply as well to the accountants' liability policy.

If the insured is covered under an occurrence basis policy, the "tail" between the date of the act or omission and the claim is of no particular concern. If coverage is under a claims-made policy, the policy period within which the act or omission must have occurred and notice given to the insurer is quite important and must be considered carefully, especially when the coverage is being shifted from one insurer to another. Under this circumstance, continuity of coverage generally can be picked up by endorsement, for an added premium. Keeping the coverage with one insurer will eliminate this problem.

If the insured does a substantial amount of work in the securities field, subject to the Securities Exchange Act, there may be a surcharge on the premium.

The policy period typically is one year but may be written on a three-year basis.

Architects' and engineers' professional liability

The professional liability exposure of architects and engineers has increased greatly in the last 10 years, although this expanding liability has been apparent for 25 years or more. It has been that long since the courts upheld the right of third parties to recover damages from architects and engineers. Before that development, architects' and engineers' liability was limited to damages sustained by the owner of the construction project. In the past few years, malpractice suits against architects and engineers have increased approximately 20 percent per year, much of this in the so-called frivolous lawsuit area.

The market for architects' and engineers' malpractice insurance, often called errors and omissions coverage, is limited. Six companies write the vast majority of this insurance, although the major multi-line insurers sometimes write this on a limited basis only. With this reduced availability, the coverage can be difficult to obtain and sharply increased adverse experience in recent years in this line is reflected in the cost. Therefore, maintaining continuity with an agent or broker and the insurance company is imperative.

The Architects' and/or Engineers' Professional Liability Policy is almost always written on a claims-made basis rather than on an occurrence basis. The distinction between these two types of insurance contracts has been discussed. The claims-made policy poses a dilemma for the architects or engineers as design error may not be revealed or translated into a claim until some years after the fact. Therefore, continuity of coverage is important as the policy can be written so that claims asserted under the current policy are covered even though the error, omission, or negligent act occurred under a prior policy that had been continuously renewed in the same insurance company up to the present policy.

Insured. Under the Architects' and/or Engineers' Professional Liability Policy, the insured is the named insured and includes any partner, officer, director, stockholder, or employee of the named insured, while acting within the scope of his duties for the named insured.

Policy. The policy is an Architects' and/or Engineers' Professional Liability Policy.

The policy limits are expressed as a single limit and an aggregate limit, for example, $500,000/$1 million. The single limit of liability applies to a single claim arising from an error, omission, or negligent act. The aggregate limit of liability applies to all claims arising from a single error, omission, or negligent act or from related errors, omissions, or negligent acts in the same policy period. However, the aggregate limit of liability can also be expressed as an annual aggregate limit, and reference to the policy language on this point, therefore, is essential.

The scope of the policy generally has been limited to the United States, its territories or possessions, and Canada, with coverage for other areas of the world added by endorsement. It is now possible to obtain the policy with worldwide coverage, but certain countries are excluded.

Coverage. The policy covers the architects' or engineers' liability arising from errors, omissions, or negligent acts. The insuring clause in a typical policy might state the policy would pay—all sums (subject, of course, to the maximum amount payable under the policy) that the insured shall become legally obligated to pay as damages if such legal liability arises out of the performance of professional services for others in the insured's capacity as an architect or engineer and if such legal liability is caused by an error, omission, or negligent act of the insured or any person or organization for whom the insured is legally liable.

As with other professional liability policies, coverage is subject to a deductible, the amount of which can be negotiated upward or downward depending on the premium.

The policy affords coverage for loss or damages as a consequence of claims asserted and, in addition, reimburses the insured for claims expenses incurred. Claims expense includes legal and other types of fees, costs, and expenses resulting from the investigation, adjustment, defense, and appeal of a claim. Not all claims expense is reimbursable; for example, legal fees generally must be those of an attorney who has been designated by the insurance company, and, therefore, policy language must be carefully checked on this point.

One can readily foresee a claim situation in which the insured, the professional architect or engineer, strongly believes there has been no error, omission, or negligent act and, therefore, no legal liability while, on the other hand, the insurance company—recognizing a potential liability—may propose to offer a settlement. The policy anticipates this situation by providing:

a. That the insurance company may not settle a claim without the "consent" or the "informed consent" of the insured, and

b. If the insured withholds consent to a good-faith settlement recommended by the insurance company, the company's liability to the insured for the loss incurred thereafter on the claim is limited to the amount proposed in settlement, if in fact there was a solid negotiated figure, plus those claims expenses incurred up to that point.

This can be a dilemma for the professional who feels strongly about his position in the matter and who must make the decision whether to risk the additional loss and expense which would be incurred if the claim results in an adverse judgment in an amount in excess of the negotiated amount.

Exclusions. Because of the nature of the services rendered by the insured, there are some exclusions worthy of mention in this policy in addition to standard exclusions. Some of these, for which there is no coverage for loss or expense, include:

a. The making of surveys of subsurface conditions or ground tests by the insured or the evaluation or analysis of any surveys of subsurface conditions or ground tests.
b. Any liability of others assumed by the insured under a contract or agreement.
c. Professional services performed by or on behalf of a joint venture of which the insured is a member.
d. All activities in connection with ski lifts, commercial amusement rides, and skateboard parks.
    Coverage for the foregoing, however, can usually be added by specific endorsement to the policy.
e. Any dishonest, fraudulent, or criminal acts or omissions or those of a knowingly wrongful nature committed intentionally by or at the direction of the insured.

The architect or engineer, partly because of the nature of the services performed, is subject to certain claims which arise from or are a consequence of the nonprofessional side of the business operation and are such that the distinction between a professional liability exposure arising from an error, omission, or negligent act and a nonprofessional exposure arising from the insured's general operations is unclear. While this somewhat gray area of exposure is discussed in more detail later in this chapter, it must be emphasized that for the architect or engineer, coverage for the operational nonprofessional type of loss is a necessity not only to pick up this exposure but also to eliminate the possibility of any failure of coverage with respect to a liability which may lie in the gray area.

PROFESSIONAL LIABILITY OF A CORPORATION

Recognizing that no professional liability discussion can be complete without reference to the liability which a corporation and its officers can incur, this chapter concludes with a brief review of corporate liability.

A corporation can incur liability for its acts, errors, omissions, negligent conduct, and so forth, just as professionals can, and these exposures require a variety of insurance coverages usually in a combination of policies, one or more of which will cover the liability sometimes referred to as the malpractice exposure or the errors and omissions (E&O) exposure. A discussion of that insurance package is beyond the scope of this chapter. However, one facet of that coverage—the professional liability exposure of the directors and officers of the corporation—will be discussed. As stated, this is a summary of a broad and complex topic and is not intended by the authors to be substituted for professional advice from both the corporation's lawyer and agent or broker.

Directors' and officers' liability insurance is a relative newcomer to the field, having been written for only the last 40 years or so. At its inception, it was purchased only by the largest corporations and written by comparatively few insurance companies. Since the 1960s however, corporate liability has expanded greatly and, with it, the liability of corporate directors and officers, and today most corporations have at least some coverage for this area of liability.

Insured. The insured under this policy are the corporation and the duly elected directors and officers of the corporation, who usually are required to be identified on the application for the coverage at the inception of the policy and sometimes named in the policy itself. The coverage also applies to all who become directors or officers after the inception date. The policy sometimes is subject to a requirement that the insured update or periodically advise the insurer of new elections or appointments, and which probably will generate an additional premium.

Policy. The policy is known as the Directors' and Officers' Liability Policy. It usually is written to include two particular areas:

a. Reimbursement to the officers and directors of covered loss and expense incurred individually.

b. Reimbursement to the corporation of covered loss and expense which it, in turn, has reimbursed to directors and officers, assuming that corporate reimbursement of such is permitted by the bylaws of the corporation and the jurisdiction where incorporated.

Directors' and officers' coverage is almost invariably written on the claims-made basis as contrasted to the occurrence basis. This distinction has been discussed earlier in this chapter, and the same rationale applies.

Coverage. The policy, subject to some variation in the language, generally covers the loss and certain expense incurred by the insured as a consequence of any wrongful acts of the directors or officers while acting in their individual or collective capacities. A wrongful act is defined generally in this kind of policy as an actual or alleged error, misleading statement, misstatement, act or omission, or neglect or breach of duty.

Loss generally includes amounts which the insureds are obligated to pay for claims made against them and includes damages, judgments, settlements, as well as the cost and expense incurred in the defense of lawsuits. Punitive damages may or may not be regarded as within the definition of loss. This must be checked carefully with the insurer. Note, however, that loss, by express policy language, does not include fines or penalties imposed by law upon the insured or insureds.

Most policies reimburse the insured or insureds only to the extent of 95 per cent of the loss incurred, either individually or corporately. The rationale for this is that, if the directors and officers individually have an exposure not reimbursable by the corporation, they will be somewhat less willing to take chances with management judgments if some of their own money is at risk. These policies also may be written with a deductible imposed either on an individual or a per loss basis.

Exclusions. Directors' and Officers' Liability Policies, while not uniform, generally exclude loss from claims arising from:

a. Libel or slander.
b. Profits from illegal trading by one or more of the insureds in securities of the corporation.
c. Dishonesty of directors and/or officers or contributed to by dishonesty of directors and/or officers.
d. Bodily injury or property damage.
e. Illegal remuneration not approved by the stockholders.

This is by no means a complete summary of the exclusions and reference to the actual policy is necessary.

While the policy excludes reimbursement for loss incurred as a consequence of dishonesty and other illegal conduct, those exclusions generally are conditioned so that officers and directors who are innocent and without knowledge of the dishonest conduct are not excluded from the coverage.

MISCELLANEOUS

Common to all of the professions discussed in this chapter is the distinction which must be made with respect to liability which arises from or is related to the professional nature of the business as contrasted to liability which arises from the general operations or nonprofessional side of the business.

Professional liability insurance for hospitals, doctors, dentists, lawyers, accountants, architects, and engineers is designed primarily for protection against liability arising from the rendering or failing to render services of a professional nature. Conversely, general liability insurance is designed to cover the same insured's liability flowing from acts of a nonprofessional nature.

The distinction between the two kinds of services rendered and the decision whether the service falls on one side of the line or the other is often difficult to draw and results in a borderline or gray area. This has led to much litigation on the point, and it is accurate to say, in some states, the questions are not yet clearly answered and, in others, the results are sometimes contradictory.

To consider this distinction in depth is beyond the scope of this chapter, but it is important to appreciate and understand that these two areas of liability coexist and must be handled correctly. For this, one must consult with the corporation's lawyer and insurance agent or broker, and this summary is not intended as a substitute.

This dilemma affects all of the professionals heretofore mentioned, as well as hospitals, nursing homes, convalescent homes, ambulance services, beauty parlor operators, and others. The difficulty stems from the necessity to determine whether a service, an act, an omission is professional in nature, the consequence of which is exposure under the professional liability insurance, or whether the service, act, or omission is nonprofessional.

The meaning of the term *professional services* becomes important because it influences borderline coverage and claim situations. How the term is defined by the courts in various states determines whether a certain act or service is incidental to the primary role of the professional and therefore within the scope of the professional liability policy, or whether it is incidental to a nonprofessional role and consequently within the scope of the general liability policy.

To adequately cover these dual exposures, two insurance policies are needed: the first to cover the professional liability exposures flowing from the rendering of professional services, and a general liability policy to protect against the negligence of the insured flowing from premises and other nonprofessional operations. As policy language, insuring clauses, conditions, and exclusions are not uniform among the various insurers, the possibility exists that an act or omission lies in the gray areas and is not included under either policy. The ideal way to handle this is to have both the professional liability and the general liability contracts of insurance in the same insurer, which eliminates the need to draw the distinction in an obscure case, assuming, of course, adequate limits on each policy. It is not always possible, however, to carry both coverages with the same insurer—which illustrates the need for the services of a competent agent or broker.

NOTES

1. Couch on Insurance 2d §1:85 (1959).

2. Douglas R. Slain, "Claims against Professionals Continue to Show Sharp Rise," *New York Law Journal*, August 30, 1979.

3. Id.

4. Prosser, *The Law of Torts*, 4th ed. (1971), p. 145.

5. 159 F.2d 169 (2d Cir. 1947).

6. William B. Schwartz and Neil K. Komesar, *Doctors, Damages and Deterrence: An Economic View of Medical Malpractice*, R-2340-NIH/RC (Rand, June 1978), p. 2. For a thorough technical analysis of the economics of the medical malpractice crisis and the impact of this crisis on the insurance industry see Simon Rottenberg, ed., *The Economics of Medical Malpractice* (American Enterprise Institute for Public Policy, 1978).

7. See *supra*, note 6, Schwartz, p. 3.

8. Id., p. v.

9. Id.

10. Id., pp. 14–15.

11. James E. Ludlam, "Ways to Head Off a New Malpractice Crisis," *Medical Economics*, January 7, 1980.

12. *New York Times*, May 28, 1959.

13. Charles Kramer, *Medical Malpractice*, 4th ed. (Practicing Law Institute, 1976), p. 5.

14. James M. Vaccarino, "Malpractice: The Problem in Perspective," *J.A.M.A.*, vol. 238 (8): 861 (1977).

15. Id.

16. Darrell L. Havener, "Observations regarding Investigation and Preparation of Medical Malpractice Litigation," in *Defense of Medical Malpractice Cases*, ed. Donald J. Hirsch (Defense Research Institute, vol. 1977), (4), p. 7.

17. See Vaccarino, "Malpractice," p. 861.

18. Sylvia Law and Steven Polan, Pain and Profit: *The Politics of Malpractice* (New York: Harper & Row, 1978), p. 11. See also *HEW Secretary's Malpractice Commission Report*, 1973, Appendix, pp. 539–40. For data on geographical maldistribution of malpractice actions against doctors, see *A Report on the Health Professions Educational Assistance Act of 1974*, Sen.-Comm. on Labor on Public Welfare, S.R. No. 93–1133, 93d Cong. 2d sess., 55–57 (1974).

19. See Law and Polan, *Pain and Profit*, p. 12.

20. See Kramer, *Medical Malpractice*, p. 6.

21. Id.

22. 70 C.J.S. Physicians and Surgeons §54(e).

23. 70 C.J.S. Physicians and Surgeons §54(a).

24. See Kramer, *Medical Malpractice*, p. 12.

25. 155 N.Y. 201, 49 N.E. 760 (1898).

26. *Beach* v. *Chollet*, 120 Ohio St. 449, 166 N.E. 415 (1928).

27. See Kramer, *Medical Malpractice*, pp. 13–24.

28. 154 Cal. App. 2d 560, 317 P.2d 170 (1957).

29. Id., 317 P.2d at 181.

30. Merton E. Marks, "Informed Consent in Medical Malpractice Cases," in *Defense of Medical Malpractice Cases*, ed. Donald J. Hirsch (Defense Research Institute, vol. 1977), (4), pp. 57–58.

31. Dennis J. Horan and Patrick Halligan, "Authority for Medical Treatment," *For the Defense*, vol. 22 (2):13 (1980).

32. *Mitchell* v. *Robinson*, 334 S.W.2d 11, 18 (Mo. 1960).

33. See Kramer, *Medical Malpractice*, p. 13.

34. *Roberts* v. *Young*, 369 Mich 133, 119 N.W.2d 627 (1963).

35. *Canterbury* v. *Spence*, 464 F.2d 772 (D.C. Cir. 1972), *cert. denied*, 409 U.S. 1064 (1972).

36. See *supra*, note 35, *Canterbury* at 785. Note, however, that some

commentators argue that *Canterbury* was overruled *sub silentio* or restricted by *Haven* v. *Randolph*, 494 F.2d 1069 (D.C. Cir. 1974).

37. *Wilkson* v. *Vesey*, 110 R.I. 1606, 295 A.2d 676, 688 (1972). See also *Harrigan* v. *United States*, 408 F.Supp. 177 (E.D. Pa. 1976); *Scaria* v. *St. Paul Fire & Marine Insurance Co.*, 68 Wis. 1, 227 N.W.2d 647 (1975); *Small* v. *Gifford Memorial Hospital*, 133 Vt. 552, 349 A.2d 703 (1975).

38. *Hunter* v. *Brown*, 4 Wash. App. 899, 484 P.2d 1162, 1167 (1971), *aff'd*, 502 P.2d 1194 (Wash. 1972).

39. *Sard* v. *Hardy*, 34 Md. App. 217, 367 A.2d 525 (1977).

40. *Zeleznik* v. *Jewish Chronic Disease Hospital*, 47 A.D. 2d 199, 205, 366 N.Y.S. 2d 163 (2d Dept. 1975).

41. See Marks, "Informed Consent", pp. 61-62.

42. 5 N.Y.S. 2d, 152 N.E.2d 249 (1958).

43. Robert C. Maynard and Eleanor D. Kinney, "The Statute of Limitations in Medical Malpractice Law," in *Defense of Medical Malpractice Cases*, ed. Donald J. Hirsch (Defense Research Institute, vol. 1977), (4), pp. 45-46.

44. 72 N.M. 285, 383 P.2d. 250 (1963).

45. *Emmet* v. *Eastern Dispensary and Casualty Hospital* 130 App. D.C. 50, 396 F.2d 931 (1967). See also *Eschenbacher* v. *Hier*, 110 N.W. 2d 731 (Mich. 1961).

46. *Billings* v. *Sisters of Mercy of Idaho*, 86 Idaho 485, 389 P.2d 224 (1964), wherein the Court permitted a malpractice action to be brought in 1962 based upon surgery which took place in 1948, and during which an undiscovered gauze sponge was left in the patient. See also *Huysman* v. *Kirsch*, 6 Cal. 2d 302, 57 P.2d 908 (1936).

47. *Frohs* v. *Greene*, 253 Or. 1, 452 P.2d 564 (1969); *Costa* v. *Regents of University of California*, 116 Cal. App. 2d 445, 254 P.2d 85 (1953).

48. *Amer* v. *Akron City Hospital*, 47 Ohio St. 2d 85, 351, N.E.2d 479 (1976).

49. *Waldman* v. *Rohrbaugh*, 241 Md. 137, 215 A.2d (1966).

50. 70 C.J.S. Physicians and Surgeons §38.

51. See Kramer, *Medical Malpractice*, p. 32.

52. *Schloendorff* v. *Society of New York Hospital*, 211 N.Y. 125, 105 N.E. 92 (1914).

53. Id. at 93.

54. *Kennedy* v. *Parrott*, 243 N.C. 555, 90 S.E.2d 754 (1956).

55. Louisell and Williams, *Trial of Medical Malpractice Cases*, §8.09 (1974).

56. See Kramer, *Medical Malpractice*, p. 35.

57. See ibid., p. 40.

58. See Horan and Halligan, "Authority for Medical Treatment," p. 13.

59. 33 Ill. 2d 326, 211 N.E.2d 253 (1965), *cert. denied*, 383 U.S. 946 (1966).

60. Edward E. Hollowell, "Potential Liability of Hospital Staff Membership," 1 *Med. Liab. Rptr.* 15 (1979).

61. 138 N.J. Super. 302, 350 A.2d 534 (1975).

62. Id., 350 A.2d at 539.

63. Id.

64. See Hollowell, "Potential Liability," p. 15.

65. See Havener, "Observations," p. 11.

66. Robert L. Lambert, "Medical Staff Is Key in Hospital Risk Management," *Pennsylvania Medicine*, November 1978, p. 20.

67. Id., pp. 21-22.

68. James E. Ludlam, "Ways to Head Off a New Malpractice Crisis," *Medical Economics*, January 7, 1980, pp. 42-48.

69. See Slain, "Claims Against Professionals."

70. Duke Nordlinger Stern, "Causes of Attorney Malpractice Claims," 3 *Prof. Liab. Rptr.* 199-200 (1979).

71. Duke Nordlinger Stern and Joanne Martin, "Let the Code of Professional Responsibility Be Your Guide (Part 1)," 3 *Prof. Liab. Rptr.* 73–74 (1978).

72. *Matter of Palmieri*, 7 N.J. 51, 385 A.2d 856 (1978).

73. *Employer's Casualty Co.* v. *Tilley*, 496 S.W.2d 552 (Texas 1973).

74. See, for example, *Parsons* v. *Continental National Group*, 550 P.2d 94 (Arizona 1976).

75. Frank G. Jones, "Responsibilities of Attorneys Defending Insurance Liability Cases," 3 *Prof. Liab. Rptr.* 128–129 (1979).

76. Duke Nordlinger Stern and Joanne Martin, "Let the Code of Professional Responsibility Be Your Guide (Part 2)," 3 *Prof. Liab. Rptr.* 91–92 (1978).

77. Jeffrey M. Smith, "Preventing Attorney Liability in Securities Transactions," 3 *Prof. Liab. Rptr.* 181–182 (1979).

78. See *Fort Myers Seafood Packers, Inc.* v. *Steptoe & Johnson*, 381 F.2d 261 (D.C. Cir. 1967), *cert. denied*, 390 U.S. 946 (1968); *Roberts* v. *Ball, Hunt, Brown & Baerwitz*, 57 Cal. App. 3d 104, 128 Cal. Rptr. 901 (1976); *Goodman* v. *Kennedy*, 18 Cal. 3d 335, 134 Cal. Rptr. 375, 556 P.2d 737 (1976).

79. See Smith, "Preventing Attorney Liability," p. 181.

80. Id.

81. *Wassel* v. *Eglowsky*, 399 F.Supp. 1330 (D. Md., 1975), *affirmed*, 542 F.2d 1235 (4th Cir. 1976).

82. See Smith, "Preventing Attorney Liability," p. 182.

83. See, for example, *Sorenson* v. *Parlikowski*, 581 P.2d 851 (Nevada, 1978).

84. Dan L. Goldwasser, *Accountants' Liability: Litigation Strategies and Tactics* (Practicing Law Institute, Litigation Course Handbook Series No. 89 (1976).

85. Id. pp. 15–16. See also *Rhode Island Hospital Trust National Bank* v. *Swartz Bresenoff, Yavner & Joacobs*, 455 F.2d 847 (4th Cir.

1972); *Aluma Kraft Mfg. Co.* v. *Elmer Fox & Co.*, 493 S.W.2d 378 (Mo. App. 1973); *Shatterproof Glass Corp.* v. *James*, 466 S.W.2d 873 (Ct. App. Texas 1971).

86. *Carr* v. *Lipshie*, 9 N.Y. 2d 983 (1961); *National Surety Corporation* v. *Lybrand*, 9 N.Y.S. 2d 554 (1939); *Stanley L. Bloch, Inc.* v. *Klien*, 45 Misc. 2d 1054 (Sup. Ct. N.Y. 1965); *Bancroft* v. *Indemnity Insurance Co. of N.A.*, 203 F. Supp. 49 (W.D. La. 1962).

87. *Investment Corp. of Fla.* v. *Buchman*, 208 So.2d 291 (Dist. Ct. App. Fla. 1968); *Gammel* v. *Ernst & Ernst*, 245 Min. 249, 72 N.W.2d 364 (Minn. 1955).

88. See Goldwasser, *Accountants' Liability*, p. 12.

89. See ibid., pp. 19–26.

90. 425 U.S. 185 (1976), *reh. denied*, 425 U.S. 986 (1976); *Kohler* v. *Kohler Co.*, 319 F.2d 634 (8th Cir. 1963); *Speed* v. *Transamerica Corp.*, 235 F.2d 369 (3d Cir. 1956); *Kardon* v. *National Gypsum Co.*, 73 F. Supp. 798 (E.D. Pa. 1947).

91. *Globus* v. *Law Research Service, Inc.*, 418 F.2d 1276 (2d Cir. 1969); *Crowell* v. *The Pittsburgh & Lake Erie Railroad Co.*, 373 F.Supp. 1303 (E.D. Pa. 1974).

92. *Blue Chip Stamps* v. *Manor Drug Stores*, 421 U.S. 723 (1975).

93. See Goldwasser, *Accountants' Liability*, pp. 22–23.

94. See ibid., p. 23.

95. See *Redington* v. *Touche Ross & Co.* 592 F.2d 617 (2d Cir. 1978), *cert. granted*, November 27, 1978), 46 U.S.L.W. 2598 (2d Cir., April 21, 1978) wherein the Court . . . that accountants who prepare and certify false and misleading financial statements for security brokers are liable to the brokers' customers under Section 17 of the 1934 act.

96. See *Escott* v. *Bar Chris Construction Corp.*, 283 F.Supp. 643 (S.D.N.Y. 1968).

97. Martin L. Wolf, "Architects, Engineers and the Statute of Limita-

tions," in *Liability of Architects and Engineers*, eds. Paul W. Brock and John J. Kircher (Defense Research Institute, May 1969), p. 48.

98. Bibb Allen, "Liability of an Architect or Engineer to Third Parties," in *Liability of Architects and Engineers*, eds. Paul W. Brock and John J. Kircher, (Defense Research Institute, May 1969), p. 5.

99. Richard M. Seybold, "Liability of Architects or Engineers to Their Clients," in *Liability of Architects and Engineers*, eds. Paul W. Brock and John J. Kircher (Defense Research Institute, May 1969), p. 31.

100. Id. See also *Scott* v. *Potomac Ins. Co.*, 217 Or. 323, 341 P.2d 1083, 1088 (1959).

101. See *Kellogg* v. *Pizza Oven, Inc.*, 157 Col. 295, 402 P.2d 633 (1965).

102. *Edward Barron Estate Co.* v. *Woodruff Co.*, 163 Cal. 561, 126 P. 351 (1912).

103. *Willner* v. *Woodward*, 201 Va. 104, 109 S.E.2d 132 (1959).

104. See *supra* note 100, Allen, pp. 28–29.

105. 3 N.Y.2d, 143 N.E.2d 895 (1957).

106. 217 N.Y. 382, 111 N.E. 1050 (1916).

107. 373 So.2d 689 (Fla. App. 1979).

108. *Paxton* v. *Alameda County*, 119 Cal. 2d 393, 259 P.2d 934 (1953).

109. *Montijo* v. *Swift*, 33 Cal. Rptr. 133 (Cal. App. 1963).

110. *Stewart* v. *Schmeider*, 376 So. 2d 1045 (La. App. 1979).

111. *Erhart* v. *Hummonds*, 232 Ark. 177, 334 S.W.2d 869 (1960); *Paxton* v. *Alameda County, supra.*

112. See *Hortman* v. *Bechker Construction Co.*, 92 Wis. 210, 284 N.W.2d 621 (1979).

113. *Wynner* v. *Buxton*, 2 Civ. No. 55474 (Cal. App., September 25, 1979).

114. *Day* v. *National U.S. Radiator Co.*, 128 So.2d 660 (La. 1961); *Clinton* v. *Boehm*, 115 N.Y.S. 425 (App. Div. 1909), *aff'd*, 90 N.E. 1165 (1909).

115. *Clemens* v. *Benzinger*, 207 N.Y.S. 539 (App. Div. 1925).

CHAPTER 16

EXECUTIVE EXPOSURES

THE AGE OF LIABILITY

DIRECTORS AND OFFICERS LIABILITY
 The growing need for D&O coverage
 The obligations of directors and
  officers
 The D&O policy
 International considerations

FIDUCIARY LIABILITY INSURANCE

KIDNAP AND RANSOM
 Introduction
 Loss prevention
 Insurance
 Type and availability of coverage
 Who can be covered
 Scope of coverage
 Conditions of coverage
 Premium considerations

POLITICAL RISK INSURANCE

Peter H. Foley
Executive Vice President
INA Underwriters Insurance Company
INA Special Risk Facilities, Inc.
New York, New York

Peter H. Foley is Executive Vice President of INA Underwriters Insurance Company, a subsidiary of INA Corporation. He oversees all professional liability coverages underwritten by the INA, including medical malpractice, directors and officers liability, and various forms of errors and omissions coverage. He also negotiates treaty reinsurance for the INA in these areas. Prior to joining the INA, Mr. Foley served with three other insurance organizations, in positions of rapidly increasing stature. He graduated from Franklin Pierce College in New Hampshire in 1974 with a degree in industrial psychology, and since then has been a Senior Casualty Underwriter with the Aetna Casualty & Surety Insurance Co., an Assistant Secretary of General Reinsurance Corporation in New York, and Vice President of Insco, Ltd. in Bermuda. Mr. Foley received an MBA with a major in Financial Management from Fairleigh Dickinson University in 1978.

THE AGE OF LIABILITY

Whether you call it the Computer Age or the Me Generation, the Sexual Revolution or the Post-industrial Era, there's never been a time like the present. The several thousand years that Man has been walking around on this planet have been categorized according to major changes—specific developments—that have reshaped his world and altered the course of history. Thus, we have the Stone Age, the Iron Age, and more recently, the Jet Age.

Now, however, the rate of change has accelerated. The flow of major, new developments comprise an ever-present variable in the equation of economics, science, and politics for the 1980's.

There are two sides to the contemporary climate of change. While our expanding technology enables us to achieve more, it also exposes us to risks that were once undreamed of. In recent years, financial and physical risks have been compounded by pressures from the social sector. Besides merely making a product or providing a service, businesses are expected to function as architects of social change. As a result, everyone engaging in business has become accountable to multiple public interest groups. If against this background of ongoing change and societal reshuffling, there is one label that best describes the present, it is the Age of Liability.

This is a fact which is, at long last, apparent to the insurance industry. Generally perceived as being ponderous and conservative, the insurance industry was shaken from its lethargy by the social change and economic inflation of the early and mid-1970s. The more progressive insurers, perceiving that change would take place, either with or without them, have developed coverages to respond to these changes. Among the more important for the businessman are:

Directors and officers liability insurance,
Fiduciary liability insurance,
Kidnap and ransom insurance,
Political risk insurance.

The major part of this chapter will be spent addressing the most complex of the four coverages—directors and officers liability (D&O). It should be noted that D&O exposure also can be directly affected by the presence and scope of the other three types of coverage.

DIRECTORS AND OFFICERS LIABILITY

The growing need for D&O coverage

"I wasn't involved" and "I didn't know" . . . if these ever were valid defenses against professional liability, that day is gone forever. For all professionals—lawyer, accountant, doctor, engineer, director, officer and even clergyman—*accountability* is the watchword. It would take an encyclopedia of social, political, and economic evolution to catalogue the reasons for this. Suffice to say a mutuality of entitlement has been spawned. Since the 1960s, government giveaways, generous court decisions, and growing antibusiness and antiprofessional sentiment has greatly increased the exposure of professionals. This was dramatically illustrated by the malpractice crisis that has jeopardized health care in this country. Premiums, when insurance is available increased by over 400 percent during a recent 18-month period.

Today, much of the same scrutiny that has been directed at the surgeon in the operating room is being focused on the corporate director and officer. To be sure, the public disclosure of payoffs has been seen by many as justification for greater SEC involvement in and pressure on the corporate board.

A deputy director for the enforcement division of the SEC once explained his findings that directors were treated like mushrooms: "They were kept in the dark and heaped with manure." This has changed. There is a new awareness that serving as a corporate director is a serious responsibility. The once "clubby" atmosphere of the boardroom has now disappeared.

While there has been litigation involving directors and officers for many years, the suit arising from the Penn Central collapse of 1970 was a watershed development. In that case, the insurance company settled on behalf of the directors and officers in 1974 for a reported $10 million. This case is often cited as the real beginning of the trend to hold directors and officers to a higher level of responsibility.

A random sampling of the headlines from recent stories in *The Wall Street Journal* illustrates how frequently directors and officers are accused of misunderstanding their responsibilities:

"Computervision Corporation Sues Former Executive at Firm He Founded" (11/14/80)

"Ex Director of Central Banking System Sues Chairman and Seven Directors" (11/7/80)

"Coastal Corporation Chief Accused of Misdeed in Suit by Shareholder" (11/7/80)

Let us look at some cases which illustrate the strength of this trend.

The *Three Mile Island, Ford Pinto, Firestone 500 Tire* and *DC-10* cases provide examples of occurrences involving liability claims against directors and officers.

The continuing and increasing number of tender offers and acquisitions, both friendly and unfriendly, open the door to allegations of liability. Liability can result from an acquisition which dilutes equity and from declining an offer where stock prices subsequently drop. The potential for liability claims is present in almost any major decision. Actions which frequently give rise to such claims are:

1. Conflict of interest, such as holding a stock interest in an acquiring company or in a customer.
2. Extension of credit where credit is not warranted.
3. Failure to file annual reports.
4. Failure to require withholding in connection with social security and income taxes.
5. Failure to attend board meetings.
6. Violations of by-laws or state statutes.

An area of pressing concern is earnings projections made by corporate officials. In 1979 the SEC, while asking that corporations make more forecasts on sales, earnings, and other important data, set forth *Safe Harbor Rules* in the hope that the rules would allow more firms to feel comfortable in making forecasts. A review of these rules suggests numerous pitfalls. For example, the forecaster is required to state assumptions material to the forecasted estimates. Consequently, the company either must spell out in detail how it arrived at its forecast, or alternatively, be prepared to do so if that forecast fails to materialize. Public companies must also make full and prompt disclosure of material facts that change its estimates to any significant extent. The SEC has stated that the burden of proof that a projection is reasonable and in good faith is upon the forecasting corporation and not the claimant in a lawsuit. As can be seen, the current construction certainly is not a "safe harbor"; it is a snare waiting to trap the unwary.

The obligations of directors and officers

Every director and officer has two basic responsibilities to the corporation:

1. *Loyalty.* Directors and officers must refrain from engaging in personal activity which would injure, or constitute taking advantage of, the corporation and must keep confidential corporate information.

2. ***Care.*** Directors and officers must exercise obedience and diligence in meeting their duty to the corporation.

A succinct statement of the duties of the director and officer can be found in Section 35 of the *Model Business Corporation Act,* which states:

> A director or officer should perform his duties as director or officer, including his duties as a member of any committee of the board upon which he may serve, in good faith, in a manner he reasonably believes to be in the best interest of the corporation, and with such care as an ordinarily, prudent person in a like position would use under similar circumstances.

When directors and officers act beyond their power—disposing of the corporation's money or property without proper authority, for example—they can be required to make good the loss. This liability is based on the common law rule that holds an agent liable for the damages of his principal when the agent violates his express or implied authority.

Liability for negligence usually results from two causes.

The first is a failure to manage the corporation's affairs with normal skill and diligence. A negligent manager may be held liable not only to the corporation's stockholders but to its creditors as well. The failure of W. T. Grant is an example.

The second is a failure to disclose with reasonable accuracy the state of condition of the corporation. This can result in liability by an officer or director to buyers or sellers of a corporation's securities and even to creditors of a corporation. The *Mattel Company* case, where several members of senior management were involved in falsifying financial statements is illustrative. The D&O suit which resulted was settled for in excess of $13 million.

There are, in general, three major types of law suits that can be lodged against a director or an officer:

1. The class action suit, which is a suit brought against a director or an officer by an individual shareholder on behalf of himself and all the shareholders of a company.
2. The derivative action, which is a suit seeking compensation on behalf of the corporation for failure of the director or officer to act in a prudent manner to the detriment of the corporation.
3. The third-party action, which is an action brought by a governmental body, a creditor, or even a former employee against a director or an officer, alleging failure to exercise responsibility in a prudent and responsible fashion.

Liability imposed upon a director or officer for breach of duty to the corporation is a *personal* exposure. As this cold fact dawns on each director and officer, one of two things often occurs—resignation from the board or pressure for more comprehensive insurance coverage.

D&O insurance evolved to meet two needs—the protection of corporate assets from being exhausted due to the indemnification of directors and officers, and the protection of directors and officers from exposure in nonindemnifiable litigation. Adequate D&O coverage can be an incentive to competent persons to join and remain on a corporate board.

The D&O policy

There are a few general features of directors and officers coverage that should be considered and understood before purchasing this protection. First, most D&O insurance is written on a *claims-made*, as opposed to *occurrence*, basis. This means that coverage is provided by the policy in effect when the claim is made, or when a notice of a possible claim is given, not when the negligent or irresponsible act occurred. Two examples may be helpful in understanding this concept.

One Example:

Insurance company A insures ABC Corporation on a *claims-made* policy for calendar year 1979.

Insurance company B insures ABC Corporation on a *claims-made* policy for calendar year 1980.

An employee of ABC Corporation is discharged on January 15, 1979, and brings suit against ABC Corporation on January 15, 1980.

Under the *claims-made* policy, Insurance company B would respond since it has issued a claims-made policy and the claim was lodged during this period.

Another example:

Insurance company C insures XYZ Corporation on an *occurrence* basis for calendar year 1979.

Insurance company D insures XYZ Corporation on an *occurrence* basis for calendar year 1980.

An employee of XYZ Corporation is discharged on January 15, 1979 and brings suit against XYZ Corporation on January 15, 1980.

Insurance company C would respond even though the claim is brought during company D's policy for the act *occurred* during insurance company C's policy period issued on an occurrence basis.

The foregoing examples are for conceptual purposes only. There are endorsements which can broaden or restrict coverage and produce a different result.

The typical D&O policy is written on a *dual-form* basis; that is, the first part of the policy insures the directors and officers for their own liability and the second part provides reimbursement to the company against loss on account of a wrongful act by a director or officer for which it is required, or permitted, (under provisions in the by-laws or statutes) to indemnify its directors and officers. Note that coverage is *not* provided under the dual-form policy for suits against the corporation, but only for those suits instituted against a director or officer. Under the dual form, there is only one limit of liability and it can be exhausted by a loss in either part. Moreover, under the dual form, there are retentions (deductibles) for both parts. In the directors and officers part there is a per director retention and an aggregate limit, and a ceiling is imposed when several directors or officers are involved. On the other hand, there is only one retention for reimbursement regardless of the number of directors or officers involved.

In a suit involving both the director and officer and the reimbursement parts, the retention in the reimbursement part would constitute the maximum amount to be assumed by the company. The insurer relies upon the retention by the company to eliminate the small nuisance cases the directors and officers, or the company on their behalf, should be able to absorb. The policy also provides for a 5 percent participation by an insured in all losses which are in excess of the retention. Often it can be eliminated for limits in excess of $1 million. For the nonprofit or small corporation, it can be totally deleted. The imposition of the 5 percent participation assures the involvement of the insured and the corporation. D&O policies are frequently written on a three-year basis but with an annual aggregate liability limit. This means that the limit of liability for an annual period constitutes the limit of liability available under the policy.

Since the usual procedure is to write coverage on a *claims-made* basis, the policy contains an extended discovery period. These are essential to protect the insured from being left with no coverage in the event of cancellation or nonrenewal. If the insurer cancels or refuses to renew the policy, the insured has the right, upon payment of a small additional premium, to a 90-day extension of coverage. The provision provides coverage for claims which may be made during the extension period (even though it is after the date of cancellation); provided, of course, that the wrongful act upon which the claim is based occurred prior to the date of cancellation or nonrenewal.

In a claims-made policy, there are notice provisions which also protect the insured. If written notice of a claim or act which is expected to result in a suit is given to the insurer prior to policy termination, the actual claim, even if filed after policy expiration, is treated as if it occurred during the policy itself. As further consideration, the firm must identify those acts which it expects may result in a claim. We recommend that incidents identifiable as having suit potential be discussed with counsel. The insurer should then be advised.

At this time there are no real differences in the D&O policies available in the marketplace. The coverage available is quite broad because of the in-depth evaluation that precedes the issuance of a policy. Any differences result from the use of endorsements attached to the basic policy. D&O policies typically are written in lay language and thus are easy to read.

The insuring clause is a major section of a D&O policy. It assures that if during the policy period a claim is made against an insured in his capacity as director or officer for any actual or alleged error or misleading statement (a wrongful act), the insurance company will pay any loss which the insured is legally obligated to pay. A major problem of conflict concerns those outside directors who sit on the board who also provide service to the corporation in their capacity as lawyers, investment bankers, or consultants. The question has not been resolved; and outside directors must be aware of this potential problem. The by-laws may provide clarification on the point.

In the first section, we also find that the definition of loss covered is any loss except fines or penalties for matters deemed uninsurable under the law. This is basically a punitive damages exclusion based on countervailing public policy.

Most policies provide coverage for new directors or officers of a subsidiary acquired or created after the inception of the policy. This coverage is automatic as long as the additions are reported within a specified period of time. Some insurance companies use the phrase "as soon as possible."

In the exclusion section, one will usually find the following excluded from the policy:

1. Libel or slander (available under other coverages).
2. Personal profit at the expense of the company (a violation of the loyalty concept).
3. Excess remuneration to which the insureds are not entitled.
4. Short swing profits as defined by the Securities Act of 1934.
5. Dishonesty of the insureds (the insurer will defend a dishonesty claim until dishonesty is proven).
6. Actions covered by other insurance or which is indemnifiable under a previous policy due to exercise of the notice provisions.

7. Suits against which the insureds may be indemnified by the corporation (coverage available under the part two corporate indemnification).
8. Bodily injury and/or property damage (coverage available under general liability or other liability policies).

The corporate reimbursement part of the policy has only three exclusions: (1) excess over other insurance, (2) other directors and officers liability insurance previously in force, and (3) bodily injury or property damage.

The application form submitted to the insurer becomes part of the policy and serves as a warranty. It usually contains the following wording:

> It is warranted that the particulars and the statements contained in the written proposal form, a copy of which is attached hereto, and the declarations form a basis of this policy that are to be considered as incorporated in and constitute part of this policy.

The importance of polling directors and officers at the time application is made to ascertain that they have no knowledge of facts which could lead to a breach of this warranty is paramount. When purchasing coverage for the first time or changing carriers, a long form application is used with the above warranty. Renewal applications do not contain the warranty wording.

How does a president, chairman, or general counsel who signs the application know that all of his officers have advised him of all facts and incidents? This question arises in a firm with numerous officers, such as a bank. A "severability" provision will protect the directors and officers of the firm as a group in this type of situation. *Severability* means that the nondisclosure by one officer of a situation that could give rise to a suit will not void coverage for the other directors and officers. This severability provision must be negotiated prior to the policy's commencement and made an endorsement to the basic policy. If it is, then the insurance company must prove that the director or officer knew of a situation which has resulted in a claim to avoid liability.

Consideration should be given to adding possible legal and investigative costs and expenses when deciding upon the level of coverage. Legal expenses in D&O litigation can be substantial in today's litigious climate. One has only to look at the hourly rates of experienced counsel necessary to defend these complex cases to understand why there have been cases where the legal costs have exceeded several million dollars.

Legislation has made the underwriting of D&O insurance easier.

The New York Stock Exchange aided in the effort. Effective June 30, 1978, it required that all listed companies have audit committees. It has been estimated that 70 percent of the nation's 1,000 largest companies now have boards with a majority of outsiders and that 97 percent of those 1,000 have audit committees comprised of outside directors. A newer committee gaining increasing acceptance is the nominating committee which recruits new directors. Committees get people involved, forcing them to ask questions. Statistics show that directors spent an average of 11 working days in 1979 for each board they sat on. In the mid-70s, it was one or two days.

Membership on a nonprofit board carries the same burden as being a member of a business board. As a result, nonprofit boards have become more businesslike. No longer is sitting on a board of a hospital or other institution simply the prestigious ornament it once was. Recent suits against directors or trustees of nonprofit organizations range from claims that funds have been mismanaged to claims of conflict of interest and ignorance. For example, in a case often cited, the trustees of a training school formed to provide health services to the poor were charged with mismanagement, nonmanagement, and self-dealing as well as breach of their fiduciary responsibility in their supervision of the institution's investments. Membership on the board of a nonprofit organization can be more dangerous than serving as a member of a business board in that typically the board members of a nonprofit organization, by design, represent many different community, societal, and economic viewpoints. These members can be quite vocal if they believe that their interests are not being served and may be quick to charge disagreeing members with mismanagement.

Today, members of both profit and nonprofit boards are approaching their responsibility with far more caution. For example, many now take notes and refrain from participating in matters where a conflict of interest could be inferred.

International considerations

It is not only the United States that is seeing a changing attitude toward director's and officer's responsibility for their actions. Canada, the United Kingdom, Germany, and Australia are also experiencing increasing regulatory and legislative change. Canadian business corporations will see legislation in effect in 1981 codifying conduct for directors and officers and specifically sanctioning lawsuits by shareholders.

In the United Kingdom, recent lawsuits have enhanced the right of shareholders to bring claims against directors for a breach of duty. Legislation defining the responsibilities of directors is an idea whose time has come. In Australia, "an executive officer of a corporation must act honestly, and exercise his duties for the company, and additionally must exercise care, diligence, and skill not less than a reasonably prudent man would exercise in relation to his own affairs in comparable circumstances." Although this sounds similar to our Model Business Corporation Act, an executive officer is defined as *any* person who takes part in the management of the company. This extends the covered group well beyond the traditional director and officer definition.

Therefore, directors and officers of international firms must not only consider their exposure in the United States, but must consider their exposure for their company's activities in other parts of the world as well. Since it is unlikely one will find a territorial definition in a D&O policy, it could be argued that the coverage is already there. Still, a company would be well advised either to purchase separate D&O coverage in each country in which it operates or expand its current policy through endorsement to include liability under foreign law.

FIDUCIARY LIABILITY INSURANCE

Prior to the passage of the Employee Retirement Income Security Act of 1974 (ERISA), liability for a breach of fiduciary responsibility under employee benefit plans was not viewed as a significant risk by most corporations. Legal guidelines prior to the passage of ERISA were vague; and, in any event, most states had no prohibition against plan provisions exculpating fiduciaries for all but willful or reckless violations. The passage of ERISA changed this situation drastically.

Although discussion of ERISA's substantive provisions on fiduciary conduct are beyond the scope of this chapter, it should be noted that ERISA contains both broad and specific rules on fiduciary conduct and provides for enforcement of these fiduciary rules by both the Department of Labor and plan participants who now are armed with a statutory scheme that favors plaintiffs. In addition to liberal venue and service of process provisions, ERISA authorizes courts to order equitable relief, if appropriate. Additionally it gives courts the discretion to award attorneys' fees and costs to either party in a lawsuit. Finally, in addition to establishing the employee benefit plan as an entity which may sue or be sued, ERISA imposes a risk of personal fiduciary liability on plan fiduciaries such as corporate officers or directors.

Faced with the potential for large liability due to the sizable amount of funds held under pension and profit sharing funds, corporations have taken two courses of action to protect themselves and plan fiduciaries. First, they generally have provided broad indemnification for inside fiduciaries for liability under ERISA's fiduciary provisions and, second, they have transferred the risk of the assumed liability to an insurer through the purchase of fiduciary indemnification insurance.

Before discussing some of the major features of fiduciary indemnification insurance, it should be noted that these policies are purchased in addition to the traditional directors and officers liability policies currently held by most corporations. Most directors and officers policies either currently contain or are being amended to contain exclusions for liability under ERISA.

Set forth below is a summary of some of the more important features of a fiduciary indemnification policy and some comments about potential problem areas. It should be noted that although ERISA is now over six years old, the insurance market for these policies is still in the developmental stage.

Most of the policies being offered are *claims-made* policies. That is, payment by the insurance company is conditioned on a claim being filed or made during the life of the policy. Claims-made policies are to be contrasted with *claims-occurred* policies which condition payment on the occurrence of the action leading to the claim during the policy period. The risk with claims-made policies is that you may not be aware of a breach at the time it occurs and by the time you do become aware of it the policy may have terminated. In the event the corporation has been unable to secure a successor policy or if the successor policy excludes past acts, there may be a gap in coverage.

It is important to have a broad definition of *insured*, the persons to whom coverage is extended. Since employee benefit plans can sue and be sued under ERISA, they should obviously be named as an insured. Coverage also should be secured for all officers, directors, employees, etc. who serve as fiduciaries under the corporation's employee benefit plans. In addition, because losses may be triggered by nonfiduciary in-house administrative personnel performing ministerial duties, coverage for them should also be obtained. Care should be taken that outside fiduciaries such as professional trustees and investment managers are excluded from coverage. These individuals should (and probably do) provide for their own coverage; and the cost of that coverage is reflected in the fees they charge.

Finally, coverage should be obtained for former and successor fiduciaries and other individuals associated with the plan, so that coverage will not cease merely because of a change in the individual who was performing a particular fiduciary function. Of course, coverage should extend to the estate, heirs, and legal assigns of any insured.

The *definition of damages* section of a policy is another area that should be carefully examined. Many policies exclude recovery for fines or punitive damages. The exclusion of fines might mean that the policy does not cover excise taxes imposed for violations of the prohibited transaction rules under the Internal Revenue Code. Since prohibited transaction violations can occur innocently, coverage for such potential exposure should be obtained. Exclusions for recovery of punitive or exemplary damages should also be looked upon unfavorably since courts are empowered to fashion broad remedies for breaches of ERISA or fiduciary rules. Finally, since a court may award attorneys' fees to a plaintiff, coverage should extend to them.

The definition of *wrongful acts* should be examined to see if it is limited to breaches of fiduciary duty. There could be situations where an error in plan administration which does not amount to a breach of fiduciary duty causes a loss to the plan. Coverage for this potential loss should be obtained.

It is essential that the policy provide coverage for *defense costs.* Perhaps because of ERISA's relatively recent enactment or because of its complexity, the courts have been reluctant to grant motions for summary judgment as to a particular party. Given ERISA's broad definition of fiduciary and broad standards of fiduciary conduct, it is likely the plaintiffs' strategy will be to name all fiduciaries in the lawsuit and hope that the fiduciaries will have a difficult time extracting themselves from the lawsuit. Because of the risk of protracted litigation, a policy that provides for defense costs is a must. It would also be preferable for defense cost coverage to be over and above the policy limits and not included within them. Further, the policy should provide that defense costs will be covered even if there is a claim for a violation of a particular law or wrongful act that is not covered by the policy. For example, many policies provide that there will not be coverage if the plan is deemed to have violated sex discrimination laws. While it may be argued that such exclusion is proper as a matter of public policy, it is not clear how the sex discrimination laws will be applied to employee benefits plans in many situations; and if a plan attempts to resist a charge that it has violated the sex discrimination laws and does so unsuccessfully, defense costs should be provided under the fiduciary indemnification insurance policy. In an area related to defense costs, care should be taken that the corporation retains some control of the selection of counsel.

The *termination provisions* of the contract also bear close examination. In the event that the insurance company retains the right to cancel the policy, a policy should be purchased which contains an extension clause allowing sufficient time to replace the expired policy with a new one. A period of at least 12 months should be sought.

Close attention should also be paid to any provision of the policy providing for *recourse* by the insurance company against fiduciaries.

The policy should not provide for any recourse against individual fiduciaries. Of course, ERISA requires that any policy purchased with plan assets allow for recourse against fiduciaries, and this chapter has assumed that policies will be purchased with corporate and not plan assets. In the event that a policy is purchased with plan assets providing for recourse against fiduciaries, an additional policy allowing the fiduciaries to remove the recourse provision can be obtained by the fiduciaries with personal or corporate assets. While this sort of arrangement is permissible under ERISA, it is only permissible if the cost of the removal of recourse liability policy purchased for the individual fiduciary is not being subsidized through higher-than-normal premiums for the policy purchased by the plan.

The foregoing explanation is not intended to be an exhaustive discussion of all the features of fiduciary indemnification policies. As insurers develop additional experience with ERISA claims, variations in policies may lessen and standard terms for such policies may emerge. What is certain in this area is that the policies must be obtained with the assistance of individuals knowledgeable in the insurance area and then reviewed by counsel familiar with ERISA's provisions to determine if the policy, in fact, provides for the coverage that is necessary to deal with potential exposure under ERISA.

KIDNAP AND RANSOM

Introduction

Hardly a week goes by without our being reminded of the ever present danger faced throughout the world from acts of terrorism. If it isn't the takeover of the American Embassy in Teheran and the holding of the staff as hostages, it's the hijacking of an airliner in Damascus, or the kidnapping of an oil executive in Argentina or a missionary in Brazil. Enormous payments have been made to terrorists by both governments and companies. The rising tide of terrorism and the cost of meeting the demands of terrorists inevitably has spawned a response by companies who still must ask their personnel to take on assignments in foreign countries—even those such as Italy and Argentina with the highest incidence of terroristic acts. This response by companies has manifested itself in two ways: first, by companies putting their employees in a position where they are least likely to be kidnapped and, second, through the purchase of insurance.

Loss prevention

Risk management of terrorism, like risk management for other exposures, requires a loss prevention approach if insurance is to be obtained at a manageable cost. As is obvious, the company that makes it more difficult for its employees to be kidnapped is a better risk than one that has no loss prevention program. A word or two about loss prevention techniques at the outset may be in order. Generally speaking, these loss prevention techniques fall into two categories—anonymity and security.

The reason for anonymity is obvious. To the extent that people don't know of a person's relationship with a company or of the significance of his position with the company, he is that much less likely to be a target. Consequently, as little publicity as possible should be given to the comings and goings of company personnel, particularly those in executive positions. Briefcases and suitcases should not bear nametags nor even be marked with initials. Access to home addresses should be strictly controlled and telephone numbers should be unlisted. Travel routes should be varied to make ambush more difficult.

Of course, such measures fly in the face of a company's normal approach to public relations. Where to draw the line between these conflicting considerations depends in part on the country involved; the company's image (i.e., is it apt to be regarded by revolutionaries as an "enemy of the people"?); and the importance to the company of making known the activities of a particular executive.

Achieving the proper level of security is even more difficult, for few companies can afford—or desire—to make their business offices armed camps. Still, there are some things that can be done. Guards can be employed, access to company offices can be strictly controlled, and employees can be required to live in buildings where strangers will find it difficult to enter.

Because a company ordinarily will not be knowledgeable in how to effect an appropriate level of anonymity and security, organizations have sprung up to provide advice on these subjects. Typically they are operated by former agents of the Federal Bureau of Investigation, the Central Intelligence Agency or some other intelligence group. A prudent company operating in foreign countries, particularly where terrorism is most prevalent, and genuinely concerned for the protection of its employees and their families, will be well advised to retain one of these organizations as part of its approach to understanding the proper level of risk management for it. Employment of such a company and the establishment of a loss prevention program will reduce the premium paid for kidnap and extortion insurance.

Insurance

The insurance approach to this exposure will be considered under five headings:

1. Type and availability of coverage.
2. Who can be covered.
3. Scope of coverage.
4. Conditions of coverage.
5. Premium considerations.

Type and availability of coverage

There are two types of coverage: property and liability, and kidnap and ransom.

Standard property and liability policies usually will cover both property damage and liability to third parties arising from acts of terrorism. Each company should insure that its existing policy, in fact, does provide such coverage. If it does not, it's possible to obtain this coverage through endorsement.

Kidnap and ransom insurance has evolved as a separate coverage. The theory behind such coverage is that it protects corporate assets and avoids shareholder problems. It is available in all but a few states, and those that have not yet approved are expected to do so. On the other hand, some countries—Italy and France for example—ban kidnap and ransom insurance on the basis that it would encourage kidnapping, and in others—Israel and West Germany among them—it is unlawful to negotiate with kidnappers or extortionists. As one would expect, it has always been possible to obtain such coverage from Lloyds. Additionally, over the past 10 years, several U.S. insurers— INA, Chubb, and The American International Group—began offering it.

Who can be covered

Coverage can be obtained for directors, officers, employees, their relatives, even for guests. Who is covered is a significant factor in determining the risk level and thus will have a substantial impact on the premium. Generally, 80 percent to 85 percent of the premium results from the coverage of directors and officers. Therefore, since the additional premium for such coverage is so small, it would seem prudent for a company obtaining such insurance to have the coverage extend to all employees. Another question which must be addressed—and the answer to which will affect the premium—is whether relatives will be covered only when they are residing in the household of an employee or irrespective of where they may be situated.

Scope of coverage

The basic coverage offered by the typical kidnap and ransom policy extends to kidnapping (the actual or alleged kidnapping of one or more covered persons) and extortion (the unlawful obtaining of money or other consideration by threatening to kidnap, injure, or kill one or more covered persons). Over and above the basic coverage, a company may obtain personal assets, reward, transit, and death and dismemberment endorsements. A personal assets endorsement, as the name suggests, extends to the personal assets of a covered employee. It usually does not cover personal assets of guests or relatives. If it has the reward endorsement, the policyholder can obtain reimbursement for monies paid to an informant up to a specified limit for information leading to the arrest and conviction of the kidnappers or extortionists. A transit endorsement provides reimbursement for monies lost by destruction, disappearance, or wrongful taking while being conveyed to those making the demand. However, it should be noted that it does not cover confiscation by government officals. Another endorsement which may be obtained is one providing a fixed sum should a covered person die or suffer dismemberment or loss of sight as a result of being kidnapped.

Conditions of coverage

For kidnap and ransom insurance to be effective, a company, prior to an occurrence, must implement security measures, not have disclosed that it has insurance and have chosen a deductible and maximums. Coverage is limited to specified amounts per loss and per policy year.

Those conditions which must be met in connection with the event itself are:

1. A demand must be made against the policy holder.
2. A person kidnapped or threatened must not be carrying the amount claimed.
3. It must be determined that a kidnapping actually occurred or a threat was genuine.
4. Local law enforcement authorities must be notified. (Experience has shown that there is a direct correlation between the timeliness of notice and the safe release of the victim, capture of the responsible persons, and return of the money paid.)
5. The insurer must be notified promptly.

Several special endorsements are available. These include:

1. The political exclusion endorsement, which reduces the premium by excluding from coverage a person who holds a public office or government post.
2. The business premises extension.
3. A property damage exclusion.
4. The independent negotiator endorsement, which provides for payment of reasonable fees and expenses to third parties who specialize in negotiating with kidnappers and extortionists.

Premium considerations

As was noted above, the insured, at the time of application, must choose a deductible and maximums, both per loss and per policy year. As is true with any insurance, the larger the deductible, the smaller the premium; the greater the coverage provided, the larger the premium. There is great latitude in the per loss maximum which will be underwritten by the insurer. The maximum has ranged from as little as $250,000 to many millions. Regardless of the number of losses in a year, the insurer ordinarily imposes a maximum limit on its liability for a particular year. Usually, that maximum is double the maximum amount permitted for a single loss.

There are no credible statistics available to serve as the basis for establishing premiums. Therefore, the rates are judgmental, based on a consideration of the following factors, all of which bear on the risk assumed:

1. The total assets of the policyholder.
2. The nature of the policyholder's principal business. Among those industries considered to have the greatest exposure are airlines, financial institutions, arms dealers, and petrochemicals.
3. The number of overseas facilities and the countries in which these facilities are located.
4. The number of covered persons and their level of responsibility.
5. Previous experience. A prior kidnapping or extortion is a significant factor, as there is a greater chance for an occurrence where there has been a successful kidnap demand or extortion.

POLITICAL RISK INSURANCE

The concept of political risk insurance has taken on a new meaning in the last several years—especially the past year. The private market has shown increasing interest in expanding the amount of insurance available to provide coverage for political risk. Limited coverage has been available under the Overseas Private Investment Corporation

(OPIC), Lloyds, and export credit insurance under the Foreign Credit Insurance Association (FCIA). With continuing political turmoil throughout the world and the basic instability of the less developed countries, pressure for expanded coverage has increased dramatically. U.S. firms have investments overseas in excess of $200 billion. These financial investments are not limited to large firms. Many small firms have invested overseas.

At the outset it may be well to define political risk. It is

> The risk of arbitrary, discriminatory acts of governments which result in financial loss to foreign owned business.

The following facts should put a proper perspective on the potential liability. At the beginning of 1970, in addition to the $200 billion in foreign investment, the exports of U.S. companies to approximately 100 countries in the developing world accounted for $10 billion. At the end of 1979, this figure had risen to over $63 billion. In the past 10 years, over 60 Third World countries nationalized the property of U.S. companies. Many of these nationalizations were without fair compensation.

The Overseas Private Investment Corporation (OPIC) was created in 1969 as a U.S. government agency for the purpose of mobilizing and facilitating the participation of U.S. private capital and skills in the development of less developed friendly countries. OPIC provides coverage for new overseas investments in eligible countries against the risks of war, revolution, nationalization without fair compensation, outright confiscation, creeping expropriation, and blocked remittance of earning and capital. It also protects contractors from losses when on-demand letters of credit or other performance guarantees are called without fair cause.

There are dramatic short comings under OPIC. Investments in developing countries are favored. An investment, to be covered, must satisfy both U.S. foreign policy objectives and the aspirations of the host country. Its major emphasis is on new, not current or existing, investments.

On the other hand, it has served a valuable purpose. At the end of 1979, OPIC had policies in force with a value of $8.8 billion and had paid out more than $370 million to 102 claimants. Projections are that at the end of 1980, the coverage of policies in force increased to approximately $9.6 billion.

Another form of insurance is the export insurance available under the Foreign Credit Insurance Association. As the name implies, it provides coverage in the event foreign buyers of U.S. goods and services fail to make payment. FCIA has been in existence since 1961, and like its counterpart, OPIC, has some of the same limitations with national interest considerations taking precedence.

While political risk insurance has been available for some time, there has been little demand for it until the last several years. With increasing international instability and the demonstrated limitations of the government programs, it is likely that Lloyds, along with several American companies, will write an even larger volume of political risk insurance over the next few years. Private companies generally are able to provide $80 to $90 million of insurance on a single project. In exceptional cases even greater coverage is possible. In one recent situation, capacity in excess of $150 million was put together.

Coverage is usually available for (1) nationalization, confiscation, or investment expropriation, (2) cancellation of import or export licenses, (3) contract repudiation or contract frustration, (4) inconvertibility of currency, and (5) unfair calling of demand deposits.

The underwriting and the premium charged, as with kidnap and ransom, depends upon the country involved, the nature of the project, and the industry. Some of the industries identified as having high exposure are natural resources, banking, insurance, utilities, and transportation. Currently, premiums range anywhere from .3 percent to 12 percent or more of insured values, depending upon the industry.

Besides pure avoidance, there are some loss-prevention steps that can be utilized to minimize the potential exposure. They are:

1. Use of local partners (private only).
2. Invaluable status—keep the propriety information at home.
3. Vertical integration.
4. Local borrowing.
5. Minimization of fixed investments.
6. Payment in convertible currency.

CHAPTER 17

MISCELLANEOUS COVERAGES

BOILER AND PRESSURE VESSEL
COVERAGE

MACHINERY COVERAGE

THE BOILER AND MACHINERY POLICY
  Definitions
  Exclusions
  Conditions
  Indirect coverage—Business
    Interruption

Inspection and suspension
State laws
Risk management techniques
Questions to ask the agent or broker

GLASS INSURANCE

CREDIT INSURANCE

VALUABLE PAPERS INSURANCE

Kenneth J. Kelly
Vice President, Secretary, and General Counsel
Hartford Steam Boiler Inspection and Insurance Company
Hartford, Connecticut

Kenneth J. Kelly began his career in the insurance industry in 1955 with the Travelers Insurance Company. He joined the Hartford Steam Boiler Inspection and Insurance Company in 1960, after graduating from the University of Connecticut Law School. He is currently Vice President, Secretary, and General Counsel of that company.

There is no such thing as a miscellaneous policy of insurance. To the best of my knowledge no businessman has ever called his broker to inquire as to whether his miscellaneous coverages were complete and up to date. In this businessman's Handbook, however, certain less prominent coverages must, for organizational reasons, be grouped in a miscellaneous chapter. There is no rationale for such a grouping. Technically, it is possible that the failure of an air-conditioning system might so overheat the occupants of a building that in order to permit entry of a cooling breeze, one individual might, in dispair, throw a packet of valuable papers through a plate glass window thereby losing the papers and the basis of one's credit. An insured might well, in this case, call his broker to inquire as to the state of his miscellaneous coverages. Aside from this somewhat tenuous connection, there is no commonalty among these various coverages and each will be discussed separately.

BOILERS AND PRESSURE VESSEL COVERAGE

The most obvious peril connected with the operation of boilers and pressure vessels is explosion. This peril is inherent in hot water boilers, steam boilers, steam piping, and in pressure vessels in general. Explosions have diminished considerably since the late 19th century when locomotive, sawmill, portable, and a variety of other types of boilers were exploding with dismal frequency. Modern safety devices as well as engineering and inspection services furnished by most boiler and machinery insurers have helped to reduce explosions of these objects to a relatively infrequent occurrence. Even one such explosion, however, can be a tragic event in terms of potential destruction and injury because of the violence of such an explosion.

A far more common occurrence in the modern era is the less destructive, but still costly, cracking, burning, bulging, or collapse of boilers and pressure vessels. One of the most common failures of boilers is the failure of "low water cutoffs," that is, that control which shuts off the burner when the water level in the boiler is low. Such a failure generally results in damage from overheating and, in the case of cast iron boilers, cracked sections.

The disruption of business caused by such damage, while less catastrophic than that caused by an explosion, can nevertheless be very costly.

Refrigerating and air-conditioning losses are the type of losses to which most businessmen are exposed and with which they are fairly familiar. The loss of an air-conditioning unit, or the loss of a vessel or other component part of an air-conditioning system, will generally not involve catastrophic property damage, but will almost certainly result

420

in a business interruption loss if such equipment should be lost during the cooling period of the year.

Refrigerating systems primarily used for cold storage purposes can fail resulting in property damage to the insured object as well as business interruption losses. The failure of such systems quite often also results in extensive damage to the goods or processes which are dependent upon the continuation of refrigeration. The expenses of cleanup and of recharging the systems can be quite expensive.

MACHINERY COVERAGE

The Machinery coverages of the boiler and machinery line developed subsequent to boiler and pressure vessel coverage and were recognized as a natural extension of such coverages. The energy and capacity for destruction inherent in objects classified as "machinery" is quite similar to that found in boiler and pressure vessels. Any piece of rotating equipment, such as a flywheel or turbine, contains energy. In the case of steam turbines there also exists energy in the form of steam pressure.

Machinery coverages include objects such as air compressors, fans and blowers, pump units, engines, turbines, as well as miscellaneous electrical equipment such as switchboards and other apparatus used for power distribution. The failure of this type of object can result in extensive property damage as well as considerable business interruption losses.

Failures of objects classified as machinery objects, while less destructive than failures normally associated with boiler and pressure vessels, occur more frequently and may also involve extended periods of idleness with concomitant business interruption and consequential losses.

It becomes readily apparent when reading through a list of the more important exposures connected with boiler and machinery insurance that the potential for extensive property damage, as well as for prolonged periods of business interruption, are hazards that lurk within the oily depths of nearly every piece of equipment of the sort enumerated. While this hazard may be under control, it is never fully tamed, and may at any moment break with great destructive force.

THE BOILER AND MACHINERY POLICY

Definitions

There are various types of policies covering the exposures discussed above. Many businessmen buy boiler and machinery insurance as a supplement to, or as an optional part of, the SMP (Special Multi-Peril Policy), or as a separate Boiler and Machinery Policy. Large companies with extensive operations utilizing many different kinds of equipment will buy Comprehensive coverage, a package type policy covering essentially all boiler and machinery exposures, generally above certain self-insured levels.

The most commonly used Boiler and Machinery Policy, for all its arcane language, is essentially a straightforward document. All of the items of equipment which might be used in the conduct of the business, and which have certain common characteristics, are grouped together in various sections. For example, boilers, fired vessels, and electric steam generators are grouped together with one common definition of "Object" and one common definition of "Accident." The declarations page of the policy will indicate which groups of Objects are covered under a particular policy. "Specific" coverage, which covers specific Objects as opposed to groups of Objects, is available under limited circumstances.

The Insuring Agreement is fairly simple. It provides that the insurer will pay for a loss from an Accident (or in some policies an "occurrence") as defined in the policy, to an Object as defined in that same policy. Such payment is subject to other provisions and exclusions of the policy. The operative words are *Object* and *Accident*.

The definition of each Object is carefully spelled out under the appropriate section of the policy which pertains to that particular Object. The definitions are designed to include essentially the energy containing portions of the Object and to exclude exposures which might be covered in another policy, such as most furnace explosions and items such as settings, refactory, and so on, not subject to pressure of contents nor containing inherent energy.

The definition of Accident is extremely broad. In essence the definition states that if the described Object breaks down, the insured may recover under the terms of the policy. The definition of Accident excludes wear and tear, break down of structures or foundations, and furnace explosions unless otherwise covered. This is not an exhaustive list of all of the exclusions in the definition of Accident. It is important to note that the breakdown of the insured Object is an occurrence for which the insured may be compensated, with certain limited exceptions.

In addition to the basic first-party property damage, the policy contains provisions for certain other coverages. The Repair or Replacement coverage, essentially an elimination of depreciation, may be added to the policy at the insured's option. The policy contains a limit on water damage and ammonia contamination of $1,000. These limits, for the property covered therein, may be increased by the insured. Some boilers, because of age or scarcity of replacement parts, may not be eligible for standard, or "broad" form coverage, but may only be covered under a "limited" type of coverage. Under the limited form of coverage the "explosion" or catastrophe type occurrence would be covered. The less catastrophic, and more common occurrence, i.e., cracking, bulging, collapse, and burning, would not be covered.

The Boiler and Machinery Policy remains somewhat unique in that it still contains some liability features which probably qualify it for the designation casualty insurance as opposed to property insurance which it basically is. The policy automatically provides coverage for damage, for which the insured is legally liable, to property of others in the care, custody, and control of the insured, and coverage for the insured's legal liability for bodily injury may also be included at the insured's option. It is important to note that such third-party liability must arise out of an Accident as defined to an Object as defined.

Exclusions

The exclusions to the Boiler and Machinery Policy are relatively few and of the garden variety found in most policies of insurance. There are exclusions for damage caused by war, insurrection, nuclear reaction, radiation, and contamination, and any increase necessitated by ordinance or law, regulating or restricting repair, use, and so on, the so-called demolition endorsement.

The more important exclusions found in the Boiler and Machinery Policy are those dealing with explosions and fire. These exclusions essentially provide that loss from fire causing an Accident or loss from fire caused by an Accident is excluded. Similarly, loss from combustion explosion outside the Object which causes an Accident or loss from combustion explosion outside the object which is caused by an Accident is also excluded. Coverage for business interruption is not generally automatically included under standard coverage, but is an option available to an insured. There are also limitations applying to loss caused by an earthquake.

Conditions

There is a provision made for the automatic coverage of newly acquired properties, that is, locations, when an insured is covered by blanket group coverage as opposed to specific coverage. New Objects added to named locations are automatically insured if they meet the definition of Object under the applicable blanket group description. Additionally, the ordinary conditions found in most policies are also found in the Boiler and Machinery Policy, that is, those conditions pertaining to notice of loss, subrogation, other insurance, and so on. There is no mandatory provision for filing a proof of loss in the Boiler and Machinery Policy, and most companies writing this line do not require the filing of a proof of loss. There are provisions pertaining to inspection of an insured Object as well as suspension of coverage discussed later in detail.

Indirect coverage—Business Interruption

The three common Business Interruption forms used in connection with a Boiler and Machinery Policy are: Actual Loss Sustained, Valued, and a Consequential Loss form. Recovery under the Business Interruption forms used with a Boiler and Machinery Policy depend upon the occurrence of an Accident as defined, to an Object as defined, in the insurance policy. The ordinary exclusions and conditions of the Standard Boiler and Machinery Policy form are carried over to the Business Interruption forms, with appropriate exceptions.

Valued form. Under the Valued form, a Daily Indemnity is specified which is the maximum amount of recovery for each day during which business on the described premises is totally suspended. In case of a partial suspension of business, a portion of the specified Daily Indemnity is paid, based upon the reduction in *current business,* as that term is defined in the Business Interruption Endorsement.

Actual Loss Sustained. Under this form, unlike the Valued form, the insured has to prove his loss. The insured's recovery is limited to the loss of net profit plus specified fixed charges and expenses that continue despite the Accident. This insurance is provided on a co-insurance basis, and obviously care must be taken in establishing values and in reporting them, where that is required, to the insurance company. A waiver of co-insurance is generally available.

Consequential damage. This indirect coverage provides indemnity for loss on specified property of the insured when such loss is due to spoilage from lack of power, light, heat, steam, or refrigeration. Such coverage is also available for specified property of others similarly damaged for which damage the insured is legally obligated to reimburse the third party. As in other indirect coverages, it is essential that there be an Accident to an Object before such indemnity is available to an insured. It is important that the goods or property be specifically identified. This coverage is written on an Actual Loss Sustained basis, and may be written either with or without co-insurance.

Deductibles. Various forms of deductibles may be obtained for indirect coverages with a concomitant reduction of premium. It is particularly essential when buying Business Interruption Coverage in connection with a Boiler and Machinery Policy that an insured carefully identify the critical Objects in the plant or business; the amount of down time that might be caused by the total or partial loss of such an Object; the net effect on total business or production occasioned by a complete or partial loss of such an Object; and then purchase business interruption insurance in adequate limits in order to protect fully against such losses. Varying limits for different classes of Objects may be obtained by an insured depending upon the critical nature of each such class of Objects.

Inspection and suspension

Two of the more important conditions of the policy are those dealing with inspection and suspension of coverage. A very large component of the total boiler and machinery premium is for the engineering and inspection services furnished by most boiler and machinery insurers. Boiler and machinery insurance in its conception was as much concerned with the safe and continuous operation of equipment as with indemnifying insureds who suffered a loss by reason of destruction of their property. The Hartford Steam Boiler Inspection and Insurance Company, the first such company in the United States, was formed by engineers who were far more acquainted with engineering and the prevention of catastrophic boiler and pressure vessel explosions than they were with the fine print of a policy of insurance. To this date, boiler and machinery insurers spent a great deal of time and human energy on developing better and safer ways to operate energy utilizing equipment. Indeed, in most parts of the world boiler and machinery insurance is included within the generic term *engineering insurance*.

The inspection condition of the policy permits, but does not obligate, the insurance company to make inspections of the insured equipment. Such inspections are made primarily for the benefit of a boiler and machinery carrier, inasmuch as an inspection that prevents an Accident also prevents a loss to that company. However, in most cases the interests of the insured and the carrier are for all practical purposes identical. Both want to prevent bodily injury and destruction of property.

State laws

There is no federal law or standard applicable to the inspection and certification of boilers and pressure vessels. There is a uniform boiler law, based on the ASME Code, which has been adopted, with some modifications, in most jurisdictions. At the present time, of the 48 contiguous states, Hawaii, Alaska, and the District of Columbia, all but 7 have laws requiring inspection of power boilers on an annual basis. Of these seven states not requiring annual inspection of power boilers, two have construction and installation requirements. Forty-one states and the District of Columbia have construction and installation requirements for heating boilers and hot water supply boilers with inspection requirements either on a yearly or biannual basis. The kinds of objects on which ongoing inspections are required vary widely from jurisdiction to jurisdiction based upon service (steam heating, hot water heating, or hot water supply), location of equipment (private residence, apartment units based on unit number, places of public assembly, places of employment, and schools), and size. Unfired pressure vessels are covered by law for construction and installation in 33 states and the District of Columbia; however, only 26 states and the District of Columbia requires in service inspection of unfired pressure vessels on an ongoing basis.

The inspection requirements for unfired pressure vessels and similar types of Objects vary widely from jurisdiction to jurisdiction. Some states cover only air tanks while others cover a wide variety of objects in many kinds of service. Some jurisdictions require these objects to be inspected annually, some require inspections biennially, and others require inspections triennially.

These inspections must be performed by authorized inspectors, that is, those holding a National Board Commission. At the present the only inspectors holding such commissions are those employed by a governmental jurisdiction or by an insurance company actively engaged in writing boiler and machinery insurance. Upon inspecting the Object the inspector will, when required by law, issue a report to the jurisdiction which will issue, where necessary, an operating certificate.

Suspension of coverage. If an inspector employed by an insurance company discovers a "dangerous condition" when making an inspection, the inspector may suspend coverage for that Object. A "dangerous condition" would clearly exist if the object were being operated in clear violation of the law, that is, without safety valves, and so on, but might also exist where no clear violation of the law is present, but the inspector feels that the continued operation of the object presents an unreasonable hazard. Insurance will be reinstated when the condition is corrected.

Risk management techniques

Risk management techniques in the boiler and machinery field of insurance are not vastly different from those employed in other fields of property insurance. The effort begins with risk evaluation, and requires a quality risk analysis by a boiler and machinery insurer's personnel in conjunction with the insured's personnel. This survey will identify the critical pieces of equipment and the potential loss exposure which must be of concern to the Risk Manager. A total equipment inventory, plus the loss experience of the risk and other similar risks, coupled with operating history and the knowledge of product and markets, will help to identify the critical areas of loss exposure.

Most boiler and machinery insurers have rather extensive loss prevention programs, for loss prevention is the genesis of boiler and machinery insurance. A substantial variety of risk management techniques are available including the already mentioned risk analysis and exposure evaluations, as well as operator and supervisory training programs, preventive maintenance programs, a program to acquire critical spare parts, and development of emergency and pre-emergency planning programs.

The choice of any of these risk management techniques depends upon the results of a proper exposure analysis. An exposure analysis should consist of the following elements as a bare minimum:

1. A concise analysis of plant or business operations ranging from the introduction of raw materials to the completion of finished products, in the case of manufacturing operations, or analyzing work flow, customer servicing, and sales in nonmanufacturing businesses.
2. A survey of utility services received by a plant or business (water, steam, electricity fuel, etc.), including the sources of the services and the effects of partial or complete loss of any of these services on production or business.
3. An audit of the number, size, and approximate age of boilers, pressure vessels, transformers, turbines, generators, air-conditioning systems, and other electrical and machinery equipment.
4. A determination of the approximate replacement value of the major or critical machines used directly in production or essential to the conduct of business.
5. An inventory of spare parts for major machines and equipment including the identification of problems relating to accessibility and ease of removal of damaged equipment, and the development of a plan to deal with the problems that are identified.
6. An analysis of the effects of curtailment or stoppage of production or business or spoilage of products resulting from failure of such equipment.
7. An analysis of the level of training and experience required of the personnel operating the equipment, with special emphasis upon the personnel operating the critical items of equipment, and the

possible effect upon operations of an error on the part of operating personnel.

Implicit in such an analysis of the exposures contained in any plant or business is an evaluation of these exposures and the impact that the failures most likely to occur might have upon operations. The businessman is now in a position to decide which risk management techniques are most appropriate for his particular business, and can determine which insurance carrier is best fitted to provide those techniques. Reliable, continuous operation of a business is far more important, and of far greater value to an insured, than a recovery of a loss under a policy of boiler and machinery insurance.

Questions to ask the agent or broker

Steven Allen is fond of remarking that in this modern era there is an inordinately large number of people who have all the answers, but a very great scarcity of those people who have the questions. That being the case, an attempt will be made to list the questions that an insured ought to ask the agent or broker in connection with the purchase of a boiler and machinery policy. It is important to remember that fire insurance and boiler and machinery insurance are the two basic forms of property insurance which will generally cover the plant and equipment of a business. There are others, but these are the two basic coverages. The insured should know what the basic fire policy and the extended coverage commonly made a part of the fire policy provide in the way of insurance. The insured should recognize that most fire policies do cover furnace explosions, that is, an explosion in a boiler's combustion chamber, and may well cover explosion of hot water boilers and other pressure vessels not containing steam. The perils covered by the Boiler and Machinery Policy have already been discussed. The insured therefore should ask the following basic questions of its agent or broker:

1. What gaps in coverage might exist between a boiler policy and a fire policy where neither would provide coverage for a loss?
2. Have duplicate areas of coverage been eliminated from the property policies?
3. Are the items critical to the operation of the plant or business fully insured?
4. Is there repair and replacement (i.e., elimination of depreciation) coverage on those critical items?
5. Is there adequate Business Interruption coverage which would permit the businessman to make up production elsewhere and to

meet all increased costs arising out of the use of an alternative location?

6. Will the insurer make recommendations for spare parts, accident prevention programs, perform periodic inspections, and conduct competent Accident investigations?

7. Will the insurer handle whatever reports have to be made to regulatory agencies, and do whatever is necessary to help the insured comply with laws or regulations which might apply to insured equipment?

8. In the event of an Accident, what sort of facilities does the insurer have to locate spare parts, or replacements parts, or new or used equipment?

9. Is the insurer capable of a sophisticated analysis of the causes of failure and able to recommend procedures to prevent future failures?

Boiler and machinery insurers are developing a wide range of professional and technical services in the areas of loss prevention, equipment reliability, and failure analysis. Such services may be of limited interest to most insureds, but it is an indication of the level of professional and technical expertise that a particular boiler and machinery insurer might be able to provide in case of need.

GLASS INSURANCE

Glass insurance is sold most readily to businesses which feel there is imminent danger of a brickbat being thrown through the front window. Many businesses simply go self-insured on the theory that vandalism or social unrest is not enough of a hazard to their business to require the protection of a glass policy. Hartford, Connecticut, which prides itself on being the "insurance city," was also the home of one James Lahey, famed window smasher. Mr. Lahey specialized in barroom windows, and many proprietors of such establishments, after having collected a number of times under their policies and in danger of having the coverage cancelled, discovered that their best protection lay in a policy of providing Mr. Lahey with a complimentary "shot and a beer." Such a policy will ward off the Laheys, and a Comprehensive Glass Policy will provide coverage for most other hazards.

The coverage under the Comprehensive Glass Policy extends to the glass described, and to the lettering and ornamentation thereon as separately described. An "all glass of type described" endorsement is available which eliminates the detailed schedule in the policy, even though a schedule must still be submitted to the insurer.

The perils covered are breakage of glass or chemical damage thereto. Coverage is extended to the repair or replacement of frames when necessitated by glass damage, securing openings as needed while awaiting repair or replacement of the glass, and removing or replacing obstructions, other than window displays, necessary to repairing the damage. The three items last mentioned are subject to a recovery of $75 each per occurrence, but additional limits may be purchased.

Exclusions are but three in number, that is, loss from fire, a standard nuclear exclusion, and loss from war, insurrection, rebellion, or revolution. The last exclusion was of particular significance during the urban riots of the 60s when the line between rioting and civil insurrection was a fine and tenuous demarcation.

The conditions of the policy are standard, the most important being the measure of loss, that is, actual cash value of the property at the time of loss, or the cost of repair or replacement with like kind, all subject to the policy limit. There is a requirement of prompt notice and a requirement for filing a proof of loss, not always insisted upon.

One of the great advantages of this type of insurance is that the insurer will generally be a large buyer of glass. This gives the insurer greater economic leverage in expediting repairs to damaged glass. This can be important to a businessman anxious to conduct business behind plate glass windows and not a plywood palisade.

Risk management. It is important that the glass to be insured be adequately described. Care should be taken with the insurance agent to discuss coverage for somewhat unique types of glass, such as stained glass, Neon and flourescent signs, and structural glass. Care should also be taken to eliminate duplication of coverages and to explore other forms of all risk coverage for such glass which might be obtained at a lesser rate than that for the Comprehensive Glass Policy.

CREDIT INSURANCE

Commercial credit insurance is not available for every business enterprise. It is available only for manufacturers, wholesalers, and service organizations. It is not available for retailers or on any aspect of business involving retail trade. This line of insurance is little known and little used. It is intended to provide protection to an insured for the "abnormal" credit loss caused by insolvency or default due to the happening of a specified event, which permits a debt owed to the insured by its customer to become a claim under the policy. There is an extensive list of these events contained in the policy, but they may be characterized as events normally associated with insolvency, that is, appointment of a receiver or creditors' committee, the seizures or sale of the debtor's property, and events not associated with insolvency such as the death, disappearance, or mental incompetence of the debtor.

The "abnormal" credit loss referred to is simply the covered loss above an agreed retention by the insured. That retention, essentially a deductible, is established as a percentage of the insured's net sales— defined as gross sales less allowances and invoice price of goods returned and accepted. This loss, the "primary" loss, attempts to remove from coverage the losses which an insured is *expected* to incur in the normal course of operating a particular type of business. The amount of the primary loss may be adjusted, usually at renewal, depending upon the experience of the business.

There is also a so-called co-insurance clause in credit policies. The purpose of the clause, as used in this policy, is not to persuade an insured to insure to value, but simply to provide additional deductible protection to the insurer. The insured is reimbursed a stated percentage of its loss depending on the credit rating of the defaulting account. The credit ratings are obtained from a recognized merchantile rating organization, and a specified co-insurance percentage, or deductible, is assigned to each rating. This use of co-insurance or percentage deductible aspects of credit insurance is falling into disuse and policies are being written subject only to the primary loss type of deductible. Claims generally must be presented to the insurer before they are three months past due under the terms of the original sale or within one year of shipment. The claims are accepted as of the date filed.

There is flexibility in the establishment of the limit of loss applicable to any one debtor and the method of reporting the details of accounts covered by the policy. These should be explored with the agent or broker to determine how much flexibility is needed by a particular insured.

Insurance companies involved in this line of insurance provide ancillary services which may be of value to an insured. An insurance company handling any volume of such claims knows the forms, methods, and procedures used in collecting insolvent accounts as well as methods of preventing such losses. Such assistance may cover the uninsured as well as the insured portion of the loss, and there may be a fee applicable to the attempted recovery of the uninsured portion of the loss.

Foreign Credit Insurance. A Foreign Credit Insurance Association has been formed in the United States in cooperation with the Export-Import Bank to provide credit insurance to exporters of goods to certain foreign countries. The terms of this coverage differ in important respects from domestic credit insurance and should be thoroughly discussed with an agent.

VALUABLE PAPERS INSURANCE

The policy affords coverage for physical loss of valuable papers.

Valuable papers are defined as written, printed, or otherwise inscribed documents and records excluding money or securities. The coverage is "all-risk," with certain exclusions, principally loss from wear and tear, errors in copying or processing, and loss due to electrical or magnetic injury unless caused by lightening.

The insurance may be written on a specific or blanket basis. The measure of loss for blanket coverage is the actual cash value of the property destroyed, or what it would cost to repair or replace the property. If the property is specifically insured, however, the measure of loss is the value assigned to specified articles. There is a condition providing for appraisal in the event the parties disagree as to the amount of the loss.

The property must be kept at the location specified, and protected as specified, but there is a limited extension of coverage while the property is temporarily removed from the specified location, and a full extension of coverage when the removal is due to imminent danger of loss provided proper notice is given to the insurer.

An insured should be concerned primarily with the choice of either blanket or specific coverage, depending on the nature of the valuable papers and the amount of premium the insured is willing to spend.

Valuable Papers coverage is sometimes written in conjunction with Accounts Receivable coverage as the two coverages do compliment one another.

CHAPTER 18

TITLE INSURANCE

THE RISKS COVERED BY TITLE INSURANCE

INTERESTS IN REAL ESTATE THAT MAY BE COVERED BY TITLE INSURANCE

SCOPE OF COVERAGE; LIMITATIONS ON COVERAGE
The standard coverage policy
The extended coverage policy

Exclusions from coverage
Endorsements

TERM OF THE POLICY; CONTINUATION OF COVERAGE

THE TITLE INSURANCE COMMITMENT

THE AMOUNT OF INSURANCE; THE COST OF TITLE INSURANCE

AVAILABILITY OF TITLE INSURANCE

John E. Flood, Jr.
Chairman of the Board
Ticor Title Insurers
Los Angeles, California

John E. Flood, Jr., is Chairman of the Board and Chief Executive Officer of Title Insurance and Trust Company and Pioneer National Title Insurance Company, and Group Vice President of Ticor, a Los Angeles based financial services company. TI, PNTI, and its subsidiary Title Guarantee-New York offer title insurance services nationwide.

Title insurance is perhaps the least understood line of insurance written in the United States. This is not because title insurance is of recent origin (the first title insurance company was chartered more than 100 years ago) nor is it due to lack of familiarity as a result of infrequent usage (millions of title insurance policies are issued annually in the United States). Title insurance comes to the attention of most Americans only upon completion of the purchase of a home, when an owner's title policy is delivered along with numerous other legal documents and papers relating to the transaction. The charge for title insurance is a single premium paid at the time of policy issuance, and since there are no billings for renewal premium payments, the insured owner is not thereafter reminded of the existence of title insurance protection of his investment in real estate. Consequently, among the vast majority of the population, there is far less awareness of the existence and scope of title insurance coverage than of automobile liability and property damage insurance and other lines.

The purchase of a home is typically the largest single investment made by a family, and title insurance should be one section in the "umbrella of insurance coverage" which protects the homeowner against financial loss.

In commercial real estate transactions, title insurance is an absolute requirement of almost all purchasers, long-term lessees, and mortgage lenders who usually have a clear understanding that there are varying degrees of title coverage generally available and that it may be possible to negotiate special coverage by an endorsement tailored to the requirements of a particular transaction.

The foundation of title insurance is the real estate law of the state in which the land described in a policy is located. Each state, through its constitution and legislature, has made its own choice of governmental policy regarding the basis on which real estate can be owned, used, conveyed, encumbered, and inherited. For example, many states adopted the common law of England as the basic system of property rights while others opted for the quite different rules of community property law. Even if a state is broadly classified as a "common-law state," the specifics of its real property law may vary considerably from that of a neighboring common-law state. The same variations exist among the states which fall into the community property category.

Since the fundamental law of real estate is so diverse among the states, it is not surprising that there is equal diversity in the recording and registration systems which have been established to perpetuate the deeds and other documents which comprise the "chain of title" to land within a political subdivision. Likewise, the methods of examining titles and evaluating their validity developed in different ways in different localities.

In some cases, an attorney would search the indexes in the recording office to identify the recorded documents affecting title to the relevant land. He would then examine that series of documents and deliver a legal opinion regarding ownership of the land and the liens and encumbrances affecting that land. If the opinion of title was satisfactory to the client, the client would proceed with his contemplated purchase or mortgage loan. In other areas, this task was divided. A layman skilled in searching land title records was employed to prepare, and certify as correct, an abstract of title. An abstract is a file which contains a copy or synopsis of each recorded document affecting title to a specific parcel of land—in short, a written history of the ownership of that land. The abstract was then delivered to an attorney for evaluation and preparation of a legal opinion.

In any enterprise involving such massive detail as the search and examination of land titles, there is great potential for human error in assembling a chain of title. In a field as complex as real estate law, even the most competent attorney may misjudge the correct application of legal principles to a particular set of facts, thereby causing a loss to be sustained by his client.

When a client did suffer loss because of abstractor or attorney error, the client might or might not be entitled to recover a judgment against the person at fault. Moreover, if a judgment was obtained, there was little assurance that assets would be available to satisfy the judgment.

It was a result of this unsatisfactory state of affairs that in the latter part of the 19th century, title insurance was made available to indemnify an investor in real estate against loss caused by error or omission in the title searching process or by judgmental error in evaluating the legal effect of the documents on which the lawyer's opinion of title was based.

Both of the early methods of title evaluation continue in use in many areas of the United States. As the nation's population increased, however, and as land was subdivided and resubdivided, the volume of real estate transactions multiplied to the point that in most urban counties searching titles from the public records was no longer acceptable in terms of cost and time requirements. Thus, the private "title plant" was born.

A title plant contains essentially the same title information that is found in the public recording offices but by means of highly refined name and property indexes, coded maps, and other devices, copies of the title documents affecting a particular land parcel may be much more accurately and efficiently retrieved from a title plant.

Initially, the title insurer relied on the work of the abstractor and the opinion of the examining attorney as the basis for insuring against loss by reason of title defects. With the advent of title plants, it became inevitable that the separate functions of search of recording indexes, examination of title documents, and the underwriting of risk would be combined and performed by a single provider of title services, whether a branch office of the title insurance company or the office of an issuing agent appointed by the title insurer. In most parts of the United States, title companies also offer a related service variously known as "escrow," "closing," or "settlement," which facilitates the exchange of money and documents involved in the completion of a real estate transaction.

In many cases, the investor's attorney, although not examining the full chain of title, reviews the title evidence produced by the title company and ascertains that the title insurance policy to be issued will include the coverages required by his client. In most states, a title insurance policy does not purport to be a legal opinion as to the condition of title. Rather, it is a contract which defines the risks assumed by the title insurer and the conditions under which the insured will be indemnified in the event of loss because of a title defect or encumbrance which is insured against by the terms of the policy. Thus an irregularity in an ancient title document, although still "affecting" the title in a strict legal sense, will ordinarily be insured against by not listing it as an exception from coverage (if in the title underwriter's judgment that irregularity will not cause loss to the insured). If a claim based on that defect is asserted, the insurer, of course, is required to eliminate the defect by quiet title action or other means, at its expense, or to compensate the insured for any loss incurred.

THE RISKS COVERED BY TITLE INSURANCE

The fundamental concept of title insurance is to eliminate the risk of loss arising from title defects or encumbrances existing at the time of issuance of a policy. Most other lines of insurance provide indemnification for loss created by the occurrence of a post-issue event, for example, fire, theft, or death. The principal function of title insurance is controlled loss prevention, while other lines of insurance provide for compensation if an unforeseen and uncontrollable occurrence causes loss during the period of policy coverage. In this sense, the loss prevention service provided by a title insurer or its agent is a benefit to the insured perhaps equal in value to the insurer's agreement to compensate the insured if a title loss occurs.

When a residential or commercial property is purchased, it is usually because that particular property uniquely meets the requirements of the purchaser in terms of such considerations as location, design, traffic flow, proximity to schools, and other amenities important to that purchaser. The purchaser seeks undisputed ownership and possession of the property chosen rather than the possibility of a monetary recovery from the title insurer. In recognition of this fact, and in serving their own financial self-interest, the issuers of title insurance make a careful evaluation of title prior to policy issuance, and do not operate on a casualty basis or in reliance on historical claims frequency data.

Before agreeing to insure a particular land title, therefore, the insurer or its agent causes a search and examination of that title to be performed. The search involves the identification of all records that may affect the title, and these are found in numerous public offices: the County Recorder's Office (for deeds, mortgages, etc.); the State Court Clerk's Office (for probate decrees, foreclosure judgments, etc.); the County Tax Collector's Office (for the status of real estate tax payments); the City Treasurer's Office (for the status of special assessments for improvements which have benefitted the property); the Office of the Clerk of the United States District Court (for bankruptcy records, federal condemnation proceedings, etc.); and the City Clerk's Office (for notice of street closures, etc.).

When the search has produced a "chain of title," that is, a listing of all records that must be considered in evaluating the title, an examination of those records is performed by a person familiar with the rules and principles of real estate law. The examiner then prepares a report on title which reflects his conclusions regarding current ownership of the land; any defect in that ownership ascertainable from records in the chain of title; the existence of liens, which are charges on the title securing payment of monetary obligations (delinquent real estate taxes, mortgages, unpaid money judgments against the title holder, etc.); and the existence of other encumbrances which affect the title to, or restrict the use of, the land (easements, leases, building restrictions, etc.).

The preliminary title report (often in the form of a contractual commitment to issue a title insurance policy on the conditions specified) indicates the title insurer's evaluation of the title as of the date shown and, in effect, is an offer by the title insurer to issue a policy consistent with the contents of the report, subject to any changes in title occurring between the date of the report and the date of policy issuance.

The preceding outline of the search, examination, and reporting process may also serve as a description of one category of risk covered by title insurance, i.e., the risk that the condition of "record title" as reported is erroneous because the search was inaccurate or incomplete or because the title examiner misread the legal effect of the records before him. This category of risk encompasses errors and omissions of a mechanical nature, as well as those of a judgmental or underwriting nature. If the search and examination processes are perfectly performed, there still remain two other categories of title risks to which a real estate investor is exposed: off-record risks which may be characterized as "hidden," and off-record risks which may be characterized as "apparent."

Hidden off-record title risks are those defects which cannot be ascertained by the most meticulous examination of the recorded title documents nor by a land survey, inspection of the land, and inquiry of the presumed owners and occupants of the land. Some examples of hidden defects are forged signatures of deeds in the chain of title, lack of legal capacity of the maker of a deed (due either to mental illness or lack of legal age to contract), misrepresentation of marital status, false personation (the true owner of the land is John Doe and another person named John Doe purports to convey or mortgage the land), obtaining possession through fraudulent means of a deed validly executed and acknowledged by the true owner (lack of legal delivery), and erroneous indexing of a deed or other title document in the public recording office. Title defects of this nature are within the coverage of title insurance and are often referred to as the "true insurance risks" assumed by a title underwriter because there is no feasible means of discovering their existence until an adverse claim is asserted against the insured's title.

Apparent off-record title risks are those matters which cannot be ascertained by examination of recorded title documents but which would be disclosed by an accurate survey of the land, an inspection of the land, or inquiry directed to the one claiming to own the land, as well as anyone found in possession of the land other than the purported owner.

For example, a survey of the land to be purchased may show that a neighboring owner has constructed a fence or wall which encloses a portion of the subject land or, even more serious, has placed a garage or a portion of his home on that land. Such encroachment, if continued for a sufficient time and under certain conditions, may be the basis for a claim by the encroaching neighbor that he has acquired valid title to the land so occupied under a legal doctrine known as "adverse possession."

Conversely, a survey may disclose to a prospective purchaser that the home he is interested in purchasing is partially located on land not owned by the seller, a title problem the purchaser would surely not want to assume. An inspection of the land by a prospective purchaser may disclose the existence of a two-story structure set back 5 feet from a side lot line, while the title report shows a recorded restrictive covenant providing that any structure on the land may not exceed one story in height and is to be set back 10 feet from each side lot line.

Finally, by way of illustration, the record title owner of a lot may be John Doe. Inspection of the property discloses that it is in the possession of Mr. and Mrs. Roe. The law requires a prospective purchaser to determine by what right a "stranger" is in possession. Inquiry might establish that the Roes hold an unrecorded lease or contract to purchase the lot. The purchaser would be required to honor the lease or contract since by law he is charged with knowledge of all facts which would be disclosed by inquiry of a person in possession, to the same extent as if those facts were disclosed by a recorded title document. The title insurance coverage available to protect against apparent off-record risks will be discussed elsewhere in this chapter.

In addition to providing indemnification for loss resulting from those title risks covered by the policy, the insurer agrees to provide for the defense of the insured in any litigation based on an alleged title defect which is insured against by the policy. The insurer's obligation to provide a defense, at its sole cost, is a valuable policy benefit in an era which has been characterized by a dramatic increase in the number of lawsuits filed across the nation and by an equally dramatic increase in attorney's fees and other expenses of litigation. Even if a plaintiff is asserting a claim which is wholly without substance, a defense must be made, and the many opportunities for pre-trial proceedings for discovery of evidence, plus the expense of trial and perhaps of appeal, could well make the cost of defense a major financial burden for a landowner. If an adverse claim relates to a matter within policy coverage, the defense will be provided by the title insurer.

Two illustrations may assist in arriving at an understanding of the extent of the insurer's obligation to defend:

1. The insurer has issued a policy which shows an easement as an encumbrance on the title, granted by a prior owner for driveway purposes over the east ten feet of the land described in the policy. Later, the person entitled to the benefit of the easement files a lawsuit alleging that the actual agreement between him and the prior owner was that the 10-foot strip was to be used not only for driveway purposes but also for installation of an overhead utility pole line, that the recorded easement grant was in error in not referring to the additional permitted use, and asking that the court establish by decree his right to install the pole line in the easement area. The insured, believing that an overhead utility line in that location will be unsightly and impair the value of his property, is unwilling to permit that additional use and tenders defense of the lawsuit to his title insurer. Since the policy excepted from coverage only an easement for driveway purposes, it impliedly insured that enforceable easements for other purposes did not exist of record at the date of the policy, and the title insurer is obligated to provide for the insured a

defense of the lawsuit. If the defense is successful, the insurer has no further obligation to the insured regarding that claim. If the plaintiff prevails in the lawsuit, however, the insurer's loss is the total cost of defense plus payment to the insured of a sum of money equal to the reduction in value of the insured's property as a result of installation of the pole line.

2. The insured purchased property under an agreement to assume an existing mortgage and to pay the balance of the purchase price to the seller in cash. In accordance with this agreement, the purchaser obtains an owner's policy which shows the assumed mortgage as an exception from policy coverage. Later, the holder of the mortgage claims a default has occurred and commences an action to foreclose the mortgage. The insured owner, asserting that the mortgage holder has wrongfully declared a default, tenders the defense of the foreclosure action to his title insurer. Since the policy showed the mortgage as a lien on the insured's title, and excepted it from coverage by correct description and recording reference, the title insurer has no obligation to defend a lawsuit in which foreclosure of the mortgage is sought even if there is a genuine dispute regarding the existence of a default. Having excepted the mortgage from coverage, the insurer has thereby excepted from coverage all claims or disputes arising out of the existence of the mortgage.

Frequently, it is difficult to determine the precise legal theory on which a lawsuit against an insured is based. Therefore, it may not be clear whether the action relates to a matter within policy coverage. In such cases, the recent trend of appellate court decisions has been to hold that the doubt is to be resolved in favor of the insured, on the ground that an insurer's obligation to defend is broader than its duty to indemnify for loss.

The dollar amount of insurance stated in the policy is not reduced as a result of expenditures made by the insurer in providing a defense.

INTERESTS IN REAL ESTATE THAT MAY BE COVERED BY TITLE INSURANCE

The law permits many different interests in real estate to be created. Almost any interest legally created may be the subject of title insurance. Interests in real estate are of two general categories: those which represent ownership or the right of possession and those which represent security for the payment of a debt or, infrequently, performance of some other legal obligation. For the first category an owner's policy of title insurance is issued, and for the second category a lender's (or loan) policy is issued. Different policy forms are required because an owner and lender are exposed to somewhat different title risks. In the event of loss or impairment of title, the method of claim settlement and the elements of damage sustained by each may be different.

The ownership or possessory interests most commonly insured are fee simple estates, leasehold estates, and easements. A fee simple estate is thought of as the highest possible degree of ownership of land because it entitles the owner to the entire property (subject, of course, to encumbrances created by him or by a prior owner of the fee simple estate). The ownership is subject to no time limitation, the owner may freely dispose of that estate during his life, and at his death ownership of that estate passes to his heirs at law or to the beneficiaries named in his will.

A leasehold estate is a limited ownership interest in land, usually entitling the lessee (tenant) to exclusive possession of the leased property for a fixed term of years, and at the expiration of that term the right of possession "reverts" to the owner of the fee simple estate.

An easement is a limited right of possession or use, for a specifically defined purpose, of land owned by another. For example, an easement can be created for a specific purpose, such as a driveway or the installation and maintenance of a utility line, over a parcel of land for the benefit of a contiguous parcel. When the property benefitted by the easement is sold or mortgaged, the title insurance policy usually describes and insures both the fee simple estate in the benefitted property and the easement serving that property. Policies may be issued insuring the ownership of an easement only, usually to governmental units that have acquired easements for roads, long-distance electric transmission lines, trunk sewer lines, and so on.

In some states, the purchase of land may be financed by means of an installment payment real estate contract rather than by mortgage. In such instances, the partial ownership interest of the purchaser under the contract may be insured at the time the contract is entered into and the down payment is made.

Each of the real estate interests described may be insured within the format of the basic owner's policy. Since a failure of title, however, may cause a lessee to suffer special items of damage, some title insurers offer a specially prepared "owner's leasehold policy" which addresses itself more precisely to a lessee's title insurance needs. Other companies offer the special coverage required by lessees by attaching an endorsement to the basic owner's policy.

The most common security interest covered by title insurance is a lien on the land securing the repayment of principal and interest to a mortgage lender. Depending on the state in which the land is located, the lien is created by a document called a mortgage, a deed of trust, or a security deed. The lender's policy of title insurance insures that the lien has been validly created by the owner of the mortgaged land, that it is enforceable in the event of default, and that the lien has the position of priority of claim on the land as shown in the policy. The mortgaged property may be the fee simple estate, the fee simple estate together with an easement benefitting that estate, or a leasehold estate in the land described in the policy.

Usually the debt secured by the insured lien is a single promissory note, but the same policy form may be used to insure a lien created by a trust indenture to secure the repayment of a series of notes or bonds bought by different persons. It should be understood that a lender's policy only insures the validity and priority of the mortgage lien; it does not guarantee, in whole or in part, that the underlying debt will be repaid nor that the value of the mortgaged estate will be sufficient to cover the debt in the event of default, foreclosure, and sale.

In many states, title insurance is available in connection with transactions involving minerals in or under land where ownership of minerals has been separated from ownership of the remainder of the fee simple estate in that land. Where such separation has not occurred, a policy may be issued to insure the validity of a lease which authorizes the lessee to enter land to explore for and extract oil, gas, or other minerals.

Occasionally all or a substantial percentage of the stock of a corporation which holds title to land is purchased. Although title insurance is not generally available to insure title to personal property, such as shares of stock, the purchaser may desire some assurance regarding title to land owned by the corporation. This assurance may be provided, not by a policy naming the stock purchaser as the insured but by issuance of an owner's policy naming the corporation as the insured, dated concurrently with the transfer of the shares. Such a policy indirectly assures the stock purchaser that if the value of the corporation's land is reduced by title defects and encumbrances insured against, the corporation will receive compensation for the loss under the title policy. It should be borne in mind, however, that such policy does not insure against impairment of, or encumbrances on, the corporation's title if created or permitted by the corporation during its ownership and if not disclosed by the public records relating to land titles.

SCOPE OF COVERAGE; LIMITATIONS ON COVERAGE

While title insurance terminology is not uniform across the United States, in most areas title insurers offer both "standard coverage policies" and "extended coverage policies." In a preceding section, three basic categories of title risks were described: (1) the risk that the condition of "record title" is not as shown in the title insurance policy, (2) "hidden" off-record risks, and (3) "apparent" off-record risks.

The standard coverage policy

The form of policy, either owner's or lender's, which affords standard coverage title insurance provides protection against loss resulting from those title risks categorized as (1) and (2). Under the standard form of policy, insurance against "apparent" off-record risks is excepted from coverage, usually by a set of printed "exceptions from coverage" appearing in Schedule B of the policy form. While the content of the printed Schedule B exceptions varies from state to state, or even from company to company within a state, the following may be considered a fairly typical set of printed (or standard) exceptions:

A. Rights or claims of parties in possession, not shown by the public records.
B. Easements, or claims of easements, not shown by the public records.
C. Encroachments, overlaps, boundary line disputes, or other matters which would be disclosed by an accurate survey or inspection of the premises.
D. Any lien, or right to a lien, for services, labor, or material heretofore or hereafter furnished, imposed by law and not shown by the public records.

Item D relates to "mechanics' liens" or "labor and material liens" which in most states have priority dating from the commencement of work or of the furnishing of materials which improve the land, even though notice of the existence of such liens may not appear in the recording office until months after the commencement date.

The extended coverage policy

An extended coverage policy, either owner's or lender's, broadens the title insurance coverage by providing protection against "apparent" off-record risks (category (3), above). A survey of the land showing property boundaries and location of all improvements, usually supplemented by an inspection of the property made by a member of the title company's staff, is the basis on which some or all of the Schedule B printed or standard exceptions from coverage may be eliminated. The survey and inspection will indicate whether there are boundary or encroachment problems, a "stranger" in possession of the property, easements in actual use although not based on a recorded easement grant, violation of building restrictions or covenants, or recent construction or repair work which gives rise to unrecorded mechanics' liens on the land.

Although the broadly stated printed exceptions will be eliminated from Schedule B of an extended coverage policy, that schedule will contain typewritten exceptions relating to specifically described title defects or adverse claims which have been brought to light by means of the survey or inspection.

The issuance of an extended coverage policy clearly involves the assumption of additional risk by the title insurer and the provision of additional processing services by the insurer or its policy issuing agent. An additional premium is usually charged for the broader coverage. In most cases, the person applying for an extended coverage policy is also responsible for the cost of furnishing acceptable survey data to the title insurer or its issuing agent.

The insurer's obligation to provide for the defense of the insured in litigation based on a title risk insured against is the same under a standard coverage policy as under an extended coverage policy.

Exclusions from coverage

The exceptions from coverage which appear in Schedule B of a title insurance policy, either as printed or typewritten paragraphs, relate to defects, liens, and encumbrances which actually or potentially affect title to the particular land described in the policy. Policies of title insurance also contain "exclusions" from coverage, usually appearing as a "Schedule of Exclusions from Coverage" or as a paragraph in the "Conditions and Stipulations" of the policy. For example, the "American Land Title Association Owner's Policy—Form B—1970" includes the following section:

Schedule of exclusions from coverage

The following matters are expressly excluded from the coverage of this policy:

1. Any law, ordinance, or governmental regulation (including but not limited to building and zoning ordinances) restricting or regulating or prohibiting the occupancy, use, or enjoyment of the land, or regulating the character, dimensions, or location of any improvement now or hereafter erected on the land, or prohibiting a separation in ownership or a reduction in the dimensions or area of the land, or the effect of any violation of any such law, ordinance, or governmental regulation.
2. Rights of eminent domain or governmental rights of police power unless notice of the exercise of such rights appears in the public records at date of policy.
3. Defects, liens, encumbrances, adverse claims, or other matters (a) created, suffered, assumed, or agreed to by the insured claimant; (b) not known to the company and not shown by the public records but known to the insured claimant either at date of policy or at the date such claimant acquired an estate or interest insured by this policy and not disclosed in writing by the insured claimant to the company prior to the date such insured claimant became an in-

sured hereunder; *(c)* resulting in no loss or damage to the insured claimant; *(d)* attaching or created subsequent to date of policy; or *(e)* resulting in loss or damage which would not have been sustained if the insured claimant had paid value for the estate or interest insured by this policy.

Note that item 1 relates to governmental actions controlling use and subdivision of real estate which are generally applicable to every parcel of land within the particular jurisdiction, that is, item 1 (and also item 2) exclude from coverage those limitations on ownership and use affecting all land, imposed by the general law of the state, and which are not unique to the particular parcel of land described in the policy. Item 3 excludes from coverage: (1) losses which result from matters within the control or knowledge of the insured, and (2) certain occurrences which are simply not within the intended scope of the insurance contract and for which an insured would not reasonably expect coverage.

Endorsements

Any form of title insurance policy—owner's or lender's, standard coverage or extended coverage—may be modified by endorsement. Many endorsements are rather routinely requested and issued in cases involving a particular transaction category for which they are designed. Infrequently, a transaction may incorporate a unique title requirement, and in such cases the investor or his legal counsel may negotiate with the title underwriter the terms of a specially drafted endorsement to provide the desired additional title insurance coverage. The laws or insurance regulations of a particular state may limit the availability of endorsement coverages.

Regarding title insurance policy forms generally, a significant degree of national standardization has developed under the auspices of the American Land Title Association, the membership of which is comprised of title insurance underwriters, title insurance agents, and abstractors. In a few states, policy forms developed by the state association of title companies are used predominantly, although ALTA policy forms may also be available on request in these areas.

TERM OF THE POLICY; CONTINUATION OF COVERAGE

A title insurance policy does not expire as a result of the passage of time. A single premium is payable at the time of issuance of the policy and the coverage continues for as long as the insured is exposed to the possibility of a monetary loss resulting from a title defect which is insured against by the policy. Regarding an insured owner, the insurance protection exists as long as title to the insured interest is retained by the insured. Even after sale of that interest, the insured is protected as long as the insured is subject to liability based on a matter within policy coverage because of covenants of warranty given when the conveyance of the insured interest was made.

A lender's policy insures the validity and priority of the lien of a mortgage and when the debt secured by the mortgage is paid in full the lender's policy expires since there is no longer a possibility that the insured can sustain a loss by reason of a defect in the title or in the lien insured. If, however, the insured lender acquires title to the mortgaged land through foreclosure or by deed given in lieu of foreclosure, the policy continues in force during the period of the insured lender's ownership and, further, coverage continues for so long as the insured lender holds a new purchase money mortgage given in connection with the lender's resale after foreclosure. By the terms of the lender's policy, the title insurance protection automatically follows the lawful ownership of the debt secured by the insured mortgage lien. The validity of an assignment, however, is not insured unless it is shown in Schedule A of a loan policy or in an assignment endorsement.

Under either an owner's or lender's policy, if the insured is an individual, the benefits of the policy enure to those who succeed to the insured's ownership at the death of the insured. If the insured is a corporation or a trustee, policy coverage continues in favor of those who become successors of the insured by operation of law as, for example, by merger of one corporation into another or by the appointment of a successor trustee. Upon sale of the interest insured under an owner's policy, the coverage of the policy is not assignable to the purchaser.

A title insurance policy provides no protection with respect to actions or events which affect the title but which first occur after the date of the policy. Thus, even though the policy benefits may enure to certain successors of the named insured, the policy coverage is not brought forward to a later date but is limited to the coverage in force as of the date of the policy. If the insured (or the successor of an insured) desires coverage to be updated and the amount of insurance to be increased because of an increase in value due to inflation or construction of improvements, a new policy may be requested. Although involving a separate transaction and a new insurance contract, such a "renewal policy" will, in most areas, be issued for a premium which is much less than the premium charged for original coverage in the same amount.

THE TITLE INSURANCE COMMITMENT

After application is made for title insurance, the first title insurance document received by the applicant and other interested persons is one which summarizes the underwriter's evaluation of title based on the search and examination of title. In a few areas, this document is called a *preliminary report* or *preliminary commitment*. The "American Land Title Association Commitment for Title Insurance—1966" is the most widely used and accepted form. No matter how denominated, the function of this form is to begin the sale or loan "closing" process.

In addition to summarizing the condition of title, the commitment provides a correct legal description of the land involved, identifies the specific form of policy or policies the insurer is prepared to issue, the amount of insurance requested, the standard and special exceptions which will appear in the policy or policies (unless removed before closing) and, in most localities, a brief description of the legal instruments required to create the estate or interest to be insured. In the case of the ALTA Commitment for Title Insurance, the terms and limits of the underwriter's commitment to insure, and the extent of insurance protection afforded if the commitment is relied on to the detriment of a proposed purchaser or mortgage lender, are spelled out in the Commitment.

With the Commitment in hand, the parties to the proposed transaction may proceed to prepare for the "closing" or "settlement." The Commitment provides information from which it can be determined whether the conditions of the underlying sale or lease agreement, or mortgage loan commitment, can be fulfilled. At this stage, the proposed insured will also be determining whether to request endorsements which will provide additional title insurance coverage. The closing agent (an attorney, an escrow company, or an escrow department of a title company or bank) is responsible for coordination among the parties, compliance with all closing instructions received from the parties, proper handling of all legal documents and funds involved in consummating the transaction, and, finally, obtaining a title insurance policy for each party to be insured, complying in form and content with the previously established requirements of the insured.

THE AMOUNT OF INSURANCE; THE COST OF TITLE INSURANCE

An owner's policy of title insurance covering the fee simple estate is ordinarily issued in an amount equal to the value of that estate, which in most instances will be determined by the purchase price. If unimproved land is purchased but immediate construction of improvements is contemplated, the policy may be issued in an amount that will reflect the value of the land and the improvements when construction is completed. An owner's policy insuring an easement only is usually issued in an amount equal to the price paid for the easement grant.

It is extremely difficult to establish a formula for determining the amount in which a leasehold estate should be insured. Some factors to be considered are the length of the lease term, the presence or absence of an obligation on the part of the lessee to construct improvements, and the cost of relocating the business operation if the lease fails and the lessee is ousted from the leased premises. In premium rate filings, some title insurance companies provide a formula as a basic guideline to the minimum amount of leasehold insurance to be issued. By and large, the lessee or his legal counsel will determine the amount of title insurance that will provide adequate financial protection.

Currently, many title insurance companies attach to an owner's policy, without additional charge, an "inflation endorsement" which provides for periodic increases in the amount of insurance, usually equal to increases shown by some defined index which measures the rate of inflation, but with a stated ceiling. In many cases, the ceiling is an amount equal to 150 percent of the original face amount of the owner's policy.

A lender's policy of title insurance is customarily issued in an amount equal to the original principal amount of the mortgage debt. It is possible, of course, that if the mortgage lien is lost or impaired for any reason, the lender's monetary loss could exceed the original principal amount of the debt by reason of the accumulation of unpaid interest or by reason of advances made by the lender to pay taxes or fire insurance premium in order to preserve the security. Some lenders, therefore, request issuance of a lender's policy in amount equal to the original principal amount of the debt plus 10 percent, or some other specified percentage.

If a mortgage loan is sold and assigned, the assignee may desire an updated lender's policy (or an assignment endorsement) in an amount equal to the then unpaid balance of the mortgage debt.

In most instances, payments made under the policy by the insurer to the insured or to a third-party claimant reduce the face amount of the policy by the amount(s) so paid. As indicated earlier, however, payments by the insurer to provide for defense of the insured in litigation do not reduce the amount of insurance in force.

The cost of title insurance varies widely among the states because in different areas different means are employed to produce a policy. As explained, title insurance is comprised of three basic components: (1) the search, which identifies all title documents to be considered; (2) the examination, which involves the evaluation of those documents from a legal and underwriting perspective; and (3) the assumption by the title insurance company of a contractual insurance liability.

In most metropolitan areas, and probably in a majority of all jurisdictions, the charge for these components is a single premium, usually referred to as an "all-inclusive rate." Under that practice a premium rate schedule will indicate the total charge applicable to the amount of insurance requested. This approach does not reflect the fact that the search and examination functions are more difficult and time consuming in some cases than in others. The result is an averaging of the cost of production, with the objective of achieving an adequate profit on the entire book of business written, and complete predictability regarding the cost of a policy in a stated amount.

At the other extreme, a separate charge is made for each component, that is, the search is in the form of an abstract of title purchased from an abstractor, the title is examined and certified by a practicing attorney who will charge a fee for this service and for handling the closing, and title insurance is purchased from a title insurance company at a flat rate per thousand dollars of coverage. The cost of the title package is unpredictable because the charges for the first two components are likely to be related to the length of the chain of title and degree of complexity of the examination of the particular title.

As a very general observation, in the purchase of a residential property of modest value, the total cost of the three separately priced components is likely to exceed the single charge computed as an all-inclusive rate applicable to the same amount of title insurance.

AVAILABILITY OF TITLE INSURANCE

Title insurance is available in every state of the United States, except Iowa, and in most territories and possessions of the United States. A very small volume of title insurance is written in Great Britain and Mexico. The six or eight largest title insurance companies in the United States are national companies. The smaller insurers typically limit their operations to one state or to a few states within a single region of the country.

While most title insurance is issued by commercial title insurance companies, in a few states title insurance may be obtained from a lawyers' title guaranty fund, an association of practicing attorneys usually organized as a business trust. Individual attorney-members are authorized to issue policies in the name of the fund. Such policies are similar in form and scope of coverage to those issued by commercial title insurers.

In a number of states, particularly in the eastern section of the United States, practicing attorneys perform the search and examination function, on the basis of which they issue certifications of title. In many cases, the attorney has an arrangement with a commercial title insurer under which the attorney is authorized to issue the insurer's policy based on the attorney's certification of title. In other cases, the attorney will not issue the policy but instead will forward the certification of title, and perhaps supplemental information, to a branch office of a title insurance company with a request for issuance of the appropriate policy. Companies operating in the latter mode maintain a list of "approved attorneys" whose certifications of title will be relied on for the purpose of issuing title insurance.

Editor's note

As the text of this Chapter will indicate, title insurance is based primarily on state law. There is great diversity in real estate law, custom, and title practices among the states. Accordingly, almost any general statement made about title insurance forms, procedures, and coverage may be subject to some qualification, usually not of a substantial nature, if applied to a particular jurisdiction. The author cautions that this explanation of title insurance is necessarily a general treatment of the subject and may not be accurate in every detail as a reflection of the title insurance business in every part of the United States.

SECTION **V**

PACKAGING EXPOSURES
INTO ONE POLICY

CHAPTER 19

ROUNDING OUT
THE INSURANCE PROGRAM

EXCESS LIABILITY COVERAGE
Use of the excess
The unlimited magnitude of liability
exposure

THE COMMERCIAL UMBRELLA
POLICY
History of the umbrella
Purpose of the umbrella
Primary coverage required by
umbrella underwriters
Limits of liability required on
underlying policies
Self-insured retention
Limits of liability
The insuring agreement

Exclusions
Conditions
Professional umbrella coverage

THE DIFFERENCE IN CONDITIONS
POLICY
What can be covered
Perils covered
The deductible
Important coverages afforded
Co-insurance
Other insurance provisions
Indirect losses
Filling in the gap: An example
Conclusions and summary

George B. Flanigan, Ph.D., CPCU
Associate Professor
University of North Carolina at Greensboro
Greensboro, North Carolina

George B. Flanigan is Professor, Department of Business Administration, the University of North Carolina at Greensboro. He is also Associate Director of the Center for Applied Research at the University. Dr. Flanigan took his undergraduate degree at the University of Illinois—Chicago Circle, and his doctorate from the University of Iowa. He received his CPCU designation in 1979. Dr. Flanigan does consulting in cash flow forecasting, valuation, and risk and insurance management. He has published in the *Journal of Risk and Insurance*, the *CPCU Journal*, the *CLU Journal*, and the *Insurance Law Journal*.

Richard Turner, CPCU
Regional Director
Cincinnati Insurance Company
Columbia, South Carolina

Richard Turner is Regional Director of Cincinnati Insurance Company. Mr. Turner graduated from the University of South Carolina in 1967, spent five years with St. Paul Insurance Companies, serving as field representative and field supervisor in Birmingham, Alabama, and, later in Nashville, Tennessee. In 1972 Mr. Turner joined Cincinnati Insurance Company as a state agent in Nashville, Tennessee, and in 1974 was transferred to South Carolina to "open the state" for the company. In 1978 Mr. Turner was promoted to Regional Director for the company. Mr. Turner received a general certificate of insurance from the American Institute of Property and Casualty Underwriters in 1969, CPCU designation in 1974, became President of the Tennessee Insurance Association in 1971, and was selected as Insurance Company Representative of the Year in 1978 by the Independent Insurance Agents of South Carolina. Mr. Turner is presently co-authoring a textbook for the American Institute and also serves as instructor in both the CPCU Program and the educational program for the Independent Insurance Agents of South Carolina.

The chapter is about treatment of potentially catastrophic loss exposures, such as floods, massive court judgments, or major burglaries. Excess liability insurance, umbrella liability insurance, and the Difference in Conditions Policy are all techniques the insurance buyer can employ to broaden, supplement, and increase his basic insurance coverages in order to better protect against these and other potentially catastrophic losses.

EXCESS LIABILITY COVERAGE

In many instances, an insurer will wish to limit its exposure to loss by writing relatively low limits of liability on general liability contracts. Sometimes this is explained by a reinsurance treaty where the reinsurer may be unwilling to exceed high limits on a given class of business. The insurer could also have certain classes of business risks excluded in its reinsurance treaties; or it may want to limit the dollar amount of exposure to a low level for such classes of risks. Possibly the insurer would limit its dollar exposure simply to protect its reinsurer from a potentially large loss and thus protect the insurer/reinsurer business relationship.

When these limits do not fit the realistic needs of a business, it becomes necessary to obtain a policy with limits in excess of the primary policy. The principal purpose of excess liability insurance is to increase the limits of liability to the level needed by a particular business.

The excess policy is used on the "hard to place" account that has a catastrophic exposure potential normal markets will not absorb. When a business encounters this problem, a market to "layer the coverage" up to the desired limits must be sought. These coverages often are found in specialty insurance markets and at a surcharged rate. When dealing in the specialty insurance market, it is wise to investigate the excess insurer. The buyer will be dealing with unknown or unfamiliar companies and should be satisfied that they are capable of paying losses should they occur.

The basic excess liability policy is a "following form" contract. Excess liability insurance policies track the primary insurance in coverage, conditions, definitions, and exclusions. The excess carrier relies on the primary carrier for coverage interpretations. The excess contract will not pick up coverages that are left out of the primary policy. It is and should be used as a means of layering limits of liability to the level needed by the insured.

The basic excess policy can be used in general liability, automobile liability, and employers' liability. It can even be used to add a layer of liability to an umbrella contract. To illustrate the use of the excess liability policy, several cases follow:

1. A business involved a forestry operation that cut trees, operated a saw mill, and ran a trucking firm. The business transported the wood from the forest to the wholesaler. It needed a Comprehensive General Liability Policy and a commercial auto policy with limits high enough to qualify for a commercial umbrella policy.

The business had difficulty finding insurance because the truck fleet included 44 tractor trailer units, some of them long haul. The business first contacted a primary umbrella company to see what primary limits of liability would be required for writing the umbrella. It was ascertained that limits of $500,000/$500,000 Bodily Injury, $100,000/$100,000 Property Damage on the comprehensive general liability, and $500,000/$500,000 Bodily Injury, and $500,000 Property Damage on the fleet were necessary.

The business acquired the Comprehensive General Liability Policy with an insurer with no problem; however, the company would not write the commercial auto policy. The agent went to the specialty market and layered the coverage with three companies. Company A wrote the primary policy with limits of $15,000/$30,000 Bodily Injury and $5,000 Property Damage. Company B agreed to the second layer with limits of $85,000/$270,000 Bodily Injury and $95,000 Property Damage in excess of Company A. This brought the limits up to $100,000/$300,000 Bodily Injury and $100,000 Property Damage. Company C agreed to write limits of $400,000/$200,000 Bodily Injury and $400,000 Property Damage in excess of Company A and Company B. This provided the limits needed for the risk.

Company	Bodily injury	Property damage
A	$ 15,000/$ 30,000	$ 5,000
B	85,000/ 270,000	95,000
C	400,000/ 200,000	400,000
Totals	$500,000/$500,000	$500,000

Company A was the primary insurer and agreed to pay all claims up to the $15,000/$30,000 Bodily Injury and $5,000 Property Damage limits. Company B's excess policy would pay only when the claim exceeded the limits under Company A's policy. Company C's policy would only respond after Company A and B's limits were exhausted.

The limits on the fleet policy were layered to meet the underlying requirements for the umbrella. By the use of the straight excess contract, the umbrella requirements were completely satisfied and a $3,000,000 umbrella policy was issued by the umbrella carrier.

2. A gasoline and oil distributor operated in only one county, used small tank trucks for delivery, and had the following insurance problem. The insurer would write the account, but it would be on two different policies rather than one, due to the way the insurer's reinsurance program was set up. The insurer had a reinsurance treaty that excluded this class of risk because of its "catastrophe loss potential." However, the company also had an excess liability department with a separate reinsurance treaty that included gasoline and oil dealers.

The company solved the problem by issuing a policy with limits of $25,000/$50,000 Bodily Injury and $25,000 Property Damage, and then the excess department issued a policy for the excess above those limits up to $1,000,000 as a combined single limit of liability. In this case, the insurer made use of an excess liability policy to satisfy the needs of its customers.

Use of the excess

The excess policy creates layers of coverage for each insurer involved. Each insurer waits to respond until the layer immediately under it has been exhausted. Rating is a matter of using the standard rates for the coverages involved and surcharging for hazardous exposures the underwriter feels exist. Often the excess policy is the only way to provide necessary liability limits.

The unlimited magnitude of the liability exposure

In recent years juries which hold businesses responsible for damages and injuries arising out of their products or activities have demonstrated an inclination to require very large payments to injured parties. Recently three cases have received a great deal of publicity. One is the now infamous 1973 Ford Pinto case (which allegedly caused deaths to occur when the gas tank exploded on collision), the Hooker Chemical Company's problem with the Love Canal (where the gradual pollution from seepage over the years required the evacuation of entire neighborhoods), and perhaps the most publicized of all, the Three Mile Island situation (which caused temporary dislocation and wage loss for thousands). The long-term damages of all of these cases are unknown.

There is less publicity for most commercial liability judgments, but they are frequent and in many cases serious. An Illinois jury recently awarded a Versailles, Illinois, farmer $15.7 million when he was seriously burned by an International Harvestor tractor that "geysered" fuel when it overheated. A Moose Lake, Minnesota, boy was awarded $3.39 million because he was paralyzed when struck by a baseball thrown by a baseball pitching machine. The award was against the manufacturer, the distributor, and the retailer of the machine.

A different sort of case occurred in California recently. A new store was about to open when it was totally destroyed by fire. The store's fire insurance company paid the loss then sued (subrogated against) the contractor who installed the sprinkler system that apparently malfunctioned and was awarded $1.2 million. In Indianapolis, Indiana, sparks from a welder's torch ignited the combustible contents of a building and ultimately the entire building was destroyed. Similarly, in a Tennessee case, a contractor erred in installing a heating system. In both cases the contractor was held responsible for the entire damage to the building and its contents.

The instances mentioned serve to emphasize the potentially unlimited magnitude of liability exposures. It can reasonably be said that "you can't have too much liability insurance."

THE COMMERCIAL UMBRELLA POLICY

The umbrella liability policy can provide an insured with high limits of liability and extremely broad coverage. It can serve as primary coverage for uninsured exposures over a self-insured retention. In the climate of today's high court awards in the liability area, the umbrella policy is a "must."

History of the umbrella

Lloyd's of London was a market for "following form" excess coverages for years before it developed the first true umbrella policy in the late 1950s. The original Lloyd's umbrella policy was extremely broad with very few exclusions. Several U.S. companies followed Lloyd's and developed their own umbrella policy. This new line of liability coverage soon became unprofitable, the market became restricted, and many losses incurred that had not been anticipated by the underwriters. Lloyd's and the domestic companies began adding exclusions to limit their liability. Today's commercial umbrella policy evolved.

Purpose of the umbrella

The umbrella is designed to give the insured needed high limits of liability protection on a very broad coverage form, and in so doing, give protection for uninsured primary exposures. As the name implies, the umbrella covers over and above the existence of any primary liability insurance contract. It extends the limits on the primary policies by the amount of the limits on the umbrella policy. Although there is no standard umbrella form, the remainder of this chapter will discuss a "typical" umbrella policy.

Primary coverage required by umbrella underwriters

Umbrella underwriters require a warranty that certain policies are in effect and will be maintained for certain underlying exposures. Underlying (or primary) policies usually required are:

1. Comprehensive General Liability Policy including personal injury, contractual liability, and products and completed operations.
2. Comprehensive Auto Liability Policy.
3. Employers' liability.
4. Any other exposures specifically relating to a particular insured such as aircraft liability, watercraft liability, and professional liability.

If the underlying policy excludes the products or completed operations hazard, the umbrella can still be written, but it will be endorsed to exclude this hazard.

A possible exception is personal injury coverage. If the underlying general liability policy does not cover personal injury liability, the underwriter may elect to either exclude this exposure or leave it on the umbrella according to how great the exposure may be.

Limits of liability required on underlying policies

The required underlying limits of liability vary from insurer to insurer on different classes of business. Minimum limits are usually $300,000 Bodily Injury and $50,000 Property Damage on the primary general liability policy and $100,000/$300,000 Bodily Injury and $50,000 Property Damage on commercial auto, although many umbrella markets are requiring higher primary limits. The requirement for employers' liability is usually the statutory limit in the insured's state workers' compensation law, usually $100,000.

Because of the tremendous catastrophe loss potential in certain types of liability exposures, high minimum limits on the underlying policies may be required. For instance, to include aviation liability for owned aircraft under the umbrella contract, it is not uncommon to require $1,000,000 per passenger seat of primary coverage. Medical malpractice is another area where high primary limits may also be required. High limits for primary coverage are generally required for a trucking risk hauling hazardous materials such as gasoline or volatile or dangerous chemicals.

Self-insured retention

The typical umbrella policy contains a "self-insured retention" which operates similar to a deductible. The common self-insured retention in most umbrella policies is set at $10,000, although on the larger accounts it may be significantly increased. This is an area of coverage that must be closely analyzed by the insured because of the defense coverage afforded in the umbrella. In some umbrellas, the retention is deducted from a court judgment or claim settlement, but "first-dollar" defense cost coverage is afforded. In others, defense cost is not covered. For example, in a case where personal injury liability was not covered under the primary general liability policy but was covered under the umbrella, a lawsuit was filed for defamation of character (an example of personal injury). The court awarded the plaintiff $6,000 and the cost to defend the insured was $2,000. If the $10,000 self-insured retention included "first-dollar" defense cost, the insured would only suffer the $6,000 loss (his defense cost would be fully covered but the $10,000 self-insured retention applies to the award). If defense cost was not included, the insured would suffer the full $8,000 of award and costs.

Limits of liability

The minimum limit of liability under the typical umbrella coverage is $1 million. Larger accounts may need up to a $50 million to $100 million policy. Today's multi-million-dollar judgments should serve to induce the consideration of limits in excess of the typical minimum.

The insuring agreement

A typical umbrella policy's insuring agreement is extremely broad, granting coverage for almost any personal injury or property damage liability claim. (It is, therefore, important to clearly understand the terms and exclusions found later in the policy.) Moreover, the insuring agreement clearly states that regardless of how many named insureds are covered under the policy or how many are actually named in a suit, the limits of the policy are those specifically stated on the declarations page of the policy.

The definition of who is insured grants coverage to the named insured in the declarations page and also any unnamed subsidiaries or organizations over which the named insured assumes active management. The "insured" includes directors, officers, or stockholders of the named insured while acting within the scope of duties for the named insured, as well as organizations or employees acting within the scope of their duties. The policy also provides coverage for any person or organization to whom the named insured is obligated by virtue of a written contract. Always check the definition of named insured since each umbrella policy may differ.

The definition of underlying limits is vital and has great significance to the umbrella concept. It specifically states that all underlying limits set forth in the policy are deemed applicable regardless of any denial of coverage that the underlying insurer may assert (for example, because of the insured's failure to comply with policy conditions) or the inability of the underlying insurer to pay by reason of bankruptcy or insolvency. This wording works like a warranty in the policy stating that the umbrella will never pay until the underlying limits are exhausted whether or not the underlying insurer actually responds to the claim.

Exclusions

Each exclusion in the umbrella policy is important because of the broad insuring agreement. Major exclusions are:

a. Any obligation under the workers' compensation law is specifically excluded. Excess coverage is afforded over the employer's liability section of the workers' compensation policy but not over the statutory workers' compensation benefits.

b. Liability arising out of injury of one of the employees by another employee in the course of their employment.

c. Owned aircraft and aircraft chartered without a crew. This coverage can be assumed by endorsement when the exposure is adequately covered on a primary policy. This exclusion does not apply to nonowned aircraft. Coverage would apply for aviation liability for the licensed pilot who occasionally borrows an aircraft. This exclusion also excludes owned watercraft over 50 feet in length. Watercraft liability for boats less than 50 feet in length and nonowned watercraft of any length are covered. Owned watercraft over 50 feet in length may be covered by endorsement.

d. An advertising liability exclusion appears in all umbrella policies. The insurance buyer should review it to determine exactly what is excluded since it may vary greatly from contract to contract.

e. Product recall. This deletes coverage for losses sustained if the insured has to withdraw his product from the market. This is a standard exclusion in nearly all general liability as well as umbrella policies.

f. Property damage to the insured's own property, or the insured's own product.

g. War.

h. Loss of use of property that has not been physically injured is excluded if the loss of use is caused by delay or lack of performance of a contract by the insured. Also excluded is any loss of use caused by failure of performance of the insured's product to the extent warranted by an insured.

There are two additional exclusions that are of such importance that they are not listed in the exclusions section of the policy but are displayed on a separate page. They are found in most umbrella policies and usually cannot be deleted—the nuclear energy liability exclusion and the exclusion for pollution.

Conditions

Another section of the umbrella policy that requires careful scrutiny by the insurance buyer is the policy conditions section. Like many other areas of the umbrella, this section can vary widely from insurer to insurer but the typical umbrella policy will contain most of the following conditions:

Notice of occurrence. This condition requires the insured to give written notice to the insurer of any claims whenever it appears that a judgment or settlement may involve payment under the umbrella policy. Further, it requires the insured to forward all information concerning the claim as well as all documents and investigation reports. This condition enables the insurer to keep track of the claim in the event that it may become involved at a later date.

Appeals. This gives the umbrella insurer the right to appeal a judgment when the underlying insurer has elected not to appeal and the judgment has exceeded the underlying limits or the self-insured retention. If an appeal is made, the umbrella insurer is responsible for all associated cost and interest on the judgment.

Maintenance of underlying insurance. This condition requires that the underlying policies described in the declarations section, including renewals or replacements, be maintained in full effect during the effective period of the umbrella policy. If the underlying limits are not maintained, the umbrella will still only respond after the underlying limits are exhausted.

Cancellation. This provision gives the company the right to cancel the policy with 30 days' written notice to the named insured.

Professional umbrella coverage

The umbrella policy does not exclude professional liability. It is automatically picked up under the umbrella insuring agreements. Umbrella underwriters, however, will not accept professional coverage over a $10,000 self-insured retention. This exposure must be covered by underlying policies or the umbrella underwriter will specifically exclude professional liability.

The most common way to cover the professional exposure is on a "following form" or excess type coverage. In other words, when the professional liability is covered under an umbrella policy, the professional coverage will track the wording of the underlying policy. For instance, if the primary policy is on a claims-made basis, the professional coverage in the umbrella policy will also be on a claims-made basis. On the other hand, if the primary policy is on an occurrence basis, the umbrella policy will be on an occurrence basis.

Underlying limits of liability required for the umbrella will vary from underwriter to underwriter and from one professional class to another. With the prevalence of high court awards in the professional liability area, underwriters are requiring higher primary limits of liability. Rating of the professional portion of the umbrella policy is not based on a percentage of the primary premium as in the other coverages. The premium charged is usually a flat rate with a minimum premium charge for the exposure.

THE DIFFERENCE IN CONDITIONS POLICY

The Difference in Conditions Policy is a relative newcomer to the insurance marketplace. Buying this policy can be difficult. There are few markets that provide this broad property contract. However, it is a valuable tool and one that the alert Risk Manager and insurance buyer can use to adequately cover existing exposures.

There is no standard Difference in Conditions Policy. Underwriters engaging in this market use very similar forms. Some are individually written on a manuscript basis to tailor coverage to fit the needs of a specific risk.

The purpose of the Difference in Conditions Policy is to protect the insured from losses which are not covered under basic property coverage. It provides coverage for the catastrophic loss. It extends the "perils covered." It is not intended to provide excess coverage over inadequate limits, although on occasion it can be tailored to provide excess coverage.

What can be covered

The policy covers the same exposures insured under a basic property insurance program—real and personal property, improvements to real property, property in transit, and loss of income. Coverage is also included for personal property in the care, custody, and control of the insured if the insured is legally liable and has agreed to provide coverage.

Certain types of property are specifically excluded from coverage either because of high loss frequency or because 100 percent insurance to value is easily available on the property in normal markets. These are:

1. Aircraft, watercraft, vehicles licensed or designed for highway use.
2. Animals, growing plants, standing timber, growing crops, trees, shrubs, or lawns.
3. Currency, money, notes, postage, stamps, securities, evidence of debt, letters of credit, railroad, or other tickets.
4. Jewelry, watches, pearls, precious and semiprecious stones, gold, silver, platinum, other precious metals or their alloys, bullion, furs and articles trimmed with fur, except the inclusion does not apply to industrial diamonds or precious metals or their alloys used for industrial purposes.
5. Property sold by the insured under conditional sale, trust agreement, installment payment, or other deferred payment plan, after delivery to customers.
6. Architect fees, cost of excavations, grading and filling, underground flues, pipes, wiring (but not wiring in conduit), drains, brick or stone or concrete foundations, piers, or other supports below the undersurface of the lowest basement floor, land values.
7. Property eligible for insurance coverage in Nuclear Energy Property Insurance Association or Mutual Atomic Energy Reinsurance Pool.
8. Data processing equipment and media (meaning all forms of converted data, program or instruction vehicles employed in the insured's data processing operations).

Perils covered

The Difference in Conditions Policy is written on an all-risks basis. This does not increase the limit of liability written on basic forms but fills in gaps on an all-risks basis.

Not all perils, or causes of loss are covered, however. Excluded perils are:

1. The perils of fire and lightning as in a Standard Fire Insurance Policy.
2. The perils of windstorm, hail, explosion, riot, riot attending a strike, civil commotion, aircraft, vehicles, and smoke as in an Extended Coverage Endorsement.
3. The perils of vandalism and malicious mischief as in a Vandalism and Malicious Mischief Endorsement.
4. The peril of sprinkler leakage as in a Sprinkler Leakage Endorsement.

It should be noted that the exclusions apply whether or not insurance for these perils is being maintained at the time of the loss.

Clearly the intent of the Difference in Conditions Policy is that the basic perils of fire, extended coverage, vandalism, and sprinkler leakage be covered under standard policies.

Two more excluded perils also deserve special mention.:

1. Earthquake, landslide, subsidence, or other earth movement.
2. Flood—meaning "waves, tide or tidal water, and the rising (including the overflowing or breakage of boundaries) of lakes, ponds, reservoirs, rivers, harbors, streams, or similar bodies of water whether wind driven or not."

Both earthquake and flood are specifically excluded from coverage, but can be included for an additional charge. In the policy declarations page there is a block for a limit and deductible for each of these perils. If the underwriter agrees to write these perils, a limit and deductible amount may be set that is different from the other amounts or limits. If a risk is located in a flood or earthquake prone area, this coverage may be difficult for the buyer to obtain.

Employee dishonesty is excluded in the typical Difference in Conditions Policy, as well as steam boiler explosion, since these coverages are usually easily obtainable through regular markets. The usual exclusions relating to mechanical breakdown, wear and tear, and other "maintenance" types of loss are also excluded. War and nuclear losses are too catastrophic to be covered, although the nuclear peril can sometimes be added by endorsement.

The deductible

The policy is intended to cover losses the insured may sustain. Consequently, the deductible is usually high and can vary from one thousand to hundreds of thousands of dollars. The high deductible, used to eliminate the frequent but still cover the severe loss, is usually negotiated between the buyer and the insurer in an attempt to fit the needs of the insured.

Important coverages afforded

Some very important perils that are not covered by the basic property policy can be picked up. Both the flood peril and earthquake peril can be covered. Normally a high deductible will be used allowing the flood deductible to be covered through the federal government's flood program.

Property in transit may be covered in the insuring agreement for high limits of liability.

Burglary is covered. Often a business has a major burglary exposure and the burglary limit needed may not be available through normal markets or the rates may be high for the limits desired. This policy can cover the catastrophe burglary exposure at a lower rate because of the high deductible and would suit and needs of the type of business that attracts the professional criminal (such as a large firearms' dealer or stereo wholesaler).

Off-premises water damage is covered, such as a break in a city water main resulting in water damage to the insured premises. This is excluded under a basic property form, but would be covered by this policy.

Building collapse, excluded under the fire policy with extended coverage, could be covered by the Difference in Conditions Policy. During the winter of 1979, a severe ice storm hit a southern city. Many buildings collapsed. This policy could have covered these losses. The policy is broad—in fact, it is "all-risks" in nature.

Co-insurance

One of the most important features of the Difference in Conditions contract is that there is no requirement that the insured carry insurance to value. The basic property policy will be written with either 80 percent, 90 percent, 100 percent insurance to value, either actual cash value or replacement cost. This gives the insured adequate coverage for the losses that are normally insured. To save on premiums the insured may want to limit the amount of insurance for all-risks coverage. There are also situations where the maximum probable loss from the all-risks perils is not nearly as great as from the basic perils.

For example, consider a high-rise motel located in an area subject to surface flooding. The value of the structure is $3 million. The buyer can cover the $3 million for fire and special extended coverage under a basic policy. But the insured is concerned with the flood exposure excluded under basic policies. If the motel is not in an approved flood zone (not eligible for the Federal Flood Insurance program), the only option is the Difference in Conditions Policy.

Other insurance provisions

An important feature of the Difference in Conditions Policy is the "other insurance" clause. The typical "other insurance" clause excludes coverage on any loss for which other coverage is available through the basic property policies. It also states that the policy will not be considered as contributing insurance. However, the clause does have a feature that allows coverage on an excess basis, allowing primary coverage (if it is available) on a limited basis. The Difference in Conditions Policy will respond as an excess coverage, after the primary limits are exhausted.

Indirect losses

Usually the policy is written to cover direct damage exposures, but it can also cover the indirect loss. When basic coverage is written on indirect losses, the Difference in Conditions Policy can be used to fill in the gaps, such as picking up the all-risks coverage on earnings, loss of rents, and other indirect losses.

Filling in the gap: An example

Captain Kidd Villas, a newly constructed apartment complex located on a sea island in a southern state, was highly susceptible to loss from a hurricane or flooding accompanying a hurricane. The permanent mortgagee required full protection from these exposures.

The complex was insured under a commercial package policy with the special extended coverage endorsement attached giving all-risks coverage. However, the all-risks contract contained some serious gaps in coverage that made it inadequate. First, as is true in most seacoast states, windstorm and hail coverage are excluded from the extended coverage endorsement when the risk is located in the beach area. Second, flood is not covered under the special extended coverage endorsement form. Third, this state was also in an active earthquake zone. Although there had not been a serious earthquake since 1890, earthquakes and tremors were recorded on a regular basis.

Recognizing these limitations, the insurance agent went to the state Windstorm and Hail Underwriting Association (a pool of companies set up to handle the exposures of hurricane losses—most coastal states have these pools which set a maximum amount they will write on a particular class of risk) and obtained coverage up to $200,000 per building. He then obtained from the Federal Flood Insurance program $250,000 per building for flood exposure.

Having accomplished the above, the agent was able to obtain a Difference in Conditions Policy to fill in the gap and obtain the rest of the coverage needed to satisfy the mortgagee. What in fact the agent was seeking was flood, wind coverage, and earthquake insurance in excess of the limits available through the pool's catastrophe insurance—with large deductibles.

The Difference in Conditions Policy can serve as a way to fill the gaps in almost any business's property contract; it can be tailored to fit the needs of almost any type of risk and fill unprotected gaps in basic insurance policies.

Conclusions and summary

Both property and legal liability exposures can result in catastrophic losses. In some cases, losses can originate from perils not insured under existing policies (flood for example) or from judgments rendered in court. Both can be covered by insurance.

Use of the "excess" insurance products examined in this chapter, in many cases requires the use of specialty markets. The excess coverage for property is the DIC or Difference in Conditions Policy. Markets are hard to find, but not impossible. In most cases, the Difference in Conditions Policy will pick up additional perils and not increase overall coverage limits. But in other cases, limits are increased.

In liability lines, pure excess insurance means exactly that. The policy provides additional limits of insurance that will come into play after primary coverage is exhausted. In some cases it will even apply after other excess policies. No new exposures are contemplated or accepted. In contrast, the umbrella liability policy adds at least $1 million of protection to existing liability policy limits and insures uncovered liability exposures for $1 million over a self-insured retention. It is prudent for all businesses to protect their assets with an umbrella liability insurance policy.

CHAPTER 20

THE BUSINESSOWNERS' POLICY

ELIGIBILITY FOR THE
BUSINESSOWNERS' POLICY

PROPERTY COVERAGES
Standard policy form
Special policy form

LIABILITY COVERAGES
Business liability
Medical payments
Definition of the insured

GENERAL CONDITIONS AND OTHER
PROVISIONS
War Risk, Governmental Action, and
Nuclear Exclusions

General conditions
Conditions applicable to Section I
Conditions applicable to Section II

BOP RATING

SUMMARY AND QUESTIONS FOR
THE AGENT OR BROKER
Summary
Questions you might ask your agent
or broker

Edward M. Glenn, Ph.D., CPCU, CLU
Vice President
Marsh & McLennan, Incorporated
Birmingham, Alabama

Edward M. Glenn earned his undergraduate degree from the University of Alabama and his graduate degrees from the Wharton School, the University of Pennsylvania. Before joining Marsh & McLennan, Dr. Glenn operated an independent consulting firm. Previously, Dr. Glenn served as a lecturer at the Wharton School, and as Senior Assistant Director of Curriculum Development for the American Institute for Property and Liability Underwriting, Malvern, Pennsylvania. Prior to attending graduate school, he served as a Supply Corps Officer in the U.S. Navy.

The Businessowners' Policy (BOP) is a standardized package policy, specifically designed to meet the insurance needs of the small to medium-sized retail store, office, or apartment complex.[1] This package approach is possible because smaller businesses share common characteristics and generally do not face the unusual types of loss exposures that would require individualized treatment. Like the Homeowners' Policy introduced about 20 years earlier, the BOP is a simplified, easy to read, indivisible package policy that features broad protection, a limited number of optional coverages, and a simplified rating procedure, all at a competitive price.

The BOP program offers eligible businessowners a choice of two policies, the *Standard Policy* or *Special Policy*. The Standard Policy is the "basic" version of the BOP, and the Special Policy is the more comprehensive or "deluxe" version. The Standard BOP covers the property insured against losses caused by the perils named in the contract.[2] Burglary and Robbery coverage is an option which may be added to the Standard Policy. The Special BOP covers the property insured against "all-risks" of loss, except those specifically excluded in the policy.[3] Otherwise both policies are essentially the same with property coverage for *(a)* Buildings, *(b)* Business Personal Property, *(c)* Loss of Income, and *(d)* Other Optional Property coverages as well as Comprehensive Business Liability coverage.[4]

The relatively new BOP program was first introduced in 1974. In 1976 the Insurance Service Office[5] (ISO) filed its BOP program. Because of its widespread use, the ISO version of the BOP program will be used as the basis of discussion and analysis. However, many insurers have developed their own BOP programs, and one should expect to encounter differences and variations, albeit slight, in terminology, eligibility rules, coverages, optional limits of liability, and the rating procedures published by different insurance companies.

ELIGIBILITY FOR THE BUSINESSOWNERS' POLICY

Eligibility for the BOP program is determined by the nature of the business (as noted below, certain types of businesses are specifically ineligible) and by the size of the building which houses the business. Insurers with independent BOP filings may impose different eligibility criteria, such as specific limitations on sales volume. The Insurance Service Office eligibility requirements have been summarized and presented in Exhibits 20–A and 20–B. Exhibit 20–A is the appropriate reference when the building is to be insured with a BOP. Exhibit 20–B is applicable to businesses who lease and therefore have no need to insure the building. When the building and business personal

Exhibit 20-A
BOP ELIGIBILITY GUIDELINES FOR BUILDINGS

Type of occupancy	Maximum height	Maximum units/area*	Retail area* restrictions
Apartment building(s) (at a single site)	Not to exceed 6 stories	No more than 60 dwelling units	Limit of 7,500 square feet mercantile space
Office buildings	Not to exceed 3 stores	No more than 100,000 square feet total area	Limit of 7,500 square feet mercantile space
Retail stores (this limitation includes all buildings at the same location)	This limitation includes all buildings at the same location	This limitation includes all buildings at the same location	Limit of 7,500 square feet for total area

* Basement areas closed to the public are not included in the area calculations.

property contained therein are owned by the same entity, both must be covered in the same BOP.

The BOP program may be used to insure apartments, office buildings, and retail stores so long as they satisfy the size eligibility guidelines and are the type of business not specifically ineligible for coverage.

The types of businesses or property which are ineligible for BOP coverage are:[6]

1. Operations centered on automobiles, motor homes, motorcycles, or mobile homes. Parking lots and garages are acceptable when they are an incidental part of an otherwise eligible operation, such as a store which has parking facilities on the premises. While dealers in watercraft, snowmobiles, or other recreational motor vehicles are technically eligible for BOP coverage, the BOP does not respond to most claims involving liability for or physical damage to owned boats or motor vehicles.
2. Bars, grills, or restaurants.
3. Condominiums—ISO's condominium program is available for this type of property.
4. Contractors—But a store "wherein the principal business is

Exhibit 20-B
BOP ELIGIBILITY GUIDELINES FOR BUSINESS PERSONAL PROPERTY

Type of occupancy	Maximum area
Office buildings	10,000 square feet (in any one building)
Retail stores	7,500 square feet

buying and selling of merchandise" is not automatically ineligible if the operation involves some contracting exposure. For example, a hardware store might sell and install fences without taking away from its essential character as a hardware store.

5. Buildings which have any portion of their occupancy devoted to manufacturing or processing.

6. Insureds whose operations involve "one or more locations which are used for manufacturing, processing, or servicing." A retail outlet for the products of an owner-manufacturer is thus not eligible, even if the manufacturing operations are conducted at another location(s).

7. Household personal property of the owner of the business.

8. Private dwellings. Garden apartments which group one- or two-family units within a single area are eligible, assuming all units are under one ownership, management, and control.

9. Places of amusement. Fairs, carnivals, amusement parks, theaters, and bowling alleys all are ineligible inasmuch as none of them serves a principal function in the "buying and selling of merchandise."

10. Wholesalers. These are normally large-scale operations. Thus, the nature of these operations differs from that envisaged for BOP.

11. Financial institutions such as banks, savings and loan associations, credit unions, stock brokers, and so on. The heavy crime exposure is beyond that of the average small to medium-sized business.

In summary, landlords may insure their buildings under the BOP program provided the building satisfies the eligibility guidelines set forth in Exhibit 20–A, and provided that the type of business occupying the building is not one of the 11 ineligible types. If the building owner and the businessowner are one and the same, then the BOP must cover both the building and its contents in the same policy. Businessowners who are tenants of an office or mercantile building may cover their business personal property, provided the maximum area restrictions presented in Exhibit 20–B are not exceeded.

PROPERTY COVERAGES

Both versions of the BOP may be used to provide coverage for a businessowner's Building, Business Personal Property or both, as well as cover Loss of Income, Other Optional Property coverages, and Comprehensive Business Liability coverage. The principal difference between the two BOP policies is that one is a named perils policy (Standard form) while the other is an all-risks policy (Special form).

Two distinctive characteristics of both BOP policies are their *replacement cost*[7] coverage for both buildings and business personal property which is provided *without a coinsurance provision*. The absence of a coinsurance clause is unusual, especially when offered in conjunction with automatic replacement cost coverage for a building *and* its contents.

The property coverage provided by the Standard BOP will be discussed in the next section, followed by a brief description of the Special BOP property section. Liability coverages, Section II of the BOP, will then be reviewed. The liability coverage offered by both versions of the BOP is the same. The ISO BOP program makes liability limits of either $300,000 or $1,000,000 available under either policy form. See Exhibit 20–C for BOP coverages at a glance.

Standard policy form

Section I, the property section, of the Standard BOP insures against direct loss caused by fire, lightning, the extended coverage perils (windstorm or hail, explosion, smoke, aircraft or vehicles, riot, riot attending a strike or civil commotion), vandalism and malicious mischief, and sprinkler leakage. For property in transit, the following perils apply:

a. Collision, derailment, or overturn of a transporting conveyance.
b. Standing or sinking of vessels.
c. Collapse of bridges, culverts, docks, or wharves.

Direct property losses are subject to a $100 deductible per occurrence under the BOP. This deductible applies separately to each location with an overall aggregate of $1,000 per occurrence for all locations. A higher deductible amount ($250) applies separately to two of the optional BOP coverages, Employee Dishonesty and Burglary and Robbery. No deductible clause applies to loss of income claims.

Building. Coverage A of Section I provides for the replacement cost of the building(s) at the premises described in the declarations for which a limit of liability is shown, including (while on the premises):

1. All garages, storage buildings, and appurtenant structures usual to the occupancy of the insured.
2. Fixtures, machinery, and equipment constituting a permanent part of and pertaining to the service of the building.
3. Personal property of the insured used for the maintenance and service of the building, including fire extinguishing apparatus, floor coverings, and appliances for refrigerating, ventilating, cooking, dishwashing, and laundering.
4. Outdoor furniture and yard fixtures.

Exhibit 20–C
BOP COVERAGES AT A GLANCE

Section I—Property insurance	Standard Policy	Special Policy
A. Building Debris removal cost as added insurance Automatic quarterly increase in coverage	Named perils coverage Replacement cost No co-insurance	"All-risk" coverage Replacement cost No co-insurance
B. Business personal property Equipment, fixtures, and inventory Limited coverage for property in transit Coverage for property of others in insured's care, custody, and control 25% peak season feature		
C. Loss of income Actual loss sustained up to 12 months No coinsurance No deductible		
D. Money and securities On- and off-premises coverage Optional property coverages: Employee dishonesty Exterior signs Exterior grade floor glass Burglary and robbery (Standard Policy only) Boiler and machinery Earthquake assumption endorsement	Not covered by Standard Policy	

Section II—Comprehensive business liability insurance	Standard Policy	Special Policy
E. Business liability Premises and operations Products and completed operations Personal injury liability Blanket contractual Broad form property damage Fire and explosion legal liability Employer's nonownership automobile liability Host liquor liability Supplemental payments Druggists' professional liability (if applicable)	Employees covered as an insured Choice of $300,000 of $1,000,000 combined single limit of liability per occurrence	Same as Standard
F. Medical payments	Up to $1,000 per person and $10,000 total per accident	Same as Standard

5. Personal property owned by the insured in apartments or rooms furnished by the insured as landlord.
6. Trees, shrubs, and plants at the described premises for not more than $250 on any one tree, shrub, or plant, including expense incurred for removing all debris thereof; however, the total liability of the company shall not exceed $1,000 in the aggregate for any one loss.

In addition to these items, the building coverage part provides for "debris removal" and for quarterly automatic increase in insurance, the exact percentage increase to be shown in the policy declarations. Debris Removal coverage is provided as an additional amount of insurance, without a specified limit, over and above the amount of insurance shown for Coverage A.

Business Personal Property coverage. Coverage B of Section I of the BOP provides for the replacement cost coverage of the business personal property owned by:

> the insured, usual to the occupancy of the insured, at the premises described in the Declarations for which a limit of liability is shown including:
>
> 1. Similar property held by the insured and belonging in whole or in part to others but not exceeding the amount for which the insured is legally liable, including the value of labor, materials, and charges furnished, performed, or incurred by the insured; and
> 2. Tenant's improvements and betterments, meaning the insured's use interest in fixtures, alterations, installations, or additions comprising a part of the building occupied but not owned by the insured and made or acquired at the expense of the insured, exclusive of rent paid by the insured, but which are not legally subject to removal by the insured.

Most insurance policies normally exclude any coverage for the property of others in the insured's "care, custody, or control." The BOP specifically grants this type of coverage as defined above.

Another advantageous feature of the Business Personal Property coverage is the "seasonal automatic increase" provision. This increases the amount of insurance specified for Coverage B by an extra 25 percent, to provide for seasonal fluctuations, without requiring the insured to specify in advance, the dates for those peak seasons. This can be a beneficial provision for a merchant.

Note that "this increase shall not apply unless the limit of liability shown in the declarations is 100 percent or more of the insured's average monthly values for the 12 months immediately preceding the date of loss, or in the event the insured has been in business for less than 12 months, such shorter period of time."

The business personal property of the insured, as well as any similar property of others in the insured's care, is covered while in transit or otherwise temporarily away from the described premises. This is another of the BOP's "extra" coverage provisions beneficial to the insured. Business personal property at newly acquired locations is also covered for up to 30 days for amounts not to exceed $10,000.

Loss of Income coverage. Coverage C of Section I provides for Loss of Income coverage. This coverage is not subject to the BOP deductible, to any co-insurance requirement, not to any maximum stated dollar limitation. Coverage is on an "actual loss sustained" basis. Loss of Income coverage is limited to the period it would take to repair, rebuild, or replace the damaged property, but under no circumstances for a period longer than 12 months.[8]

Coverage C states:

> This policy covers the actual business loss sustained by the insured and the expenses necessarily incurred to resume normal business operation resulting from the interruption of business of the untenantability of the premises when the building or the personal property is damaged as a direct result of an insured peril. The actual business loss sustained by the insured shall not exceed:
>
> 1. The reduction in gross earnings less charges and expenses which do not necessarily continue during the interruption of business, and
> 2. The reduction in rents, less charges and expenses which do not necessarily continue during the period of untenantability.

The insured is required to resume normal operations as promptly as possible and to use all reasonable means to preclude any delays in reopening. The BOP further states that the insurer will not be liable for any increase of loss caused by interference of strikers or by cancellation of any lease or contract unless that loss results directly from the interruption of business. Finally, the insured is expected to minimize any income loss by resuming full or partial operations at the insured location or elsewhere if practical.

Property not covered. The Standard BOP does not provide coverage for:

1. Exterior signs *unless* insured under the optional coverages.
2. Growing crops and lawns.
3. Aircraft, automobiles, motor trucks and other vehicles subject to motor vehicle registration, or watercraft (including motors, equipment, and accessories) while afloat.
4. Bullion, money, and securities.

Property subject to limitations. The Standard BOP limits the coverage for two principal classes of property:

1. Valuable papers and records meaning books of account, manuscripts, abstracts, drawings, card index systems, and other records (except film, tape, disc, drum, cell, and other magnetic recording or storage media for electronic data processing) are covered for an amount not exceeding the cost of blank books, cards, or other blank material plus the cost of labor incurred by the insured for transcribing or copying such records.
2. Film, tape, disc, drum, cell, and other magnetic recording or storage media for electronic data processing are covered for not exceeding the cost of such media in unexposed or blank form.

While the BOP provision includes this coverage without a specific dollar limitation, it does not cover the cost of research, which will, in all likelihood, be necessary to reproduce the records in question.

Exclusions. The Standard BOP does not provide coverage for losses:

1. Occasioned directly or indirectly by enforcement of any ordinance or law regulating the construction, repair, or demolition of buildings or structures.
2. Caused by or resulting from power, heating, or cooling failure unless such failure results from physical damage to power, heating, or cooling equipment situated on premises where the property covered is located, caused by the perils not otherwise excluded. Also, the company shall not be liable under this exclusion for any loss resulting from riot, riot attending a strike, civil commotion, or vandalism or malicious mischief.
3. Caused by any electrical injury or disturbance of electrical appliances, devices, fixtures, or wiring caused by electrical currents artificially generated unless fire as insured against ensues and then this company shall be liable for only loss caused by the ensuing fire.
4. Caused by, resulting from, contributed to, or aggravated by any of the following:

    a. Earth movement, including but not limited to earthquake, landslide, mudflow, earth sinking, earth rising, or shifting;
    b. Flood, surface water, waves, tidal water or tidal waves, overflow of streams or other bodies of water, or spray from any of the foregoing, all whether driven by wind or not;
    c. Water which backs up through sewer or drains;
    d. Water below the surface of the ground including that which exerts pressure on or flows, seeps or leaks through sidewalks, driveways, foundations, walls, basement or other floors, or through doors, windows or any other openings in such sidewalks, driveways, foundations, walls or floors;

e. Delay or loss of market;

unless fire or explosion as insured against ensues, and then this company shall be liable for only loss caused by the ensuing fire or explosion.

Optional coverages. The Standard BOP makes several types of property coverages optionally available to the eligible businessowner. The businessowner may select any of these options by paying the appropriate additional premium. Any optional BOP coverages included must be designated on the declarations page.

Employee Dishonesty coverage. When the declarations page indicates that Employee Dishonesty coverage is included, the insured has coverage for any losses of money and other forms of business personal property caused by the dishonest or fraudulent acts of the insured's employees. The declarations page indicates the BOP's limit of liability for this loss.

There are several conditional aspects of this form of crime coverage, and the businessowner should ask his or her agent to review these conditions prior to purchasing this optional form of coverage. One important condition excludes coverage for any losses due to dishonest or fraudulent acts by the insured, any partner, officer, director, or trustee. Another condition freezes the amount of loss to that sustained at the time of its discovery, that is, once discovered, the BOP will pay for the loss up to that date, but not for any further loss caused by the known culprit.

Exterior Signs coverage. The declarations page will indicate the amount of insurance applicable when this optional coverage is in effect. This coverage insures all exterior signs located on the premises whether they are the property of the insured or belong to others and are in the care, custody, and control of the insured. The usual perils and exclusions provisions of the Standard BOP do not apply to this coverage, except for the War Risk, Governmental Action, and the Nuclear Exclusion. This coverage applies for "all-risks" of loss excluding wear and tear, latent defect, rust or corrosion, or mechanical breakdown.

Exterior Grade Floor Glass coverage. This optional coverage provides replacement cost coverage for:

> all exterior grade floor and basement glass, including encasing frames and all lettering or ornamentation thereon, which are the property of the insured or the property of others in the care, custody, or control of the insured in the building described in the Declarations, for direct physical loss excluding wear and tear, latent defect, corrosion or rust.

It also includes reimbursement for the expense of

boarding up damaged openings, installing temporary plates, and removing or replacing obstructions when necessary.

As was the case with Exterior Signs coverage, the usual perils and exclusions of the Standard BOP do not apply, except for the War Risk, Governmental Action, and Nuclear Exclusions. BOP glass coverage is one of the broadest, most comprehensive glass coverages available.

Burglary and Robbery coverage. When Burglary and Robbery coverage is selected, it provides insurance against losses to:

1. Business personal property (excluding money and securities) on the described premises for an amount not to exceed 25 percent of the limit of liability of Coverage B—Business Personal Property.
2. Money and securities while in or on the described premises or within a bank or savings institution for an amount not to exceed $5,000.
3. Money and securities while enroute to or from the described premises, bank or savings institution, or within the living quarters of the custodian of such funds for an amount not to exceed $2,000.

Certain types of property are subject to limited Burglary and Robbery coverage:

1. Fur and fur garments are covered for not exceeding loss in the aggregate of $1,000 in any one occurrence.
2. Jewelry and watches, watch movements, jewels, pearls, precious and semiprecious stones, gold, silver, platinum, and other precious alloys or metals are covered for not exceeding loss in the aggregate of $1,000 in any one occurrence. This limitation shall not apply to jewelry and watches valued at $25 or less per item.

Insurers frequently require that certain types of businesses have an acceptable burglary alarm system in order to obtain the optional Burglary and Robbery coverage.

Boiler and Machinery coverage. When this coverage is selected, it provides coverage for loss to an *Object* (boiler, pressure vessels, and air-conditioning equipment, as defined in the policy) when caused by an *Accident* as defined in the policy. Coverage is for all "objects" owned, leased, or operated under the control of the insured. This optional BOP coverage gives the insurer the right (but not the obligation) to inspect the equipment insured and to suspend coverage (only in writing) if dangerous conditions are found. Pro rata premium credit will be granted during any suspension.

Other optional coverages. Some insurers offer other types of optional property insurance coverages. Two of the most common of these are for accounts receivable and the earthquake peril, both available by endorsement.

When Accounts Receivable coverage is available and included in a BOP, it is normally subject to a separate deductible provision and separate limit of liability. This form of coverage will pay all sums owed a business by its customers, provided those sums become uncollectible due to loss or damage to the firm's records of its accounts receivable.

The Earthquake coverage may be added to most BOPs by endorsement. Some insurers, however, limit the availability of this extension of coverage to the Special BOP. When added to a BOP, the Earthquake Assumption Endorsement provides coverage for the business's building(s), business personal property, and loss of income. The limits of liability are the same as those for any other peril that might cause a covered property loss, but the deductible is a percentage of the applicable limits of liability, usually 2 percent.

Special policy form

The Special BOP is similar to the Standard. The few differences that do exist between these two BOPs, however, are significant. The policy wording that provides coverage for buildings, business personal property, and loss of income is identical in both policy forms. But, the Special BOP makes these coverages available on an all-risks basis while the Standard BOP provides named perils coverage. The Special BOP also automatically includes Money and Securities coverage, available only on an optional basis with the Standard BOP. Finally, and primarily because of the difference between the all-risks and named perils approach to coverage, there are differences between the Special and Standard BOP in terms of the property excluded from coverage and property subject to limitations. The following pages will focus on the differences found in the Special BOP.

Property covered. As noted above, coverages A, B, and C of the Special BOP define the building(s), business personal property, and loss of income to be insured in precisely the same way as does the Standard BOP. The Special BOP covers these categories of property against "all-risks" of direct physical loss, rather than on a named perils basis, subject only to the exclusions specifically set forth in the policy. The Special BOP lists 16 different possible causes of loss for which the policy will not respond:

1. Occasioned directly or indirectly by enforcement of any ordinance or law regulating the construction, repair, or demolition of buildings or structures.
2. Caused by or resulting from power, heating, or cooling failure or due to change in temperature or humidity unless the change

results from physical damage to the building or to equipment contained therein caused by a peril not otherwise excluded; also the company shall not be liable for any such loss resulting from riot, riot attending a strike, civil commotion, or vandalism or malicious mischief.

3. Caused by any electrical injury or disturbance of electrical appliances, devices, fixtures, or wiring caused by electrical currents artificially generated unless fire as insured against ensues and then this company shall be liable for only loss caused by the ensuing fire.

4. Caused by pilferage, appropriation, or concealment of any property covered or any fraudulent, dishonest, or criminal act done by or at the instigation of any insured, partner or joint venture, including any officer, director, trustee, employee or agent thereof, or any person to whom the property covered may be entrusted.

5. Caused by leakage or overflow from plumbing, heating, air conditioning, or other equipment or appliances (except fire protective systems) caused by or resulting from freezing while the described building is vacant or unoccupied, unless the insured shall have exercised due diligence with respect to maintaining heat in the buildings or unless such equipment and appliances had been drained and the water supply shut off during such vacancy or unoccupancy.

6. Caused by:

    a. Wear and tear, marring or scratching;
    b. Deterioration, inherrent vice, latent defect;
    c. Mechanical breakdown of machines, including rupture or bursting caused by centrifugal force;
    d. Faulty design, materials, or workmanship;
    e. Rust, mold, wet or dry rot, contamination;
    f. Dampness or dryness of atmosphere, changes in or extremes of temperature;
    g. Smog, smoke from agricultural smudging, or industrial operations;
    h. Birds, vermin, rodents, insects, or animals;

    unless loss by fire, smoke (other than smoke from agricultural smudging or industrial operations), explosion, collapse of a building, glass breakage, or water not otherwise excluded ensues, then this policy shall cover only such ensuing loss. If loss by water not otherwise excluded ensues, this policy shall also cover the cost of tearing out and replacing of any part of the building covered required to effect repairs to the plumbing, heating or air-conditioning system or domestic appliance but excluding loss to the system or appliance from which the water escapes.

7. Due to any and all settling, shrinking, cracking, bulging, or expansion of driveways, sidewalks, swimming pools, pavements, foundations, walls, floors, roofs, or ceilings.

8. Caused by explosion of steam boilers, steam pipes, steam turbines, or steam engines (except direct loss resulting from the explosion of accumulated gases or unconsumed fuel within the firebox, or combustion chamber of any fired vessel or within the flues or passages which conduct the gases of combustion therefrom) if owned by, leased by, or operated under the control of the insured, or for any ensuing loss except by fire or explosion not otherwise excluded, and then the company shall be liable for only such ensuing loss.

9. To steam boilers, steam pipes, steam turbines, or steam engines caused by any condition or occurrence within such boilers, pipes, turbines, or engines (except direct loss resulting from the explosion of accumulated gases or unconsumed fuel within the firebox, or combustion chamber of any fired vessel or within the flues or passages which conduct the gases of combustion therefrom).

10. To hot water boilers or other equipment for heating water caused by any condition or occurrence within such boilers or equipment, other than an explosion.

11. To property in the open caused by rain, snow, ice, or sleet.

12. Caused by, resulting from, contributed to, or aggravated by any of the following:

   a. Earth movement, including but not limited to earthquake, landslide, mudflow, earth sinking, earth rising, or shifting;

   b. Flood, surface water, waves, tidal water or tidal waves, overflow of streams or other bodies of water, or spray from any of the foregoing, all whether driven by wind or not;

   c. Water which backs up through sewers or drains;

   d. Water below the surface of the ground including that which exerts pressure on or flows, seeps or leaks through sidewalks, driveways, foundations, walls, basement or other floors, or through doors, windows or any other openings in such sidewalks, driveways, foundations, walls or floors;

   unless fire or explosion as insured against ensues, and then this company shall be liable for only loss caused by the ensuing fire or explosion; but these exclusions shall not apply to loss arising from theft.

13. Due to voluntary parting with title or possession of any property

by the insured or others if induced to do so by any fraudulent scheme or false pretense.

14. Due to unexplained or mysterious disappearance of property or shortage of property disclosed on taking inventory.
15. Due to delay or loss of market.
16. To property sold by the insured under conditional sale, trust agreement, installment payment, or other deferred payment plan, after delivery to customers.

The all-risks Special BOP automatically includes coverage for theft losses with a $250 theft loss deductible. This deductible is consistent with the $250 deductible applicable to certain closely related optional coverages under the Standard BOP, for example, Employee Dishonesty, Burglary and Robbery.

Money and Securities coverage. Coverage D of the Special BOP provides on- and off-premises insurance coverage for money and securities used in the insured's business. The amount of insurance applicable to this category of coverage is selected by the insured and set forth in the space provided in the declarations page.

Optional coverage. The automatic inclusion of Theft and Money and Securities coverage under the Special BOP eliminates the need for the Burglary and Robbery coverage option available under the Standard BOP. In all other respects the Special BOP offers the same optional coverages as does the Standard BOP—Employee Dishonesty, Exterior Signs, Exterior Glass, and Boiler and Machinery. Some insurers offer Accounts Receivable and Earthquake coverage with their Special BOP, others do not.

Property not covered. The same three categories of property are specifically excluded under the Special BOP as under the Standard policy:

1. Exterior signs *unless* insured under optional coverages.
2. Growing crops and lawns.
3. Aircraft, automobiles, motor trucks, and other vehicles subject to motor vehicles registration, or watercraft (including motors, equipment, and accessories) while afloat.

A fourth exclusion under the Standard BOP (bullion, money, and securities) is specifically covered under the Special BOP, Coverage D, discussed earlier.

Property subject to limitations. The Special BOP has two different sets of limitations. The first of these limits the coverage for valuable papers and records, and so on, including film, tape, and other forms of electronic data storage media to the cost of blank cards or other media form. In the case of a manual records system, the coverage also recognizes the cost of labor needed to transcribe or copy such records, but not to reproduce the electronic data processing types of storage media. These limitations are the same as those found in the Standard BOP.

The second set of limitations are exclusive to the Special version of the BOP. Coverage for the following categories of property is limited, as indicated, whenever a loss is caused by a peril not excluded under the policy. However, the limitations do not apply to losses caused by fire, lightning, any of the extended coverage perils or sprinkler leakage. The limitations are:

1. Glass constituting a part of the building is not covered against loss for more than $50 per plate, pane, multiple plate insulating unit, radiant heating panel, jalousie, louver, or shutter, nor for more than $250 in any one occurrence.
2. Glass, glassware, statuary, marbles, bric-a-brac, procelains, and other articles of a fragile or brittle nature are not covered against loss by breakage. This limitation shall not apply to bottles or similar containers of property for sale or sold but not delivered, not to lenses of photographic or scientific instruments.
3. Fur and fur garments are covered for not exceeding loss in the aggregate of $1,000 in any one occurrence.
4. Jewelry and watches, watch movements, jewels, pearls, precious and semiprecious stones, bullion, gold, silver, platinum, and other precious alloys or metals are covered for not exceeding loss in the aggregate of $1,000 in any one occurrence. This limitation shall not apply to jewelry and watches valued at $25 or less per item.

LIABILITY COVERAGES

The liability coverage provided by the Standard BOP is exactly the same as that provided by the Special BOP. While some insurers may permit higher limits of liability under the Special BOP, there is no difference in the types of liability covered nor in the definitions and other provisions used in Section II of either form of BOP. The liability coverage is quite broad. The only decision the insured needs to make with respect to this section is whether to select the $300,000 or the $1 million limit of liability made available through the BOP program.

Business liability

Coverage E of the BOP states that it

> . . . will pay on behalf of the *insured* all sums which the *insured* shall become legally obligated to pay as damages because of *bodily injury,*

property damage, or *personal injury* caused by any *occurrence* to which this insurance applies.

The BOP liability insuring agreement thus provides comprehensive general liability insurance on an occurrence basis. This includes the usual liability coverage for a business's "premises and operations." Coverage for "completed operations" and "products" liability are also specifically included as well as "personal injury" liability. The latter protects the insured against alleged false arrest, libel or slander, and wrongful entry or eviction or other invasion of privacy. A Special Fire Legal liability provision provides up to $50,000 of coverage per occurrence for all damages resulting from fire or explosion which damages structures rented to or occupied by the named insured.

The liability coverages outlined are specifically set forth in the policy. In addition to those, the BOP covers other forms of liability by virtue of the wording contained in the Business Liability Exclusions. These include Employers' Nonowned Automobile Liability,[9] Blanket Contractual Liability,[10] and Host Liquor Law Liability.[11]

Most insurers also provide Druggists' Professional Liability coverage when the insured operates a retail drugstore. This coverage specifically protects the named insured, including partners, executive officers, and so on, and the individual pharmacists employed by the named insured. This coverage applies to all claims arising out of goods or products prepared, sold, handled, or distributed by the drugstore.

Another extension of coverage nearly always found in the BOP is Broad Form Property Damage coverage. This coverage is especially valuable to those businesses that service or install items away from their business location. In essence, this coverage relaxes the usual "care, custody, and control" exclusion to specifically cover damage to property caused by the negligent installation or replacement of some part of some piece of equipment or system. The cost of the negligently installed item is excluded from coverage.

Limits of liability. As noted, the insured may select liability insurance limits of either $300,000 or $1 million.[12] These limits of liability are "per occurrence" limits, not reduced by any "supplementary payments" (discussed below). However, the "per occurrence" limit selected is also an *aggregate limit* for *all occurrences* during the policy period stemming from the completed operations and/or products liability hazards. And, as noted, Fire Legal Liability claims are further limited to no more than $50,000 per occurrence.

As with other forms of liability insurance, the insurer is obligated to defend any claim or suit against the insured seeking damages covered by the BOP even if the suit is false, fraudulent, or groundless. However, the BOP also gives the insurance company the right to make investigations and settlements of claims as it (the insurer) deems expedient. Finally, once the BOP limits of liability have been exhausted by payment of a judgment or by settlement, the insurer is released from any further obligation to defend the insured or to make payments on his or her behalf.

Supplementary payments. The BOP, like other liability contracts, offers to make certain supplementary payments, which, if necessary, do not count toward the policy's limit of liability. These types of payments are:

1. All expenses incurred by the company.
2. All cost taxed against the insured in any suit defended by the company and all interest on the entire amount of any judgment which accrues after entry of the judgment and before the company has paid or tendered or deposited in court that part of the judgment which does not exceed the limit of the company's liability.
3. Premium on appeal bonds in any such suit.
4. Premiums on bonds to release attachments in any such suit for an amount not in excess of the applicable limit of liability of this policy.
5. Expenses incurred by the insured for first aid to others at the time of an accident for bodily injury to which this policy applies.
6. Reasonable expenses incurred by the insured at the company's request in assisting the company in the investigation or defense of any claim or suit, including actual loss of earnings not to exceed $50 per day.

Medical payments

The BOP automatically includes medical payments coverage (Coverage F) in the amounts of $1,000 per person and $10,000 for all persons requiring medical attention or a result of a single accident. It should be noted that this coverage is provided on an "accident" as opposed to the "occurrence" basis.

Definition of the insured

The "named insured" is the person or organization set forth as such on the declarations page (item 1). However, the liability insurance coverage applies separately to each "insured" against whom a claim is made or a suit filed, but this does not increase the total amount of insurance available as a result of any single occurrence. It merely allows all "insureds" to have access to the BOP liability coverage. The

BOP's limit of liability with respect to any particular occurrence is the same regardless of the number of insureds named in a suit.

The BOP defines the word *insured* quite broadly, to mean and include any of the following:

1. If the named insured is designated in the declarations as an individual, the person so designated but only with respect to the conduct of a business of which he is the sole proprietor, and the spouse of the named insured with respect to the conduct of such a business.
2. If the named insured is designated in the declarations as a partnership or joint venture, the partnership or joint venture so designated and any partner or member thereof but only with respect to his liability as such.
3. If the named insured is designated in the declarations as other than an individual, partnership or joint venture the organization so designated and any executive officer, member of the board of trustees, directors of governors or stockholder, thereof while acting within the scope of his duties as such.
4. *Any employee* of the named insured while acting within the scope of his duties as such.
5. Any person or organization while acting as real estate manager for the named insured.

GENERAL CONDITIONS AND OTHER PROVISIONS

The BOP program does not utilize the exact language or format of the Standard Fire Policy's (SFP) well-known 165 lines of conditions and exclusions. The essence of those provisions and others, however, is contained in both policy versions of the BOP program. These conditions and other provisions are found in the BOP sections labeled War Risk, Governmental Action and Nuclear Exclusions, General Conditions, Conditions Applicable to Section I (Property), or Conditions Applicable to Section II (Liability), which appear in the policy in that order, following the description of coverages. Some of the more important of these provisions and conditions will be discussed briefly.

War Risk, Governmental Action, and Nuclear Exclusions

Virtually all insurance policies exclude coverage for losses caused by war risks, governmental action, and nuclear catastrophes. This section of the BOP, as with most other insurance policies, is intended to exclude losses caused by hostile or warlike action in time of peace or war, insurrection, rebellion, revolution, civil war, usurped power, risk of contraband, illegal transportation or trade, nuclear radiation, and radioactive contamination.

General conditions

This section of a BOP policy contains 13 different provisions which deal with general matters and thus would normally be found in most insurance policies. Several of these provisions have been reworded to simplify the language, but the meaning and substance of these provisions remains unchanged. These provisions deal with:

1. "Concealment or Fraud," which voids the policy.
2. "Subrogation."
3. "Waiver or Change of Provisions," which can only be done by written endorsement.
4. "Liberalization," which states that any future extension or broadening of BOP coverage will benefit this particular policy as though the policy were altered by written endorsement.
5. "Replacement of Forms and Endorsements," which states that the insurer may convert "old" contract forms to "new" at the policy's anniversary date, even if it is a continuous policy (one without a specific termination date).
6. "Inspection and Audit," which gives the insurer the right but not the obligation to inspect the business insured.
7. "Assignment," which provides that the insured cannot assign his or her interest in the BOP to another party without the written consent of the insurer. If, however, the *named insured* should die within the policy period, the coverage provided by the policy would apply to:
   a. To the named insured's legal representative, as the named insured, but only while acting within the scope of his duties as such; or
   b. To the person having temporary custody of the property of the named insured but only until the appointment and qualification of the legal representative.
8. "Premium," which states that the premiums for the BOP policy are to be computed in accordance with the insurer's applicable rules, rates, and minimum premiums then in effect and that the policy may be continued by payment of successive one year premiums.

Some of the other "general conditions" found in the BOP are not the same as comparable provisions found in other types of insurance contracts. Each of these, therefore, deserves a brief comment. The *cancellation* provision of the BOP gives the named insured the right to cancel the policy as of some future date, if specified in writing in advance of the desired effective date of cancellation. The insurer may cancel by giving the named insured and the mortgagee at least 30 days' advance notice, in writing. This is a much improved provision for the named insured *vis-a-vis* the SFP (five days' notice) and the SMP (ten days' notice). The return premium is computed on a pro rata basis if the insurer cancels the policy. If the named insured should cancel, the return premium is 90 percent of the unearned premium, as determined on a pro rata basis. This approach is different from the traditional short-rate return premium calculation, yet the result is very nearly the same.

Two other provisions found in the General Conditions section of the BOP define the *Policy Period, Territory* and *Time of Inception.* The usual time of inception for a BOP is 12:00 noon, but if the BOP is replacing a policy that expires at 12:01 A.M., the BOP inception shall be 12:01 A.M. to coincide with that and thus avoid any lapse of coverage. The policy territory includes the 50 states of the United States of America, the District of Columbia, and Puerto Rico.

The two remaining provisions in this section of the BOP are concerned with *Other Insurance* and *Insurance under More Than One Coverage Part or Endorsement* of the BOP. The BOP Other Insurance provision declares the BOP property coverage to be excess rather than pro rata with other applicable policies. The BOP general liability coverage is implicitly primary coverage (to permit excess liability or umbrella coverage to be utilized in the customary manner), except for property in the care, custody, or control of the insured which is also excess coverage. The final provision states that in the event there is a loss covered by more than one part of an endorsement to the BOP, then the insurer's limit of liability is the amount of the loss. This provision is included to enforce the fundamental principle of indemnity.

Conditions applicable to Section I

This section of the BOP enumerates 14 different provisions which are applicable to the BOP Property coverage. These provisions include the usual insurance clauses which set forth:

1. The "Duties of the Named Insured after a Loss."
2. "Appraisal," which outlines procedures to be followed in the event the insured and the insurer fail to agree on the amount of a loss.
3. The Company Options provision which gives the insurer the following rights:

If the Company gives notice within thirty (30) days after it has received a signed, sworn statement of loss, it shall have the option to take all or any part of the property damaged at an agreed value, or to repair, rebuild or replace it with equivalent property.

4. The Abandonment of Property which states that the insurer need not accept abandoned property.
5. The Payment of Loss Clause of the BOP stipulates that property losses are to be paid within 30 days (as opposed to 60 days in the SFP) of the date that an acceptable proof of loss has been presented.
6. The Suit Clause states that:

No suit shall be brought on this policy unless the insured has complied with all the policy provisions and has commenced the suit within one year after the loss occurs.

7. The Mortgage Clause of the BOP is essentially the same as the one contained in other property insurance contracts. This provision applies to the buildings insured, but not to any business personal property.
8. The Recoveries Clause states that if any recoveries are realized on loss or damaged property, the insured

. . . shall be entitled to all recoveries in excess of the amount paid by the Company, less only the actual cost of effecting such recoveries.

9. The Loss Clause states that the amount of insurance provided in a BOP will not be diminished by a loss—generally true of all property insurance.
10. The No Benefit to Bailee Clause states:

The insurance shall not inure directly or indirectly to the benefit of any carrier or other bailee.

11. The No Control provision states that the coverage provided by a BOP will not be prejudiced

a. By any act or neglect of the owner of any building if the insured is not the owner thereof, or by any act or neglect of any occupant (other than the insured) of any building, when such act or neglect of the owner or occupant is not within the control of the insured; or
b. By failure of the insured to comply with any warranty or condition contained in any endorsement attached to this policy with regard to any portion of the premises over which the insured has no control.

Three other clauses found in this section of the BOP require a little more attention. The first of these is the Replacement Cost provision. It is reproduced below in full. The reader should note how the first half of this provision (part a) defines the limits of replacement cost while the second half (part *b*) states that property damage must actually be repaired or replaced before the insurer is obligated to pay the replacement cost of any damages. The full Replacement Cost provision reads as follows:

a. With the exception of loss of Money and Securities, loss shall be adjusted on the basis of the replacement cost value of the property insured hereunder, but the limit of liability of the Company shall not exceed the least of:

1. The full cost of replacement of such property at the same site with new material of like kind and quality without deduction for depreciation; or

2. The cost of repairing the insured property within reasonable time; or

3. The limit of liability applicable to such property shown on the Declarations; or

4. The amount actually and necessarily expended in repairing or replacing said property or any part thereof.

b. The Company shall not be liable for payment of loss on a replacement cost basis unless and until actual repair or replacement is completed. The insured, however, may elect not to repair or replace, in which event loss settlement shall be made on an actual cash value basis rather than on a replacement cost basis. Should the insured elect this option, the insured's right to make further claim on a replacement cost basis shall not be prejudiced provided the Company is notified in writing within 180 days after loss of the insured's intent to make such further claim.

Another provision in this section of the BOP gives the insurer the right to settle losses with the owner of the property lost or damaged, even if that person is not a party to the contract (the Privilege to Adjust with Owner provision).

The final provision in this section of the BOP deals with the subject of vacancy and unoccupancy. Vacancy means that the building is empty; it has no contents or activities customary to its usual type of occupancy. An unoccupied building would lack the people and activities, but it would not be empty; it would have contents. The BOP Vacancy or Unoccupancy provision grants blanket permission for unoccupancy, but limits coverage during periods of vacancy to no more than 60 days.

Conditions applicable to Section II

There are three provisions contained within this section of the BOP. The first of these is concerned with Action against the Company. This provision states that:

No action shall lie against the Company unless:

a. There shall have been full compliance with all of the terms of this policy; and

b. The amount of the insured's obligation to pay shall have been finally determined either by judgment against the insured after actual trial or by written agreement of the insured, the claimant and the Company.

Any person or organization or the legal representative thereof who has secured such judgment or written agreement shall thereafter be entitled to recover under this policy to the extent of insurance afforded by this policy.

The two remaining provisions set forth the Insured's Duties in the Event of Occurrence, Claims or Suits and that the BOP *shall not* serve as proof of financial responsibility under that type of law in any state.

BOP RATING

The underwriting (the process of selecting and properly classifying insurance prospects or applicants) and rating of BOP business is critically dependent upon the information gathered by the agent or broker. There should, therefore, always be at least one personal fact-finding visit and inspection made by your agent or broker.

The businessowner should expect the agent or broker to seek certain information about the business which is necessary to complete the BOP application and to develop the BOP premium. This includes the basic background information about the business—name of business and its owners, type of business, square footage of the building and the percentage of the building occupied by the business, the grade of fire protection at this location, building and contents replacement cost values, value of outside signs (if any), area of external glass, form of BOP desired, effective dates (if purchased) and other information about the handling and storage of money, burglar alarms, door locks, and so on.

The most noteworthy feature of the BOP rating procedure is its sheer simplicity. The entire indivisible package premium is developed from the amounts of insurance to be placed on the building (if applicable) and the business personal property. If any of the optional coverages are desired, they can be added for a separately determined additional charge. Of course, the rates for the special BOP are higher than those for the standard BOP.

One final point which should be noted about BOP premiums is the possibility for premium credits or debits, based on certain underwriting factors. These factors are shown in Exhibit 20–D. Special credits *and* debits may be applied to accounts which carry a premium of $500

Exhibit 20–D
UNDERWRITING CHARACTERISTICS WHICH MAY JUSTIFY PREMIUM MODIFICATIONS

1. *Management*—Cooperation in matters of safeguarding and proper handling of property covered.
2. *Location*—Accessibility and environment.
3. *Building features*—Air conditioning and unusual structural features.
4. *Premises and equipment*—Care, condition, and type.
5. *Employees*—Selection, training, supervision, and experience.
6. *Protection*—Not otherwise recognized.

or more. These credits and debits are intended for use when the special characteristics of the business in question do not seem to be fully recognized in the basic BOP rate structure. The maximum premium deviation for all credits/debits combined is limited to 15 percent.

SUMMARY AND QUESTIONS FOR THE AGENT OR BROKER

Summary

The BOP is an excellent product for its intended market. It offers the consumer-businessowner the advantage of broad coverage (replacement cost without coinsurance; loss of income; property of others in the insured's care, custody, and control; transit, peak season, broad business liability coverage, including employees as additional insureds and much more) in an easy to read policy all at a competitive price.

Questions you might ask your agent or broker

1. Is my business eligible for the BOP?
2. Is my business eligible for the Special BOP? If not, why not? Is there something I can do to enable my business to overcome that (those) problem(s) and thus become eligible?
3. What coverages does the BOP provide? Which are mandatory and which are optional?
4. What legal limits of liability insurance are available to me?
5. Will my BOP include coverage for the property of others in my care, custody, and control?
6. Are the building (if applicable) and business personal property values you used adequate for my needs? How did you develop the figures you used for the:
   Building?
   Inventory?

Furniture and fixtures?

Improvements and betterments?

7. What rating factors (types of construction, occupancy, etc.) were used to calculate this premium?

8. Are you giving me any rate credits? Any rate debits? Why or why not? If so, how much credit/debt and why?

NOTES

1. The Special Multi-Peril Policy (SMP) is another business package insurance program. The SMP program predates the BOP and has a much broader range of application. The SMP program serves the insuring needs of larger organizations, of businesses ineligible for the BOP, and whenever the complexity of a business requires individualized treatment.

2. Property insurance policies which follow this approach to coverage are commonly called named perils contracts.

3. Policies which take this approach to coverage are popularly known as all-risks contracts, even though they do have exclusions.

4. Note that the BOP coverage does not include workers' compensation or business automobile liability insurance; these coverages are sufficiently different as to warrant separate policies.

5. The Insurance Service Office is a national network of offices which collect loss information and use that data to develop rates for most kinds of property and liability insurance. Insurance companies that subscribe to this service may use the ISO rates and their policy forms, or independently file with the various states, their own policy

forms and "deviated" schedule of rates.

6. *Fire Casualty and Surety Bulletins;* Fire and Marine Section, Commercial Multi-Peril, pp. PB-2 and 3.

7. The replacement cost provisions are discussed more fully under the heading "Conditions applicable to Section I." It should be noted, however, that some companies permit the BOP to be written on an *actual cash value* basis if that is the request of the insured. If the insured would not plan to rebuild the building the business occupies then Replacement Cost coverage makes no sense; see the later discussion.

8. Some independently filed BOP plans limit the loss of income time period to eight (8) months under their Standard BOP.

9. See Standard ISO BOP, Business Liability Exclusion No. 1.

10. See Standard ISO BOP, Business Liability Exclusion No. 4.

11. See Standard ISO BOP, Business Liability Exclusion No. 7.

12. Some insurance companies offer other limits of liability, often $500,000 as well as the limits cited in the text.

CHAPTER 21

THE SPECIAL MULTI-PERIL POLICY

DEVELOPMENT OF THE PACKAGE
CONCEPT
Reduced cost
A single policy contract
History of the package
The present SMP policy

A SUMMARY OF SMP COVERAGES
Property insurance
General liability insurance
Optional coverages available
Crime coverage
Boiler and machinery insurance

BUSINESSOWNERS' PROGRAM—A
COMPARISON

DETAILED REVIEW OF COVERAGES
AVAILABLE
Property insurance—Section I
General liability coverage—Section II
Crime coverage—Section III
Boiler and machinery
insurance—Section IV

CONCLUSION

John C. Morrison
President
INA Special Risk Facilities, Inc.
New York, New York

John C. Morrison, CPCU, was named President and Director of INA Special Risk Facilities, Inc., in June 1977. Prior to joining INA Special Risk as Executive Vice President in February 1977, Mr. Morrison was Vice President of American International Reinsurance Company, Inc., and Vice President and Director of captive insurance operations for American International Company, Ltd., Hamilton, Bermuda. From 1971 to 1976, he was President of Commerce and Industry Insurance Company of New York, part of American International Group, Inc. Mr. Morrison serves as Director and President of INA Special Risk Facilities, Inc., and INA Underwriters Insurance Company. He is also a Director of Bankers Standard Fire and Marine Company; Bankers Standard Insurance Company; California Union Insurance Company; INA International Investors, Ltd.; INA of Texas; INAMAR, Ltd.; Indemnity Insurance Company of North America; Pacific Employers Insurance Company; Petroleum Insurance, Inc.; and Montgomery & Collins, Inc. Additionally, Mr. Morrison serves as Senior Vice President of Indemnity Insurance Company of North America and Executive Vice President of Indemnity Insurance Company of North America and Executive Vice President of Pacific Employers Insurance Company. A graduate of Yale University (B.S., 1948), Mr. Morrison is a member of the Yale Club of New York City, the University Club, and is affiliated with the New York City chapter of the Society of Chartered Property and Casualty Underwriters (CPCU).

DEVELOPMENT OF THE PACKAGE CONCEPT

The Special Multi-Peril Policy (SMP) is a "combination" or "package" policy consisting of both *mandatory* and optional coverages. Like every other viable commercial product, the package policy was developed to fill a need; in this case, the several needs of the small to medium-sized commercial policyholder:

1. Lower cost.
2. More complete coverage in a single policy contract.
3. Some flexibility of choice as to optional coverages.

Flexibility of choice makes it necessary for the policyholder and his agent or broker to carefully review his insurance needs to be sure those coverages are selected which will respond adequately to his needs.

Reduced cost

Reduction in cost is probably the most important feature of the SMP program. This cost reduction results from two factors:

First, processing cost reductions are realized by both the insurance company and the agent or broker when they handle one policy instead of two to ten (as they would in the absence of a package policy).

Second, another cost reduction occurs because generally the loss experience of the SMP "class" is better than the experience for similar coverages written under a series of separate policies.

Both the cost and loss savings are passed on to the policyholder.

Only certain kinds of businesses are eligible for the SMP. Moreover, many underwriters attempt to screen the businesses which do qualify and to select only the better risks for SMP treatment.

The selection process is repeated at renewal time, when the loss experience and inspection reports of the individual policyholder are taken into account in deciding eligibility for continued SMP treatment and premium discount. Consequently, it is necessary, in order to retain these reduced insurance costs, for an SMP policyholder to maintain his premises in orderly condition, and be receptive, concerned, and alert to loss prevention recommendations and efforts.

The SMP or Commercial Package, as a statistical class, is not a well-defined and constant group of similar risks but rather an ever-changing group of similar risks. The selection process of insurers tends to ensure that the group will statistically show a better than average loss ratio.

500

Those policyholders who, because of this kind of business and underwriting selection, are eligible for the SMP program, probably will enjoy cost reductions in the range of 15–30 percent. These are "up front" reductions in initial premium. SMPs are written by both dividend and nondividend paying insurance companies, and some, therefore, may be subject to additional savings through the dividend process.

A single policy contract

The other main advantage of the SMP is one single policy covers most of the business operation's insurance exposures. One policy means only one expiration to worry about, one premium payment (or a planned series, if a payment plan is used), one insurance policy file, and, consequently, low probability the insurance program will have gaps in coverages. Also, one policy combining several coverages gives the policyholder's account a higher profile with the insurance company's underwriter. Theoretically, a well-written SMP, together with a workers' compensation policy and appropriate automobile coverages, should cover all of the insurance needs (other than employee benefits) for most small to medium-sized business enterprises. Nevertheless, the flexibility provided by the optional coverages and, in fact, the choices of coverages requires a careful and complete analysis of the policyholder's exposures. For example, in the mandatory property section, an insured must decide whether the desired coverage is "all-risks" or just Fire and Extended coverage. If the insured chooses the latter coverage, then he must decide whether there is a need for protection against sprinkler leakage or other water damage or earthquake protection. All of the foregoing decisions pertain to the *mandatory* property section of the package. There are then the *optional* sections to be reviewed, and coverage must be selected as needed.

A SMP is not a package which automatically gives all the needed coverages. It requires thoughtful decisions, review, and updating as situations change.

History of the package

In one sense package policies have been a part of the insurance scene for many years. Even the simple fire and extended coverage policy is a "package" in that the extended coverage endorsement combines a number of separate perils (wind, hail, explosion, impact by vehicles or aircraft, and riot and civil commotion) into an indivisible package which can be purchased or not, but cannot be subdivided.

Other packages of coverages or perils have come along over the years, including the Homeowners' Policy in the personal lines field.

The first real multi-line packages, combining property and casualty exposures, did not appear until the early 1960s. Part of that delay can be attributed to inertia within the insurance business, but to a large degree, regulatory restraints prevented multi-line combinations. For years, many state laws governing insurance companies required that they be licensed as single-line companies and as such those licensed for property could not write casualty lines and vice versa. These regulations were gradually relaxed during the 1950s as it became apparent that the Homeowners' Policy and other single-line packages were working well and gaining broad buyer acceptance. The interest in multiple-line packages for the commercial field intensified largely due to the complaints of commercial insurance buyers who were looking for cost reductions and complaining about the number of policies and details with which they had to cope. Insurers, together with agents and brokers, focusing on these desires of potential policyholders, developed the package concept. The few innovative and aggressive insurance companies who developed these new packages merchandised them in the spirit of free enterprise to get ahead of their competitors and attract more business.

The Special Multi-Peril Policy, introduced in most states in 1960, was the first *standard* package policy. The package as originally introduced continued with only minimal modification until 1977 when a fairly comprehensive revision was made. This did not change the concept but broadened eligibility rules and simplified policy forms.

The present SMP policy

Today's SMP policy program consists of eight different classification groups, each group having its own package discount. The group in which a business is placed affects the premium it pays. For the most part, the same policy forms are employed for each of the eight groups.

The 1977 revision to the SMP program sets eligibility rules so most insureds can qualify for the program. Only a few classes are excluded. They are:

1. Boarding and rooming houses and other residential premises containing fewer than three apartment units.
2. Farms and farming operations.
3. Automobile filling or service stations; automobile repairing or rebuilding operations; automobile, motor home, motorcycle dealers; parking lots or garages unless incidental to an otherwise eligible class.

4. Grain elevators, grain tanks, and grain warehouses.
5. Properties to be rated under *(a)* Rating Plan for Highly Protected Risks, *(b)* Schedule for Petroleum Properties, *(c)* Schedule for Rating Petrochemical Plants, *(d)* Schedule for Rating Electric Generating Stations, or *(e)* Schedule for Natural Gas.

Eligible insureds are grouped into eight trade group classifications which determine the size of the applicable discount:

1. Apartment houses.
2. Contractors.
3. Motel-hotel operations.
4. Industrial and processing plants.
5. Institutions.
6. Mercantile operations.
7. Offices.
8. Service firms.

The package discounts which apply to each group vary by group and by state. Discounts are periodically recalculated to reflect the loss experience of the group or class as a whole. For example, it is possible for a group to have a package factor of 1.00 (no discount) or, if experience warrants, a factor of .65 (a discount of 35 percent).

It is unlikely there will be significant coverage and eligibility revision in the SMP program for several years. There will, periodically, be minor changes and updates. Eligibility is now quite broad, the coverage options are stabilized, and cost savings have been established. Likely adjustments will be modification of package discounts for individual business groups.

A SUMMARY OF SMP COVERAGES

Property insurance

Property insurance, a mandatory coverage, is included under Section I of the SMP. This coverage may include real property (buildings and structures) and personal property (stocks of merchandise, machinery and equipment, and supplies), depending upon the insurable interest of the policyholder. For example, if an insured both owns and occupies a building, both Real and Personal Property coverages must be included. If an insured is a tenant only, just personal property must be insured. All building and personal property insurance should be purchased under one SMP to avoid problems at the time of a loss.

General liability insurance

General liability insurance is covered under Section II of the SMP. It, too, is a mandatory coverage. General Liability coverage protects the policyholder against his liability to others for loss or injury caused by or resulting from the policyholder's premises and operations. It covers such exposures as lawsuits arising out of slips and falls on the business premises, injuries due to operation of equipment, and certain liabilities assumed under contracts or agreements. It also includes liability arising out of the use or consumption of products produced or sold. Generally, however, if the products liability exposure is severe, most underwriters will exclude it under the SMP, requiring a separate products liability policy.

The SMP does not cover claims for injury to employees which must be covered under a separate workers' compensation policy. Neither does the SMP cover liability arising out of the operation of automobiles or trucks, which must be insured under an Automobile Liability Policy. There are other special situation exposures not protected under Section II of the SMP, such as liability for errors or omissions by professionals. For example, Section II of an SMP covering an architect or engineer's office or a doctor, lawyer, or accountant's property would not cover their exposure for professional errors. Instead, a separate Professional Liability Policy is necessary.

The insurance buyer must fully describe his property and operations to an experienced and dependable insurance agent or broker and rely upon his professional advice to be sure of proper protection. The basic SMP, with mandatory Section I and Section II coverages, must be supplemented by workers' compensation, automobile coverages, and desired employee benefits programs. Then special situations or desirable additional coverages may be identified and added.

Optional coverages available

Under Section I of the policy, an important option is insurance for loss of profit. This may take the form of rental value insurance for apartment or other tenant occupied buildings or it may be business interruption or use and occupancy insurance for industrial or mercantile operations. It is a valuable option to consider in that it reimburses an insured for lost income, less any expenses that can be discontinued. Additionally, there are options as to perils insured against. The insured can select the basic Fire and Extended coverage, the optional perils endorsement, or the all-risks forms. Other options include tuition fees insurance for schools and colleges, coverages for buildings during the course of construction (all but insignificant additions or new buildings must be specifically added by endorsement), and various forms of special coverage such as Fine Arts, Valuable Papers and Records, Cameras and Equipment, Musical Instruments and Physicians' and Surgeons' Equipment, none of which is covered under the basic SMP property form.

There are no optional coverages available under Section II of the SMP. Decisions have to be made, however, as to the limits of liability desired and whether there are special exposures which require special-purpose policies. A businessman should consider purchasing an umbrella liability policy giving protection above the general liability limit and also excess of limits under automobile and other liability policies. As described in Chapter 19, the umbrella policy provides broad and inexpensive coverage which should be carefully considered in arranging an adequate insurance program.

Crime coverage

Crime coverage, available under Section III, is entirely optional. It consists of five kinds of protection against loss caused by criminal acts. These five categories, each of which can be selected separately, are:

1. *Employee dishonesty*—covers loss resulting from the deliberate dishonest or fraudulent acts of employees (other than the insured or a partner).
2. *Loss inside the premises*—covers loss of money and securities from the premises by robbery or burglary from a safe and for destruction or unexplained disappearance of money and securities.
3. *Loss outside the premises*—covers loss of property in the custody of a messenger or armored car.
4. *Counterfeit currency or money orders*—covers loss due to the insured's acceptance of counterfeit instruments.
5. *Depositors forgery*—covers loss due to forgery of checks written on the insured's bank account.

Boiler and machinery insurance

Boiler and Machinery coverage (Section IV) is optional and, if selected, receives the SMP package discount. Almost all fire and extended coverage policies exclude damage resulting from explosion of boilers or other pressure vessels. Consequently, this coverage is needed if the insured property contains any heating or process boiler or steam generator that operates under pressure.

Protection is also included for the insured's liability for damage to property of others, as well as associated defense costs. This is important because the liability coverage under Section II excludes liability arising out of these kinds of explosions.

Machinery coverage provides insurance against the damage and costs resulting from the breakdown of machinery on the premises. The equipment to be insured must be listed. It usually makes sense to insure breakdown only of those machines that are abnormally expensive and time consuming to repair or whose presence is critical to the operation as a whole. The coverage also extends to damage to surrounding property, which is excluded in basic fire and extended coverage policies. It is wise to ascertain if the insurance company has a good boiler and machinery inspection service, for these inspections can be as important as the coverages themselves.

BUSINESSOWNERS' PROGRAM—A COMPARISON

The evolution of commercial package (SMP) policies and programs can be traced back to the development of the homeowners' "package" covering the personal property and personal liability of individuals. From this point, the idea of combining property and liability coverages was later applied to commercial type business operations, ranging in size from small to very large. There was no differentiation in the rating or coverage approaches.

One independent insurer filed a program which was a simplified version of the SMP in 1974, designed to provide coverages for the small business operation. This simplified approach with a simple rating structure, fixed coverages, and fixed limits of liability was called the Businessowners' Policy or BOP. The BOP in essence was designed for the small business operation with standard and uncomplicated insurance needs.

Property coverage under the BOP is available for buildings, business personal property, and loss of income (includes coverage for business interruption, extra expense, and rents). The perils insured are (1) "named perils"—fire, extended coverage, vandalism and malicious mischief, sprinkler leakage, and transportation; or (2) "all-risks." Other coverages which can be included are Employee Dishonesty, Plate Glass, Earthquake, and Boiler and Machinery coverages.

The Liability coverage is written at a limit of $300,000 with an option to increase the limit to $1 million. Coverage is provided for the premises/operations exposure, products and completed operations, fire legal liability, personal injury liability, broad form property damage liability, host liquor liability, and nonowned automobile liability. Medical payments coverage may be added as an option for the limits for $1,000 each person, $10,000 each accident.

There are specific eligibility requirements for the program. Certain types of business operations such as restaurants, bars, and grills; operations centered on automobiles, motor homes, motorcycles; and so on, are not eligible. Other categories, such as apartments, stores, and office buildings have a maximum square footage limitation above which they are ineligible.

The businessowners' program is limited to small and simple business operations. Its simplified rating approach and coverage format makes this a viable mechanism for providing the insurance needs and coverage for business operations of that type. The special multi-peril program remains as a more complete and flexible approach for providing insurance coverage to the larger or more complex business.

DETAILED REVIEW OF COVERAGES AVAILABLE

To effectively analyze an SMP program, it is necessary to consider each of the basic sections of the policy individually, focusing upon the coverages and options available. In this manner, one can understand the individual components, each of which is analogous to the monoline coverages outlined in previous chapters. In order to avoid repetition, familiarity by the reader with monoline coverages and concepts is assumed. If this is not the case, a review of Chapters 4 through 8 and 17 is suggested.

Property insurance—Section I

Section I of the SMP is designed to provide coverage for all of the property exposures of an insured. A careful analysis of needs in this area is important so a comprehensive insurance program can be established. There are two broad categories of property which need to be considered: real and personal. The package policy is sufficiently flexible to include almost all of the various types of property coverages an eligible business operation may need to insure. The foundation of most Section I coverages is the Standard Fire Policy.

Virtually all *real property* is included in the definition of *building(s)* on the SMP coverage forms. This includes buildings; structures; additions; fixtures; permanent equipment and machinery used for maintenance and service of the building; material and supplies intended for use in construction; alterations or repairs; yard fixtures; fire extinguishing apparatus; refrigeration, ventilating, cooking; dishwashing and laundering equipment; and floor coverings, all of which are located at the designated premises.

Basic exclusions from building coverage are swimming pools, fences, piers, docks, wharves, walks, cost of excavation, building foundations, and underground pipes.

Coverage is available through the SMP for business *personal property* which is usual to the occupancy or operation of the insured. Included also are tenants improvements in buildings not owned by the insured and a limited extension to the personal property of others. For the most part, personal property coverage is limited to the designated premises. Some basic exclusions are animals and pets; watercraft; automobiles, vehicles, or trailers licensed for highway use; aircraft; personal property while waterborne; household and individual personal property; accounts, bills, currency, deeds, evidence of debt, money, and securities. Valuable papers, money, and securities coverage is available under Section III or by means of various crime endorsements.

The type of personal property covered under Section I consists of, but is not limited to, stocks of merchandise and of raw materials, supplies and fittings, furniture and fixtures, equipment or machinery. Latter portions of this chapter will review methods of providing coverage for other types of personal property such as accounts receivable; valuable papers; goods of others in the care, custody, and control of the insured; and miscellaneous property which have special coverage needs.

Coverage for both buildings and personal property is provided by combining several different peril forms. The basic forms are the *General Building Form* and the *General Personal Property Form.* Under these two forms, insurance coverage is on a named peril basis. These perils include fire; lightning, windstorm, or hail; explosion; smoke; aircraft or vehicle damage; riot, riot attending a strike, or civil commotion; vandalism or malicious mischief. Coverage is limited by exclusions of electrical injury, interruption of power, earth movement, flood, or enforcement of ordinance or law regarding use, construction, or repair of a building.

These basic coverage forms can be supplemented at additional cost by the addition of other coverage endorsements which broaden the protection. An *Optional Perils Coverage Endorsement* is available for both building and personal property coverage. Additional perils covered by this form are breakage of glass (which is part of the building and subject to limitations); falling objects (loss or damage to personal property in the open not included); weight of ice, snow, or sleet; water damage (coverage is included for accidental discharge of water or steam from plumbing, heating, or air conditioning, but discharge from automatic sprinkler systems is excluded from coverage); and loss caused by collapse of the building structure itself.

At the insured's or insurer's option, *Vandalism and Malicious Mischief* can be excluded, deleting this peril from the General Form.

The *Sprinkler Leakage Endorsement* provides coverage for damage to property from leakage or discharge of water (or other substance) from an automatic fire protection system. It includes coverage for loss or damage resulting from collapse of a tank which is part of the system. This endorsement has specified limits of liability, co-insurance percentages, conditions, and exclusions, and must be separately requested and priced when developing the SMP contract.

As an alternative to the named perils approach, an insured may consider coverage on an all-risks basis. The *Special Building Form* and *Special Personal Property Form* provide this at additional cost. These forms cover "all-risks" *but* are subject to a number of exclusions. The exclusions are loss caused by enforcement of local or state ordinances regulating construction; electrical injury to electrical appliances caused by artificially generated current; flood, earthquake, sewer backup, or water below the surface of the ground; wear, tear, gradual deterioration, rust, corrosion, mold, wet or dry rot, inherent or latent defect; smog; smoke, vapor, or gas from agricultural or industrial operations; mechanical breakdown, including rupture or bursting caused by centrifugal force; settling, cracking, shrinkage, bulging, or expansion of pavements, foundations, walls, floors, or ceilings; animals, birds; vermin or other insects, explosion of steam boilers, steam pipes, or engines. Also excluded are vandalism and malicious mischief damage to any building vacant or unoccupied for more than 30 days; continuous or repeated seepage or leakage of water or steam from plumbing, heating, and air conditioning, or other equipment; theft of any property *not* an integral part of a building at time of loss; unexplained or mysterious disappearance of property; and loss caused directly or indirectly by an interruption of power.

An *Earthquake Extension Endorsement* can be added to afford coverage for damage to property caused by earthquake. This coverage is on a designated premises basis subject to mandatory deductible percentages.

The peril options are supplemented with several special arrangement forms intended to meet the needs of certain insureds. One set of forms, the *SMP Condominium—Additional Policy Provisions Endorsement*—is available to provide named peril or all-risks property coverages for condominium operations. These forms follow the General and Special forms discussed earlier with special terms and conditions included to meet the needs of the condominium association.

Another set of forms, the *SMP Builders' Risk Completed Value Form* (named perils) and the *SMP Special Builders' Risk Completed Value Form* ("All-Risks"), is designed to provide property insurance coverages for builders' risk exposures. Another most useful provision of the SMP program is the availability of reporting form endorsements which convert basic property coverage forms to a reporting basis.

These forms, the *Reporting Endorsement—Specific Rate* and the *Reporting Endorsement—Average Rate,* are convenient for businesses that have a fluctuation of personal property values and difficulty in determining a correct amount of insurance. By using a reporting form, an insured can establish a limit of insurance sufficient to cover maximum values at a given time. The insured reports actual values at stated periods, and a premium is charged on the average value at risk during the year. The insured has the benefit of adequate coverage during peak periods and a fair premium charge based on actual values.

There are various deductibles available. Generally credits in premium rate follow those applied to property coverage if written separately rather than under an SMP program.

Another important consideration is valuation of the insured property at the time of a loss. Unless specifically endorsed or stated in the coverage form, all property will be valued at *actual cash value.* The precise definition of actual cash value depends upon the type of property under consideration. There are variations in the application of actual cash value, depending on whether real, personal, finished good, or stock (inventory) type properties are being valued.

Generally, actual cash value is defined as the cost to repair or replace the damaged property less an amount for actual physical depreciation, *not* as book value. This basis of adjustment may be modified, however, by the attachment of the *Replacement Cost Coverage Endorsement.* Under this endorsement, insured property involved in a loss will be adjusted on the basis of the amount necessary to repair or replace the damaged property, subject only to the limit of liability and without regard to the actual age of the property at time of loss. This endorsement *does not* delete any co-insurance requirement and is not extended to certain types of property (stock, property of others, valuable papers, and records, fine arts, etc.). Proper insurance to value should always be maintained in accordance with the basis of coverage and ultimate loss adjustment.

Business interruption insurance. In addition to the basic coverage and variations available under the Mandatory part of Section I, there are important *Optional* coverages available under the SMP program.

Business interruption insurance includes a broad category of specific "loss of use" or "time element" insurance coverages designed to indemnify the insured for a loss of earnings (as defined in the coverage form), tuition fees, rents, or the extra expenses involved in continuing operations in the event an insured premises is damaged by an insured peril. These coverages have been discussed in Chapter 6. Under the SMP program a number of these business interruption forms are available.

Coverage may be added by the use of a *Gross Earnings Endorsement* (covers gross earnings less noncontinuing expenses) for the actual loss sustained by an insured from the interruption of business. As with all gross earnings forms, coverage is subject to a co-insurance or contribution clause of 50, 60, 70, or 80 percent of the annual gross earnings for the firm. Any failure to maintain an adequate amount of insurance as respects the selected co-insurance percentage would result in a claim payment penalty for a sustained loss.

Coverage for ordinary payroll expense either may be excluded or limited to a period of 90 consecutive days following damage to the insured premises. If not specifically covered, it will not be paid unless proven to be essential to continuing or speeding resumption of operation.

Business Interruption coverage also may be written on an *Earnings Endorsement.* It is the intent of this form to cover the actual loss sustained by the insured (earnings less noncontinuing expenses) with no co-insurance requirement. Recovery is restricted to a percentage of the limit of liability applicable on a monthly basis. The insured may select 16.67 percent, 25 percent, or 33.33 percent depending on how long he estimates it would take to repair the premises. Coverage will be for the perils against which the building and/or its contents are insured.

Extra Expense Endorsement. Some firms may find it advantageous to purchase insurance protection for extra expenses incurred to continue their operations should their premises be damaged or destroyed. The *Extra Expense Endorsement* available under the SMP program provides this coverage. Coverage is limited on a monthly basis (i.e., not more than 40 percent of the endorsement's limit for any one month or less) and generally follows the perils insured in Section I. This coverage should be considered in lieu of or in addition to business interruption insurance for those businesses where a shutdown is unacceptable. In such situations, the insured will incur expenses for temporary facilities and resources that will enable customers to be serviced. Remember the "expense" portion of business interruption policies only covers expediting expenses incurred to the extent that they *reduce* the loss of net profit. Accordingly, it may be desirable to have both Extra Expense *and* Business Interruption coverage in some situations.

The *Combined Business Interruption and Extra Expense Endorsement* provides coverage for both business interruption and extra expenses exposures with a single limit of liability. There are specified percentage options available to an insured that can be applied depending upon the estimated length of time required for restoration.

The *Tuition Fees Endorsement* provides coverage for lost tuition revenues which an educational institution might suffer in the event the physical facilities were damaged and unusable as a result of an insured peril. The basis of recovery is the actual loss sustained from the date of loss to the opening of the school year commencing after restoration is completed. Coverage is available on an 80 percent or 100 percent co-insurance basis.

The *Loss of Rents Endorsement* is available to provide coverage for loss an insured may sustain due to the untenantability of a designated premises resulting from damage by an insured peril. Coverage is usually subject to the application of a pre-selected contribution clause which functions as a co-insurance clause. In other words, the insurance company will not be liable for a greater proportion of any loss than the stated limit of liability bears to the amount which is produced by multiplying the previous 12 months of rental values by the specified percentage of contribution.

Mercantile Open Stock Burglary Endorsement. Because personal property of a business may be subject to loss caused by burglary, robbery, or theft, there are several extension endorsements to Section I of the SMP available to provide crime coverages. These endorsements are available under Property Insurance Section I or, in some cases, under Section III which deals exclusively with crime coverages. Coverages under the SMP closely parallel those available on a separate (monoline) basis.

The Mercantile Open Stock Burglary Endorsement may be included with the General Personal Property Form to provide coverage for merchandise, furniture and fixtures, and equipment of the insured at a designated premises against loss caused by burglary or robbery of a watchman while the premises are not open for business. If personal property is covered by the Special Personal Property form ("all-risks"), this endorsement is not needed.

Mercantile Open Stock Burglary and Theft Endorsement. This endorsement provides coverage for loss or damage to merchandise, furniture, fixtures, and equipment at a designated premises for (1) burglary or robbery of a watchman while the premises are not open for business, and (2) theft or attempted theft, whether or not the premises are open for business. Here again, this endorsement is not needed if the Special Personal Property form has been selected.

Church Theft Endorsement. This endorsement is designed to provide coverage for a church against theft or attempted theft of money, securities, or other property while at the church, in a bank or night depository, or in the care or custody of an authorized person. The form is subject to definitions and exclusions which should be reviewed. Coverage can be provided at an agreed value for specified articles and/or limit for all other property.

Liability for Guests' Property Endorsement. Subject to specific exclusions and limitations, *Liability for Guests' Property Endorsement* provides coverage for "Innkeepers' liability" for loss or damage to property of guests while within the insured premises or in the possession of the insured.

Mercantile Robbery and Safe Burglary Endorsement. This form provides coverage for loss of money, securities, and other property both inside and outside the insured premises, in addition to burglary of a safe.

Broad Form Storekeepers Endorsement. Designed to provide limited fidelity and burglary coverage for the small mercantile store, this endorsement is used when the insured employs less than five employees.

Inland marine coverages. There are several optional inland marine coverage endorsements which can be added to Section I. These are designed to provide coverage for both owned property and property of others in the care, custody, or control of the insured. Coverage is on an all-risks basis, subject to specific exclusions, terms, and conditions. These endorsements follow closely the usual inland marine property floater contracts. The specific endorsements available are *Radium Floater, Fine Arts Floater, Camera Floater, Musical Instruments Floater, Neon Sign Endorsement, Glass Coverage Endorsement,* and *Physicians and Surgeons Equipment Endorsement.*

Accounts Receivable and Valuable Papers and Records Endorsements. These endorsements provide coverage on an all-risks basis, similar to inland marine floater endorsements, and are examined individually.

The *Accounts Receivable Endorsement* is available to provide coverage for all sums due from the insured's customers, plus interest and collection expenses provided the insured is unable to make collection because of a direct loss or damage to the accounts receivable records. Both reporting and nonreporting forms are obtainable, depending upon the needs of the insured.

The *Valuable Papers and Records Endorsement* provides insurance coverage for valuable papers and records of the insured while on the designated premises. Included are documents and records, books, maps, films, drawings, abstracts, deeds, mortgages, and manuscripts. Money and securities are excluded. The perils insured against are "all-risks" of direct physical loss. A separate limit of liability is allowed for specified articles, and a blanket limit is available to provide coverage for all others not specified. There is a limited extension provision for coverage of such property while away from the designated premises (10 percent of the combined limits not to exceed $5,000).

General Liability coverage—Section II

Coverage for basic liability is *mandatory* and provided under Section II of the SMP. Generally, coverage is written on a comprehensive general liability (CGL) basis for any occurrence arising out of the ownership, maintenance, or use of the insured premises and for operations which are necessary or incidental to the named insured's business. Coverage is on a combined single limit basis. Separate limits for bodily injury and property damage are available if desired. The form provides coverage for both the products and completed operations exposures unless excluded.

It is imperative that the insurance company underwriter be consulted to determine what forms are being utilized in their standard package policy for Section II liability coverages. An insurance company may have their own form filed to provide coverage for the premises/operations exposures. In addition, there may be other optional endorsements available to broaden the scope of coverage. Broad form liability, personal injury coverage, employers nonowned automobile, automobile fleet coverages, professional liability, comprehensive medical payments coverage, contractual liability, independent contractors, and elevator collision are examples of coverages which may or may not be available depending on the individual account and the insurance company providing the policy.

Crime coverage—Section III

This section of the SMP is designed to provide coverage for money and securities, negotiable instruments, and employee dishonesty. Basic property forms exclude crime coverages, and there is only limited coverage for these exposures available under some of the miscellaneous crime endorsements (Broad Form Storekeepers or Mercantile Robbery and Safe Burglary Endorsements). Some businesses, however, need broader coverage, higher limits, or may not be eligible for coverage under the limited endorsements.

There are three basic forms for coverage under this section: *Comprehensive Crime Coverage Endorsement, Blanket Crime Coverage Endorsement,* or *Public Employers Blanket Endorsement.* The principal difference between the Comprehensive Crime and Blanket Crime coverage is that under the blanket form, coverage for *all* insuring agreements is mandatory. Under the comprehensive crime form, the insured may opt for the specific coverage agreements and varying limits of liability depending on their needs. In addition, coverage for employee dishonesty on a blanket position basis is available only under the Comprehensive Crime Endorsement. The blanket position coverage under this endorsement allows the stated limit of liability to be applied to each employee. Therefore, for example, if three employees acted in collusion to steal $30,000, a $10,000 blanket position coverage would cover the loss in full. In contrast, the commercial blanket limit of liability applies on an occurrence basis for any one loss, regardless of the number of employees involved. In the previous example, a $30,000 Commercial Blanket Bond would be required to cover the loss in full.

The following are the coverages or insuring agreements available under the Comprehensive Crime Endorsements:

IA. *Employee Dishonesty (Commercial Blanket).* This agreement provides coverage for the loss of money, securities, and other property as a result of any dishonest or fraudulent acts by the insured's employee(s). The limit stated is the amount which can be applied to each occurrence, regardless of the number of employees which may be involved. All employees of the insured are covered.

IB. *Employee Dishonesty (Blanket Position).* Coverage under this agreement is identical to that provided under IA. However, the limit of liability is applied on a per employee rather than per occurrence basis. All employees of the insured are covered.

II. *Money and Securities—Loss Inside the Premises.* This provides coverage up to the specified limit of liability for loss of money and securities by destruction, disappearance, or wrongful abstraction inside the insured premises or at any banking premises.

III. *Money and Securities—Loss Outside the Premises.* Coverage under this agreement is the same as under II, except that coverage is for money and securities while outside the premises, being transported by a messenger, in the home of a messenger, or while in an armored vehicle.

IV. *Money Orders and Counterfeit Paper Currency Coverage.* This agreement provides coverage for the insured against loss due to the acceptance, in good faith, of any counterfeit money or money orders in the course of business.

V. *Depositors Forgery Coverage.* Coverage under this agreement is provided for the insured or bank, when a savings or checking account is maintained, for the loss which results from forgery of checks, drafts, or other negotiable instruments.

Coverage under these agreements is not always all inclusive. The forms must be reviewed for specific limitations and exclusions and the consideration of deductibles should not be overlooked. It is important to note the form provides coverage for loss by extortion unless specifically excluded. Coverage under Section III is intended to closely parallel the monoline crime coverages available under separate policies or under the Comprehensive Crime or Three-D Policy (Dishonesty, Destruction, or Disappearance). However, the SMP discount may make it sensible to include crime coverage here.

Boiler and machinery insurance—Section IV

Depending on the nature of the exposures, an insured may have a need for insurance covering boilers, refrigeration equipment, electrical apparatus, and other kinds of machinery. This type of coverage was discussed in Chapter 17.

Some insurance companies will not insure this coverage but will obtain a cooperative arrangement with another insurer specializing in this area to provide the underwriting, pricing, and loss control services. Such coverage still may be endorsed to the insured's package policy at a discount.

The *SMP Boiler and Machinery Coverage Endorsement* provides the basic language and coverage for this section of the multi-peril policy. Included are all boilers, unfired pressure vessels, and piping in use or connected and ready for use. Usually coverage is provided on the basis of a survey completed by the insurance company. The specific limits, locations, and terms are outlined on a separate *Declarations Endorsement*. Coverage on other types of machinery and apparatus can be provided through the use of an *Additional Object Groups Endorsement*. This equipment must be scheduled.

Business Interruption coverage may be available under Section IV on a valued daily indemnity basis or a valued weekly indemnity basis. Extra Expense coverage also may be available for the period of restoration. In addition, coverage may be available for Prevention of Occupancy and Consequential Damage. Coverage is written on an actual cash value basis unless the insured opts for repair and replacement cost, which is added by endorsement.

CONCLUSION

The SMP program has proved to be a viable mechanism in meeting most of the basic insurance needs of the small to medium-sized business. This does not, however, preclude its use with a large firm, but larger businesses may have insurance requirements beyond the scope of the SMP program. The major advantage of the package insurance policy, combining several separate insurance coverages, is a single policy contract at a reduced cost and the flexibility of the available insurance coverage options.

It is imperative that insurance needs be carefully assessed both from the standpoint of exposure to loss and limits of liability. Many exposures can severely impair the business operations of a firm and render it inoperative. These situations have to be anticipated and the insurance benefits compared to the cost.

The impact of the SMP program has been significant. The increase in premium dollars written by the insurance companies in the commercial package policy area is evidence of its popularity and success. Indications are this coverage approach will continue to grow in popularity, permitting the insurance buyer to continue to benefit from the advantages the SMP program offers in meeting his insurance needs.

CHAPTER 22

INSURANCE FOR FARMERS

THE FARMOWNERS' (FARM
PACKAGE) POLICY
Basic Perils coverage
Broad Perils coverage
All-risk coverage
Property requiring specific insurance
Additional features and extensions
Liability coverage

WORKERS' COMPENSATION AND
EMPLOYERS' LIABILITY

CROP HAIL INSURANCE

LIVESTOCK MORTALITY INSURANCE

SAFETY, LOSS CONTROL, AND
INSURANCE TO VALUE

James A. Carter
President and Chief Operating Officer
Lumbermens Mutual Insurance Company
Mansfield, Ohio

James A. Carter is President and Chief Operating Officer of the Lumbermens Mutual Insurance Company, Mansfield, Ohio. Prior to his current position he was President, Chief Executive Officer, and a Director of INA Farm Center, Inc., which specialized in agricultural insurance and reinsurance marketing. Mr. Carter has had over 26 years of experience in property and casualty insurance underwriting, marketing, and management. He is a graduate of The Citadel, The Military College of South Carolina, with a Bachelor of Arts in English Literature, and is the author of various articles on general subjects, insurance, and management.

Few groups in history have made a more vital contribution to the nation or to the world than America's farmers. Not only is our food dependent upon their skill and dedication to their chosen livelihood, but our entire standard of living is highly dependent upon agriculture.

Therefore, no other label fits today's American farmer quite so well as *businessman;* a businessman whose astute use of modern technology enables him to manage a growing and profitable operation characterized by greater production and increased yield.

As a farmer, you are well aware of risks. You face them every day. By simply operating a farm your life becomes an ongoing battle with a most formidable opponent—the unpredictable elements of nature. You also own very valuable property, and there are many things that can happen to it—either by minor accident or major disaster—making your chances of getting through even one year unscathed highly improbable.

Fortunately, there are alternative measures available to you, and one of these measures is arranging with your insurance advisor to protect yourself against a large portion of such risks by insurance in return for a reasonable premium charge.

That is what this chapter is all about—the insurance protection available to you, the American farmer, a businessman.

Over the years insurance practices for dealing with farm and non-farm risks have differed considerably because of differences in hazards and because of the influence of history on farm insurance.

For nonfarm risks, "standard" policies have existed for decades. However, this has *not* been true for farm risks. A major reason for this is that much farm insurance historically has been written by small mutual companies or associations operating only in a state or a county, and serving the more isolated farmers who in the past banded together for the mutual protection of their property and operations.

These companies have not been closely controlled by state insurance regulation, and they, therefore, produced their own contracts which served their membership's desires and perceived needs. Many of these companies continue to exist and prosper serving a segment of American agriculture. At the same time the national mutual and stock insurance companies over the past few years have developed "standard" farm insurance contracts.

In order to confine this chapter to a manageable treatment of the subject, discussion will be restricted to "packaged" contracts for property and liability insurance and the specialized contracts for livestock and growing crops generally offered by the national and regional mutual and stock insurance companies of America.

THE FARMOWNERS' (FARM PACKAGE) POLICY

Just as there is a Homeowners' Policy for the residential home-owner and a Commercial Package Policy for the commercial establishment, there is a Farmowners' or Farm Package Policy available to you as an American farmer. This contract essentially provides you with two broad areas of protection. It provides coverage for your property, and it also gives you protection in case of public liability losses and suits arising out of your personal pursuits and farming operations. There is a broad range of coverages available under this policy, and it can be modified or tailored to meet most of your property and public liability insurance requirements as a farmer, whether large or small. It does not cover your crops in the field while growing and maturing. However, insurance protection for your crops is available, and it will be discussed.

The policy insures against physical loss to your dwelling; personal property in that dwelling; and other farm property, including farm machinery, livestock, stored crops; farm structures; outbuildings; and farm personal property.

There are three levels of property coverage available; the Basic, the Broad, and the All-Risk Perils forms. Differences in protection and cost should be carefully evaluated with your insurance advisor. In many states the entire package is competitively rated and priced. Some company's policies also contain dividend provisions returning a portion of the insurance company's profit, if any, to you, the policy-holder.

Basic Perils coverage

Generally, Basic Perils coverage insures your dwelling; personal property in the dwelling; other farm property such as farm machinery, livestock, farm structures, stored crops; and farm personal property against the following perils: fire and lightning, windstorm, and hail, explosion, riots, vandalism and malicious mischief, damage to property from vehicles or falling aircraft, damage to property which is being moved to a safe place for protection from a covered peril, accidental damage from smoke, accidental damage to electrical appliances resulting from artificially generated electrical currents, sonic boom, and theft.

The following specific property also usually is insured against certain additional perils:

☐ Injury or damage to livestock or other farm personal property (except mobile farm machinery and equipment) from overturn or collision of the vehicle in which it is being transported.

- ☐ Damage to mobile farm machinery and equipment from overturn.
- ☐ Damage or injury to mobile farm machinery and equipment, other farm property, and livestock from earthquake.
- ☐ Injury to livestock on or off the premises from flood.
- ☐ Damage or injury to mobile farm machinery and equipment, other farm personal property, and livestock from bridge or culvert collapse.
- ☐ And, damage or injury to mobile farm machinery and equipment, other personal property, and livestock in the event the vessel in which such property is being transported is stranded, sunk, burned, or involved in a collision.

Not covered in the Basic Perils form are the following:

1. Loss caused directly or indirectly by frost or cold weather, ice (other than hail), snowstorm or sleet, whether or not driven by wind.
2. Loss or damage to the interior of your buildings and the property in the building caused by rain, snow, sand, or dust, all whether or not driven by wind, *unless your covered building has sustained actual damage to roof or walls by the direct force of wind or hail*. If there has been damage to the roof or walls of the covered building by the direct force of wind or hail, coverage is provided for loss to the interior of that building or the property in the building if caused by rain, snow, sand, or dust entering the buildings through the openings in the roof or walls.
3. Loss by water from sprinkler equipment or other piping, unless there is damage to such equipment or piping as a direct result of wind or hail.
4. Loss to livestock or poultry by fright, by freezing, or smothering in blizzards or snowstorms, or by their running into streams or ditches or against fences or other objects.
5. Loss to crops, grain, hay, or straw outside of buildings.

Coverage for the perils of *aircraft and vehicles* excludes loss to driveways, walks, fences, lawns, trees, shrubs, and other plants if caused by any vehicle or aircraft owned or operated by you or an occupant of your covered premises. *Injury to electrical appliances, devices, fixtures, and wiring from electrical currents artificially generated* excludes loss to television picture tubes.

Theft generally does not cover:

1. Loss caused by your relatives residing with you.
2. Loss caused by your tenant, his employees, or members of his household.
3. Loss to money, securities, and other valuable personal articles if

the portion of the dwelling customarily occupied exclusively by you is rented to others.

4. Loss to any other residential premises or property therein or thereon owned or rented by you to a member of your family residing with you except when in actual use as your or their temporary residence.
5. Loss in or to a dwelling in course of construction of lumber and material therefor until completed and ready for occupancy.
6. Loss of property left unattended in any motor vehicle unless the loss is the result of forcible entry into a fully enclosed body or compartment (not including a glove compartment), and there is visible evidence of such forcible entry and the doors and windows were locked—except when on your insured residential premises or when you are required to surrender the keys to a bailee.
7. Loss by mysterious disappearance or unaccountable shortage.
8. Loss due to the acceptance of counterfeit money, fraudulent post office or express money orders, or checks, or promissory notes which are not paid upon presentation.

Broad Perils coverage

Broad Perils coverage generally include the same protection for your dwelling, its contents, and other farm property as featured in the Basic Perils.

Additionally, the Broad Perils form generally insures your dwelling and its contents against the following perils not in the Basic form:

1. Damage resulting from falling objects.
2. Steam or a hot water heating system rupture.
3. Damage to buildings or property within them resulting from weight of ice, snow, or sleet.
4. Collapse of buildings.
5. Glass breakage in the dwelling.
6. Water escape resulting from leakage or overflow in plumbing, heating, or air-conditioning systems.
7. Freezing of plumbing, heating, and air-conditioning systems.

Reimbursement also would be provided for any additional living expenses incurred as a result of damages caused by the covered perils.

From the peril of *falling objects*, there is excluded:

1. Loss from earthquake, landslide, or other earth movement.
2. Loss to the interior of buildings or the property covered therein caused by falling objects unless the building first sustains actual damage to roof or walls from such falling objects.
3. Loss to lawns, trees, shrubs, and plants.

From the peril, *weight of ice, snow, or sleet,* there is excluded loss to outdoor equipment; fences; retaining walls, if not a part of the covered building; driveways; walks; lawns; trees; shrubs and plants, except as the direct result of the collapse of the building.

From the peril, *collapse of building,* there is excluded:

1. Loss by earthquake, landslide, or other earth movement.
2. Loss to outdoor equipment.
3. Loss to fences; retaining walls, if a part of the covered building; driveways; walks; lawns; trees; shrubs; and plants.

From the peril, *glass breakage,* there is excluded loss while the covered building is vacant beyond a period of 30 days except that a building in the course of construction shall not be deemed to be vacant.

From the peril, *water escape,* there is excluded the cost of repairing or replacing the plumbing, heating, or air-conditioning system, or domestic appliances or parts thereof unless the loss is caused by earthquake, landslide, or other earth movement, or the result from freezing.

Excluded from the *freezing of plumbing, heating, and air-conditioning systems* peril are:

1. Loss resulting from earthquake, landslide, or other earth movement.
2. Loss while the covered building is vacant or unoccupied unless due diligence shall have been exercised with respect to maintaining heat in the building, or unless the plumbing, heating, or air-conditioning systems, and the domestic appliances have been drained and the water supply shut off during vacancy or unoccupancy.

In addition to the exclusions enumerated before, the policy does not cover loss caused by flood, except as provided under Basic Perils; nor loss caused by surface water; waves or tidal wave; overflow of stream or other bodies of water of a spray from any of the foregoing. However, such a loss or damage as a result of fire or explosion is covered.

Also excluded from Broad Perils are:

1. Loss by misappropriation, secretion, conversion, infidelity, or any dishonest act on the part of you or any other party of interest, your or their employees or agents and others to whom the property may be entrusted except carriers for hire.
2. Loss caused by order of any civil authority.
3. Loss from hostile or warlike action in time of peace or war.

4. Loss from insurrection, rebellion, revolution, and so on.
5. And, loss from nuclear reaction as defined in the policy.

All-risk coverage

The All-Risk Perils form includes all of the coverages for your dwelling, its contents, and other farm personal property which are available in the Basic and Broad Perils forms.

Additionally, your dwelling and mobile farm machinery are insured against all risk of direct physical loss or damage from any perils not in the Basic or Broad Perils forms, with only the following exceptions:

1. Damage to any insured item caused by regular wear and tear, dampness of atmosphere or extreme temperature.
2. Damage to the dwelling caused by termites or other insects.
3. Damage from deterioration, rust, wet or dry rot, mold, settling, or the shrinkage or expansion of the foundation, walls, floors, or ceilings.
4. Damage to physical property outside the dwelling such as pavements, swimming pools, and foundations caused by freezing, thawing, or the pressure of weight of water.
5. Routine breakdown of farm vehicles.
6. Damage to tires, unless the loss results from fire, windstorm, or theft.
7. Damage caused by animals or birds owned by you or your employee, unless the loss is the result of fire, explosion, or smoke.

Property requiring specific insurance

In any previous definition of property covered, *certain property is specifically excluded* from the definition under the policy, regardless of whether the Basic, Broad, or All-Risk form is used for coverage.

Excluded property includes:

1. Aircraft.
2. Vehicles designed and licensed primarily for use on public roads.
3. Recreational vehicles, except for specific coverage previously mentioned.
4. Property otherwise insured under specific policies such as live animals covered under mortality insurance.
5. Race horses while on the grounds of public racetracks.
6. Growing crops, trees, plants, shrubs, and lawns.
7. Portable buildings; property stored in or being processed in public facilities.

8. Outdoor radio and television equipment, silos, windmills, windpumps, and their towers.
9. Light poles and wiring and fencing and corrals.
10. Property belonging to a tenant.
11. Property rented to others except while on the insured premises or in the dwelling customarily occupied exclusively by the insured.

To be covered any property falling in any of these categories must be specifically insured by another policy or by endorsement to the Package Policy.

There are also certain monetary limitations for specific property.

1. Money is limited to $100.
2. Securities, tickets, and manuscripts or any combination thereof are limited to $500.
3. Firearms and jewelry of various descriptions as well as furs is limited to $500.
4. Boats and their equipment are limited to $500 (this coverage applies only while the boats and their equipment are in an enclosed building on your insured premises).
5. Stamps and coin collections are limited to $1,000.
6. And, property while being transported is limited to $1,000.

These limits may be increased by endorsement.

Additional features and extensions

The following additional features or extensions of coverage are available:

1. Increased coverage for valuable personal articles such as jewelry, furs, and antiques.
2. Extended theft coverage, including mysterious disappearance.
3. Additional coverages for perils involving livestock, including accidental shooting, attack by wild animals, drowning, and electrocution.
4. Coverage against the fraudulent use of credit cards in the event they are stolen.
5. Coverage against loss of income as the result of physical damage to property caused by an insured peril.
6. Coverage against extra expenses incurred in continuing farm operations elsewhere or with rented equipment while damaged property is being repaired.
7. Higher deductibles which can result in lower premiums.

Liability coverage

Regardless of whether you choose the Basic, Broad, or All-Risk form of coverage for your property (Section I), you also will be insured against liability arising out of your personal and farming activities up to the limits set forth in Section II—Liability of your policy.

This means that if a person is injured or property is damaged as a result of your farm operation, any claim for which you are legally liable is covered up to the limits of the policy. Personal liability resulting from strictly personal activities also is covered.

Medical expenses for guests who are accidentally injured on your property will also be paid, regardless of who is responsible.

In certain cases, when someone else's property is damaged while in your care, custody, and control, this policy provides for either payment or replacement.

It should be kept in mind that in all cases, coverage is limited by the coverages selected and the amount of coverage purchased.

Furthermore, you will be defended in lawsuits, whether successful or groundless, and, in most cases, all court costs and judgments will be paid, subject to the limitations and exclusions stated in this policy.

You also may purchase, under Section II of the policy coverage for loss by death of any cattle, horse, dog, sheep, or goat owned by you and caused by collision between such animal and a vehicle not owned and operated by you or any of your employees, if the collision occurs while the animal is within a public highway and is not being transported.

Bodily injury and property damage coverage also may be extended to include personal injury liability—that liability arising out of one or more of the following offenses committed in the conduct of your personal activities or farming business; false arrest, detention, or imprisonment or malicious prosecution; the publication or utterance of a libel, or slander, or of any defamatory or disparaging material; or a publication or utterance violating an individual's right of privacy, except that such acts related to advertising, broadcasting, or telecasting is excluded from coverage. Wrongful entry, eviction, or other invasion of the right of private occupancy is covered.

Exclusions to personal injury coverage are:

1. Liability assumed under contract or agreements.
2. Willful violation of a penal statute or ordinance.
3. Injury to your employee arising out of his employment by you.
4. An utterance made by or at the direction of you with knowledge of the falsity of the utterance.

Liability coverages under the policy also may be extended to insure against claims arising out of injury to you, your family, your farm, and other employees in certain limited nonfarm business pursuits in which you or members of your family may be engaged.

Because of the trend toward larger and more sophisticated farming operations, a word of caution is appropriate regarding proper liability coverages. Sometimes too little thought is given to what liability coverages are appropriate or what policy should be used to cover a farming operation which may be involved in other complex and diversified activities. The casual approach of, "It's a farm so a Farmers' Comprehensive Liability Policy or coverage as provided under the Package Policy is appropriate," can be unsound in today's world.

It behooves you and your insurance advisor to survey comprehensively all businesses owned or operated by you prior to determination of what type of liability coverage is best. A roadside stand to sell your farm products would be covered under the basic coverage of Section II of the Package Policy; however, the operation of a processing plant, a farm implement dealership, a crop dusting or spraying service, or other related commercial operations may not be covered.

In summary, the involvement of any activities which may be classified as not personal or not farming requires careful review by you and your insurance advisor to determine if a more comprehensive liability policy, explained in Chapter 8, is not more appropriate than a Farmers' Comprehensive Liability Policy or liability as provided under Section II of the Farmowners' or Farm Package Policy.

Some vehicles which are licensed primarily for use on public highways or roads are excluded from the coverages discussed in this chapter. Your automobiles, trucks, and other licensed motor vehicles must be insured under separate policies. You should refer to Chapters 9 and 10 which describe in detail protection needed and available for automobiles and trucks as well as for garage operations.

WORKERS' COMPENSATION AND EMPLOYERS' LIABILITY

Also, depending on your operations, you may have a workers' compensation and employers' liability exposure of a very serious nature which goes beyond that coverage contemplated under the extension of Section II of the Package Policy for employers' liability. In some states you, as a farmer, are required by law to be covered by workers' compensation insurance. If you do not have workers' compensation insurance in such states you lose any common-law defenses against an insured employee in case an employee sues you for an injury arising from his employment by you.

In any event, consideration should be given to insuring this risk under a Standard Workers' Compensation Policy including employers' liability. Even if agricultural employees are exempt from workers' compensation laws in the state in which you operate, you may be inadequately covered if you have only employers' liability under the Package Policy or a Farmers' Comprehensive Liability Policy. For example, if one of your farm employees, while engaged in nonagricultural work related to your operations, is injured, he might sue and secure a judgment against you. If the court were to rule that his injury came within the workers' compensation law, employers' liability under a Farmers' Comprehensive Liability Policy or the Package Policy would not respond.

Additional information on workers' compensation and employers' liability insurance may be found in Chapter 11.

CROP HAIL INSURANCE

You will recall from the discussion of the Farmowners' or Farm Package Policy that crops in the field are excluded from coverage. However a Crop Hail Policy is available which protects your crops against direct loss from the perils of hail, fire, and lightning once there is a normal stand clearly visible above the ground.

If the crop is one which begins with the transplanting of plants grown elsewhere—such as tobacco—coverage becomes effective at a specific time after the crop has been set in the field. For example, insurance becomes effective on a tobacco crop on the 15th day after the crop has been set in the field. The Crop Hail Policy is not only a specific perils policy but it also names the specific crops and specific location of such crops for identification in case of loss. Crops and fields not designated have no coverage even though owned by you.

The policy becomes effective one minute after midnight on the day immediately following the date that you and the insurance company representative sign the application. That application becomes a legal and binding part of the contract of insurance. If damage occurs during the day between the signing of the application and the attachment of the coverage, no insurance will apply. The premium collected will be returned if notice is given to the company within 72 hours after such damage. The company must also be advised of any other insurance written on the described crops including Federal Crop Insurance Corporation Coverage. Unless notification of such other insurance coverage is given, the Crop Hail Policy does not cover the crop. Each of these conditions is set forth in detail in the Application-Declarations of the contract which you sign.

The Crop Hail Policy has special provisions applying to specific crops and also to each state or group of states in which the crop or crops are most prevalent. Generally there are specific termination dates set forth in the policy for coverage of each crop.

Certain optional coverages are also available:

1. The optional extension of fire coverage to certain crops excluded in the basic policy.
2. Coverage for wind with hail in certain situations.
3. Coverage applying only to an amount in excess of a certain percentage of the loss.

Other than specific exclusions applying to various crops and various states, there is only one general exclusion in the policy—nuclear incidents.

A very important consideration for you in obtaining your crop hail insurance is adjustment of claims for loss. The adjustment of crop losses is a very special activity, considerably different from that of the adjustment of other property and casualty losses. Investigate the company's experience in writing of crop insurance and in the adjustment of crop claims.

Brief mention of the Federal Crop Insurance Corporation, an activity of the federal government, in the crop insurance area is appropriate. This activity, subsidized by federal taxes, provides all-risk protection in various sections of the country for various crops. For further information on this subject, contact the local agent of the U.S. Department of Agriculture.

LIVESTOCK MORTALITY INSURANCE

In our discussion of the Farmowners' (Farm Package) Policy, you will recall that certain limited coverages are provided for livestock or farm animals. However, there is a specific policy, the Livestock Mortality Policy, which provides life insurance for farm animals and livestock.

The Livestock Mortality Policy insures against loss by death only. But the coverage extends to loss by death resulting from intentional destruction for humane reasons to avoid or terminate incurable and excessive suffering provided the destruction of the animal is accomplished according to the terms of the policy. These terms must be explicitly followed for coverage to apply:

☐ A veterinary surgeon acceptable by the company must certify in advance of the destruction that it is necessary to terminate incurable and excessive suffering.

☐ With respect to horses injured in the course of a race, a qualified veterinarian appointed by the state to serve at the racetrack where the injury occurs may certify that the suffering was incurable and so excessive that immediate destruction was imperative for humane reasons as an alternative to the employment of a veterinary surgeon acceptable to the company.

Livestock mortality does not insure against loss by reason of a covered animal becoming unsuitable for a particular use or purpose, including the use specified in the policy, whether as a result of disease or injury or otherwise. Also, it does not cover death by intentional destruction because of such unsuitability.

The insurance company has the additional right, at any time, in its discretion, and at its sole expense to assume control of the treatment of any covered animal which is sick or injured. The insurer, at its expense, also may move the covered animal to any place at which treatment is available and have such treatment administered by a veterinarian of the insurer's choice. In the event that the animal recovers from the illness or injury as a result of the treatment and is returned to the insured, no claim for loss of the animal shall be made by reason of the insurer's exercise of his rights.

Specific conditions apply to livestock mortality and its coverage:

1. At the time the insurance becomes effective you must be the sole owner of each covered animal. Coverage for any animal ceases immediately upon sale of the animal or any interest in it.
2. Any covered animal cannot be operated on for castration or spaying without the permission of the company. Further, upon recovery of the animal from such operation, you are required to forward to the company a veterinary certificate for review. The company reserves the right to revise coverage under the policy within 30 days of the operation.
3. Failure to obtain company permission for an operation will terminate coverage for the animal at midnight prior to the day of the operation.

Specific exclusions to this coverage are:

1. Loss resulting, directly or indirectly, from neglect or failure to provide proper veterinary care and attention.
2. Willful or malicious injury by you, your agent, your employees or bailees (except bailees for hire).
3. Loss which results from fraudulent, dishonest, or criminal acts or omissions done by you or at your instigation or by your employee or any other person having the care, custody, or control of the animal including independent contractors.
4. The destruction of any animal because the animal has contracted

or been exposed to any contagious or communicable disease, whether such destruction is by order of any government or otherwise.

5. Confiscation, nationalization, requisition, or destruction by or under the order of any government or public or local authority or any person or activity having jurisdiction in the matter.
6. Loss to any animal which has been "unnerved" (the operation of neurotomy for lameness).
7. Loss caused by or resulting from hostile or warlike action, by any government or sovereign power using military forces, or by any agent of such government, power, authority, or forces.
8. Loss caused by insurrection, rebellion, revolution, riots, civil commotion, and so on.

The policy does not cover:

1. The death of any covered animal if the animal is used for any purpose other than that specified in the policy.
2. Death directly or indirectly occurring as a consequence of a surgical operation, unless conducted by a qualified veterinary surgeon and certified by him to have been necessitated solely by a peril insured against, and to have been carried out in an attempt to preserve the animal's life.
3. Death directly or indirectly occurring as a consequence of an inoculation, unless conducted by a qualified veterinary surgeon and certified by him to be of prophylactic nature or necessitated by a peril insured against.
4. Loss by nuclear reaction or nuclear radiation or radioactive contamination, or by any weapon of war employing nuclear fission or radioactive force.
5. Loss by death or destruction of any animal because it is unfit for or incapable of fulfilling any particular functions or duties.
6. Loss as a consequence of delay, loss of use, or loss of market.

Livestock mortality insurance is provided only upon the receipt and acceptance of a completed and signed application including a veterinary certificate of examination. Veterinary certification is also necessary for renewal.

SAFETY, LOSS CONTROL, AND INSURANCE TO VALUE

Now that the more standard property and liability contracts of insurance used generally by the larger national and regional mutual and stock companies have been reviewed, two very important related subjects need to be discussed. These are loss control and insurance to value.

Though the American farmer always has prided himself on his independence or uniqueness when compared to other commercial enterprises, social legislation continues to bring him more and more under the umbrella of federal and state regulation in the conduct of his business. Notable are the requirements of certain states or the federal government that agriculture is subject to the provisions of the Occupational Safety and Health Act of 1970 (OSHA); workers' compensation laws, and laws restricting the hiring of younger people.

Beyond any moral and humane desires to protect against loss of life and limb is the legal necessity to comply with various safety and employment laws. Also, since insurance contracts are contracts of indemnity, there are many hidden costs in lost time and lost productivity not covered by insurance. For these reasons safety and loss control is important.

In the farmer, the merger of man, machines, and environment is seen in its purist form. With continually increasing complexity of farm operations and machines used in farming, the farm has become a complex combination of hazards requiring careful management to protect against liability losses. This growing complexity of liability hazards has been accompanied by rapidly increasing values in real and personal property.

Certain services by your insurer are contemplated in the premium charges and other services may be purchased for additional costs. Other services are available from unrelated farm insurance experts— both governmental and private. The National Safety Council has a division devoted solely to agriculture and agriculture-related safety management. Available through this national organization are a number of specialized pamphlets and the Farm and Ranch Safety Management kit. Their address is 425 N. Michigan Avenue, Chicago, Illinois 60611. Also through the Extension Service of the U.S. Department of Agriculture, Agriculture Experimental Stations, and through land grant colleges in the various states, written and personal assistance is available. The increasing importance of safety and loss control in farming operations has been acknowledged by the National 4-H Council and the Future Farmers of America in their youth programs and activities.

The location of your property and operations is generally not within a metropolitan area where professional fire fighters and equipment are available. For this reason individual efforts to prevent fires and to contain them once started is of paramount importance to you. The sources cited also may be used to obtain expertise, literature, services, and equipment to aid you in controlling fire peril.

Lightning is one of the more dangerous weather perils to property and is a principal cause of loss. Yet protection and expert assistance is available to reduce loss from this peril.

The constant increase in liability judgments arising in part from the liberal interpretation of negligence can no longer be escaped by the American farmer. It is important that you be aware of and use all means to prevent loss which may be caused by your operations, the products you sell, and the environment in which you operate. Such loss prevention is an integral part of your risk management program.

Any treatment of insurance involves two aspects: the necessity of the insurance company to secure an adequate premium to cover small losses as well as the large ones; and the need for adequate recovery by the insured to cover the increasingly larger losses caused by rapidly increasing values in real, personal, and farm property.

As mentioned earlier, there are a number of companies which use various methods to limit losses and to require participation by the farmer in such losses. Two such methods are the Deferred Loss Payment Clause and the Percent to Value Provisions found in some smaller mutual companies. However, for our purpose, only the provisions of the Farmowners' (Farm Package) Policy will be discussed.

Emphasis on the subject of insurance to value is especially necessary in a discussion of farm insurance. For despite the growing sophistication of farming as a business, the typical farmer needs help in improving and updating his insurance program. It is fair to say that this subject has not received the degree of attention from farmers that it has by other commercial enterprises.

Surveys continually show that large numbers of American farmers are seriously underinsured. The underinsured farmer continues to be the most vulnerable to the ravages of inflation should he fall victim to fire, windstorm, or some other disaster which causes serious damage to his real, personal, and farm properties. A recent survey, completed by a national insurance company in which 80 farmers participated, showed 68 of the farmers to be underinsured. The various dwellings, personal property, farm structures machinery, equipment, and livestock involved were valued in excess of $15.5 million. Yet insurance coverage carried amounted to just over $6 million—considerably less than half their value. This same company, at the request of one farmer, surveyed his property which had not been reviewed professionally for insurance for over eight years. The value of his dwelling was established at $55,000, yet it was insured for only $25,000. His farm buildings were valued at $78,000 but were covered for only $45,000. His machinery, livestock, feed, and grain valued at $300,000 were insured for a mere $82,000. Nothing in the survey indicated this to be an unusual case.

The Farmowners' or Farm Package Policy provides for replacement cost on your dwelling up to the limits of the policy. This means that if the amount of insurance carried is at least 80 percent of the rebuilding cost at the time of loss, it would be fully insured subject to the limits of the policy. However, in case the insurance were less than 80 percent of the current rebuilding cost, your insurance policy would only respond for the actual cash value, which is defined as replacement cost minus depreciation. Blanket personal property is also fully insured for the amount of the loss if 80 percent of the value is insured; otherwise, the insured becomes a co-insurer in case of loss. Outbuildings are insured on an actual cash value basis.

Ideally, your insurance should be adequate to cover the cost of repairing, rebuilding, or replacing a key structure (a dwelling or outbuilding vitally important to the farm operation) with materials of like kind and quality without any reduction in the payment for depreciation. Therefore, for best protection of your assets, your dwelling and all key farm structures should be insured for 100 percent of their replacement value. Your outbuildings and farm personal property, such as machinery, equipment, livestock, grain, and feed, should be insured for 100 percent of actual cash value. Household and personal effects should be inventoried and insured for 100 percent of replacement or actual cash value (whichever your policy provides).

There is no doubt that in the current climate the possibility of establishing a six-figure legal claim has extended beyond urban and surburban environs to the rural environment of the farmer, and he is viewed as an equal to business in this respect. Also inflation, increasing complexity, and sophistication has raised real, personal, and farm property values to a level which makes protection of your assets against physical loss of vital importance to your future.

The insurance contracts and services discussed in this chapter provide the best protection available to you today for your farming operations. The listing of perils covered and types of property and losses excluded can serve as a check list for you to "buy back" any exclusion or limitation you need. Farmers work hard enough at their farming activities. Lack of insurance should not interfere with that valuable work.

PROVIDING FOR BUSINESS CONTINUATION THROUGH INSURANCE AND SELECTED EMPLOYEE BENEFITS

PROVIDING FOR BUSINESS CONTINUATION THROUGH INSURANCE AND SELECTED EMPLOYEE BENEFITS— FOR THE SOLE PROPRIETOR

HEALTH INSURANCE
  Blue Cross–Blue Shield
  Comprehensive Hospital-Surgical-
    Major Medical coverage
  Optional coverages available with
    group plans

HOW TO BUY

DISABILITY
  Policy considerations

LIFE INSURANCE
  Mutual or stock company
  Term or permanent
  Beware of the twister

  Nonforfeiture provisions
  Options and riders
  Use of dividends

RETIREMENT

DISPOSING OF THE BUSINESS
  Disability
  Death
  Retirement
  Necessary provisions in the buy-sell
    agreement

THE ESTATE PLAN OF THE SOLE
PROPRIETOR

Arthur Gowell, CLU
Trust Officer
Burlington County Trust Company
Moorestown, New Jersey

Arthur Gowell majored in economics and insurance at the Wharton School, University of Pennsylvania. He has more than 30 years' experience in life insurance sales and sales management, and presently is a trust officer at Burlington County Trust Company, Moorestown, New Jersey. Mr. Gowell has taught courses for life underwriters in business life and health insurance, and has been a frequent contributor to insurance journals. He received his Chartered Life Underwriter designation in 1958 and his Masters Degree in Financial Services in 1979.

Gordon K. Rose, CLU
Vice President for Student and Faculty Services
The American College
Bryn Mawr, Pennsylvania

Gordon K. Rose is Vice President for Student and Faculty Services at The American College, Bryn Mawr, Pennsylvania. He received his B.S. Degree from Penn State University in 1950 and the CLU designation from the American College in 1957. After 18 years in life insurance sales, sales management, and insurance company home office executive positions, he joined The American College in 1969. He has instructed CLU courses for the past 15 years. Mr. Rose is active in the Griffith Foundation for Insurance Education and a member of the Board of Trustees. He is a member of the American Society of CLU, ICEDS, and ARIA.

The sole proprietor knows the meaning of "It was the best of times—and the worst of times." Being in business for oneself generates a proud sense of accomplishment in creating and building as personal judgment dictates. The sole proprietor is the boss. He makes the decisions (to the extent permitted by tax law, zoning law, and a host of regulatory agencies) and enjoys the fruits of his labor to the fullest. The sole proprietor generally finds, however, that the business is inseparable from life. Long hours and full responsibility limit the time available for family and vacations. Frequently, limited financial resources hinder the ability to grow and adverse economic conditions often hit the sole proprietor most severely.

Legally, there is no distinction between "John Smith, owner" and "Mr. John Smith, private citizen." Business assets are personal assets; business liabilities are personal liabilities; and the only differentiation is the existence of different checkbooks. It follows then that much "business insurance" is really personal insurance. Whether the premium check is written from the business or personal checkbook seldom makes a difference to the bottom line.

Most small-business owners who walked away from large corporations to strike out on their own enjoyed substantial fringe benefits while working for those corporations. As described in detail in Chapters 26 and 27, benefits typically included health insurance protection, considerable group life insurance, salary continuation in the event of disability, and probably a pension and/or profit sharing plan. These same individuals, now entrepreneurs, probably don't insure themselves properly.

If the sole proprietor fails to provide for these benefits through his business, his bottom line indeed may be a false and misleading one. It makes little sense to seek the freedom of sole proprietorship if this freedom is achieved at the cost of endangering the security of the owner and his family.

This chapter explores basic insurance coverages needed by the sole proprietor and how best to obtain them.

HEALTH INSURANCE

Blue Cross–Blue Shield

"The Blues" usually provide the lowest cost protection, but not always. As basic hospital expense protection, Blue Cross is simple and "painless." Show the card on admission and at discharge pay only the phone bill and TV rental. Blue Shield is another matter. Often, the schedule of payments to physicians for various treatments or operations are limited and the patient can end up owing a substantial amount to the physician. Moreover, Blue Cross and Blue Shield plans are not uniform across the country. It is worthwhile to ask a group insurance specialist to compare "the Blues" with commercially available plans in your area.

One solution is to purchase Blue Cross for hospital expenses and supplement it with a commercial "wrap-around" plan providing surgical and major medical benefits. Many Blue Cross–Blue Shield plans do not provide major medical coverages for groups of less than a minimum number of people. Where this is the case, the combination suggested is particularly appropriate.

Comprehensive Hospital-Surgical-Major Medical coverage

In the past, Comprehensive Hospital-Surgical-Major Medical coverage was widely available for individuals. Today, most insurers find this coverage unprofitable and no longer write it. It is, however, possible to obtain such coverage as "group insurance," even on the sole proprietor alone. Many insurers will write a "group plan" on as few as two or three individuals. Deductibles range from $50 to $1,000 or more per covered person per year. A typical plan would provide, after a $100 annual deductible, reimbursement of all medical expenses at 80 percent of the next $2,000 and 100 percent thereafter up to a maximum of $1,000,000. Typical exclusions would be dental expense, eyeglasses, hearing aids, cosmetic surgery, and any expenses otherwise reimbursed—such as through veterans benefits or no-fault auto insurance.

Medical expense reimbursement is the first insurance protection which should be purchased by the sole proprietor. Substantial medical expenses for the business owner or a family member can drain business and personal assets.

Many group health plans are written in conjunction with a minimal amount of group life and group accidental death benefits—usually $5,000 or $10,000. The rates for this part of the coverage are relatively inexpensive and should be accepted gladly.

Optional coverages available with group plans

Optional group coverages include disability income—usually for a limited benefit period and dollar amount, group dental care and group vision care. Rates are fairly high for these "add-ons." The business owner should be able to self-insure them, since these claims are usually moderate in amount.

HOW TO BUY

Rates and coverages change rapidly in this field. It is recommended that you ask your agent or broker to obtain several proposals, and review them carefully. It is a good idea to ask for the names of other nearby businessmen with the same coverage and check with them as to the adequacy of claims service. Shop again if your rates are substantially increased after a year or two.

Most small group plans place limitations on benefits paid during the first year for "pre-existing conditions." This part of the policy should be examined carefully. A pre-existing condition usually is one for which treatment has been received within a period of 90 days prior to the effective date of your coverage.

Premiums for the sole proprietor are not deductible as a business expense but are allowed as a regular medical expense if personal deductions are itemized. Premiums paid for employees are fully deductible by the employer and are not taxable income to the employee. Many employers follow the practice of paying only the employee's share of group insurance premiums and of having the employee contribute, through payroll deduction, the cost of coverage for dependents.

DISABILITY

Since most of us suffer illness or have accidents at one time or another, the second most important peril to insure is the temporary or permanent loss of earning power. Long-term disability has been .called "living death"; its financial impact can be severe. In addition to losing earning power, the disabled proprietor probably adds continuing medical expenses to his normal living costs.

Costs of disability income policies vary widely. The good ones are expensive, but choose the best. Policy definitions are important and directly affect the cost of protection.

A "noncancellable" policy is one which may be renewed to age 65 or 70 at a premium that will never be increased. A "guaranteed renewable" policy is one in which the insurer reserves the right to increase premiums on a "class" basis (all similar policies). A policy which is "renewable at the option of the company" is one in which the company may refuse to renew and you probably will lose it if you suffer a disability which is apt to recur. You probably would then be unable to replace it, because of your health.

The "insuring clauses" are important. The definition of "disability" can range from "inability to perform most of the duties of your own occupation" (the best) to "insured must be house-confined and under the regular care of a physician" (the worst). Ask to see several contracts and assure yourself that you are dealing with a quality insurer and a competent agent.

The provisions which most affect your premium are those relating to the "waiting period" and the "benefit period." The waiting period is that period of time which must pass between the onset of disability and the beginning of benefit payments. It can range from seven days to one year. Many businessmen choose a 30-day waiting period as a reasonable compromise. If you can afford to self-insure for three to six months, the choice of a longer waiting period can generate a meaningful savings. The factors that should be taken into account are discussed in Chapter 24.

The benefit period can range from six months to "until age 65." The longer the benefit period, the more complete the protection. Cost considerations cause many businessmen to limit the benefit period to two years or five years, which in fact covers more than 90 percent of all disabilities.

Policy considerations

Amount of coverage.   Most applicants cannot obtain as much disability coverage as they would like. Insurers usually limit benefits to 50 or 60 percent of earned income and often reduce that figure by the amount the insured receives from the disability portion of social security. For example, if the businessman has net profits of $24,000, he has an earned income of $2,000 per month. Social security will usually pay a benefit of at least $500 per month beginning the sixth month of disability. The insurer will most likely limit this businessman to a $1,000 per month benefit for the first 6 or 12 months, and $500 per month thereafter.

Optional benefits.   There are many such as accidental death benefits, additional benefits while hospital-confined, accident benefits beginning the first day or extending past age 65. These extra-cost fringes substantially increase the total cost. Most businessmen are well advised to stick to basic protection.

Policy exclusions and limitations.   Since medical history is an important factor in determining the chances of future disability, insurers ask for complete details on past injuries and illnesses. The insurer may charge an additional premium, or may add a rider to the policy excluding benefits for disability resulting from a particular cause or condition, depending on the type or severity of a previous health problem.

Association group coverage.   Many businessmen receive offers of disability coverage from trade associations, credit card companies, and others. Although this source can be used to *supplement* basic coverage, it should not be used in place of it. These plans generally are neither noncancellable nor guaranteed renewable. Also if you apply for individual coverage after acquiring such supplemental coverage, an insurer will further reduce the amount it will issue. If, on the other hand, the regular coverage is purchased first, it can be supplemented with whatever amount of group benefit is available. Be sure to examine any policy for a provision which may limit or require coordination of benefits with other insurance which may be carried.

Business overhead expense. Business overhead expense insurance is a good buy and a must for most businessmen. Simply stated, it provides monthly benefits during disability—usually after 30 days and extending for 12 to 18 months in amounts equal to your business expenses. It is a reimbursement plan, which means that benefits are paid only for expenses actually incurred. Eligible expenses include rent, utilities, salaries (except your own), lease payments, and interest (but not principal) payments on a mortgage or an installment purchase.

Since operating expenses continue while the owner is sick, this protection keeps the doors open and keeps current bills paid until the owner is able to resume work. If it is a one-man business, or one where the personal services of the proprietor are required to produce sales, overhead expense protection will at least prevent accumulation of overdue bills.

One additional type of disability policy should be mentioned. It provides for partial or total return of premiums if there are few or no claims. Usually it is only written on the "to age 65" benefit period, and the premium is substantially higher than for a regular policy. In evaluating such a policy, consider how much money you would accumulate if you deposited the additional premium in a separate savings plan.

Unnecessary coverage. Avoid contracts which provide limited benefits, such as income only when hospital-confined, accident only coverage and policies which pay only for certain "dread" diseases such as cancer. They are high-profit items in the insurer's portfolio.

Taxation. The business overhead disability policy premiums are deductible as a business expense. On the other hand, benefit payments are considered taxable income when received, but this income is offset by deductions for the expenses which the income is used to pay. Premiums for disability income not purchased for business overhead expense are not deductible by the sole proprietor either on Federal Tax Return Schedule C or as an itemized personal deduction. Nor are the benefit payments considered taxable when received.

LIFE INSURANCE

Few of us come close to insuring the value of our lives. When buying life insurance, the aim of the sole proprietor, the corporate executive, or the young employee is the same: to enable his family to continue to live in their own world if the breadwinner dies. The difficult question is what amount is needed to achieve that aim. Each of us is apt to perceive our needs in a different way. A one- to two-hour interview with a capable and conscientious agent or broker can be most helpful. Insureds will probably get a higher degree of knowledge and professionalism from a CLU, but there are some non-CLUs who are equally proficient. Ask questions about the agent's experience, continuing education, and professional association affiliations. Do not be pushed or pressured into an immediate decision, but, on the other hand, do not unduly postpone your decision. The risk is too great.

Mutual or stock company

With a few exceptions, life insurers are either "par" or "nonpar." The first, "mutual" companies, generally charge initially higher premiums, then pay annual dividends usually on an increasing scale. The policyholder "participates" in the profits of the insurer. Generally, net premiums (after dividends) will be lower after about ten years than the "nonpar" or "stock" companies. These have stockholders, and savings in mortality and interest are paid to the stockholders.

In recent years, this difference has been blurred by the appearance of stock insurers who issue policies which pay dividends and by mutual insurers who issue policies which use the dividend to increase the amount of insurance. It boils down to a comparison of individual policies.

Term or permanent

Once a decision as to the amount of insurance is made, the next determination is the type of policy to purchase. Often, the number of dollars available force the decision. Where a buyer is under age 35, term insurance rates are very attractive. After age 35, term insurance costs accelerate at an increasing rate. After age 45 or 50, term insurance is seldom an attractive buy, and after age 65 or 70, either the insurers will not continue term insurance or, if they do, the rates become so high that the buyer will choose to drop the policy.

Again, in this area, there have been many innovative changes. High interest rates have encouraged term life plus annuity investment combinations. These invariably look good on the computer printouts which are used to illustrate them, but be cautious. Often a high interest rate will be projected for 20 to 40 years in the future while the less advantageous income tax treatment of such an arrangement will be ignored by the agent.

Term insurance is similar to property or liability coverage. Each year a premium is charged which will cover the risk for that year. At the end of each year another premium must be paid to keep the coverage in effect. Term insurance is often written as Yearly Renewable Term on which the premium increases each year. Or it may be 5-, 10-, or 20-year term where the premium remains level for the stated period. One-year and five-year term are usually renewable automatically, at a higher premium, generally to age 65 or 70. Ten or 20-year term is usually not renewable without providing the insurer with new evidence of the buyer's insurability.

Most term policies are "convertible"; the policyowner can change it to whole life or some other permanent policy plan. This is an important privilege. Be sure that it is included if available.

Another form of term insurance is "decreasing term." Originally, it was developed to provide an income to a family until the children were grown. This is a decreasing need since each year the insured survives shortens the period for which income is needed. This plan is widely used as "mortgage insurance," designed to reduce at the same rate as the principal balance of a given mortgage.

In a period of high inflation, decreasing term life insurance does not meet a valid purpose. If the cost of living is increasing, a policy with a death benefit that decreases is working against the policyowner's objectives.

The alternative to term insurance—and the plan which most professional agents will urge you to consider—is whole life (ordinary life). Premiums are level and payable for life, and the policy accumulates a "cash value." The cash value is analogous to the equity in a home. It represents that portion of the policy which you own; it belongs to you if you decide to terminate the protection. Some agents and many investment advisors counsel clients to avoid cash value policies. They argue that (1) you can buy term insurance and "invest the difference" on your own to your long-term advantage, or (2) that you cannot adequately protect your family and business without purchasing low-cost term life insurance.

Insurance agents and insurers have been inventive in finding ways to make a whole life policy act like a term policy. One such method, called minimum deposit, involves the borrowing of the cash value each year and applying this sum to the payment of premiums. It is an appropriate plan, under certain circumstances. To be attractive, the buyer should be above the 40 percent tax bracket so as to maximize the advantage of the income tax deduction for interest paid on the policy loans which support the plan. Unless the insured increases his out-of-pocket payments as time goes on (to cover the increased interest expense), the plan will become unattractive in its cost/benefit relationship.

A variation of the "minimum deposit" plan is called variable-pay life. The insured chooses a schedule of payments, increasing every few years, but has the option to vary the premium payment schedule as conditions dictate.

These variations are possible *because* of cash values which can give greater flexibility than term life insurance.

Beware of the twister

The twister is an agent who makes a living by inducing an insured to cash in existing policies in favor of the agent's proposed "better deal." An individual approached on this basis should be wary. Expect that the figures will "prove" the worthiness of the proposal, for if they did not the twister would not show them to you.

Practically every state requires that an agent proposing a replacement of an existing policy tender a prescribed "disclosure statement." This purports to give the information needed to make an intelligent decision. Unfortunately, the forms are confusing—"figures do not lie, but liars can figure."

When replacement of existing policies is suggested, the cardinal rule is this: Obtain the proposal in writing and have it reviewed by an agent of the present insurer or by an independent advisor.

Nonforfeiture provisions

There are options available to an insured who decides to stop paying premiums on a permanent life insurance policy.

One option is "paid-up insurance." An insurance policy can be re-written, endorsed, and divided in a fashion whereby the insurer essentially takes back the original policy; issues a new one for less than the original amount; and calls the new one "paid up."

Another option is to use the cash value to purchase term insurance for an "extended term" of years. For example, a whole life policy purchased at age 35 and paid for ten years would then carry itself as term insurance for about an additional 15 years.

In a third option, the cash value can be (1) taken as a cash payment or (2) borrowed at a favorable interest rate or (3) even turned into a monthly life income at retirement.

Options and riders

There are a variety of options available. They should be used if, and only if, they are of true value.

Disability waiver of premium.   The "waiver of premium" option is often included automatically. It usually is a good buy. It provides that if you are disabled and unable to work (usually for six months but sometimes for only three or four months), the insurer will pay the policy premiums for you as long as the disability lasts and will reimburse you for any premiums which you paid during the waiting period. If the policy is a term policy, check when (if ever) the insurer will convert the term to a permanent plan during disability and continue to waive the premiums.

Accidental death benefit.   Many buyers want "double indemnity," feeling they are so healthy that their premature death, if it occurs, is bound to be only through an accident. Unfortunately, statistics do not support the premise. Most buyers would be better off using the cost of the accidental death benefit for the purchase of additional basic protection.

Guaranteed insurability.   Typically, this gives the insured an option to add as much as $25,000 more life insurance at three-year intervals to age 40, without evidence of insurability. For those few who become uninsurable, or substandard, it is a valuable privilege. Many agents will, however, point out that for a few dollars more, the insured can purchase term insurance which can be converted at will, and which provides the full death benefit immediately rather than only as options mature.

Family insurance riders.   This is a worthwhile extra if the buyer wishes to provide death benefits for his wife or children. It is far less expensive than using separate policies, but provides term insurance only. Eventually the family will have to replace this rider or allow it to expire.

Use of dividends

With a participating policy, the insured has a choice in the use of the annual dividends. At one time almost everyone let them accumulate (at interest) with the insurer. There are two disadvantages: first, the guaranteed rate of interest is seldom more than available in a passbook savings account; second, the interest on the dividend accumulations are considered taxable income to the policyowner. (Dividends on the other hand are a tax-free return of part of the premium.)

A more appropriate use is to buy "paid-up additions." This means that a dividend, of say $50, might purchase $100 or $150 of additional permanent insurance. The dividend has not been spent as the paid-up insurance can always be surrendered for its cost at the very least. In many insurance companies, the paid-up additional insurance also contributes to the annual dividend, thus having a compounding effect. A further advantage is that the annual increase in the total death benefit will to some extent offset inflation.

Another common use of dividends is to reduce premiums. If the insured's income is increasing, there seems little value in using the dividends in this manner. In the long run, it will work out better to buy paid-up additional insurance and then, at retirement, to start applying the value of the paid-up additions to current premiums. With a good low-cost insurer, this could result in making a whole life policy only a 15- or 20-payment policy. Ask your agent to provide an illustration of what is often called quick pay whole life.

Increasingly an option called the "fifth dividend option" is used. Each year, a part of the current dividend is used to purchase one-year term insurance. The amount is usually equal to the cash surrender value of the basic policy at the end of the next year. This generally requires only a part of the dividend, and the balance may be used in any of the other ways discussed.

An example may help to make this clear. A particular whole life policy issued at age 40 with a face amount of $50,000 might have a gross annual premium of $1,000. By the fifth year, the annual dividend would be about $90 and the cash value of the policy about $2,650. About $13 of the dividend would be used to increase the death benefit by more than $2,650 for the following year. The balance of the dividend, $77, may be used to reduce premiums, purchase paid-up additional insurance, or be left on deposit with the insurer.

The "fifth dividend option" is appropriate if the policyowner plans to borrow the cash value for one reason or another. Since such a loan would be deducted from the face amount of the policy at death, the fifth dividend option would "insure" the loan.

Taxes. Life insurance premiums for the sole proprietor are not tax deductible, with one exception. If purchased as part of a Keogh retirement plan, which is discussed at greater length in Chapter 24, most of that part of the contribution used for life insurance premiums will be a deductible business expense.

Substandard life insurance. Approximately 99 out of 100 life insurance applicants qualify for coverage on some basis. Five to 10 percent however, may be offered a substandard or "rated" contract. This simply means that while fully covered, an extra premium is charged because of a physical impairment or an occupational hazard. Should you find yourself with this type of contract, always ask your agent or broker to obtain additional quotes from one of the many brokerage agencies who specialize in substandard risks.

RETIREMENT

A sole proprietor has three ways to build a retirement program. The first is by investing aftertax dollars. The second is through an Individual Retirement Account (IRA), which permits annual contributions of 15 percent of income, to a maximum of $1,500. Contributions may be as much as $1,750 if your spouse shares in the IRA.

The advantages of the IRA are: there is no need to include employees, there is no complicated annual reporting, and the annual contribution is deductible for federal income tax purposes.

Third is the Keogh plan. Generally, this plan permits annual contributions of 15 percent of income, to a maximum of $7,500. Here, however, all employees who have three years of service must be included and they (or the employer) must contribute the same percentage of their salary as the sole proprietor. In a Keogh plan, the employees' shares are immediately and fully vested.

If you are able and willing to save more than $7,500 per year, consider incorporating. A pension consultant could then design a plan or plans which would accommodate your objectives.

Contributions to an IRA or Keogh plan are tax deductible. There is also no current tax liability on the annual investment earnings. Taxes are paid on the benefits as they are received after retirement when, presumably, you will have extra exemptions and be in a lower tax bracket. You may *not* borrow against or take money out of these plans without incurring taxes and penalties, but you may discontinue them, if necessary.

IRA contributions are often used to purchase bank CD's, money-market funds or flexible premium annuity contracts. Keogh money is often "split-funded"—partially in life insurance and the balance in mutual funds, a bank or annuities. The consensus is that the business owner should be conservative in the investment of retirement funds. The tax deduction provides immediate gain. Growth-type investments generally create capital gains, and since there is little or no favorable capital gains tax treatment available in retirement plans, one might wish to make these investments outside a tax-qualified plan. Also, if there are employees involved, one should not risk employee dissatisfaction which would result from poor investment performance.

DISPOSING OF THE BUSINESS

Planning for the disposition of his sole proprietorship at his disability, death, or retirement is of paramount importance to the small businessman. Since there is no legal distinction between business and personal assets and in most cases the proprietor's business is the largest and most valuable asset in his estate, disposal of a business requires forethought and careful planning to prevent loss of business value.

Disability

If there is a key employee who is capable and willing to take over the business, an agreement should be prepared to describe the event that will trigger a buy-out. It might be, for example, a disability which has lasted for a stated period (one or two years) and which is expected to be permanent. It is possible to purchase disability buy-out insurance, but the cost and the problem of allocating payment of premiums may make such a solution impractical. The simplest solution is to agree that the key employee will purchase the business out of profits over an extended period at an attractive rate of interest. The danger is that if the business fails under his management, there probably will be no practical way to enforce the agreement. The fact that the business owner is still alive, and presumably available to give advice, should help.

Essentially, the business owner must rely on personally-owned disability income insurance to provide for his family, if he is unable to work. That is why it is so important to have enough high-quality income replacement protection.

Death

An executor under a Will is primarily concerned with gathering the decedent's assets so that they can be distributed to his heirs. Unless given specific authority in a Will, an executor will not wish to continue the operation of a business. He is usually not familiar with the business, and if he runs it badly, his mistakes may make him personally liable for losses sustained. Further, if there is no Will and there are minor children surviving, most courts will insist that a business be liquidated by the administrator so that the children's share can be set aside and invested with more safety.

As with disability, the ideal solution requires the existence of a key employee who can and will continue the operation. A buy-sell agreement can be designed which will give the key employee control of the business in exchange for payment to the executor of a fair price. Since the employee is unlikely to have such a sum available, the solution is life insurance on the proprietor, owned and paid for by the employee. It is wise to have a trustee hold the agreement and the policy so that the transaction will proceed without problems at the proper time.

Since the employee often is not able to afford to pay what could be a substantial annual premium, several alternatives are suggested:

1. The employer can bonus the premium to the employee, letting the employee pay only the tax on the bonus. In effect, the employer is purchasing tax-deductible insurance on himself and agreeing to give the business to the employee at the owner's death.
2. "Split-dollar" insurance is a second alternative. The employer pays, each year, that portion of the premium which corresponds to the annual increase in cash value. At death, the cash value is paid to the employer's estate. The employee pays the balance of the premium, a much smaller portion, and owns the death benefit in excess of the cash value. The "fifth dividend option" may be used to keep the death benefit level.
3. A combination of the above methods. If the full purchase price cannot be financed through life insurance, the agreement may provide for installment payments of the balance.

Retirement

Normally, a proprietor will start planning some years in advance for sale at retirement. If permanent life insurance owned by an employee has been used to fund a buy-sell agreement to be effective at the death of the proprietor, the cash value of the policy can be a downpayment on the purchase of the business at the proprietor's retirement. In any event, it is obvious that advance planning is the key. Unfortunately, all too often a business owner will spend 12 to 18 hours a day planning the growth of his or her most important asset, yet will fail to take the time to make effective plans to protect that asset from the losses which inevitably occur at disability, death, or retirement.

Necessary provisions in the buy-sell agreement

A buy-sell agreement between the sole proprietor and an employee may cover any or all of the three perils—disability, death, or retirement.

Care should be taken to assure that:

1. A trustee is named to hold the life insurance policy and the buy-sell agreement.
2. The agreement extends to and includes any additional policies subsequently purchased. This will cover the growth in value of the business.
3. Upon the death of the proprietor, the estate is required to sell and the employee is required to purchase the business interest, at a determined price (see paragraph 4 following). It is important that there be a detailed agreement as to exactly what assets and

liabilities comprise the business interest. Remember how difficult it may be to distinguish between personal and business property.

4. The value (initially stated at a given figure) is agreed upon and updated each year. This is simpler than the use of complicated formulas referring to sales and profits. Also, the provision for agreed-upon value should provide that if a new figure has not been endorsed within a fixed period, such as two years, the value will be determined according to a formula, or by use of one or more qualified appraisers.

5. The employee agrees that the insurance policy be applied to the purchase price and that any balance still due on the purchase price be paid in installments for a fixed period at a given rate of interest.

6. In the event the agreement is terminated by mutual agreement, the proprietor is given the right to purchase the insurance policy from the employee.

7. The buyer agrees to indemnify the estate of the proprietor for all business debts.

8. The conditions under which the agreement will terminate are:
   a. Mutual agreement.
   b. Termination of employment of the employee.
   c. Bankruptcy or insolvency of the proprietor.
   d. Death of the employee prior to the death of proprietor.
   e. Simultaneous deaths.
   f. The option of the proprietor if the employee fails to continue the life insurance or assigns it or borrows against it.

A schedule should be attached to the agreement listing any life insurance policies which are to be used to support the agreement.

THE ESTATE PLAN OF THE SOLE PROPRIETOR

Special clauses must be included in a Will to enable an executor to exercise judgment in continuing, selling, or liquidating the business portion of the estate. Other factors are important, especially if the business is to be continued by the family.

Who owns the business? A sole proprietor is a sole owner, but if the spouse has participated in the business to a material degree, it is possible to reduce the taxable value in the estate of the proprietor by attributing a part of the business value to the spouse.

Will the business be left to one of the children? If so, can the other heirs be adequately provided for with other estate assets? Life insurance can be used to provide fair treatment.

Will the surviving spouse depend upon the business for income? If so, will that unduly penalize the child or children who plan to continue to run the business?

Taxes are a major impediment to estate creation. Each of us owes it to our heirs to plan our estate in such a way as to reduce estate and inheritance taxes as far as possible. Professional counseling must be employed to develop appropriate planning for each of these contingencies.

The sole proprietor must be concerned about protecting both his or her business *and* family. The absence of a package of corporate employee benefits requires the proprietor to realistically assess the degree to which the family's future security depends upon the continued profitability and the preservation of the asset value of the business. A well-thought-out plan including medical expense reimbursement, personal disability income protection, business overhead expense disability coverage, life insurance, retirement planning, and provision for the sale of the business at death will provide such security. Without such a plan, the proprietor is shifting the risk of loss to the family and heirs, rather than to an insurer. The first step is to seek professional help from a member of the "Estate Planning Team"—an attorney, a CLU, a CPA, or a trust officer.

PROVIDING FOR BUSINESS CONTINUATION THROUGH INSURANCE AND SELECTED EMPLOYEE BENEFITS— FOR PARTNERSHIPS

THE USE OF THE PARTNERSHIP VEHICLE

DESCRIPTION OF THE PARTNERSHIP VEHICLE
Continuity of life
Centralization of management
Limitation of liability
Free transferability of interests

THE DECISION TO USE A PARTNERSHIP
Tradition
Business
Taxation

THE PARTNERSHIP AS AN AGGREGATE

TAX CONSIDERATIONS IN SELECTING THE PARTNERSHIP VEHICLE
Starting up
Operating
Termination

INCOME SPLITTING

COMPENSATION AND FRINGE BENEFITS

KEOGH PLAN

BUY-SELL AGREEMENTS
Partner valuation
Book value
Sales of interests
Capitalization of income
Capitalization from assets
Purchased goodwill

DISABILITY INSURANCE FOR THE PARTNERSHIP

MISCELLANEOUS INSURANCE
Group term life insurance
Health insurance
Fringe benefits insurance

Richard W. Ledwith, Jr., CLU
President
The Ledwith Insurance Corporation
Philadelphia, Pennsylvania

Richard W. Ledwith, Jr., received his B.S. degree from the Wharton School of Business of the University of Pennsylvania in 1961. After his graduation, he entered the life insurance business, where he has been one of the top producers in the industry for the last 19 years. In 1969, he attained his Chartered Life Underwriter degree from the American College of Life Underwriters. He is the President of The Ledwith Insurance Corporation, which represents over 30 major life insurance companies. He is a life member of the Million Dollar Round Table, and has received numerous awards as a leading producer for many different companies. He specializes primarily in the areas of Estate Planning, Business Insurance, Qualified Retirement Plans, and Group Insurance.

Robert S. Price, Esquire
Partner
Pepper, Hamilton & Scheetz
Philadelphia, Pennsylvania

Robert S. Price received his A.B. degree from Kenyon College in 1958 and his LL.B. from Yale Law School in 1961. Since his graduation, he has practiced law in Philadelphia, specializing in taxation, employee benefits, and tax-exempt financing. He is a partner in Pepper, Hamilton & Scheetz and has written on a number of subjects in his fields of expertise.

THE USE OF THE PARTNERSHIP VEHICLE

While a business may start out as a sole proprietorship, its successful pursuit frequently requires the proprietor to hire others and eventually bring them into the ownership. At that time, a decision must be made as to how the ownership will be shared. It may be shared either by forming a partnership or a corporation (with or without a Subchapter S election by the corporation). That choice is often made in favor of a corporation because of the prestige associated with that form of organization, as well as limited liability benefits afforded the shareholder. However, a rational decision can be made only as a result of careful analysis of the benefits and burdens of each form. The facts of each case alone determine the relative appropriateness of the two forms of organization; no general rule works in all cases.

DESCRIPTION OF THE PARTNERSHIP VEHICLE

Perhaps the first step towards making a rational decision whether or not to select the partnership form is to understand just what a partnership is. Section 6(1) of the Uniform Partnership Act defines a partnership in this way: "a partnership is an association of two or more persons to carry on as co-owners a business for profit." Unfortunately, the Internal Revenue Code of 1954, as amended (the "Code") is much more expansive in its definition of a partnership. Section 761(a) of the Code says that "the term 'partnership' includes a syndicate, group, pool, joint venture or other unincorporated organization through or by means of which any business, financial operation or venture is carried on, and which is not . . . a corporation or a trust or estate." The regulations implementing this section warn that the concept of a partnership for tax purposes is broader than the common law concept and may include groups not commonly thought of as partnerships. So that, where a "handshake" agreement, or informal written agreement is made, it may not be very clear what choice has been made. An agreement that does not conform to the partnership statute adopted by the state in which the business is located can present serious questions. Too often a partnership is present where none was thought to be, or an association taxable as a corporation is present where a partnership was thought to be.

The following factors have been treated as evidence that a trade or business is being operated as a partnership. In a partnership, the parties:

a. Jointly contribute capital or services, and jointly own that capital.
b. Share the profits and losses.

c.   Share control.
d.   Have a partnership agreement and adhere to it.
e.   Hold out to others that the endeavor is a partnership.
f.   Keep separate books and records for the business.
g.   Hold title to property of the business, and conduct it in the partnership's name.

The importance of these facts is that they establish that the business is a partnership and is not one of a number of possible alternative arrangements such as a sole proprietorship with a sharing of expenses, a pooling arrangement, or an employer-employee, principal-agent, creditor-debtor, seller-buyer, or lessor-lessee relationship. Each of these other categories may produce federal income tax results quite different from those of a partnership relationship and, of course, may have very different employee benefit programs.

Most important, those facts will also establish that the business is actually a partnership and not an association taxable as a corporation. Both a partnership and a corporation require associates and an objective to carry on business for joint profit. However, an association may be taxable as a corporation, even though it has not gone through the incorporation steps set out in the applicable state law. It is particularly important that there be no question that a business that is intended to be a partnership not be an association taxable as a corporation. The tax treatment of a corporation, and of its benefit program, is so different from that of a partnership that confusion over which category an organization is in can lead to costly litigation and unexpected taxes to pay. An association is taxable as a corporation if at least three of the following four additional characteristics are present.

Continuity of life

Generally, an association has continuity of life if it will not dissolve or change its identity upon the withdrawal of a member. A partnership subject to a statute following the Uniform Partnership Act or Uniform Limited Partnership Act does not have continuity of life because the continued existence of the organization after the withdrawal of a member depends on the agreement of the remaining members to continue it.

Centralization of management

Generally, an association has centralization of management if continuing and exclusive authority is vested in some but not all of its members to make business decisions for the organization without ratification by the other members. As in the continuity of life context, even if the members agree to delegate management powers to one or more members, if the ultimate authority remains in all of them, there is no centralization of management.

Limitation of liability

Generally an association has limited liability if under applicable state law, *none* of its members is personally liable for the debts of the organization. (In contrast, in a general partnership each partner is liable for the acts of his fellow partners in the course of the partnership's business.)

Free transferability of interests

Generally, an association has free transferability of interests if a member, without the consent of any other member, may substitute a nonmember in his place and transfer all of the attributes of his interest to that new member.

THE DECISION TO USE A PARTNERSHIP

Once there is an understanding of the nature of a partnership, the question is whether that is the best form for the activity of the organization. The partnership form is used for a variety of reasons:

Tradition

The business or profession has always operated as a partnership.

Business

The flexibility required is best provided by a partnership.

Taxation

The best tax results will arise from the use of the partnership form.

The first and second of these reasons are discussed next, but the third reason requires such extensive discussion that it is covered separately later in this chapter.

The partnership has been the traditional form of operation in many businesses, particularly in the professions. Indeed, though it is generally not true today, state laws at one time prohibited the performance of certain professions by corporate employees. A partnership was the only available form for professionals who wished to conduct their efforts as a group. As a result, conservative professionals tend to insist that the partnership form be retained. For other businessmen, the simplicity of the partnership form has led to its use because they prefer to do business on a "handshake" basis, without the formalism and recordkeeping required by a corporation.

In contrast with these often emotional reasons for selecting the partnership form are certain rational business reasons for using it. The partnership form is simple and easy to use. It is not burdened with the organizational formalities and state taxes that accompany a corporation. It does not have to register to do business in foreign states. Since a general partnership interest isn't a security, sale of a general partnership interest generally avoids the disclosure and registration requirements that federal and state laws apply to stock interests.

Also, the partnership form may provide a minority share partner with greater protection than can be afforded to him in a corporation. For example, the minority shareholder can be dismissed as an employee by the officers of the corporation who are elected by the majority interest. The result of this dismissal is a termination of income, without the requirement that the enterprise itself be terminated. The minority shareholder may have his capital tied up in the enterprise without receiving any income from it; a result that a well-drafted partnership agreement can easily avoid. Finally, the losses from a partnership may be used by the partners against their other income, subject to the "at risk" limitations, a critical advantage in the early years of a business venture.

In sharp contrast are several very valid business reasons for using the corporate form. Certain businesses, such as banking, are required by statute to be conducted in the corporate form. Also, where large infusions of publicly solicited equity capital are needed, the corporate form is so much more convenient that it is almost always used. A related consideration is the limited liability available to an investor in a corporation who risks no more than his investment. His position is unlike that of a general partner who is personally liable for the obligations, as well as to the misdeeds, of his partners incurred in the course of the partnership's activities.

While considerations of personal liability are generally advanced as the primary reason for incorporating, as a practical matter, the difference between partnerships and corporations is not as great as first appears. As noted in Chapter 25, a closely held corporation generally finds that personal guarantees by its stockholders are required by the corporation's lenders. Also, limited partnerships can restrict the personal liability of a limited partner to the amount he has committed to invest, provided that he is not actively involved in managing the partnership. Finally, adequate casualty insurance coverage can protect the partners from the consequences of most misdeeds, if not from the consequences of the economic failure of their venture.

THE PARTNERSHIP AS AN AGGREGATE

The Internal Revenue Code treats a partnership for tax purposes as an aggregate of its partners. It is useful to understand the general differences between entity and aggregate treatment before considering the tax reasons for choosing either the partnership or the corporate vehicle.

A partnership is an economic and legal entity. It files its own tax return, selects its own taxable year (with certain limitations), and makes certain other elections as a partnership. However, the theory of the Code is that the partnership itself is not a tax-paying entity. The partnership is merely an aggregation of individuals who are jointly conducting a business. Each partner is taxable on his distributive share of the income or loss derived from the partnership, which is merely a conduit through which that income or loss is passed. In addition to reporting his share of that income or loss, each partner must separately report his share of capital gains and losses, charitable contributions, dividends, and certain other items.

The share of income or loss and these other items that a partner must report is governed by the partnership agreement. However, that allocation of gain or loss and other items must have substantial economic effect to be controlling. If an allocation is set aside on audit, a partner's share of such items will be determined in accordance with his interest in the partnership, taking all facts and circumstances into account.

TAX CONSIDERATIONS IN SELECTING THE PARTNERSHIP VEHICLE

The tax considerations fall into three categories: those relevant to starting up the business, to its operation, and to its termination.

Starting up

If appreciated property is to be contributed to the business, it can generally be done so to either a partnership or corporation free of tax. However, where more than 20 percent of the corporation's stock will be received by one or more stockholders in return for services, this nonrecognition of appreciation provision will not apply. In contrast, if the partnership form is utilized, the recognition of gain on appreciated property contributed to the partnership may be avoided. Also, the transfer of property to a corporation subject to liabilities in excess of the tax basis of the property transferred may trigger gain to the transferor. Recent changes in the Code eliminated the worst features of this tax trap, but care must still be exercised as to what liabilities are assumed by the corporation.

The partnership agreement may also provide for special allocations, so long as they have economic substance and their principal purpose is not to avoid tax. Thus, unlike a corporation, a partnership agreement may allocate to a partner a share of profits and losses disproportionate to his capital interest, if those tests are met. In addition, tax questions that arise from "thin capitalization" do not trouble a partnership. Unlike in the corporate context, there is no tax difference whether a partner contributes to his partnership, in his capacity as a partner, in equity or debt form. Finally, a corporation has considerably more flexibility in choosing a fiscal year for tax purposes than a partnership.

Operating

Since a partner includes in his basis for his interest his share of the partnership's liabilities, he may be able to receive tax-free distributions of cash in excess of his share of partnership income and his capital interest. Where the distributions are in kind, rather than cash, the partnership format may be of particular value, especially when compared with the complexities associated with removing no-longer-needed assets from a corporation without incurring tax.

There are also a number of minor differences that flow from the conduit nature of the partnership. A partnership passes through to each partner the charitable deductions it makes. Since the limitation on deductions for an individual is much higher than that applicable to a corporation, the partnership form enables greater deductions to be taken. Similarly, the pass-through of the investment tax credit enables a partner to use it against his other income, where a corporation may be unable to use the credit fully and promptly. The pass-through of tax-exempt interest to the partners has made the partnership a useful form for specialists in state and local finance. While the interest is also exempt to a corporate recipient, it loses its exempt character when paid to a shareholder-employee as a dividend or as salary.

Of minor concern is the higher level of social security and unemployment tax jointly paid by the corporation and the employee, as compared to the level paid only by the self-employed partner. Of equally minor concern, in most situations, will be the fact that the investment indebtedness interest limitations and tax preference items for minimum tax purposes also pass through to the partners. There are no similar corporate provisions in the case of investment indebtedness interest, and a corporation aggregates the tax preference items and has somewhat different provisions with which to cope. A corporation also has to cope with questions as to whether the compensation it pays to its shareholders is reasonable, whether it has unnecessarily accumulated its income, and whether it is a personal holding company. In a given situation, these considerations can be crucial.

Termination

Because the partnership is continually adjusting the basis of each partner's interest to reflect the income and distributions of the partnership, termination usually is not an event that generates severe tax consequences. However, in the case of a corporation, the reverse is true. The income that has been accumulated and subjected to tax at the corporate level will be taxed again at the shareholder's level, though generally at capital gains rates. Therefore, in the selection of the form to be used, consideration should be given to whether the business is really expected to be a long-term, ongoing venture. Conversely, consideration should also be given to the possible unwanted termination for tax purposes of a partnership because of the sale or exchange of 50 percent or more of the total interest in the partnership's capital and income within a 12-month period. Careful planning can avoid such a termination or minimize the adverse effects of such a termination. However, where the termination of a business after a short time is contemplated from the beginning, it is apparent that the corporate form presents greater complexities. At that time, the need to minimize tax on the disposition of appreciated assets of the corporation also requires strict adherence to certain sections of the Code that do not apply to a disposition made by a partnership.

INCOME SPLITTING

Once the parties to a business have determined to use a partnership, there are a number of ways to maximize its usefulness. They are discussed in this and the following sections. A simple method for reducing the effect of the progressive tax rates is to split a business's income among the members of a family, particularly among the children. However, the employment by the business must be bona fide and the salary must be reasonably related to the work done, or it will not stand up under scrutiny by the Internal Revenue Service. This rule applies whether a partnership or a corporation is used. If the employment is bona fide, the coverage of family members in fringe benefit plans and by social security can be quite beneficial.

Under the appropriate circumstances, a family partnership (or a Subchapter S corporation) can be used to split the income even where there is no bona fide employment of family members. Since service derived income cannot be assigned but is attributable to whoever performed the service, the circumstances are appropriate where capital is a material factor in producing the income to be split. It is this capital or property that can be given to, say, a son or daughter. He or she may contribute it to the partnership in return for an interest in the profits of the partnership, that reflects that capital. If the child is in a lower income tax bracket, the overall tax burden on the family is reduced. Where the child is an adult, the transfer must result in a complete divestiture of beneficial interest in the transferred property. Where the child is a minor, the use of a trust or other format permitted under state law is required. The estate and gift tax consequences of the gift of a partnership interest must, of course, be carefully considered.

COMPENSATION AND FRINGE BENEFITS

If a partnership's business is one in which both personal services and capital are material income-producing factors, each partner's personal service income to which the maximum tax of 50 percent applies is limited to the reasonable compensation for services rendered. Of course, a corporate employee who is also a shareholder in a business that needs a good bit of capital may find that his compensation too may be attacked as unreasonable. In the partnership situation, the auditor's aim is to deprive the partner of the use of the maximum tax. In the corporate context, the auditor's aim is both to deprive the stockholder of the use of the maximum tax and to deprive the corporation of its deduction by characterizing the payment as a dividend rather than salary. The customary defense against the unreasonable corporate compensation argument is that the salary is reasonable when compared to the salaries of other employees doing similar work. This argument may be less helpful to a partnership which obviously utilizes large amounts of capital.

Since a partner is treated as a self-employed person, he is not eligible for many of the deductible fringe benefits available to his own employees, or to corporate employees.

The contributions to accident and health plans, disability insurance, medical reimbursement, group term life insurance, and wage continuation plans (the "fringe benefits" that are available to corporate employees that are discussed in Chapter 26) are not deductible by a partner except as he may be able to claim a deduction as a medical expense on his personal return. However, Congress has increasingly required that these health and welfare plans not discriminate in favor of the highly compensated. They must also comply with the burdensome provisions of ERISA. Thus, the increased costs of coverage and compliance have reduced their utility, even in the corporate context.

KEOGH PLAN

There is, however, one fringe benefit provided specifically for sole proprietors and for partners: the H.R. 10 or Keogh plan. In 1962, Congress passed the Self-Employed Individuals Tax Retirement Act. That act, also known as H.R. 10 or Keogh after its principal proponent, permits a partnership to set up a qualified retirement plan that includes partners. However, that plan will be subject to certain restrictions or limitations that do not apply to a corporate plan. As part of the decision whether to incorporate or use the partnership form, a crucial question is whether these restrictions or limitations are unduly onerous.

In general, the advantages of a Keogh plan parallel the advantages of a qualified corporate plan. The contributions made on behalf of a partner (and, of course, his employees) are deductible. Despite this deductibility, the income tax consequences to the individual on whose behalf the contributions were made are deferred until distribution, when the recipient presumably is retired and may be in a lower tax bracket. There may also be favorable tax rates applicable to the retirement benefit if it is received in a lump-sum distribution. Also, earnings attributable to the investment of those contributions grow tax-free. They, too, are not subject to tax until distribution. Exhibit 24–A shows how quickly assets can be accumulated through a Keogh plan in contrast to the accumulation that is possible through aftertax savings.

The restrictions and limitations of a Keogh plan, compared to the restrictions and limitations of a corporate plan, are as follows:

A corporation may deduct a contribution to a defined contribution plan of up to 15 percent of an employee's compensation. When coupled with a money purchase pension plan, up to 25 percent of compensation may be contributed and deducted. There is also an absolute dollar limit, that is annually adjusted for inflation, on the maximum contribution on behalf of an employee. That limitation was originally $25,000 but has been substantially increased due to inflation. In contrast, no more than $7,500 or 15 percent of an individual's earned income, whichever is less, may be contributed under a defined contribution Keogh plan. There are provisions permitting defined benefit Keogh plans that may permit somewhat higher contributions. However, when contrasted with a combination of defined benefit and

Exhibit 24-A

Assumptions:
   Annual contribution $7,500 per year.
   Retirement age 65.
   Participant is in 50 percent federal income tax
      bracket.
   Average rate of return is 8 percent.

Age of entry in plan	Values at retirement—age 65	
	No plan*	With plan
30	$287,244	$1,395,766
35	218,731	917,594
40	162,419	592,158
45	116,135	370,671
50	78,092	219,933
55	46,824	117,342

* Illustration assumes participant is in a 50 percent federal income tax bracket and must pay tax each year of $3,750 on the $7,500 to be saved without a qualified Keogh plan.

defined contribution corporate plans, there is a great gap between what can be contributed and deducted for an individual by a corporation and what can be contributed and deducted for a self-employed individual by a partnership. Yet the greater contribution limitation is not necessarily determinative of which form to use. Many businesses cannot afford to make contributions greater than those permitted under a Keogh plan. In that situation, it may be sufficient, and in contrast to what can be accomplished in a personal savings plan, a Keogh plan can be quite valuable. Exhibit 24–B shows for a hypothetical two-man partnership, with one and two employees, the annual savings available through a Keogh plan.

There are a number of other limitations that may apply to a Keogh plan but not to a corporate plan. The most restrictive of these limitations apply to those Keogh plans that cover individuals who are deemed to be owner-employees. An owner-employee is a self-employed individual who is either a sole proprietor of the business or a partner owning more than a 10 percent interest in either the capital or profits of the partnership. If a Keogh plan covers an owner-employee, these additional limitations apply.

Briefly, these limitations are that a Keogh plan may take into account a self-employed persons's earned income, whether or not he is an owner-employee, only up to $100,000. The integration of a plan with social security, which has the effect of skewing contributions towards the more highly compensated participants, is computed differently in a plan that covers owner-employees. A Keogh plan which

Exhibit 24-B

Assumptions:
Two equal partners.
$60,000 annual income per partner.
All eligible employees earn $12,000 per year.

		No Keogh plan	Keogh plan No employees	Keogh plan One employee	Keogh plan Two employees
1.	Partner A annual income ...	$60,000	$60,000	$60,000	$60,000
2.	Partner A share of contributions for employees	0	0	759	1,539
3.	Earned income from partnership	$60,000	$60,000	$59,241	$58,461
4.	Deductible contribution to partner A Keogh account ...	0	7,500	7,500	7,500
5.	Adjusted gross income	$60,000	$52,500	$51,741	$50,961
6.	Personal exemptions and estimated excess itemized deductions	8,000	8,000	8,000	8,000
7.	Net taxable income	52,000	44,500	43,471	42,961
8.	Federal income tax	15,758	12,333	11,834	11,499
9.	Estimated tax savings by establishing Keogh plan ($15,758 less line 8)	0	3,425	3,924	4,259
10.	Net annual savings to partner A by establishing Keogh plan (line 9 minus partner A's share of contributions for employees)		$+3,425	$+3,165	$+2,720

Notes:
Plan contribution equals 15 percent of earned income or $7,500, whichever is less.

With no employees, partner A contributes 12.5 percent of earned income to plan; with one employee, 12.66 percent; and with two employees, 12.83 percent.

Federal income tax assumes partner A files joint return, has no other dependents, and itemizes deductions.

covers an owner-employee must also limit voluntary contributions to the smaller of $2,500 or 10 percent of earned income, and no voluntary contributions are permitted unless the plan covers a participant who is not an owner-employee.

Contributions made for employees in a plan covering an owner-employee must be immediately vested and nonforfeitable when made. If the plan covers no owner-employees, it may use the usual vesting requirements even though self-employed employees are covered by the plan. Also, distributions may not be made to an owner-employee before he attains age 59½ and must begin before the end of the taxable year in which he attains age 70½, unless he dies or becomes disabled. There is also a limitation on how long those payments may be spread out.

The same funding instruments used by corporate plans are available to Keogh plans. However, the limits on the amount of contributions that may be made tend to keep the size of the dollars to invest relatively small. As a practical matter, this reduces the range of funding vehicles available. Many small partnerships have avoided this difficulty by adopting master or prototype plans put forth by trade associations, banks, and insurance companies. An insurance company plan, or a plan with some insurance features, is frequently chosen.

If part of the contribution is used to purchase an insurance policy for each participant to provide a death benefit, the maximum premium so used may never exceed 49.9 percent of the total contributions. Even with this restriction, the use of insurance can provide a significant death benefit for each participant in the plan. When this benefit is provided through the plan, a partner effectively receives life insurance on a deductible basis and can reduce his personal insurance that he pays for with aftertax dollars. Also, the entire death benefit and the side fund account in the plan can be excluded from a deceased partner's estate for federal estate tax purposes, if certain tests that apply to distribution of that benefit are met. This insurance may, if properly designed, continue to provide a death benefit even in the event of the insured's total and permanent disability prior to retirement.

A special provision of the Code authorizes an owner-employee to purchase whole life insurance, endowment or annuity contracts without worrying that he will make an excess contribution in a year when the required premium exceeds the allowable contribution. However, the premium, including all contract extras such as waiver of premium, cannot exceed $7,500. It also must not exceed the average of the amounts that were deductible by the business with respect to the owner-employee's earned income for the three taxable years preceding the year in which the contract was issued. Exhibit 24–C shows how insurance can be used in a Keogh plan to provide a deceased partner's family with the benefits he might have received had he lived to his normal retirement date.

When the beneficiary of a self-employed individual receives a payment through the maturing of a policy held by a plan, that portion of the payment which is pure insurance (the face value of the policy less its cash value) is treated as tax-free insurance proceeds.

Many insurance companies have sophisticated computerized facilities to aid in the economical design and administration of Keogh plans. Many have a variety of plans and funding vehicles to choose from. Frequently their plans will be prototypes that have already been approved by the Internal Revenue Service.

Exhibit 24-C

Assumptions:

Annual contribution $7,500 per year.

Thirty-five percent or $2,625 of contribution allocated to insurance.

All dividends are used to purchase paid-up additional insurance.

Average rate of return on balance is assumed to be 8 percent.

	Age of entry in the plan		
	30	40	50
Death benefit in 1st year:			
Insurance policy*	$ 215,768	$142,232	$ 88,165
Side fund	4,875	4,875	4,875
Total	$ 220,643	$147,107	$ 93,040
Total death benefit if no insurance	7,500	7,500	7,500
Death benefit in 10th year:			
Insurance policy*	$ 235,994	$155,384	$ 99,771
Side fund	76,272	76,272	76,272
Total	$ 312,266	$231,656	$176,043
Total death benefit if no insurance	117,341	117,341	117,341
Death benefit at age 65:			
Insurance policy	$ 403,951	$213,049	$111,673
Side fund	907,248	384,902	142,955
Total	$1,311,199	$597,951	$254,628
Total death benefit if no insurance	1,395,766	592,158	219,932

* Notes:

Insurance policy illustrated is a Connecticut Mutual Life Insurance Company, Econolife-80.

Dividends are based on the 1980 scale and are neither guarantees nor estimates for the future.

The type of insurance policy will vary depending on plan specifications and the underwriting practices of the insurance carrier selected.

P.S. 58 tax cost of insurance is not included. Moreover, if the insured does not die prior to retirement, the cash surrender value is less than face. However, he has saved the cost of buying life insurance outside of the plan.

Where a partnership does not chose to adopt one of the plans provided by an insurance company, or to provide an insured death benefit, an insurance company's services may still be useful. A growing form of insurance company participation is the use of guaranteed income contracts, where the insurance company receives funds from the trustee and guarantees a rate of return on its investment of those funds. This is a swiftly evolving field and the nature of the guarantees has been changing, particularly as to the terms under which the trustee may reclaim his funds. Often an insurance company will set the rate of return for an initial period of years and thereafter will reset the rate prior to the beginning of each plan year and guarantee it for that period. Some contracts guarantee no loss in principal. Others allow for withdrawal of the lesser of market or book values.

Finally, it should be noted that there has been continual agitation to increase the dollar limitations on Keogh plan deductions. These limitations are so easily avoided by incorporation that it would seem obviously sensible to make the corporate and partnership limitations comparable. This increase would obviate the need to distort the business vehicle election. Yet the Treasury continues to resist increases in the limitations; presumably on the theory that it is better to lock the barn door even when most of the horses have left through the hole in the back wall.

BUY-SELL AGREEMENTS

Some partnerships provide for the retirement of a partner by making him guaranteed distributions after his retirement. If pursuant to a written plan, payable during retirement, and with no requirement that services be performed, these payments to a partner will be treated as retirement income for social security purposes. However, this sort of arrangement presumes the continuation of the partnership by the remaining partners. In a large professional partnership, this assumption is not unreasonable. It may be less reasonable in a smaller or business partnership.

When a partner withdraws from a smaller or business partnership, for reasons of age, death, or disability, his surviving partners may be unwilling or unable to pay him much for his interest. To assure a withdrawing partner that the remaining partners both can and will purchase his interest, particularly on his death, buy-sell agreements funded by life insurance are often used. They both set the value of the interest and provide funds for its purchase. When the proceeds of the insurance are not available on a withdrawal because it is for reasons other than death, the agreements usually provide that a more leisurely payment schedule will apply.

Few smaller or business partnerships recognize that the odds on a partner dying before he reaches 65 are quite high, as shown in Exhibit 24–D.

These rather high odds make the existence of a buy-sell agreement and a method of valuation a necessity. In the absence of a buy-sell agreement, the death of a partner in a small partnership may leave his surviving partners to face some unpleasant possibilities. The deceased partner's heirs may have the right under local law to require

Exhibit 24-D
ODDS OF AT LEAST ONE DEATH BEFORE AGE 65
(expressed as number of chances out of 100*)

One business owner		Two business owners		Three business owners	
Age	Chances	Ages	Chances	Ages	Chances
30	28.3	30–30 ...	48.5	30–30–30 ...	63.1
35	27.5	35–35 ...	47.4	35–35–35 ...	61.8
40	26.4	40–40 ...	45.8	40–40–40 ...	60.2
45	24.8	45–45 ...	43.5	45–45–45 ...	57.6
50	22.4	50–50 ...	39.8	50–50–50 ...	53.3
		30–35 ...	48.0	30–35–40 ...	61.7
		35–40 ...	46.6	35–40–45 ...	59.9
		40–45 ...	44.7	40–45–50 ...	57.0
		45–50 ...	41.7		

These figures are based on the Commissioners 1958 Standard Ordinary Mortality Table of insured lives and cannot be considered predictions for particular individuals or joint combinations of individuals. However, they are illustrative of results for a large group of single or joint lives as the case may be.

the partnership to liquidate, where there is no written agreement to the contrary. The deceased partner's heirs may try to buy out the surviving partners, which raises the question of whether a fair value can be agreed upon; assume the decedent's partnership position; or sell the partnership interest to a third party. All of these possibilities contain the seeds of conflict.

In contrast, a properly drawn buy-sell agreement sets the value of the deceased partner's interest for federal estate tax purposes; provides for the orderly transfer of that interest to the surviving partners; assures that there are sufficient funds to purchase the deceased partner's interest, to the benefit of his heirs; and minimizes the disruptive effects of the partner's death on the partnership.

Many valuation methods are used, and the following are the most common.

Partner valuation

The value of a partnership is usually fairly easy for the partners to determine themselves when they are of approximately the same age and health. Since they do not know who will be the first to die, each partner in setting his estimate of what a partnership share is worth will be fixing the price at which he will both buy and sell. Once set, that price generally is usually permitted to stand until it is mutually revised. However, this method may be more difficult to use where there are differences in age and health.

Book value

While not usually indicative of the true value of the partnership to its owners, this method has the virtue of simplicity.

Sales of interests

Where partnership interests have been sold to others, the price paid, with or without adjustments, may be used.

Capitalization of income

This method capitalizes the operating income of the partnership generally averaged over a period of years at a percentage that increases with the riskiness of the partnership's business.

Capitalization from assets

Reasonable income from the tangible assets of the partnership is computed first; say, at 10 percent. Then the operating income in excess of that return is computed. This income is assumed to have been derived from goodwill and is capitalized at the same or a different percent. The sum of the value of the tangible assets and the goodwill is the value of the partnership.

Purchased goodwill

Where the partnership has purchased a business developed by others, the value of the partnership may be based on that purchase price, with adjustments to reflect changes in the business since that purchase.

Some partnerships, particularly where capital is not a material factor, or where it is easily liquidated, have taken another approach. They have set a minimal value on the partnership interest, after providing for the return of the deceased partner's capital. They have required each partner to acquire sufficient amounts of life insurance to provide for his family responsibilities. In that way each partner provides his own protection on a pay-as-you-go basis. The partnership is not used to provide a death benefit, and the partners forego any beneficial adjustments that the use of life insurance to purchase the decedent's interest might have provided to their bases for their partnership interests.

Once the valuation problem has been resolved, the nature of the buy-sell agreement itself can be considered.

There are two general approaches to structuring buy-sell agreements, which are also discussed in Chapters 23 and 25. First, under the "entity" agreement, the partnership owns the insurance policies used to fund the buy-sell agreement, pays the premiums, and names itself as the beneficiary. The proceeds of the policy are then used to redeem the deceased partner's interest in the partnership. The second approach is the "cross-purchase" agreement. Under this approach, the partners agree among themselves to purchase the partnership interest from the deceased partner's estate, without involving the partnership. Each individual funds his obligation by taking out a policy on the life of his fellow partners. He names himself as owner and beneficiary, and pays all premiums. In neither instance will the premiums be deductible. One major advantage that flows from the ownership of the policies by the partnership is that it may characterize the payments it makes either as distributions of income or as payments for goodwill, to the extent the payments exceed the deceased partner's share of the partnership's net asset value. This flexibility may be of considerable value.

Where there are numerous partners, the number of policies that would be involved have pushed partners towards using the entity approach. For example, if there are only two partners, only two policies are needed. However, if there are 4 partners, the cross-purchase arrangement requires 12 policies. On the other hand, ownership of the policies by the partnership may be hazardous if there is reason for concern over whether the partnership's creditors will get first crack at its assets. Some partnerships have used an unincorporated association to purchase the policies to avoid this risk.

Consideration must also be given in drafting the buy-sell agreement to the effect the structure used and the method of payment chosen will have on the bases of the surviving partners in their partnership interests. For example, insurance proceeds that are to be used to pay for the partnership interest should not go directly to the decedent's estate or spouse as a credit against the purchase price of that interest. The direct payment would not increase the bases of the surviving partners.

Whatever the terms of the buy-sell agreement, the value of using life insurance to fund it is clear. There are three obvious advantages:

a. The heirs of the deceased partner receive an immediate lump-sum payment for their interest in the partnership. They do not have to rely on the future profitability of the partnership to pay for their interest as is necessary where there is a deferred buy-out arrangement.

b. Even when a partner lives until he retires, additional retirement benefits can be obtained for a retiring partner by converting the insurance policy to an annuity and amending the deferred buy-out arrangement to reflect these benefits.

c. If he dies before retirement, the insurance approach is less expensive than an unfunded buy-out.

When a partner dies and the partnership has not funded for an immediate buy-out of the deceased partner's interest, a deferred buy-out usually takes place. Under this arrangement, the partnership agrees to buy the deceased partner's business interest over a period of time. This deferred buy-out is therefore paid for out of the earnings of the partnership with aftertax dollars. The surviving partners are therefore put in the awkward position, especially in the case of the smaller partnership, of trying to continue to operate profitably with one less partner and, also, buy out his interest with aftertax dollars. (See Exhibit 24–E.)

The savings through the use of life insurance to fund the buy-sell agreement obviously increase the earlier the partner dies. Exhibit 24–F demonstrates these savings.

In summary, it is most important that a buy-sell agreement exist, that it be carefully drafted, that a valuation method be built into it, and that it be funded with insurance.

DISABILITY INSURANCE FOR THE PARTNERSHIP

One of the most serious problems that can confront a partnership arises when a partner becomes totally and permanently disabled.

Exhibit 24–E
TEN-YEAR DEFERRED BUY-OUT FROM "AFTERTAX"
EARNINGS

Assumptions:
Each partner's share valued at $100,000.
Each partner is age 40.

	25 percent tax bracket	50 percent tax bracket
Total earnings before taxes to produce $100,000 net	$133,333	$200,000
	25 percent tax bracket	*50 percent tax bracket*
Add interest at 6% on unpaid installments, $10,000 per year (6% on average indebtedness of $50,000 is $3,000 before taxes)	$ 30,000	$ 30,000
Total pre-tax income required ...	$163,333	$230,000

Exhibit 24-F

Assumptions:

Each partner's share valued at $100,000.

Each partner is age 40.

$100,000 Econolife (Whole Life) policy with a $1,848 gross annual premium (nondeductible).

Death at end of —	25 percent tax bracket pre-tax earnings needed to pay premiums	(Less dividend additions)	50 percent tax bracket pre-tax earnings needed to pay premiums	(Less dividend additions)
5 years	$12,320	$ 9,187	$18,480	$13,780
10 years	24,640	15,684	36,960	23,556
20 years	49,280	21,911	73,920	32,866
25 years	61,600	20,967	92,400	31,450

Notes:

The total cost will depend on the time of death.

Dividends purchase paid-up additional insurance, which reduces the surviving partners' ultimate cost.

The policy becomes fully paid up with dividend additions in 25 years.

Dividends are based on the 1980 scale and are neither guarantees nor estimates for the future.

Prior to disability, he was a source of income for the partnership, but after his disability, he becomes a financial burden to the partnership. A properly drafted Partnership Agreement should clearly state what the obligation of the partnership is to the disabled partner, what constitutes disability, what is the amount and duration of benefits to be paid to the disabled partner, and finally, at what point in time the disabled partner's interest may be purchased by the active partners.

The following statistics will serve to emphasize the need for the partnership to deal with the disability problem with the utmost care. Few people realize that before his or her normal retirement, one out of every seven Americans will be disabled five years or more; the chances of a 35-year-old becoming disabled for three months or longer, because of an accident, are about one in three; nearly 30 percent of those disability cases caused by an accident will be permanent; and the chance of disability striking before normal retirement age is greater than the probability of death before that age.

With a partnership made up of three men, age 60, 35, and 30, the chances of at least one of the three suffering a disability of 90 days or more before he reaches age 65 are more than nine in ten. The more people in a business, and the younger those people are, the closer those odds come to ten in ten. Despite these overwhelming statistics, many partnerships still fund their disability payments to disabled partners out of partnership income. Over a time, this can become a sizable commitment and cause considerable unrest among the active partners.

One solution is to shift this risk from the partnership to a commercial insurance carrier. Many professional partnerships, such as law firms, accountants, and architects, have local association group disability plans, some of which offer an attractive benefit and cost package. Care should be taken in reviewing the benefits provided and the total cost to make sure that it meets the requirements of the partnership. In particular, the definition of disability in each plan should be read carefully and compared to the definitions in other available plans. Nothing can be more frustrating to professional partners than to be told that a partner is not disabled under a policy definition when his partners are certain that their partner's skills have departed due to his disability.

The individual policy which was discussed in Chapter 23 has become increasingly popular. As stated earlier, it is noncancellable and guaranteed renewable, and the definition of disability is usually superior to the group contract. Typically, there is a waiting period prior to disability benefits commencing. This might be either 30, 60, 90, 180, or 365 days. In general, the longer the waiting period, the lower the premium.

The larger partnership might well be advised to select a waiting period of 90 days, and to plan to fund the first 90 days of benefits out of partnership income. The smaller partnership might find this too great a financial burden, and would therefore be better advised to select a contract with a shorter waiting period, such as perhaps 30 to 60 days. In addition, the type of business in which the partnership is engaged will determine how quickly a partner's disability will be reflected in reduced income—and a reduced ability to self-insure. Where there is a time lag due to the large volume of accounts receivable, the capacity to self-insure is greater. These are the primary points which should be considered in selecting a disability income contract.

However, there are several other factors which should also be evaluated. The duration of the disability benefit can vary from one year to age 65, or for life. It is often worthwhile to compare the value of a longer benefit period to a partnership with its cost, which is often only a small increase in the premium. Many companies also offer a Residual Benefit which, in effect, provides that a portion of the disability benefit will be paid to the partially disabled partner in proportion to the loss of earnings which he has sustained. Many companies require that a period of total disability must precede the Residual Benefit before it can become operative. Other companies will allow a Residual Benefit without a preceding period of total disability.

The individual contract may also offer an option to increase the disability benefit regardless of the partner/insured's medical condition. In some instances, this benefit can allow a partner/insured to double his coverage over a period of years irrespective of his medical condition.

The selection of a disability benefit policy is more difficult than it would first appear. The partnership would be well advised to secure the advice of a competent disability agent or broker. In addition to evaluating the partnership's needs and recommending which of the different plans to select, he will also advise the partnership in the event of a claim. Unlike life insurance where there is no question as to whether a person is dead or alive, disability claims are rarely clean. For example, consider the partner who is attempting to return to work on a part-time basis after recovering from a heart attack. At first he comes to work one or two half-days per week. Gradually, over a period of months, he increases this to a full 40-hour week. When was he considered no longer disabled? The agent or broker is that individual most qualified to answer this question, and to go to bat for the partnership.

A disability plan may be extended to incorporate a buy-out. The disability buy-out program allows a partnership to continue functioning on a productive basis when one or more of its partners becomes totally disabled. In its simplest terms, a disability buy-out program provides that when a partner has been totally disabled for a specified period of time, the partnership will become obligated to begin purchasing the disabled partner's interest in the partnership. This buy-out provision should be covered in the Partnership Agreement. However, it should be pointed out that this provision is optional. It is not as necessary as the buy-sell provisions or the disability income provisions discussed previously.

There are a number of commercial carriers that write disability buy-out insurance. A typical program provides that in the event a partner is totally disabled for a period of one year, the insurance carrier will begin to make payments to the partnership in an amount sufficient to purchase the disabled partner's interest in full by the end of the second year of total disability. In the event that the disabled partner returns to work prior to the completion of the buy-out period, the benefits will stop. At this time, he may either buy back into the partnership or his remainder interest in the partnership will continue to be purchased out of the partnership income.

This type of insurance is relatively inexpensive and the partnership would be well advised to secure several proposals so that it can properly weigh the benefits against the comparatively small premium outlay.

MISCELLANEOUS INSURANCE

Finally, there are a number of other types of business insurance that may have some use in a partnership context.

Group term life insurance

Because group term life insurance covering the lives of the partners is not deductible by them, they often fail to investigate that form of insurance and deprive themselves of favorable insurance underwriting and rates. The cost a partnership pays for a partner's group term life insurance will be taxed as current income to him. Despite this disadvantage, the purchase of group term life insurance for all employees of a partnership may result in an otherwise uninsurable partner acquiring coverage at standard rates, if his group is large enough to benefit from such underwriting.

Health insurance

The description in Chapter 23 of the types of health insurance available to a sole proprietorship may also be relevant to a given partnership.

Fringe benefit insurance

The description in Chapter 26 of the types of insurance that employers can provide to key employees may have limited application to a partnership. Of course, to the extent that the partnership has common-law employees whom it wishes to reward through such fringe benefits, that description is entirely relevant. However, in a partnership, key employees are generally rewarded by admission to the partnership. Thereafter, the ability of the partnership to reward a key individual by providing him with tax deductible fringe benefit insurance vanishes. When such benefits are nevertheless provided, it is most likely to be for special reasons that are founded on the relationships among the partners, not for the usual economic and tax reasons.

In summary, it is hoped that this chapter has alerted the concerned partner to the need for a partnership document that clearly sets forth that his organization is, in fact, a partnership and has identified for him those areas where insurance protection is either useful or necessary for his partnership. If he pursues these concerns with knowledgeable lawyers, agents, brokers, and other benefits consultants, both he and his partnership will greatly benefit.

PROVIDING FOR BUSINESS CONTINUATION THROUGH INSURANCE AND SELECTED EMPLOYEE BENEFITS— FOR CORPORATIONS

NATURE OF CLOSE CORPORATION
BUSINESS CONTINUATION

TRANSFER OF OWNERSHIP

BUY-SELL AGREEMENTS
  Advantages
  Details
  Funding the buy-sell agreement
  Beyond the buy-sell agreement

LIFE INSURANCE PRODUCTS

PARTIAL CORPORATE REDEMPTIONS

VALUATION OF CLOSELY HELD
CORPORATIONS
  Market value
  Intrinsic value—earnings
  Intrinsic value—other considerations

YOUR VALUE

William J. Kane, CLU, MSFS
President
Miami Valley Estate Planning Corporation
Dayton, Ohio

William J. Kane is President of Miami Valley Estate Planning Corporation. He received his BBA at St. Bonaventure University in 1949, and is a graduate of National Trust School, Northwestern University (1964), Stonier Graduate School of Banking, Rutgers University (1966), and American College (1979) as Master of Science in Financial Services. Mr. Kane has been a Specialist in Trust New Business Development for 17 years.

This chapter is a description of some of the alternative solutions to the problem of disposing of the business interest of a stockholder/officer at death, disability, or retirement. It includes an explanation of the use of buy-sell plans among the co-stockholder/officers by the entity or cross-purchase methods. The reason for this approach is that the vast majority of business corporations are, in reality, proprietorships or partnerships with a corporate charter. Lenders usually require personal guarantees or pledges of personal assets by the stockholder/officers when these corporations borrow. The owners are usually the active managers and rely not on dividend income from their ownership but on salaries. In most cases the ownership of the close corporation is the largest single holding of the owner or owners. Owner-managers of closely held corporations are, of course, interested in employee benefits for themselves and their nonowner employers. These benefits are discussed in Chapters 26 and 27. Consequently, this chapter is exclusively devoted to close corporation business continuation and valuation problems.

NATURE OF CLOSE CORPORATION BUSINESS CONTINUATION

The ownership of the corporation is represented by shares of stock. This facilitates the transfer of ownership by sale of these shares, whether by an owner during his lifetime or by his estate or heirs after his death. At the death of a majority shareholder the chemistry of the business changes immediately, even though legal title can be moved smoothly. The surviving working owners usually either buy out the heirs, sell out to the heirs, accept the heirs, or if the heirs sell to others, accept the purchasers into the business.

There are, however, many potential sources of conflict because of the differing interests of the parties. Those owners who are the business managers want to be paid, in salary, for their efforts and also want to accumulate or reinvest earnings in the business. The nonmanagerial owners generally want dividends, particularly if they are not, do not want to be, or are incapable of earning salaries from the company. If the new majority owners attempt to force themselves on the surviving shareholders-managers, conflict, disruption, and hard feelings may result. If the heirs do not participate actively in the business, they are usually leaving their financial futures in the hands of the surviving shareholders until they can find a buyer for their interest. To find the right buyer, with cash, who will pay the full value at the right time (which is soon after an owner's death) is difficult for a majority holder's heirs and even more so for the heirs of a minority holder.

TRANSFER OF OWNERSHIP

There are seven basic ways that a business interest can be transferred:

1. *Will.* A Will may leave the shares, in specific numbers, to specific heirs, after the owner's death.
2. *The laws of intestacy.* If a shareholder dies without a valid Will, state statutes will determine who are the heirs and who will receive the shares.
3. *Gift.* The shareholder may make a gratuitous transfer during his lifetime.
4. *Sale.* The shareholder may sell shares at their fair market value—to a willing buyer who is under no compulsion to buy—in an "arm's-length" agreement.
5. *Agreement.* The shares may be transferred under a business purchase agreement (commonly known as a buy-sell agreement).
6. *Reorganization.* The shares may be shifted by changing their number or even their characteristics as a representative of a class of stock.
7. *Redemption.* The corporation may buy back the stock.

The assumption made in the following discussion is that the owner-managers of the close corporation are not related, and that they wish to buy the shares of any other owner who dies. If this assumption does not apply and the owner-managers are related, a Will, intestate succession, gifts and/or a reorganization can keep control within the family. Anyone in this position should contact his or her tax attorney for advice. The balance of this chapter addresses buy-sell agreements and the valuation of stock in close corporations.

BUY-SELL AGREEMENTS

There are two different forms of buy-sell agreements: a Stock Redemption (or Entity) Agreement and a Cross-Purchase (or Criss-Cross) Agreement.

The Stock Redemption (or Entity) Agreement is between the stockholders and the corporation. The corporation agrees to or has first option to purchase the shares of the corporation owned by a stockholder at his death or, in some cases, his disability.

A Cross-Purchase (or Criss-Cross) Agreement is between the stockholders themselves. The surviving shareholders have first option to buy the stock of the deceased (or sometimes the disabled) shareholder.

Advantages

The advantages of a buy-sell agreement are:

1. They set an agreed-upon price for the stock or a formula to set that price.
2. They provide a known market for the stock—the survivors will or have an option to purchase or will be required to purchase the deceased's shares.
3. The business will continue without interruption. There will be no delay in the transfer of the shares and the voting control the shares represent.
4. The family of the deceased will receive the agreed-upon value for their share of the business, not a lower forced sale value.
5. The surviving owners will not be forced to share the business with the deceased's family members who may not be able to work easily with surviving management or who may have different financial objectives.
6. The known succession of ownership will give all the shareholders the comfort that their personal and their family's best interests are protected.
7. The cash received by the deceased's estate for the sale of stock under the buy-sell agreement will provide the estate with liquidity and reduce any pressure to sell other estate assets to pay estate taxes or other costs.

Details

There are certain similarities in both forms of buy-sell agreements.

First, there is an agreed-upon price or a price determined in accordance with an agreed-upon formula. Second, who gets the shares is spelled out; how many shares go to whom (the corporation or other shareholders). Third, the method of payment is established (i.e., cash in full; part cash part notes payable; or payment in installments).

There are also certain differences between the two forms of buy-sell agreement. In the Entity Form, the corporation is a party to the agreement. In the Cross-Purchase Form, only the shareholders are parties. If life insurance is used in the Entity Form, there is only one policy per shareholder; while in the Cross-Purchase Form, each shareholder holds a policy on the life of each other shareholder who is a party to the agreement. In the Entity Form, the resultant purchase by the corporation will not vary the relationships of surviving owners. In contrast, in the Cross-Purchase Form, the control may or may not vary, depending on the agreement.

Local law may or may not permit shares to be purchased by a corporation, except from its retained earnings or other surplus. This restriction can create problems for an Entity Form Agreement. There are no such local law problems in a Cross-Purchase Agreement. Premiums for insurance to fund the agreement are not deductible under either form. However, if the corporation pays bonuses in the amount of the premiums to shareholders to pay premiums under the Cross-Purchase Agreement, the corporation can, if the compensation (including the bonuses) is still at a reasonable level, deduct the cost. In either case the life insurance proceeds will flow to the proper place, the estate of the deceased shareholder, without income tax consequence. In the Entity Form, the surviving shareholder's proportionate interest in the corporation would increase after the shares are purchased, but his "cost basis" for his shares would not. In the Cross-Purchase Form, the shareholder's cost basis in his shares would increase by what he paid for the new shares.

Funding the buy-sell agreement

Buy-sell agreements can be funded to fulfill the promise to buy by four basic sources:

1. The business. In the Entity Form the business may provide the purchase price from either current operating funds, borrowed funds, or retained earnings accumulated prior to the shareholder's death. All are expensive sources of dollars. To use current operating funds may wreck the business. To borrow may strain the corporation. It may use up borrowing power for the wrong purposes and reduce income by incurring expensive interest costs. Retaining earnings may cause a worse problem—the earnings may be found to be unreasonably accumulated, which triggers a large tax penalty. Additionally, if there are two deaths in rapid succession, the ready funds could be exhausted and the heirs of the second decedent or the surviving shareholders could be left owning a depleted corporation.

2. Note purchases. Either the corporation, in the Entity Form, or the surviving shareholders, in the Cross-Purchase Form, may use notes to pay for the shares. However, notes leave the deceased's heirs at the mercy of the performance of the surviving stockholders in operating the business profitably. Also, in most cases, the deceased's estate tax bill is due to the Internal Revenue Service, and his inheritance tax bill is due to the state of his domicile, *in cash* at the end of nine months (barring extensions). This means that the heirs may have to initially raise monies from other sources—something that they and the deceased may not have contemplated.

3. *A combination of cash and notes.* This partial funding method is an improvement on the above methods, but its success depends upon the amount of down payment, the amount and terms of the notes, and the business abilities of the surviving owners.

4. *Fully funded Agreement.* This method uses life insurance on the life of the deceased shareholder to fund the agreement. In either the Entity Form or the Cross-Purchase Form, the corporation or the other shareholders can pay in full, in cash, and promptly. The heirs receive the agreed value of the business; the shares are promptly transferred; and the surviving shareholders have the certainty that they will have the business. This is the most satisfactory arrangement.

In summary, a buy-sell agreement funded with life insurance can peg the value of the shares, provide a full value to the family in cash, assist in settling the shareholder's estate, and give the deceased's family independence from the surviving shareholders for their future economic security.

Beyond the buy-sell agreement

Certain life insurance products are better suited than others to provide the funding for a buy-sell agreement. Careful comparison shopping is required. Also, the valuation of a corporation, as discussed later in this chapter and in Chapter 24, can be a very complex matter. Consideration should also be given to the fact that there are ways to transfer the value of a corporation to his family, if that is what the corporation's owner wants, other than through a buy-sell agreement with a third party. Internal Revenue Code Section 303, 302 and 306 can provide ways to use corporate dollars to pay estate settlement costs (at least in part). These items will be discussed later in some detail.

LIFE INSURANCE PRODUCTS

The life insurance products most commonly used for buy-sell agreements are:

1. *Term insurance*—which covers the risk of death without a buildup of value in the policy for the owner. It is a temporary solution to a permanent problem but is also the least expensive solution in terms of the outlay of dollars per year.
2. *Permanent insurance*—which is usually Whole (or Ordinary) life

with a cash value buildup. A limited payment life (meaning there are no further premiums due at the end of the stated payment period) is also a form of permanent insurance covering the lifetime of the insured.

3. *A combination of the above*—which is used when the premium payor cannot, or does not want to, handle the cost of permanent insurance for the entire purchase amount agreed upon in the buy-sell agreement.

Corporate-owned life insurance, usually in a permanent form, is frequently used to provide funds to redeem the stock of a deceased shareholder even where no formal buy-sell agreement exists.

PARTIAL CORPORATE REDEMPTIONS

Under Section 303 of the Internal Revenue Code, if the value of the decedent's corporate stock exceeds 50 percent of this Adjusted Gross Estate (total value less administrative costs, funeral expense, and court costs), the corporation may redeem enough shares to pay the sum of all death taxes due plus funeral and administration expenses of the estate.

The proceeds of a key man life insurance policy owned by the corporation at the key man's death would make "instant cash" available to provide these funds to the estate. If the deceased holds "preferred" stock at death, which would be taxed for federal income tax purposes at ordinary income rates if redeemed by the corporation (so-called Section 306 or "Tainted" stock), the use of Section 303 would prevent the redemption from being treated as ordinary income.

If the deceased's estate does not meet the ownership percentage test under Section 303 (50 percent of Adjusted Gross Estate), the estate may still qualify for capital gain treatment on the sale of the stock. Under current law the estate's tax basis in the shares will be stepped up to fair market value on the shareholder's death. If all of his shares are redeemed by the corporation at this fair market value, there will be no taxable gain under Section 302. This section can also be used if the Section 303 limitations (death taxes, funeral expenses, and administrative expenses) are fully used or if Section 303 does not apply to *all* of his stock in closely held businesses. In other words, Section 302 can be used in conjunction with Section 303. However, in order to use Section 302, one of the following tests must be met:

1. The redemption must be substantially disproportionate in that it reduces ownership by a substantial percentage (generally at least 80 percent of the percentage previously owned); or

2. The redemption is in complete redemption of all of the share-holder's shares.

Because there is no "pegged value," as there would be with a properly drawn buy-sell agreement, the use of the Sections 302 or 303 may involve valuation problems with closely held stock.

VALUATION OF CLOSELY HELD CORPORATIONS

Valuation is one of the most written about and discussed subjects in business and estate law. The Treasury Department issued a ruling (Revenue Ruling 59–60) spelling out those factors which will be considered in valuing shares for estate and gift tax purposes. The broad preamble of this ruling suggests that all financial data, as well as all relevant factors affecting fair market value, should be considered in the valuation of close corporation stock. Here are only some of the relevant factors according to the Internal Revenue Service:

a. Nature and history of the business.
b. The condition and outlook for the specific industry and the general economic outlook.
c. The financial condition and book value of the business.
d. The earning and dividend paying capacity of the corporation.
e. Previous sales of stock and the size of the block of shares to be valued compared to the total outstanding.
f. Comparison of stock prices of corporations in the same or similar lines of business being actively traded in a free and open market—either on an organized exchange or over the counter.
g. The existence of goodwill or the presence of other tangible value.

The ruling indicates that the nature of the business will determine the weight applied to each of the above factors, that is, investment company shares will have their assets weighed the most in determining value, while in a product or service company, earnings will count more.

This ruling suggests that there will be relatively little precision to the appraisal. The most important factor would seem to be the existence of a recent, competent, and independent appraisal, setting the value of the shares in a business buy-sell agreement. An alternative to setting the price is to have a valid binding agreement as to the valuation formula to be used in the agreement.

There are several methods that can be used to establish the proper value of the shares in either a buy-sell agreement or at the time of a purchase or a gift. These same methods can apply to estate values as well.

Market value

The first valuation method is to value the shares through reference to some degree of market activity in the stock, not withstanding the fact that control could be held by a family group. The general rule is that the best indication of value is the market price ascertained in a free and open market. In examination of the market, it has to be determined whether or not the market is free of abnormal pressures and influences which would make actual transactions unreliable even as a benchmark to value. Some of these abnormal factors are:

1. Inability to acquire control through the unavailability of sufficient stock in the marketplace.
2. The effect of a boom or depression on the market price.
3. Misinformation which changed the market price.
4. A manipulated or "rigged" market—one controlled by the major shareholders for their own benefit.

Once it has been determined that there are no abnormal pressures or influences, the existence of an "open market" must be tested. There has to be sufficient activity (volume and transactions current to the valuation date) for the prices to be proper for valuation purposes. If the stock is traded through an exchange or over the counter, these prices will prevail for valuation. If there is an open market, other factors—intrinsic in nature—do *not* have to be taken into account. If only bid and ask prices are available, the mean price is used.

The greater the market activity, the more the weight given to market prices. A negative factor, however, is sales that are between family members. Sales between insiders are not always a negative factor.

Intrinsic value—earnings

If the fair market value cannot be determined by reference to market transactions or to values set by arm's-length agreements (buy-sell agreements, etc.), then Intrinsic Factors have to be taken into account. These factors are earning capacity, book value, dividend paying capacity, and the existence of goodwill and other intangibles creating value. Each factor has to be examined in the context of the history of the business, its economic outlook, and the outlook of the industry. The lack of marketability is also an important factor.

The prime factor is earnings. Stock market analysts use price earnings ratios as one of their major indicators. A buyer is specifically concerned with future earning power of the company. The past earning power is considered to estimate future earning power under the following rules:

1. Revenue Rule 59–60 states that five or more prior years' earnings should be taken into account to predict earnings.
2. Earnings trends—the progressive increase or decrease in net income should be given more weight than just averaging the earnings for a five-year period.
3. If prior years have shown a loss and if it is not a manipulated loss, losses should be computed into the average.
4. Determination of earnings in the year in which the valuation date occurs and for later years is most appropriate.
5. Abnormal economic periods should be considered.
6. Abnormal or nonrecurring factors such as change in accounting methods, unusual capital gains or losses, or heavier than usual contributions to retirement plans have to be weighed.
7. The salaries of shareholder officers and their affect on earnings have to be weighed.
8. The loss of a key man can have a dramatic effect on future earnings.

Once the average earning power is computed, the proper multiplier to capitalize that power must be determined and applied. The risk factor has major bearing on the multiplier selected. The more the risk, the smaller the multiplier. The best guide is comparable multipliers of publicly traded companies. If this is not possible, comparable companies not publicly traded can be used. Once comparable companies have been located, the average price-earnings multiplier of their shares can be applied to the earnings of the stock to produce a valuation.

Intrinsic value—other considerations

The Revenue Ruling indicates that another primary consideration is the dividend-paying *capacity* rather than previous *actual* dividends. This method is quite close to an earnings factor.

The book value–net asset value factor also comes into play. The book value of an operating company can only be considered after it is determined that the asset values on the books are close to their fair market value.

As mentioned, the lack of marketability is an intrinsic factor. Lack of marketability can arise with either a minority or majority interest. Too large a block or too small a block can result in a limited ability to sell but for different reasons. Legal or contractural restrictions on sale may also contribute to a lack of marketability. There is no general rule on how large a marketability discount a court will apply to a stock's value.

A combination of all factors has been looked to by the courts. For example, in one case the court gave the following weight to certain factors: Earnings accounted for 50 percent of value; dividends, 30 percent; and book value, 20 percent. Then a 12 percent discount was allowed for lack of marketability. In another case, 50 percent was allowed for earnings and 25 percent each for dividends and for book value, and a 10 percent discount was applied.

Minority interests, due to a lack of value to others, have received discounts ranging from 20 percent to 66 percent of the net asset value per share.

YOUR VALUE

This brief discussion of the valuation process undertaken by two courts should give you reason to pause and carefully consider how to stay out of that morass. A well drafted buy-sell agreement, which establishes an arm's-length price, either at death or during lifetime, can prevent 99 percent of the problems presented here.

In addition, with the same stroke of the pen, the parties to the agreement can spell out how to cope with the other great problem— "living death." This is the long-term disability of one of the co-owners. The waiting period before buy-out begins; the price to be paid; the method by which that price is to be paid; and other pertinent details such as the right to buy back in an event of recovery during the buy-out period, can be described in detail so that there are no surprises in the event of a long-term disability.

If the whole risk cannot be covered by insurance, then a series of installment notes should be provided to cover the difference between the insurance and other available funds and the agreed-upon purchase price.

In summary, planning in these areas well may mean the salvation of an owner's family and his corporation. No owner-manager wants non-productive shareholders making financial demands that distract from corporate activities. A properly drawn buy-sell agreement, including a fair market, arm's-length valuation of stock, is critical. The buy-sell agreement provides for the payment to a deceased's estate of cash in a timely fashion. It also relieves his heirs of business worries and frees the surviving owners from interference from heirs.

No attempt has been made to suggest exactly how you should organize your buy-sell agreement. Each case is individual, and an expert estate planner, CLU, accountant, and/or tax attorney is necessary to determine your personal needs and your corporation's needs. The key point is that adequate planning can insure the accomplishment of your goals relative to both your family and your corporation's continuation. Planning, by definition, means "in advance." Failure to plan properly or in advance led to the pitfalls discussed in this chapter.

CHAPTER 26

PROVIDING FRINGE BENEFITS FOR KEY PERSONNEL

THE OBJECTIVES OF THE BENEFIT PROGRAM

PENSION AND PROFIT-SHARING PLANS

EMPLOYEE STOCK OWNERSHIP PLANS

FUNDING THE PLAN

THE INDIVIDUAL RETIREMENT ACCOUNT

THE SIMPLIFIED EMPLOYEE PENSION PLAN

TAX-DEFERRED ANNUITIES AND THE NONPROFIT ORGANIZATION

DEFERRED COMPENSATION PLANS
  Tax aspects
  Funding the plan through life
    insurance
  Funding the plan through annuities
  Funding the plan through mutual
    funds
  Including majority stockholders

GROUP LIFE INSURANCE
  Prefunding through group
    permanent insurance
  Prefunding through a retired lives
    reserve plan

CAFETERIA PLANS

EMPLOYER FINANCED INSURANCE
  Paying the premium as a bonus
  Split-dollar insurance

INTEREST FREE LOANS

EXECUTIVE HEALTH PLANS

MEDICAL REIMBURSEMENT PLANS

PLANNING FOR THE RECEIPT OF FRINGE BENEFITS AT RETIREMENT

PLANNING FOR THE RECEIPT OF FRINGE BENEFITS AT DEATH

SELECTING THE AGENT OR BROKER AND CHOOSING THE PROGRAM

INTRODUCTION TO AND FOLLOW UP WITH THE EMPLOYEES

SUMMARY

Wendell J. Bossen, CLU
Executive Vice President
Inter-Ocean Insurance Company
Cincinnati, Ohio

Wendell J. Bossen, CLU, Executive Vice President, Inter-Ocean Insurance Company, has had more than 22 years in the sale and marketing of life insurance. His specialty is corporate sponsored benefits and estate planning. Mr. Bossen is a frequent contributor to numerous publications on executive fringe benefits and their relationship to personal estate planning.

Mel J. Massey, Jr., Esquire
President
Advanced Underwriting Consultants
Indianapolis, Indiana

Mel J. Massey's firm, Advanced Underwriting Consultants, Indianapolis, Indiana, advises life insurance company home offices and their field agents on pensions, estate planning, and business insurance. He is a graduate of Case-Western Reserve University Law School, a Chartered Life Underwriter (CLU), and has 19 years' experience in these "advanced underwriting" areas. He has written numerous booklets, brochures, sales courses, and magazine articles on business insurance, estate planning, pension, and employee benefit plans.

THE OBJECTIVES OF THE BENEFIT PROGRAM

The success of most businesses, large and small, is dependent on their ability to attract and retain key personnel. The intensity of competition for high performance people places demands on management to develop a compensation climate that provides proper recognition for performance on a current basis along with creative use of fringe benefits to amplify both the present and future value of the total compensation system.

Since most key employees likely will be compensated at levels that attract income tax rates in the upper brackets, properly designed fringe benefits paid by the employer with pre-tax dollars have the potential to sharply influence the net value of the compensation package. It is not unusual for the actual cost of a fringe benefit to be worth twice that dollar value to the employee and, in some instances, even more.

While the economic advantages to both the employer and employee are a strong motivation, they should not obscure the fact that the objectives of a benefit program are:

1. To provide additional security for the employee.
2. To enhance the value of the compensation program.
3. To improve attitude and job performance.
4. To add an additional drop of glue to the retention of key people.

The benefit program must work in harmony with the overall objectives of the business, as well as the needs of its employees, or its worth will be largely diluted and reduced to a tax-deductible waste of money. A number of questions and considerations must be addressed to design a program of benefits that will maximize the impact of the dollar investment while achieving the desired results.

A prerequisite to the design and scope of a fringe benefit program is the identification of those employees whose performance is vital to the success of the business. Some thought also must be given to determining whether today's key employees, and the positions they occupy, are likely to be the same in the future. This is an especially important consideration in the case of a new business. The talents critical in the initial stages may well lose much of their importance afterward.

It can be difficult to maintain a high degree of objectivity in identifying key people. Evaluations of personality must be set aside in favor of evaluations of performance. You must be aware that gratitude and performance may not be forthcoming from the same person. There definitely is a place in this evaluation, however, for recognition of an heir apparent, particularly in the smaller, closely held business. Grooming a key employee as a potential buyer for a business interest can be enhanced with selective fringe benefits.

It should be noted here that one of the key employees, if not the key employee, in a closely held corporation may be the principal stockholder. While retention may not be an issue in the case of a principal stockholder, all of the other needs will generally be present along with those unique to ownership. The stockholder-employee has an obligation to himself to maximize those fringe benefits available to him as additional compensation for risking capital.

It is also important for you to distinguish between key positions and key people. An important position with many competent people available to fill it requires different treatment than a super-achiever whose contribution far surpasses a formal job description. He may be a key person even if he is not currently in a job that is critical to the success of the business. Positions can be more easily accommodated by a structured fringe benefit program, while an individual super-achiever might require recognition by use of selective benefits. In the case of the super-achiever, it is important to avoid unwarranted rewards to an entire group in order to recognize a single stellar performer.

The characteristics that are unique to the key people in a given business will help determine the type of benefits that will have the most appeal to them and give the best dollar value to the employer. Age, sex, education level, family status, and income are some of the characteristics that will influence the employer's choices. Young, well-educated people, for example, may perceive themselves as having upward mobility within their field. They are generally less influenced by benefits projected far into the future with gradual vesting provisions. They are more influenced by benefits that free up income currently for improved living standards or personal investment. Middle-aged, high-income people, on the other hand, might be more inclined to sacrifice current benefits for those that make the future, particularly retirement, more secure.

While the profile of the existing group is important to design, management must determine whether it is representative of the people it wants or is likely to attract in the future. A sharp variance between these profiles could dictate compromise or, more likely, built-in flexibility to accommodate change.

Each industry, and each business within that industry, possesses characteristics that will affect the choice and condition of benefits. Turnover rate, availability of personnel, training cost, profit stability, and potential for growth are variables which deserve consideration in program design. An unusually high turnover rate might be reduced by benefits that accelerate with years of service. Instability of profits could require that some benefits, particularly those of a future value, be tied to business performance.

Perhaps the worst fringe benefit program is the one designed for somebody else. Unless it addresses the current position and future objectives of your business, it will stand little chance of reaching its potential in attracting and holding high performance employees. On the other hand, proper design will not only help achieve those objectives but it will help to communicate your objectives to your employees in the process.

It is not necessary to plan for every possible future contingency, but it is highly desirable to incorporate adequate flexibility to weather changes with a minimum of disturbance.

Basic fringe benefits for your general personnel may be considered a necessary cost in providing employee security and maintaining a competitive posture as an employer. Extended fringe benefits for key employees, however, are performance oriented. Thus, they can be considered an investment in the attraction, retention, and motivation of those people who will be most instrumental to success of your business. Viewed in this manner, these costs can be expected to be returned in improved performance and attitude. In spite of this, there naturally will be a limit to the amount of money available for commitment to this purpose, and it is imperative the result of these expenditures be maximized.

When available funds prevent implementation of a benefit package that recognizes all key personnel, priorities will have to be established. First consideration will generally go to those who are vital to the success of the business today, especially if their skills are in demand elsewhere. Second consideration should go to those qualified people who must be attracted to continue growth, and, finally, consideration should be given to those who have contributed years to the effort.

Specific benefits can and should be tailored to the problem to which they are addressed. While the variations are endless, the following are some general categories of benefits.

PENSION AND PROFIT-SHARING PLANS

A wag once suggested that no man's life, liberty, or property is safe while the legislature is in session. Despite congressional "reforms" in other areas, one effective tax shelter that remains for working Americans is a retirement plan. Regardless of the plan an employee is eligible for, an IRA (Individual Retirement Account), an HR-10 Plan (Retirement Plan for Self-Employed Individual), Tax-Deferred 403(b) Annuity, or a regular pension plan, the working individual gains much from establishing and participating in such a plan. These plans are discussed in greater detail elsewhere, but certain basic principals must be discussed here:

1. *Contributions are deductible.* Within certain limits, employer contributions are deductible. For this reason, not only is an employer more likely to establish a retirement plan, but also the amounts contributed have greater impact because of the deduction.
2. *Earnings of the plan accumulate tax-free.* Tax-free accumulation means bigger benefits. The following table shows the advantage of accumulating and compounding dollars at a tax-free 6 percent rate over the accumulation of the same dollars at the resulting 3 percent rate if they are first subject to tax (assuming a 50 percent tax bracket):

	$1,500		$7,500		$15,000	
Years	3%	6%	3%	6%	3%	6%
5	$ 8,202	$ 8,962	$ 41,010	$ 44,812	$ 82,020	$ 89,620
10	17,712	20,958	88,560	104,790	177,120	209,580
15	28,735	37,009	143,677	185,047	287,355	370,095
20	41,514	58,489	207,570	292,447	415,140	584,895

If the retirement benefit is taken as an annuity, the tax-free accumulation advantages are carried further.

3. *Retirement benefits are advantageously taxed.* A retirement annuity is taxable only as each annuity payment is drawn. By this time, the executive may be in a lower tax bracket. If the employee is a participant in a qualified plan (a corporate pension or profit-sharing plan, or an HR-10 plan), he may elect a lump-sum distribution if the plan permits such distribution, and choose to be taxed under a special ten-year forward averaging provision of the law, provided he has participated in the plan five or more years.

There may even be income tax advantages to an employee's beneficiaries if he dies before retirement. If a portion of the pre-retirement death benefit is considered to be life insurance, that portion will be income tax free, whether it is received in a lump sum or as an annuity.

4. *A retirement benefit is apart from all other property.* A retirement benefit is shielded by law from business or personal disasters that may befall the employee in later years. It cannot be touched by creditors and, in some states, by former spouses. The congressional intent was to provide the *employee* with a retirement benefit.

The basic motive of an employer in establishing a pension plan may be different than his motive in establishing a profit-sharing program. Again, Chapter 28 provides greater details. However, a pension plan usually provides a defined benefit on retirement for the executive and the other covered employees. The benefit is usually either a percentage of the employee's compensation or is based on a formula which takes into account his years of service and his compensation.

A profit-sharing plan usually has a dual purpose—to furnish a profit incentive to the covered employees during their working years and also to provide retirement benefits. To achieve the profit incentive, the firm ties its contributions to the plan to its profits. The contributions made from profits are invested and reinvested, and at retirement, the employee's benefit in his proportional share of the accumulated fund.

EMPLOYEE STOCK OWNERSHIP PLANS

An Employee Stock Ownership Plan (ESOP) is similar to a profit-sharing plan, but the funds of the plan are largely invested in the stock of the employer corporation. Furthermore, the employer may contribute its stock to the plan and take either a tax deduction or a tax credit for its contribution. The fund also can be leveraged to buy still more shares of employer stock.

Stock ownership plans may purchase the shares of present stockholders, including the majority stockholder. Thus, the major stockholder can reduce his interest over a period of time without running the risk of his gain being taxed as ordinary income, as would occur if the corporation partially redeemed his shares.

One important advantage of an ESOP is that the employees own stock in the employer corporation and are able to build the value of the stock and the size of their retirement fund through more effective work efforts. Furthermore, the corporation has a continuing source of money for expansion and other corporate needs.

Distributions to employees from an ESOP at retirement may be in cash or securities. If it is in securities that are not readily tradable, the employee may request the employer redeem the securities from him. Because this same privilege extends to the employee's estate or beneficiary at death, many corporations insure the lives of the key employees who would receive the largest distributions to make sure there is enough cash to make the redemptions.

FUNDING THE PLAN

Insurance company contracts have been used almost from the beginning to fund retirement plans. In plans with fewer than 15 to 25 participants, it has been customary to use individual insurance and annuity policies; the economics of pension plans with more participants seem to favor group contracts.

In recent years, the difference between individual and group contract funding has been obscured by the advent of the group-type, no front-end-load annuity as an individual policy. Today, the contrast between the group and individual annuities of the same insurer is often not as great as the difference between the individual annuities of different companies.

Both pension and profit-sharing plans continue to be funded with a combination of an individual or group life insurance policy and a side investment fund. The purpose of the life insurance is to provide a pre-retirement death benefit inside the plan. While such death benefit could be provided with group term insurance outside the plan, certain tax benefits developed later in this chapter accrue largely to the executives or managers when the insurance is inside the plan.

Changes also have occurred in group contracts used to fund pension plans. In the past, the cost of pension administration performed by the insurance company was deducted from the earnings of group deposit administration contracts. Today, many insurance companies bill the pension fund or the employer separately for the plan administration they perform. Thus, investment comparisons may be more readily made between money left with the insurance company and funds invested elsewhere.

Insurers also are offering to invest pension monies in segregated accounts which are apart from insurers' general accounts. The insurer may not guarantee the value of the assets or the return in a segregated account. Instances where the insurer *will* guarantee the values and the return are discussed in Chapter 24. In either case, the charges for investment management are generally spelled out in the contract and not determined in a discretionary manner by the insurer.

In general, if the employer's profits fluctuate widely from year to year, the employer may be best served by a profit-sharing plan. No contribution need be made in a year with no profits, and if the plan permits it, the board of directors may even determine the amount that may be contributed, within certain limitations. As mentioned previously, the employer's motivation is important. If the employer's principal purpose is to shelter money in years when income taxes on its profits would be oppressive, it probably should limit its consideration to a profit-sharing plan.

Many employers earn steady profits. Furthermore, their key employees may be past age 45 or age 50. A defined benefit pension plan generally will produce larger benefits for them. Because of the shorter funding period, larger deductible contributions may be made and a greater percentage of those contributions will be spent for their benefit. In any corporation with that type of key personnel, a defined benefit illustration should be a part of every retirement plan proposal. Through the use of computers, the illustration can be prepared at little added expense.

THE INDIVIDUAL RETIREMENT ACCOUNT

Many times a pension or profit-sharing plan is out of the question in a particular company. Perhaps it is too new, too small, or not profitable. Fortunately, there are two retirement plans which might be employed in the business.

The first is an Individual Retirement Account or Annuity (IRA). Each employee decides for himself whether or not he wants to participate. If he does, he can make a deductible contribution up to 15 percent of compensation, or $1,500 annually. In a given year, he may raise, lower, or not make a contribution.

On a pick-and-choose basis, his employer may help him with his contribution by bonusing part or all of the contribution. Normally, this is followed by payroll reduction with the employer sending the employee's contribution to the plan sponsor.

THE SIMPLIFIED EMPLOYEE PENSION PLAN

A Simplified Employee Pension Plan (SEP) is a more recent variation of an IRA. The employer may contribute as much as $7,500 or 15 percent of compensation per employee, whichever is less, if the contribution is allocated among the eligible employees on a nondiscriminatory basis. If the employer's contribution falls short of 15 percent of compensation or $1,500 in a given year, each employee may elect to make up the difference and deduct the contribution. Eligible employees are those who have worked for the employer in three out of the last five years and are age 25 or older. Union employees may be excluded if there has been good faith bargaining.

Life insurance may not be used to fund an IRA or a SEP plan. A flexible premium annuity may be used to fund such plans. Annuities with no or a low front-end-load are among the popular ways the plans are funded.

Both IRAs and SEPs are easy to administer. The only duty the employer has in either plan is to add any money it puts up for the plan to the employees' W-2 forms. In a SEP plan, the employer gives copies of the government form it signs to the employees, along with the literature supplied by the plan sponsor.

TAX-DEFERRED ANNUITIES AND THE
NONPROFIT ORGANIZATION

The need for executive and technical talent is not limited to the for-profit enterprise. Schools and hospitals are among those nonprofit organizations with large executive and technical staffs.

Most such institutions have pension plans. The most common type is the so-called money purchase pension plan; the employer contributes a percentage of the employee's compensation, which the employee may match in whole or part. The employee's pension is what these sums will purchase in benefits at retirement.

Employees of certain charities qualified under Section 501(c) (3) of the Internal Revenue Code, and public schools may provide additional sums for retirement through nonqualified annuities under the provisions of Section 403(b) of the Code. Included in the definition of Section 501(c) (3) organizations are religious, charitable, scientific, literary, and educational organizations.

Whether a tax-deferred annuity is purchased for an employee of such organization is usually a decision the employee makes. This is because the premium for the annuity usually comes from compensation he would otherwise receive. Via an agreement between employer and employee, the employee's compensation is reduced and the employer uses the reduced amount to buy the annuity.

The employee may exclude the employer-paid premium from his gross income to the extent it does not exceed an *exclusion allowance* for the year. The exclusion allowance is computed by taking 20 percent of the employee's includable compensation, multiplied by his years of service, and subtracting the total tax-exempt "annuity premiums" which the employer paid in prior years. Today the exclusion allowance may be calculated by a computer, which makes it easier to determine the maximum annual contribution.

For a number of years, the tax-deferred annuity market has been a sizable source of business for life agents. Many employees of Section 501(c) (3) organizations and public schools are capable of saving additional sums of money—especially those who are higher paid or do not have or have completed their child-raising responsibilities, or have spouses who also work. The employee who signs up for a tax-deferred annuity gets an immediate tax break. He defers tax on the premium and on the growth in the annuity until after his retirement, when he may be in a lower tax bracket.

Over the past 20 years, many different annuity products have been purchased as tax-deferred annuities. In recent years, the most widely used annuity has been the flexible premium type with a low or no front-end-load.

DEFERRED COMPENSATION PLANS

Despite the wide range of employee benefits in American industry, many people are not in a position to profit from so basic a benefit plan as a qualified retirement program. Such a person may be an executive who works for a company or organization without a retirement plan or, perhaps because of his age at the time of his employment, is not greatly aided by his employer's plan or, maybe, the employer's retirement program is weighted in favor of lower paid workers.

One answer to improving key employees' position is a deferred compensation plan. Basically, it is an agreement to pay future benefits in return for present service. It can be tailored to meet the needs of an individual employee. It may be used by an employer to attract or retain skilled people. It also may allow highly compensated individuals to accumulate enough money for retirement.

A deferred compensation agreement should be prepared to fit the needs of each particular employer and employee; there is no set format an agreement need take.

For example, an employer may have a valued employee who is disturbed by the fact that the employer has either no pension plan or an inadequate plan. To hold this person, the employer may agree to pay the employee, say, $3,000 per month for 15 years, commencing at retirement, if the employee continues to work for the employer until his retirement. To show good faith and to help meet and measure the obligation to the employee, the employer often purchases an insurance policy and/or annuity contract.

Tax relief is another major reason for deferred compensation agreements; for not only can an employee save for retirement, but also he can lower his current income and consequently his current income taxes.

Under a deferred compensation agreement, an employer may agree to pay the employee, for example, $10,000 less per year in current compensation. The employer retains the $10,000, investing the deferred account in life insurance, annuities, mutual funds, or other investments. At the employee's termination of employment, he will be paid the value of the account in installments over a period of years.

Among the employees who can benefit from deferred compensation are the important engineer, the star salesman, the profit-making manager of a branch operation, the general manager of a firm, and the full-time executive secretary of a club, trade, or civic association.

A deferred compensation plan is not limited to the employer-employee relationship but may be arranged between an independent contractor and his principal. For example, in the hospital setting a pathologist or radiologist may have an independent contractor relationship with the hospital, provided his fees are received through the hospital. On the other hand, the doctor who is paid directly by his patients is not an independent contractor of the hospital. His contract relationship is with each individual patient.

Hospital-associated doctors are not the only persons who can take advantage of deferred compensation. Other deferred compensation candidates are physicians who perform services for union-and community-sponsored clinics and convalescent homes, attorneys, accountants, manufacturers' representatives, and other professionals who serve any type of organization for compensation.

Tax aspects

The Internal Revenue Service, if not the tax law, recognizes three types of deferred compensation plans: (1) plans for employees and independent contractors of state and other local governments, (2) plans for employees and independent contractors of tax-paying corporations, and (3) plans for employees of tax-exempt organizations.

Those who work for state, county, and city governments by law may enter into deferred compensation agreements with those governments and defer the lesser of $7,500 or 33.33 percent of their compensation for a taxable year. The deferred amounts are reduced by any amounts contributed to tax-deferred annuities on behalf of the workers. For one or more of the participant's last three years before normal retirement age, the lesser of $15,000, or the amount that could have been deferred, but was not deferred under the above ceiling, may be deferred. Deferred compensation must not be made available to the public employee or independent contractor any earlier than his separation from service or the occurrence of an unforeseeable emergency (as defined by IRS regulations).

Numerous state and local government deferred compensation plans are in effect with new plans and participants being added daily. In some cases, plans are solicited by the governments themselves; that is, the government not only owns but selects the investments of the deferred accounts. In other cases, an organization of insurance agents or agents acting independently solicit the employees of the participating government. In the latter case, the investment normally used to fund the deferred compensation agreements is a group or individual annuity of the flexible premium, low or no front-end-load type. The contracts are owned by the government.

The tax rationale for deferred compensation plans generally, and the plans of tax-paying corporations, partnerships, and proprietorships in particular, goes back almost 50 years. The following sentence digests the many court decisions and revenue rulings—"so long as the taxpayer does not earn the income prior to the date of the deferred compensation agreement, that the parties intend to be bound by the terms of the agreement, and that no funds are set aside for the taxpayer's benefit, the fact the deferred compensation agreement was made to suit the tax needs of the employee is not enough to result in the promised pay being included in gross income today."[1]

The fact the employer maintains a deferred account, which remains the property of the employer, to meet and measure its obligation to the employee or independent contractor does not place the employee in receipt of income until the dates of actual payment. In the correct deferred compensation agreement, the employee-taxpayer is an unsecured creditor, sharing with other unsecured creditors the risk of bankruptcy of the employer.

Funding the plan through life insurance

There is little sense for an organization to make deferred pay promises and then be surprised when the event occurs and not be able to meet its obligation. Three types of assets generally have been purchased to meet and measure deferred compensation payments—life insurance, annuities, and mutual fund shares.

Most deferred compensation agreements promise the employee the same benefit if he lives to retire or if he dies prematurely. Few employers promise a substantial pre-retirement death benefit without insuring the obligation.

The particular policy an employer purchases will depend upon its general financial condition. Obviously, term or whole life insurance could be purchased. A particularly appropriate policy is a life paid up at retirement policy. The premiums are paid by the employee's retirement date, and the corporation is free to make the promised payments out of current earnings or accumulated surplus. The employer should own the insurance policy and be the beneficiary both before and after retirement. The employee should not be given any rights to the policy either in the policy itself or in the deferred compensation agreement; otherwise the employee may be subject to premature taxation. Furthermore, the provisions of the insurance policy should not be translated into the agreement. If the dollar amounts in the policy are repeated in the agreement, the employee will have the taxable economic benefit of the policy's benefits as if he were the owner of the policy.

At retirement, the employer has the option of retaining the policy and paying the deferred compensation out of current revenue or other funds, or surrendering the policy and using the cash values as the basis for the payments to the retiree. From the viewpoint of net cost, the former method is to be preferred because some day the employer will receive the insurance proceeds tax-free, substantially reducing the cost of the plan.

Funding the plan through annuities

An annuity contract is another way to remove the fear, "will I get it when I retire?" Both the employer and the employee know the annuity will generate a monthly income from which the deferred compensation payments can be made. The employer has the choice of writing its own check for the deferred compensation amounts or having the insurance company, acting as its agent, send the annuity check directly to the retired employee or his beneficiary. In the latter instance, the insurance company would make the payments *subject* to the employer's right to rescind the payment order. As in the case of the insurance policy, the employer will, at all times, be the owner of the annuity contract and the sole payee.

For the tax-paying employer corporation, annuity income is taxable under the regular annuity rule of the tax law. The portion of each installment which represents the annuity premiums or deposits is received tax-free as an investment return; the balance of the installment is taxable income to the employer. Most deferred compensation agreements provide for a reduction in the corresponding payments due the employee to reflect the taxes paid on the annuity income. However, some agreements then will "gross up" the deferred compensation payments to mirror the deduction the employer gains through those payments.

Funding the plan through mutual funds

Fund shares have a definite place in deferred compensation plans. Regardless of the type of mutual fund purchased, they promise diversification and professional management of the investments in the deferred account. Many employers are hard pressed to handle their own normal business operations, much less worry about the management of an investment account.

The deduction for corporate dividends received is a major reason why tax-paying corporations should consider using mutual fund shares to meet and measure deferred compensation obligations. The Internal Revenue Code permits a corporation to deduct from income 85 percent of dividends received on stock it owns in another corporation. Thus, 85 percent of a mutual fund distribution that is attributable to dividends is deductible from the corporation's income. It includes in income only the 15 percent balance of the dividends.

In the top 46 percent corporate tax bracket, only 6.9 percent of the corporation's dividend income is lost to income taxes. For a corporation in the lowest 17 percent bracket, only 2.55 percent of the dividend distribution will be lost to taxes. The portion of the fund distributions attributable to capital gains is taxed as capital gains regardless of the period the shares are owned by the employer-corporation.

At the employee's retirement, the employer may elect to have the mutual fund pay it monthly sums under a withdrawal plan. Under a withdrawal plan, a fixed amount is withdrawn from the fund each month regardless of the dividend income or the capital gains realized by the fund. Two tax problems may result with this type of distribution when quarterly distributions are used to purchase additional shares: (1) determining the value of the new shares for purpose of profit and loss, and (2) avoiding a wash sale (purchase and sale of the same shares within 30 days). A common method for identifying the shares redeemed under a withdrawal plan is the first-in, first-out (Fifo) method. It avoids the possibility of a wash sale, but in a rising market, Fifo produces a lower basis and a greater capital gain on the shares redeemed because it assumes the shares sold were those first acquired.

Although an employer may set aside or earmark funds in a deferred account for later payout to an employee under the terms of a deferred compensation agreement, the employer has no tax deduction until the employee is in receipt of income. Of course, deferred compensation payments also must qualify as an ordinary and necessary business expense and be reasonable compensation for services rendered by the employee in the current and past years.

Given a properly drafted deferred compensation agreement, the employee should be in receipt of income when he receives the installments after his retirement, termination of employment, disability, death, or other occasion called for in the agreement. If the deferred compensation payments are made to the employee's widow or other beneficiary, the beneficiary may exclude the first $5,000 received from gross income. The balance will be taxable to the beneficiary as income.

At the death of the employee, the present value of the future payments under the type of deferred compensation agreement described in this chapter will be included in the employee's estate for estate tax purposes. In certain circumstances, a plan providing a death benefit only will escape inclusion in the employee's estate.

Including majority stockholders

Whether deferred compensation should be arranged for the majority stockholder-employee is an important question because it is considerably easier to sell deferred compensation for the principal owner than for any other employee.

There seems little question that an employer-corporation can purchase a life insurance policy on a stockholder-officer for purposes of deferred compensation without the premium payments being considered a constructive dividend to the officer. What is questioned is the ability of the corporation to deduct the deferred benefits when paid to the majority stockholder-employee or his beneficiary.

The Internal Revenue Service may challenge deferred compensation payments as being constructive dividends (and not deductible by the corporation) and require the corporation to demonstrate that the payments were intended to result in a business benefit to it and not made to insure the financial security of the major stockholder or his widow.

In many closely held corporations, the reasonableness of the compensation paid the majority stockholder-employee has been the subject of controversy between the corporate employer and the Internal Revenue Service. If the corporation had difficulty justifying the compensation paid during the stockholder-employee's working years, justifying deferred compensation after retirement will be much more difficult when the basis for the deferred benefits will be the services the employee performed during his working years.

Before a deferred compensation plan is established for a majority stockholder-employee, the attorney for the corporation should be consulted and a determination made by him as to whether the proposed deferred compensation will be deductible.

GROUP LIFE INSURANCE

Since the first group life insurance contract was written a little more than 65 years ago, there has been a tremendous growth in the popularity of group insurance. Today it has largely replaced industrial insurance as the life insurance coverage for the working man. Not only are workers covered in insurance amounts ranging from $2,000 to one or two times compensation, but in recent years one or more classes of officers, executives, and managers have been insured for amounts as high as $250,000, $500,000, or more.

The employer usually can deduct the premiums it pays for group term life insurance. The employee excludes from his or her gross income the cost of the first $50,000 provided by the employer. Amounts of insurance provided by the employer in excess of $50,000 are taxable to the employee. The value of the employer-provided insurance is measured by Table I, contained in Treasury regulations. Table I is based on modern group insurance premiums and, thus, does not overstate the employer's cost in providing the group life benefit. In addition, the insured employee who works beyond age 64 is taxed as if he were age 64, and after retirement, an employer-provided group term insurance benefit costs and retiree nothing, although a benefit of many thousands of dollars may be payable at his death.

Most group term insurance plans terminate coverage when the employee reaches retirement age. Formerly, this was age 65. The Age Discrimination in Employment Act pushed back to 70 the mandatory retirement age. Most group plans have been amended and insurance coverage now terminates at 70 for those who continue to work. Cost is the reason more employers do not continue group term coverage on employees and retirees past 70; this is the time when the greatest mortality is experienced.

Many employees, especially executives and managers, need life insurance after as well as before retirement. These persons have created substantial estates through stock acquisition and appreciated assets which, at death, are subject to administration costs, debts, and estate taxes. Retirement does not diminish the need for life insurance to provide liquidity.

The estate owner has the option of converting his group term insurance at retirement. Unfortunately, the premium for the converted policy is quite high, approximately $60 per thousand. The retiree with a $500,000 policy would be faced with a $30,000 premium burden through his retirement years. In addition, the group insurance carrier levies a $32,000 charge-back to the group insurance contract of the former employer.

Fortunately, tax law permits two methods for prefunding post-retirement group insurance. First is group permanent insurance; the second one is a Retired Lives Reserve.

Prefunding through group permanent insurance

Group permanent insurance is a method for purchasing insurance which is paid up at the employee's retirement. The tax law requires that the employee pay the premium for the portion of the insurance premium which buys the group permanent benefit. In some plans, the participating employee pays his premium via payroll reduction. In other plans, the employer pays the group permanent premium and adds that premium to the employee's W-2 at year-end.

In recent years, following a change in the law, insurance companies have offered allocated individual insurance policies to fund group permanent plans. In companies with ten or more employees eligible for group insurance, the group permanent plan often is superimposed on an existing group term insurance plan. In ten-plus groups, the group permanent coverage may be limited to specific classes of employees.

Group permanent insurance also may be limited to one or more classes of officers, executives, managers, or supervisors. The Treasury regulations require that amounts of insurance granted a class be determined by a formula which precludes individual selection. Ostensibly, if a viable formula is present, large amounts of group permanent insurance may be provided the executives and managers of an employer.

In many of these plans, the employee's only cost is the tax he pays on the amounts included in his gross income, which is much easier than paying the entire insurance premium out of current income. The employee includes in his gross income *(a)* the cost of employer-paid term insurance in excess of $50,000; *(b)* the premium or portion of the premium for the group permanent benefit; and *(c)* in case of a participating policy where the employee retains the dividend but pays nothing toward the permanent benefit, the annual dividend.

Prefunding through a retired lives reserve plan

While the matter is not literally free from doubt, current tax law appears to permit an employer to deduct its accrual of funds in a reserve account to pay future group term insurance premiums. Using this provision, a number of major American corporations have placed more than $1 billion in Retired Lives Reserves with insurance companies to fund group term insurance for employees after retirement.

Prefunding through a Retired Lives Reserve is an excellent way to provide post-retirement group insurance.

1. The employer may deduct its deposits to the fund.
2. Interest at a high, current rate is applied to the fund by the insurance company.
3. As a result, the deposits made by the employer are low. The employer pays about $6 per thousand for an employee age 35. Compare this with the $60 per thousand the same employee would pay if he waited to age 65 and converted his group insurance.
4. The earnings of the fund are not taxable to the employer or employee.
5. The fund is never taxable to the employee.

6. At retirement age, the employer's insurance obligation to the employee normally ends.
7. During his working years, the employee includes only the value of group insurance in excess of $50,000 in his gross income; after retirement, the group term benefits cost him nothing.

A Retired Lives Reserve plan is subject to the same tax rules which govern other group insurance plans.

If the employer group contains fewer than ten employees eligible for insurance, the insurability of the participants must be determined without physical examinations and other evidence outside nonmedical questionnaires. The amounts of insurance must be either a uniform percentage of salary or be based on coverage brackets under which no bracket exceeds the next lower bracket by more than 2½ times and the lowest bracket is at least 10 percent of the highest bracket. If a Retired Lives Reserve benefit is provided for the entire group, however, individual employees may waive part or all of their coverage.

If the employer group contains ten or more eligible employees, insurability may be determined on the basis of medical examinations. As previously mentioned, the amounts of insurance must be determined on the basis of a formula which precludes individual selection. If post-retirement group insurance is provided, coverage does not have to be provided all employees but may be limited to a class or classes of employees.

A Retired Lives Reserve program is an excellent way for an employer to provide post-retirement group insurance to those employees who need to carry group insurance past retirement. The expense to the employer is small; the benefit to the employee is large, and he is only out-of-pocket the tax he pays when the group term benefit in excess of $50,000 is included in his income *before* retirement.

CAFETERIA PLANS

As its name suggests, a cafeteria plan is a written plan whereby the employee may choose the benefits he wants from a package of two or more employer-provided benefits. The benefits may be nontaxable such as accident and health benefits, disability benefits, group term live insurance up to $50,000, and group legal benefits to the extent such benefits are excludable from gross income. The plan also may provide taxable benefits such as group term insurance in excess of $50,000, and cash or other property.

The employer contributions under the plan are excludable from the employees' income to the extent the participant elects nontaxable benefits. Prior to 1979, the employee had to include in his income employer contributions to the extent he could have elected taxable benefits, even if few or no taxable benefits were elected.

The plan must not discriminate in favor of highly compensated individuals as to contributions or benefits if the employer contributions for nontaxable benefits are to remain excludable from the highly compensated individual's gross income. A plan is not discriminatory if the total benefits for highly compensated employees, measured as a percentage of compensation, are not significantly greater than the total benefits for the other employees.

Because the law permitting cafeteria plans was passed relatively recently, it is impossible to describe a typical plan.

EMPLOYER FINANCED INSURANCE

Many times a key employee's needs for insurance cannot be met through a group insurance plan. Perhaps the amounts required are larger than may be justified through group insurance. Or the insurance is needed for a purpose for which group insurance cannot be used— for example, to fund a buy-sell agreement, the uses of which were discussed in Chapters 23 and 24.

There are two ways the needed insurance may be provided with the help of the employer. The first is through an insured bonus; the second is through a split-dollar insurance plan.

Paying the premium as a bonus

On an individual basis the employer may pay the premiums on a life insurance policy owned by an executive or by a member of the executive's family or by a trust created for the benefit of the family. The major advantage to the employee is that the insurance is purchased with the employee out-of-pocket only the tax he pays for having the bonus included in his gross income. In some cases the employer pays a second bonus to cover the tax.

If premiums are paid for an employee, the premium bonuses are "wages" and subject to payroll taxes—social security tax, federal and state unemployment compensation taxes, and federal and state withholding taxes.

The employer may wish to pay the withholding and social security taxes for the employee. Whether the employer pays a net or gross bonus, the employer's action must be reflected on the employee's W-2 form. In addition, if the bonused employee is a stockholder of the company, the bonus should be cast as additional compensation in a board of directors' resolution.

Split-dollar insurance

An employer may join the employee in purchasing a life insurance policy which the employee or a family member or trust may own and control. As it is an individual arrangement, the employer and employee may share the cost of the insurance and its benefits in the manner they determine.

Under one traditional method, the employer pays the portion of the premium equal to the cash value increase and claims the cash value if the employee dies or the plan is terminated. Thus, the employer's only cost is the lost use of its money until the cash value is returned.

Another widely used method is for the employer to pay the entire premium with the employee's family or trust receiving the insurance proceeds in excess of the premiums paid.

For most split-dollar plans sold in the employer-employee setting since 1964, there is a cost to the employee for the insurance benefit received. He must include in his gross income the value of the insurance benefit determined through use of government PS-58 insurance rates, plus the portion of any insurance dividend used for his benefit, less any contribution he personally made to the plan.

Split-dollar insurance can be an executive incentive plan, providing a valuable benefit to the employee on a selective, informal basis, often with little cost to the employer. The plan gives the executive the insurance coverage he needs at a time when he may be at least able to afford it. Furthermore, the employer may permit the employee to take over the policy after retirement, and he may pay the annual premium out of the cash value increase each year.

INTEREST FREE LOANS

One of the most attractive "perks" available to a highly compensated employee is an interest-free loan from his employer. Assuming the loan is bonafide and payable on demand, the fact it is made on an interest-free basis is not a taxable event.

It should be kept in mind that the IRS does not agree with this view which was first accepted almost 20 years ago by the Tax Court. Furthermore, the Tax Court has held against taxpayers (1) where term loans were made; and (2) where interest-free loans were made to an employee by an employer-corporation which itself borrowed sizable sums from banks.

It is likely not a good idea to use interest-free loans from an employer to buy life insurance. If the employee subsequently borrows on the insurance policy, and many of them do, he may not be able to deduct the interest. In addition, insurance purchased with an interest-free loan from the employer has the appearance of a split-dollar insurance plan. Thus, the IRS could include in the executive's gross income an economic benefit computed at PS-58 rates. It may be better to use a formal split-dollar agreement rather than take the corporate loan route. There is a greater degree of tax certainty with a split-dollar plan.

EXECUTIVE HEALTH PLANS

Medical care expense and disability expense are perils an employer cannot ignore. One out of every seven Americans is hospitalized each year; one out of two men, now age 35, will be disabled for at least 90 days before age 65, and of those disabled for at least that period, the average period of disability is 2½ years.

Every business should provide medical expense and sick-pay benefits for all its employees; every business *must* provide those benefits for its executives or run the risk of bankruptcy or liquidation. The role that insurance can play in providing these and other fringe benefits is discussed at great length in Chapter 27. Therefore, this chapter will be confined to the following observations:

The Internal Revenue Code helps by making the benefits deductible by the employer and partially excludable from the employee's income.

1. Payments made as insurance premiums for medical care insurance and disability income insurance are generally deductible and excludable from the incomes of the covered employees.
2. Payments made to employees as sick pay, either directly or through employer-paid insurance, are deductible to the employer but may be income to the disabled employee. There is a $100 per week sick-pay income exclusion, but the exclusion is not available if the employee's adjusted gross income (including the disability income payments) exceeds $20,200 annually.

For the health plan benefits to be tax deductible by the employer and largely tax-free to the covered employees, they should be set forth in a written "plan for employees." In more than a dozen decisions, the Tax Court has established the parameters of such a plan.

1. The plan must be documented, usually by a board of directors' resolution, and communicated to the covered employees, usually in a letter or a booklet.
2. The plan must be for employees. It cannot be a plan to benefit stockholder-employees in their role as stockholders. Conversely, a plan may be established for a class of employees, such as officers,

executives, managers, or supervisors, and still gain the tax advantages of the law. While the fact all the participants were stockholder-officers did not disturb the Tax Court in several decisions, most employers are well advised to include one or more non-stockholders in the plan.
3. The plan benefits must be reasonable when related to the services rendered and the other compensation paid the employees.

MEDICAL REIMBURSEMENT PLANS

For taxable years of the employer which begin after 1979, medical reimbursement plans of an employer must be nondiscriminatory if the reimbursements are to be excludable from the gross income of the officers, executives, and managers of the employer. A discriminatory plan is one that pays greater benefits on a dollar-for-dollar basis for key employees than for other employees. In addition, a plan is discriminatory if the benefits are in proportion to employee compensation.

The nondiscriminatory rule does not apply to insurance benefits provided by an insurance company where there is a shifting of risk to the insurance company. Thus, individual and group policies may provide major medical and other insured benefits to a class of officers, executives, or managers without the benefits being taxable to these employees.

Most major medical insurance policies will not pay, among other medical and dental bills, the cost of eyeglasses, contact lenses, cosmetic surgery, and orthodontia; however, there are advantages to an employer operating a discriminatory medical reimbursement plan. Personally paid medical expenses are only deductible to the extent they exceed 3 percent of the taxpayer's adjusted gross income. The taxpayer's out-of-pocket cost is the full amount of his medical expenses plus the tax on the income used to pay all expenses below the 3 percent deduction.

With a discriminatory plan, the participant's cost is reduced to the tax on the income below the 3 percent deduction. If the taxpayer's medical expenses exceed 3 percent, the employer pays them and the employee has his medical bills paid "tax-free."

PLANNING FOR THE RECEIPT OF FRINGE
BENEFITS AT RETIREMENT

As his retirement date approaches, the employee turns his attention to the various elections available to him under his employer's fringe benefit programs. The income tax advantages of a fringe benefit program do not exist as a matter of right; they are achieved only through planning.

For the purpose of this discussion, assume the employee has a deferred compensation plan, pension and profit-sharing benefits, and group life insurance.

Along with social security, a pension is the basic source of retirement security in today's world. The employee starts here to compute his retirement income. He first determines the amount of income he and his spouse will both need and desire after retirement.

Perhaps his retirement income need will govern the date of his retirement; permitting, if he wants to do so, an early retirement at age 62, or requiring a later retirement at age 70. On the other hand, the state of his health or his desire to get on with some post-retirement activity may dictate an early retirement.

After his retirement age is established, the employee then reviews the payment options under his pension plan. If he is married at the time of his retirement, his automatic pension option is a monthly income for the joint lives of the retiree and his/her spouse (possibly with a reduced payment for the survivor). Three other income options are frequently permitted in pension plans: a monthly income for life, a monthly income for life with a certain number of months guaranteed, and a monthly income for a specified period (no lifetime payment guaranteed). To get one of these three other options, the married employee will have to elect it prior to the time the pension benefit begins.

Some pension plans permit the employee to take a lump-sum distribution of the pension benefit; others do not. Capital gains treatment may be available for the portion of the distribution with respect to employee service prior to 1974. For plans established after 1973 and for employees whose entire period of service is post-1973, only the special ten-year forward averaging rules are available.

There may be a tax advantage to capital gains and/or ten-year forward averaging treatment, but a decision to take a lump-sum distribution should be tempered by monthly income needs as well. A monthly income option will produce not only a greater but also a more consistent income than an invested lump sum in most cases. This follows from the fact the monthly income under an option consists of both principal and interest and is guaranteed.

If the employee has benefits from both a pension and a profit-sharing plan, he first should determine that his retirement income needs are satisfied before considering a lump-sum distribution of a profit-sharing benefit. Profit-sharing benefits can be converted, either through the plan or through other methods, to a monthly income at retirement under one of the four income options listed for pension plans.

Logically, the employee who does take a lump sum could use the net proceeds, after paying the tax, to invest or to exercise any unexercised stock options he holds at retirement.

The usual deferred compensation agreement calls for the payment of the deferred compensation benefit over the first years of the employee's retirement—often payments are spread over the first 10 or 15 years. With other retirement benefits, this gives the retired employee a greater retirement income in the early years of his retirement than later.

He might be able to level his entire retirement income with the help of the pension plan administrator. Specifically, it might be possible to receive a reduced pension benefit for the first 10 or 15 years and an increased pension thereafter.

The trend in recent years in planning employee fringe benefits has been to extend receipt of some or all of the group insurance benefits. This policy has also been applied in many cases to hospitalization plans. Today, most group hospitalization plans coordinate with Medicare benefits for retirees and others eligible for Medicare. In addition, many firms pay the retiree's Medicare premiums or provide and pay for a Medicare supplement. The premiums are not income to the retiree if they are paid under a "plan for employees" (see heading "Executive Health Plans").

Group life insurance may also be continued after retirement, but in a reduced amount. It has been customary to reduce coverage 50 percent immediately upon retirement. Group coverage may (1) continue at that level until death; (2) reduce still further at later ages; or (3) terminate entirely at some age, for example, age 70. As previously mentioned, many employers have installed group permanent or retired lives reserve plans for some or all of their employees, so as to continue needed insurance after retirement.

Either before or after retirement, the employee should give thought to the disposition of what is often a sizable group life insurance benefit. Group life insurance, like personal insurance, can be made payable to a life insurance trust. If the trust is revocable, which means the insured can change his mind later, administration expenses will be saved in the employee's estate and his spouse's estate, if she dies after him, and estate and inheritance taxes may possibly be saved in the spouse's estate.

A group insurance benefit also may be assigned to a spouse or to an *irrevocable* life insurance trust. The use of the trust may allow the insurance benefit to escape taxation in the spouse's estate if he or she dies after the insured, as well as save taxes at the insured's prior death.

The assignment of group insurance is the making of a gift. The premium the employer pays annually is the measure of the gift. Because a group insurance premium normally increases annually, it is possible for the premium gift to be subject to gift tax, despite the $3,000 annual gift tax exclusion.

It is best before an employee assigns his group insurance to ask his attorney's advice on the matter. The attorney also can help fit the group insurance into the remainder of the employee's estate plan.

PLANNING FOR THE RECEIPT OF FRINGE BENEFITS AT DEATH

Spouse's benefits are an important part of any fringe benefit program. Because it is sometimes the highly regarded employees who die early, many employer's have installed fringe benefit programs providing worthwhile survivor's benefits. It takes proper planning and coordination of those benefits to minimize taxes and maximize the surviving spouse's income.

The present value of future deferred compensation payments of the type discussed in this chapter are usually included in the gross estate for estate tax purposes. In addition, the deferred benefits will be income to the spouse or other beneficiary as they are received.

A surviving spouse may be able to deduct the proportionate part of the estate tax generated by the inclusion of the deferred compensation benefits in the employee's estate. The deduction for the estate tax paid is not automatic; it would be lost if the deferred compensation benefit qualified for the marital deduction. To avoid its qualification, the employee should name his or her spouse as the primary beneficiary and the children as secondary beneficiaries of the benefit.

Alternately, the benefit could be made payable to the executive's nonmarital deduction trust. The employee may consider it desirable to direct that benefit to a corporate trustee who is better able to invest and manage the deferred compensation for the benefit of the surviving spouse and family.

As previously mentioned, a surviving spouse or other beneficiary may exclude from gross income the first $5,000 of any death benefit received from the employer. That exclusion could be used by the first $5,000 received in a lump-sum settlement of an employee's pension or profit-sharing benefit or, as suggested here, used by the first $5,000 received as a deferred compensation benefit.

Although payment options vary from plan to plan, there are generally two ways a spouse can take a death benefit under a pension or profit-sharing plan. First, the death benefit may be paid as a monthly income, either for a number of years or over the spouse's lifetime. Second, the death benefit may be paid in a lump sum.

Taxes are not the most important consideration when choosing the way to receive the benefit. The spouse's and the family's needs are the primary consideration. If the benefit is taken as an annuity, the income is not only guaranteed but, because it is paid from both principal and income over a period of time, the spouse may receive a larger income than would be provided by principal or interest alone.

Taxation, too, may make annuity payments preferable to a lump-sum distribution. If the surviving spouse takes a lump-sum distribution and elects capital gains and/or ten-year forward averaging tax treatment, the lump sum will be included in the deceased employee's gross estate. That inclusion may generate a sizable estate tax liability. An estate which uses up the full unified estate tax credit, after claiming the maximum marital deduction, is subject to a minimum estate tax rate of 32 percent.

On the other hand, estate taxation may not be a problem if an employee's estate is small. Or, if the spouse's income is small, he or she may advantageously take a lump-sum distribution, elect five-year income averaging, and, simultaneously, exclude the lump sum from the taxable estate.

Numerous pension and profit-sharing plans serviced by the insurance industry are split funded; that is, they are funded with both whole life insurance and a separate investment fund. At death, the participant's beneficiary will receive the face amount of the life insurance and, depending on the type of plan and its provisions, some portion or all of the investment fund.

The insurance-at-risk portion of the life insurance is received income tax free. The balance of the payment (cash value portion of the life insurance and the investment fund amount) may be paid under the lump-sum distribution rules if the plan permits such distribution and the beneficiary so elects.

If a lump-sum is elected for the total sum, the insurance-at-risk portion will escape inclusion in the gross estate. The remainder will be in the estate if capital gains and/or ten-year forward averaging tax treatment is elected.

A major advantage to an employee of a split-funded plan is the ability of his spouse or other beneficiary to split the pre-retirement death benefit and minimize taxes. If the beneficiary takes the insurance-at-risk portion as a lump sum and annuitizes the balance, neither portion will be in the estate. Only the annuity will be subject to income tax as the installments are received over the annuity payment period.

The spouse may exclude from her taxable income the first $5,000 of death benefit she receives, regardless of the payment option elected. The $5,000 exclusion is probably a greater benefit if it is used against a benefit like deferred compensation, which is taxable at ordinary income rates rather than used to offset a lump-sum distribution from a pension or profit-sharing plan that may benefit from lower capital gains and/or ten-year forward averaging tax treatment.

Escaping taxation in the employee's estate is only half the battle. If it is likely that a pre-retirement death benefit will someday be taxed as an asset of the surviving spouse's estate, and her estate will be large enough to be subject to tax, perhaps it should be made payable to the employee's nonmarital trust. The benefit will not be included in the surviving spouse's estate at death. If a trust is not used, and if the employee provides that his spouse will receive a monthly income from the policy at his death, he can keep the remaining unpaid balance at her subsequent death out of her estate by naming the children or a children's trust as the secondary beneficiaries.

Estate planning for an employee is not something done once and forgotten. Times change; circumstances change. An employee's plan must be adapted to changing fringe benefits and property ownership. For this reason, planning with the help of an attorney, accountant, trust officer, life agent, and pension plan administrator is a continuing activity which will end only when there is no one left to plan for.

SELECTING THE AGENT OR BROKER AND CHOOSING THE PROGRAM

Management should select an agent or broker to handle the company's fringe benefit program who is an expert in his field. He should be regarded as a consultant and not as a distributor of the insurance products that will be used to provide those fringe benefits. Unless that distinction is made, there will be a tendency for the agent to sell and management to buy pre-packaged solutions; solutions that will be appropriate to management's problems only by chance. This distinction does not ignore the fact that a commission will be earned. However, recognition of this distinction is essential to a good working relationship between the company and its agent or broker.

Once management is convinced of the competence of its agent, it must candidly discuss with him the present status of the business, its personnel situation, and its objectives. This discussion may prove to be most revealing in determining the ability of management and the agent to work together toward a common goal. An agent's reluctance to listen and probe, coupled with his persistent return to selling a product, might signal to management that it has made a poor choice of agent. Similarly, a guarded and incomplete disclosure of its problems by management will tell a competent agent that he will have difficulty giving appropriate advice. There must be a feeling of confidence that each is committed to a common goal.

After management and its agent have had a comprehensive discussion of the current status and objectives, the agent can be expected to make recommendations on the type and design of benefits. These benefit recommendations should be tested by a number of questions.

- How do the benefits relate specifically to your business and your employees?
- Are they on target or merely general solutions?
- What flexibility is provided for both anticipated and unexpected changes in business structure or conditions?
- What is their tax treatment to the employer and the employee and how sure is that tax treatment?
- How much of an advantage do the benefits provide the employee over anything that he can get independently?
- Are they difficult to administer?
- Can they be easily understood?
- Are the long-range cost commitments commensurate with the expected results in performance, retention, and attitude?
- Who will service the benefits and keep them current?
- Is their cost competitively priced?

A proposed benefit that will have to be withdrawn in the future without a replacement of equal value, whether for reasons of economics or stability, is apt to have a negative effect on morale. It is therefore, important to resolve as many of these questions as possible at this stage.

INTRODUCTION TO AND FOLLOW UP WITH THE EMPLOYEES

After a decision has been made as to scope and design of the fringe benefits for key personnel, the time will arrive for a crucial step: their introduction to eligible employees. If management and the agent or broker have been working as a team to this point, this presentation can be a rewarding climax to their efforts. It is surely deserving of their best performance. The explanation of the benefits and their value to the employee is, with few exceptions, best handled by the agent. Points that for reasons of modesty and good taste may be uncomfortable for management to make are easily made by the agent. Some presentations may be made on a group basis, while those employees whose value and position is highest may deserve one-on-one attention.

The employer who assumes that the installation of a valuable and suitable fringe benefit program automatically means that those benefits will be cherished is in for a disappointment. It is natural for management to expect gratitude. It is equally natural for the high performance employees to feel that they have earned the program or even that it is inadequate. At best, an initial gratitude will fade as the details become cloudy with the passing of time.

Again, the management-agent team must follow up to maintain the plan's effectiveness as an important component of the compensation program. Periodic review of benefits with key employees helps to keep the value of those benefits fresh in their minds. It can also be an assist to management as an independent source of feedback on employee morale and the need for additional fringes in the future.

SUMMARY

Fringe benefits aimed at key employees are not a benevolent gesture on the part of management. They are a strategically placed investment, intended to return a profit in the form of productivity and retention. Proper design following a candid evaluation of the situation by management, objective advice by the agent or broker, and continued follow-up can assure the return of and on the investment.

NOTE

1. Congress affirmed the existing interpretation of the law in the Revenue Act of 1978 as it affects the deferred compensation agreements of tax-paying enterprises. In doing so Congress did not place deferred compensation plans of tax-exempt organizations in either the public employees or tax-paying corporation categories. The IRS interprets this as an indication of the desire of Congress to have the IRS make final and enforce its proposed regulation of February 1978, which would (in the case of tax-exempt organizations) include in the employee's gross income the amount the employer defers in the year it is deferred, if the agreement was employee-motivated and arranged at the instigation of the employee.

It is generally conceded the IRS will have difficulty enforcing this regulation if it becomes final because (1) it flies in the face of 50 years of court decisions and almost 20 years of its own contrary rulings; and (2) it is difficult to determine when an agreement is employee-motivated. The second IRS hearing on the proposed regulation took place on November 27, 1979; it likely will be many months before IRS action in this matter is known.

CHAPTER 27

FRINGE BENEFITS FOR GENERAL PERSONNEL

GROUP INSURANCE BENEFIT PLANS

REGULATION OF INSURED EMPLOYEE BENEFITS

CHOOSING AMONG AVAILABLE BENEFIT PLANS

BASIC GROUP BENEFIT PLANS AVAILABLE
  Group life insurance benefits
  Group health insurance benefits
  Group disability income coverages
  Group dental insurance

HEALTH MAINTENANCE ORGANIZATIONS (HMOS)
  Basic benefits and exclusions

RISK MANAGEMENT TECHNIQUES

EMERGING FRINGE BENEFITS
  Group legal
  True group auto
  Vision care

EMPLOYER PACKAGING ASSISTANCE AVAILABLE

KEY QUESTIONS TO ASK YOUR AGENT OR BROKER

Charles H. Stamm, III, Esquire
Vice President and General Counsel
Connecticut General Life Insurance Company
Hartford, Connecticut

Charles H. Stamm is Vice President and General Counsel of Connecticut General Life Insurance Company, and General Counsel of Connecticut General Insurance Corporation and Aetna Insurance Company. Mr. Stamm joined Connecticut General as an attorney in 1963 and was appointed General Counsel in 1970. He is a Phi Beta Kappa graduate of Princeton University and received his Juris Doctorate from the Yale Law School in 1963. Mr. Stamm is a Director of the Association of Life Insurance Council and a member of the Hartford County, Connecticut, and American Bar Associations. He is also a member of the Government Relations Committee of the Insurance Association of Connecticut and has served on several committees of the Health Insurance Association of America. In addition, Mr. Stamm is active in a number of corporate and civic activities.

The small business has some unique characteristics when considering fringe or employee benefits. It competes with big business and unions in the labor market, but by virtue of size cannot extend the same level of flexibility and security. The performance of each dollar spent is critical. Benefit plans have to be simple to administer, easy to understand, well communicated, reasonable in coverage levels, and comprehensive in scope. The advantage a small business has of being able to establish a team spirit can quickly become a disadvantaged if one employee is disgruntled and perceived by his peers to have been unfairly treated.

A small business needs actively to use a third-party employee benefit resource. Employees cannot look to the business to provide their security forever. The owner can die or the business fail. Smaller employers do not have the luxury of personnel departments and claims counselors. If the functions of guarantees, communications, and claims decisions are transferred to a third party, the employer will retain the ability to join with the employee against "them." He can take the credit for the good and can avoid the blame for the bad.

Finally, the principal purpose of a small business is usually to fulfill its owner's objectives. This added dimension leads to the consideration of how benefits can be tailored to fill the specific needs of the owner. Where there are unique needs and desires, even of a personal nature, the fringe benefit program can often respond in a cost effective and tax-sheltered manner.

Fringe benefits have been described as all work-related benefits not paid in cash. In general, fringe benefits respond to needs for:

☐ Medical and dental care for employee and family.
☐ Income replacement in the event of short- or long-term disability.
☐ Life insurance security in the event of premature death.
☐ Retirement income security when old age precludes the ability to continue earning.

Fringe benefits are expensive. In 1977, supplemental economic benefits amounted to 36.7 cents for every dollar paid in salary according to the Chamber of Commerce of the United States. The Industrial Revolution, legislation, unionization, and competition are some of the factors which have stimulated the growth of employee benefit plans in the United States and Canada. There is no question that employee benefit plans have raised the living standards of working people over the past few decades. The purpose of this chapter is to better acquaint employers with benefit plans available for their employees.

GROUP INSURANCE BENEFIT PLANS

The Social Security Administration refers to employee benefit plans as "those non-governmental-sponsored plans that provide either for income maintenance when employment is temporarily interrupted or permanently terminated, or for payments to alleviate the burden of the heavy medical expenses occasioned by illness or injury."[1] This definition clearly includes the Group Life, Health, Disability, Dental and Health Maintenance Organization benefits highlighted in this chapter.

A broader categorization of total benefits available has been developed by the Chamber of Commerce. As part of employee benefit plan fringe benefits it includes:

□ Legally required payments.

□ Pension and other agreed-upon payments.

□ Payments for nonproduction time while on the job.

□ Payments for time not worked.

Although group insurance is probably the best known of all the available employee benefits, many people do not understand its scope and true purpose. In the following sections, we will attempt to bridge this knowledge gap.

REGULATION OF INSURED EMPLOYEE BENEFITS

The design of group insurance plan benefits must take in account the recent mandates and restrictions imposed upon employers by the Federal Pregnancy Disability Act and the Age Discrimination in Employment Act.

The Pregnancy Disability Act amended Title VII of the Civil Rights Act of 1964 to extend the prohibition against sex discrimination in employment to include discrimination on the basis of pregnancy, childbirth, or related medical conditions. The act requires treatment of affected women equal to that of unaffected workers for all employment-related purposes including receipt of benefits under fringe benefit programs.

By virtue of 1978 amendments to the Age Discrimination in Employment Act, the class of workers protected against age discrimination was extended to include those between ages 65 and 70. The act has been interpreted by the Equal Employment Opportunities Commission, its administering agency, to permit reduction of fringe benefits for older employees only where such reductions are demonstrated to be cost justified on an actuarially sound basis. The basic rule is that employer expenditures for such benefits on behalf of an older worker should be no less than similar expenditures made on behalf of a younger worker.

Although the precise effect of these enactments on various types of coverage commonly found in group benefit plans is subject to question, insured plans are designed to expose employers to as little risk as possible from these laws.

Group benefit plans are within the federal definition of employer welfare benefit plans and, as such, are also regulated by certain provisions of the Employee Retirement Income Security Act of 1974 (ERISA). The impact of ERISA is discussed in greater detail in the next chapter. From the employer's perspective, the primary effect of ERISA on insured welfare plans is required employer reports to governmental agencies and disclosure to employees describing the terms and operation of the plan. In addition, those responsible for the operation and administration of the plan are subject to fiduciary rules which govern their conduct and impose civil and criminal sanctions for breach of their fiduciary responsibilities.

The design of employee benefit plans is also influenced by minimum benefit requirements imposed by the insurance laws of the state where the policy is to be issued. For example, many states require group medical policies to include coverage for treatment of alcoholism or mental illness. Similarly, some states require that services rendered by midwives, chiropractors, naturopaths, and other licensed providers be covered to the same extent as the same services if rendered by a physician.

CHOOSING AMONG AVAILABLE BENEFIT PLANS

From a self-interest standpoint, employees and their dependents are most interested in the specific benefits available to them. However, there are a number of reasons why the ultimate plan is critical to the individual making the benefit choice—the employer. It is the employer who truly owns the group insurance policy.

Once an employer decides to offer an insurance benefit plan, the results of the decision are hard to undo, in that most plans are expected to continue in force for many years. It is important that the employer weigh a number of basic factors before implementing a group insurance program. A summary of some basic considerations are:

1. Cost benefit reasonableness.
   □ Has provision been made for expected annual cost increases?
   □ Will it be difficult to reduce coverage (i.e., costs) once established?

□ Will the benefit be contributory (the employees will share part of the cost) and what is the cost/benefit reasonableness if the plan will be contributory?
  □ Can and will the employees be willing to absorb part of the cost of the benefit?

2. Overall level of benefits provided.
  □ The benefit is never expected to bring employee total security.
    □ It must be weighed with other benefits available to the average employee from:
      1. Individual life insurance.
      2. Social security.
  □ What benefit plans offered by business competitors?
  □ What are the union offerings and requirements, if applicable?

3. Administrative efficiency of benefit plan.
  □ Are there provisions for prompt and efficient payment of claims?
  □ What are the provisions for communication of benefits and procedures to employees?
    □ Booklets.
    □ Bulletins.
    □ Forms.
  □ Are administrative expenses assumed by employer?

4. Flexibility of benefits in today's changing environment.
  □ Can new benefits be integrated into the program?
  □ Is there the ability to adjust inadequate benefit levels?
  □ Is there the ability to adjust to a changing employee group—
    □ Where the change is in the composition of the group?
      1. Male/female percentage changes.
      2. Size in relationship to turnover and output changes.
  □ Where the change is in the needs of the average employee?

The impact of group insurance plans selected is so great to all concerned parties (employer, employees, and dependents) that basic policy features and exclusions available to employers will be examined next.

BASIC GROUP BENEFIT PLANS AVAILABLE

Although numerous combinations and variations exist in the insurance marketplace, at least one of the following standard plans constitutes a part of almost any benefit offering: (1) group life, (2) group health, and (3) disability.

In addition, group dental plans and Health Maintenance Organizations have gained popularity and will be reviewed.

Group life insurance benefits

Nearly 20 cents of every premium dollar spent for life insurance goes toward the purchase of group insurance. At the end of 1976, group life insurance accounted for 43 percent of the life insurance in force on residents of the United States. *By the end of 1978, group life insurance totaled nearly $1,244 billion,* with the average coverage per employee being $16,753.

Employees almost universally expect some free life insurance and the opportunity to purchase additional insurance on a cost-sharing basis. The perceived need is strongest for younger parents with families. Usually, up to one times salary is provided on a noncontributory (employer pays all) basis.

There are four basic categories of group life insurance: (1) group term, (2) group permanent, (3) group paid-up, and (4) group survivor income.

Group term. Group term insurance is by far the most popular, as well as the oldest, group life insurance vehicle. In simple terms, the plan consists of one-year renewable life insurance issued on an individual basis. More than 96 percent of the group life insurance in force in the United States in 1979 was written on this basis.

The major advantage of group term over the other group and individual life plans described is low premium rates. Various disability clauses and provisions are also available under most plans.

Major drawbacks from an employee's perspective include the temporary nature of the product and the high cost of conversion to ordinary insurance. The plan may be terminated at any time, either as a result of job loss or termination of the master policy. Another major disadvantage is that term policies offer only pure protection; they do not build up cash values. These are the trade-offs for the advantageous low-premium feature.

Group permanent. The desire of employers to obtain group life contracts which create individual cash values has resulted in group permanent life plans. Group permanent insurance offers cash values as well as continuing death protection after retirement, depending upon the percentage of the policy paid up prior to retirement.

Group permanent insurance clearly offers advantages to retirees, but it also contains disadvantages to the employee since the annual premium is normally taxable. Partly due to this negative tax characteristic, group permanent insurance had accounted for less than 1 percent of total group life insurance at the end of 1977.

Group paid-up.   Group paid-up insurance is a more popular cash value plan which does not have the severe tax disadvantages of permanent. Basically, premiums are split between employer and employee, with the employee contribution allocated to paid-up life insurance. Thus the plan is really a combination of both term and permanent features with minimized tax liability.

Group survivor income.   This group life product is very similar to group term with the difference existing in the way death benefits are paid to beneficiaries. Installment payments are made for as long as a qualified survivor lives after the death of the insured, up to a maximum age, typically 62.

The chief advantage of this plan lies naturally with dependent provisions which ease the adjustment period after the death of a family's breadwinning employee. The assumption is that the lump-sum payments characteristic of the other plans, could be spent or invested unwisely. Under survivor income, lump-sum settlements are replaced with a lifetime income stream.

Group life summary.   According to a 1979 survey conducted by the American Council of Life Insurance, the majority of the public (53 percent) still views group life as supplemental coverage to personal life insurance.[2]

The four categories are basic plans. At least one of these plans is found in almost every employee group insurance benefit package. Variations and modifications exist which will help meet the employer/employee needs of any specific group. Group insurance brokers, representatives, and/or agents can match and custom-tailor plans to satisfy specified needs.

Group health insurance benefits

Almost all employees expect protection from catastrophic hospital and surgical bills. This is perhaps the strongest need from the employee's point of view because of expensive existing medical care delivery systems. Additionally, there is considerable expectation that health insurance should cover an increasing part of the total medical bill, including prescription drugs, doctor visits, and outpatient treatment for mental illness. Group health insurance plans normally indemnify the employee, or the employee's covered dependent, against certain specified medical expenses arising because of illness, injury, or pregnancy. Preventive medical expenses, such as routine examinations and tests are generally not provided by such group health plans.

Typically the basic types of benefits or policy features provided under group medical expense policies cover hospital charges, surgical fees, and certain nonsurgical medical expenses. Many commercial carriers offer Major Medical coverage and some offer hospital indemnity insurance.

1. Hospital expense benefits.[3]   Hospital expense coverage reimburses the insured, in whole or in part, for hospital charges that result from illness or accident. A summary of benefits available through most insurers are:

□ *Outpatient.* Basic plans generally define the limits of this benefit to be charges made by a hospital for treatment of injuries in an emergency setting. This care, including the hospital's charges for outpatient surgery, must be rendered usually no later than the end of the day following the accident.

□ *Room and board.* Hospital charges are covered up to a stated daily maximum amount, or for a semiprivate room, for a stated maximum number of days during any continuous period of confinement. A continuous period usually simply means one or more confinements for the same or a related cause.

For a higher premium rate, intensive care and coronary care coverage is sometimes available under separate contract.

□ *Other hospital charges.* Outpatient treatment defined as ancillary charges falls under this category. These charges would normally include the use of an operating room, drugs or medicines, diagnostic laboratory, or x-rays and any other services furnished by the hospital at the direction of the attending physician.

In addition to the basic hospital coverages listed above, most insurers offer benefits in various combinations and prices to cover the following areas:

□ Anesthesiologists' charges.
□ Ambulance benefit.
□ Mental illness benefit.
□ Intensive and progressive care.
□ Ambulatory surgical facilities.
□ Maternity benefits.
□ Nursing home care.

2. Surgical expenses.   Reimbursement for surgical procedures are payable to the insured regardless of whether the surgery was performed during a hospital stay, on an outpatient basis, or in a physician's office.

Payment may be either on a scheduled or nonscheduled basis. Schedules are simply listings of stated surgical procedures with a maximum dollar value payable for each. Some schedules may show unit values for each procedure.

If anesthesiologists' charges are included in the schedule, this benefit is excluded under the hospital expense benefit.

The policyowner normally has the option of including or excluding obstetrical benefits in the schedule. If included, dollar maximums are specified for pregnancy-related procedures such as those associated with the normal delivery of a child, miscarriage, abortion, cesarean section, or abdominal operation for ectopic pregnancy.

3. Nonsurgical medical expense benefits. Treatment by physicians, other than surgeons, is also covered under basic group benefit plans. Some plans only cover hospital treatment while others extend to home or office visits. The in-hospital coverage is also commonly referred to as a "physician's fee" benefit.

A number of limitations and exclusions are normally contained in contracts for this benefit to avoid misuse and duplicate coverage. Obstetrics, dentistry, eye refraction, and the fitting of glasses are customarily not included.

4. Major medical expense benefits. The benefits described in the above three categories are basic coverage with specific limitations. Major medical policies go beyond these limitations to protect against the heavy medical expenses of severe injuries or prolonged illnesses.

Benefit percentages payable range from 75, 80, or even 100 percent above a stated minimal deductible. Amounts payable range from $10,000 maximum to as high as $1 million or unlimited, depending on the policy.

Two types of major medical insurance plans exist:

1. *Superimposed major medical.* As the term implies, these plans fit over an insurer's existing basic hospital-surgical-medical expense plan or a Blue Cross–Blue Shield basic plan. In effect, the superimposed plan takes over where the basic plan leaves off.
2. *Comprehensive major medical.* Instead of splitting limitations and coverages between two separate plans, comprehensive policies cover nearly all types of medical care services under one agreement. Normally the cash deductible is lower ($50 or $100) for comprehensive than for superimposed which normally carries a $100 minimum deductible.

Exclusions. The following items are normally not covered under major medical plans:

1. Expenses resulting from injury or illness caused by war.

2. Expenses resulting from injury or illness covered under workers' compensation.
3. Care or treatment given in any government facility, unless the insured is legally required to pay for it.
4. Cosmetic surgery, unless necessary because of injury.
5. Dental work, unless necessary because of injury.
6. Expenses for treatment resulting from intentionally self-inflicted injury.
7. Normal pregnancy.

Other restrictions, as well as benefit maximums, deductible requirements, coordination of benefits, reasonable and customary charges, and exclusions for preexisting conditions, vary from contract to contract, but are representative of almost every plan.

Group disability income coverages

Short- and long-term group disability coverage is available. Short term by far exceeds long term in popularity.

Although the impact of a long-term disability on an employee can be catastrophic (especially if the employee is not eligible for disability payments from social security), there are not nearly as many employers who provide long-term disability coverage as provide other benefits. The great majority of short-term disability plans are noncontributory, while long-term coverage usually are either contributory or noncontributory. However, long-term disability plans, often referred to as LTD, are becoming increasingly popular. One reason for the slow growth of short-term plans is that many employers have uninsured salary continuation plans.

Typical benefit structure. Short-term plans normally do not adequately cover employees in high-income brackets. The coverage typically does not exceed $250 or $300 per week. This would be adequate for most ordinary employees, however.

Benefit ranges vary by size and make up of the group. Also, benefits are a competitive factor among competing insurers. Most long-term benefits are similar to the following schedule:

Basic weekly earnings	Weekly benefit
Less than $100	$ 50
$100 but less than $200	75
$200 but less than $300	125
$300 and over	150

Typical maximum benefit periods. Thirteen or 26 weeks, with a few as high as 52 weeks, is the normal benefit period for short-term plans.

Long-term periods are influenced by need, size of the group, and the insurer's underwriting philosophy. For smaller groups (below 25 or 50), it is common for the sickness limits to be restricted to five years and, at times, as little as two years, while the accident coverage might be to age 65.

Group dental insurance

The nation's fastest-growing employee benefit. Because dental insurance is practically impossible to obtain on an individual basis, it is an extremely valuable employee benefit.

The growth of group dental insurance has been spectacular. In 1965, only about 3 million Americans were covered by dental insurance. At the end of 1975, enrollment reached 35 million. Now, more than 60 million individuals are covered under some form of dental benefit plan.

And the trend continues. By 1985, enrollment is estimated to reach 100 million.

A number of factors have contributed to this growth:

□ People are more aware that oral health is favorably related to general well-being and that attractive teeth are appealing.

□ Dental techniques have been improved so dental treatments are less painful yet often more costly.

□ Unions have often bargained to include dental coverage.

□ The dental profession is now working actively with insurers in developing dental benefit programs.

Who administers dental plans? Plans are overwhelmingly insured by group life and health carriers—about 60 percent of the total insured population. Approximately 25 percent are enrolled in plans sponsored by state dental associations. Some 10 percent are in Blue Cross–Blue Shield-administered programs with the balance in independently sponsored programs.

Why include dental insurance? While there are several good reasons for adding dental insurance to your health care package, three are particularly important:

1. The prevalence of dental disease.
2. The rising cost barrier to dental care.
3. The potential for containing cost and improving quality.

Prevalence of dental disease. Dental disease is almost universal. Ninety-five percent of the population are affected by tooth decay, 20 percent have lost all their teeth, and 44 percent of all young adults have developed gum disease. Last year, about half our population visited a dental office, yet nearly one third of those under 17 have never been to a dentist.

The impact on productivity is dramatic. Because of dental disease, more than 100 million working hours are lost in business and industry each year. Research has shown that dental conditions account for 12.6 days of restricted activity and 4.7 days of bed disability per 100 persons per year.

Critical to the interpretation of these statistics is the fact that most dental disease can be prevented by regular care and early treatment.

Cost. One of the biggest barriers that keeps people from seeing their dentist is cost. In 1977, expenditures for dental services in the United States were $10 billion, more than three times the amount spent in 1967. This increase has come about as the result of inflation, an aging population, and advances in the quality of dental care. For example, in previous years, the trend was to use the relatively quick and inexpensive extraction procedure to combat dental disease. Now the trend is to save a person's natural teeth which usually involves more sophisticated and costly techniques.

Improving quality/containing cost. A properly constructed and administered dental insurance program can reduce claim costs by as much as 15 percent through:

☐ Minimizing the fee barrier to regular dental checkups. Early detection of minor problems can eliminate costly future problems.

☐ Spotting unnecessary expenses and/or treatment that cannot be expected to have lasting effect.

☐ Controlling coverage duplication.

☐ Monitoring and managing charges that are higher than reasonable and customary.

☐ Recommending alternate treatment plans.

As a dental insurance buyer, you have the power to positively influence the cost and quality of dental care through your choice of the plan design and insurance company to administer the program.

Plan design. Dental plans are different from medical care plans. The development of a well-designed and administered dental plan starts when the employer recognizes the important differences between the practice of medicine and the practice of dentistry.

□ Dental care is largely within the control of the individual. That is, the patient frequently chooses whether or not to have dental care. In the case of medical care, treatment is much less elective.

□ Dental care is selective in that there are alternate procedures for treating disease and restoring teeth.

□ Dental expenses are generally smaller, more predictable, and budgetable.

Because of these differences, informed dental plan buyers should look for separate and highly specialized dental plan administration.

Typical covered services.[4] Plans naturally vary in total amount of coverage, but all services fall into one of the following eight categories:

1. *Diagnostic*—oral examination, x-rays, and laboratory tests to determine the existence of dental disease or to evaluate the condition of the mouth.
2. *Preventive*—prophylaxis, fluoride treatment, and other procedures designed to prevent dental decay and to maintain dental health.
3. *Restorative*—fillings, crowns, and inlays used to restore the functional use of the patient's natural teeth.
4. *Oral surgery*—surgical extraction of teeth and other surgical treatment of diseases, injuries, and defects of the jaw.
5. *Endodontics*—treatment of the diseases of the dental pulp within existing teeth, such as root canal therapy.
6. *Periodontics*—treatment of the diseases of the surrounding and supporting tissues of the teeth.
7. *Prosthodontics*—replacement of missing teeth and structures by artificial devices such as dentures and bridgework.
8. *Orthodontics*—prevention and correction of dental and oral anomalies through the use of braces, retainers, and other correctional devices.

Typical group dental plan exclusions.[5] Because of the possibility for misuse, some plans may have as many as 30 exclusions. The most common exclusions are:

1. Charges for services or supplies that are cosmetic, including charges for personalization of characterization of dentures.
2. Charges for the replacement of a lost, missing, or stolen prosthetic device.
3. Charges for the repair or replacement of an orthodontic appliance.

4. Charges because of an accident related to employment or disease covered under workers' compensation or similar laws.
5. Any portion of a charge for a service in excess of the reasonable and customary charge.
6. Charges for an appliance where an impression was made before the patient was covered; a crown or fixed bridgework for which a tooth (or teeth) was prepared before the patient was covered; root canal therapy if the pulp chamber was opened before the patient was covered.
7. Charges for services or supplies not reasonably necessary for the dental care of the covered individual.
8. Charges for services rendered through a medical department, clinic, or similar facility provided or maintained by the patient's employer.
9. Charges for services or supplies for which no charge is made that the employee is legally obligated to pay for which no charge would be made in the absence of dental insurance.
10. Charges for services or supplies that do not meet the accepted standards of dental practices, including charges for services or supplies which are experimental in nature.
11. Charges for services or supplies received as a result of dental disease, defect, or injury caused by an act of war, declared or undeclared.
12. Charges for any services for which benefits are payable under any health care program supported wholly or partly by funds of the federal government, or any state, or political subdivision.
13. Charges for any duplicate prosthetic device or any other duplicate appliance.
14. Charges for a plaque control program.

HEALTH MAINTENANCE ORGANIZATIONS (HMOS)

In general terms, Health Maintenance Organizations (HMOs) provide their members with comprehensive health care services in return for a fixed prepaid amount, called a capitation. Participating employers offer membership in an HMO as an alternative to traditional health insurance, with the employee choosing which he or she prefers. More specifically, HMOs are an organized system which handle both the delivery and financing of health care. They provide and/or assure the delivery of a wide range of comprehensive services, to a voluntarily enrolled population, within a specific geographic area for a fixed, prenegotiated, and periodic payment.

Many private insurers have participated in the development and/or operation of HMOs. In 1976, 22 commercial companies were involved in some 50 operational HMOs, 12 of which were federally qualified.

Basic benefits and exclusions

In order for an organization to qualify as an HMO under the HMO Act of 1973, the following basic benefits must be provided:

1. Physician services.
2. Inpatient and outpatient hospital services.
3. Emergency health services.
4. Short-term outpatient evaluative and crisis intervention mental health services (not to exceed 20 visits).
5. Medical treatment and referral to appropriate ancillary services for drug and alcohol abuse.
6. Diagnostic lab and diagnostic and therapeutic x-ray services.
7. Home health services.
8. Preventive health services, including voluntary family planning, infertility services, and preventive dental and eye care for children.

The following supplemental services, mandatory under the 1973 act, are now optional by a 1976 amendment:

1. Intermediate and long-term care.
2. Vision, dental, and mental health care not included in basic benefits.
3. Long-term physical medicine and rehabilitative care.
4. Prescription drugs.

The benefits listed above are the minimal requirements. Individual HMO services will naturally vary.

The following services are typical exclusions for most HMOs:

1. Services covered by government or employer programs.
2. Strictly custodial care.
3. Not medically necessary cosmetic surgery.
4. Adult dental procedures that are not authorized by a doctor of the specific HMO.
5. Auto injuries covered under no-fault.
6. Nonemergency services received without approval by a doctor of the specific HMO.

Because unnecessary care (hospitalization, surgery, etc.) increases the HMOs expenses but *not* its income, it has a strong incentive to avoid such care. It also has an incentive to keep its members healthy and, thus, minimize the expenses resulting from avoidable serious illness. As a result, HMOs provide periodic examinations, health education, and other preventive services.

The federal government and others feel HMOs will be a significant factor in helping solve the nation's problem of seriously escalating health care costs. President Carter's 1981 budget calls for tripling federal funding to support HMO expansion. It is estimated that this funding would increase the number of federally qualified HMOs from 105 in 1980 to 139 by the end of 1981. In the longer range the federal Department of Health and Human Services seeks to increase the number of HMOs in the United States to 462 by 1988, and triple the national enrollment to over 22 million people.

The law requires that employers who have a minimum of 25 employees residing in the HMO service area, offer at least one of each of the two types of qualified HMOs:

1. *Closed panel HMO*—A group of physicians who work at a single site and are employees of the HMO, or are members of a medical group which, in turn, contracts with the HMO to provide medical services.
2. *Individual Practice Association (IPA)*—Arrangement in which doctors continue to work out of their own offices.

These are the required minimal arrangement offerings. In the marketplace today, four major HMO models can be identified:

1. Staff Group Practice Plans.
2. Capitated Group Practice Plans.
3. Capitated Individual Practice Plans.
4. Fee-for-Service Individual Practice Plans.

Although the model titles are somewhat self-explanatory, an employer should contact an agent or broker if specific characteristics and help in selection is sought.

A 1978 survey conducted by the National Association of Employers on Health Maintenance Organizations concluded that firms whose employees were HMO participants experienced a slightly smaller increase in health care costs during 1978 than firms not offering the option. The difference amounted to an approximate 2 percent savings on increasing health costs. One of the study's conclusions was that although most large corporations are offering an HMO option, few seem to be interested in developing their own.

In summary, HMOs are an effective tool in minimizing escalating medical costs. This information highlights what is available to employers in most localities. Representatives of HMOs can provide specific HMO characteristics for a given locale.

RISK MANAGEMENT TECHNIQUES

A businessman will want to control risk by insulating the company from sharp increases in benefit cost. This is accomplished by establishing a relatively level annual outlay, perhaps as a percentage of annual direct compensation. Such cost insulation is accomplished by providing benefits through an insurance company. Providing benefits in this manner allows small and moderate-sized businesses to enjoy the protection available to very large businesses through the pooling of risk. The concept is that all employers will pay a risk premium so that each may avoid these increases in annual cost.

Cost can also be controlled by certain aspects of benefit design. Perhaps the best example is the use of a deductible for medical and dental insurance. Employees are expected to pay the first $50, $100, or $200 of otherwise covered expenses in a calendar year. This shifting of expense from the insurance program to the employee can considerably reduce the annual premium of the insurance policy. Another technique is the use of co-insurance where the employee is required to pay from 10 percent to 25 percent of the medical expenses (usually up to a "stop loss" limit after which the plan pays 100 percent of expenses). Use of deductibles and/or co-insurance should fit within the employer's overall objective of providing benefits that meet needs under a well-thought-out benefit policy.

Some employers feel that they can control costs by "self-insuring." Most feel this means adopting a pay-as-you-go approach on the assumption that their employees will not have as many claims as other companies and, therefore, there is no need to pay a risk premium. This idea may be acceptable for low-risk situations, such as very limited short-term disability coverage. However, it is not at all advisable in most employee benefit situations as a normal pattern of cost will develop in the long run and excessive cost may hit at any time.

A more acceptable definition of self-insurance would mean self-funding or building of reserves against future claims. This can be accomplished with the aid of an actuary and through the establishment of a trust to insulate the funds from regular company assets. This type of program is usually cost effective only for very large companies who can afford the staff to coordinate the plan and evaluate the actuary's report. The small businessman purchases this type of expertise, along with the ability to share risk, at the time an insurance policy is purchased.

EMERGING FRINGE BENEFITS

Group legal, auto, and vision care are three currently available benefits that are destined for rapid growth in the next five years. Some

view these as the only viable new fringe benefits that unions have to
offer today.

Group legal

Group legal plans have experienced a noticeable growth over the
past few years, especially in the areas where labor unions and bar
associations agree to cooperate.

The term *Group Legal Services* commonly identifies programs
which provide legal assistance for large numbers of the middle-in-
come public associated with groups. Other terms such as Prepaid
Legal Service Plans, Legal Protection Insurance, and Group Legal
Services Insurance have been used to describe Group Legal Service
Plans. Coverage is typically for legal advice, consultation, office work,
various judicial and administrative proceedings, and major legal expenses.

The types of legal plans available vary widely. The most common
plans feature either the *open-panel* design in which the individual is
free to use a lawyer of his/her choice for legal services, or the *closed-
panel* design in which a select group of lawyers is designated to provide services to eligible individuals. Alternate plans can be designed
to present a modified open- or closed-panel approach or a combination
approach in which predetermined services are provided under an
open-panel concept and other services are offered via a closed-panel
design.

The types of group legal plans being marketed include:

☐ *Private plans* sponsored by credit unions, legal aid societies,
   armed forces, teacher associations, consumer co-ops, municipal
   employees, labor unions.
☐ *Bar* sponsored plans.
☐ *Taft-Hartley* trust plans.
☐ *Insurance* company plans.
☐ *Student* plans.

Generally, the plans have attempted to modify and attune their
benefits to the particular employee group. As a result, benefits and
costs vary according to the needs of the employee group being
serviced.

Studies show that the very wealthy and the very poor have ready
access to legal representation—but that the vast majority of the mid-
dle-income Americans do not have ready access to attorneys because
of the heavy financial burden it may place upon them.

It is projected that in the 80s group legal will witness the kind of
growth that characterized group health insurance in the 30s and 40s.

Labor unions are seeking means to respond to their members' legal needs through prepaid group plans. Employers in the medium- to large-size category have also expressed a desire for legal protection insurance.

It is anticipated that interest in the employee benefit field will increase as a result of increased demands for legal services and the favorable tax treatment accorded employees under the Tax Reform Act of 1976.

Summary. State and federal legislation and the support of proponent consumer groups will foster the growth of group legal plans. It is difficult to estimate the timing of this growth, but it is assumed that this fringe benefit will be widely available by 1985.

True group auto

In order for an auto policy to be "true group," the following characteristics must generally be present:

☐ Minimum percentage participation requirement.

☐ Contributions for premiums by both employers and employees.

☐ Group underwriting and experience rating.

The shared premium expense, quite naturally, is viewed as a very desirable fringe benefit by employees. However, like group legal, the legislative environment, particularly regarding tax incentives, must change before a large market for true group auto (TGA) can develop. Currently, only a few insurers have been experimenting with the concept. However, large growth is anticipated in the next five years.

Vision care

Group vision care appears to be destined for the type of rapid growth over the next five years that group dental care had experienced over the past five years. Unions have negotiated vision benefit contracts in many industries, and this trend will likely continue. Like dental coverage, employees view optical care as a highly desirable fringe benefit.

Reasonable and customary scheduled plans as well as panel approaches are available throughout the group insurance industry. Schedules are updated to reflect a range of current cost levels of vision services throughout the country. Flexibility for the policyholder is generally provided through various combinations of available benefit packages.

Typical benefits available provide payments for the following expenses incurred: (1) eye examinations, (2) lenses, and (3) frames.

Limits on number of examinations and materials are also generally stipulated.

Typical exclusions include the following:

1. Sunglasses.
2. Replacement of eyeglasses beyond specified examination limitations.
3. Care or materials not listed in a provided schedule.
4. Medical or surgical treatment of the eye.
5. Certain types of tinted lenses.
6. Contact lenses, except in certain specified situations.
7. Lenses or frames which are not medically necessary and are not prescribed by an optometrist or opthalmologist.

EMPLOYER PACKAGING ASSISTANCE AVAILABLE

In order to help the employer determine and establish the best benefit mix or package for his or her employees, insurance companies provide sales and service representatives to assist in the following areas:

□ Presentation of the plan to employees.

□ Enrollment into the plan.

□ Establishment of administrative procedures.

□ Maintenance of participation (if plan is contributory).

□ Resolution of any questions.

KEY QUESTIONS TO ASK YOUR AGENT OR BROKER

The following questionnaire contains specific questions about the insurer's practices, experience and ability to service the case.[6]

General:
1. If you are notified on March 1, 1979, that you have been selected as insurer, by what date could you deliver the master contract and booklet/certificates?
2. What is the location of your closest servicing office? Please describe the staff.
3. What is the location of your closest group claims office? Please describe the staff.
4. Do you have a loss control program? Please describe in detail.
5. How are "reasonable and customary" charges determined under your major medical contract? Please provide details.

Rates:
1. Will you provide a two-year rate guarantee? How would rates vary as guarantee period lengthens?

2. Please describe your renewal practices. Include statement as to whether or not you will provide 60 days' advance notice of rate change.

Retention:
1. Define paid claims for *(a)* life and *(b)* health insurance.
2. How do you establish reserves for incurred but unpaid claims?
3. What is the percentage of interest credit you allow on *(a)* claim reserves, *(b)* premium in excess of incurred claims and retention, *(c)* contingency reserves, and *(d)* any other reserves?
4. Please show the effect on your premiums if incurred claims were *(a)* 10 percent higher and *(b)* 10 percent lower, than those included in your illustration.
5. How do you establish reserves for approved waiver of premium claims? Amount?
6. Please describe the basis on which you determine premium taxes.
7. Please describe your formula provision for charging claims arising from a catastrophe. Please give your definition of a catastrophe.
8. How do you handle terminal experience refunds upon cancellation of the contract *(a)* on an anniversary date and *(b)* off the anniversary date?
9. What is your charge per $1,000 of group life insurance converted? Does your company charge for health insurance conversions? Explain.

NOTES

1. *Social Security Bulletin,* November 1977, p. 19.
2. *Monitoring Attitudes of the Public Report,* 1979, p. 28.
3. *Group Life and Health Insurance,* vol. I, 1979, pp. 213–18.
4. *Group Life and Health Insurance,* vol. I, 1979, p. 265.
5. *Group Life and Health Insurance,* vol. I, 1979, p. 269.
6. Health Insurance Association of America, *A Course in Group Life and Health Insurance,* 1979, p. 118.

CHAPTER 28

INSURED PENSION AND PROFIT SHARING

DEFINED CONTRIBUTION PLANS—IN GENERAL

DEFINED BENEFIT PLANS—IN GENERAL

THE ADVANTAGES AND DISADVANTAGES OF THE DEFINED CONTRIBUTION PLAN

THE ADVANTAGES AND DISADVANTAGES OF THE DEFINED BENEFIT PLAN

THE TAX QUALIFIED PLAN CONCEPT

ERISA—EMPLOYEE RETIREMENT INCOME SECURITY ACT
  Reporting and disclosure

Minimum standards
Other ERISA requirements
Fiduciary duties
Plan termination insurance

INSURED PENSION PLANS

INSURED GROUP PENSION PRODUCTS
  Deposit administration contracts
  Immediate participation guarantee
  Separate accounts

QUESTIONS TO ASK THE AGENT OR BROKER

Charles H. Stamm, III, Esquire
Vice President and General Counsel
Connecticut General Life Insurance Company
Hartford, Connecticut

Charles H. Stamm is Vice President and General Counsel of Connecticut General Life Insurance Company, and General Counsel of Connecticut General Insurance Corporation and Aetna Insurance Company. Mr. Stamm joined Connecticut General as an attorney in 1963 and was appointed General Counsel in 1970. He is a Phi Beta Kappa graduate of Princeton University and received his Juris Doctorate from the Yale Law School in 1963. Mr. Stamm is a Director of the Association of Life Insurance Council and a member of the Hartford County, Connecticut, and American Bar Associations. He is also a member of the Government Relations Committee of the Insurance Association of Connecticut and has served on several committees of the Health Insurance Association of America. In addition, Mr. Stamm is active in a number of corporate and civic activities.

Thomas F. Shea, Esquire
Counsel
Connecticut General Life Insurance Company
Hartford, Connecticut

Thomas F. Shea is Counsel of Connecticut General Life Insurance Company. Mr. Shea received a Bachelor of Science with honors and a Juris Doctor from the University of Connecticut. He has extensive experience in the field of Pension and Profit Sharing while employed in the Group Pension and Legal Departments of Connecticut General. He is a member of the American Council of Life Insurance legal section and has served on the Funding, Small Case, and Fiduciary Task Forces of that organization. He is also a member of the American Bar Association, Connecticut Bar Association, and Hartford County Bar Association.

The ability of a person to work and earn can be compared to a piece of machinery. When new, it needs to be "broken in" and fine tuned. Then follows a period of high productivity requiring only periodic maintenance. As time goes by, parts start to wear, efficiency becomes impaired, and eventually the machine has to be replaced. So too with the most important asset of a small business, its people. This reality is the fundamental motivation behind the drive for "financial security." Custom as well as competition dictate that it is the employer's responsibility to provide what has become the primary source of this security—the pension plan.

The long-term success of any pension plan depends, in no small part, on decisions made before the plan is established. The sponsor-to-be should be clear as to the objectives his plan is intended to fulfill. Normally, plans are established for a complex set of reasons including the financial situations and expectations of the company's employees, trends in the industry at large, the impact of the company's direct competition, union pressure, management's personal philosophy regarding the direct and indirect compensation of its employees, and the businessman's own personal financial requirements.

An initial analysis, including a study of what the company can afford to pay, should be conducted with the assistance of competent professionals. It should produce the raw data base necessary to make specific decisions as to the type of plan, the desired benefit/contribution level, coverage rules, and the like.

There are two basic kinds of pension plans: defined contribution and defined benefit plans.

DEFINED CONTRIBUTION PLANS—IN GENERAL

As the name implies, under a defined contribution plan the yearly amount of the employer's contribution is determined, usually as a percentage of each participating employee's current compensation. Each year while an employee is employed and covered, that amount of money is paid into an individual accumulation account maintained for the employee under the plan. At retirement, the employee becomes eligible to receive the proceeds credited to his account. These proceeds consist of total contributions made plus investment earnings on these contributions minus administrative charges made against the account.

An employee participant who terminates employment prior to retirement may be eligible to receive a portion of the amount credited to his account balance, to the extent he has satisfied the plan's "vesting" rules. A defined contribution plan will often provide that the full account value is paid to the participant's beneficiary if the participant dies prior to his termination of employment, even if he has not met the vesting requirements. Normally, a defined contribution plan will permit the employee to receive his account balance, or the vested portion of the balance if he terminates employment before retirement, either in a lump sum, in installments over a set period of years, or in a lifetime pension, possibly with a pension to the surviving spouse as well. The distinguishing feature of a defined contribution plan is that the amount of retirement benefit which will be provided cannot be determined until the participant retires or otherwise becomes eligible for a distribution. The value of the participant's account from both contributions and investment return cannot be ascertained until that time.

A plan that uses a fixed percentage of the participant's annual compensation as the primary determinant of the amount of contribution payable on his behalf, whether or not there are profits, is called a *defined contribution money purchase pension plan*. A defined contribution *profit-sharing plan* operates in much the same fashion except that the plan sponsor's yearly contribution is determined on the basis of the company's profits, if any, for the year in question. The amount payable from those profits may be based on a set formula or may be determined by the company's board of directors, at its sole discretion. Each participant's share of this contribution is allocated on the basis of his compensation and often his years of service with the plan sponsor. (The plan sponsor is normally the employer, but this is not always the case.)

A subclass of defined contribution plan is called a *thrift plan*. Under a typical thrift plan, plan participants elect to have a certain percentage of their compensation deducted and deposited to an individual account. The plan sponsor usually agrees to match all or a portion of the employee contribution.

Another hybrid plan is called a *target benefit plan*. Here the pension amount, payable at retirement, is determined by formula for each eligible participant. Each year a level annual premium is calculated and credited directly to the participant's account, using assumptions on future experience, including rate of investment return. At such time as a benefit is to be distributed, the accumulated balance in the participant's account is made available. To the extent actual plan investment experience differs from that assumed in the annual premium structure, the amount distributed will be greater or lesser than the amount necessary to provide the "target" annuity benefit produced by the formula. Like other defined contribution plans, the investment risk is borne by the individual participant, not by the plan sponsor.

DEFINED BENEFIT PLANS—IN GENERAL

A defined benefit plan is generically different from a defined contribution plan in that the retirement *benefit* amount is predetermined as contrasted with the individual contribution amount. Under a defined benefit plan, a formula is used to determine the level of benefit to be provided to each retiree. When an employee becomes a participant, the yearly pension he can ultimately expect to receive at retirement is calculated in accordance with that formula. Some formulas are based on a flat dollar amount; for example: $15/month pension for each year of service. However, most formulas are based on a percentage of compensation with some recognition made of the length of the employee's service. For example: a formula may determine an employee's pension by multiplying 2 percent of the average of the employee's last five years' earnings times the number of years of his employment. From time to time after he begins to participate, the participant's ultimate pension payable at retirement will be recalculated using the plan formula then in place. The contribution the employer will make under a defined benefit plan is the amount actuarially necessary to provide the pension each participant will be entitled to when he retires, under that calculation.

There are a number of different ways to pay for or fund a defined benefit plan. This chapter focuses on the "group unallocated" method. Under this method, contributions are not preset and billed for individual accounts as is the case with the defined contribution plan. Instead, the actuary considers the employee group covered by the plan as a whole and develops a recommended level annual cost which, in his judgment, will generate sufficient assets over the lifetime of the plan to pay for each employee's benefit at retirement.

Each contribution made by the plan sponsor as a result of the actuary's recommendation is invested in a fund that is selected by the plan sponsor, but is legally owned by an entity such as an insurance company or trustee. The fund must be separated from other assets of the corporation and must be held exclusively for the covered employees and their beneficiaries, by the insurance company or trustee.

THE ADVANTAGES AND DISADVANTAGES OF THE DEFINED CONTRIBUTION PLAN

A businessman considering establishing a retirement program for his employees must of necessity carefully weigh the advantages and disadvantages of the defined contribution and defined benefit arrangements.

Because of the individual account concept, the defined contribution concept is relatively easy to explain and operate. The liability of the employer is fixed and can be stated simply as a percent of payroll, in the case of a money purchase plan, or as a portion of company profits in the case of a fixed formula profit-sharing plan. While defined contribution plans are subject to certain federal pension regulations, the level of regulation is not as onerous as that for defined benefit plans. The nature of a defined contribution plan also allows individuals to make certain choices and arrangements which generally are not available under the defined benefit arrangement. For example, a participant may borrow against the vested portion of his account or elect that a percentage of the sponsor's yearly contribution be applied to purchase life insurance on his behalf. A participant may be offered a choice of investment alternatives for his account (e.g., common stocks, fixed income investments, company stock) thus enabling each participant to determine the degree of risk he wishes to assume in planning for retirement.

A disadvantage of the defined contribution plan is its limited ability to provide benefits based on employment periods prior to the plan's adoption. Basically, it provides benefits only for service periods after the plan has been established. Because the participant's account balance at retirement is based on his salary history, or the employer's profit history, from his participation day forward, the account balance or its equivalent in yearly pension would typically have no direct relationship to earnings before retirement. This kind of plan, therefore, can function as a structured earnings-replacement-after-retirement program only in a general sense. An additional negative from the perspective of the plan participant is that it is he, not the plan, who bears the risk of the plan's investment performance. Earnings (or losses) on plan assets are reflected directly in his individaul account balance.

THE ADVANTAGES AND DISADVANTAGES OF THE DEFINED BENEFIT PLAN

The defined benefit plan affords the plan sponsor great flexibility in designing a pension benefit package. For example, the formula for determining benefits can easily be structured so that employees' service prior to the establishment of the plan can be recognized. If the plan sponsor wishes to use his plan as a vehicle for replacing a portion of wages earned immediately prior to retirement, a defined benefit plan is uniquely equipped to satisfy this objective. A measure of predictable retirement security for the remaining lifetime of the retired employee can be facilitated through the use of a defined benefit plan. In contrast with the defined contribution plan, a participant who terminates before retirement with a vested interest in all or a portion of his accrued pension is not normally permitted to take his benefit immediately in cash (although this kind of provision is possible if the plan sponsor so desires). Instead, the plan provides the participant with a yearly pension payable starting on his normal retirement age (generally age 65). From the participant's perspective, another advantage is that he has no risk from the plan's investment performance. Any shortfalls in available funds must be made up by the plan sponsor. Retirement planning is facilitated for the participant since he can count on a fixed level of income, with protection for his spouse, if desired.

A disadvantage of this type is that it is more difficult to explain and more difficult to operate. First, in the area of pension cost development, the plan sponsor will require the ongoing assistance of a competent actuary. Second, the average plan participant tends to understand the concept of an individual account balance better than the concept of an accruing pension based on many variables. Third, the liability of the plan sponsor is not as clear-cut under a defined benefit plan as under a defined contribution plan, because it is not a direct and calculable percentage of compensation. Lastly, the federal regulations for defined benefit plans are burdensome. For example, plan sponsors of defined benefit plans must participate in the federal government's "plan termination insurance system" to cover shortfalls in assets on termination, while plan sponsors of defined contribution plans are exempt from this requirement.

THE TAX QUALIFIED PLAN CONCEPT

Federal regulation applies to private pension plans. For decades, Congress has sought to encourage the establishment and maintenance of such plans by offering tax incentives which favor both the employer and its employees.

Provided that certain requirements are met, contributions, within prescribed limits, made to provide benefits can be deducted by the employer from gross income for tax purposes. The investment growth of the plan assets is not taxable income to the employer or to the plan's trust or insurance fund. The plan participant or his beneficiary is not taxed on contributions to the plan on his behalf until a benefit is actually distributed to him—usually after retirement when in most cases he will be in a lower tax bracket. Moreover, there are estate tax exclusions for certain death benefits and comparable gift tax exclusions for certain transfers.

A "qualified pension plan" (i.e., a plan designed to qualify for favorable tax treatment under the Internal Revenue Code) must meet a number of basic requirements, whether it be a defined contribution or defined benefit type. These requirements ensure that in return for the various tax advantages, the plan is operated for the exclusive benefit of *all* the employees covered and not simply the long service, highly paid group. These requirements include or require the following:

1. The plan must be in writing. This is partly to establish its existence and partly to permit plan participants to examine the plan document to determine their rights.
2. The assets of the plan must be in a fund entirely separate and distinct from the assets of the plan sponsor. This segregation of plan assets can be accomplished by having the assets held by a trustee appointed under a trust agreement or held by an insurance company under an annuity contract.
3. The plan sponsor must establish and operate the plan with the expectation that it will be a permanent arrangement. While the plan sponsor can terminate the plan at any time, he must be prepared upon termination to demonstrate that the plan did not operate to benefit only a favored few employees over the short term.
4. The plan must cover either a prescribed percentage of employees or a classification of employees that the IRS determines not to be discriminatory in favor of higher paid employees.
5. Complex rules exist to ensure that a plan's contribution and benefit structure will not operate to favor the higher paid employees.
6. A qualified plan cannot provide benefits that are determined arbitrarily. A plan can meet the rule that its benefits must be "definitely determinable" if either the benefits payable to the employee participants or the contributions required by the plan sponsor can be determined actuarially.
7. The plan must be operated so that all funds are held for the exclusive benefit of employees and their beneficiaries. There can be no diversion of plan funds for any other purpose.
8. The terms of the plan, along with the fact of its establishment, must be disclosed to employees by written notice.

ERISA—EMPLOYEE RETIREMENT INCOME SECURITY ACT

In 1974 the federal law governing employee pension and welfare benefit plans was codified and expanded by the Employee Retirement Income Security Act (ERISA), the most comprehensive and technical employee benefits legislation ever enacted by Congress. While ERISA regulates virtually all employee benefit plans, its focus is on pension plans. Requirements were established in the areas of employer reporting, employee disclosure, minimum eligibility, and vesting and fiduciary standards, which apply to both defined benefit and defined contribution plans. A procedure for insuring earned benefits under defined benefit plans was also created.

Reporting and disclosure

Summary Plan Description (booklet). Each participant covered under a pension or welfare benefit plan must receive a booklet (a Summary Plan Description) that contains specified information about the administration of the plan and the benefits provided thereunder. The booklet must be written in clear understandable language. It should describe the benefits available, the conditions that must be met to receive these benefits, and any circumstances that would cause a participant to be denied his benefits. The booklet identifies those responsible for the operation of the plan and communicates the remedies available for redress of denied claims.

Annual Report. An Annual Report containing certain financial information must be filed with the Internal Revenue Service and the Department of Labor by the administrators of employee pension and welfare benefit plans. This obligation is currently met by filing one of the "5500 series" of forms supplied by the Internal Revenue Service. Simplified reporting is available for smaller or insured plans. A Summary Annual Report, a synopsis of the information contained in the Annual Report, must be furnished to each participant and beneficiary annually.

Application for Determination. Generally it is in the plan sponsor's best interest to secure prior approval from the Internal Revenue Service that a pension or profit-sharing plan meets the requirements for qualification for favorable tax treatment. This is currently accomplished by the plan sponsor filing an Application for Determination using one of the "5300 series" of forms. Simplified filing is available through the use of pre-approved prototype, and master plans available through insurance companies and other financial institutions such as banks and mutual funds.

Employee Statement of Benefits. Annually, upon request, and at termination of employment, each participant must receive a statement of earned benefits.

Other reports, notices. There are numerous other reporting requirements that must be satisfied when certain events occur (e.g., plan amendment, plan termination).

Minimum standards

Technical rules apply under ERISA in the areas of:

Participation, where there are limitations on the eligibility standards, in terms of age and years of service, that a pension benefit plan may impose.

Vesting, where there are limitations on the permissible conditions a plan may impose, in terms of age and years of service, after which a participant must be entitled to all or a portion of the pension accruing for him under a defined benefit plan or the account value accumulating for him under a defined contribution plan.

Joint and survivor protection, where under certain circumstances, a plan must provide for death benefits payable to the participant's spouse, should the participant die after he was eligible to retire or after he retired from active employment.

Minimum funding standards, where the employer must maintain acceptable level of contributions to the plan, to avoid having to pay a penalty tax to the IRS and running the risk of the IRS's termination of the plan.

Other ERISA requirements

Maximum benefits. There are maximum allowable benefits for an individual covered by a defined benefit plan. There is a maximum allowable annual contribution for an individual covered by a defined contribution plan, and an overall maximum for an individual covered under both types of plan. These limits are updated yearly to reflect changes in the cost of living.

Commencement of benefits. The plan must provide that benefits commence within a specified period, usually normal retirement age.

Plan termination. Covered employees' benefits vest to the extent assets are available upon the termination of the plan regardless of length of service.

Fiduciary duties

ERISA codified the fiduciaries' duties relating to employee pension and welfare benefit plans. Generally, those persons or institutions who have discretionary authority over plan management and administration or disposition of plan assets are considered to be fiduciaries. Under ERISA, fiduciaries must discharge their duties with respect to a plan:

1. Solely in the interests of the participants and beneficiaries.
2. For the exclusive purpose of paying benefits and defraying reasonable expenses of the plan.
3. With the care and skill that a prudent man familiar with such matters would use in a similar enterprise.

A fiduciary must diversify plan investments in accordance with ERISA dictates so as to minimize the risk of large investment losses. Further, he must see that the plan is administered in accordance with governing instruments. Finally, a fiduciary may not engage in a prohibited transaction. Generally, prohibited transactions include dealings with certain "insiders" or parties in interest with respect to the plan.

ERISA imposes civil and criminal penalties for breaches of fiduciary duty. There are circumstances where one fiduciary may be liable for actions of another fiduciary, where he knew or should have known that the other fiduciary was acting improperly.

Plan termination insurance

Defined benefit plans are generally required to participate in the federal government's plan termination insurance program. Plan sponsors who have these plans pay a specified per-participant annual charge, which is used to provide pension benefits (up to certain guaranteed levels) to participants covered under plans which terminate with insufficient assets. Defined contribution plans are exempt from termination insurance because the nature of the plan is to provide an actual account balance, not a future level of promised pension benefit.

INSURED PENSION PLANS

Simply stated, a pension plan is nothing more than a pool of assets into which contributions are made during the years of high productivity and from which withdrawals are made during retirement. A critical factor in a pension plan is the interest or growth of the assets. This is determined by the way the money is invested. The range of alternatives is great and can include savings accounts, bonds, stocks, and sometimes even real estate. The challenge is to achieve a proper balance between security with the inherent risks of investments with greater potential rewards.

In answer to this need, insurance companies have developed products that guarantee principal and, in addition, pay an annual rate of return that may be guaranteed for a number of years. Mutual funds of all varieties offer a way of obtaining management expertise over an investment portfolio as well as accurate reporting of each participant's account.

Life insurance can also be included in a pension plan. Though the rate of return is low, the safety and added advantage of a pre-retirement death benefit has appeal. Disability can also be insured so that even if an employee is disabled and contributions are no longer made, the ultimate pension benefit is still available at retirement. Many of these considerations are also discussed in Chapter 24.

If the amount of money to be invested by a plan is relatively small, or the number of participants is few, a plan may be ineligible for some of the products and services described below. This means that other funding methods may have to be used.

Many insurance companies, banks, and securities dealers provide Prototype Pension Plans. The wording in these documents has been preapproved by the Internal Revenue Service, thereby making the final plan approval quicker and simpler, limiting the IRS review to the options selected. Prototypes reduce the costs of installing a plan yet still give a wide range of flexibility in selecting trustees and administrators (often the business owner), vesting schedule alternatives, participation requirements, retirement date choices, and funding alternatives.

There are local and national pension service organizations which, for a modest fee, will handle ongoing plan administration and employee communication. Their services include tax form preparation, production of descriptive booklets, actuarial certifications, cost estimates, and annual accountings. Even the smallest employers can provide retirement plans for themselves and their employees on a reasonable cost basis. The combination of Prototype documents, equity and insurance funding alternatives, and purchase of administrative services can result in plans that are competitive with those of the major businesses in the United States.

As an employer's work force grows larger, over 25 lives for example, additional options become available. One choice available to a plan sponsor is to purchase a full service arrangement from an insurance company. Here, the insurance company will issue one or more contracts to the plan sponsor (or the trustee) and agree to accept and invest the contributions made to fund the plan's benefits. It is possible for the plan sponsor to purchase a wide range of technical services under this kind of insured arrangement. Contracts designed for defined contribution type plans are available, as are contracts designed to provide unallocated investment fund management for defined benefit type plans. The plan sponsor may even secure and pay for select specified services from the insurance company.

Another choice is to select a trustee—often a bank—to administer the plan and its trust. While there are advantages to this arrangement, one consequence is that the plan sponsor will have to arrange for the provision of some plan services (e.g., preparation of booklets, annual reports, etc.) from other sources.

INSURED GROUP PENSION PRODUCTS

Deposit administration contracts

A common funding method for defined benefit plans is the group unallocated or deposit administration (DA) method. The plan sponsor's contributions for the covered group are held in a fixed income and/or equity fund and invested by the insurer in ratios selected by the plan sponsor and his advisors. Amounts held in the fixed income fund are credited with a guaranteed rate of interest. The value of the plan sponsor's equity fund will vary as the value of the underlying investments vary. Under the terms of the DA contract, no more than a stated "contract charge" for expense recovery purposes is withdrawn each year by the insurance company from plan assets. When an employee covered by the plan becomes eligible for a pension benefit, the premium necessary to purchase that benefit, as described in the contract's guaranteed annuity purchase provision, is charged against plan assets. Because of this purchase feature, any further liability for the pension benefit is shifted from the plan sponsor and the plan to the insurance company. Should the financial experience (interest, expense and mortality guarantees offered under the contract) under the DA contract prove to be more favorable than assumed, rate credits or dividends are issued to the plan by the insurance company at its discretion.

Immediate participation guarantee

A widely used variant of the DA method is the immediate participation guarantee (IPG) method. The IPG is similar but not identical to a trust in practical application.

Under the IPG, the plan sponsor's contributions are accumulated in an unallocated fund or funds managed by the insurance company, as under the DA approach. Where the DA contract's interest, expense, and mortality guarantees provide a stabilizing effect on fluctuations in the plan's financial experience, no such guarantees are generally present under an IPG contract. Actual interest earned by the plan's assets is credited to the plan's account. Actual expenses chargeable to the plan are withdrawn from the account, and pension benefits are not typically purchased or guaranteed by the insurance company. Under the typical IPG contract the insurance company merely acts as the plan's paying agent, disbursing periodic payments as required by the plan from assets as payments become due. In a nutshell, the IPG concept permits the plan and the plan sponsor to participate immediately in the actual experience of the plan (i.e., the interest earned, expenses incurred, and retirement benefits paid) be this experience favorable or not.

The DA method, by contrast, credits and charges the plan under a structure of assumptions relative to expected and guaranteed interest, expenses, and mortality experience. The chief advantage of the DA approach is that dramatic shifts in financial experience from one year to the next are, for the most part, avoided due to the stabilizing effect of the contractual guarantees.

The primary advantage of the IPG contract is that actual plan experience in the areas of mortality, expense, and investment result is immediately reflected in or borne by the fund. Conversely, this feature may be a disadvantage where the plan experiences losses or unfavorable investment results over the short term.

Separate accounts

In addition to investing in group contracts (which basically involve participation in an insurance company's general fixed income portfolio), plan sponsors normally have the option of causing assets to be invested in one or more separate accounts. The separate account is similar to a bank collective trust in that it pools investments of various plans within an account separate from other insurer assets, and usually concentrates on a specific type of investment. Typically an insurer might offer separate accounts of the following types:

1. A growth-oriented equity account (common stocks).
2. A short-term account (certificates of deposit, commercial paper).
3. A private placement account (nonpublic obligations of corporate borrowers).
4. A real estate account (real properties, mortgages).

The multiplicity of separate account vehicles offers the plan sponsor a wide range of investment alternatives.

On the defined contribution side, insurance company contractual arrangements offer all necessary services, including the accounting systems required to operate the individual participant accounts—the chief administrative burden of this kind of plan. The insurance company's expense recovery policy will normally be described in the contract document or separate service agreement. As previously mentioned, all earnings on assets held by the insurance company under defined contribution arrangements are credited directly to the participants' accounts. For the participant who wants to receive his account balance in the form of a pension benefit at retirement, the insurance company servicing the plan will typically make available a nonparticipating guaranteed annuity purchase facility for this purpose.

QUESTIONS TO ASK THE AGENT OR BROKER

1. What are the historical levels of performance of the investments or contracts recommended?
2. What experience in servicing pensions does the organization have? Is there a local contact?
3. What personal services in communications and question answering will the agent or broker give?
4. Are the fees reasonable for the services being rendered?
5. How may of the identified personal and business needs will be fulfilled by the recommended plan?
6. How many of the ERISA communication requirements will be assumed by the insurer? At what cost?

UNIQUE EXPOSURES

CHAPTER 29

COMPUTER FACILITY (DATA PROCESSING) INSURANCE

DEVELOPING THE DISASTER PLAN

DATA PROCESSING EQUIPMENT
INSURANCE
  Understanding the lease clauses
  General data processing policies
  The Difference-in-Conditions Policy
  User or employee negligence

DATA STORAGE MEDIA INSURANCE
  Determining media values

ACCOUNTS RECEIVABLE INSURANCE

BUSINESS INTERRUPTION
INSURANCE

EXTRA EXPENSE INSURANCE

DATA PROCESSORS' (THIRD-PARTY)
ERRORS AND OMISSIONS LIABILITY
INSURANCE
  Sources of loss

RECOMMENDED CAUSE OF ACTION

APPENDIX: RISK AND INSURANCE
SURVEY FOR DATA
PROCESSING

Guy R. Migliaccio
Senior Vice President
Marsh & McLennan, Incorporated
New York, New York

Guy R. Migliaccio is a Senior Vice President of Marsh & McLennan, Incorporated, and has been a member of the Computer Security Institute's Advisory Council since its inception in 1974. He is involved with many of the Fortune 500 list of companies, advising them on insurance and risk matters related to their data processing operations. He is a graduate of the City University of New York with a degree in marketing and management.

DEVELOPING THE DISASTER PLAN

Most data processing centers throughout the world are easy targets for fraud, embezzlement, and sabotage. The catastrophic effects resulting from such perils as floods, hurricanes, tornadoes, earthquakes, fire, smoke, or acts of violence can be equally disastrous. At best, fire, vandalism, and other causes of loss have repercussions which can last for months and even years. Losses can result in destruction of vital records, lengthy downtime, with corresponding erosion of goodwill among clients, customers, suppliers, and others. At worst, such emergencies result in a loss of business, severely curtailed profits, or, in extreme cases, a company's withdrawing from business altogether.

Data processing system users are frequently unmindful of these possibilities and assume that their vital reports will flow forever from the computer center. They further assume that if a catastrophe occurs, data processing management will have developed sufficient loss control contingency procedures and will have purchased an insurance policy to enable recovery from the disaster.

Unfortunately, due to lack of time or tight budgets, the computer center management usually has neither a viable contingency plan nor a proper and adequate insurance program. This chapter will summarize the kinds of losses to which computer facilities are subject and examine the kinds of insurance available.

The chapter is divided into six major sections, each of which represents a separate area of exposure and subject for insurance. These areas sometimes overlap, and it is not always clear where one area begins and the other ends. Damage to the computer system could involve one or all six of these areas. A properly developed disaster plan, however, should protect essential equipment and records, and include an insurance program that neither permits a large loss to go uncovered nor allows the costly purchase of unnecessary policies.

The six major insurance coverages developed in this chapter are for Data Processing Equipment, Data Storage Media (called Data Processing Media in insurance terms), Accounts Receivable, Business Interruption, Extra Expenses, and Data Processors' Errors and Omissions Liability.

DATA PROCESSING EQUIPMENT INSURANCE

Although some firms own their electronic data processing equipment, most lease it and sometimes falsely believe that the manufacturer or leasing firm assumes responsibility for loss or damage to the computer under terms of the lease. This may or may not be the case.

However, the fact that the manufacturer or lessor has insurance on its equipment does not automatically free the user of liability. The high cost of the equipment provides an incentive to the lessor's insurance company to exercise its subrogation recovery rights (claiming damages from the third party that caused the catastrophe), and that company is not likely to feel bound by the lessor's good intentions toward the user. A "waiver of subrogation" should be negotiated between the user and the lessor's insurance company to avoid any attempt at recovery. Prior to loss, this subrogation waiver does not cost the user one cent. Following a loss, if the user has not procured a waiver, the cost could be enormous.

Understanding the lease clauses

The vast differences in wording and terms of equipment leases require the user to analyze the wording and terms carefully to determine the extent of the liability which is being assumed. Here are some examples of common liability assumption clauses found in computer lease agreements:

"The manufacturer (or lessor) relieves the user for loss or damage to the equipment caused by fire, lightning, and smoke." This clause relieves the user for these three perils, but not for loss or damage caused by other perils. In this instance, the user would be well advised to purchase a supplemental "all-risks" or Difference-in-Conditions Policy which excludes fire, lightning, and smoke, which should be available at a reduced cost (fire is usually the most expensive peril to insure against).

"The manufacturer (or lessor) relieves the user of liability for all risks of loss or damage to the equipment, except where the user has contributed to same by his negligence." This clause is drawn from the standard Comprehensive General Liability Policy, which does provide coverage for negligent acts of the insured or his/her employees that result in bodily injury or property damage to third parties. The general liability policy does not normally cover damage to the property of others in the care, custody, or control of the insured. Without this type of coverage, one lessee was held liable for damage to the lessor's equipment caused by burglars. The lessor contended that the lessee exercised less than ordinary care by providing inadequate security measures. Judgment was rendered in favor of the lessor for $175,000. The insured's policy did not cover this award, and the insurance company was not obligated to provide a defense.

"The manufacturer (or lessor) relieves the user of liability for all risks of loss or damage to the equipment except for loss or damage caused by nuclear reaction, nuclear radiation, or radioactive contamination." This clause is the most desirable from the user's standpoint since it relieves the user of liability for virtually all damage, including losses resulting from the moving of equipment, negligent handling, flood, etc.

General data processing policies

When a business owns its equipment or holds a lease that makes the business completely and directly responsible for all causes of loss or damage, the broadest protection available is called for. The reader should be cautioned at the outset not to look to customary forms of insurance for the protection needed in the area of data processing. For example, a standard fire policy does not cover:

☐ Accidental breakage.
☐ Collapse of roofs.
☐ Water damage.
☐ Loss while in transit.
☐ Vibration.
☐ Earthquake.
☐ Flood.
☐ Electrical injury.
☐ Burglary or theft.

The limitations and exclusions are virtually endless.

Fortunately, several insurance companies offer policies that insure against all risks of direct physical loss or damage to data processing equipment. Such policies do not normally exclude:

☐ Earthquake.
☐ Flood.
☐ Burglary.
☐ Theft.
☐ Unexplained or mysterious disappearance.
☐ Electrical injury.

The broadest forms available exclude only:

☐ Errors in machine programming.
☐ Latent defect.
☐ Wear and tear.
☐ Gradual deterioration.
☐ War and nuclear destruction.
☐ Dishonest and criminal acts by employees.

It is important to elaborate on this last exclusion. Experience has shown that many computer fraud or sabotage losses are caused by employees. For example, employees have been known to:

□ Use bogus input to send generous tax refund checks to their relatives.

□ "Knife" a tape, with the cost to a company of hundreds of thousands of dollars to reconstruct the destroyed data.

□ Send truckloads of merchandise into limbo.

□ Supply priceless secrets to business competitors.

As a precautionary and insurance measure, if management questions the background, attitude, or performance of any employees in the data processing operation, consideration should be given to dismissing them or transferring them out of the department to ensure that they will not have access to either the equipment or the records.

All data processing policies covering equipment offer a choice of replacement cost new (the cost to replace at the present time) or actual cash value (replacement cost new less physical depreciation). In view of the rapid obsolescence of computers, a policy should cover losses on a current replacement cost basis. This requires that the amount of insurance not be based on original cost. It also requires a frequent updating of the amount of insurance, especially during times of high inflation, in order to avoid a co-insurance penalty.

If the equipment is no longer manufactured or available, the policy should state that in the event of loss, the amount of the insurance will equal the value of the equipment. In insurance jargon, this is known as Agreed Amount or Stated Value. A data processing policy may also provide a blanket amount of insurance over several locations where computers are installed as well as coverage for equipment in transit.

One further crucial point: When purchasing equipment insurance, it is important not to accept a policy that shows the serial numbers of listed equipment. Too frequently, a malfunctioning piece of equipment is returned to the manufacturer and a substitute sent in its place. If that substitute item were damaged on your premises, the insurance company could deny liability because the serial number would not match the one shown in the policy. Therefore, if you must accept a policy that lists equipment, be sure it describes the type of equipment in general terms only, such as "one IBM 360-50 CPU." Do not include the serial number.

The Difference-in-Conditions Policy

The data processing policy offers broad coverage for users of electronic data processing equipment. For some firms, though, it may be advantageous to include data processing equipment under the basic property insurance program that protects the other assets of the firm, and then to purchase additional insurance under a Difference-in-Conditions Policy. This policy, commonly called DIC, is usually a tailor-made, typewritten form providing whatever is available under data processing policies, but has some additional advantages:

☐ Newly acquired equipment is automatically covered without special notice to the insurance company.

☐ The all-risks coverage applies to all property, not only electronic data processing equipment, and can be extended to include media, extra expense, business interruption, and accounts receivable on a blanket basis.

☐ The rate per $100 of insurance purchased is often lower because of less adverse selectivity against the insurance company and largely unregulated rate filings.

DIC coverage is usually available with a deductible of $5,000 or higher and is most advantageous with a deductible that exceeds $25,000. It is more beneficial to the larger firm that has a greater capability to carry high deductibles (risk retention) and that already has a sound basic or underlying insurance program. Smaller firms are best advised to purchase a data processing policy that carries a lower deductible and is not contingent on an underlying or basic program of insurance.

User or employee negligence

Some leases impose legal liability for loss or damage due to the negligence of the user or employees. Although the standard Comprehensive General Liability Policy does not cover this exposure, coverage may be secured in several ways:

☐ A separate legal liability policy may be purchased to cover liability for damage to leased equipment. Defense of claims, even frivolous ones, is provided by the insurance company without additional charge.

☐ The existing Comprehensive General Liability Policy may be extended to include legal liability for damage to the leased equipment in the care, custody, or control of the user. Again, this coverage is normally excluded and must be added by special endorsement.

☐ An umbrella excess liability policy may be purchased to insure legal liability above a self-insured retention of $10,000 or $25,000. Make sure the costs of defending a suit against you by the insurance company are on a first-dollar basis.

The umbrella policy is recommended because of the additional benefits derived. Not only will it cover losses of electronic data processing equipment not included in the standard Comprehensive General Liability Policy, but it will also cover losses that are excluded in all forms of primary liability insurance policies, including automobile insurance. Losses that are covered by the primary insurance benefit from higher limits because the umbrella policy provides excess coverage.

DATA STORAGE MEDIA INSURANCE

The cost of reproducing or replacing lost or destroyed data storage media (referred to as data processing media in insurance jargon), including duplication of research, by far exceeds the amount recoverable under standard policies. Unless specifically stated, data processing policies do not cover any form of media. Other types of contents insurance will cover media, but only to the extent of blank value and simple transcription expenses. At the time of loss, it is like offering a parched individual a thimbleful of water. However, if agreed upon, data processing policies will cover all risks of loss or damage to active media, including programs or instructions, and all information stored thereon.

A data storage media policy pays the actual cost to reproduce or replace the media. A separate or blanket limit of insurance can be designated for all remote locations where media are stored. The coverage is subject to the same exclusions for loss due to "electrical or magnetic injury of electronic recordings." This exclusion is not mandatory. An insurance broker or agent familiar with data processing loss exposures can have the exclusion eliminated for a nominal charge. However, unless the policy terms and conditions are tailored, this painful exclusion never fails to appear.

Other considerations when obtaining data storage media coverage include:

☐ Many businesses maintain their own key-punch equipment to convert information from original source materials into data processing media, and then have a messenger transport the media to an outside service bureau. In this case, it is important that the policy clearly state that loss of media in transit and while on the premises of the service bureau is covered.

☐ Most policies have severe limitations regarding transit and outside locations. Be sure that media at all remote locations are covered, including those en route.

Determining media values

The determination of media values is one of the most perplexing parts of an insurance survey. It entails a careful and complete analysis of all data processing functions in order to arrive at a realistic value that avoids either overinsurance or underinsurance. While there are no prescribed guidelines for arriving at adequate insurance limits, some techniques have been devised. The Electronic Data Processing Media Estimate in the Appendix of this chapter outlines one such technique.

The policy form used by some companies includes a condition requiring the insured to keep a duplicate copy of each master program or instruction tape in a fireproof safe or vault in another building or in a fire area separate from the originals. Any failure to abide by this condition would deny coverage to the insured.

Data storage media represent only one form of valuable documents and records for most businesses. It is unwise to single out media for insurance coverage while ignoring other forms of valuable records, including accounts receivable. The most advantageous way to purchase all-inclusive records insurance is to amend the definition of data processing media in the policy to include all valuable records and papers.

ACCOUNTS RECEIVABLE INSURANCE

To many firms, the loss of accounts receivable records represents a potential disaster. Even with total confidence in the honesty and sincerity of debtors, dependence upon customers' goodwill to voluntarily settle their accounts will inevitably lead to problems, and to doomsday in businesses where help from customers cannot be anticipated.

Fire is the major peril to your records, and fire insurance will not reimburse a business for its loss. There is much cause for concern. Fire insurance pays only for the *cost of blank* tapes, blank drums, or other materials, *plus the* actual *cost* of the *labor to transcribe* such records. It *does not* provide coverage for records destroyed or damaged unless duplicate copies are available to make copying or transcribing possible. The fire policy *will not reimburse* uncollected money resulting from loss or damage to accounts receivable records.

The purchase of accounts receivable insurance is a prudent measure even when a business has taken every precaution possible to avoid loss. The premium is relatively low, the policy conditions are liberal. Any internal loss-prevention program is subject to human error—there may be a time lag in record duplication; new operations may create new problems; a sudden fire or explosion may destroy records during the working day when they are unprotected (60 percent of all fires reported occur from 7 A.M. to 6 P.M.); and off-premises exposure may be more or less uncontrollable.

Accounts Receivable Policies are of the all-risks type, have a minimum of exclusions, and may be purchased separately or as a part of a general electronic data processing policy. Moreover, Accounts Receivable coverage is for consequential rather than direct damage. While most policies require monthly reporting of the accounts receivable balance, nonreporting forms are also available.

The policy will specify the type of cabinet, safe, or vault (called receptacles) in which the records must be kept when the premises are not open for business and when the records are not actually in use. It is possible to avoid this requirement by doubling the rate. It is also possible to obtain rate credits of as much as 40 percent for receptacles that afford a high degree of protection.

Accounts receivable insurance will reimburse you for:

☐ The amount of money due from others, provided you are unable to collect as a direct result of loss of or damage to the receivable records.

☐ Interest charges on any loan to offset impaired collections. (Coverage of this type is quite broad and includes interest charges until insurance is settled or until outstanding balances are collected.)

☐ Extra collection costs made necessary by loss of accounts receivable.

☐ Other expenses reasonably incurred in reestablishing records. These can include travel, advertising, overtime, auditors, etc.

The following risk management approaches should be considered:

☐ Purchase limits of liability high enough to cover the maximum amount that would be required to cover complete losses or to reconstruct records.

☐ Exclude certain assured large accounts if they exceed 20 percent of the average monthly amount of accounts receivable.

☐ Review branch locations that customarily forward records to the main premises. Coverage for branches is limited to 10 percent of the policy limit, or $250,000, whichever is less. If more insurance is required, it must be specifically requested.

☐ Submit multiple locations for average rate treatment.

☐ Include transit coverage for an additional premium.

☐ Obtain discounts of 25 to 50 percent by duplicating records and storing them at another location.

BUSINESS INTERRUPTION INSURANCE

When owned or leased computer equipment is damaged, a company may suffer a substantial loss of net profit from current operations. This loss may result from either a reduction in operating income or extra expenses incurred to continue normal data processing operations.

Business Interruption coverage is available by endorsement to the data processing policy that covers equipment and media. It covers loss or damage to equipment, media, or the premises that results in a provable and definite reduction in income. Be sure that the policy does not limit the business interruption coverage to damage to equipment and media only, but embraces the premises housing the data center as well. For example, if the data processing center is on the sixth floor of a building, and the first five floors are burned out, the computer operation will obviously be interrupted.

Business Interruption coverage can be written to provide a stated dollar-amount recovery for each day of total interruption and a pro-rated amount for partial interruption. Extra expenses (to be discussed more fully in the following section) are covered under Business Interruption, but only to the extent that the business interruption loss is reduced. This is an important point because many insureds have been falsely led to believe that business interruption insurance is a substitute for extra expense insurance.

Other misconceptions often result in insuring data processing business interruptions separately from other operations of the firm. Some limitations or disadvantages of this trend are:

☐ The policy may duplicate coverage, particularly when only the premises housing the electronic data processing facility are damaged and the equipment and media remain intact.

☐ No business interruption recovery is provided for loss resulting from damage to the production capability of the firm unless it interferes with the data processing operation.

☐ It is difficult to measure accurately the loss of income directly resulting from damage to the data processing operation when other damaged property cannot be included.

One way to overcome these limitations is to insure the business interruption losses due to electronic data processing as well as business interruption losses due to other operations of the firm with the same insurance company. As a general rule, it is advisable to take out as many kinds of insurance as possible with the same company. For example, fire policies exclude damage from exploding boilers but cover damage from an ensuing fire. Boiler policies exclude fire but cover boiler explosion damage. However, if the fire caused the boiler to explode, the boiler policy would not cover the explosion. Following a loss, it is often difficult to determine whether the fire started first and caused the boiler explosion or whether the boiler exploded first causing the fire. While the two separate insurance companies are each busy denying liability, your claim remains unsettled. If, however, both boiler and fire policies are with the same insurance company, it has no recourse but to pay the claim.

EXTRA EXPENSE INSURANCE

A business with a well-integrated data processing operation seldom maintains backup personnel and facilities to perform manually or mechanically those functions normally performed electronically. It is therefore essential that electronic data processing operations be continued at any price following a loss.

If duplicate master program tapes are available, an outside service bureau or backup facility can sometimes continue normal operations, but usually at great expense. Time on available equipment may be purchased at high cost, often at abnormal hours and with substantial overtime to employees. In addition, costs for transportation of data and personnel will surely be increased.

Because of the reduced efficiency, additional personnel will probably be required. If an entire data processing operation can normally run for $600 an hour, it is safe to estimate that following a loss, temporary operation off premises can cost as much as $1,200 an hour. If the system runs eight hours per day, the increased cost per five-day week would be $24,000. Since the simplest IBM equipment can sometimes take 12 weeks to replace, the extra expense loss for 3 months in this example can be estimated at $288,000. And that is the extra expense loss only. It does not include reproduction of media and presumes that the user is not held liable for equipment damage.

It is a fair assumption that few data processing operations have only business interruption exposure; most have both business interruption and extra expense exposure. The purchasing of both coverages is recommended. Once again, extra expense insurance can be added by including it on the data processing policy that covers equipment, media, and business interruption. Under a pure form of Extra Expense coverage, the insured is reimbursed for all expenses incurred to continue data processing operations without having to prove any resulting income. Normally, this insurance provides a stated limit of liability and covers a period of time judged adequate for the repair and replacement of the lost or damaged property, including the computer facility itself. The exclusions are essentially the same as those applying to equipment, media, and business interruption.

It is sometimes difficult to convince a user of the need for extra expense insurance. For example, ABC Corporation insists that its longstanding oral, reciprocal agreement with XYZ Corporation for mutual backup is viable. For proof, ABC points to the situation eight months ago when it was down for five hours and XYZ provided the required time. But when an operation is down 24 hours a day, 7 days a week, for 12 to 24 weeks, the verbal agreement may well crumble. Businesses are well advised to consider purchase of this coverage. One note of caution—extra expense insurance is not a substitute for basic risk control. If alternate facilities and compatible equipment as well as program and transaction media are not available, operations must cease and an insurance payment is not possible.

It is difficult to determine the amount of extra expense insurance required, since there is no set formula for doing so. For an approximation, however, the following factors must be analyzed:

☐ Normal departmental costs.
☐ Availability and costs of backup facilities.
☐ Increased personnel costs.
☐ Increased transmission costs.
☐ The probable maximum period of interruption.

All of the figures should be projected against a background that includes the most adverse circumstances, remembering that nothing will go right following a disaster. To help measure potential extra expense losses more accurately, consult the Risk and Insurance Survey in the Appendix to this chapter.

DATA PROCESSORS' (THIRD-PARTY) ERRORS AND OMISSIONS LIABILITY INSURANCE

Many computer installations sell excess machine time to outside customers or perform certain data processing services for them. If only the excess time is sold, machine operations and programming are normally performed by the customer's employees. In other cases, the data processing department's own employees provide all such services for the customers, sometimes utilizing customer-furnished media.

Data processing services sold to outside customers usually expose the operation to liability for financial loss due to error, omission, negligence, malicious acts, dishonesty of employees, as well as machine malfunction. Service contracts usually attempt to restrict the liability of the servicing operation, although the legality of such restrictions is questionable. It is therefore advisable to carry insurance against such liability. Since this insurance cannot be provided under the special data processing policy (because it involves third-party claims), separate policy coverage is required.

Data processors' errors and omissions liability insurance is available from a few U.S. insurance carriers as well as from Lloyd's of London. The coverage is impossible to purchase unless the insured agrees to the following exclusions:

☐ Any dishonest or criminal acts of employees.

☐ Libel, defamation of character, and slander.

☐ Loss or damage to property of others in your care, custody, or control.

☐ Liability assumed under any contract.

☐ Advice or opinions on financial statements.

☐ Loss from preparation of income tax forms.

☐ Losses caused intentionally by the insured.

☐ Personal injury, bodily injury, and property damage.

Sources of loss

The work of a data processing center involves four basic functions: (1) systems design, (2) programming, (3) data capture, and (4) computer processing. Any of these functions can be a source of loss. There is one additional source, malfunction of the computer or its peripheral equipment. The following examples illustrate this very strong possibility:

☐ Recently, a market research firm hired a service bureau to collect some market data. The research firm reached a number of conclusions which were the basis for the client's decision to open regional warehouses. However, due to an error in the service bureau's tabulations, the market research conclusions were unsound and the client firm went bankrupt. The client subsequently brought suit against both the market research firm and the service bureau, seeking compensation for opening the warehouses in the wrong geographic areas.

☐ A publisher of a weekly magazine hired a service bureau to handle distribution and mailing to its thousands of subscribers. Erroneously a delivery of 30,000 issues was made to an individual homeowner who would normally receive one copy. The 30,000 issues should have been delivered to a wholesale distributor who handled a large metropolitan area for the publisher. By the time the magazines were correctly rerouted, the newsstands and other outlets where the magazine was sold would not accept them.

☐ A large New York City bank that processes paychecks for many large unionized manufacturers was unable to deliver the paychecks on time due to software problems. Union contracts clearly spelled out the penalty for tardy paychecks. It cost the bank tens of thousands of dollars to maintain goodwill.

The policy of the largest insurer of Data Processors' Errors and Omissions Liability excludes the critical exposure of losses resulting from faulty systems design and programming errors.

Increasingly, multiple users have access to and can activate the computer from remote terminals. The response time to the user is so rapid that the computer appears dedicated to each user. Some insurance companies deem this to be no different than if the client sent its own employees to the service bureau to operate and activate the computer. They claim that an essential element of the coverage is that the processing be done for others, with clients having no part in the process. Fortunately, not all of the few insurance companies that write Data Processors' Errors and Omissions Liability have taken this position. Firms primarily doing accounting or financial processing will have an easier access to coverage than those involved with simulating techniques, or engineering or scientific applications.

The premium for this coverage is calculated at a rate per $1,000 of gross receipts billed to clients for data processing services. Basic limits are $10,000 per claim, with a $20,000 aggregate for losses in any one annual period, subject to a minimum mandatory deductible of $1,000. Both the limits and deductible may be increased within narrow parameters. It is extremely difficult and costly to purchase limits in excess of $5 million.

If a service bureau has a unilateral Hold-Harmless Agreement in its contract, under which it disavows any responsibility for its errors and omissions, it might be possible to modify the Comprehensive General Liability and/or Umbrella Liability Policy to include coverage for Hold-Harmless Agreement exposure. This appears to be the most economical way to approach the high premiums normally levied for this coverage, and it will probably afford the easiest access to higher limits of protection.

RECOMMENDED COURSE OF ACTION

Data processing centers represent a risk classification that has one of the highest concentrations of value with which the insurance industry has ever had to contend. The loss from a fire in one computer facility involving only 650 square feet of space (56 square meters) amounted to $5 million. The compactness of future systems will greatly increase the easy possibility of theft.

In spite of this high probable loss, the underwriter generally receives a low premium because data processing centers are generally located in office buildings where fire and extended coverage rates are low. Fire rates do not accurately reflect the heavy concentration of value or the delicate hardware and software involved. It is conceivable that a fire one or two floors beneath an electronic data processing room generating heat of 140 degrees F (60 degrees C) may erase or distort language on tape, without smoke or flames ever touching it.

With sensitivities this high, many insurance underwriters attempt to avoid this type of risk and write manufacturing plants which carry a higher rate and afford a better spread of risk. Underwriters, by doing this, can make a smaller commitment for their company and generate premiums which are just as substantial. Moreover, some recent, large, well-publicized losses have cast gloom over the data processing insurance industry.

The situation for insurance buyers is not hopeless, however, and there is no reason why adequate coverage cannot be purchased with the exercise of good insurance sense. The following suggestions should prove helpful:

☐ Take the account approach—You can improve your bargaining position with underwriters by combining your property and casualty coverages, wherever possible, with the same company. This account leverage is an important ally when placing data processing coverage.

☐ Think in terms of deductible—Sometimes even a modest deductible may induce an underwriter to accept business that he might otherwise have rejected. Remember that deductibles also reduce premium costs.

☐ Utilize loss prevention systems—Fire detection and extinguishing equipment is evidence to the underwriter that you are as interested in minimizing loss potential as he is. The expenditure rarely exceeds one percent of the total values at risk.

☐ Develop contingency plans—A disaster plan that protects essential records and prepares your firm for continued operations under emergency conditions is also essential.

The more dependent upon computers a business becomes, the greater its financial risk. Disruption of data processing can bring the operation of any organization, no matter how large or small, to a screeching and complete halt. The costs of repairing or replacing data processing equipment and media are phenomenal. The income lost and the expenses incurred during a slow up or work stoppage can spell ruin. To be forewarned is to be forearmed.

APPENDIX: RISK AND INSURANCE SURVEY FOR DATA PROCESSING

This questionnaire has been designed to identify and isolate the loss exposures, if any, that may be present in your data processing operation. The first section asks general questions while Enclosures 1 and 2 focus on specific types of losses. It is imperative that knowledgeable and responsible electronic data processing personnel be involved throughout this evaluation since much of the information sought requires intimate knowledge about the environment in which the computers are housed, the hardware, the software, the operating procedures, and the functions that the data processing section performs.

Some answers must be rough estimates. However, since these estimates are critical in reaching a proper evaluation, they should be very carefully considered by responsible personnel familiar with the overall operation.

Basic assumption: When completing this questionnaire, please assume a major disaster in or around the data processing room that destroys the operation completely and requires reconstruction of the environment, on-premises media, and replacement of the hardware. Complete the estimates based on this worst-possible-situation assumption, taking into account whatever off-premises backup of media and hardware is available.

Note: A questionnaire is a track on which to run. It is designed to develop data in a logical sequence for subsequent analysis and interpretation. Some questions are merely starting points to lead to other questions.

QUESTIONNAIRE*

Data Processing Equipment (Hardware)

1. Please attach a list of all EDP equipment with a brief description of each item of equipment, e.g., console, power unit, tape drive, etc.

Manufacturer	Model no.	Serial no.	Owned	Leased	Description	Replacement cost

2. If there is any leased equipment, please attach a copy of each lease agreement in effect.
3. What is your best estimate of the time it would take to replace the equipment now being utilized? _____

Data Processing Media (Software)

4. Are duplicate programs maintained? _____
5. If yes, where are they stored? (Describe fully, including comments regarding safe and vault storage if applicable.)

_____

_____

_____

_____

6. How frequently are duplicate programs updated? _____

7. What is your best estimate of cost to reconstruct or reproduce your media? (See Enclosure 1 for assistance in arriving at a cost estimate.)
   Cost to reproduce programs: $_____
   Cost to reproduce other data: $_____
8. What is your best estimate of the time it would take to reconstruct or reproduce your media?
   Programs: _____
   Other data: _____

Data Processing Extra Expense/Business Interruption

9. List the functions presently performed by your data processing unit:

_____ _____

_____ _____

_____ _____

_____ _____

* Questionnaire prepared by Chubb & Son, Inc., underwriting managers for the Federal Insurance Company.

10. List functions contemplated within the next 12 months:

    _____   _____

    _____   _____

11. Is your system on-line or batch?
    If both, estimate percent of each: Batch _____ %
    On-Line _____ %

12. What are your machine-time requirements?

	Current	*Estimate 1 year hence*
Hours per day:	_____	_____
Days per week:	_____	_____

13. Have you made alternate arrangements for the use of compatible equipment configurations in the event of loss or damage to your data processing equipment?
    With whom? _____ Where? _____
    Written or oral? _____
    Assuming the complete disruption of present DP facilities, would such arrangements meet with your operational requirements?

    _____

    _____

14. Please estimate expenses above the normal that your firm would incur in the event that all DP operations had to be performed off-site, including temporary conversion to manual systems necessary for current operations. (See Enclosure 2 for assistance in arriving at this estimate.) $_____

15. Would loss of your DP center cause a loss of income to your firm?

    _____

    If so, please estimate the loss per month: $_____

Environmental Information

16. Street address of building where the DP installation is located:

    _____

17. The DP room is on the _____ floor of this _____ story building.

18. Building construction is _____

19. Briefly indicate the general type of occupancies or occupancy in the building, i.e., offices, manufacturing, mercantile, etc.: _____

    _____

20. Is the DP room equipped with a smoke and heat detection system? Do you employ automatic extinguising systems such as sprinklers, CO_2, Halon 1301, etc.? Please specify: _____
    Does activation of either system or both systems in combination:
    a. Sound a local alarm _____
    b. Sound an alarm at a constantly attended remote location _____
    c. Automatically shutdown air-conditioning _____

    d. Automatically de-energize computers _____

    e. Automatically close dampers leading to room _____

21. Is the DP room physically separated by a masonry wall from the media storage area? _____

22. Is the DP room covered by a watchman's service during nonoperating hours?

    If so, what is the frequency of rounds? _____

23. What is your best estimate of the time and cost to replace the immediate environment housing the DP operation?

        Time: _____

        Cost: _____

24. Do you perform data processing services for others?

    For whom? _____

    Description of services: _____

Recapitulation of Loss Estimates

Environment	Time required to replace	Dollar cost required to replace
Hardware	_____ mos.	$_____
1. Owned	_____ mos.	$_____
2. Leased	_____ mos.	$_____
Media		
1. Programs	_____ mos.	$_____
2. Data	_____ mos.	$_____

* Maximum time estimate: _____ mos. at

    $_____ per mo. (business interruption) = $_____

* Maximum time estimate: _____ mos. at

    $_____ per mo. (business interruption) = $_____

ENCLOSURE 1: DP MEDIA ESTIMATE

A. This enclosure is intended to guide you in estimating the cost to restore your DP media to the state existing prior to the loss.

B. For the purposes of this enclosure, media shall be defined as all forms of converted data, and/or programs, and/or instruction vehicles employed in your DP operations, e.g., magnetic tapes, punch cards, data cells, disks, drums, etc. Source materials not converted into some form of DP record should not be included in your estimate.

C. In estimating your media values, the following factors should be included:

   1. The total bank value of media prior to processing. This figure should be adjusted to include an estimate for media materials expected to be utilized in the next 12 months.

   2. The total cost of reconstructing media (cost of programs should be kept separate from other data if possible), to include consideration of the following:
      a. Programmer's time.
      b. Key-punch time.
      c. Card to tape, drum, disk, etc., time.
      d. Machine time.

   3. Additional manual procedures necessary to produce input for the reconstruction of the destroyed media but not previously included in your operations, such as batch preparation.

   4. Research and clerical procedures necessary to obtain data lost because of the destruction of backup materials or source documents.

   5. If compatible equipment is not available, so that the equipment to be used will take a greater number of running hours to produce the same result as your present equipment, multiply the estimated number of additional hours by the "prime-time" rate.

D. The totals of paragraphs C-1 through C-5 represent an estimate of your maximum media values.

ENCLOSURE 2: DP EXTRA EXPENSE ESTIMATE

A. This enclosure is intended to guide you in estimating the cost above the normal cost of operating your DP center that would be incurred following complete disruption of your DP operations.

B. 1. List the jobs that must be done and the number of machine-hours for each to arrive at the total machine-hours per month. Note: If more than one type of equipment is used, list the hour requirements for each separately.

   2. List the name and location of facilities with which you have made backup contracts. If none, list facilities that might be available.

   3. List the prime-time hourly rates and number of hours available at each location; include local and state taxes on such rentals. Note: If more than one type of equipment is needed, indicate whether the backup locations have the dual equipment necessary. If not, show alternate locations that do have such equipment and the hourly prime-time rates.

4. Multiply the totals from 1 and 3 to arrive at basic equipment expense. Note: If compatible equipment is not available, and the equipment to be used will take a greater number of running hours to produce the same result at your present equipment, multiply the estimated number of additional hours by the prime-time rate and add the result to 4 to arrive at the total machine-time requirements.

5. Estimate and list monthly expenses such as:
   a. Announcements—mail, radio, television, papers, etc.
   b. Transportation to backup facilities of:
      (1) Supplies.
      (2) Personnel (to and from).
      (3) Other.
   c. Communications, such as telephone, telegraph, leased lines, couriers, etc.
   d. Special protective services such as guards, containers for transporting vehicles, etc.
   e. Overtime or other salary adjustments for insured's personnel.
   f. All costs of additional employees for temporary conversion to manual systems necessary for current operations including:
      (1) Advertising or employment agency fees.
      (2) Salaries.
      (3) Equipment rentals.
   g. If not included in hourly rate under 3 above, also list costs at temporary location for:
      (1) Rent or rehabilitation costs.
      (2) Light, heat, power, janitorial devices.
      (3) Cost of additional insurance such as fire legal liability, if required by processor.
   h. Total monthly expenses.
   i. Add 10 percent for contingencies.
   j. Total.

Important:

   k. Deduct expenses that discontinue at original location due to loss.
   Note: These costs will be items such as heat, light, power, air conditioning, protective services, and rental of leased equipment, but only if contract for same contains an abatement clause.
   The result is the amount of net monthly extra expense and should be multiplied by the number of months necessary to place the insured's own equipment back on line and debug it, i.e., restore it to the same condition that existed before the loss.

CHAPTER 30

BUSINESS LEGAL EXPENSE INSURANCE AND TENDER OFFER DEFENSE EXPENSE INSURANCE

BUSINESS LEGAL EXPENSE
INSURANCE
  The need
  Highlights of the coverage
  Exclusions
  Eligibility
  Plans available
  Examples of how this insurance has
    been utilized
  Business legal expense insurance
    summary

TENDER OFFER DEFENSE EXPENSE
INSURANCE
  Background on tender offers
  Covered expenses
  Benefits limits available
  Optional coinsurance
  Deductibles and policy period
  Significant exclusions
  Significant definitions in the policy
  How the insurance works
  The significance of the range of limits
    and deductibles
  Special considerations
  The premium
  Public policy considerations

Sydney Aronson
Chairman
NAS Insurance Services
Santa Monica, California

Sydney Aronson is the Chairman of NAS Ltd., a Chicago-based excess and surplus line insurance firm. He works at its Santa Monica, California-based division, NAS Insurance Services, which is a correspondent and coverholder for Underwriters at Lloyd's, London. A graduate of the University of Michigan, he is an Adjunct Professor at California State University, Northridge. For the last 15 years he has been active in the development of new insurance coverages in the health field as well as specialty commercial programs.

No business should consider an unusual exposure as uninsurable merely because no insurance policy exists today. Many of the insurance policies discussed in this book did not exist 20 years ago. But some astute business brought a problem to a creative agent or broker and, together with an insurer or with Lloyds of London, an insurance coverage was developed.

This chapter presents two such creative coverages. The first, business legal expense insurance, may well be suited to the small- to medium-size business facing a growing array of currently uninsured legal expenses. The second, tender offer defense expense insurance, addresses a specific exposure of businesses listed on an organized securities exchange.

BUSINESS LEGAL EXPENSE INSURANCE

The Need

It's harder and harder to run a business or professional practice these days. Mounting government regulations and constant tax law changes compound paperwork and force businesses to adopt more complex systems.

As each new law enters the books, the legal exposures of a business grows: from ERISA regulations, OSHA regulations, civil rights legislation, to new tax codes and laws governing the employment rights of senior citizens.

It is no wonder that virtually every judicial district and court system is jam-packed with suits. Many courts are several years behind.

The tide of suits, claim the experts, comes from three main sources. One is the greater complexity of doing business, which naturally makes for more suit-causing events. Second is the greater sophistication of the general population. Events that previously would be passed by are today often the subject of a suit. And third, they say, is the flood of lawyers coming out of the law schools, looking for work and eager to try their mettle. In some states the number of licensed lawyers has increased by 50 percent in the last ten years.

And, unfortunately for the small- or medium-size business or professional group, along with mounting lawsuits have come escalating legal fees and costs. Today, for the small business, the defense cost of just one suit can be as catastrophic as a fire or major accident. In some cases, lawsuits have bankrupted businesses. Costs have skyrocketed so high that many businesspeople and professionals hesitate to consult with attorneys when threatened by a suit or when they feel the need to take plaintiff action.

Some businesspeople or professionals believe they are protected from most legal exposures by their liability policies—errors and omissions, product, general, etc. The standard liability policies do provide important protection—but there are vast areas that may not be covered. Some of these include:

- Litigation of contract claims.
- Suits for fraud or libel.
- Suits or complaints from customers.
- Debt collection.
- Legal problems with IRS or other federal or state agencies.
- Suits from disgruntled employees.
- Suits from suppliers, distributors.
- Suits related to labor and union problems.
- Suits involving alleged violations of environmental statutes or regulations.
- Consumer legal actions.
- Suits involving occupational safety violations.
- Suits alleging discrimination of any kind—age, race, religion, creed.
- Suits involving restraint of trade violations.

The list highlights only some of the legal exposures common to small businesses that are usually not covered by standard liability policies. And because suits of these kinds are becoming more the rule than the exception, there is a great need for legal insurance to shelter businesses and to keep them viable.

Business legal expense insurance reimburses a business, professional, or professional group for its business-related legal expenses in an unforeseen lawsuit. A claim need only be an unforeseen legal expense which qualifies as an income tax deductible expense under Section 162 of the Internal Revenue Code.

Highlights of the coverage

100 percent reimbursement for defending a suit.   Complete coverage of legal defense expenses to the limit of the plan chosen.

100 percent reimbursement for legal consultation.   An unforeseen legal problem or the threat of a suit often requires consultation with an attorney. Complete coverage up to the limit of the plan chosen.

80 percent reimbursement for plaintiff action.   If, after consultation with an attorney, a business decides it has a case against someone and should sue, the plan pays 80 percent of the legal expenses for plaintiff action, up to the plan limits chosen.

Arbitration Proceedings Coverage.   As an option, for an additional 20% of the standard premium an insured can receive 100% reimbursement for arbitration proceedings, up to the limit of the Plan chosen.

Free choice of attorney.   Unlike liability coverage where the insurance carrier is in charge, chooses the lawyer, and controls the defense, this plan permits the insured to utilize any attorney or law firm it chooses—and the attorney and the insured are in complete control of their own case.

Unlimited usage.   There are no limitations on how often the plan may be used, up to the limits chosen. After a policy year is completed, an insured can apply again for the full limits of protection for another policy year.

Tax deductible.   Premiums are a tax-deductible business expense.

Lawsuits can surface at any time but may be the result of something that happened three, five, or ten years ago. These legal timebombs are a threat to any business. Business legal expense insurance has full *prior acts* protection—back to the day the business started.

As insurance costs and the costs of business mounts, more and more businesses can only afford liability policies with hefty deductibles. *Business legal expense insurance covers the legal defense expenses that are subject to these deductibles,* up to the limits of the plan chosen.

In addition to sheltering the business from these defense costs, the combination of a Business Legal Expense Insurance Policy with a Liability Policy with a deductible is often less expensive than a Liability Policy without a deductible. Here, at less cost, the insured business is able to cover not only its liability exposure but has widened its range of protection with the broad coverage unique to business legal expense insurance.

It is becoming more common for suits against a business to name the corporate directors in the suit as well as the business. *When this happens, the Business Legal Expense Insurance Policy provides for legal defense expense coverage for the directors as well as the business.*

Exclusions

There are certain exclusions, such as:

1.   Claims involving the use and operation of an automobile or vehicle. The purpose of this exclusion is to prevent the coverage from

being used to take the place of automobile and other liability insurance.

2. Class action suits.
3. Suits against physicians or medical groups related to malpractice.
4. Defense of criminal prosecution.
5. Any matter which the insured has conspired with another to have instituted.
6. Legal expenses that are provided by an attorney or group of attorneys to the insured, on behalf of an insuror obligated to reimburse the insured under the terms of a liability policy or another type of indemnification agreement. (This exclusion does not apply, however, to any out-of-pocket legal expenses incurred by the insured which are less than or equal to the insured's deductible under such agreement up to the amount reimbursable under the policy.)

Eligibility

Any sole proprietorship, partnership, corporation, professional, or professional group is eligible if they have 100 employees or less. The business or professional group is the insured, and the insurance covers its business-related legal expenses.

Plans available

Currently, businesses can choose from seven plans. They are:

	Annual limit						
	Plan A annual limit	*Plan B annual limit*	*Plan C annual limit*	*Plan D annual limit*	*Plan E annual limit*	*Plan F annual limit*	*Plan G annual limit*
Actual defense costs insured limit	$5,000	$10,000	$15,000	$20,000	$25,000	$35,000	$50,000
Plus: Legal consultation, action prior to court action	150	300	300	300	300	300	300
Plus: Plaintiff Action, in addition to legal consultation as cited above	250	500	500	500	500	500	500

This insurance is also available to firms with more than 100 employees or for firms with special situations. Special situations refer to firms that might not qualify for the standard policy at standard rates due to unique circumstances, high claims experience or special exposures. In the case of both the larger firms and special situations, individual submissions will be accepted and can be individually under-written.

The insurance is also available to associations as a benefit of membership, to associations desiring unique legal insurance programs for their members, and on an association/group basis.

Examples of how this insurance has been utilized

Business legal expense insurance provides the financial muscle that the small and medium businesses need (and often lack) to deal with suits—and to benefit from consultation with their attorneys without extra concern over consultation costs. It helps provide peace of mind about the ongoing operation of a business—and makes it possible for businesses to use the power of their attorneys when needed. The following actual cases from the files give some idea of the various ways the insurance has been utilized:

Business sued by state in anti-trust action

Sued by the state for restraint of trade, a construction company faced civil penalties and an injunction. They fought the suit and were reimbursed for $9,472.98 in defense costs.

Disgruntled customer sued plumbing and heating company for negligence

The customer, a condominium developer, accused the company of negligence and breach of an implied contract in the installation of plumbing and heating for the condominiums. The plumbing company was able to defend itself, being fully insured for the $9,293.24 in defense costs.

Slapped with fraud suit, a sports equipment maker fired back with plaintiff action

Sued by its bank for breach of contract and fraud, the manufacturer took the offensive and filed suit against the bank for collection of money owed them. The company was reimbursed $4,138.13 for defense costs and $500 for the plaintiff action.

Corporation and principals charged with theft of trade secrets

A bio-engineering firm and its principal officers and directors were sued for misappropriation of trade secrets and breach of fiduciary duty by a former employer. The corporation was reimbursed $10,000 for defense costs which included the principal officers and directors named in the suit.

Architectural firm disputed tax bill with state

When the architects filed their state tax return, they didn't expect a dispute from the tax board. But that's what they got. The firm called its attorney and he settled the argument for them. The architects were reimbursed $300 for legal consultation costs.

Business countersued former attorneys in fee collection action

An insurance brokerage, dissatisfied with its attorneys' services, was even more outraged to learn it was being sued for failure to pay legal fees. The business cross-filed a lawsuit charging malpractice. To date it has been reimbursed $2,090 for defense and prosecution costs.

The case of the collapsed sidewalk

A firm of consulting engineers was sued for allegedly providing incorrect specifications on a cut and fill project. Among other things, a collapsed sidewalk brought on a suit. The firm's Liability Policy had a $5,000 deductible, which was covered by the firm's Business Legal Expense Insurance Policy.

Business legal expense insurance summary

As these claims show, a substantial case can be made for business legal defense expense insurance. It can stand on its own. It also works hand in glove with a business's or professional's Standard Liability Policy to provide protection in line with modern requirements.

TENDER OFFER DEFENSE EXPENSE INSURANCE

Background on tender offers

A new insurance coverage that will grow in importance over the next decade is tender offer defense expense insurance.

Today cash tender offers have become the most popular acquisition device for takeovers of one publicly held corporation by another. In fact, there are several instances where smaller corporations, using the tender offer technique, have managed to takeover corporations which were much larger.

While tender offers are common today, they were used most sparingly and mainly for different purposes in the past. In the early 1920s, corporations often used tender offers to buy back their own shares in the open market from existing shareholders. No corporate chief executive in those days would dream of making a hostile tender for the control of another company. It just wasn't done. But, today it is . . . and very commonly.

The reasons are, of course, varied. For many corporations, it is more sensible and economical to acquire a going company than to start a business from scratch. The need for diversification to help shelter earnings from the ups and downs of business life is another. The "cheap" dollar relative to foreign currencies brings many a Japanese, European, and Near Eastern business into the American scene ready to acquire relative bargains—and footholds in the American and multinational market. To many foreign business the relative political stability of the American scene is also very attractive. Sharp changes in interest rates help trigger tender offer activity as do variations in inflation rates.

While some boards of directors, top management, and shareholders have welcomed the opportunity to be acquired, many have not. They view certain takeover attempts as clearly contrary to their interests. They prefer to fight—and herein lies the problem. The costs of a tender offer fight are often enormous, can drain corporate assets, and have a very damaging effect on earnings.

Marshall Field's fight against an attempted takeover by Carter Hawley Hale, Inc., cost Marshall Field over $3.5 million in investment banker, accounting, and public relations expenses. Legal and litigation costs in this case are not known but clearly were significant. For instance, when MCA, Inc. attempted to acquire Coca-Cola Company of Los Angeles, the legal fees alone were in excess of $2.5 million. By the time the Pullman-McDermott-Wheelabrator Frye fracas finally settled down the combined fees paid by these companies totaled over $17 million. The Home Insurance-Northwest Industries-City Investing case depleted treasuries some $6 million. The Mead Corporation-Occidental Petroleum battle lasted nine months, resulting in bills of $15 million.

Commenting on the reasons for these staggering defense costs, Wheelabrator vice president Mark Stern told *The Wall Street Journal:* "When the stakes are high, you don't want to lose everything by trying to cheap it out. You have to let the meter run."

Defense costs for the large corporations in handling tender offers are understandably high—and, normally, less for the smaller and medium-size corporations trying to fend off an unwanted suitor. However, many business analysts see these corporations as choice targets of the future because, all things being equal, it is often more financially rewarding to go after this group than the larger corporations. Often, the "raider" believes that he can finance the tender internally without having to incur the high interest rates charged for the tender of large corporations.

The Spring 1980 edition of *Mergers and Acquisitions* reports on a survey of the *Fortune* 1,000 corporations by the National Association of Accountants. It showed that 40 percent of these corporations considered themselves vulnerable to takeover attempts.

Having tender offer defense expense insurance enables corporate officers and boards of directors to make decisions about tender offers on their merit alone. It helps relieve financial pressures created by the cost of defense and their impact on earnings and performance. By providing significant financial shelter, it helps create an atmosphere where decisions can be made with due deliberation, in a fiduciary manner, and with full consideration of all parties involved.

Tender offer defense expense insurance provides publicly held corporations with coverage to help defray legal and other defense expenses related to their successful resistance of tender offers.

Eligible corporations include those whose stock is traded on the New York and American Stock Exchanges, regional stock exchanges, the national over-the-counter market, regional over-the-counter markets, and other firms whose common stock is registered under Section 12 of the Securities Exchange Act of 1934.

Covered Expenses

Covered expenses include:

☐ Outside attorney fees and costs.
☐ Outside accounting fees and costs.
☐ Investment banker fees.
☐ Cost of shareholder and other communications.

These include outside public relations advisors and activities, transfer agent, and registrar of securities expenses, proxy solicitation, mailing and printing expenses.

All multiple tender offers occurring within the certificate period (policy year) are included.

Payment for covered expenses incurred requires the passage of only 90 days during which there have been no subsequent takeover attempts. There are no limits to the number of tender offers covered during the policy year—up to the maximum of covered expenses provided by the policy.

Benefits limits available

Corporations may purchase various maximum amounts of insurance per tender offer, and in the aggregate, for covered defense expenses for successful resistance to tender offers. These maximum amounts are: $250,000, $500,000, $1 million, $2 million, $3 million, $4 million, and $5 million.

Tender offers generally qualify if they are subject to the filing requirements of Section 13(d) and 14(d) of the Securities Exchange Act of 1934.

Optional coinsurance

There is an *optional* coinsurance feature on the first million dollars of coverage only. The coinsurance provides for 80 percent to be paid by the insurance and 20 percent of covered expenses paid by the insured corporation in the event of a claim.

Deductibles and policy period

There is a minimum deductible of $50,000 per tender offer. Corporations desiring higher deductible amounts have a broad range from which to choose. They are: $50,000, $250,000, $500,000, $1 million, $2 million, $3 million, $4 million, and $5 million.

The optional coinsurance feature applies when the deductible is under $1 million. When the deductible is for $1 million or more, there is no coinsurance.

The policy provides coverage for 12 months.

Significant exclusions

Benefits are not payable for certain expenses, such as:

☐ Investment banker (or others) fees for seeking alternative offers.

☐ An insured event which occurs within 30 days after the effective date of the first policy year (does not apply to renewals).

☐ An insured corporation's opposition to any tender offer not subject the filing requirements of Sections 13(d) and 14(d) of the Securities Exchange Act of 1934.

☐ The insured corporation's cost for tender offers initiated by the insured company or an agent or affiliate of the insured.

☐ Any expense incurred prior to the receipt of a tender offer.

☐ The insured corporation's opposition to any tender offer which is not successfully resisted by the insured.

☐ An insured corporation's opposition to a tender offer which would not enable the offeror to control the insured corporation.

There are certain other exclusions which are detailed in the policy.

Significant definitions in the policy

Insured event: Means the initial publication or sending or giving of a tender offer.

Tender offer: Means any publicly announced offer or solicitation made during the certificate period to all the beneficial owners of any class of the assured's voting securities to purchase all or part of a specified number or percentage of the issued and outstanding voting securities of that class during and for a specified time period and for a specified or determinable consideration.

Successful resistance: Successful resistance shall be deemed to have occurred at that point in time when 90 days have elapsed following the expiration of the most recent tender offer period, or any extensions thereto, during which there has been no takeover attempt *and* there has been since the insured event: *(a)* no change in, and no agreement to change, the ability to designate or elect a majority of the members of the board of directors of the assured; *and (b)* no change in, and no agreement to change, the ability to direct or cause the direction of the management and the policies of the assured.

Takeover attempt: Means any communication, negotiation, or activity toward the acquisition of control of the named assured.

Control: Means the ability either to designate or elect a majority of the members of the board of directors of the assured or to direct or cause the direction of the management and policies of the assured.

Affiliate: Means any person or corporate body who directly or indirectly through one or more intermediaries is under the control of, or is under common control with, the assured.

How the insurance works

The Case of Company B

Company A tendered for company B—which had a policy with a limit of $1 million, a $50,000 deductible and 20 percent coinsurance. B's directors considered the tender, found it contrary to their shareholder's interests, and decided to fight. The best outside attorneys in the tender offer field were engaged. A prominent investment banker was enlisted in the ranks, as was a top outside accounting firm. An experienced public relations firm was brought in and the battle was joined. When the smoke cleared, and following the 90-day period when there were no other takeover attempts, company B presented its expenses.

Legal costs amounted to $600,000. Accounting charges were $200,000. The investment banker rang up $300,000 and the public relations effort cost $200,000. In all, the fracas cost $1.3 million. Company B footed the $50,000 deductible and 20 percent of the remaining bill, which equaled $250,000. The remaining $1 million of incurred expenses was covered by a claim check to the insured corporation.

The Case of Company Z

Company Z has $5 million in tender offer coverage with no coinsurance and a $50,000 deductible. Suddenly it finds itself the object of desire by an unwanted suitor, company X. Company Z's board reviews X's tender offer, finds it without merit and decides to fight. In marches the army of outside lawyers, accountants, investment bankers, and public relations experts, and the battle ensues. Company Z emerges victorious. It keeps control, but suddenly another company named Y decides it, too, would like to get its hands on company Z and comes up with a much sweeter offer. Company Z's board pow-wows again and decides that the new offer has no merit. Again the troops are called out and again company Z is victorious. Ninety days pass during which the air is free of takeover attempts. The bills now come in. The fight against the first tender offer from company X cost $3 million. During the struggle against company X, some legal and other work was gotten out of the way, so the cost of resistance to company Y's offer was only $2,050,000. Total expenses came to $5,050,000. Company Z had to pay $50,000 of these expenses . . . and the insurance covered $5 million.

If company Z wanted to self-insure a significant portion of the risk, and, as an example, had a policy with a deductible of $2 million, then in this case company Z would have covered $2 million of these expenses itself and the insurance would have paid $3,050,000.

The significance of the range of limits and deductibles

The range of limits (or maximum amounts of coverage) from $250,000 to $5 million provides opportunities for the small to the very large corporations to create a tender offer protection program within their budgets and anticipated exposures.

The range of deductibles, from $50,000 to $5 million, gives corporations the opportunity to self-insure significant portions of the risk and also pattern premiums close to their budgets.

By careful utilization of both limits and deductibles, a corporation can hone in on the amount of protection its board deems necessary for it to be able to consider tender offers relatively free from anxiety over the impact on earnings of the cost of defense.

Special considerations

Tender offer defense expense insurance is pure indemnity coverage. It is most like major medical insurance which reimburses a patient for medical bills, less a deductible and coinsurance amount. The patient chooses the doctor—and with tender offer coverage, the insured corporation chooses the lawyer and other professionals it wants.

Besides the right to choose and direct defense, the insured corporation also controls expenses in an indemnity/tender offer coverage situation. And, most often, because of the high stakes involved, the amount of tender offer coverage purchased is the amount reimbursed.

This is all in distinct contrast to liability coverages such as directors and officers insurance, with which most insurance buyer/risk managers, boards of directors, chief financial, and chief executive officers are familiar. There is a natural tendency to compare coverages, particularly the consideration of premium. But, of course, in a liability claim, the insured has no control, the carrier provides the defense with lawyers of its own choosing, and, most important, has full control of expenses. The limits on a liability policy do not relate to the limits on an indemnity policy—particularly in the tender offer sphere. Rather than just a legal adversary situation, a tender offer fight often becomes a "war" with armies of professionals battling other armies. The battle is pursued through the courts, in the press, in millions of mail solicitations, in charges, countercharges, suits, countersuits, in "raiders" attacks, in "white knights" riding to the rescue—all costly and likely to use up every penny of tender offer coverage.

The premium

Each corporation presents a different tender offer profile, a different degree of vulnerability to a takeover attempt—so each premium is different. The cost to one firm may differ sharply with another, even though they may share many common characteristics. At this writing, the minimum premium is in the $8,000 range for a minimum limit policy with a $50,000 deductible and 20 percent coinsurance. For similar policies with a $1 million limit, the minimum premium is $25,000. There have been quotations in the $30,000 to $40,000 area, a few for more and a few for less. Policies with a higher deductible amount would, of course, have substantially reduced premiums.

Public policy considerations

There are no public policy limitations on the purchase by a corporation of tender offer defense expense insurance.

As a general rule, a policy of insurance will not be deemed to be contrary to public policy unless the loss insured against is so directly related to an immoral, fraudulent, or illegal activity that it encourages or promotes it.

Any question of public policy with respect to the purchase of tender offer defense expense insurance arises from the potential conflict of interest a target company's board of directors may face in weighing the preservation of its own position as incumbent management against the fiduciary obligation it owes to its shareholders.

To date, the courts have given almost complete deference to the business judgment of the target's directors in taking almost any action to defeat an unfriendly takeover. One of the reasons for this is the fact that in a very high proportion of the situations in recent years, such resistance has proved beneficial to shareholders. In a number of cases, the resistance has given management time to develop competing offers at higher prices or the resistance has caused the bidder to raise the bid. Even where the target's defensive actions succeeded in keeping it independent, the market price, after a period of time, has often been higher than the rejected offer price.

In the many suits brought by target shareholders against directors for the rejection of a takeover bid, no director has yet been held liable. The courts have found for the directors on various grounds, including inadequacy of price, illegality of the offer, illegality of the acquisition of control of the target by the offeror, and concern about the impact of the takeover on the employees of the target and the community in which it operates.

Management has not only the right but the duty to resist by all lawful means persons whose attempts to win control of the corporation, if successful, would harm the corporate enterprise. Moreover, the courts have generally recognized management's right to defend its control and its policies at corporate expense. The cases which have considered this issue have turned on the question of whether the expenditures were made to further some legitimate corporate policy as distinguished from expenditures made primarily to enable management to perpetuate itself in office.

The purchase of tender offer defense expense insurance allows a target corporation's board to look more objectively at a tender offer. If the target's board decides, for whatever reason, that resistance to the tender offer is in the best interests of the corporation, then an insured target may well have the necessary resources to resist successfully. Such insurance would be especially useful for those targets whose treasuries would be drained considerably as a result of prolonged resistance and who might otherwise have to accept an offer which may not be in the best interests of the target's shareholders. Additionally, if a bidder is aware that its target may have tender offer defense expense insurance, the bidder may very well offer more than it might have otherwise in order to avoid the resistance which the bidder knows can now be offered by the target due to target's purchase of insurance. Such flexibility and benefits which seem to flow from the purchase of tender offer defense expense insurance would thus further legitimate corporate policy, especially in view of the great discretion with respect to resistance to tender offers given to target's boards of directors.

The benefits which the purchase of such insurance offers far outweigh any possibility that management may use the purchase of such insurance as a weapon to defend against a tender offer, acceptance of which might be in the best interests of the corporation. If a shareholder believes that directors or officers have damaged the corporation or have personally gained some profit or advantage as a result of their decision to resist a tender offer, then the shareholder's proper remedy is a derivative action. The day may come, however, when directors are subject to suit for failing to maintain such insurance in much the same manner that a suit could be anticipated today if directors failed to obtain fire insurance and the corporation's factory burned down.

At this writing these coverages are underwritten at Lloyds, London.

CHAPTER 31

ENVIRONMENTAL IMPAIRMENT LIABILITY INSURANCE

STATUTORY AND REGULATORY
REQUIREMENTS
  Resource Conservation and
    Recovery Act (RCRA)
  Comprehensive Environmental
    Response, Compensation, and
    Liability Act (Superfund)
  Motor Carrier Act
COMMON LAW LIABILITY
  Strict liability

Nuisance
Negligence

INSURANCE AVAILABILITY AND
MARKETS

RISK ASSESSMENT TECHNIQUES
  Inherent hazard potential
  Environmental pathways
  Potentially exposed population
  Facility-specific considerations
  Summary of the risk

REDUCING RISKS

Lynne M. Miller
President, Risk Science International,
A Division of Frank B. Hall & Co., Inc.
Washington, D.C.

Lynne M. Miller is President of Risk Science International. She presently directs programs for evaluating environmental risks of companies applying for EIL Insurance. In addition to helping develop the risk assessment procedures, she has worked closely with the underwriters and brokers on EIL. She holds a B.A. in Biology from Wellesley College and an M.S. in Environmental Science from Rutgers University.

Both Mr. Murphy and Ms. Miller have lectured extensively on the techniques used to assess environmental and health risks from exposure to hazardous chemicals.

The authors wish to acknowledge the valuable contributions of Robert M. Wenger, Corporate Counsel at Clement Associates.

Michael J. Murphy
Chief Operating Officer
Risk Science International
Washington, D.C.

Michael J. Murphy is Chief Operating Officer of Risk Science International, a Division of Frank B. Hall & Co., Inc. He has assisted in the development of risk assessment techniques used to assess environmental impairment liabilities. Mr. Murphy holds a B.S. from the University of Buffalo and holds an M.S. in Natural Sciences from the Roswell Park Memorial Institute, a cancer research center in Buffalo, New York.

The problem of handling and disposal of toxic and hazardous compounds is emerging as a major environmental and public health concern of the 1980s. Hardly a week passes without the media carrying accounts of leaking waste barrels from mismanaged disposal sites, contaminated drinking water from faulty underground storage tanks, polluted air from uncontained compounds, and health impairment from exposure to various toxic compounds.

Federal and state governments have taken steps to respond to the public's insistence that something be done to protect adequately health and resources. Laws have been passed requiring industry to change its practices to ensure safer management of hazardous materials. Because of increased public awareness and legal responsibilities, companies are assessing more carefully than ever their practices for handling chemicals.

Progressive corporate planners, risk managers, and loss control specialists are identifying the potential long-term health and environmental risks from hazardous chemicals and are taking steps to minimize these risks. Some of these risks can now be shared with the insurance industry. Most companies are not insured against long-term or gradual pollution, but several insurers now offer environmental impairment liability (EIL) insurance, which provides coverage for claims arising out of gradual pollution occurrences. The market is broadening to meet the increasing demand for this new coverage. One reason for this increased demand is recent insurance requirements for certain hazardous waste facilities. But, irrespective of insurance requirements, companies are recognizing their increased liability under common law.

This chapter provides highlights of insurance requirements mandated by statute and summarizes theories of common law. Specific markets for EIL insurance are considered. Techniques are discussed that are being used by underwriters and corporate planners in assessing the potential for gradual environmental impairment arising from specific operations or facilities.

STATUTORY AND REGULATORY REQUIREMENTS

Three major federal statutes require companies whose activities involve hazardous substances to be financially responsible for adverse consequences of their actions and mandate or encourage them to have private insurance coverage for environmental damage. These statutes are the Resource Conservation and Recovery Act (RCRA),[1] the Comprehensive Environmental Response, Compensation, and Liability Act (Superfund),[2] and the Motor Carrier Act.[3]

Resource Conservation and Recovery Act (RCRA)

RCRA establishes a federal program to provide cradle-to-grave regulation of hazardous waste. Under RCRA, the Environmental Protection Agency (EPA) is directed to list and identify the characteristics of the hazardous wastes that are subject to regulation. Standards are established for generators and transporters of hazardous waste that will ensure proper recordkeeping and reporting, the use of a manifest system to track shipments of hazardous waste, the use of proper labels and containers, and the delivery of the waste to properly permitted treatment, storage, and disposal facilities. To ensure that these facilities are designed, constructed, and operated in a manner that protects human health and the environment, EPA is directed to promulgate technical, administrative, monitoring, and financial standards for them. EPA believes "liability insurance is the most appropriate mechanism for assuring the public that there will be a pool of funds available from which third parties can seek compensation for claims arising from the operations of hazardous waste management facilities."[4] Civil and criminal penalties are imposed for violations of RCRA. The first comprehensive set of regulations to implement RCRA was issued on May 19, 1980. Through April 1981, there have been at least 15 major modifications, clarifications, and additions.

Regulations promulgated on January 12, 1981[5] establish liability and insurance requirements for sudden and nonsudden occurrences as follows:

Sudden occurrences. An owner or operator of a hazardous waste treatment, storage, or disposal facility must maintain liability insurance for sudden and accidental occurrences that cause injury to persons or property in the amount of at least $1 million per occurrence, with an annual aggregate of at least $2 million, exclusive of legal defense costs. Existing facilities must have this insurance by October 1981. New facilities must have this insurance 60 days before hazardous waste is first received.

Nonsudden occurrences. An owner or operator of a surface impoundment, landfill, or land treatment facility that is used to manage hazardous waste must maintain liability insurance for nonsudden and accidental occurrences that cause injury to persons or property in the amount of at least $3 million per occurrence, with an annual aggregate of at least $6 million, exclusive of legal defense costs. An owner or operator of an existing facility must have this insurance by the following dates:

April 1982—for facilities with annual sales totaling $10 million or more in 1980.

April 1983—for facilities with annual sales of $5–$10 million in 1980.

April 1984—all other facilities.

New facilities must obtain this insurance 60 days before hazardous waste is first received.

The regulations allow owners or operators to obtain insurance covering both sudden and nonsudden occurrences in the amount of at least $4 million per occurrence, with an annual aggregate of at least $8 million, exclusive of legal defense costs.

Owners or operators who can demonstrate that the levels of sudden or nonsudden insurance are higher than necessary for their facility may request a variance from the regional administrator of EPA for an adjusted level of liability coverage. Conversely, the regional administrator can request higher levels of sudden or nonsudden insurance if warranted by the degree and duration of risks at a facility. The regional administrator can also extend the nonsudden requirement to treatment and storage facilities that pose risks of nonsudden damage.

The regulations do not allow companies to insure themselves. EPA is studying the mechanism of self-insurance; the January 12, 1981 regulation stated that EPA expects to decide whether to add self-insurance provisions to the liability requirements within "several months."[6] As of May 1981, no formal decision on self-insurance had been made by EPA; however, a decision is expected in August 1981. Individual state insurance requirements may be broader or have higher limits than federal requirements. Companies should determine the status of their state's hazardous waste programs to determine the minimum insurance coverage that must be obtained.

Comprehensive Environmental Response, Compensation, and Liability Act (Superfund)

Superfund was enacted in December 1980. It requires owners or operators of present and past hazardous substances disposal facilities to notify EPA of their existence by June 1981. Superfund establishes a fund, financed by taxes on petroleum and certain chemicals as well as by direct federal appropriations, to be used by the President for response to a release or substantial threatened release of a hazardous substance, pollutant, or contaminant which may present an imminent and substantial danger to the public health or welfare. Furthermore, it imposes, with few exceptions, strict liability on persons who are involved with hazardous substances for (1) all government response costs and (2) damages for injury to, destruction of, or loss of natural resources.[7]

The potential liability for companies under Superfund is enormous. Section 107(c) establishes specific limits for release of hazardous substances as high as $50 million.

In addition, Section 107(e) expresses the intent of Congress that companies not transfer liability. It states, "no indemnification, hold harmless, or similar agreement or conveyance shall be effective to transfer from the owner or operator of any vessel or facility or from any person who may be liable for a release or threat of release . . . the liability imposed." However, Section 107(e) *does* allow parties to insure against these liabilities.

Superfund requires companies to be financially responsible for their actions. Section 108 requires owners and operators of vessels over 300 gross tons that carry hazardous substances and that use any port or place in the United States or the navigable water or any offshore facility to maintain financial responsibility of $300 per gross ton or $5 million (whichever is greater). Insurance is one way to show evidence of financial responsibility; other mechanisms are guarantee, surety bond, or qualification as a self-insurer. Failure to comply with the requirement for financial responsibility can result in a fine of $10,000 per day.

In addition, Superfund requires the development of financial responsibility requirements for facilities involved in the "production, transportation, treatment, storage, or disposal of hazardous substances" (Section 108(b)). These requirements are to be promulgated no sooner than December 1985. By December 1983, classes of facilities are to be selected for which financial requirements will first be developed.

Because of the enormity of the potential liability established by Superfund, Congress recognized that companies whose activities involve hazardous substances will need to examine critically their present insurance coverage. In recognition of the fact that the market for EIL insurance is in its infancy, Section 301 mandates a study and report to Congress in December 1981 (interim report) and December 1982 (final report) on whether adequate and reasonable private insurance protection is available to owners and operators of vessels and facilities subject to liabilities under Superfund and whether the insurance market is sufficiently competitive to assure purchasers of features such as a reasonable range of deductibles, coinsurance, and exclusions.

Motor Carrier Act

Section 30 of the Motor Carrier Act is designed to assure the public that a motor carrier maintains an adequate level of financial responsibility sufficient to satisfy claims covering public liability and environmental restoration liability. The final regulations to implement this section are expected to be promulgated by June 1981. On January 26, 1981, the U.S. Department of Transportation proposed the schedule of limits shown in Table 1.[8]

Financial responsibility under Section 30 may be established by insurance, guarantee, surety bond, or qualification as a self-insurer.

COMMON LAW LIABILITY

Companies whose activities involve hazardous substances have understandably focused their recent attention on RCRA, Superfund, and the Motor Carrier Act. As discussed above, these laws establish practices and standards to which companies must adhere, and they impose civil and criminal penalties for violation. A major purpose of these laws is to make these companies liable for and financially responsible to the public for damages caused by their activities. RCRA and the Motor Carrier Act impose specific insurance requirements on certain companies, and provisions of Superfund suggest a congressional intent that companies involved with hazardous substances establish financial responsibility through private insurance.

The regulations implementing these laws are just now evolving; it will probably be several years before the final regulatory apparatus is in place. Apart from statutorily imposed liabilities, anyone who operates a business dealing with hazardous substances must recognize that there are well-established common law principles and theories that can form the basis for recovery by plaintiffs for personal injury and property damage.

Superfund creates a new federal cause of action on behalf of the federal and state governments for damage to natural resources, but it does not establish a similar cause of action for individuals for personal injury or property damage.

However, Superfund, as well as RCRA, have savings provisions that make it clear that no provision in either act should be construed to affect in any way the obligations or liabilities of any person under any other law, including common law.

Superfund implicitly states that private citizens must continue to rely on existing common law and statutory remedies to provide legal redress. In fact, Section 301(e) mandates a study due December 1981 to evaluate the adequacy of such existing remedies.

The following are examples of common law theories where there is a substantial body of existing state law upon which lawsuits could be based:

Table 1
INSURANCE REQUIREMENTS UNDER THE MOTOR CARRIER ACT

Type of carriage	Commodity transported	Single limit requirement		
		July 1, 1981	July 1, 1982	July 1, 1983
For-hire:	Property (nonhazardous)			
Large motor carrier		$750,000	$750,000	$750,000
Small motor carrier		500,000	600,000	750,000
Tow-truck operations		500,000	500,000	750,000
For-hire and private:	Oil or hazardous substances as listed in 40 CFR Parts 110, 116, and 261 transported in cargo tanks, portable tanks, or hopper-type vehicles with capabilities in excess of 3,500 water gallons			
Large motor carrier		5 million	5 million	5 million
Small motor carrier		1 million	2 million	5 million
Tow-truck operations		1 million	1 million	5 million
	or			
	In bulk Class A explosives, poison gas, liquified gas, or compressed gas			
	or			
	Large quantities of radioactive materials as defined in 49 CFR 173.389			
For-hire and private:	All oil, hazardous materials, hazardous substances, and hazardous wastes not mentioned in (2) above			
Large motor carrier		1 million	1 million	1 million
Small motor carrier		500,000	750,000	1 million
Tow-truck operations		500,000	500,000	1 million

Strict liability for ultrahazardous activity

This theory has its roots in an 1865 English case, *Rylands* v. *Fletcher*.[9] In that case, the defendant was found liable for the escape into his neighbor's mine shafts of water stored on the defendant's land, even though the defendant was found not to be negligent. This case established the theory, which is very much alive today, of imposing strict liability for the escape of substances from one's land that are likely to cause great harm.

Nuisance

Plaintiffs who are neighbors of a facility that is involved with hazardous substances could base a lawsuit on nuisance, alleging that the activities of the facility have resulted in a substantial and unreasonable interference with the use or enjoyment of their land.

Negligence

In environmentally based damage cases, there is a growing trend of holding the offending company strictly liable for the consequences of its actions involving hazardous substances. In such cases, the plaintiffs can recover without showing negligence on the part of the defendants. However, in those jurisdictions and in those cases where strict liability is not a viable theory on which to base recovery, plaintiffs can allege that the defendants were negligent—that there was a failure to warn to take other precautions or a failure to choose a reputable disposal facility. Also, it is well established that where a statute sets standards of care or conduct, such as in RCRA and Superfund, deviation from those standards may constitute conclusive evidence of negligence, i.e., *negligence per se*.

Evolving case law on apportionment of damages is also important to companies whose activities involve hazardous substances. If more than one company has generated the hazardous wastes disposed of at the site, it may be impossible to determine which company's waste caused injury or damage. When faced with such a problem, courts have gone different ways. In a 1973 Texas decision, *Borel* v. *Fibreboard Corporation*, the court held a group of asbestos insulation manufacturers jointly and severally liable for the asbestosis of an employee of an insulating contractor on the theory that they all contributed to his disease.[10] In a recent California case, *Sindell* v. *Abbott Labs*, the plaintiff alleged that she contracted cancer because her mother took diethylstilbestrol (DES), a drug frequently prescribed at one time for threatened miscarriage, during her pregnancy.[11] The plaintiff could not prove which company manufactured the drug that her mother took. The court apportioned damages according to the market share of the manufacturers.

Companies must also be concerned with the possibility that small individual claims may mushroom into enormous lawsuits if class actions are certified, a significant possibility in environmental impairment cases that mobilize neighbors and communities, as, for example in the *Love Canal* and *Three Mile Island* cases. In addition, these cases tend to be highly visible and extremely emotional, two factors that cannot be overlooked when juries are involved, especially when a verdict for the defendant company may depend on the resolution of highly technical scientific issues in a charged atmosphere.

Changing law concerning the statute of limitations also must be of concern to companies. The rules of traditional tort law used to require lawsuits to be initiated within several years of the time the incident in question actually occurred. However, it can no longer be assumed that the passage of time is a bar to claims based on past practices of companies. Courts are holding that the clock does not start to tick until the plaintiff knows or should have known that his legal rights have been violated.

Because of potential common law liability, companies should continually take steps to minimize the actual or potential risks associated with their business and to make certain that their insurance coverage against gradual occurrences is consistent with these risks.

INSURANCE AVAILABILITY AND MARKETS

Companies that handle hazardous substances must evaluate their need for nonsudden or gradual EIL insurance because of requirements imposed by statute and because of potential liability under common law. Many companies assume incorrectly that they are covered for gradual environmental impairment in their Comprehensive General Liability (CGL) policy.

Until the early 1970s, protection against both sudden and gradual occurrences was afforded in most CGL policies. However, large pollution claims and the heightened awareness of pollution hazards resulted in the exclusion of gradual environmental releases from CGL policies. A typical CGL policy issued today will exclue "bodily injury or property damage arising out of the discharge, dispersal, release or escape of smoke, vapors, soot, fumes, acids, alkalis, toxic chemicals, liquids or gases, waste materials or other irritants, contaminants or pollutants into or upon land, the atmosphere or any water course or body of water; but this exclusion does not apply if such discharge, dispersal, release, or escape is sudden or accidental."

While most companies carry CGL insurance, they face a significant gap in liability coverage for nonsudden or gradual environmental impairment.

Until recently, only a limited market has been available for gradual EIL insurance. In 1974, Wohlreich and Anderson Inc., a U.S. affiliate of the Howden Swann Group, Ltd., was the first to offer EIL insurance in the United States. In 1980, Shand, Morahan, and Company, Inc., of Evanston, Illinois, began offering environmental impairment liability insurance and the American International Group began offering pollution legal liability insurance. These three insurance facilities are presently the major markets for EIL Insurance in the United States. However, the demand for this insurance has increased markedly, and a number of insurance companies are planning to offer EIL coverage in the near future.

The policies currently available are all on a claims-made basis. While there are some significant differences in coverage under the policies issued by these three insurers, all are intended to cover claims arising from gradual pollution damage to off-site property or persons resulting from the operations of the insured. All policies provide a broad definition of the types of gradual pollution conditions or environmental damage that is covered. They include: emission, discharge, dispersal, disposal, release, escape or seepage of smoke, vapors, soot, fumes, acids, alkalis, toxic chemicals, liquids or gases, waste materials or other irritants, contaminants or pollutants into or upon land, the atmosphere, or any watercourse or body of water. The policies of Wohlreich and Anderson and Shand, Morahan and Company also include in the definition of environmental impairment the generation of smell, noises, vibrations, light, electricity, radiation, changes in temperature, or any sensory phenomena.

The policies currently available generally meet the needs of companies requiring gradual occurrence coverage under the RCRA regulations. In fact, higher limits are available than the $3 million to $6 million limits required by RCRA.

Because EIL coverage is so broad and the potential for multimedia environmental contamination is often so great, the underwriters must assess carefully the operations of the company making application for insurance. Underwriting tools include a completed application form, financial reports, and supporting materials such as maps of the location and a description of the facilities and operations. This information is used by the underwriters to provide an indication of the premium. Before a firm premium is quoted or coverage is bound, the underwriters usually require an independent risk assessment of the facility, based on an on-site inspection and an evaluation of the potential for environmental impairment. Depending on the insured's operations, the risk assessment may require a cursory effort of only a few days or may require an in-depth effort of several weeks.

RISK ASSESSMENT TECHNIQUES

The risk assessment addresses the potential for gradual environmental impairment arising from the operations of the insured. The scientific disciplines essential for a proper evaluation of impairment potential include toxicology, public health, ecology, chemistry, and engineering. Toxicologists will consider the inherent hazard of the material generated, handled, or disposed of—for example, are these compounds known or suspected of causing chronic health damage? Public health specialists will consider the potentially exposed human population and identify high-risk groups. Ecologists will consider the interrelationship of the animal and plant population to the environment and pathways of exposure. Chemists will consider emissions and wastes from industrial processes as well as the fate of individual compounds. Engineers will consider facility design and the potential for release of materials from the facility.

A unique approach to risk assessment is one by Risk Science International (RSI), scientific consultants located in Washington, D.C. Differing from the traditional engineering approach to insurance surveys, RSI's multidisciplinary procedure for evaluating the potential for gradual environmental impairment arising from specific operations or facilities is based on an analysis of four major factors:

1. The inherent hazard of materials generated, handled, transported, stored, or disposed.
2. Environmental pathways that may result in human exposure.
3. The nature of potentially exposed populations and the characteristics of their exposure.
4. Management practices and other activities specific to a particular facility.

The analysis is directed at assessing the likelihood that health or environmental risks will occur. This is accomplished by identifying pathways of movement for those materials known or suspected to be hazardous that might be brought into contact with biological populations in the surrounding areas, and result in gradual injury to those populations.

Inherent hazard potential

A critical step in the assessment of potential risks that may be associated with a facility applying for EIL insurance is the toxicological evaluation of the various chemicals used, produced, and disposed of. Such evaluations are made on each chemical for which some degree of human exposure is likely to occur, whether from use during production, from air and water emissions, or from waste disposal. Such evaluations serve two major purposes: (1) they permit characterization of the likely nature of the toxic damage that may result if human exposure occurs; and (2) when coupled with information on the conditions and magnitude of the human exposure, they permit assessment of the likelihood that toxic injury will occur in an exposed population.

The assessment procedure considers separately the hazards from acute and chronic exposures. Short-term or acute toxic effects from chemicals usually occur when exposure is relatively large and sudden. Long-term or chronic toxic effects usually occur when the period of exposure is long and the level of exposure is below the level that produces immediately observable toxicity. Additionally, for a selected group of toxic chemicals, delayed toxicity may result even from exposures of relatively short duration. The toxic effects from short-term and long-term exposure to a compound will depend on the physical, chemical, and biological properties of that compound and other materials and processes with which they may interact. These properties are considered in the assessment of inherent hazard. Factors considered for acute exposure include several parameters of toxicity, reactivity, volatility, ignitability, corrosivity, and physical state.

The inherent hazards from long-term exposure or from short-term exposures that may cause delayed effects are examined in more detail separately because these are often the most critical factors in evaluating the potential for nonsudden environmental impairment. Factors considered include the potential for the compound to cause cancer, birth defects, genetic damage, and other chronic toxic effects in humans or animals.

Environmental pathways possibly leading to exposure

The media and means through which humans, animals, or other species are exposed to chemical substances introduced into the environment are termed environmental pathways. Typical pathways include air, soil, water, and biological organisms moving into and out of the site. The pathways by which a chemical substance moves through the environment depend upon both the physicochemical properties of the substance and the physicochemical properties of the environment.

To evaluate the pathways that materials will travel in the event of gradual release, several parameters must be considered. These include the elevation of the facility, its proximity to surface water and groundwater, local geology, type and porosity of soil, drainage patterns, precipitation, and evidence of contamination. Additionally, the movement of some materials can be influenced by their interactions with the surrounding environment. Such processes as photochemical action, adsorption to soil particles, and chemical interactions with water and other materials in the media can affect movement and also create new hazardous materials of concern. Reducing risks associated with pathways of escape involves identifying the most likely and most potentially damaging pathways and emphasizing control action on these pathways.

Potentially exposed population

Knowledge about certain characteristics of a potentially exposed population is important for assessing the health impact. Thus, a worker population consisting only of healthy adults may be especially vulnerable to certain types of chemical hazards only, while a residential community with a substantial population of infants, children, pregnant women, and invalids may be vulnerable to a much broader range of effects and substances. Areas with large numbers of food-producing animals are also of concern because of the potential for accumulation of toxic emissions in the food chain and economic loss from toxicity in such animals.

In summary, assessment of risk requires not only estimating the likelihood that exposure to a toxic chemical will result in damage, but also determining the size and nature of the population in which the damage might occur. Such knowledge increases the power with which the likelihood of toxic injury can be predicted.

Facility-specific considerations

The design, construction, operation, and maintenance of the facility all affect the release of potentially hazardous materials from a site. An evaluation should consider operating and design plans; compliance with federal and state standards for air emissions, aqueous discharge, and hazardous waste management; spill plans and equipment; site security; and violations and past damage incidents. The specific factors to be considered will depend on the type of facility being evaluated.

For all facilities, it is important to examine critically the inspection and maintenance routines as well as the methods used by management to train workers to recognize and deal expeditiously and effectively with hazard occurrences. It is equally important to consider the efficiency of emergency procedures, which will influence estimates of safety and health risks to local residents.

Another consideration is how seriously management ensures that line managers are aware of the need to reduce health and environmental risks and to take action to increase the safety of their plants.

Summary of the risk

The potential for gradual environmental impairment is evaluated in terms of the four factors discussed above. Information gathered on inherent hazard potential of materials, environmental pathways, and management practices is used to estimate the likely magnitude of exposure and relative risks to populations and ecological systems. An important part of any risk assessment is a consideration of how exposures can be decreased or minimized.

REDUCING RISKS

An assessment of health and environmental risks is a valuable tool for underwriters of EIL insurance. This risk assessment is also an important first step for corporate planners. Once areas of exposures have been identified, companies can assess the potential liabilities and financial impact of such exposures. Corporate planners can then examine the impact of alternative strategies for decreasing the exposures and then meaningfully allocate resources for risk reduction.

Any risk reduction strategy must be evaluated in the framework of regulatory requirements. For example, if a company disposes of hazardous waste, it must ensure that its operations are in compliance with RCRA. But risk reduction strategies must go far beyond regulatory requirements; all areas resulting in financial exposure and common law liability must be considered.

A broad range of options could be considered, depending on the nature of the risk:

Alter the manufacturing process so that less toxic raw materials are used or less toxic by-products are produced.

Minimize the source of chemical emission with control equipment.

Recycle materials that present a risk from disposal.

Alter storage and disposal practices for hazardous materials.

Improve management practices; for example, institute a training program on environmental issues.

Change facility structure; for example, pave surfaces where materials may be spilled or improve site security.

Even the most comprehensive program of risk identification and reduction will not ensure that all future exposures will be eliminated. The techniques of assessment are continually being refined, and new control technologies are being developed to handle industrial compounds. Furthermore, a compound that today is believed not to pose a substantial hazard may be considered hazardous in the future. Thus, while planners are attempting to recognize the exposures that may result from their companies' operations, many are also examining EIL insurance as an essential mechanism to cover areas of excessive risk today and uncertain future risks.

NOTES

1. Enacted into law October 21, 1976 (PL 94-580) and subsequently modified by the Quiet Communities Act of 1978 (PL 95-609) and the Solid Waste Disposal Act Amendments of 1980 (PL 96-482).
2. PL 96-510, December 11, 1980.
3. PL 96-296, July 1, 1980.
4. 46 FR 2827.
5. 40 CFR 265.147: amended 46 FR 27119, May 18, 1981.
6. 46 FR 2828.
7. Natural resources is defined by Section 101(16) to mean "land, fish, wildlife, biota, air, water, ground water, drinking water supplies, and other such resources belonging to, managed by, held in trust by, appertaining to, or otherwise controlled by the United States (including the resources of the fishery conservation zone established by the Fishery Conservation and Management Act of 1976), any state or local government, or any foreign government."
8. 49 CFR Part 387.
9. L.R. 3H.L. 330 (1868).
10. 493 F.2d 1076 (5th Circuit, 1973).
11. 163 Cal. Rptr. 132 (Sup. Ct. 1980) cert. denied, 66 L. Ed. 2d 140 (1980).

APPENDIX: RISK MANAGEMENT CHECKLISTS

APPENDIX: RISK MANAGEMENT CHECKLISTS

RISK MANAGEMENT SURVEYS

Most business owner-operators concentrate their personal efforts on making their business assets productive and profitable while keeping their operational expenses as low as possible. Business profits fuel our economy and give us all a better way of life.

Insurance is one major expense item for most businesses but a necessity if assets are to be kept productive and profit levels protected. Any technique that can reduce expense without sacrificing the quantity and quality of output or reduce protection levels on assets generates a welcome addition to profit.

Each chapter of this *Handbook* has offered risk management techniques and suggestions on ways to save dollars that would otherwise be spent unnecessarily on insurance premiums, uninsured losses or ineffective benefits. Chapter 1 introduced risk management concepts, and Chapter 2 provides information on where risk management services may be obtained. In the aggregate these chapters suggest the following questions for your considerations: Does your business need a Risk Manager? Can risk management techniques save your insurance dollars? Must you rely on insurance alone to protect your assets? Are your profits protected adequately? This section contains two risk management surveys to help you find answers to these questions.

The first, most appropriate for smaller businesses, is a "short" operational risk profile questionnaire developed by Robert E. Bill Associates, Inc., of Farmingdale, New York, and Sarasota, Florida. Answering these questions *before* you visit your agent or broker will not only save time but will undoubtedly generate further dialogue between you and your agent or broker that could lead to better and more economical asset and profit protection for your business.

The second survey is known as the *Aetna Plan Questionnaire* copyrighted by Aetna Life and Casualty Company. It is far more detailed and is more useful for the larger businesses or organizations, however, it can certainly be useful to all businesses.

We commend the completion of these surveys to you as a path to a keener awareness of operation loss exposure and potential areas of expense savings. If this effort leads you to consider engaging an outside "objective" source to look at your risk management and/or insurance program, you may wish to contact a CPCU, a property and liability insurance specialist. The CPCU designation is granted by The American Institute for Property and Liability Underwriters in Malvern, Pennsylvania, whose current CPCU curriculum emphasises risk management. The Institute's sister organization, The Insurance Institute of America, also in Malvern, Pennsylvania, has a specialized course in risk management and another exclusively for loss control. Another fine source is the Risk and Insurance Management Society (RIMS) in New York.

To be effective these questionnaires must be answered fully and objectively. Bad loss information must be revealed for it points to the need for risk avoidance, loss control and other risk management techniques that frequently can generate greater profits in the future.

We acknowledge with appreciation the permission which we have been given by Robert E. Bill, President, and Patrick J. Maher, Senior Vice President, of Robert E. Bill Associates to reproduce the Robert E. Bill Risk Profile, and John D. Faunce, Manager, Commercial Lines Division, Aetna Life and Casualty Company, to reproduce the *Aetna Plan Questionnaire*.

718

RISK PROFILE

Yes	No	
_____	_____	1. Do you have a brochure or other written material which describes your business operations or products?
_____	_____	2. Is your business confined to one industry?
_____	_____	3. Is your business confined to one product?
_____	_____	4. Do you own buildings?
_____	_____	5. Do you lease buildings *from* others?
_____	_____	6. Do you lease buildings *to* others?
_____	_____	7. Do you plan any new construction?
_____	_____	8. Are your fixed asset values established by Certified Property Appraisers?
_____	_____	9. Do you own any vacant land?
_____	_____	10. Are any properties located in potential riot or civil disturbance areas?
_____	_____	11. Are any properties located in potential flood or earthquake areas?
_____	_____	12. Do your properties have Security Alarm Systems; i.e., Fire-Sprinkler Discharge—Burglary—Smoke Detection, etc.
_____	_____	13. Are there any unusual fire or explosion hazards in your business operation? (Welding, painting, woodworking, boilers or pressure vessels, etc.)
_____	_____	14. Do you take a physical count of inventory at least once each year?
_____	_____	15. Do you lease machinery or equipment other than automotive?
_____	_____	16. Do you stockpile inventory, either raw or finished?
_____	_____	17. Could you conveniently report inventory values on a monthly basis?
_____	_____	18. Do you buy, sell, or have custody of goods or equipment of extremely high value? (Radium, gold, etc.)
_____	_____	19. Do you use any raw stock, inventory, or equipment which requires substantial lead time to reproduce?
_____	_____	20. Do you export or import?
_____	_____	21. Do you buy or sell on consignment?

Yes	No	
_____	_____	22. Do you buy or sell goods which must be shipped via waterway?
_____	_____	23. Do you handle any material with a high damageability factor; i.e., subject to loss from temperature changes, dampness, prolonged shelf life, etc.?
_____	_____	24. Do you handle any goods or merchandise in the form of pairs or sets?
_____	_____	25. Are most incoming shipments made via common carrier?
_____	_____	26. Are most outgoing shipments made via common carrier?
_____	_____	27. Are your purchase terms F.O.B. your plant?
_____	_____	28. Are your selling terms F.O.B. the customer?
_____	_____	29. Do you consider your trade area to be local?
_____	_____	30. Do you have goods or equipment located on the premises of subcontractors, bailees, or others?
_____	_____	31. Is your business seasonal?
_____	_____	32. Does your business generate accounts receivable?
_____	_____	33. Do you work with drawings, manuscripts, plans, or other records which, if lost or destroyed, could cause serious loss?
_____	_____	34. Do you have or use EDP equipment or facilities?
_____	_____	35. Do you sell on a contract basis with long-term obligations to your customers?
_____	_____	36. Do you buy from any single source suppliers with only one production or warehousing location?
_____	_____	37. Does one firm account for more than 1 percent of your gross sales?
_____	_____	38. If you suffer a major property loss, would you take every available emergency measure to continue servicing your customers during the period of repair or restoration to avoid losing the market?
_____	_____	39. Is your business subject to regulation by federal, state, or local authority?
_____	_____	40. If more than one location, are they interdependent?

Yes	No		
———	———	41.	Do you have property of others in your custody?
———	———	42.	Does your business regularly call for the execution of written contracts?
———	———	43.	Do you conduct business outside the United States?
———	———	44.	Do you operate a company infirmary or hospital?
———	———	45.	Do you operate an employee restaurant?
———	———	46.	Do you have occasion to use boats or aircraft, other than scheduled commercial?
———	———	47.	Do any employees hold a pilot license?
———	———	48.	Do you hold meetings or conventions outside the United States?
———	———	49.	Do you subcontract work to others?
———	———	50.	Do you require subcontractors to furnish evidence of liability and workers' compensation insurance?
———	———	51.	Do you perform subcontract work for others?
———	———	52.	Are your sales achieved by direct salesmen?
———	———	53.	Do you install or test your products on the customer's premises?
———	———	54.	Do you provide a written warranty as to use or fitness of the products you sell?
———	———	55.	Do you manufacture or sell finished products?
———	———	56.	Do your operations involve any risks of pollution or contamination?
———	———	57.	Do you sell or provide service directly to the customer?
———	———	58.	Do you lease automotive equipment?
———	———	59.	Do you provide autos for the use of officers or salesmen?
———	———	60.	Do you regularly operate vehicles beyond a 50-mile radius of their home garages?
———	———	61.	Do you operate any vehicles which are subject to the jurisdiction of the ICC?
———	———	62.	Do you normally mortgage new automotive equipment?
———	———	63.	Is it *usual* to have persons other than employees riding in your vehicles?

Yes	No		
_____	_____	64.	Do you require some form of driver training or participation in safety activities?
_____	_____	65.	Do you require pre-employment physical examinations?
_____	_____	66.	Do you routinely check with previous employers to determine the work record of new job applicants?
_____	_____	67.	Is there an active safety committee to prevent employee injuries?
_____	_____	68.	Do employees have regular occasion to travel and work in other states?
_____	_____	69.	Do employees have occasion to work or be aboard ship or on navigable waters?
_____	_____	70.	Do groups of employees have frequent occasion to travel together?
_____	_____	71.	Are any employees based outside the United States?
_____	_____	72.	Has there been an OSHA inspection of your premises?
_____	_____	73.	Have you established appropriate internal systems and procedures for compliance with OSHA?
_____	_____	74.	Are there any outstanding citations from OSHA?
_____	_____	75.	Has your company ever sustained an employee dishonesty loss?
_____	_____	76.	Can your company accumulate more than $1,000 of cash at a single location?
_____	_____	77.	Is countersignature required on outgoing checks?
_____	_____	78.	Are incoming checks immediately recorded and stamped for deposit?
_____	_____	79.	Are bank deposits made daily?
_____	_____	80.	Do you use armored car service?
_____	_____	81.	Do you employ outside auditors?
_____	_____	82.	Is your company a public corporation subject to SEC jurisdiction?
_____	_____	83.	Do you employ security personnel including watchmen?
_____	_____	84.	Do you have need for Surety Bonds?
_____	_____	85.	Do you advertise nationally?

Yes	No		
———	———	86.	Do you provide a group medical program for employees?
———	———	87.	Do you provide a group life program for employees?
———	———	88.	Do you provide a disability income program for employees?
———	———	89.	Do you provide a qualified Pension or profit-sharing plan for employees?
———	———	90.	Are most employees union members?
———	———	91.	Have you been doing business with the same insurance broker for more than five years?
———	———	92.	Do you have a formal or declared risk management program?
———	———	93.	Is each division or location a separate profit center?
———	———	94.	Is your company currently paying taxes at a surtax level?
———	———	95.	Are the company asset schedules heavily depreciated for book value purposes?
———	———	96.	Is your net quick ratio at least two to one?
———	———	97.	Is cash flow a problem?
———	———	98.	Would a $100,000 uninsured loss be ruinous?
———	———	99.	Does the company have substantial investment in research and development?
———	———	100.	Is management of a mind to retain risk or self-insure when circumstances are favorable?
———	———	101.	Is short-term credit available if needed?
———	———	102.	Has your company ever sustained any unusually large or unique losses, either insured or uninsured?

Ætna
LIFE & CASUALTY

**ÆTNA PLAN
QUESTIONNAIRE**   Date _____ 19 ____

1	Exact operating name of firm.	
2	☐ Corporation ☐ Partnership ☐ Joint Venture ☐ Individual ☐ Other	
3	Post office address and zip code of firm.	
4	a. Is this firm owned or controlled by another? Name of parent company? b. Does this firm own or control other firms? Names? c. Information as to degree of control.	
5	Describe nature of client's business. *Also indicate whether manufacturer, contractor, distributor, wholesaler, retailer or a combination of these.* How many years in this business?	
6	Describe any new or discontinued operations within the last 3 years.	
7	Names and titles of Owners, Executives, Trustees, etc. a. Co-owners or partners b. Executive officers *(If inactive, so state)* c. Trustees, executors receivers, etc. d. Employed family members.	
8	a. Does the firm have any overseas operations? Give exact name or names under which foreign branches operate. b. Give locations and functions of foreign operations.	
9	Do you bid on federal or state contracts? What types?	

BUILDINGS OR PREMISES

		Location 1	Location 2	Location 3	Location 4
10	Indicate all locations which you own, lease or use. (Be sure to include branches, sales offices, dwellings owned by firm, vacant land, parking lots and locations in foreign countries.) Obtain for each location a copy of any lease agreements. Include zip codes for each location.				
	Exact use of each location.				
11	If property is owned by firm or a related interest, in what name is title held?				

QUESTION NO. 12 APPLIES ONLY TO LOCATIONS OWNED BY CLIENT OR A RELATED INTEREST					
12	a. Latest Building Appraisal (Obtain copy) Date				
	Insurable Value				
	Replacement Cost				
	b. What is your estimate of present building value?				
	c. If property is mortgaged, to whom?				
	d. Are fire or other insurance policies held by mortgagee? Kind — Amount?				
	e. Would any zoning ordinance prevent the repair or replacement of any building damaged by fire or other peril?				

1

BUILDINGS OR PREMISES (Continued)

QUESTIONS NO. 13 THROUGH 26 APPLY TO ALL LOCATIONS

			Location 1	Location 2	Location 3	Location 4
13	What part of the premises do you use or occupy? Describe the tenancy of the portion you do not occupy.					
14	If you are owner or general lessee, do you rent 90% or more of the premises (or any entire single building) to tenant who operates elevators, furnishes power, etc? Describe or diagram.					
15	Area and Frontage	Show (a) Area of buildings and (b) Frontage of property as required for Liability insurance rating purposes.				
16	Construction of Building	Outside walls				
		Floors				
		Roof				
		Number of stories				
17	Hotels, Motels Apartments	Number of rental units?				
		Closed season From — To				
18	Automatic Sprinkler System	Type of system—Wet or Dry?				
		Type of alarm (Describe)				
		Approx. age of system				
		Part of building equipped				
19	Fire Protection	Type of fire alarm?				
		Number of fire extinguishers? Who maintains them?				
		Fire Department service Contract? Cost?				
20	Boilers and Pressure Vessels	Number and description of heating or power boilers				
		Kind of fuel used				
		Description and use of other pressure vessels				
		Which of above items would cause business interruption if damaged?				
		Estimated daily loss if business is interrupted				
21	Power Machinery* (including refrigeration and air conditioning equipment)	Number of items and description				
		Indicate any item whose breakdown would cause business interruption				
		Estimated daily loss if business is interrupted				
		* Large items of machinery eligible for machinery insurance: motors, engines, turbines, generators, transformers, compressors, pumps, flywheels, switchboards, etc.					
22	Cold Storage or Controlled Atmosphere Rooms	Where located				
		Use				
		Value of perishable contents				
		Auxiliary Generators				
23	Plate or Ornamental Glass	Number of plates, size and description*				
		Value of lettering				
		* Indicate whether Exterior, Interior, Carrara, Bent or other special glass.					
24	Signs	Outside signs (Number, type and value)				
		Inside signs (Number, type and value)				

ESCALATORS AND ELEVATORS

		Location 1	Location 2	Location 3	Location 4
25	Number of Escalator landings?				
26	Number of Elevators?				
27	If this risk is in a jurisdiction requiring mandatory elevator inspection, is the present insurance carrier performing the inspections?		☐ Yes		☐ No

NOTES

SKETCH SHEET

This space may be used for a sketch or map of premises showing position of building, streets, driveways, sidetracks, etc.

CONTENTS

		Location 1		Location 2		Location 3		Location 4	
28	Date or dates on which you take stock inventory?								
29	If a manufacturer, what is profit in finished goods on the premises at any one time?								
30	Is there a chattel mortgage on any property? Give details.								
		Month	Amount	Month	Amount	Month	Amount	Month	Amount
31	Stock — Average value*	XXX		XXX		XXX		XXX	
	Peak value								
	Low value								
32	Unattached Furniture and Fixtures — Value of all *unattached* furniture, fixtures, office equipment and supplies?								
33	Permanently attached Furniture, Fixtures, Improvements, Betterments — Value of all *permanently attached* furniture and fixtures?								
	Value and type of improvements and betterments made by client to non-owned premises?								
34	Machinery If appraisal is available, obtain copy — Value of power machinery indicated in question 21?								
	Value of all other machinery?								
35	Electronic Data Processing Media — Value?								
	Owned or leased?								
	If leased, who is responsible for damage?								
	Cost to replace stored data?								
	Time to replace stored data?								
	Any use by others?								
	Who is liable for loss or destruction of data of others?								
36	Dies Patterns Molds, Tools Owned by Client — Value of dies?								
	Value of patterns, molds, forms, lasts and models?								
	Value of tools?								
37	Property of Others in Client's Custody — Description and value of property? i.e.: finished goods — raw material — dies — patterns — property left for repair or processing — employees property — leased equipment								
	How was value determined?								
	Who is responsible for such property and to what extent?								
38	Radioactive Materials — Value and kind of radioactive materials?								
39	Client's Property in Custody of Others — Description, value and location of your property (merchandise, equipment, dies, etc.) in custody of sub-contractors or others for processing, service or repair or leased to others, loaned, rented or on consignment? Who is responsible?								

*The word "value" wherever used in this questionnaire refers to insurable value, i.e., replacement cost new less depreciation.

4

CONTENTS (Continued)

40	**Indicate the value of any of the following property owned by the client:**	

Contractors equipment (attach schedule) $_____   Salesmen's samples $_____

Scientific instruments $_____   Exhibits $_____

Cameras and projection machines and equipment $_____   Radium $_____

Were these values included in answers to previous questions?   ☐ Yes   ☐ No

41	Valuable Papers	Description, value and exact location where valuable papers are kept? Nature of the valuable papers?

			Location 1	Location 2	Location 3	Location 4
42	Accounts Receivable	Number of accounts				
		Average, total outstanding, each month? Maximum, total outstanding, each month?				
		Maximum outstanding balance on any single account?				
		Are accounts receivable records kept in fireproof container?				
		Are duplicate records kept? Where? How long? What percent of the records?				
43	Deferred (Time) Payment Sales	Estimated annual amount of deferred payment sales				
		Maximum unpaid balance any one customer				

SHIPMENTS

	Method of Transportation	Amount Shipped Annually		Amount Received Annually		Max. amount any one shipment
		Prepaid	F.O.B.	Prepaid	F.O.B.	
44	Own Trucks					
	Public Truckmen					
	Rail					
	Domestic Air Freight					
	Parcel Post					
	Registered Mail		XXX		XXX	
	Coastwise Steamer					
	Intercoastal Steamer					
	Overseas - waterborne or air					
	First Class or Certified Mail		XXX		XXX	
	Armored Car or Messengers		XXX		XXX	
	What percent of values are shipped under Released Bill of Lading?					

NOTES

5

MONEY, SECURITIES, ETC.

			Location 1	Location 2	Location 3	Location 4
45	Money (Currency, Coins, Bank Notes, Bullion, Travelers Checks, Registered Checks, Money Orders Held for Sale to the Public) Show Maximum Amounts	Cash other than payroll on premises				
		Payroll cash on premises				
		Total kept in each safe overnight including undistributed payroll (Identify Each Safe By Number)				
		Cash kept at home of custodian overnight				
		In custody of each bank messenger or paymaster				
		In custody of each truck driver, salesman or collector				
		How often are bank deposits made?				
46	Armored Car Service	Are cash receipts picked up by armored car?				
		Is payroll delivered by armored car?				
47	Other Checks and Stamps (Including Trading Stamps) Maximum Amounts for Each	Total on premises at one time				
		Are checks immediately recorded and stamped for deposit only, or photographed?				
		Which locations issue checks? Maximum amount per check?				
		Total kept in each safe overnight (Identify Each Safe By Number)				
		In custody of each bank messenger and paymaster				
		In custody of each truck driver, salesman or collector				
48	All Instruments or Contracts Representing Either Money Or Property Including Tokens and Tickets Maximum Amounts	Total kept in each safe (Identify Each Safe By Number)				
		In custody of each bank messenger				
		In safe deposit vault or at other locations (Specify)				
49	Valuable Merchandise or Other Property Maximum Amounts	Total kept in each safe (Identify Each Safe By Number)				
		In custody of each truck driver or salesman				
		In safe deposit vault or at other locations (Specify)				
50	Number of Custodians Away from Premises at Same Time	Bank messengers and paymasters				
		Truck drivers, salesmen and collectors				

SAFES AND VAULTS

	Safe or Vault	Name of Maker	Serial Number	Shape of Door, Thickness of Steel in Door and Walls Excluding Insulation. Special Labels if applicable.	Location (Use location numbers previously shown and indicate where in building safe is situated.)
51	No. 1				
	No. 2				
	No. 3				
	No. 4				

6

PROTECTION

<table>
<tr><td>52</td><td>Watchmen, Guards Protective Equipment

Main Location Only*</td><td>
WATCHMEN on duty within premises when closed _____ (Number)   ☐ Signal central station hourly   ☐ Punch clock hourly
GUARDS on duty within premises when open _____ (Number)   with each messenger _____ (Number)
paymaster _____ (Number) Any over 64 years?   ☐ Yes   ☐ No
LOCKED SATCHEL (approved) used by messenger ☐ Yes ☐ No   by paymaster ☐ Yes ☐ No
PRIVATE CONVEYANCE used by messenger ☐ Yes ☐ No   by paymaster ☐ Yes ☐ No
BURGLAR ALARM: Make: _____ Protects: ☐ Safe ☐ Vault ☐ Premises
   Installation _____ Class _____ Certificate No. _____ Expiration date _____
Describe any other protection (hold-up alarm, tear gas systems, bandit resisting enclosures, etc.)
_____
_____
*Use separate page where necessary to show information relative to watchmen, guards and protective equipment at other locations.
</td></tr>
</table>

<table>
<tr><td rowspan="8">53</td><td colspan="2">Check any of the following statements which apply to the operation:</td></tr>
<tr><td>a. Audit by independent public accountant - Quarterly _____ Semi-annually _____ Annually _____</td><td></td></tr>
<tr><td>b. Audit by employee who is equivalent of public accountant, who has no other duties and makes written and signed periodic reports of such internal audits</td><td></td></tr>
<tr><td>c. Audit reports rendered directly to individual owner, all partners or Board of Directors</td><td></td></tr>
<tr><td>d. Require countersignature of checks</td><td></td></tr>
<tr><td>e. Joint control of securities</td><td></td></tr>
<tr><td>f. Reconciliation of bank account by someone not authorized to deposit or withdraw</td><td></td></tr>
<tr><td>g. If there is Fidelity coverage do new employees complete personal application supplied by the Insurer including, at least, a record of previous employment?</td><td></td></tr>
</table>

CLASS 1 AND/OR CLASS 2 EMPLOYEES

<table>
<tr><td rowspan="14">54</td><td colspan="2">**OFFICIALS**</td><td colspan="2">**ACCOUNTING**</td><td>Asst. Managers</td><td></td><td>Custodians</td><td></td><td rowspan="2">Salesmen of Auto Dealers</td><td></td></tr>
<tr><td colspan="2">Chairman</td><td colspan="2">Auditors</td><td>Branch Managers</td><td></td><td>Watchmen</td><td></td><td></td></tr>
<tr><td colspan="2">President</td><td colspan="2">Asst. Auditors</td><td>Dept. Managers</td><td></td><td></td><td></td><td>Demonstrators</td><td></td></tr>
<tr><td colspan="2">Vice President</td><td colspan="2">Cashiers</td><td>Superintendents</td><td></td><td></td><td></td><td>Canvassers</td><td></td></tr>
<tr><td colspan="2">Treasurer</td><td colspan="2">Bookkeepers</td><td>Factory Supts.</td><td></td><td>**SALES**</td><td></td><td>Collectors</td><td></td></tr>
<tr><td colspan="2">Asst. Treasurer</td><td colspan="2">Paymasters</td><td>Purchasing Agents</td><td></td><td>Sales Managers</td><td></td><td>Drivers</td><td></td></tr>
<tr><td colspan="2">Secretary</td><td colspan="2">Timekeepers</td><td>Messengers (Outside)</td><td></td><td>Asst. Sales Mgrs.</td><td></td><td rowspan="2">Drivers' Helpers (Other than brewers)</td><td></td></tr>
<tr><td colspan="2">Asst. Secretary</td><td colspan="2">Adjusters</td><td></td><td></td><td>Floorwalkers</td><td></td><td></td></tr>
<tr><td colspan="2">Comptroller</td><td colspan="2"></td><td>**STOCK**</td><td></td><td>Buyers</td><td></td><td>Chauffeurs</td><td></td></tr>
<tr><td colspan="2">Asst. Comptroller</td><td colspan="2">**MANAGEMENT**</td><td rowspan="2">Shipping or Receiving Clerks</td><td></td><td>Asst. Buyers</td><td></td><td></td><td></td></tr>
<tr><td colspan="2"></td><td colspan="2">Managers</td><td></td><td rowspan="2">Salesmen (Outside who collect)</td><td></td><td></td><td></td></tr>
<tr><td colspan="2"></td><td colspan="2"></td><td>Stock Clerks</td><td></td><td></td><td></td><td></td></tr>
<tr><td colspan="6"></td><td colspan="2">**Total Class 1 and/or 2 Employees**</td><td></td></tr>
<tr><td colspan="6"></td><td colspan="2">**Total All Employees**</td><td></td></tr>
</table>

NOTES

7

PUBLIC LIABILITY

			Sold Under Applicant's Label		Annual Sales
		a. List and describe all products manufactured, handled, distributed and sold and the intended use.	Yes	No	
		(1) _____			
		(2) _____			
		(3) _____			
		(4) _____			
		(5) _____			
		Secure copies of advertising material, catalogues and labels describing above products and use.			
		b. Description of Completed Operations (if exposure exists)			Annual Receipts
		(1) _____			
		(2) _____			
		(3) _____			
		(4) _____			
55	Products and/or Completed Operations	c. Products manufactured or prepared by others bearing name or label of client.			
		d. Products manufactured or prepared by others which do NOT bear name or label of client.			
		e. Do you issue any warrantee of products? Describe or submit copy.			
		f. Are prizes or premiums given away or sold? Describe.			
		g. Do you have written or verbal hold harmless agreements with your wholesalers or retailers? Secure copy or give details.			
		h. Are any imported products sold? (If any describe and submit contract.)			
		i. If question 8, page 1 indicates a foreign exposure, describe all products manufactured, handled, distributed, sold, the intended use and the countries where this activity occurs.			
		j. If applicant manufactures any product intended for use in aircraft, missiles, rockets, etc., give details.			
		k. Describe any experimental products and state when they are expected to go on the market.			
		l. List products which applicant no longer manufactures which varied from those now being produced.			
56	Contractors	Indicate type of contracting work and estimated annual receipts from each type. Describe XCU exposures.			
57	Work Done Under Contract	Description and cost of work done for you by others under contract.			
	except alterations and additions to client's premises	Do you require certificates of insurance? If so, submit copies.			

8

		PUBLIC LIABILITY (Continued)	
58	Alterations and Additions to Client's Premises	Are alterations or additions contemplated or in progress? Who will do work? Describe and indicate cost.	
59	Liability Assumed Under Contract	Have you assumed liability of others under: a. Lease agreements for real estate? b. Lease agreements for signs, refrigerators, etc.? c. Sidetrack agreements? d. Contracts for electric power, steam, etc.? e. Permits for wires, overpass, pipe line, etc., across private or public property? f. Other contracts (i.e., construction and installation agreements, compliance certificates, etc.) IMPORTANT: Obtain copies.	
60	Away From Premises Where Questions Apply Obtain Details	Does your firm: a. Own or maintain advertising signs? b. Sponsor athletic teams or any other unusual advertising medium? c. Own, hire or use boats? d. Loan or rent equipment to others? e. Exhibit at fairs, exhibitions or trade shows? f. Install, service, remove or demonstrate any products? Receipts.	
61	Nuclear Materials	Does your firm: a. Operate any nuclear reactors, fabricate fuel or handle nuclear waste materials? b. Supply services, materials, parts or equipment in connection with a nuclear facility? c. Transport nuclear materials?	
62	Miscellaneous Liability	Describe any other operations involving liability exposures. (Examples: Ownership or operation of industrial village, industrial railroad, swimming pools, bathing beaches, grandstands, gymnasiums, bowling alleys, ski-tows, toboggans, sale of electricity to others, dams, reservoirs, tanks or storage of flammables including gasoline, LPG and other similar liquids or gases.)	
63	Liability for Malpractice Not Applicable to Private or Public Hospitals or Clinics	Do you maintain a hospital, infirmary or first aid station for your employees? Are members of public admitted? Describe.	
		Number of doctors: (a) on your payroll (b) under contract (c) on call	
		Number of nurses: (a) Registered (b) Not registered	
		Any other hazards such as beauty parlor, barber shop or other professional service?	

NOTES

9

		Location 1	Location 2	Location 3	Location 4
	Estimated annual payroll (for all officers and employees according to classification which best describes duties):				
	a. Office work only (including draftsmen whose duties are confined to office work).				
64	b. Outside salesmen, collectors or messengers (who do not deliver merchandise).				
	c. Chauffeurs, drivers and their helpers (including driver-salesmen).				
	d. All others*.				
	e.				
	*Governing classification usually applies to all other employees. If not, show division on lines d and e.				
65	Does each job applicant complete a ☐ Prior Employment History Questionnaire? ☐ Medical History Questionnaire?				
66	Are pre-employment physical examinations given or required?				
	Are periodic checkups given or required?				
67	Give age and duties of any employee under 18.				
68	Number of employees in each age category? _____ Under 30 _____ 30 to 40 _____ 41 to 55 _____ 56 to 65 _____ over 65				
69	What percent of employees work part-time or employed elsewhere? What do these employees do for you?				
70	Is there a safety committee? If so, who are its members?				
	How often are safety meetings held?				
71	If there is a Loss Control Program, does it include ☐ Full time Director? ☐ Written procedures and records? ☐ Formal employee training programs? ☐ Accident investigation, recommendations for corrective action and follow-up? ☐ Periodic checks on safety equipment? ☐ "Light work" rehiring/retraining program for injured employees?				
72	Have you ever been cited for OSHA violations? If so, when and for what?				
73	Are Workers' Compensation Certificates of Insurance required on work done for you under contract?				
74	Do employees belong to a union?				
75	Do any of your employees work in other states? (Permanent or itinerant?)				
76	Do your employees ever go aboard boats in line of employment? Describe.				
77	Do you sponsor employee recreational facilities or extraneous activities?				
78	Any liquor liability exposure?				
79	Are restaurant facilities provided for employees?				

NOTES

10

BUSINESS INTERRUPTION AND OTHER TIME ELEMENT EXPOSURES

80	Business Interruption	Total annual ordinary payroll (excluding Officers, Executives, Department Managers, employees under contract and other important employees whose pay would continue during period of business interruption).	
		Annual Gross Sales less discounts, returns, bad accounts, prepaid freight.	
		Annual cost of raw materials entering into article produced, or cost of merchandise sold.	
		Annual cost of heat, light and power.	
		Estimated percentage of increase or decrease in profits for coming year.	
		Is continued full-time operation of your plant dependent upon any one supplier or customer?	
		Is your business dependent upon outside heat, light or power? Give details.	
81	Extra Expense	If your premises are damaged, what percentage of your business could be continued at another location?	
		Estimate of "extra expenses" in order to carry on business at another location.	
		If your premises are damaged, what percentage of your business could be continued at your present location?	
		Estimate of "extra expense" in order to continue business at your present location.	
82	Leasehold and Rents Tenant	Is there a written lease?	
		Present monthly rent.	
		Estimated cost of similar facilities elsewhere.	
		Was an advance rental or cash bonus paid?	
		Are premises sublet at a higher rental?	
83	Rental Income or Value Owner	Annual Rental Income from tenants?	
		Annual Rental Value of part of premises occupied?	

NOTES

11

84 DESCRIPTION OF OWNED AUTOMOBILES AND TRAILERS

Insured's Vehicle Number	Model Year	Original Cost New	Make	Body Type and Model	Identification Number	Town-State Principally Garaged	Use *	Radius **	Weight ***	Value if not ACV

*USE
"S" (Service) — Transportation of Personnel, tools and equipment and usually parked at job site.
"R" (Retail) — House to House Delivery.
"C" (Commercial) — All other.
If more than one use, indicate uses and percentages.

**RADIUS — Measured as straight line from point of principal garaging.
***WEIGHT GVW or GCW in pounds.
GVW — Recommended maximum weight of vehicle and load.
GCW — Recommended maximum weight of vehicle, trailer and load combined.

LIST ALL PERSONS WHO DRIVE OWNED AUTOMOBILES

Vehicle Number	Name and Address	Married Y-N	Date of Birth	License Number	State	Sex M-F	Years Licensed	Good Student	Driver Training	Miles one way to work or school	Pleasure Business Farm

For drivers of Private Passenger Vehicles

12

AUTOMOBILE (Continued)

85	Are any Statutory Filings Required? ICC, State Utility Commission, Financial Responsibility.	
86	Are operations periodic or seasonal, resulting in the lay-up of any vehicles for 30 consecutive days or more? Indicate vehicles by item number.	
87	Are owned vehicles used to transport employees or others? Describe.	
88	Name officers, partners or employees who are permitted personal use of company owned vehicles.	
89	Are owned vehicles used for towing special equipment (air compressors, concrete mixers, etc.)?	
90	Are vehicles rented, leased or loaned to others? Explain.	
91	Has liability been assumed under any contract relating to vehicles?	
92	Hired Cars	Estimated annual cost of hire: a. Private passenger cars	
		b. Truckers	
		c. Public transportation automobiles, moving van associations and freight forwarders.	

NOTES

AIRCRAFT

93	Do you own any aircraft? Give make, year, cost and use.	
94	List name and title of any officer or employee who pilots the aircraft for use in your business.	
95	Do you hire, lease or charter aircraft? How frequently?	
96	Do any of your officers or employees own or hire aircraft for use in your business? Describe.	
97	How many officers or employees regularly use commercial aircraft for business travel?	

Answer Supplementary Questions if Applicable then Turn to Loss Experience — Page 17

SUPPLEMENTARY QUESTIONS FOR AUTOMOBILE DEALERS, GARAGES, ETC.

Check ☐ Franchised Dealer   ☐ Non-Franchised Dealer   ☐ Storage Garage or Public Parking Place
       ☐ Service Station   ☐ Equipment and Implement Dealer

A.	Make of cars, trucks, motorcycles or other vehicles handled? If foreign made, submit copy of contract or dealer franchise.	
B.	Makes and amounts of any agricultural or construction equipment, snowmobiles, auto homes, campers or other recreational vehicles handled? Describe.	
C.	Do officers, co-partners, salesmen or employees have separate insurance coverage on their privately owned automobiles?	
D.	Do you own any cars or trucks which are not used principally in connection with your dealership, garage, service station, etc.?	
E.	Do you rent cars to others: a. With drivers? b. Without drivers?	
F.	Do you loan cars to customers? To what extent?	
G.	Do you own or hire vehicles or trailers used as "haulaways" for conveyance of automobiles or tank trucks for delivery of gas or oil?	
H.	Do you "drive away" cars from factory or distribution point? Describe.	
I.	Do you finance your own automobiles or retain any security interest? Explain.	
J.	Do automobiles owned by you engage in any pre-arranged or organized racing or speed contest? Explain. Do you sponsor racing cars?	
K.	Do you do spray painting? Where?	
L.	Do you have inside gasoline pumps?	
M.	Do you call for or deliver customer's cars? How many per day?	
N.	How many sets of plates do you hold? Dealers _____ Regular _____ Transporter _____ Junk Dealer _____	

		Location 1	Location 2	Location 3	Location 4	Location 5
O.	Estimated annual payroll: a. Clerical office employees. b. Proprietors, partners, officers, salesmen, general managers, service managers & chauffeurs. ($2000 each) c. All other employees.					
P.	Owned Autos: Maximum number and value at any one time? New					
	Used					
Q.	Consigned Autos: Maximum equity at any time? (If under "Floor Plan," is Dealer's equity insured?)					
R.	Do you ever use an open lot or unattended building for storing or selling cars? Is lot enclosed?					
S.	Customer's cars left for repair or storage Max. Number					
	Max. Value					
T.	If the risk is a franchised or a non-franchised dealer, is Limited Liability Coverage for certain insureds desired? ☐ Yes ☐ No					

14

SUPPLEMENTARY QUESTIONS FOR LAUNDRIES AND CLEANERS
(If client conducts both operations, complete both columns)

			Laundry	Cleaner
A.	Gross receipts past 12 months			
B.	What percentage is cash and carry?			
C.	What percentage is . . .	Retail?		
		Wholesale?		
D.	Number of orders handled weekly?			
E.	Approximate number of orders in custody at one time? (By locations.)			
F.	Average number days in custody	Cash and carry		
		To be delivered		
G.	Average value per order			
H.	What kind of solvent is used?		XXXXXX	
I.	Is cleaning room separated from remainder of plant? How?		XXXXXX	
J.	Is boiler room separated from remainder of plant? How?			
K.	Do you store furs or other goods on instruction from customers? Give details.			
L.	Have you sustained any fire, theft or other losses to customers' goods during last 3 years? Describe.			

NOTES

15

SUPPLEMENTARY QUESTIONS FOR EMPLOYEE BENEFITS

A.	Life Accident and Group Insurance	Check coverages now in effect:
		☐ Business Life
		☐ "Key Man" Life
		☐ "Key Man" Accident
		☐ "Key Man" Health
		☐ Salary Budget Income Protection Plan (A&H)
		
		☐ Group Life
		☐ Group Accident and Health
		☐ Group Hospitalization
		☐ Profit Sharing Plan
		    Funding Agency _____
		☐ Pension Plan
		    Funding Agency _____

B.	Group Proposal	If Group Insurance Proposal is contemplated, obtain the following: 1 — Copy of Employee Announcement Booklet and Employee Certificate. 2 — Copy of current premium statement. 3 — Last 2-3 years premiums and claims. (If over 100 insured employees, U.S. Dept. of Labor Form A-1 will provide data.) If separate analysis of investment return and/or plan features is contemplated, plan and trust documents, contracts and asset information should be obtained.

SUPPLEMENTARY QUESTIONS FOR FIDELITY COVERAGE

A.	Fidelity Exposure	The exposure Formula is derived from two principal elements of exposure to large dishonesty losses: (1) — Current Assets and (2) Gross Sales or Income. For businesses which perform service functions such as transporting the property of others, or which perform work on or process the property of others, the value of that property should be included in the "Total Current Assets" and the "Goods on Hand" totals. For firms acting in an agency capacity which have custody of cash, securities, etc., belonging to others, or have disbursing or collecting responsibilities (insurance agents, for example), the average amount of such items on hand at one time should be included in "Total Current Assets" and the annual volume of such items should be included in "Annual Gross Sales or Income".

How Much Honesty Insurance Should The Firm Carry?
(Refer to the Exposure Index Formula)

B.	**Formula**
	
	1. Enter the firm's total current Assets (cash, deposits, securities, receivables, goods on hand, etc.,) .... $_____
	
	  A.* Enter the value of Goods on Hand (raw materials, materials, materials in process, finished merchandise or products) .... $_____
	
	  B.* Enter 5% of A .... $_____
	
	  C. Enter Current Assets less Goods on Hand, i.e., the difference between 1 and 1A .... $_____
	
	  D. Enter 20% of C .... $_____
	
	2. Enter Annual Gross Sales or Income .... $_____
	
	  A. Enter 10% of 2 .... $_____
	
	3. Total is Firm's Dishonesty Exposure Index .. $_____
	
	4. Suggested Minimum Amount of Honesty Insurance (Apply total in line 3 to table in right-hand column to determine suggested minimum amount of Honesty Insurance) .... $_____
	  * If separate figure for Goods on Hand is not available, omit 1A and 1B and insert the total Current Assets figure in line C.
	
	NOTE: The suggested amounts are minimum amounts and must not be interpreted as the maximum amounts which may be needed to provide indemnity to the full extent of losses which may occur.
		Suggested Minimum Amounts of Honesty Insurance
		
		Exposure Index
			Amount of Bond

Exposure Index	Amount of Bond
Up to — $ 25,000	$ 15,000 — $ 25,000
$ 25,000 — 125,000	25,000 — 50,000
125,000 — 250,000	50,000 — 75,000
250,000 — 500,000	75,000 — 100,000
500,000 — 750,000	100,000 — 125,000
750,000 — 1,000,000	125,000 — 150,000
1,000,000 — 1,375,000	150,000 — 175,000
1,375,000 — 1,750,000	175,000 — 200,000
1,750,000 — 2,125,000	200,000 — 225,000
2,125,000 — 2,500,000	225,000 — 250,000
2,500,000 — 3,325,000	250,000 — 300,000
3,325,000 — 4,175,000	300,000 — 350,000
4,175,000 — 5,000,000	350,000 — 400,000
5,000,000 — 6,075,000	400,000 — 450,000
6,075,000 — 7,150,000	450,000 — 500,000
7,150,000 — 9,275,000	500,000 — 600,000
9,275,000 — 11,425,000	600,000 — 700,000
11,425,000 — 15,000,000	700,000 — 800,000
15,000,000 — 20,000,000	800,000 — 900,000
20,000,000 — 25,000,000	900,000 — 1,000,000
25,000,000 — 50,000,000	1,000,000 — 1,250,000
50,000,000 — 87,500,000	1,250,000 — 1,500,000
87,500,000 — 125,000,000	1,500,000 — 1,750,000
125,000,000 — 187,500,000	1,750,000 — 2,000,000
187,500,000 — 250,000,000	2,000,000 — 2,250,000
250,000,000 — 333,325,000	2,250,000 — 2,500,000
333,325,000 — 500,000,000	2,500,000 — 3,000,000

16

LOSS EXPERIENCE — ALL LINES

Loss experience is vital to underwriting and pricing an account. The more information secured, the more quickly an underwriting judgement can be made and the most competitive price developed. Also, underwriting judgement is based on other factors such as:

MANAGEMENT ATTITUDE

Does client have a written Safety and Loss Control Program? ☐ Yes ☐ No

Is the program working? ☐ Yes ☐ No

Who is responsible for the program _____

PHYSICAL CONDITION OF PREMISES AND EQUIPMENT

Housekeeping is ☐ Good ☐ Fair ☐ Poor

Premises maintenance is ☐ Good ☐ Fair ☐ Poor

Equipment maintenance is ☐ Good ☐ Fair ☐ Poor

LOSSES — PAST THREE YEARS

Coverage	Date of Loss	Amount	Description of Loss
Buildings Fire and Allied Lines			
Contents Fire and Allied Lines Incl. Open Stock Burglary			
Valuable Papers			
Accounts Receivable			
Shipments — Transportation			
Other Inland Marine Lines			

17

740

Coverage	Date of Loss	Amount	Description of Loss
Money and Securities			
Employee Dishonesty — Check Forgery			
Public Liability Other Than Products (BI - PD)			
Products Liability (BI - PD)			
Workers' Compensation			
Auto (BI - PD)			
Auto Physical Damage			

LOSSES — PAST THREE YEARS — Continued

Experience Rating: — Premiums and Losses for each of the previous five years are required for risks which qualify.

18

INDEX

A

Abnormal credit loss, 431
Abstract of title, 437
Accident prevention, 225–26
Accidental death benefit, 548
Accountants professional liability, 373–75
  breach of contract, 374
  fraud, 374–75
Accounts receivable coverage, 432, 482, 513
  data processing insurance, 668–69
Actual cash value (ACV), 89–90, 102–3, 121, 510
Actual loss sustained, 144, 424
Adverse possession, 440
Aetna Plan Questionnaire, 717–40
Affirmative warranty, 91
Age Discrimination in Employment Act, 625
Aggregate deductible, 104
Aggregate excess insurance, 285
Agreed amount endorsement, 102–3
Aircraft hull all-risks policy, 347
All-inclusive rate, 451
All-risks coverage, 73–74, 97–98, 120
  difference in conditions policy, 465, 467, 468
  special multi-peril policy, 509
  transit insurance, 128
Alter ego cases, 163
American conditions clause, 325
American Institute for Property and Liability
    Underwriters, 717
American International Group, 708
American Land Title Association Commitment
    for Title Insurance, 449
American Management Association, 5
American open cargo policy, 330–31
American Steamship Owners P & I
    Association, 337
Apparent off-record title risk, 440
Appraisal, 111
Approved pilot clause, 68
Architects and engineers professional liability,
    375–79
Aronson, Sidney, 683
Assault and battery, 275–76
  professional liability, 365–66
Attorney, liability claims against, 70, 369–73,
    381–83
Audit of premises, 208
Automatic sprinkler system insurance, 13, 150,
    508–9
Automobile, definition, 233, 251
Automobile liability, 64, 220–44
  bodily injury claims, 197, 221
  business auto policy; see Business auto
    policy
  commercial auto risks, 220
  compulsory insurance, 223

Automobile liability (cont.)
  garage risks, 221
  general liability-automobile policy; see
    General liability-automobile policy
  group insurance, 641
  leasing, 220, 222, 224
  liability risk, 221
  noninsurance risk handling methods, 224–28
  physical damage to vehicle, 221
  property damage, 221
  public auto category, 220–21
  statutory requirements, 223–24
Automobile medical payments, 252
Aviation insurance, 24, 68, 96, 197, 341–50
  charters and rentals, 346
  ground rules, 342
  liability, 343–47
  physical damage to craft, 347–50

B

Bambury, Joseph A., Jr., Esquire, 113
Basic automobile liability insurance coverage,
    252
Basic premium, 282
Benefit period, 543
Bid bonds, 313, 314
Bidek, Charles T., 247
Bill, Robert E., 716, 717
  Risk Profile, 716–22
Binder, 86
Birnbaum, Sheila L., 289
Blanket coverage
  business interruption insurance, 152
  direct damage to building contents, 121
  property damage, 104–5
Blanket crime policy, 156, 173–74
Blanket rating formula, 105–6
Blanton, James C., 247
Blick, George L., 311
Blue Cross-Blue Shield, 540–41
Bodily injury, 195–98
  commercial auto liability, 221
  definition, 275–76
  garage policy, 258–60
  truckers liability, 248–49
Boiler and machinery insurance, 71, 125
  business interruption, 424–25
  businessowners' policy, 481
  conditions, 423–24
  definitions, 421–23
  exclusions, 423
  inspection and suspension, 425
  questions for agent, 428–29
  special multi-peril policy, 505–6, 516
  state laws, 425–26
  use and occupancy, 136

Boilers and pressure vessels coverage, 420–21
Bond, 157
BOP; *see* Businessowners' policy
Borel v. Fibreboard Corporation, 707
Bossen, Wendell J., 593
Bowers, James W., 183
Breach of contract, 365, 374
Breach of express or implied warranty, 67
Broad form comprehensive general liability
  endorsement, 190
Broad form property damage (BFPD)
  endorsement, 190, 202–3, 487
Broad form storekeepers' coverage, 513
Broker, 22
  fixed-fee arrangement, 25
  liability of, 70
  rating, 24–25
  selection of, 25–26
Builders risk completed value forms, 509
Buildings and fixtures insurance, 84–111, 117
  BOP coverage, 474–77
  BOP eligibility guidelines, 473–74
  definition, 93
  general property form, 93–97
  special multi-peril policy, 507–8
Burglary and robbery insurance, 61, 481,
  512–13
Bus van insurance, 221
Business auto policy (BAP), 228–44
  covered autos, 233
  deductibles, 237, 238–39
  exclusions, 230
  liability insurance coverage, 229–30
  medical payments coverage, 231
  no-fault coverage, 230–31
  options, 236–40
  physical damage coverages, 232
  premium computations, 240–43
  questions to be asked of broker, 243
  uninsured motorist coverage, 231–32
Business continuation insurance
  partnership; *see* Partnership
  sole proprietor; *see* Sole proprietorship
    business continuation insurance
Business interruption insurance, 61, 133,
  136–52
  blanket, 152
  contingent, 143–44
  data processing insurance, 670–71
  endorsements, 150–51
  leasehold interest, 152
  major clauses in forms, 144–50
  rental value, 151–52
  special multi-peril policy, 510–11
Business legal expense insurance, 78
  coverage, 685–86
  eligibility, 687
  examples of utilization, 687–89
  exclusions, 686–87
  need for, 684–85
  plans available, 687
Business overhead expense insurance, 544
Business personal property insurance; *see*
  Personal property insurance

Businessowners policy (BOP), 67, 74, 506–7
  building coverage, 474–77
  cancellation provisions, 480–81
  conditions, 489–94
  eligibility, 472–74
  exclusions, 479–80
  insured, definition of, 488–89
  liability coverages, 486
  loss of income coverage, 478
  medical payments, 488
  optional coverages, 480–82
  personal property coverage, 477–82
  personal property eligibility guidelines, 473,
    474–75
  policy period, 491
  questions for agent, 496–97
  rating, 494–95
  special policy form, 482–86
  standard policy, 472, 474, 475–82
  territory, 491
  time of inception, 491
Buy-sell agreements, 75, 76, 552–53, 571–75,
  583–86, 591
  funding, 586
  life insurance products, 586–87

C

Cafeteria benefit plans, 610–11
Canterbury v. Spence, 362
Captive insurance companies, 17–18, 35, 286
  cargo insurance, 332
Cargo insurance, 249, 254–55
  all-risk insurance, 326–27
  average clauses, 325
  deviation clause, 327–28
  exclusions, 326–27
  factors affecting cost, 330–31
  forms, 323–24
  franchises, 325–26
  general average, 327
  import/export, 329
  international competition, 331
  perils covered, 324–25
  rating, 329–30
  risk management techniques, 331–33
  salvage, 327
  valuation, 328
  warehouse to warehouse, 327
Carman, Charles H., 311
Carter Hawley Hale, Inc., 690
Carter, James A., 519
Carton, Patrick F., 113
Cash value policies, 546
Casualty insurance, 23
Catastrophic loss coverage, 464
Chain of title, 436, 438, 439
Church theft insurance, 513
Civil authority interruption of business
  insurance, 148
Claim adjustments, 21–22, 131–33
  costs, 132–33
  time limitations, 132
Claim and recovery of sequestration, 316

Claim reserve, 208
Claims-made basis liability policy, 384–85, 402, 403, 408
Claims-occurred policies, 408
Class action suit, 401
Class rating formula, 105
Clement Associates, Inc., 709
Close corporation business continuation
  buy-sell agreements, 583–86
  nature of, 582–83
  transfer of ownership, 583
  valuation, 588–91
Coca-Cola Company of Los Angeles, 690
Co-insurance, 90, 95
  businessowners' policy, 475
  contribution clause, 138, 139
  credit policies, 431
  difference in conditions contract, 467
  floater policies, 130
  tender offer defense expense insurance, 691
Commercial automobile risks; *see* Automobile liability; Business auto policy; *and* General liability-automobile policy
Commercial blanket bond, 156
Commercial policies, 156
  coverages, 157–60
  employees, 161–62
  exclusions, 163–67
  inventory exclusion clause, 162, 164–66
  joint insureds, 176
  libel or slander, 176–77
  limits and liabilities, 173–75
  notice and proof of loss, 167–73
  riders, 177
  subrogation, 176
  suit limitations, 171
  valuation, 175
Commercial property floater policies, 129–30
Commercial umbrella policy; *see* Umbrella liability policy
Completed operations liability, 67, 186, 203, 291, 298–301
Composite rates, 209
Comprehensive automobile liability policy, 65, 252
  underlying policy requirements, 459–60
Comprehensive coverage; *see* All-risk coverage
Comprehensive dishonesty, disappearance and destruction policy (Three-D policy), 156
Comprehensive Environmental Response, Compensation, and Liability Act (Superfund), 701, 702–4, 706
Comprehensive general liability (CGL) policy, 67
  applicable limits, 293–95
  automatically covered risks, 184–86
  aviation insurance, 343
  basic policy, 188–89
  bodily injury, 195–98
  checklist, 214
  cooperation duty of insured, 213–14
  conflicts of interest, 212–13
  coverage of policy, 191–207
  declarations, 188

Comprehensive general liability (CGL) policy *(cont.)*
  endorsements, 189–90
  environmental impairment liability, 708
  extra coverage for additional liability risks, 186–87
  insurer defense obligation, 211–12
  notice, 210–11
  occurrence, 294–96
  personal injury, 205–7
  policy jacket, 190–91
  policy territory, 293
  property damage, 198–205
  products hazard clause, 296–98
  products liability, 291–92
  rate bases, 207
  underlying policy requirements, 459–60
Comprehensive hospital-surgical-major medical insurance, 541
Compromise transfer, 20
Compulsory automobile insurance, 223
Computer facility insurance; *see* Data processing insurance
Condominium insurance, 509
Conflict of interest, 370–71, 372
Consequential damage, 424
Construction and related contract bonds, 313–15
Consumer Product Safety Act, 11
Contents, insurance of; *see also* Real property insurance
  care, custody, and control, 115–16
  claims, 131–33
  contractual exposure, 116
  coverage, 120–25
  fixtures, 117
  identification of, 116–17
  inventory, 118
  off-premises property, 119–20
  ownership concept, 115
  package policies, 122–23
  policy forms, 120–31
  special assets, 119
  supplies and equipment, 118–19
  valuable papers, 119–20
Contingent liability coverage, 185
Continuous negligence rule, 364
Contractual liability, 186–87, 197–98, 202
Contribution clause, 137, 138, 139, 145–46, 147, 150
Contributing property coverage, 143
Corleto v. Shore Memorial Hospital, 367, 368
Corporate redemptions, 587–88
Corporation professional liability, 70–71, 387–89
  directors' and officers' liability insurance; *see* Directors' and officers' liability insurance
Cost-plus insurance, 243
Counterfeit paper currency coverage, 160, 505, 515
Court fiduciary bond, 316
Covered auto symbols, 233–36
CPCU, 717

Credit insurance, 72, 430–32
co-insurance clause, 431
foreign, 432
Crime insurance, 505, 512, 513
Criss cross (cross purchase) agreement, 76,
583–84
Crop bail insurance, 529–30
Cross purchase (criss-cross) agreement, 76,
583–84

D

Damages, definition, 408–9
*Darling v. Charleston Community Memorial
Hospital*, 367, 368
Data processing insurance, 78, 130, 148
accounts receivable insurance, 668–69
business interruption insurance, 670–71
difference in condition policy, 665–66
disaster plan, 662
equipment insurance, 662–67
errors and omissions liability, 672–74
extra expense insurance, 671–72
general policies, 664
lease clauses, 663
risk and insurance survey, 676–81
user or employer negligence, 666–67
Data storage media insurance, 667–68
DC-10 case, 400
Decreasing term insurance, 546
Deductibles, 14, 95, 103–4
aggregate, 104
auto insurance, 237, 238–39
business interruption coverage, 424–25
hull insurance, 334
occurrence basis, 104
per claim basis, 104
special multi-peril policy, 510
Defective products, 66–67
Deferred compensation plans, 602–7
annuity funded, 605
life insurance funded, 604–5
majority stockholders, 607
mutual funds, 605
tax aspects, 603
Defined benefit pension plan, 646, 648,
649–50
advantages and disadvantages, 649–50
deposit administration funding method,
656–57
federal regulations, 650
group unallocated funding method, 648, 656
immediate participation guarantee funding
method, 656–57
termination insurance, 654
Defined contribution money purchase pension
plan, 646
Defined contribution pension plan, 646–50
advantages and disadvantages, 648–49
termination insurance, 654
Defined contribution profit-sharing plan, 647
Demolition coverage, 100
Dental insurance, 633–36
Deposit administration (DA) contracts, 656
Deposit premium, 209
Depositors forgery policy, 62, 160, 505, 515

Derivative action suit, 401
Difference in conditions (DIC) policy, 73, 97,
130
co-insurance, 467
coverage, 464–65
data processing insurance, 665–66
deductible, 466
indirect loss, 468
other insurance clause, 467
perils covered, 465–67
Direct property loss, 4
Direct writer, 22
Directors' and officers' (D&O) liability
insurance, 388–89
executive officer, defined, 407
fiduciary liability insurance, 407–10
international considerations, 407
kidnap and ransom, 410–14
law suits against, 402
legal expenses, 405
need for coverage, 399
nonprofit board, 406
obligations of directors and officers, 400–402
policy, 402–7
political risks insurance, 414–16
subsidiaries, 404
Disability buy-out insurance, 551, 578
Disability insurance, 542–44
business overhead expense, 544
group, 632–33
partnership, 575–78
pension plans, 655
policy considerations, 543–44
taxation, 544
Disability waiver of premium, 548
Discovery period provision of liability policy,
403
Discovery rule, 355, 364
Dishonesty, defined, 157
Dishonesty insurance; *see also* Commercial
policies
definitions, 157–59
employees, 161–62
history of, 157–59
notice and proof of loss, 167–73
risk management, 177–78
types of policies available, 156–57
Divestiture, 8, 20
Dividends
fifth dividend option, 549
paid-up additions, 548
premium reduction, 549
Divorce actions, 371
Dram shop exposure, 197
Drive other car (DOC) coverage, 237
Druggists' professional liability coverage, 487
Dual-form basis liability policy, 403

E

Earnings insurance, 141–43
privacy of financial information, 142–43
Earthquake insurance, 99, 482, 509
Easement, 443, 450
Eblen, Frank L., 219
EDS Federal Corporation, 98

EIL insurance; *see* Environmental impairment liability insurance
Electronic data processing (EDP) policy, 78, 130
  business interruption insurance, 148
Employee
  definition, 161
  liability insurance, 193–94
Employee benefits, 76–77
Employee dishonesty insurance, 157, 161, 480, 505, 515
Employee Retirement Income Security Act (ERISA), 24, 71, 651–54
  fiduciary responsibility insurance, 407–10, 653–54
  minimum standards, 653
  regulation of group benefit plans, 626
  reporting and disclosure, 652
Employee stock ownership plan (ESOP), 598
Employer-financed insurance, 611–12
Employers' liability, 268–86; *see also* Workers' compensation insurance
  captive insurance company, 286
  farmers' insurance, 528–29
  historical perspective, 268–69
  risk management techniques, 279–86
  self-insurance, 285–86
  standard workers' compensation and employers' liability policy, 274–79
  statutory requirements, 289
Endorsements, 59, 60
Engineers' professional liability; *see* Architects' and engineers' professional liability
Entity plan, 76
Environmental impairment liability (EIL) insurance, 700–713
  availability and markets, 708–9
  common law liability, 704, 706–7
  reducing risks, 712–13
  risk assessment techniques, 709–12
  statutory and regulatory requirements, 700–704
Environmental Protection Agency (EPA), 701, 702
Equal Employment Opportunities Commission, 625
ERISA; *see* Employee Retirement Income Security Act
Errors and omissions (E&O) insurance, 70, 185
  data processing, 672–74
Estate planning, 554
Estoppel, 87, 88
Excess loss premium factor, 283
Excess liability coverage, 456–59
Excess and surplus lines markets, 100–101
Executive benefit plans, 77, 594–621
Executive health plans, 613–14
Executive liability; *see* Directors' and officers' liability
Executive officer, defined, 407
Expenses to reduce loss, 147
Experience rates, 208–9, 242, 280–81
Explosion, collapse, and underground (XCU) property damage, 190, 204–5
Export-Import Bank, 431

Express warranty, 290
Exterior signs coverage, 480
Extinguishment, 89
Extra expense insurance, 137, 144, 511
  data processing, 671–72

F

Fair access to insurance requirements (FAIR) plan, 100
Family insurance riders, 548
Farm/ranch owners' insurance, 74
Farm and ranch safety management kit, 533
Farmers' insurance, 521–35
  crop hail insurance, 529–30
  farmowners' (farm package) policy, 521–28
  insurance to value, 534–35
  livestock mortality insurance, 530–32
  loss control, 533
  safety, 532–33
  workers' compensation and employers' liability, 528–29
Farmowners' (farm package) policy, 521–28
  additional features and extensions, 526–27
  all-risk perils form, 525
  basic perils coverage, 521–23
  broad perils coverage, 523–25
  liability coverage, 527–28
  property requiring specific insurance, 525–26
Faunce, John D., 717
Federal Crime Insurance Program, 62
Federal Insurance Administration, 98, 100
Federal Riot Reinsurance Program, 100
Federal Vocational Rehabilitation Act, 272
Fee simple estates, 442–43
Fellow-servant exclusion, 238
Ferrara v. Galluchio, 363
Fidelity bonds, 62
Fiduciary bonds, 317
Fiduciary liability insurance, 407–10
  claims-made policies, 408
  defense costs, 409
  ERISA, 407–10
  recourse, 409
  termination, 409
Fifth dividend option, 549
Financial guaranty bonds, 317
Financial institution bonds, 157
  employee, 161
  exclusions, 163
  notice and proof of loss, 167
Financial responsibility laws, 223
Financial statements, 5
Fire insurance policies
  New York standard fire policy, 93
  perils insured, 95–96
  pro rata clause, 149
  standard; *see* Standard fire policy
  Texas standard fire policy, 93
Fire legal liability, 190
  businessowners' policy, 487
Fire losses, 12
  hazard reduction, 12–13
Firestone 500 Tire case, 400
Fixed-fee brokerage arrangement, 25

Fixtures; *see* Buildings and fixtures insurance
Flanigan, George B., 455
Floater policies, 129–30
Flood, John E., Jr., 435
Flood, defined, 130–31
Flood Disaster Protection Act of 1973, 130
Flood insurance, 98–99, 130–31
Floor plan policies, 129
Flowers, Theodore W., Esquire, 83
Foley, Peter H., 397
Following form contract, 456
Ford Pinto case, 400, 458
Foreign credit insurance, 431–32
Foreign Credit Insurance Association (FCIA),
    72, 415, 431
Forgery, 61
    insurance, 62, 160, 505, 515
Forms, 59, 60, 61
Franchise, 325–26
Fraud, 374–75
Fraudulent concealment rule, 364
Free of particular average (FPA) conditions,
    325
Fringe benefits, 579, 594–621
    cafeteria benefit plans, 610–11
    choosing program, 619–20
    definition, 624
    dental insurance, 633–36
    employer-financed insurance, 611–12
    employer packaging assistance, 642
    executive health plans, 613–14
    general personnel, 624–43
    group auto insurance, 641
    group insurance benefit plans, 625–36
    group legal insurance, 640–41
    interest free loans, 612–13
    introduction and follow-up with employees,
        620–21
    key employees, 594–621
    medical reimbursement plans, 614
    pensions; *see* Pension plans
    planning for receipt at death, 617–19
    planning for receipt at retirement, 614–17
    questions for agent or broker, 642–43
    regulation of insured employee benefits,
        625–26
    risk management techniques, 639
    selecting agent or broker, 619–20
    vision care, 641–42
Future Farmers of America, 533

G

Garage liability form, 65
Garage risk, 221
    garage liability form, 65
    garagekeepers' insurance form, 65
    medical payments coverage, 264–65
    policy, 67, 258–65
Garagekeepers' insurance, 65, 260–62
General building form, 508
General liability-automobile policy, 250
    coverage provided, 252–53
    exclusions, 253
    insured, 252
    policy construction and rating, 250–51
    terms defined, 251–52

General liability insurance, special forms, 187
General liability risks; *see* Comprehensive
    general liability policy
General personal property form, 508
General property form, 93–97
    co-insurance, 95
    deductibles, 95
    exclusions, 96–97
    extensions of coverage, 94
    perils insured against, 95–96
    property covered, 93
    property not covered, 94
    valuation, 97
Glass damage insurance, 71–72, 429–30, 480
Glenn, Edward M., 471
Goulard, James E., 321
Gowell, Arthur, 539
Grant, W. T. Company, 401
Gross earnings form, 61, 136–41, 145, 511
Gross profit insurance, 40
Group auto insurance, 641
Group dental insurance, 633–36
Group disability income coverages, 632–33
Group health plans, 541–42, 629–32
    exclusions, 631
    hospital expense, 630
    major medical coverage, 630, 631
    nonsurgical medical expenses, 631
    surgical expenses, 630
Group insurance benefit plans, 625–36
    dental, 633–36
    disability income, 632–33
    emerging benefits, 639–42
    health, 629–32
    life insurance, 628–29
    regulation of, 625–26
    risk management, 639
Group legal services, 640
Group paid-up insurance, 629
Group permanent insurance, 608–9, 628
Group survivor income insurance, 629
Group term life insurance, 579, 607–8, 628
Group unallocated pension funding method,
    648, 656
Group underwriting, 77
Guarantee bond; *see* Surety bond
Guaranteed cost insurance, 280–81
Guaranteed insurability, 548
Guaranteed renewable policy, 542
Guarantees, 290
Guaranty bond; *see* Surety bond

H

Hand, Learned, 356
Harrington, John M., 3
Hart, B. C., Esquire, 183
Harwood, W. B., Jr., 321
*Hauenstein v. St. Paul Mercury Indemnity
    Co.*, 200
Hazardous waste disposal, 700
    common law liability, 704, 706–7
    liability insurance, 701
Health insurance
    Blue Cross–Blue Shield, 540–41
    comprehensive hospital-surgical-major
        medical coverage, 541

disability, 542–44
group health plans, 541
partnership, 579
sole proprietorship, 540–44
Health Maintenance Organizations (HMOs),
  77, 637–38
Henkel, Carroll E., 3
Hidden off-record title risk, 440
Highly protected risks (HPR), 23
Hodosh, Frederick R., 57
Holdback, 111
Hold-harmless agreements, 18–19, 31, 186,
  197–98
Home Insurance Company, 690
Hooker Chemical Company, 458
Hospital's professional liability, 366–69
Host liquor liability, 189–90
HR-10 Plan (Retirement Plan for
  Self-Employed Individual), 596
Hull insurance, 333–41
  assured and loss payable clauses, 334
  claims, 336
  collision liability, 335–36
  coverage, 337
  deductible, 334
  deliberate damage, 335
  duration of risk/policy term, 334
  general average, 335
  limits of liability and claims, 338–39
  loss of hire, 340
  markets, 340
  negotiations, 341
  perils, 334
  pilotage and towage, 336
  premiums, 337
  protection and indemnity insurance, 337
  rate, 334
  salvage, 335
  strikes, 340
  sue and labor, 335
  total loss, 335
  trading warranty, 337
  war risks, 339

I

Ignition key control, 262
Immediate participation guarantee pension
  funding method, 656–57
Implied warranty, 290
Inchmaree clause, 334
Incidental contracts, 186, 198
Income loss, 4
Income splitting, 564–65
Increased cost of construction endorsement,
  100
Indemnity, 88, 89
  agreements, 18–19
Independent contractors coverage, 185
Indirect property damage, 4, 59, 60
  blanket coverage, 152
  business interruption insurance; *see*
    Business interruption insurance
  gross earnings coverage, 137–43
  leasehold interest coverage, 152
  rental value coverage, 152

Individual Retirement Account (IRA), 550,
  596, 600
Inflation endorsement, 450
Inflation guard endorsement, 102
Informed consent, theory of, 361–63, 366–67,
  368–69
Inland marine insurance, 119, 513
Inman v. Binghamton Housing Authority,
  377–78
Innkeepers' liability, 513
Inside the premium coverage, 160
Insurable interest, 88–89
Insurance agents, liability of, 70
Insurance charge, 282
Insurance companies
  claim adjustment, 21–22
  direct writing, 22
  rating bureaus, 27
  selection of, 21
Insurance contracts
  actual cash value, 89–90
  claims settlement, 131–33
  co-insurance, 90–91
  extinguishment, 89
  indemnity, 88
  insurable interest, 88–89
  representation, 91–92
  subrogation, 92
  valued policy, 91
  warranty, 91–92
Insurance Institute of America, 717
Insurance limits relative to value, 101–5
Insurance markets, 22–24
Insurance policies; *see also* specific kinds
  cancellation, 87–88
  contractual requirements, 85–86
  guaranteed renewable, 542
  lapse, 86–87
  noncancellable, 542
  property, 120–31, 132
  real property; *see* Real property insurance
  renewable at option of company, 542
Insurance Services Office (ISO), 93, 472
Insurance to value, 101–3, 534–35
Insured, 192–93
  definition, 408
Insured group pension products, 656–58
Insured lien, 443–44
Insuring clause, 404
Interest free loans, 612–13
Intermediate trucking, 248
Internal Revenue Code, 409, 558
  business legal expense insurance, 685
  executive health plans, 613–14
  mutual funds, 605–6
  pensions of nonprofit organizations, 601
  Section 303, 587
Interstate Commerce Commission, 248, 249,
  255
Inventory, 118, 122
Inventory exclusion clause, 162, 164–66

J

Job safety, 9–10
Johnson, Joseph E., 3

Joint insureds, 176
Judicial bond, 316

K

Kane, William J., 581
Kelly, Kenneth, 419
Kensicki, Peter R., 33
Keogh retirement plan, 549, 550, 566–71
  split-funding, 550
Key employee, 595
  characteristics, 595
  fringe benefits, 596–621
Key man life insurance, 587
Kidnap and ransom, 410–14
  insurance, 411–14
    conditions, 413
    coverage, 412–13
    endorsements, 413–14
    premiums, 414
  loss prevention, 410–11
Kling, Leo, 135

L

Layering coverage, 456
Lease bonds, 317–18
Leasehold estate, 443, 450
Leasehold interest coverage, 152
Leasing of automobiles, 220
  liability, 222, 224
Ledwith, Richard W., Jr., 557
Legal expense insurance; see Business legal
  expense insurance
Legal insurance, group, 640–41
Legal liability loss, 4, 62
Legal malpractice, 369, 381–83
  commingling of client's funds, 371–72
  conflict of interest, 370–71
  securities transactions, 372–73
Liability for guests' property coverage, 513
Liability insurance, 62–75, 184–215
  comprehensive general liability policy; see
    Comprehensive general liability policy
  umbrella, 73
Liability losses, 62–67
Libel, 176–77
License and permit bonds, 313
Lien, 443–44
Lien discharge bond, 316
Life insurance, 545–50
  buy-sell agreements, 586–87
  key man, 587
  mutual or stock company, 545
  nonforfeiture provisions, 547
  pension plans, 655
  substandard, 549
  tax deductibility of premiums, 549
  term or permanent, 545–46
  whole or ordinary life, 546
Liner negligence clause, 334
Liquor liability, 197
Livestock mortality insurance, 530–32
Living death, 591
Lloyd's Form B, 203
Lloyd's of London, 23, 69, 101, 337, 415, 459,
  684, 697

Local trucking, 248
Long-haul trucking liability
  bodily injury, 248
  cargo exposure, 249
  cargo insurance, 254–55
  governmental regulations, 255–56
  jurisdictional requirements, 248
  marketing of insurance, 257–58
Longshoremen's and Harbor Worker's
  Compensation Act, 275, 279
Loss, 4
  appraisal, 111
  cooperation, 110
  holdback, 111
  notice, 108–9
  occurrence of, 106–7
  prevention, 410–11
  proof of, 109–10
Loss control, 8–14, 34
  commercial auto liability risk, 225–26
  farmers insurance, 533–34
Loss conversion factor, 283
Loss engineering, 106
Loss financing; see Risk financing
Loss inside premises, 505
Loss outside premises insurance, 505
Loss of profit insurance, 504
Loss profitability studies, 16
Loss of rents coverage, 512
Loss reserve, 208
Loss-of-use property damage, 199, 203–4
Lost instrument bonds, 317
Love Canal, 458, 707

M

Machinery coverage, 421
MacPherson v. Buick Motor Company, 377–78
Magnet properties coverage, 143–44
Maher, Patrick J., 717
Maintenance bonds, 313, 315
Major medical coverage, 630, 631
Malicious mischief insurance, 96, 508, 509
Malpractice; see also Negligence and
    Professional liability
  accountants, 373–74
  assault and battery, 365–66
  attorneys, 369–73
  compared to other civil tort problems,
    356–57
  hospitals, 368
  liability suits, 357–59
  professional custom, 355
Manual rates, 208
Manufacturers' and contractors' coverage, 185,
  255
Manufacturers' output policy, 125–27
  premiums computation, 126–27
Marine extension clauses, 328
Marine insurance, 23–24, 60, 68–69
  inland transit, 119, 513
  ocean transit, 119, 321–41
Marshall Field and Company, 690
Massey, Mel J., Jr., Esquire, 593
Mattel Company, 401
Maximum premium factor, 282

MCA, Inc., 690
Mead Corporation, 690
Medical reimbursement plans, 614
Mercantile open stock burglary policy, 61, 512, 513
Mergers and Acquisitions, 690
Migliaccio, Guy R., 661
Miller, Lynne M., 689
Minimum deposit plan, 546–47
Minimum premium ratio, 283
Minimum restoration period, 132
Mobile equipment insurance, 233
Model Business Corporation Act, 401, 407
Modified transfer, 20
Money orders insurance, 160, 505, 515
Money and securities coverage
  businessowners' policy, 485
  special multi-peril policy, 515
Morrison, John C., 499
Mortgage insurance, 546
Motor Carrier Act of 1980, 701, 704–5
Motor vehicles insurance; *see* Automobile liability
Murphy, Michael J., 689
Mutual life insurance companies, 545
Mutual P & I Associations (clubs), 337

N

Named peril coverage, 97, 120
National Council on Compensation Insurance, 27
National Flood Insurance Association, 130
National Flood Insurance Program, 98
National 4-H Council, 533
National Safety Council, 11, 533
Natural resources, defined, 703n
Navajo Circle, Inc. v. Development Concept Corporation, 378
Needle, Robert, Esquire, 267
Negligence, 62–64, 70–71
  continuous negligence rule, 364
  defective products, 67
  definition, 356
  directors and officers, 401
  hazardous waste liability, 706–7
  informed consent theory, 361
  professional liability, 354, 359
  workers' compensation, 66–67
Net sales value of production, 140–41
New venture or new construction, 5–6
New York standard fire policy, 93
Newly acquired automobile, 251
No-fault auto insurance, 223–24, 230–31
  truckers' liability, 250
Noncancellable policy, 542
Nonforfeiture provisions, 547
Noninsurance transfer, 18–20
  acquisition/divestiture, 20
  additional insured, 19–20
  automobile liability, 224–28
  indemnity, 18–19
  modified, 20
Nonnegligent liability, 64
Nonprofit board, 406
Nonprofit organization pension plans, 601

Northwest Industries, 690
Notice provisions, 167–73, 403–4
Nuclear contamination insurance, 99
  business interruption insurance, 150
Nuisance, 706

O

Object, definition, 422
Occidental Petroleum, 690
Occupational Safety and Health Act (OSHA), 8, 533
Occurrence, 194–95, 199, 251, 294–96
  definition, 295
Occurrence basis deductible, 104
Occurrence basis liability policy, 384–85, 402
Ocean marine insurance, 321–41
  cargo, 323–33
  hull, 333–41
Off-record risks, 440–41
Operations coverage, 185
Ordinary (Whole) life insurance, 546, 586–87
Other insurance clause, 467–68, 491
Outside the premises coverage, 160
Overseas Private Investment Corporation (OPIC), 414–15
Owners', landlord's, and tenants' (OL&T) coverage, 255
Owner's leasehold policy, 443
Owner's protective policy, 187

P

Package policies, 122–23, 501–2
Paid loss retrospective plan, 284
Paid-up insurance, 547
Partnership
  as aggregate, 562
  buy-sell agreements, 571–75
  centralization of management, 559–60
  compensation, 565–66
  continuity of life, 559
  decision to use, 560–62
  definition, 558
  description of, 558–59
  disability insurance, 575–78
  family, 565
  free transferability of interests, 560
  group term life, 579
  income splitting, 564
  Keogh plan, 566–71
  limitation of liability, 560
  purchased goodwill, 573–74
  taxation, 560, 562–64
  termination, 564
  use of, 558
  valuation, 572
Payment bonds, 313, 315
Payroll insurance, 141, 145
Pennsylvania Workers' Compensation Act, 269
Pension plans, 596–98
  deferred compensation, 602–7
  defined benefit, 646, 649–50
  defined contribution, 646–50
  ERISA; *see* Employee Retirement Income Security Act
  funding, 598–600

Pension Plans (*cont.*)
group insured, 656–58
nonprofit organizations, 601
profit-sharing, 598, 599
questions for agent or broker, 658
retired lives reserve plan, 609–10
self-employed, 77
separate account investment, 657–58
tax-deferred annuities, 601
tax qualified plan concept, 650–51
Per claim deductible, 104
Performance bond, 314–15
Perils, 59
automobile insurance, 239
basic fire, 95
extended coverage, 95–96
marine insurance, 324–25, 334
optional, 96
uninsurable, 84
Perils of the seas, 68, 322–23
Period of suspension, 136
Perry, Sherryl R., Esquire, 353
Personal injury, 205–7
defined, 206
excluded claims, 206–7
Personal injury protection insurance, 224
Personal property insurance
BOP coverage, 477–82
BOP eligibility guidelines, 473, 474–75
seasonal automatic increase provision, 477
special multi-peril policy, 508–9
Personnel losses, 4
Physical damage coverage, 248, 250
garage insurance, 262–64
Physicians' and surgeons' liability, 69, 359–66, 369, 380–81
Pike v. Honsinger, 360
Political risk insurance, 414–16
Pollution, 196
Pregnancy Disability Act, 625
Preliminary commitment, 449
Premises coverage, 184–85
Premises medical payment coverage, 189
Premises and operations liability coverage, 299
Premiums
advance call, 337
audits, 208, 243
benefit period, 543
businessowners' policy, 494–95
commercial auto insurance, 240–43
disability waiver, 548
dividends use, 548–49
marine insurance, 329–31, 337
payment as bonus, 611
retrospective rating, 282–83
sole proprietor insurance, 542
taxes, 549
title insurance, 451
rates; *see* Rates
waiting period, 543
workers' compensation insurance, 280–81
Price, Robert S., Esquire, 557
Product, defined, 297
Product recalls, 204
Products liability coverage, 185–86, 291
completed operations coverage, 291, 298–301

Products liability coverage (*cont.*)
comprehensive general liability policy, 291–92
products hazard coverage, 291, 296–98
sistership exclusions, 301–3
Products liability law, 290
Professional custom, 355–56
Professional liability, 69, 70, 185, 354–90
accountants, 373–75, 383–84
architects and engineers, 198, 375–79, 385–87
assault and battery, 365–66
attorneys, 70, 369–73, 381–83
breach of contract, 365
corporation, 387–89
general liability policy, 389–90
history, 355–57
hospitals, 366–69, 380–81
physicians and surgeons, 359–66, 369, 380–81
umbrella policy, 463–64
Professional services, 390
Profit loss insurance, 140
Profit-sharing plans, 598, 599
Prohibited transactions rules of Internal Revenue Code, 409
Promissory warranty, 91–92
Proof of loss provision, 132, 167–73
substantial compliance rule, 170
Property conservation programs, 11–13
Property insurance
general form; *see* General property form
personal property; *see* Personal property insurance
real property; *see* Real property insurance
Property losses, 59
direct; *see* Real property insurance
indirect; *see* Indirect property damage
Property in transit, 60
Proposed bond, 314
Pro rata clause, 149
Protection and indemnity (P&I) insurance, 69, 337
Protective coverage, 185
Prototype pension plans, 655
Public automobile category, 220–21
Public carriers, 221
Public official bond, 316

Q–R

Questionnaire for risk manager, 5
Quick pay whole life, 549

Raab, Frank, E., Jr., 267
Radioactive contamination, 99
Rates
audit, 208, 243
automobile insurance, 240–43
composite, 209
experience, 208–9, 242
manual, 208
retrospective, 209, 243
schedule plan, 242
Real estate interests, insurance of, 442, 443
Real property insurance, 59, 60, 84–111
all-risks coverage 97–101

Real property insurance (*cont.*)
 direct damage to contents; *see* Contents,
  insurance of
 general property form, 93–97
 insurance limits relative to property
  valuation, 101–5
 legal concepts, 85–88
 rates, 105–6
 recovery of loss, 106–11
 special multi-peril policy, 507–8
 standard fire policy, 92–93
Recipient property coverage, 143
Record title condition, 439
Recourse liability policy, 71
Rental value coverage, 151–52
Replacement cost insurance, 122, 475, 510
Replevin bond, 316
Reporting endorsement, 510
Representation, 91–92
Respondeat superior doctrine, 366
Resource Conservation and Recovery Act
 (RCRA), 700–702
Restatement of Torts 2d, 373–74
Resumption of operations clause, 145
Retention of loss, 14–18, 84–85
 captive insurance companies, 17–18
 cargo insurance, 332
 deductibles, 103–4
 outside funding, 17
 service organizations for, 18
 umbrella liability insurance, 460–61
Retirement, 550–552
 fringe benefits, 614–17
 pensions; *see* Pension plans
Retrospective rating, 209–10, 243
 definition of terms, 282–83
 workers' compensation insurance, 282–84
Riot insurance, 100
Risk control, 4
 avoidance, 8–9
 combination technique, 13–14
 reduction, 9–10
 separation of stock, 13
Risk-creating business operations, 185
Risk financing, 4
 retention; *see* Retention of loss
 transfer, 18–21, 224–28, 332
Risk and Insurance Management Society
 (RIMS), 717
Risk management, 4–8
 boiler and machinery insurance, 426–28
 cargo insurance, 331–33
 broker selection, 25–26
 checklists, 716–22
 dishonesty insurance, 177–78
 employers liability, 279–86
 existing operations, 6–8
 glass insurance, 430
 group insurance, 639
 identification, 4–5
 markets, 22–24
 new ventures and new construction, 5–6
 questionnaire, 5
 rating, 24–25
 retention, 14–18
 risk control methods, 8–14, 225
 role of, 4–8

Risk management (*cont.*)
 techniques, 34–35, 279–86
 terrorism, 410–11
 transfer, 18–22
Risk management consultant, 34, 35
 directory of firms and services, 39–55
 how to use, 35–39
Risk retention; *see* Retention of loss
Risk transfer, 18–22
 cargo insurance, 332
 noninsurance techniques, 18–20, 224–28
Robert E. Bill Associates, Inc., 716
Robert E. Bill Risk Profile, 717, 718
Rose, Gordon K., 539
Roybal v. White, 364
Rutherford, Thomas D., Jr., 83
Rylands v. Fletcher, 706

S

Safe harbor rules, 400
Safety department of insurance companies, 256
Safety programs, 9–10
 examples of safety memoes, 29–30
*Salgo v. Leland Stanford Jr. University Board
 of Trustees*, 361
Salvage, 109, 327, 335
Schedule rating plan, 242
Seasonal automatic increase provision of
 Businessowners' policy, 477
SEC Registration Guide, 56, 372
Securities Exchange Act of 1934, 372, 383
Securities Exchange Commission, 383
 10-K report, 5
Self-insurance, 269, 285–86
 umbrella liability policy, 460–61
Severability provision of liability policy, 405
Sex discrimination laws, 409
Shand, Morahan and Company, Inc., 708, 709
Shea, Thomas F., Esquire, 654
Shepherd, Charles N., 321
Shields, Francis E., Esquire, 353
Simplified employee pension plan (SEP), 600
Sindell v. Abbott, 707
Sistership exclusion, 204, 301
Skillern, Frank L. Jr., 155
Slander, 176–77
Smith, Robert S., 219
Snowmobile liability, 197
Sole proprietorship business continuation
 insurance
 buy-sell agreement, 552–53
 continuation insurance, 75, 76
 death, 551–52
 disability, 542–44, 551
 disposing of business, 550–53
 estate plan, 553–54
 health insurance, 540–42
 life insurance, 545–49
 retirement, 550, 552
Sound equipment insurance, 240
Special building form, 509
Special fire legal liability insurance, 487
Special multi-peril policy (SMP), 74, 187, 422
 boiler and machinery insurance, 505–6, 516
 cost, 500
 crime coverage, 505, 512, 513, 514–16

Special multi-peril policy (SMP) (*cont.*)
  deductibles. 510
  general liability, 504, 514
  history of package, 501-2
  optional coverages, 504-5
  present policy, 502-3
  property insurance, 503, 507-13
  single policy contract, 501
Special personal property form, 509
Specific excess insurance, 285
Specific rating formula, 105
Split-dollar insurance, 552, 612
Split-funding, 550
Sprinkler leakage endorsement, 509
Stamm, Charles H. III, Esquire, 623, 645
Standard fire policy, 107-9, 115, 121-23, 489
  New York, 93
  Texas, 93
Standard premium, 209, 282
Standard workers' compensation and
    employers' liability policy; *see also*
    Workers' compensation insurance
  conditions, 277
  coverage provided, 274-75
  defense, settlement, and supplementary
    payments, 275
  definitions, 275
  endorsements, 279
  exclusions, 276
Stated amount insurance, 239-40
Statutory liability loss, 4
Stern, Mark, 690
Stock life insurance companies, 545
Stock redemption (entity) agreement, 76,
  583-85
Stock reporting form, 124-25
Storekeepers' liability policy, 67
Strict liability in tort, 67
Strikes, 339
Subdivision bonds, 313
Subrogation
  cargo insurance, 332
  data processing equipment insurance, 663
  dishonesty insurance, 176
  principle of, 92, 194
  workers' compensation insurance, 278
Substandard life insurance, 549
Superfund (Comprehensive Environmental
    Response, Compensation, and Liability
    Act) 701, 702-4
Surety bond, 67, 312-19
  construction and related contract, 313-15
  court fiduciary, 316-17
  decision to bond, 318
  insurance policy compared, 312-13
  license and permit, 313
  miscellaneous, 317-18
  judicial bonds, 316
  public official bonds, 316

T

Takeover attempts, 689-97
  definition, 693
Target benefit plan, 647
Tax bonds, 317

Tax Court, 612, 613
Tax-deferred annuities, 597, 601
Tax multiplier, 283
Tax qualified pension plan, 650-51
Temporary substitute automobile, 251
Tender offer defense expense insurance, 78,
  689-97
  benefit limits, 691, 694
  co-insurance, 691
  covered expenses 691
  deductibles, 691-92, 684
  definitions in policy, 692-93
  examples, 693-94
  policy period, 691-92
  premium, 695
  public policy considerations, 695-97
Term life insurance, 545-48, 479, 586-87
Terrorism, 410
Texas standard fire policy, 93
Third-party action suit, 401
Three-D policy, 156
Three Mile Island, 400, 458, 707
Thrift plan, 647
Time element coverage, 136-52
  business interruption; *see* Business
    interruption insurance
  extension clause, 151
  gross earnings form, 136-41
  leasehold interest coverage, 152
  rental value coverage, 151
Title insurance, 72
  availability, 451-52
  corporation stock purchase, 444
  cost, 449-51
  endorsements, 447
  exclusions, 446-47
  extended coverage policy, 445-46
  history of, 436-38
  insurance commitment, 449
  insurer's obligation to defend, 441-42
  lien as security interest, 443
  mineral rights, 444
  real estate interests, 443
  risks covered, 438-42
  search and examination process, 439
  standard coverage policy, 444-45
  term of policy, 447-48
Title plant, 437-38
Tort, 62, 69
Transfer loss financing, 18-21, 35
Transit insurance, 127-29
Transportation perils, 60
Trucks and trailers insurance, 65, 241-42, 248
  long-haul trucking; *see* Long-haul trucking
    liability
True group auto insurance, 641
Tuition fees insurance, 511-12
Turner, Richard, 455

U

Umbrella liability insurance, 73, 74
  conditions, 463
  exclusions, 462-63
  history of, 459
  insuring agreements, 461

Umbrella liability insurance (*cont.*)
  limits of liability, 460, 461
  primary coverage requirements, 459–60
  professional coverage, 463
  purpose, 459
  self-insured retention, 460–61
Uniform Commercial Code, 115–16, 120
Uniform Partnership Act, 558, 559
Uninsurable risks, 84, 196, 205
Uninsured motor vehicle, 232
Uninsured motorists (UM) insurance, 224,
    231–32
  truckers' liability, 249
United States v. Carroll Towing Co., 356
U.S. Department of Transportation, 704
Use and occupancy insurance, 137

V

Valuable papers and records insurance, 72,
    432, 513
Valuation at loss, 121–22
Valued form, 424
Valued policy, 91, 101
Vandalism insurance, 96, 508, 509
Variable-pay life insurance, 547
Vessel owner's liability policy, 337
Vicarious liability, 220
Vision care insurance, 641

W

Waiting period, 543
Waiver, 87
Wall Street Journal, 399
War risks, 339

Warranties, 91–92, 290
Watercraft liability, 197
Whole life (Ordinary life) insurance, 546,
    586–87
Wilner, Diane S., 289
With average (WA) coverage, 325–26
Wolf, Penrose, Esquire, 353
Wohlreich and Anderson Group, Ltd., 708, 709
Workers' compensation insurance
  captive insurance company, 286
  death benefits, 273
  disability classification, 273–74
  diseases covered, 271
  earnings loss indemnity, 272
  employee-employer relationship, 269–70
  employment covered, 27
  farmers insurance, 528–29
  guaranteed cost insurance, 280–81
  historical perspective, 268
  injuries covered, 270–71, 273
  medical benefits, 271–72
  participatory plans, 281–82
  retrospective rating, 282–84
  self-insurance, 285
  standard workers' compensation and
      employers' liability policy, 274–79
Workers' Compensation Bureau, 280
Workers' compensation tabular retrospective
    plans, 283–84
Wrongful acts, definition, 409

X–Z

XCU (explosion, collapse, and underground
    property) coverage, 190, 204–5

Ziomek, Thomas J., Esquire, 83

*This book has been set VIP, in 10 and 9 point
Caledonia, leaded 2 points. Section numbers
are 30 point Univers # 63 and section titles
are 24/22 Univers # 63. Chapter numbers are
27 point Univers # 63 and chapter titles are
20/18 Univers # 63. The size of the type page
is 46 x 27 picas.*